SEE THE USA THE EASY WAY

136 Loop Tours to 1200 Great Places

Reader's Digest

The Reader's Digest Association, Inc.
Pleasantville, New York / Montreal

SEE THE USA THE EASY WAY

▼

STAFF

Project Editor: Fred DuBose
Project Art Editor: Marisa Gentile Raffio
Project Research Editor: Barbara Guarino Lester
Art Associate: Angel Weyant
Research Associate: Linda Ingroia
With special assistance from Art Editor Judith Carmel and
　Senior Research Editor Maymay Quey Lin

CONTRIBUTORS

Editors: Alexis Lipsitz, Marianne Wait
Copy Editor: Patricia M. Godfrey
Editorial Assistant: Richard Mazurek
Art Associates: Tomaso Milian, Ed Jacobus
Writers:

Jack Bettridge	Joan Duffy	Guy A. Lester	Judith Schwartz
Tom Black	David Dunbar	Cathy Logan	Richard Schweid
Will Blythe	Leslie Gilbert Elman	Ronni Lundy	Sara Solberg
Paul Burka	Jocelyn Fujii	Mike Macy	Susan Spano
Lola Butcher	Susan Greenburg	Betsa Marsh	Bill Thomas
W. Hodding Carter	Mary Jean Jecklin	Rick Marsi	Bryce Walker
Justin Cronin	Cory Kilvert	Mike Michaelson	James S. Wamsley
Donna Dannen	Rebecca Kimmons	Howard Millard	Carol Weeg
Kent Dannen	Katy Koontz	Megan Newman	
John Davidson	Linda Laird	Jane Ockershausen	
Carol Dawson	Dale Leatherman	Rosemary G. Rennicke	

Picture Editor: Marion Paone
With special assistance from Picture Researcher Yvonne Silver
Indexer: Sydney Wolfe Cohen
Maps: GeoSystems, an R.R. Donnelley Company

READER'S DIGEST GENERAL BOOKS

Editor in Chief: John A. Pope, Jr.
General Books Editor, U.S.: Susan Wernert Lewis
Affinity Directors: Will Bradbury, Jim Dwyer, Kaari Ward
Art Director: Evelyn Bauer
Editorial Director: Jane Polley
Research Director: Laurel A. Gilbride
Group Art Editors: Robert M. Grant, Joel Musler
Copy Chief: Edward W. Atkinson
Picture Editor: Marion Bodine
Head Librarian: Jo Manning

Library of Congress Cataloging in Publication Data
See the USA the easy way : 136 loop tours to 1200 great places.
　　p.　　cm.
　　Includes index.
　ISBN 0-89577-682-0
　1. United States–Tours.　I. Reader's Digest Association.
　E158.S39　1995
　917.304'929–dc20　　　　　　　　　94-36959

Printed in the United States of America

Symbols and Features

ROADS

Limited access-free	
Limited access-toll	
Divided highway	
Primary route	
Secondary route	
Other road	
Unpaved road	
Under construction	
Interstate route	00
U.S. route	000
Canadian autoroute	00
Trans-Canada route	
State or province route	00
Other route	000
Mileage between points	16
Interchanges	
Service areas	
Tunnel	
Pass	
Closed in winter	Closed in Winter

TOWNS AND CITIES

0 - 2,500	Sagamore ○
2,500 - 5,000	Portage ○
5,000 -25,000	Ellwood City ◎
25,000 - 100,000	Johnstown ◎
100,000 - 500,000	Pittsburgh ◎
Over 500,00	Dallas ◎
State capital	✪
National capital	✪
City tints	
Urban areas	

SITES

See the USA destination point	3
Port of entry	
Mountain peak	Mt. Ritter + 13,157
Campground	▲
State park (with camping)	Jamaica S.P. ▲▲
State park (without camping)	Thetford Hill S.P. ▲
Ski area	
Point of interest	MUIR WOODS NATL. MON. ■
Dam	＼

OTHER MAP FEATURES

Auto ferry	
Passenger ferry	
Trail	
International boundary	
State boundary	
Time zone boundary	
Continental Divide	
Perennial drainage	
Intermittent drainage	
Intracoastal waterway	
Tour route	
Water	
National park	
National or state forest	
Other park areas	
Indian reservation	
Military or government areas	
Glacier	
Swamp	

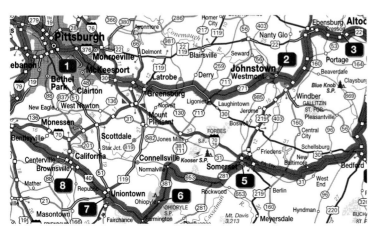

About This Book

The 136 circle tours in SEE THE USA THE EASY WAY are designed to be taken for as long as you choose—a weekend, a week, or even longer. You'll start at an "anchor site"—usually a major city, but sometimes a national park or a small town—and follow the map to the most interesting places in one of six regions: historic towns, gardens, parks, lakes and rivers, nature preserves, scenic drives, colorful small-town festivals, and more. A blue ribbon on the map for each tour traces your route and includes a number for each of the places where you'll stop; the number is keyed to a text entry that describes what you'll see.

As it takes you along the highways of all 50 states, SEE THE USA THE EASY WAY helps you avoid many of the inconveniences that sometimes come with travel. Hundreds of tips, each tailor-made for a specific attraction, tell you when to make reservations, how to save money, and what to look for, along with a host of other hints to make your trip trouble-free. These tips, set off in easy-to-spot red type, appear in every tour.

The Travel Adviser (p. 10) gives you the information you need to make your trip a success—how to pack, find travel bargains, take a break from driving, and stay safe and healthy on the road. The Travel Directory (p. 328) contains lists that help you find the kinds of attractions that may interest you most, from nature sites to grand houses; included are charts with the addresses and phone numbers of state tourism bureaus and national parks.

CONTENTS

Massachusetts: U.S.S. Constitution

New York: Ellis Island

Kentucky: Shaker Village

Michigan: Greenfield Village

New Mexico: Acoma Pueblo

Oregon: Cape Perpetua

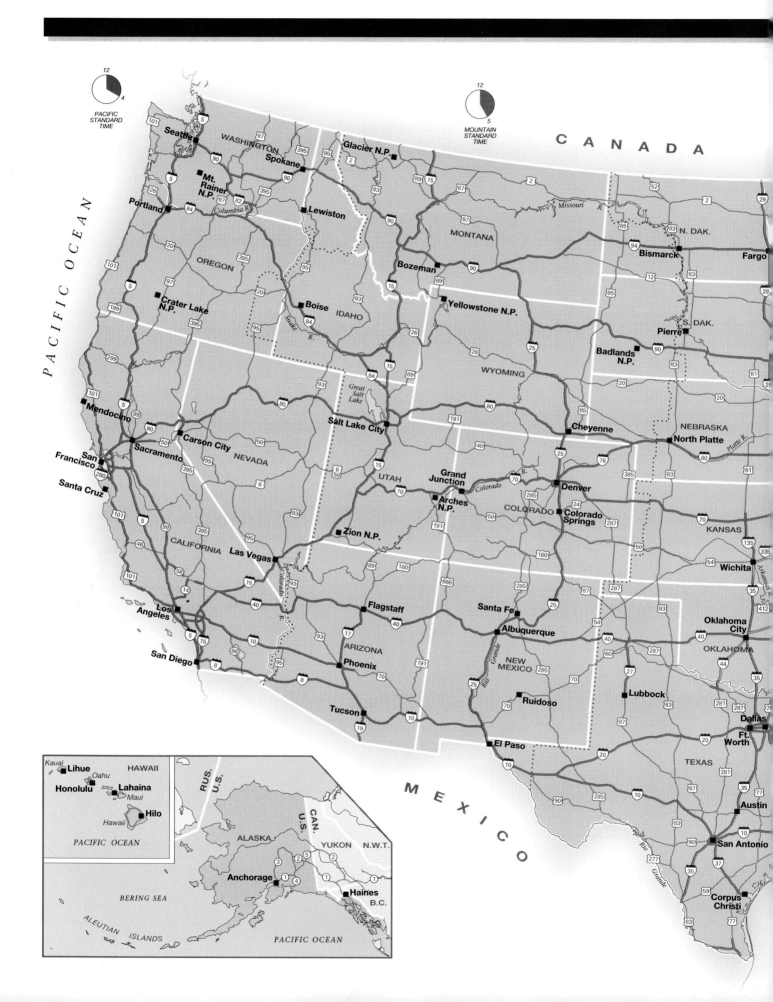

The map below shows you the starting points—marked with red squares—of the 136 circle tours in this book. Their distribution on the Interstate highway system shows you how to reach the parts of the country that you choose to explore.

Plan in Advance

I f you're willing to devote some time and effort to planning a trip a few months before you leave, you'll reap the rewards that can make your vacation postcard-perfect. Wrapping up as many details as you can will ensure that your trip is more enjoyable and less hectic. So plan early, make your reservations early, and enjoy the excitement and anticipation of things to come.

Start With a Phone Call

Contact tourist information sources, such as national parks, state tourism offices, and city convention and

visitor centers (see pp.332–333), for as much information as possible about the destinations you are most interested in: ask about sights, weather, costs, and seasonal crowds. Many places are closed for part of the year or during holidays; call ahead for schedules. Be sure to

ask for a map and a calendar of events.

The more lead time you give yourself to explore all available options before you leave home, the better you will be able to custom-tailor a trip that suits everyone's needs and interests. You'll also be able to take advantage of money-saving early-booking discounts and will have the best chance of reserving rooms in the hotels or motels of your choice. (In the most popular national parks, lodging is often booked up to a year in advance. For alternative lodgings in nearby national forests, see p.13.)

Whenever possible use toll-free numbers to request information. (For information on specific attractions, call 800-555-1212 to find out if an establishment has a toll-free number.) If writing,

use postcards to save postage, and give a deadline date for when the information is needed.

▼

WHAT PITFALLS SHOULD I AVOID WHEN PLANNING A TRIP?

☆ *Don't overschedule your itinerary to the point that you end up rushing through all the sights just so you can check them off your list. Allow ample time to fully enjoy each attraction that you choose to see, even if it means saving other desirable sights for another trip.*

☆ *Be aware that much travel information is already dated by the time you receive it. If your heart is set on a particular event or attraction, call to double-check that the information you have is up-to-date.*

☆ *In spite of your best-laid plans, expect the unexpected—from weather conditions grounding your flight to road construction that snarls traffic for miles around your attraction. Adopting a flexible attitude ahead of time and keeping a sense of humor while on the road will enable you to take minor glitches in stride.*

▲

Bear in mind that the brochures and pamphlets you request can take weeks—even months—to arrive, especially in peak travel seasons; so plan accordingly. Depending on the time of year you intend to travel, it's wise to get your information-gathering campaign under

way at least two to six months before your departure date.

Seek Out Information

Your local library can be a valuable source of free travel information. Check the card catalog for travel, history, and even fiction titles related to your destination; scan back issues of travel magazines and the Sunday travel sections of your newspapers for money-saving tips and other travel advice.

Consult the *Readers' Guide to Periodical Literature* for a list of magazine articles that have been published about your destination. Your local library probably has the magazines on its shelves or on microfilm.

Also consult the *Encyclopedia of Associations* and the *Oxbridge Directory of Newsletters* for special-interest organizations and newsletters, which are available for practically every need and topic—tours for the elderly, for singles, for the disabled; educational trips, wilderness trips, bicycle trips, historic-home tours, archeology tours, and more. (See box on opposite page.) You can also call or write an organization that interests you and ask for information or a newsletter.

Find a Good Travel Agent

Professional travel agents don't cost you a cent and can help you save time and get the most for your money. Through computer tie-ins, agents have fingertip access to vast

amounts of current information on tours, local events, airfares, car rentals, resorts, package tours, hotels, travel insurance, and most other travel needs.

Ask friends and relatives for their recommendations, and then comparison shop for a travel agent, as you would for anything else. Look for such factors as the agent's number of years in the business and specialization in whatever kind of travel you're planning. It's also a good idea to select an agency that is a member of the American Society of Travel Agents (ASTA).

Make a trial visit to the agency and ask for information about sight-seeing, lodging, and car rental. Discuss your budget and your interests. Ask what weather conditions and other details will apply at your destination when you plan to travel. If you feel that the travel agent is less than knowledgeable or is not giving you enough time or effort, take your business elsewhere.

Consider a One-Stop Resort

Budget-minded travelers and families might prefer to take advantage of the all-inclusive packages offered at many resorts. These packages are good values and neatly eliminate the problem of hidden costs.

When selecting an all-inclusive package vacation, make sure the resort will suit your needs. Call or write the resort and ask the following questions:

• What types of visitors does the resort appeal to: families, singles, honeymooners, or older travelers?

• What activities and entertainment are included in the price?

• Are there special activities for children?

• Are other options available at extra cost?

• Will you be able to select from a full menu at meals, or are you restricted to a limited one?

• Is dining sit-down or buffet style?

• Are dining tables private or communal?

• Does your family have a preference regarding dining hours?

• Are alcoholic drinks included, or are they extra?

Map Out an Itinerary

Before you leave, sit down with the entire family and work out an itinerary that outlines where you plan to be each day and what you would like to see there. Consider a variety of attractions and activities that will offer something of interest to each age group—museums, nature trails, theme parks, historic sites, and special events or festivals. Then make a list of the sights you agree are must-sees and a separate list of sights that you consider secondary.

Use a color highlighter to mark your primary sights on a

good road map. Then highlight the driving routes that connect the attractions, taking care not to overlook the back roads that can make your trip more leisurely and enjoyable. Interstate

highways will get you there faster, of course, but often lack the color you'll find off the beaten path.

Add up the mileage between sites to get an idea of how long you'll be driving each day. Allow time for dining and rest stops, and try to alternate an active day with one that is more relaxed.

Highlight your secondary sights on the map so you'll have ready alternatives in case you have to bypass a primary attraction for any reason. Or simply change your mind en route about what you want to see—spontaneity can add to any trip.

Tips for RV Travelers

Travel by recreational vehicle (RV) is becoming an increasingly popular and economical way for families to travel the countryside,

SPECIAL-INTEREST ORGANIZATIONS

The following nonprofit special-interest organizations—a sampling of those listed in the Encyclopedia of Associations—*offer free or low-cost travel-planning information.*

■ **American Automobile Association (AAA)**
1000 AAA Dr.
Heathrow, FL 32746
713-524-1851 or 800-336-4357

■ **American Camping Association**
5000 State Rd. 67 North
Martinsville, IN 46151
317-342-8456

■ **American Canoe Association**
7432 Alban Station Rd., Suite B-226
Springfield, VA 22150
703-451-0141

■ **American Hiking Society**
P.O. Box 20160
Washington, DC 20041
703-385-3252

■ **Archaeological Conservancy**
415 Orchard Dr.
Santa Fe, NM
505-982-3278

■ **Bikecentennial: The Bicycle Travel Association**
P.O. Box 8308
Missoula, MT 59807

■ **Earthwatch**
680 Mt. Auburn St., Box 403
Watertown, MA 02272
617-926-8200

■ **Friends of the Family, Inc.**
The Entertainment Complex
Suite 109
1727 Orlando Central Pkwy.
Orlando, FL 32809

■ **The Itinerary Magazine**
Box 2012
Bayonne, NJ 07002

■ **Mobility International USA**
Box 3551
Eugene, OR 97403

■ **Recreation Vehicle Industry Association**
1896 Preston White Dr.
Reston, VA 22090
703-620-6003

■ **The Sierra Club**
730 Polk St.
San Francisco, CA 94109
415-776-2211

■ **Society for the Advancement of Travel for the Handicapped (SATH)**
347 Fifth Ave.
Suite 610
New York, NY 10016
212-447-7284

■ **Travel Companion Exchange**
P.O. Box 833
Amityville, NY 11701
516-454-0880

■ **Travel Industry & Disabled Exchange**
5435 Donna Ave.
Tarzana, CA 91356

offering savings on dining and lodging, comfort, convenience, and independence.

If you don't own an RV, you can rent one (check your local Yellow Pages), but be sure to take it out for a test-drive first. Handling an RV is quite different from driving a car, and you will need to become familiar with the vehicle before attempting long-distance driving.

There are three seasons for rental rates: high (mid-July to mid-August); shoulder (before and after high season, from April to mid-July, mid-August to mid-October); low (January to the end of March). Go Camping America (800-477-8669), a nonprofit organization sponsored by RV manufacturers, will send you a list of sources where travelers can rent RV's,

along with a free camping planner.

RV clubs are growing in size and number across the country, and can offer useful advice for RV travelers. If you're interested in joining an RV club, check the *Encyclopedia of Associations* in your library or look for newsstand magazines on RV travel.

If You Have a Disability

The key to easy travel for people with disabilities is to anticipate situations and make appropriate plans. The Americans with Disabilities Act has made travel much more accessible for the disabled. Now all new public establishments must conform to requirements. However, many older ones may

still not be able to accommodate travelers who have disabilities.

Before making reservations, call ahead to airports, planes, hotels, restaurants, and sight-seeing destinations to find out what access and equipment are available.

If you use a wheelchair and are traveling by plane, let the airline know in advance if you want to keep your personal chair until the last minute before boarding. If it goes into the cargo hold last, it should come out first.

Let the airline know in advance if you will need help when boarding and disembarking. Ask for motorized aid to the gate if needed.

Arrive early for flights. If you are taking connecting flights, leave one to two hours between flights in case delays create the need to rush.

If you are taking an assistance dog along on your trip, inform everyone you make reservations with.

Plan an Early Start

When making your itinerary final, schedule an early start to each travel day so that you can keep one step ahead of the crowds at every point—even in grocery stores, laundromats, and post offices, where standing in line can waste a good deal of vacation time. (For families traveling with

small children, keeping early hours has the added advantage of maintaining a normal schedule—making life easier all around for everyone.)

At the most popular sight-seeing stops, you'll get the best vantage points if you arrive early. Theme parks and other major attractions sometimes open earlier than scheduled during peak visiting periods. Arrive ahead of time and you may get in sooner than planned. Or call the site the day before you arrive and ask if earlier hours are in effect.

Plan to arrive at your lodgings for the evening by 4 P.M., before the driver gets tired and the kids get cranky. You'll also avoid contending with traffic during twilight hours, when vision is limited, and trying to find your way around in an unfamiliar area after dark.

Terminating your travel day early gives you stress-free time to relax and review your

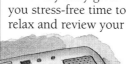

itinerary for the next day—preventing debate, delay, and confusion the following morning—and leaves you with a full evening ahead of you to enjoy unplanned-for local discoveries and activities.

Take Note of All Holidays

When you're on the road, keep in mind that banks and post offices are closed for official holidays. Retail stores and other businesses may be closed or have shorter hours.

Special events, however, such as pageants, festivals, fairs, harvest celebrations, and parades, may be taking place on and around holidays, providing a prime glimpse of local color not as readily apparent at other times of year. Check local newspapers or contact the state or local tourist bureau for more information (see p.333).

A month-by-month listing of major holidays appears below. For most holidays, specific dates change each year. When a holiday falls on a Saturday or Sunday, it is usually observed the preceding Friday or the following Monday (exceptions are July 4 and Christmas Day).

January
New Year's Day
Martin Luther
King, Jr., Day
February
Presidents' Day

▼

HOW CAN I MAKE THE TRIP MORE ENJOYABLE FOR CHILDREN?

✰ *Get the children involved at the trip-planning stage. Let each child have a say in picking activities, so that the itinerary will reflect everyone's preferences.*

✰ *Certain activities, such as guided tours or museum hopping, may be too demanding for a child's attention span. Constant changes of locale can be unsettling, and nonstop sight-seeing can become a tedious blur. Vacation locales where the family can base itself in one place and explore from there—theme parks, resorts, and summer homes—are better bets.*

✰ *Allow children some private time each day to unwind from the excitement of the day. Remember, too, that kids need to take breaks from one another. Just as at home, quarrels will arise if they have to share close quarters for too long. Let them split up whenever feasible to follow their own pursuits.*

▲

Take the Road Less Traveled

Visits to uncrowded destinations will relieve you of the agony of long lines, heavy traffic, and parking dilemmas. They may also save you money: smaller sights usually mean smaller or even nominal fees—and many may be free.

State and city tourism centers can provide information on less-visited areas in the vicinity of major area attractions (see p.15). In contrast to the tourist congestion at major national parks, national forests offer an uncrowded, scenic alternative that is ideal for enjoying outdoor activities, complete with inexpensive lodging and camping facilities. (See box at upper right.)

State parks and wildlife refuges also offer a wealth of outdoor opportunities throughout the country, with far fewer visitors than in the national parks.

If you don't want to restrict yourself to designated state and national tourist areas, look beyond the parks. Taking day trips to local events along your route or planning your trip around a personal interest will make a much more rewarding, fun-filled holiday.

Many states have designated scenic byways. They offer a change of pace, a picturesque tour, and a glimpse of the smaller towns along the way.

Routes that parallel major rivers are often especially rich in historic houses, museums, mills, and other sites that recall America's earlier years. Take the time to travel along these smaller, slower, more scenic roads for at least part of your trip.

Automobile clubs, such as the American Automobile Association, will provide their members with detailed road maps that highlight scenic roads. State tourism offices also provide route information.

If You Travel Off-Season

Most major tourist attractions have high (peak), low (off-peak, off-season), and shoulder seasons (immediately before and after the peak season). July and August are the peak tourism times in most national parks. (See p.14.) Find out during which months the site or attraction you're interested in draws the largest crowds. Also inquire whether certain days of the week or even times of day are slower than others. Then, if possible, plan your visit at a time when the crowds are thinnest.

If you're not traveling with school-age children and aren't limited to their vacation schedules, try to avoid travel during the summer months, spring vacation break (usually around Easter, when seaside resorts are crowded with college students), and holiday weekends. If you do plan to visit popular destinations in the summer, be sure to go as early or as late in the season as possible—not at mid-season, when the crowds are usually at their peak.

The only drawback to off-season travel is that some sights and facilities may not be open. But there are also certain advantages:

Resorts that are open year-round offer substantially lower off-season rates, for example. And while you may not be able to ski in Vermont in July, you will be able to take the ski lift to the top of a scenic mountain for a spectacular vista or enjoy antiques hunting, museums, music festivals, and arts and crafts shows without having to deal with crowds.

Avoid the Crowds

As a general rule, July and August are the peak visiting months in national parks and at other major tourist sites. Attendance also soars during holiday weekends and scheduled special events. Listed on the right are some of the most popular sites in the National Park System, with their peak months. Try to schedule your visit during the shoulder seasons to avoid the worst of the crush, or escape the crowds altogether by choosing lesser-known but excellent alternative sites, some of which are described on the facing page.

Peak Visitation Periods

National Parks

Site	State	Peak Crowds
Acadia	Maine	August
Badlands	South Dakota	August
Bryce Canyon	Utah	August
Everglades	Florida	March
Glacier	Montana	July
Grand Canyon	Arizona	August
Great Smoky Mountains	Tennessee–North Carolina	July
Hawaii Volcanoes	Hawaii	September
Mammoth Cave	Kentucky	July
Mount Rainier	Washington	August
Olympic	Washington	August
Rocky Mountain	Colorado	August
Shenandoah	Virginia	August
Yellowstone	Wyoming	July
Yosemite	California	August
Zion	Utah	August

National Recreation Areas, Seashores, and Monuments

Site	State	Peak Crowds
Amistad NRA	Texas	May
Cape Cod NS	Massachusetts	August
Cape Hatteras NS	North Carolina	July
Delaware Water Gap NRA	Pennsylvania–New Jersey	July
Gateway NRA	New York–New Jersey	July
Golden Gate NRA	California	August
Gulf Islands NS	Florida	June
Joshua Tree NM	California	April
Lake Mead NRA	Arizona	August
Mount Rushmore NM	South Dakota	July

National Historic Parks, Military Parks, Sites, and Memorials

Site	State	Peak Crowds
Boston NHP	Massachusetts	August
Fort Point NHS	California	May
Gettysburg NMP	Pennsylvania	July
Independence NHP	Pennsylvania	July
Martin Luther King NHS	Georgia	January
Statue of Liberty	New York	August
Lincoln Memorial	Washington, D.C.	July
Salem Maritime NHS	Massachusetts	July
White House	Washington, D.C.	April
Valley Forge NHP	Pennsylvania	May

NHP National Historic Park, NHS National Historic Site, NM National Monument,
NMP National Military Park, NP National Park, NRA National Recreation Area, NS National Seashore

Alternatives to the Most Popular Sites in the National Park System

National Parks

Alternative Site	State	Highlights
Arches	Utah	Brilliantly colored giant arches, pinnacles, pedestals
Big Bend	Texas	Spectacular mountain and desert scenery on the Rio Grande
Biscayne	Florida	Coral reefs, mangrove shoreline, keys
Canyonlands	Utah	Colorful rocks, spires, gorges, mesas, petroglyphs
Capitol Reef	Utah	Multicolored sandstone cliffs and high-walled gorges
Great Basin	Nevada	Ancient bristlecone pine forest, southernmost glacier in U.S.
Guadalupe Mountains	Texas	Most extensive exposed fossil reef on earth, desert, canyons
Katmai NP and Preserve	Alaska	Mountain wilderness, brown bears and bald eagles
Kobuk Valley	Alaska	Great Kobuk Sand Dunes, black bears, wolves, foxes, caribou
Lake Clark	Alaska	Two active volcanoes, 50-mile-long lake, red salmon
North Cascades	Washington	Alpine peaks, glaciers, mountain lakes and streams
Voyageurs	Minnesota	Forested lake-country wilderness

National Recreation Areas, Seashores, and Monuments

Alternative Site	State	Highlights
Bighorn Canyon NRA	Montana	Dramatic canyon scenery, 71-mile-long reservoir
Big South Fork NRA	Tennessee	Sandstone cliffs, natural arches, waterfalls, hardwood forests
Canyon de Chelly NM	Arizona	Ruins of ancient Indian villages on canyon walls in caves
Cape Lookout NS	North Carolina	Barrier islands, beaches, salt marshes, dunes
Congaree Swamp NM	South Carolina	Pristine tract of southern bottomland hardwoods
Coulee Dam NRA	Washington	Largest dam on Columbia River, Franklin D. Roosevelt Lake
Craters of the Moon NM	Idaho	Volcanic cones, craters, lava flows, sagebrush grasslands
Devils Postpile NM	California	Volcanic basalt columns up to 60 feet high
Dinosaur NM	Colorado	Canyons, mountains, fossil remains of dinosaurs
Gila Cliff Dwellings NM	New Mexico	Well-preserved dwellings in natural cliff cavities
John Day Fossil Beds NM	Oregon	Fossil beds from last 40 million years of Age of Mammals
Russell Cave NM	Alabama	Archeological site of 8,000 years of human life

National Historic Parks, Military Parks, Sites, and Memorials

Alternative Site	State	Highlights
Coronado NM	Arizona	Route of Coronado expedition in 1540
Federal Hall NM	New York	Site of George Washington's presidential inauguration
Fort Bowie NHS	Arizona	Base of military operations against Geronimo
Fort Clatsop NM	Oregon	Winter camp of 1805 Lewis and Clark expedition
Fort Scott NHS	Kansas	Union supply base during Civil War
Frederick Douglass NHS	Washington, D.C.	Restored home of 19th-century writer and abolitionist
Fredericksburg & Spotsylvania NMP	Virginia	Civil War battlefields and buildings
Horseshoe Bend NMP	Alabama	Battle site of Gen. Andrew Jackson and Creek Indian Nation
Klondike Gold Rush NHP	Alaska	Historic district of downtown Skagway and the Trail of '98
Nez Perce NHP	Idaho	Religious sites, historic sites from westward expansion
Pecos NHP	New Mexico	Remains of Pecos Pueblo and 17th-century Spanish mission
Tuskegee Institute NHS	Alabama	African-American college founded by Booker T. Washington

Pack Light, Pack Right

One key to a successful journey is carrying as little luggage as possible and still having everything you need to be comfortable. Think hard about what you should take along, and learn how best to pack it. The basic rules of packing are perfectly simple: make lists and check them off as you pack, don't wait to pack at the last moment, and always pack light.

Stick to the Basics

Half the battle of packing for a trip lies in choosing the minimum amount of clothing that will give you the maximum amount of wear. Stick to the basic clothes you will need to see you through the activities you have planned and the weather you expect to encounter.

If you will be away for a week or longer, pack enough clothes for each adult to last seven days—thus eliminating or minimizing trips to the laundry or dry cleaner during your time away. Children and infants generally need more —nine or ten days' worth for children, and 14 or so days' worth of clothing for infants.

Choose hand-washable, wrinkle-resistant separates that can be mixed and matched to create different outfits. Darker colors and patterned fabrics will disguise any stains that might appear.

Lightweight cotton is a comfortable choice for warm-weather trips, but 100 percent cotton wrinkles easily. Cotton-polyester blends will travel better and dry faster.

Bring comfortable, well-worn shoes. If you need new shoes for your vacation, buy them well in advance so that you'll have enough time to break them in.

It's also a good idea to bring clothes that you wear a lot at home and feel comfortable in, rather than to purchase a whole new wardrobe for the trip. A vacation is no time to have to make do with clothes that don't quite fit, match, or look the way they did in the store.

Double-Duty Clothes

Pack double-duty clothes that can serve more than one occasion. A lightweight raincoat with a zip-in lining is an excellent item to have if you're traveling to a place where the weather is changeable. A cardigan sweater is as useful during the day as it is at night; a solid-color jacket or blazer works as well with daytime jeans as with a skirt or slacks and tie for evening.

Remember that basic styles travel better than a high-fashion wardrobe. A light wool challis dress that can be worn by day and dressed up with pearls or a scarf at night gives far more wear (and takes up no more suitcase space) than a cocktail dress that will be worn for only one occasion.

Don't pack anything that you rarely wear at home. Chances are, you won't want to wear it on your vacation either.

Practice Your Packing

Do a trial pack a few days before the trip to find out whether your suitcases will hold what you plan to take, and how much each suitcase is going to weigh. Don't wait until you're loading the car to discover that your bags are heavier than you can handle.

Then start to eliminate items. Stop only when you get down to what you truly need and can comfortably carry. It bears repeating that most travelers pack far too many clothes and other unnecessary items for their vacations. What they remember after the trip is not their choice of outfits but the never-ending inconvenience of lugging too many bags in and out of the car.

Make a list of everything you pack. Keep one copy in your suitcase and leave another copy at home. (It will be useful for your insurance company if your bag is lost or stolen.) Make a separate list of items that must be packed at the last minute.

When you return, update your list and store it in your suitcase. It will make organizing your next trip that much easier.

Be sure to leave room in your suitcase for souvenirs—or take another small bag along for the purpose.

Check all gear— camera and accessories, picnic, camping, and sports equipment—at least a week before your trip, and repair, replace, or purchase as needed.

Pack It Right

Place everything you plan to take on a bed. Then sort the items into groups: heavy items, soft items (socks, T-

---

shirts, underwear), shirts, slacks, and so on. Weed out duplicates.

▼

WHAT ARE SOME GOOD WAYS TO PACK FOR CHILDREN?

☆ *Have children select some of their favorite clothes to bring along to give them familiar comfort on the road.*

☆ *A handy packing method for small children that will prevent them from upsetting the entire suitcase each day is to pack a complete set of clothes for each day in a large, see-through plastic bag with a twist tie; pack these bags into the child's suitcase. Or pack all of your socks in one see-through bag, all of your underwear in another, and so on.*

☆ *For small children, keep a few surprise toys tucked away for difficult moments.*

▲

When you've assembled and organized all the items you need to take, pack them into your suitcase in the following order:

• The heaviest items you take, such as shoes, hair dryers, and travel irons, go in first, on the bottom of the suitcase. Always put your shoes in clear plastic bags or old socks, placing them sole to sole, to prevent them from getting scuffed and to keep your clothes from getting dirty.

• Roll up soft items like socks and underwear and stuff into shoes to save space.

• Secure heavy or fragile items by surrounding them with

soft items, such as sweaters.

• Follow with other nonclothes items and with wrinkle-resistant items like jeans.

• Lay clothing out flat. Close all zippers and buttons. Fold sleeves in. Fold at waist, on seams, and on other natural creases. Fold to uniform thickness and as small as possible.

• Layer folded slacks, shorts, dresses, shirts, and blouses, ending with the clothes that wrinkle most easily.

• To minimize wrinkling, pack blouses, shirts, slacks, and dresses individually in large plastic bags. (When you unpack, hang wrinkled clothes in the bathroom and steam them by running a hot shower.)

You might also want to pack an assortment of plastic bags to use for laundry, wet bathing suits, and the like, or for storing leftover snacks.

Choose the Right Luggage

Soft duffel bags are ideal for holding wrinkle-resistant clothes and other crushproof items, and can easily be packed into smaller spaces in the car where standard suitcases can't fit.

Luggage with wheels and a pull strap saves a lot of effort if you will be traveling through airports. Choose a hard-sided suitcase if you'll be checking luggage; it

will protect the contents better.

Check with your airline about its baggage regulations and restrictions. Generally, U.S. carriers allow a maximum of three pieces of luggage for each adult.

Some airlines have weight restrictions for bags: carryons, 40 pounds maximum; checked luggage, 70 pounds maximum.

Carry-on luggage must fit under the seat or in the overhead bins. A typical carry-on measures 9" by 14" by 22"—or length plus width plus height equals 45".

The rule of thumb for checked luggage is

that length plus width plus height not exceed 62". Some airlines require that the second piece be smaller: 50" maximum.

Pack the Car With Care

Pack the car the night before you leave. This will save you time in the morning and give you a clear idea of space limitations.

Put the large suitcases farthest back in the trunk. Try to distribute the weight of the bags evenly. Then pack duffel bags and other soft luggage around hard-sided

suitcases to keep them from shifting around.

Pack the heaviest items in the trunk, the lightest on top of the car. This will help keep the car stable.

Bag items you'll need in the car (see box above). Loose items in the car tend to be easier to lose and may pose a hazard when the car comes to a sudden stop.

Avoid carrying a loaded food cooler in the trunk. The temperature there can become too high for safe food storage.

Keep a pet carrier in the passenger section of the car so that you can soothe the pet during travel.

Don't Forget the Obvious

Since you're far more likely to forget your toothbrush and toothpaste than you are your expensive new camera, scan the following checklists as you complete your packing. The lists will serve as a reminder and may spare you the annoyance of having to pay resort prices to replace essentials you left sitting at home. You may also discover a few items you hadn't thought to take along on your trip that might make life a bit easier on the road.

Documents & Essentials

- Cash, traveler's checks, checkbook
- Credit cards and other membership cards (see box, p.16)
- Driver's licenses, car registration, car insurance card
- Address book with vital telephone numbers
- Airline and other tickets, vouchers, travel itinerary
- Car, house, and luggage keys
- Watch
- Emergency medical records

Along with your other documents, carry an emergency medical record index card for each traveler in your group, with the following information:
  Name
  Address
  Date of birth
  Doctor's name, address, telephone number
  Medical conditions
  Blood type

Prescription medications
Allergies
Medical insurance company's name, address, telephone number
Person to notify in case of emergency

Medical Kit

- Prescription medication
- Medical-alert tag if you have a serious medical condition
- Aspirin, aspirin substitute
- Antidiarrhea medication
- Laxative
- Adhesive bandages, gauze pads, adhesive tape
- Elastic bandage
- Antibiotic ointment
- Insect repellent
- Sunscreen
- Sunburn, rash, poison ivy ointment, such as hydrocortisone cream
- Muscle-ache ointment
- Motion-sickness remedy
- Cough syrup, cold remedy, dosage spoon
- Decongestant
- Antacid
- Thermometer
- Scissors
- Tweezers
- Cotton balls
- Eyedropper
- Premoistened towelettes
- First-aid booklet

Personal Care & Sundries

- Personal grooming and medicinal products that may not be readily available
- Eyeglasses, sunglasses, contact lenses, and copy of prescription
- Antibacterial soap

- Toothbrush, toothpaste
- Mouthwash
- Deodorant
- Feminine hygiene products
- Shampoo, conditioner
- Comb, brush, hair accessories
- Portable hair dryer
- Hand/body lotion, lip balm
- Cosmetics, perfume
- Shower cap
- Small mirror
- Shaving kit
- Swabs, tissues
- Travel iron
- Travel sewing kit
- Travel alarm

Women's Clothes

- Undergarments
- Panty hose
- Sun hat
- Socks
- Dresses (dressy, casual)
- Skirts
- Pants (dressy, casual)
- Blouses (dressy, casual)
- T-shirts
- Long-sleeved shirts
- Shorts
- Shoes (dressy, casual)
- Nightwear, robe, slippers
- Swimwear (suit, cover-up, flip-flops)
- Scarves, jewelry, belts
- Jacket, sweater
- Waist pack or knapsack

Men's Clothes

- Underwear
- White T-shirts
- Socks
- Shirts (dressy, casual)
- Long-sleeved shirts
- Slacks (dressy, casual)
- Sporty T-shirts
- Shorts

- Ties
- Belts
- Shoes (dressy, casual)
- Nightwear, robe, slippers
- Swimwear (suit, cover-up, flip-flops)
- Jackets (dinner, casual)
- Sweaters
- Waist pack or knapsack

Children's Clothes
- Underwear
- T-shirts
- Socks
- 1 set dressy clothes
- Shoes (dressy, casual)
- Shirts
- Jeans
- Slacks
- Shorts
- Swimwear (suit, cover-up, rubber thong sandals)
- Nightwear, robe, slippers
- Sweat pants and tops
- Jacket, sweater
- Waist pack or knapsack

Toys & Miscellaneous
- Favorite toy or blanket
- Quiet toys
- Story tapes and cassette player, preferably with earphones
- Reading books
- Picture books
- Game/puzzle books
- Coloring books, washable markers (in plastic washable bag)
- Puzzles (not jigsaw)
- Pad, drawing paper, pencils, pencil sharpener (in plastic lockable bag)
- Toy cars

WHAT TO CARRY IN TRANSIT

The following items, selected from the preceding checklists, should be kept with you at all times when in transit, either on your person or in a carry-on bag. In the event that you and your checked baggage become separated, this will spare you the considerable time and aggravation involved in replacing credit cards, airline tickets, and other essential cards and documents. In case you arrive at your hotel before your baggage does, you can minimize your inconvenience by having a few basic toiletries and a change of clothes at hand to see you through one night.

- Cash, checkbook, traveler's checks
- Bank and oil-company credit cards
- Long-distance calling card
- Driver's license and car insurance card
- Auto, travel, and other club membership cards
- Half-price hotel membership card
- Address book with vital telephone numbers
- House, car, luggage keys
- Airline tickets, hotel vouchers, travel itinerary
- Eyeglasses, sunglasses, contact lenses
- Medical insurance card
- Emergency medical record card and medical-alert tag
- Prescription medications
- Watch, travel alarm
- Basic toiletries
- Change of clothes

- Playing cards
- Magnetic checkers
- Small games (but not with many small pieces)
- Car pillow
- Night-light

Foul-Weather Wear
- Raincoat
- 2 pairs gloves
- Scarves
- Boots
- Thermal underwear
- Sweaters
- Rain poncho
- Rain boots
- Rain hat
- Umbrella

Picnics & Barbecues
- Grill cooking utensils
- Grill
- Skewers
- Vegetable peeler
- Sharp knife (well wrapped)
- Quick-starting charcoal briquettes
- Matches or lighter
- Grill-cleaning brush
- Large and small saucepans; fry pan or griddle
- Aluminum foil, plastic wrap
- Cooler and ice packs
- Pump drink dispenser
- Matches in waterproof container
- Paper plates, cups
- Napkins, moist wipes
- Plastic food-storage bags
- Plastic utensils

- Plastic garbage bags
- Can/bottle opener
- Airtight plastic containers
- Fuel if using cooking stove
- Dishpan, soap, and sponge
- Scouring pad
- Scrub brush or cloth
- Dish towel
- Serving spoons
- Baking soda

See also Snacks to Keep in the Car, p.33. For tips on food safety when you picnic or barbecue, see Prevent Food Contamination, p.33.

Camping
Add these to the Picnics & Barbecues checklist:
- Tent and set-up supplies (Don't forget instructions as well.)
- Flashlights, lanterns, extra batteries
- Ground cloth for tent floor
- Cooking stove and fuel (if not using a grill)
- Water jugs
- Portable toilet, toilet paper, disinfectant
- Sleeping bags or air mattresses
- Blankets, pillows
- Towels, washcloths
- Dining canopy
- Tools (in addition to your car toolbox): folding shovel, hammer, ax, saw
- Work gloves
- Compass
- Binoculars
- Canteen
- Whistle (for emergencies)
- Rope and string, clothes-pins
- Fishing gear and license
- All-purpose nylon tarp

For a list of tools and other items to pack in the car in case of emergency, see Car Emergency Checklist, p.17.

Look for Travel Bargains

To keep your vacation as economical as possible, you will need to do some comparison shopping in advance. You can get the most for your vacation dollars by knowing what questions to ask when booking a hotel room or choosing a tour, and by taking advantage of programs and organizations that can help you streamline expenses. You'll find that bargains are available in many quarters, often just for the asking.

Explore All Options

The cardinal rule to follow in seeking out travel bargains is to never jump at the first discount offered, regardless of how attractive it sounds. You can sometimes do better than publicized "sale" prices by comparison shopping, traveling off-peak, and using all membership discounts at your disposal.

When comparison shopping for any kind of reservation—airline, hotel, car rental, tour—first ask for the lowest rate available. Then ask if there are any package rates that would cover two or more of your needs, such as a fly-drive package. Finally, ask if further discounts apply for any of your memberships or credit cards, and what restrictions apply.

Be careful, however, not to let the lure of bargain prices end up compromising your vacation. Take advantage of bargains only when they coincide with your interests.

Make Use of Memberships

Travel discounts may be available to you through a wide range of organizations, clubs, and programs, including:

- AAA and other auto clubs
- AARP and other senior organizations
- youth and student organizations
- half-price hotel clubs and frequent-guest programs
- travel clubs
- frequent-flier airline programs
- credit cards and charge cards
- museum and club memberships
- professional association memberships

Take time to become familiar with the benefits you are entitled to through your current cards and memberships, and consider investigating other organizations or programs that offer travel perks you may wish to take advantage of.

Join a Travel Club

Travel clubs offer access to sizable discounts on transportation, lodging, dining, and certain attractions. The cost of membership will be money well spent in terms of the savings you will ultimately reap.

To join a club, check the pamphlets that come with your credit card or oil-company statements; they often contain travel-club promotions. Or call the company directly and ask for the names and numbers of participating clubs.

Some clubs provide members with a toll-free number to call for information about last-minute trips and flights, while other clubs mail out listings. When selecting a club, compare the types of travel offered and consider your own scheduling needs—whether you are able to travel at a moment's notice or require more time in advance to make your plans. Find out also whether a club that interests you uses gateway cities to which you have easy access.

Half-price hotel rates are available through a number of clubs and associations for an annual fee or through the purchase of an annual directory. Each of these organizations has a list of participating hotels, motels, and resorts at which your membership entitles you to 50 percent off the list rate. Each hotel determines its discounts according to its anticipated occupancy for the date in question. You must show your membership ID at check-in.

Many club memberships offer such benefits as two-for-one dining and discounts on car rental and entertainment.

NO-FEE TRAVELER'S CHECKS

No-fee traveler's checks are available through a variety of sources, including auto, travel, and other club memberships. Traveler's check fees are also waived for some credit- and charge-card holders as a membership perk. Examples of better-known organizations that offer no-fee checks are listed below, along with any restrictions that apply:

- American Automobile Association (AAA)
- Thomas Cook Travel offices
- Mature Outlook
- American Express: no fee to Gold Card holders when purchased by mail; no fee to Platinum Card holders at any time
- Diner's Club: fees reimbursed for traveler's checks purchased at any Citibank
- Montgomery Ward Y.E.S. Discount Club: fees reimbursed for traveler's checks purchased anywhere

HOW TO GET THE BEST CAR-RENTAL DEAL

■ Contact rental companies, using their toll-free telephone numbers, to request rates. Ask about special weekend rates and whether your credit cards or club memberships entitle you to any discounts. Ask if the weekly rate is less expensive than renting for a few days at the daily rate. Compare prices.

■ Check with travel agents and airlines about money-saving fly-drive packages.

■ Check with your hotel for possible car-rental tie-ins.

■ Join frequent-renter programs for free upgrades and other benefits.

■ If possible, travel off-peak, when rates are lower. Ask rental offices about peak time where you plan to visit.

■ Try to rent on weekends instead of weekdays; it's cheaper.

■ Be aware that car rentals are often cheapest at airport locations and at popular destinations, where companies face stiff competition.

■ Reserve early for advance-booking discounts; there is no penalty for cancellation or change in booking. Have the company confirm and guarantee your rate, in case rates go up.

■ Be wary of high-pressure techniques at car-rental counters for CDW (collision damage waiver), extra-driver charges, and other options. Refuse CDW coverage if your own insurance or credit card already covers you.

■ Save money by renting a smaller car instead of a luxury model.

■ If possible, return the rental car to the location where you picked it up, to avoid drop-off fees.

■ Return the rental car with a full tank of gasoline if your contract requires it, or you'll pay top price at the agency's pumps. (Gas at off-highway locations is generally cheaper than at highway service stations; use self-service pumps for even lower rates.)

Note that special hotel rates and packages can sometimes be as good as or even better than the 50-percent-off program. Be sure to check all of the options before you make your room reservations. (See *Get the Best Room Rate*, p.22.)

Discounts of up to 65 percent off the list rates in hundreds of hotels in major cities are available through a booking service called Hotel Reservations Network. No membership is required to take advantage of this program. Call 800-96-HOTEL to ask for a specific hotel or for hotel suggestions.

Look for Senior Discounts

Seniors are often entitled to a wide range of discounts on air and hotel rates, restaurants, museums, theaters, transit, concerts, and more. Since many establishments do not openly advertise senior discounts, always ask before you pay.

AARP, the National Council of Senior Citizens, and other organizations for seniors offer travel discounts and other related services. Members are entitled to price cuts on fly-drive programs, car and RV rentals, airfares, and discounts of up to 50 percent at selected hotels.

The National Park Service's free Golden Age Passport, available to people 62 and older, gives free entry to all sights in the National Park System, and 50 percent off park fees for camping and using other facilities. Passes can be picked up in person at any national park, where proof of age will be required.

Many states offer seniors a variety of discounts, such as free access to state parks, museums, and public transportation, and discounts on lodging and restaurants. Contact the state tourism office (see p.333) for more information.

Discounts for the Disabled

Many establishments and attractions offer discounted rates for disabled travelers, but—as in the case of senior discounts—they may not be widely advertised. Again, ask about eligibility when making reservations or before paying.

The National Park Service's Golden Access Passport, available to permanently disabled persons, offers free entry to all national parks and a 50 percent discount on all facility fees. Call or write any national park (see p.332) for further information.

Get the Best Deal on Airfares

The large assortment of airfare bargains and discounts offered through travel agents, club memberships, and unpredictable airfare wars can be bewildering. Keep abreast of current prices and any short-term promotions that may be in effect through the travel section of your newspaper, or use a travel agent who has computer access to airfare information to search out the best deal. (See *Find a Good Travel Agent*, p.10.)

Ask your agent or the airline reservations clerk for the cheapest possible airfare, to avoid any confusion about the kind of ticket you want. (The latest special or the so-called supersaver fare may not be the best price available.)

Savings are often significant on midweek or off-peak flights, as well as on flights to an alternate, less-trafficked airport located near your destination—Oakland, for example, instead of San Francisco. Some of these alternate airports are hubs for lower-priced carriers; others are in "discount cities" that cost the airlines less for landing fees.

Opt for a stopover flight rather than nonstop if the price is right. Keep in mind that to get the best fares, you are usually required to stay over Saturday night.

Pay for discount tickets as soon as possible. If the price goes down before you travel, most airlines will reimburse the difference. If you must re-book, it's most likely that you will be charged only a moderate service fee.

Frequent-flier membership. Join the major airline frequent-flier clubs. Membership is free, and most offer mileage credits not only for miles flown but for hotels, rental cars, and even long-distance telephone calls. Some airlines will give you free mileage credits just for signing up. Children can join these programs too.

Airline coupon books for seniors. Discount air coupon books are offered by many airlines for travelers 62 and older. Each airline has its own policy, so be sure to find out exactly how the coupons work and whether any restrictions apply. In all cases, remember to comparison shop: You may get a better deal on a standard advance purchase or on short-term specials.

Ticket consolidators. These agencies, advertised in the Sunday travel section of some newspapers, sell un-booked air tickets at reduced rates. You can save a lot if you're willing to chance waiting for last-minute confirmation of your booking on a particular flight. (Also note that most consolidator tickets are nonrefundable or carry a hefty cancellation penalty.) Be cautious: If at all dubious about the

outfit you're about to do business with, contact the Better Business Bureau to check on the agency.

Voluntary "bumping." Air passengers flexible enough to volunteer to be "bumped" if the airline needs your seat often are thanked with free tickets to most destinations the airline travels to (on your next trip). Ask at check-in about the airline's policy and make your offer if the trade-off is attractive.

Airport transit. Larger hotels in popular destinations often provide free shuttle bus service to and from the airport, which can result in a tidy savings on taxi fare. Always inquire when making reservations.

If You're Going by Train or Bus

Amtrak offers a number of discounted fares—for children, seniors, travelers with disabilities, and armed forces personnel and their dependents. You

may also save money if you do your traveling on weekdays or during off-peak hours.

Amtrak's "All-Aboard America" program is another bargain for

travelers who want to ride the rails. Call Amtrak or your travel agent for details.

Major long-distance bus companies also offer hefty discounts for seniors, children, travelers with disabilities and their traveling companions, and military personnel. In addition, special fixed-price passes are often available for a given time period, such as 7, 15, or 30 days. Contact the carrier directly for details.

For further information on train and bus travel options, see *Spare the Car and Driver*, pp.34–37.

Get the Best Room Rate

Use the following steps to get the best rate (see box at right) at the hotel or motel of your choice:

• If you travel often, join frequent-guest plans of the major hotel chains.

• Call the hotel's direct number—not the chain's central reservations 800 number—to get the lowest rate.

• Ask for any special rates in effect for the dates you plan to visit—package rates that may include meals and a rental car, plus sight-seeing discounts and special rates and programs for children.

• Inquire about any seasonal specials and discounts for your club memberships. (Some half-price hotel clubs require you to identify yourself as a member from the

UNDERSTANDING HOTEL LANGUAGE

When booking accommodations, you may be confronted by confusing terminology. Use this glossary as a translator.

Confirmed reservation: The hotel has booked a specific category of room for specific dates. Check with the establishment regarding limitations. There is a cutoff time of arrival beyond which the hotel is not legally required to honor the reservation.

Guaranteed reservation: If you pay in advance by giving your credit-card number when you make a hotel-room reservation, your room is guaranteed even if you arrive late. But be forewarned that if you don't show up at all, the hotel still will charge the room to your credit-card account.

Double room: Room with 1 or 2 double beds for 2 people.

AP (American Plan): Room rate includes 3 meals a day, from a limited menu.

MAP (Modified American Plan): Room rate includes 2 meals a day (usually breakfast and dinner), from a limited menu.

FAP (Full American Plan): Room rate includes 3 meals a day, with unlimited menu selection.

EP (European Plan): Room only, no meals.

Continental Plan: Room rate includes a light breakfast (toast or rolls with coffee or tea, and sometimes juice). Cold cereal and milk, fruit, or pastry may also be offered.

Frequent-guest programs: Offered by some major hotel chains. Frequent guests receive frequent-flier mileage credit or accumulate points that can be redeemed for hotel stays, merchandise, or other bonuses.

First class: Not necessarily the top category available. Ask if there are any categories that rate a higher class.

Rack rate: List price for a room before any discount.

Corporate rate: Discount rate offered to business travelers (but be aware that it is usually available to anyone who asks for it).

start. This may limit the information you receive on other specials, so make a second call to inquire about 50-percent-off availability.)

• Ask for the corporate rate—available even to individual travelers, which is usually 10 to 15 percent off the rack rate.

• Ask for specific dollar costs—not percentage of discounts, which can be misleading. Be aware that advance bookings often get discounts of up to 30–65 percent.

• Ask the reservations clerk if children under a certain age can stay for free in the same room with their parents. (Some hotels offer a second room at half price to families.)

• Check rates at hotels outside major cities; they are often substantially lower.

• If you do stay in a city, visit on weekends, when rates are usually lower. Resort sites, on the other hand, generally cost less on weekdays.

• Rates at seasonal vacation centers are lower off-season. (See *If You Travel Off-Season*, p.13.)

Lodging Alternatives

Remember that hotels and motels aren't your only lodging options. (For information on camping and RV travel, see *Tips for RV Travelers*, p.11.) The following alternatives may be less expensive and just as conve-

nient, depending on your needs.
Bed-and-breakfasts. Often homey and charming, B&B's are usually less expensive than hotels and may offer a more memorable stay. Breakfast and sometimes snacks are included. The owners can usually recommend local restaurants, shops, and attractions.

For further information, look for bed-and-breakfast guidebooks in your bookstore, or contact the chamber of commerce or tourist office at your destination.
YMCA/YWCA. Most cities have a conveniently located YMCA or YWCA, that offers cheap rates for basic sleeping accommodations, which often include the use of the swimming pool or other facilities.

Contact the local Y chapter through directory assistance for further information.
Hostels. Next to camping, youth hostels are perhaps the cheapest places to stay. They are open to travelers of all ages, may offer meals or kitchen facilities, and can be great

places to meet other travelers.

For information, write: *Hosteling International—American Youth Hostels, 733 15th St. NW, Washington, DC 20005.*

For travelers over 60 (and their companions over 50), these no-frills accommodations, usually on college campuses, include room and board plus a course or two—many offered in interesting, peaceful locations.

For more information, write: *Elderhostel, 75 Federal St., Boston, MA 02116.*
College Dormitories. Don't overlook this pleasant and budget-wise lodging alternative. Some dormitories offer meals and the use of a swimming pool or other campus facilities.

For more information, write *Campus Travel Service, P.O. Box 5486, Fullerton, CA 92635,* or contact the college directly.

Bargain Hunting on the Road

Don't relax your bargain-hunting efforts

once you leave home. With a bit of forethought, you can significantly reduce your daily expenditures on such items as entertainment, transportation, food, and other services.

▼

WHAT KINDS OF DINING BARGAINS SHOULD I LOOK FOR WHEN TRAVELING?

☆ *Ask about senior discounts and children's menus when making reservations or before ordering.*

☆ *Take advantage of the early-bird specials offered at many restaurants. This can be particularly rewarding at high-priced eateries, where you can enjoy the same fare at a substantial savings.*

☆ *You can eat at lower prices at an otherwise expensive restaurant by having lunch there instead of dinner.*

☆ *Get two meals for the price of one in a wide selection of restaurants—an added bonus offered through half-price hotel clubs.*

☆ *Salad bars can provide a healthful and inexpensive meal. Simply add soup and an appetizer for a filling, balanced dinner.*

▲

Check local newspapers and the tourist center for information on free concerts, festivals, street fairs, lectures, and walking tours. Also note that museums, zoos, and other attractions often have a free-admission day during the week. Always inquire as to what discounts are

available before you pay admission.

Some cities offer discounts of up to 50 percent for same-day performances and sports events. Last-minute discounts are often available at the box office.

Buses and subways in big cities may offer discounts for seniors, children, disabled, military, families, and tourists. Fare-saver booklets, which allow all-day or multiple-day discounts, are often available. Ask at the visitor center or call the public transit office direct.

If you need to continue your ride on another bus or train, ask about free or low-price transfers.

At the hotel, save money by finding a nearby restaurant, laundromat, hairdresser, dry cleaner, and so on. In-house services are expensive.

Instead of calling from your room, use your telephone calling card at a public phone. Hotels charge a premium for telephone calls.

Avoid eating at hotels or airports, where food is often overpriced. Hotel room service is also expensive, with an extra charge usually added to the restaurant's already inflated prices. In-room minibars are convenient but exorbitant. Find, instead, a nearby supermarket or convenience store where you can buy snacks and drinks to keep in the room. (See also *Good Food for the Road*, pp.32–33.)

Be Safe and Secure

Don't let an unexpected—and unwelcome—situation ruin your vacation. First, take steps to protect your home while you're away. Then, whether you're on the highway or at the airport, in a hotel or camping out, keep yourself and your belongings safe by anticipating potential dangers, following commonsense preventive measures, and being prepared to handle a problem if one does occur.

Don't Fall for Travel Scams

Personal safety starts even before you leave home. Be alert to travel scams.

Incidents of postcard and phone-call "prizes" and "bargains," in which the caller asks for your credit card number to "verify your prize" or to "send a voucher," are taking place every day. Never give your credit card number to someone you don't know. If you haven't initiated the contact, don't respond.

Remember: If it seems too good to be true, it probably is. There are more than enough travel agents and well-known organizations to help you plan your trip. Confine your business dealings to these professionals, along with state tourist boards and other reputable organizations.

Trust your instincts. If you feel that a particular travel-service provider may not be dealing with you in good faith, contact the Better Business Bureau or the Society of American Travel Agents to check on the company or agency.

Burglar-Proof Your House

Unless someone will be house-sitting for you while you're away, you'll need to take steps to burglar-proof your home before you leave.

• Let your immediate neighbors and the local police know the exact dates that you'll be away.

• Never leave a message on your answering machine announcing the fact that you're out of town.

• Lock all doors and windows on all floors.

• Lock the garage and unplug the garage door opener.

• Have a friend or relative stop in every few days to check the house. Make sure that the person has a copy of your itinerary, along with phone numbers where you can be reached in case of emergency.

• Don't make your vacation plans known to more people than necessary.

• Leave drapes and curtains open so that the house doesn't look vacant. This will also make it easier for the neighbors to check for problems.

• Have a neighbor collect your mail and newspapers every day, or have all deliveries stopped.

• Ask a neighbor to put out garbage cans or bags for pickup in front of your house on collection day.

• Have someone mow and water the lawn or shovel snow from paths.

• Have a friend or neighbor park his car in your driveway on occasion.

• Never hide extra house keys anywhere outside the house.

• Set timers on indoor and outdoor lights and radios for random intervals.

• Keep valuables out of sight, preferably under lock and key.

Watch Your Luggage

Lost or stolen luggage can spoil a vacation faster than almost any-

thing. (See *What to Carry in Transit,* on p.19, for a list of vital documents and personal items that should be kept on your person or in a carry-on bag to minimize inconvenience if you become separated from your luggage.) You can increase the chances of your bags staying with you throughout your trip by following a few simple steps:

• Tag all luggage inside and out with your name, address, and telephone number (use a business address on the outside tag to avoid announcing an empty house to potential thieves) and your destination address. Put a copy of your itinerary in each bag. If you're checking luggage at the airport, make sure the agent attaches the correct destination tag to all your bags.

• Remove all old tags and loose straps (keep the straps in a handy place for reattachment when you retrieve your bags). Attach a brightly colored ribbon to the handle, or mark an X in bright adhesive tape on both sides of the luggage, to make it stand out for easy retrieval. Wrap an elastic strap around the width of your bags to hold them intact during handling and to discourage unauthorized opening.

• Never leave luggage unattended, and count your bags every time you get off a train or out of a taxi.

If your luggage is lost at the airport or bus or train station, make sure to report the problem before you leave the premises, and get a copy of the claim you've filed.

Safeguard Your Cards and Cash

You may want to rely on credit cards and traveler's checks instead of cash when you travel. Knowing that your money can be replaced in

case of theft will save you worry. Carry enough cash, however, to get through an emergency, and have plenty of small bills on hand for tips, tolls, snacks, and inexpensive purchases. Bring traveler's checks in small denominations.

Keep a list of their numbers with you in a separate location from the checks, and leave another copy at home. Notify the issuer at once of loss or theft.

Credit card companies offer protection if you've bought faulty goods or services and in some instances will reimburse you after a theft. Make a record of your credit card numbers and the telephone numbers of the issuers (get these from your monthly statements). Keep one copy at home and one copy with you in a safe place separate from your cards.

If your cards are stolen, call each credit card office immediately and report the loss. You won't be held responsible for charges made after you notify the company.

Always ask for your receipt carbons. Rip up and discard the carbons yourself to prevent your credit card numbers from being stolen.

When using a telephone calling card at a pay phone, try to avoid having to read your card number aloud. Thieves linger at public phones in airports and other busy public areas to overhear and steal card numbers. Look for phones that can be activated by sliding your card through.

Consider Travel Insurance

If you'll be making large prepayments on a tour or other travel service, consider taking out trip-cancellation insurance before you leave home. It will protect you against the possible loss of down payments if you have to cancel your plans because of an emergency. Buy directly from an insurance company —not from the tour operator or travel agency. (If the operator or agency goes under, you may not be covered for your loss.)

Not all travel insurance policies offer the same coverage, so be sure to carefully check the small print. Some insurance policies cover only a portion of your expenses (land travel but not airfare, for example). If applicable, make certain that the policy doesn't disqualify the holder for a medical emergency because of any preexisting conditions.

Be sure to pay by credit card. If a dispute over coverage should arise, your card issuer may be able to help you recover at least some of your money.

When You're Traveling by Car

Don't let a problem with the car—or a mishap on the road— cause you injury or loss of precious vacation time.

• Have the car checked thoroughly a week or two before you leave: brakes, headlights, taillights, belts, hoses, tires and spare tire, wipers, and fluid levels. Make sure the air-conditioning and heater are in working order.

• Carry spare car keys, a driver's license for each driver, insurance and registration cards, and your road-service membership card. Pack emergency tools and supplies in the trunk. (See also *Car Emergency Checklist*, p.17.)

• If you plan to be driving a rented vehicle or an RV that you haven't driven in a while, become familiar with the dashboard and go for a practice drive before starting out on your trip.

• Take short breaks at regular intervals to stretch and get fresh air. Pull over immediately if you become drowsy while driving and get out and stretch your legs for a few minutes. If possible, have another driver take over. When you resume driving, keep the windows open and sing along with a lively music station on the radio to keep yourself alert.

• Never drive if you have been drinking or have taken any medication that makes you feel drowsy.

• Make sure all passengers are wearing seat and shoulder belts whenever the vehicle is in motion. Infants and small children should always travel in car safety seats.

• Don't leave any heavy or sharp objects loose in the car, where they could become dangerous in a sudden stop or an accident. Also keep items off the dashboard and rear window ledge.

• Keep at least three car lengths away from the car ahead of you. Always stay within the speed limit.

• If at all possible, avoid driving in poor weather conditions.

IF YOUR CAR BREAKS DOWN

Be aware that scams are sometimes played out on motorists with no car problems. Older drivers and women traveling alone may be especially vulnerable. Carjackers may hit a car from behind, then pull a weapon when the driver gets out of the car. If you're suspicious, remain in your car and motion the other driver to follow you to a more public area, a police station, or a fire station.

Motorists posing as good Samaritans have also been known to falsely inform a driver that his tailpipe is smoking and to encourage him to pull over right away. You should be on your guard in such a situation, especially if the motorist pulls over to offer "help." Again, wait until you can get to a service station or some other populated area before you get out of the car to investigate the problem.

In the event that you do experience car trouble, it's important to remember certain *precautions. Take the following steps to ensure that you get help safely:*

■ If possible, drive far enough to pull off on a well-lit, well-traveled shoulder. Even if you have a flat tire, drive until you reach a safe area before you change it.

■ Turn off the ignition and turn on the hazard flashers.

■ Put flares behind the car to alert other drivers.

■ Raise the hood and place a "Call Police" sign in the window or tie a white cloth to the car radio antenna. If someone offers to help, roll down your window just enough to ask him or her to call the police.

■ Stay inside the car with the doors locked until a police car or towing service arrives. If the car is in the roadway, stand well away from it.

■ Lean on the horn if you find yourself in a threatening situation.

Rearrange your itinerary if necessary.

• Slow down in rain as well as snow, ice, and fog. When road oil mixes with rainwater, it can create a dangerous slick.

• Test your brakes after driving through a deep puddle.

• If you are driving in fog, rain, or snow, turn your headlights on. Use low beams in fog. Some states also require motorists to turn on headlights whenever windshield wipers are on.

• Don't risk a chain-reaction pileup in a heavy fog, even if you think that you've slowed down enough. Pull well off the shoulder, turn the flashers on, and wait for the fog to lift.

• Always drive with your doors locked and windows almost all the way up.

• Never pick up hitchhikers.

• If you spot someone with car trouble, don't get out to help. Go to a phone and call the police.

• If you are pulled over by the police, make sure you see the officer's badge and identification papers before unlocking your door or rolling down the window. (See also *If Your Car Breaks Down*, p.25.)

• Park in well-lit, well-traveled areas. (Backing into a parking space may make out-of-state plates less obvious.)

• When you leave the car, lock the doors, close the windows, and lock maps, cameras, and valuables in the trunk. Never leave keys in an unattended car.

Pick Lodgings With Care

A bargain motel isn't worth the savings if your security is compromised. Book a hotel or motel in a safe area, and take the following precautions to protect yourself and your belongings during your stay:

• When you arrive, ask to see your room before registering. It's easier to change rooms before your luggage has been delivered and the check-in formalities have been completed.

• If your room is located on an isolated corridor, ask to have it changed. Avoid street-level rooms. If you do have to stay in one, keep the window drapes closed. Make sure that the windows have locks, that the doors have peepholes and multiple locks, and that a front desk clerk is on duty 24 hours a day.

• Check that the door and window locks and the telephone are in working order and that there is a working smoke detector in the room. Find out where the nearest fire exit is located. (See also *In Case of a Hotel Fire*, p.27.)

• Store your valuables in the hotel safe. (Better yet, don't bring valuables along on your trip.) Carry your room key with you at all times; most motel

and hotel doors lock automatically.

• If someone walks by as you're about to unlock your door, wait until they pass.

▼

HOW CAN I FEEL SAFER IN A BIG CITY?

☆ *Avoid risky or deserted areas, especially at night. Travel in a group in busy, well-lighted areas.*

☆ *City driving can be harrowing. Opt for public transportation or taxis to get around, and take taxis at night. If you must drive, keep the car doors locked and the windows rolled up.*

☆ *Have small bills handy to avoid having to open your wallet or purse in public places.*

☆ *Don't wear expensive-looking jewelry, especially necklaces.*

☆ *Move purposefully; don't look like a tourist. Study a map and know where you're going before leaving the hotel.*

☆ *Women should carry purses around their neck and over one shoulder; men should carry their wallet in a front pocket, not a hip pocket. Consider wearing a money belt or waist pouch.*

☆ *Be especially watchful of your wallet in crowds and when exiting buses and trains.*

☆ *Be wary of street scams, such as sidewalk card games and "deals" on "expensive" watches.*

☆ *Look around you before using an automated teller machine. Pass it up if you are at all uncomfortable about your safety.*

▲

• If you go out for a while, leave the TV on

and the curtains closed. Don't put the sign on the door for the maid to clean up. If your room has already been cleaned before you go out, hang the "Do Not Disturb" sign on the door.

• Keep the name, address, and telephone number of the places you've stayed in case you happen to leave something behind.

Keep a Close Eye on Children

If you'll be traveling with children, make sure that they're protected against potential dangers.

• Pin a card in the child's pocket with the child's name, your name and address, and the telephone number of your hotel.

• Never leave children unattended, even in rest rooms.

• Instruct children on what to do if they become separated from you. Teach them how to identify police officers and to go to them if they get lost or need help.

• When you're walking on city streets, hold small children by the hand at all times.

• Always use a car safety seat for infants and small children. If you're flying, bring an airline-approved child seat and call the airline ahead of time to notify it that you will be using the seat.

• Dress small children in flame-resistant nightclothes.

• Leave a night-light on for the child's com-

fort in strange surroundings and to prevent falls.

Be Alert If You're Traveling Alone

Solo travelers should heed all of the precautions recommended in this chapter and exercise an even greater degree of caution in certain circumstances, to ensure a safe and enjoyable trip.

• Plan your itinerary as specifically as possible and leave a copy with a relative or friend. Also arrange for your rental car or shuttle service at your destination before you leave home.

• If you're flying, leave your car in a well-lit parking area at the airport, or have someone drop you off.

• If you'll be driving to your

motel or hotel, call ahead and ask for exact routing on well-lit, well-traveled roads. Keep the gas tank more than half full so that you don't have to stop for gas after sundown. If you do need to make a rest stop at night, choose a well-lit, populated service station or rest area. Try to park where your car can easily be seen.

• When you arrive at the hotel, be alert to anyone lingering in the lobby with the intent of listening while you check in. Should anyone overhear your room number, you can ask to have it changed.

• If you order room service, meet and tip the waiter or bellhop in the corridor. Never open your door before checking through the peephole to confirm it's someone you know or a service you ordered. If you didn't order anything, call the desk clerk and ask if he or she sent hotel staff to your room.

• Women should use discretion in getting into an elevator with a sole male occupant. If you become uneasy once inside, push the button for the next floor and get out.

• At night, take taxis for safe, easy transportation. When you return, ask the driver to wait until you have gone inside. Have your key in hand before you arrive at your room to avoid fumbling through your handbag at the door.

• If you must drive at night, park in a visible, lighted place. Look around before getting out of the car. Have your car keys ready when returning to the car, and glance under the car and in the backseat before getting in.

• If someone appears to be following you when you're walking to your car, walk past it to find help.

• Move with confidence and keep alert when walking on the street. If you sense you're being followed, do an about-face, cross the street, or duck into a store.

• Carry a whistle and don't hesitate to use it or to scream if you find yourself in a threatening situation.

Be a Smart Camper

When camping, be sure to follow these safety guidelines:

• Don't hike, raft, or swim by yourself. Use the buddy system.

• Unless you're using bottled water, boil all water for drinking and cooking or use water-purification tablets. Even the clearest-looking water can carry contaminants.

• Obtain permits whenever required at visitor centers, headquarters, or ranger stations.

• Pick up and follow safety instructions available at park entrances. Ask a ranger if you have any questions.

• Wild animals are unpredictable and should be viewed only from a distance. Never attempt to feed a wild animal.

• Rabies is becoming an increasing menace. Avoid any animal that appears to be acting strangely and report it to a ranger.

• Take protective measures to prevent Lyme disease and avoid snake and insect bites and poisonous plants. (See *If You Need First Aid*, p.31.)

• Keep campsites clean. Never leave food or garbage out

where it can attract bears and other animals. Store food in containers provided by the park or in your vehicles with the windows closed, or hang food from poles or from a tree at least 50 yards from the campsite. Pack up all trash.

• Stay on trails.

• Never leave campfires unattended. Obey all fire regulations.

• Be prepared for any sudden changes in the weather.

• Carry a topographic map or nautical chart and plenty of food and water.

• Keep well hydrated in hot weather, and slow your pace in high altitudes.

• Carry a light or wear reflective clothing when walking near a road at night.

• Wear a whistle at all times. If you become lost, stay in one place and blow on the whistle to alert others to your position. Children especially should be taught to stay in one place until they are found.

• Keep valuables locked up and out of sight in the trunk of your vehicle when you leave the immediate campsite area.

• Don't wash your dishes in lakes or

streams; harmful bacteria may be present.

Be Safe When You Swim

Most water-related accidents are easily avoidable. Even if you're a strong swimmer, be cautious and use common sense:

• Never leave children unattended in or near pools, lakes, or other water. A small child can drown in just a few inches of water in a matter of minutes. Children and nonswimmers should always wear life jackets or some other flotation device.

• Never swim alone, and wait an hour or so after eating before swimming to avoid cramping.

• Natural lakes and swimming holes are likely to be colder than expected, even in summer. Always check the water temperature and depth before jumping in, and make sure there are no rocks or hidden objects underneath the surface.

• At the beach, obey all warning signs and enter the water only when there is a lifeguard on duty. Undertows and polluted water can pose unseen dangers. In case of lightning, get out of the water and off the beach immediately.

• Limit your exposure to the sun and apply sunscreen or wear a hat to avoid a painful sunburn. (See *If You Need First Aid*, p.30.)

IN CASE OF A HOTEL FIRE

■ If you smell smoke or hear a fire alarm, call the front desk or 911.

■ Go to the door of your room. If it feels cool, open it carefully. If the hallway is clear, proceed to the fire exit and walk down the fire stairs to the ground level.

■ If smoke conditions worsen as you go down the stairs, walk up to a higher floor and wait for help to arrive. Never under any circumstances use an elevator during a fire.

■ If your room door is hot, stay inside. Stuff wet sheets or towels under the door, and hang a sheet out the window to alert firefighters.

■ If smoke enters the room, crouch low and drape a sheet or towel over your head in front of a slightly opened window.

■ If the windows do not open, avoid breaking the glass unless the smoke becomes thick. An open window draws more smoke into the room.

Stay Healthy and Hearty

G ood health is as important as ever when you're on the road. Don't let a medical emergency or something as simple as a sunburn or an upset stomach turn your dream vacation into a trip to forget. Instead, take the following precautions to keep everyone feeling shipshape. If a problem does occur, refer to the traveler's first-aid chart in this chapter as a first step.

Check Your Health Insurance

Before leaving home, check with your health insurance company to make sure that your policy is up to date and that you'll be covered during your trip: remember that some policies have geographical and other restrictions.

Carry your insurance card and the telephone number of your insurance company with you.

If You Have Health Problems

If you have a serious or chronic medical condition, talk with your doctor before you leave home. Ask about any special precautions you may need to take, such as wearing a medical-alert tag for certain conditions or carrying a short medical record.

If you have a heart condition, always carry a copy of a recent electrocardiogram.

Be a Mover and a Shaker

Don't take the start of your vacation as your cue to stop exercising. Physical activity will help counteract the stress of traveling, speed your recovery from jet lag, loosen up stiff muscles after sitting in an airplane or an automobile, and give your energy level a boost.

These days most hotels and motels have pools, and many have gyms and other fitness facilities. Depending on the kind of exercise you prefer, find out if a hotel has tennis courts, jogging paths, exercise classes, or a health club or sauna.

Take advantage of your hotel gym whenever you have the time. And go for a swim whenever you can: fitness experts consider swimming to be the best all-around exercise you can do.

You can also exercise right in your hotel room with no equipment at all. Jumping rope burns more calories than jogging, and calisthenic exercises can be done at any time; just fold a bath towel or a blanket to use as a cushion.

Walking is one of the best forms of exercise, and even walking slowly while taking in the sights does your body good (see *Take Some Walking Tours,* p.36). If you want to take a stroll a few blocks from your hotel and back, ask the desk clerk to recommend a route that's in a safe neighborhood and is not too congested.

Another good way to exercise is to climb the hotel stairs. This will raise your heart rate within a few minutes, even at a moderate pace. Just be sure to warm up first and to cool down afterward.

▼

HOW CAN I SOOTHE MY ACHING FEET?

☆ *Start by wearing comfortable shoes. Opt for sneakers or sturdy walking shoes with thick rubber soles and built-in arch support. Don't wear new shoes; go with a pair that's already broken in.*

☆ *Bring along two pairs of comfortable shoes; let one pair air out while you're wearing the other.*

☆ *Avoid standing in place for a long time.*

☆ *At the end of the day, dissolve Epsom salts in cool water and give your feet a 10-minute soak. Then elevate your feet (above your hips) for a few more minutes.*

▲

However you choose to exercise, try to do 10 minutes of gentle stretching in your room at the end of a full day of activity.

Prevent an Aching Back

Sitting for a long time in a car or plane is difficult enough for people without a history of back trouble. But if you suffer from chronic back pain, an uncomfortable seat can make it worse.

Here are some tips to keep you from getting "down in the back" when you travel:

• Adjust your seat in a car, plane, train, or bus until you feel support for your lower back. Or slip a small pillow or a rolled-up towel between your lower spine and the seat back.

• Get up and walk around in an airplane or train. When you're driving, stop and take a break now and then.

• Luggage with built-in wheels and a slide-out handle is easier on your back. If you prefer to tote a duffel bag instead of a suitcase, look for one equipped with wheels.

• When you carry luggage, be sure to balance and divide it equally in both hands. If you have one heavy bag, frequently switch it from one hand to the other.

• If you plan to sleep on plane, bus, or train rides, prop a large pillow against the window to keep your head in an upright position; dropping your head forward can give you pain in the upper back and shoulders.

- If you drive in cruise control when traveling long distances, you'll be able to more easily shift your weight and move around to alternate your back position.
- Make sure your car seat is positioned so that your arms and shoulders are relaxed and comfortable as you maneuver the steering wheel.

If You're Going by Plane

- Inform the airline when making your reservations whether any traveler has special physical or dietary needs, such as a low-salt, low-fat, or vegetarian meal.
- Ask for a seat in the middle of the plane if you're prone to motion sickness.
- Don't sit for long periods of time. Get up, stretch, and take a walk about the cabin.
- Eat light, drink plenty of liquids (airplane air is dehydrating), and keep any intake of alcoholic beverages moderate.
- Adults and older children can ease ear pain on takeoff and landing by chewing gum. Young children should suck on a pacifier or a bottle.
- If you have a cold or a sinus infection and cannot avoid flying, take a decongestant before the flight.
- Remember to keep all your prescription medications with you;

never check them with your luggage.
- Take copies of your prescriptions on your trip, and keep all medications in their original, labeled bottles to avoid mix-ups.
- If you suffer from allergies and will be staying in a hotel, ask for a nonsmoking room, available at no extra charge. "Environmentally clean" rooms, equipped with air and water filters, are now available at some hotels for an extra charge.

Fend Off Food Poisoning

The possibility of food poisoning increases when you're on the road and have to rely on portable coolers and roadside restaurants to keep and handle food safely. Follow these tips to avoid food poisoning:

- If there is any question about a food's freshness, don't eat it.
- If you carry a portable cooler in your car, follow safe refrigeration methods (see *Choose the Right Cooler*, p.33).
- Avoid restaurants that are near-empty at dining hours and that look as if they've seen their day.
- Always wash your hands with soap and hot water when handling food and just before eating.
- Specify that you want only well-done meat and poultry.
- Avoid oysters, clams, and other shell-

▼

WHAT'S THE BEST WAY TO COPE WITH JET LAG?

☆ *Get a good night's sleep before the flight.*

☆ *It's important to avoid alcohol, caffeine, and smoking before and during the flight.*

☆ *If possible, travel during your normal waking hours; avoid late-night flights.*

☆ *When you board the plane, set your watch to the time at your destination so that you'll adjust to the new hour.*

☆ *Eat light and drink plenty of fluids before and during the flight.*

☆ *If you're flying west, try to stay outside for several hours in the late afternoon of your arrival. Sunlight will help your body adjust to the new time zone.*

☆ *If you're flying east, get outside early during the first morning in your new location, and avoid late-afternoon exposure to sunlight.*

☆ *When you arrive at your destination, don't give in to the temptation to take a nap or go to bed early. Adjust your sleeping and eating to local time and get a full night's sleep.*

▲

fish, which can easily become contaminated.
- If you come down with food poisoning despite the precautions you've taken, you'll recover faster if you keep your stomach empty and sip water or suck ice chips. When you start to feel better, eat easily digested foods, such as toast and plain salted crackers. If your symptoms are severe

or last for more than two days, you should see a doctor.

Keep Pets Healthy Too

Pets may be better off left at home with a friend or in a kennel. Ask your vet and other pet owners for kennel recommendations and visit the facility before deciding to leave your pet there.

Be aware that many places, including some national parks, prohibit pets. And if you plan on taking your pet on an airplane, you must reserve space in advance.

If you decide to take your pet along on your trip, the following precautions should ensure a safe and healthy holiday for both owner and pet.
- Check with your vet beforehand to make sure your pet is up-to-date with shots.
- Have the pet vaccinated against Lyme disease. If your pet will be spending any time in a kennel, have it immunized against kennel cough.
- If your pet is on medication, carry the prescription along with the medicine.
- If your dog is a long-haired breed, give it a clipping before you leave home.

Short hair makes it easier to check for fleas, ticks, cuts, and rashes. It will also allow the dog to dry faster after a swim or a walk in the rain.
- Make sure your pet wears a snug but not too tight collar with all vaccination tags, as well as a tag with your home address.
- Attach a good-quality flea collar.
- In wooded areas, check your pet often for tiny deer ticks, which can spread Lyme disease.
- Never spray an animal with an insect repellent made for humans. And never use a product—on pets or on humans—that contains more than 30 percent DEET.
- In the car, keep smaller pets confined to a well-ventilated pet carrier. Keep larger pets restricted with pet safety gates sold for car use or with pet seat belts sold at pet-supply shops.
- Never carry a pet in the back of an open pickup truck.
- Keep windows partially closed to prevent a startled pet from jumping out.
- Never leave a pet alone in a car on a hot day. The temperature can reach life-threatening levels even in the shade. Exposure to extreme cold can also endanger a pet's life.
- Feed your pet only the food it is used to, at its usual times of day. Withhold food for two to three hours before a long car trip.
- Make sure your pet has access to fresh water at all times.

If You Need First Aid

Stress, overindulgence, fatigue, exposure to sunlight, outdoor hazards, winding roads, and abrupt changes in food and water can cause vacationers to feel under the weather. Here are some of the more common problems travelers may encounter, and how best to handle them.

Motion Sickness

This is a common complaint, especially among children.

Symptoms
- Nausea
- Headache
- Heavy perspiration
- Dizziness

Prevention
- Keep your stomach empty or eat very lightly.
- Avoid alcohol, cigarettes, and caffeine; make sure no one smokes in the car.
- If you're thirsty, sip carbonated drinks or suck ice chips.
- Sit in the front seat of the car. Look out the front window and concentrate on the horizon.

- Taking Dramamine 15–30 minutes before starting out should prevent nausea but may cause drowsiness.
- Gingerroot in prescribed doses, available over the counter, is reputed to prevent motion sickness.
- Anti-motion-sickness wrist bands, available in drugstores, may help. Skin patches are also available and may prevent nausea (as with any medication, check with your doctor first).

Treatment
If you become sick, stop the car in a safe pull-off and step outside and wait until the feeling passes. Lie down for a few minutes, then try the tips given above.

Heat Exhaustion

Also called heat prostration, heat exhaustion is generally caused by overexertion in the hot sun.

Symptoms
- Headache
- Blurred vision
- Pale, clammy skin
- Nausea, vomiting
- Dizziness
- Weakness
- Sweating

Prevention
- Avoid overactivity in hot weather and during midday hours, when the sun is strongest.
- Keep cool: wear lightweight, light-colored, loose clothing and a sun hat.
- Drink lots of liquids.
- Avoid alcohol and caffeine.
- Eat light.

Treatment
- Lay the victim down in a cool place and loosen his clothing.
- Apply cool compresses.
- Have the victim sip cool salt water and eat salted crackers.

Sunburn

Ultraviolet rays can cause an uncomfortable sunburn on anyone, and even skin cancer in persons with fair skin.

Prevention
- Avoid exposure to the sun during peak hours (10 A.M.–3 P.M.).
- Limit duration of exposure at any time.
- If you take prescription medication, ask your doctor if you need to follow any further precautions or if you should avoid the sun completely. Some medicines can increase your sun sensitivity.
- Use a sunblock with an SPF (sun protection factor) rating of 15 or higher. Fair-skinned people and travelers exposed to strong sun should opt for the highest rating available. Apply sunscreen liberally and frequently to exposed skin, especially after swimming or if you perspire heavily.
- Wear waterproof sunscreen and a T-shirt when swimming.
- To protect your eyes, wear sunglasses that block ultraviolet rays.
- Shade your face with a sun hat.
- Don't wait for your skin to turn red before getting out of the sun; it usually takes a few hours for the burn to show.

Treatment
- Take a cool bath or apply cool compresses and a moisturizing lotion. Vinegar or aloe vera gel may also help soothe the burn.
- Apply burn-relief cream or spray.
- Take an aspirin.
- Do not break blisters. When they break naturally, apply an antiseptic and cover with gauze.

Stomach Upset

Stress and changes in daily habits can often cause stomach upset.

Treatment for Diarrhea
- Take one of the several over-the-counter diarrhea remedies available.
- Drink lots of bottled water and fruit juices. Avoid tap water and ice cubes made from it.
- Eat light, and avoid alcohol, spicy food, caffeine, and milk products.

Treatment for Constipation
- Drink plenty of water and fruit juice.
- Eat raw vegetables, fruits, prunes, and whole grains.
- Exercise regularly.
- If necessary, take an over-the-counter remedy.

Insect Stings & Bites

If you know you are allergic to insect bites and stings, ask your doctor for an antidote to bring with you.

Prevention
- Cover all exposed skin, including feet.

- Wear light-colored clothes; avoid florals and bright colors.
- Don't use cologne, perfume, or perfumed soaps or lotions.
- Use insect repellent, especially in the hours between dawn and dusk, when insects are at their worst.
- Keep food and garbage in tightly covered containers.

Treatment
- Remove the stinger (only a bumblebee leaves one) by scraping it out with a knife, razor blade, or fingernail. Do not squeeze or press the stinger, which could release more venom.
- Wash the bite area with soap and cold water and cover with a gauze pad.
- Apply cold compresses for swelling, which can last a few days.
- Apply calamine lotion or hydrocortisone cream to relieve itching. A dab of vinegar may also help.
- Dissolve a little baking soda in a glass of water. Dip a cloth into the solution and place on bite for 15–20 minutes.

Allergic Reactions

Symptoms of an allergic reaction to an insect sting are
- Severe swelling in any part of the body
- Coughing, wheezing
- Severe itching
- Nausea, vomiting
- Difficulty breathing
- Anxiety
- Weakness, dizziness
Get medical help immediately.

Snakebites

There are few poisonous snakes in the U.S. Consult a reference book and become familiar with what they look like.
Symptoms
- Pain
- Swelling and bruising around the bite
- Difficulty swallowing
- Nausea, vomiting
- Diarrhea
- Blurry vision
- Seizures or convulsions
- Slurred speech
Prevention
- Wear high boots and long heavyweight pants when walking in wilderness areas.

- Avoid reaching or stepping into covered or out-of-sight spots.
Treatment
- Try to kill the snake with a heavy blow to the head. Keep it for identification.
- Keep the victim calm and still and remove all jewelry close to the bite in case of swelling.
- Try to keep the bitten area below the victim's heart.
- Pour water over the snakebite and pack with ice.
- Immobilize the area with a splint.
- Get the victim to a hospital as soon as possible and take the snake carcass along. If you were not able to kill the snake, try to give a thorough description.
- If it will take more than a few hours to get help, place a constricting band of cloth or rope 2 inches above the bite— closer to the heart than the bite mark— or 2 inches above the swelling. The band should be snug but loose enough to allow you to slip your fingers under it. If the swelling spreads, move the band to keep it 2 inches above the swelling.
- If there is no swelling, loosen and retighten the band every 20 minutes.
- Give the victim fluids but NO alcohol.

Poisonous Plants

"Leaves of three, let it be." Though not all three-leaved plants or vines contain the irritating oils of poison ivy, sumac, or oak, distinguishing the different plants is not easy. Better to be safe than sorry.
Symptoms
- An intensely irritating, oozing rash and blisters (allergic victims may have a more severe response) that can develop within hours or days after even a slight brush with these plants
Prevention
- Avoid all three-leaved plants and vines. The oil found in the guilty three plants can be active year-round. Poison ivy leaves are not always red or shiny.
- Wear socks, heavy shoes, long pants, and long sleeves.
- Keep your pet on a leash and out of wooded areas.
- If you notice that you have brushed against a poisonous plant, change clothes and handle contaminated clothes with

gloves. Wash separately from your non-contaminated clothes.
- Wash the contaminated skin as soon as possible with soap and water or rubbing alcohol; then rinse.
Treatment
- Apply cool compresses and, after drying the skin thoroughly, calamine lotion or a baking soda paste.
- If jewelweed is growing nearby, crush the leaves and flowers and rub them on the affected area.
- Take an antihistamine to relieve the itch. If you have an extreme reaction, see a doctor.

Lyme Disease

This serious disease is spread by the deer tick in heavily wooded or grassy areas. It feeds on mammals, including humans, for 12–24 hours. Ticks hatch in the spring, and peak months for infection are June and July.
Symptoms
Early Stages
- Fever
- Headache
- Extreme fatigue
- Stiff neck
- A characteristic rash that looks like a bull's-eye with an expanding red circle surrounding a lighter area may develop.
Advanced Stages
- Visual disturbances
- Facial paralysis
- Tingling and numbness
- Arthritis
- Irregular heartbeat
- Seizures
Prevention
- When traveling in wooded or grassy areas, wear long pants and a long-sleeved shirt, and tuck your shirt into your pants and your pants into your socks.
- Use insect repellent containing no more than 30 percent DEET on exposed skin, and spray on pant legs and shirt sleeves.
- Check often for ticks, especially on children and pets.
Treatment
- If you do discover a tick, use tweezers to remove it, making sure that the insect's head is completely removed from your skin. Save the tick in a jar for identification and see a doctor.

Good Food for the Road

E ating healthful food is more important than ever when you're traveling. With a little planning, it's easy enough to avoid the heavy, high-fat fast foods that are the most common fare along the interstate highways. At the same time, don't forget to sample the wonderful variety of local culinary specialties as you drive from state to state.

Be Aware of Your Choices

It's not difficult to find good, healthful food when you're on the road, even when fast-food establishments seem the only restaurants in sight. Today most chains offer low-calorie dishes as an alternative to fatty hamburgers and calorie-laden French fries.

For a wider range of choices, of course, you can venture off the interstate to find good local restaurants. Many of these establishments offer a menu of the regional cuisine, which can make your trip all the more fun. Large chain cafeterias are also a good bet, offering quick service and a wide selection of hot and cold foods.

Wherever you may choose to eat when traveling, go easy on spicy or heavy foods that could give you an upset stomach or make you feel sleepy while driving.

▼
HOW CAN I GET A HEALTHY FAST-FOOD MEAL?

☆ *If you crave a hamburger, stop at a place where the meat is grilled or broiled instead of fried. In place of cheese, add lettuce and tomato.*

☆ *Make use of the salad bar, or dress a baked potato with low-calorie accompaniments.*

☆ *Skip the soda and go with milk or juice instead. If you must have a milkshake, make sure it's low in fat.*
▲

Have a Light Breakfast

You'll find it easier to get going in the morning if you start out with a satisfying but light breakfast. Eggs, toast, and jams and jellies are fine, as are low-sugar hot or cold cereals, fresh fruit, and fruit juices. But you should bypass such heavy selections as pancakes, sausage, and bacon.

Stick to Your Schedule

Travelers need to be flexible in their eating habits (as in everything else), but sticking to your normal mealtime schedule for most of your trip will help you feel your best. Follow these tips:

• Keep the same evenly spaced three-meal-a-day schedule that you have at home.

• Take healthy snacks along to avoid the temptation of vending-machine junk food at rest stops.

• Take advantage of fresh vegetables and fruits sold at roadside stands in season. (Be sure to rinse all fresh produce, just as you would at home.)

• Try to drink at least eight glasses of water a day.

• Keep babies on their regular diets at regular hours. Bring formula that doesn't need refrigeration. If you're mixing powdered formula, use bottled water.

Follow These Food Tips

• Bring your lunch with you whenever possible. You'll eat more healthfully and save time and money too. And you can stop any time you come across an attractive picnic spot.

• Avoid a high-protein lunch, especially one with red meat as the main course. Such meals can cause an afternoon slump—not an ideal condition for a driver. Try to eat a high-carbohydrate meal—pasta, for example—with a smaller portion of a high-protein food, like canned tuna or salmon, on the side. This will help keep you from getting sleepy after lunch.

• If you do eat meat, try to have it no more than once a day. Choose chicken, turkey, or fish (baked, broiled, or grilled—not fried) instead of red meat as your choice of protein.

• Whatever you eat, keep portions moderate when traveling.

• Remember that prices in restaurants are usually cheaper at lunch time; you may want to have your main meal then—but keep it light.

• Eat plenty of fruits and vegetables, raw or lightly cooked. They'll keep your hunger satisfied without weighing you down.

• If you find yourself hungry for a snack along the road, avoid such sugary foods as cookies and doughnuts and have bananas or other fruits instead.

Enjoy Regional Cooking

One of the joys of travel is sampling local cuisine from state to state. America's classic dishes are noted for their wide-ranging flavors. Most of the time you'll want to eat the food you're used to, but trying new things can help make your trip more interesting and will introduce you to new pleasures.

Try the specialties in any part of the country: clam chowder, Boston baked beans, and Indian pudding are common in New England; farther south, you can sample crab cakes in Maryland, Smithfield ham in Virginia, and barbecued pork and Savannah red rice from the Carolinas to Georgia.

In the Deep South, Hoppin' John (rice

and black-eyed peas), hush puppies, and pecan pie are still served, and Louisiana is famous for its spicy Cajun dishes.

Try barbecued brisket or the fabled chicken-fried steak in Texas, blue corn tortillas in the Southwest, and cioppino, a hearty seafood stew, in California. In the Pacific Northwest, succulent salmon dishes are the favored fare.

In the Midwest, look for classic American pies: apple and lemon meringue, still made from scratch.

Prevent Food Contamination

Bacteria and other microscopic pests can develop quickly in summer temperatures and create mild to serious stomach upset (see *Fend Off Food Poisoning*, p.29). Since contaminated food will not necessarily smell, look, or taste different, it is critical to take special precautions when grilling, picnicking, or carrying food in the car.

Rely mainly on foods that do not require refrigeration. Unopened canned food can be carried safely without refrigeration; but once a can is opened, it must be refrigerated in a plastic container or discarded if there are any leftovers. The easiest solution is to prepare only as much food as will be needed for each meal.

Fish, meat, poultry, eggs, and dairy prod-

ucts must be refrigerated at temperatures below 40° F. Try to purchase these foods on a day-by-day basis as needed, and store them in a properly operated cooler.

If you make or purchase hot foods that you plan to eat later, wrap them in aluminum foil or a heavy towel and carry them in a styrofoam carrier that keeps the food at no less than 140° F. *Grill safety.* There are a few rules you should follow if you're cooking outdoors on a grill. First, clean the surface of the grill thoroughly. Keep the grill away from dry grasses and bushes. Make sure it is secure so it can't topple over, and try to keep it sheltered from the wind.

Extinguish coals thoroughly and dispose of ashes safely. *Safe food handling.* Wash your hands frequently when handling food, being especially careful with raw meats.

Keep foods cold or hot—not warm—and thaw meat in a refrigerator or cooler, not at room temperature.

Do not partially cook meat and then finish grilling later. And cook the meat until no pink remains in the center.

Do not place cooked meat back on the plate that was used to hold the raw meat. Use a fresh plate or wash the original plate thoroughly before reusing. The same rule goes for utensils.

When serving food, never set it out for longer than one hour unless the plates of food are sitting on ice.

If you have food left over after a meal, don't save it unless you have a proper cooler to keep it in.

Choose the Right Cooler

Coolers are always handy to have along on a trip—but make sure you choose the safest and most convenient kind.

When purchasing a chest, look for one that has sturdy handles and hinges and a latch that closes securely. It should have a drain on one side

with an attachable cap. A removable freezer pack that attaches to the inside cover is a plus.

Choose a cooler that's easy to carry, and consider what size will best suit the type of trip you most often take. Avoid ending up with one that's too large to be convenient or too small to be practical.

To keep your food fresh while traveling, follow these tips.

• Wash the cooler with soap and water before filling it to remove any bacteria.

• Fill the cooler with ice half an hour before packing it.

• Pack the food just before you leave home, or pack fresh cold food each morning on the road.

• Pack foods that have been well refrigerated, and try to carry only the edibles and drinks you will need for one to two days. While a quality insulated cooler, used according to the product's instructions, should store food safely for a few days, your best

bet is to refill the cooler each day.

• Take care to open the chest as infrequently as possible.

• Add plenty of fresh ice every one to two days, if possible, though a well-insulated chest can keep ice up to four days.

• Frozen bottles or boxes of juice will provide added cooling, as well as refreshing cold drinks.

• Fill a plastic milk jug with water, leaving a little room for expansion, and freeze overnight. Use it as an ice pack, then as cool drinking water.

• Keep your cooler in the passenger section of the car, not in the trunk.

• Outside the car, place the cooler out of direct sun, in a shady spot, if possible.

Spare the Car and Driver

Don't let a vacation become an endurance test for the driver. Once you've planned your itinerary, consider alternate methods of transportation—trains, buses, boats, ferries—to reduce driving distances or to get off the road for a day. This will give the driver a deserved break, and everyone will appreciate the change of pace.

Consider a Rental Car

You may have a more relaxing vacation if you simply leave your car behind and rent one when you reach your destination. Consider the time- and money-saving value of taking a train, plane, bus, or boat—and then renting a car for sight-seeing. Many airlines have fly/drive packages that include a discounted car-rental tie-in.

If you're traveling to another city before you rent a car, take a taxi or public transportation to the airport or station in your hometown, and leave your own car at home; this will save you the cost of parking fees that accumulate at the airport or train station while you're away on your trip. Public transit often leaves you right at the terminal's door, saving you the inconvenience of having to park and carry luggage from the lot to the terminal.

Alternatives to Car Travel

Then again, you may decide to do without a car altogether. Many people enjoy their trips more if they go by bus, motorcoach, or train.

Buses. National bus lines link all major and many smaller cities in the U.S., including such popular tourist attractions as parks, zoos, theme parks, resorts, and historic sites. A wide range of discounted rates, packages, and passes is available;

check with the individual bus lines or your travel agent.

For long-distance bus rides, choose a recognized carrier and check that the bus company is properly licensed. Be sure to ask about on-board rest rooms, rest stops, air-conditioning, and food service.

Motorcoach tours. Motorcoach companies offer scenic and package tours—which include hotels and restaurants—as well as resort and special-

interest destinations.

Tour buses are generally more comfortable than public transit buses, with softer seats and more leg room.

In major cities, these vehicles can be an inexpensive, sociable, and relaxing way to spend a few hours sight-seeing and becoming familiar with the city's layout.

Trains. The timeless appeal of a train ride, with changing views and on-board amenities, endures. And it's one travel alternative that children are guaranteed to enjoy.

Amtrak, the national passenger railroad system, offers a wide variety of tours and

customized, complete travel packages to many of the country's most popular vacation destinations, including four of America's national parks: the Grand Canyon, Yosemite, Yellowstone, and Glacier.

Amtrak's "All Aboard America" program offers discounted regional round-trip fares for tickets that are good for up to a year. They allow you up to 45 days of travel with three stopovers within designated regions.

Another convenience is the east coast Auto Train, which wisks you and your car from New York City or Washington, D.C., to Orlando, Florida.

Amtrak also offers shorter rides throughout the eastern states; some include jaunts on restored trolleys.

Rides on restored historic or reproduction railcars are a fun way to get off the road for a few hours and enjoy a nostalgic trip past scenic and historic sites. Most rides are offered only in season (usually April–October or Memorial Day–Labor Day). Ask the state tourist board (see p. 333 for details).

Finally, don't delay. Many of the discounted seats fill up quickly, so try to secure a reservation as soon as possible.

▼

HOW CAN I MAKE A LONG CAR TRIP MORE COMFORTABLE?

☆ *Travel on weekdays, when traffic is lighter. Avoid driving in and around large cities at commuting hours (usually 7–9 A.M., 4–6 P.M.).*

☆ *Make sure that the driver takes frequent breaks—and don't just switch drivers, but walk around and stretch first.*

☆ *Break for train, bus, and boat tours.*

☆ *Be flexible about your schedule and itinerary so that bad weather doesn't ruin your good time.*

▲

Take a Break From Driving

Call tourist boards (see p.333) or your travel agent to find out if scenic or tour trains, buses, boats, or other diversions are available at your destination. If so, stop at the visitor center when you arrive and confirm the routes, rates, and schedules.

Many national parks have buses or trams, complete with observation platforms, that tour the park. These vehicles reduce pollution and noise, relieve traffic congestion, and give all the riders a shared opportunity to enjoy the sights.

In urban areas, put your car in a parking garage and use public transportation. Buses and rapid transit systems link major areas of a city efficiently and inexpensively.

Take a Scenic Boat Ride

There are scores of boat rides, lasting from an hour or two to all day or longer, that will get you off the highway for an enjoyable trip through scenic waters and, in many cases, take you to some important historic sites. Many boat tours serve meals or offer theme cruises.

Glass-bottom-boat rides let you view exotic, multicolored fish swimming in the crystal-clear waters below.

Following is a sampling of some of the best boat trips in the country.

Arizona. Ride a steam paddle wheeler on Lake Powell.

California. Lake Tahoe Cruises runs stern-wheeler cruises.

Take a harbor tour in Long Beach or cruise from Long Beach to Catalina Island.

Spend a few hours whale-watching on one of many excursion boats along the coast.

Florida. Sea Escape operates one-day cruises from Miami or Fort Lauderdale.

Georgia. The *Magnolia* paddle wheeler travels the Savannah River on narrated historic tours and dinner cruises.

Travel through the Okefenokee Swamp National Wildlife Refuge via canoes or motorboats.

Illinois. Riverboats ply the Sangamon River north of Lincoln's New Salem State

Historic Site near Petersburg.

Louisiana. In New Orleans take the ferry across the Mississippi from Canal Street Wharf to Algiers.

Cruise the Mississippi and bayou from New Orleans on the *Voyageur.*

Week-long trips with a choice of itineraries are offered on the historic riverboat *Delta Queen* or the newer *Mississippi Queen*—the largest steamboat ever built. Board in New Orleans, Pittsburgh, Memphis, St. Paul, and other cities.

Massachusetts. The Massachusetts Steamship Authority operates ferries from Plymouth to Provincetown, and to Martha's Vineyard and Nantucket.

Take a day trip from Boston along the Cape Cod shore to Provincetown.

Go whale-watching on one of the excursions offered along the coast.

Missouri. The Belle of St. Louis paddle wheeler cruises the Mississippi River.

New York. Take scenic trips on the St. Lawrence River from Alexandria Bay on Empire Boat Tours.

From New York City, board the Circle Line for a boat cruise around Manhattan.

Oregon. From Gold Beach, ride jet boats on the Rogue River.

South Carolina. The only way to visit historic Fort Sumter is via the Fort Sumter Tours boat, with 2 1/4-hour cruises, including an hour-long stop at Fort Sumter National Monument.

Tennessee. A riverboat company in Nashville offers sight-seeing and dinner cruises on the Cumberland River.

You can see Chattanooga's Civil War battlefields, museums, and aquarium while riding the *Southern Belle* stern-wheeler steamboat on the Tennessee River.

Vermont. On Lake Champlain take the *Spirit of Ethan Allen* stern-wheeler.

Virginia. The *Carrie B*, a reproduction of a Mississippi riverboat, cruises to the site of the famous Civil War battle between the ironclads *Monitor* and *Merrimac.*

Island Cruises gives a wildlife safari boat tour through the Chincoteague National Wildlife Refuge.

Washington. From Seattle, take the Washington State ferry to British Columbia.

Wisconsin. From Wisconsin Dells, tours offer short trips with sight-seeing stops.

Enjoy a Trip by Train

Many destinations operate rail trips on restored historic or reproduction railcars. Riding the rails can be a fun, nostalgic way to take a break from driving and at the same time visit sites that are not accessible by car. Most rides are only offered seasonally (usually April–October or Memorial Day–Labor Day). For more information, write or call the state tourist board. Following is a sampling of some of the country's most popular rail trips:

Alaska. In Skagway: Alaska Railroad excursions, including White Pass and Yukon Route from Skagway to Fraser.

Arizona. From Williams: the Grand Canyon Railroad, crossing plains and forests to canyon rim.

California. From Fish Camp: the Yosemite Mountain–Sugar Pine Railroad in Sierra National Forest.

CAR TRAVEL WITH CHILDREN

Children have a difficult time being cooped up in a car for long periods of time. Take the following steps to make their ride as comfortable as possible.

■ Stop at sights that will be interesting to the child and stay for periods of time that will hold the child's interest.

■ Make frequent rest stops and allow children play time at the stops so that they can expend some of their energy.

■ Make sure the child has a bag of toys for in-car amusement.

■ If there is more than one child, try to alternate their seats regularly so

that no one feels cheated.

■ Assign children responsibilities, such as keeping their own toys bagged or making sure their seat areas stay neat and clean.

■ Purchase convenience items that will make driving more comfortable, such as seat and back cushions, arm rests, blankets and pillows, cup and coin holders, and sun shields.

From Fort Bragg take the California Western "skunk trains."

Colorado. From Durango: the Durango to Silverton Narrow-Gauge Railroad.

Illinois. From Monticello: the Monticello Railway Museum's Wabash Depot vintage train.
From Freeport: the Silver Creek & Stephenson Railroad antique logging train.

Indiana. From the northwest corner of the state at the Monon Passenger Station: French Lick Scenic Railway.

Iowa. From Boone: the Boone and Scenic Valley Railroad, winding through the scenic Des Moines River valley.

Maryland. From Cumberland: the Western Maryland Scenic Railroad to Frostburg.

Michigan. From about 100 miles south of Grand Rapids: the Kalamazoo, Lake Shore & Chicago Railway's Wine Country Scenic Train (with stopovers for wine tastings).

Minnesota. From Duluth to Two Harbors: the North Shore Scenic Railroad, with narrated excursions along the beautiful north shore of Lake Superior.

Missouri. From Jackson: the St. Louis Iron Mountain & Southern Railway.

Nebraska. From Fremont to Nickerson: Fremont & Elkhorn Valley Railroad.

Nevada. From Virginia City: Virginia & Truckee Railroad through mining areas.

New Mexico. From Chama: Lumbres & Toltec Scenic narrow-gauge railroad to Colorado.

Ohio. From Cleveland to Akron: the Cuyahoga Valley Line Railroad, running along the Cuyahoga River.

South Dakota. From Hill City: the Black Hill Central Railroad's 1880 Train.

Texas. From Rusk: the Texas State Railroad through Rusk/Palestine State Park.

Vermont. From Bellows Falls: the *Green Mountain Flyer.*

Wisconsin. From North Freedom (northwest of Madison): The North Freedom Mid-Continent Railway Museum's steam-train ride.

Go Rafting or Canoeing

Enjoy the scenery and wildlife on an easy rafting day trip. Or rent a canoe and spend a few hours on a lake or river.
Following are some selected trips. For specific information and phone numbers, consult *Paddle*

America, a guide to trips and outfitters in all 50 states, published by Starfish Press of Washington, D.C. Another good source is *Paddler Magazine,* published in Oceanside, California. The National Association of Canoe Liveries & Outfitters (NALCO), in Butler, Kentucky, can tell you what to look for in any state.

New England. Take a touring kayak—a comfortable, stable paddle craft—on the Maine Island Trail, a series of islands along the coast. Or canoe or raft on the Allagash, Housatonic, or Connecticut rivers.

Mid-Atlantic. The Battenkill River in New York has spectacular fall foliage, covered bridges, and inns where you can dock to spend the night. In New Jersey, you can stop at parks and historic villages on the Batsto and Oswego.

Southeast. The scenic South Fork Shenandoah River, flanked by the Appalachians, offers views of wildlife and the occasional gentle rapids. In Geor-

gia, the Chattahoochee is gentle, while the Chattooga is about as rough as rivers get.

Deep South. Rent a pirogue (dugout) to explore the swamp country of the Atchafalaya Basin in Louisiana. In Mississippi, float along on placid Black Creek or Bogue Chitto River.

Midwest. Explore the beautiful Boundary Waters Canoe Area in Minnesota. In Illinois, the Kawkakee River is sparkling clean and excellent for fishing.

Southwest. The Guadalupe River cuts through the scenic Texas Hill Country with occasional mild rapids. For the brave, the Colorado River in Arizona offers some of the country's wildest white-water rafting.

West. The Russian River runs through redwood forests in California. In Oregon, the Chutes is good for flat-water canoeing and rafting. Idaho, a paradise for rafters, has more white water than any other state.

Bring Your Bicycle Along

Bring your bike along, secured in a rack on the top or trunk of the car, and take a break by enjoying an occasional bike ride in the country. Many towns have designated bicycle paths along old railway lines and defunct canals. These often follow meandering rivers and pass by historic homes.

You can always rent a bike at your destination if you don't want to take your own. Or consider joining an organization that sponsors bicycle tours and build your entire vacation around biking.

Take Some Walking Tours

A great way to explore a city is to park the car and stroll. Many cities, especially those with a concentration of historic sites, have designated trails; Boston's Freedom Trail is an example. In Washington, D.C., the Mall and Capitol Hill are best seen on foot, while in New York City a walk along Upper Fifth Avenue will give you a close-up view of grand 19th-century mansions and some of the world's greatest museums.

Many other cities, large and small, have official historic districts or charming neighborhoods that you can wander through alone or with a guide: Charleston, Savannah, and New Orleans, in the South; Chicago, Milwaukee, and the small town of Columbus, Indiana (full of buildings and churches designed by some of the world's best-known modern architects), in the Midwest; San Antonio, Austin, and Santa Fe in the Southwest; Seattle and Portland in the Northwest; and California showplaces like San Francisco and Monterey.

Amtrak Routes

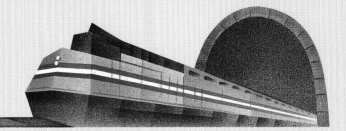

Eastern Routes

Adirondack: New York to Montreal, through the Hudson River valley, Albany, and Lake Placid region; along Lake Champlain.

Northeast Corridor: Boston to Washington, D.C., through Providence or Springfield, New Haven, New York, Philadelphia, and Baltimore.

Old Dominion: New York to Newport News, through Williamsburg with bus service to Norfolk and Virginia Beach.

Tidewater: Washington, D.C., to Newport News, with bus service to Norfolk and Virginia Beach.

Virginian: New York to Richmond.

Silver Star and Silver Meteor: New York to Tampa and Miami, through Columbia or Charleston.

Palmetto: New York to Savannah and Jacksonville.

Carolinian: New York to Raleigh and Charlotte.

Auto Train: take your car or van; Washington, D.C., to central Florida.

Empire Service: linking New York with Niagara Falls and Toronto, through Albany, Syracuse, and Buffalo.

Lake Shore Limited: linking Boston and New York with Chicago, through Albany, Syracuse, Rochester, Buffalo, Cleveland, Toledo, and South Bend; with connecting service to Detroit.

Capitol Limited: Washington, D.C., to Chicago, through Harper's Ferry, Pittsburgh, Cleveland, and Toledo.

Broadway Limited: New York to Chicago, through Trenton, Philadelphia, Harrisburg, Pittsburgh, Youngstown, and Akron.

Pennsylvanian: New York to Pittsburgh.

Cardinal: New York to Chicago, through Philadelphia, Baltimore; Washington, D.C.; Charlottesville; Charleston, West Virginia; Cincinnati; and Indianapolis.

Crescent: New York to New Orleans, through Philadelphia, Baltimore, Washington, D.C., Charlottesville, Charlotte, Atlanta, and Birmingham.

Midwestern Routes

Chicago Hub: linking Chicago with Detroit, Milwaukee, St. Louis, Kansas City, and Indianapolis.

City of New Orleans: Chicago to New Orleans, through Champaign, Memphis, and Jackson.

The River Cities: serving Kansas City, St. Louis; linking with the *City of New Orleans* in Carbondale.

Southwest Chief: Chicago to Los Angeles, through Kansas City, Topeka, Albuquerque, and Flagstaff.

California Zephyr: Chicago to Oakland/San Francisco, through Omaha, Denver, Winter Park, Glenwood Springs, Salt Lake City, Reno, and Sacramento.

Western Routes

Texas Eagle: Chicago to San Antonio and Houston through St. Louis, Dallas, and Austin; through cars from the Texas Eagle connect at San Antonio to Los Angeles via Sunset Limited.

Coast Starlight: Los Angeles to Seattle, through Santa Barbara, San Francisco/Oakland, Sacramento, Eugene, Portland, and Tacoma. Connections with San Diegan trains in Los Angeles and Santa Barbara; with Amtrak thruway bus service at Seattle to and from Vancouver, British Columbia.

Desert Wind: Chicago to Los Angeles, through Omaha, Denver, Winter Park, Glenwood Springs, Salt Lake City, and Las Vegas.

Empire Builder: Chicago to Seattle or Portland, through Milwaukee, St. Paul-Minneapolis, Glacier National Park, and Spokane; with Amtrak thruway bus service to and from Vancouver, British Columbia.

Pioneer: Chicago to Seattle, through Omaha, Denver, Cheyenne-Borie, Rock Springs, Ogden, Pocatello, Boise, Portland, Tacoma.

San Diegans: San Diego to Santa Barbara, through Orange County, Los Angeles, and north to Santa Barbara and Oxnard.

San Joaquins: San Francisco/Oakland to Bakersfield, through Martinez/Merced and Fresno; with Amtrak thruway bus service to Sacramento and Southern California.

Southern Route

Sunset Limited: Los Angeles to Miami, through Phoenix, Tucson, El Paso, San Antonio, Houston, New Orleans, Mobile, Jacksonville, and Orlando.

▼

For details, call Amtrak at 800-872-7245.

NEW ENGLAND

Autumn in Massachusetts

*H*istory *was made* on a grand scale in this small but fiercely proud region. The New World planted its roots here, in the river valleys and along the Atlantic Coast. Today, in the gentle green foothills, sparkling white church steeples reach for the sky and tidy clapboard houses sit surrounded by neat picket fences. The 13 driving tours in this section of the book take you on a pilgrimage into the past—and onto the roads that offer some of the most beautiful scenery in the country, in every season.

You'll thrill to our beginnings—in the spare meeting rooms of Boston's Faneuil Hall, where revolutionaries called out for independence, and on the venerated greens of Lexington and Concord, where they fought the good fight. But a journey into history is only one facet of a visit to Maine, New Hampshire, Vermont, Massachusetts, Rhode Island, and Connecticut. On these tours you'll explore the mighty granite peaks of the White Mountains and watch the surf pound the rock shores of Acadia National Park. You'll cross a covered bridge, stroll the Cliff Walk in Newport, and see 18th-century life at Strawbery Banke. Best of all, you'll travel to New England's tranquil little towns, with a charm rarely matched— perhaps the most appealing of all the many wonders of this lovely corner of the continent.

Acadia N.P.

Montpelier
White Mountains
Cornish
Portland
Bennington
Portsmouth
Boston
Sturbridge
Hartford
Newport
Plymouth
Mystic

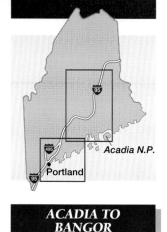

Maine

From the breathtaking beauty of the rugged coast to the history and charm of handsome ports and former fishing villages, Maine is a treasure trove of delights waiting to be explored.

ACADIA TO BANGOR

1 ACADIA NATIONAL PARK

Soaring peaks, dramatic glacier-carved valleys, clear lakes, and the sheer headlands and hidden inlets of the rock-bound coast make up one of the oldest and most beautiful national parks in America. Most of Acadia is situated on thickly forested **Mount Desert Island,** famous for its stunning scenery.

Drive or bike the 27-mile-long **Park Loop Road** on the eastern side of the island to witness many of the area's natural wonders. At pink-tinged **Sand Beach,** horseback riders share some of the park's 50 miles of carriage roads with bicyclists and hikers. At **Thunder Hole,** waves crash into a narrow chasm and explode in sound and spray. Take a break for the tradition of afternoon tea and popovers on the lawn at the park's **Jordan Pond House.** Back on Park Loop Road, you'll find it hard to miss **Cadillac Mountain**—at 1,530 feet the highest point on the U.S. Atlantic seaboard. A paved road winds to the top. Visitors standing on the summit at dawn are said to be among the first in the nation to greet the sun's rays.

Outside the park are the specialty shops, restaurants, and galleries of fashionable **Bar Harbor.** Whale-watching boats depart daily in July and August. Lovers of wildflowers will find paradise in the **Wild Gardens of Acadia,** home to some 400 native species. Nearby, the **Robert Abbe Museum of Stone Age Antiquities** offers a fascinating look at the early American Indians of this area, with prehistoric artifacts from arrowheads, baskets, and stone implements to ornaments made of bone.

▶ *Be prepared for changeable weather at Acadia. Summer temperatures can dip down to 45°F, and rain is not uncommon. And don't forget to bring your binoculars so that you can view the seals and otters offshore.*

2 ELLSWORTH

Once one of the largest lumber-shipping ports in the world, Ellsworth features a handsome business district filled with shops of every kind. Beyond the downtown area you'll find beautiful old houses lining residential streets.

The 1820's **Colonel Black Mansion,** in its restored red-brick splendor, houses an impressive collection of furnishings, carriages, and sleighs from three generations of the Black family. Visit in midsummer to see the formal garden and lilac hedges in full bloom.

For a less manicured view of nature, tour the **Stanwood Homestead Wildlife Sanctuary,** known as Birdsacre. Here pioneer ornithologist Cordelia Stanwood lived and worked, leaving a legacy that visitors, both winged and wingless, enjoy today. The

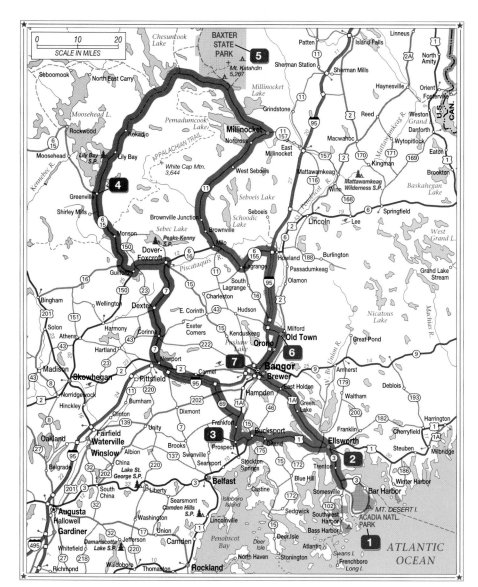

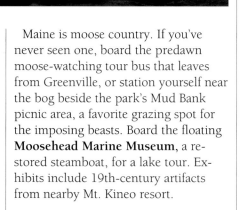

Keeping watch *over Blue Hill Bay is the 1858 Bass Harbor Head Lighthouse on Mount Desert Island in Acadia, where forested mountains give way to granite cliffs met by the sea. The park's rugged landscape was saved from development by a group of concerned summer visitors, who purchased parcels of land and donated them to the government to create what became the first National Park in the East.*

130-acre preserve, home to 100 species of birds, offers nature trails and picnic areas. The museum, housed in Stanwood's Cape Cod–style home, features country-style Victorian furniture and ornithology displays.

3 PROSPECT

Once an active fort built to protect the Penobscot River valley and Bangor from British invasion during the border disputes of the 1840's, **Fort Knox State Historic Site** measures some 250 feet by 150 feet and has granite walls eight feet thick. The 20th century slips away as you explore its underground passageways and covered alleyways. The soldiers' quarters, batteries, powder magazines, and a bakery are open to the public. In summer history buffs reenact a Civil War muster.

4 GREENVILLE

On the south end of Moosehead Lake, Maine's largest, Greenville is a gateway to a watery paradise. From here canoeists and campers explore the lake, where 420 miles of shorefront are virtually uninhabited. Many head to **Lily Bay State Park** on the eastern shore, for its waterfront campsites, boat-launching ramps, and swimming beach.

Maine is moose country. If you've never seen one, board the predawn moose-watching tour bus that leaves from Greenville, or station yourself near the bog beside the park's Mud Bank picnic area, a favorite grazing spot for the imposing beasts. Board the floating **Moosehead Marine Museum**, a restored steamboat, for a lake tour. Exhibits include 19th-century artifacts from nearby Mt. Kineo resort.

Patient observers *are likely to glimpse the elusive moose in the lush Maine wilderness.*

▶ *While in Greenville, stop for supplies and fuel before continuing on to the partially unpaved road to Baxter State Park.*

5 BAXTER STATE PARK

Surrounding Mt. Katahdin, Maine's highest point, this 200,000-acre park encompasses woods, waterways, and 46 peaks. Miles of trails traverse the interior, and one—the Appalachian—continues straight on through to Georgia. Though the Mt. Katahdin trails are the most popular, many of the other peaks provide equally spectacular views and may be less crowded. Enter the park at Old State Road near Tougue Pond.

6 OLD TOWN

This city on the Penobscot River is perhaps best known for the canoes built by the **Old Town Canoe Company**, one of the last makers of traditional wooden canoes. Guided tours in summer offer a look at how these boats are crafted.

Visitors crossing a narrow bridge from Old Town find themselves in another world: the Penobscot Indian Nation. Indian Island and the surrounding 4,900 acres constitute the reservation. The **Penobscot Nation Museum** preserves Penobscot culture and artistry, including a 30,000-entry dictionary.

7 BANGOR

In its early days Bangor was a booming, even raucous, lumber port. Merchants set up shop in what is now the **West Market Square Historic District.** Several buildings from the 1830's still stand here and in the residential **Broadway Historic District** as well.

A host of wealthy businessmen imported the best materials and craftsmen to create such houses as the 1845 **Isaac Farrar Mansion.** The finest marble and stained glass are set off against rich mahogany paneling and ornate carvings. Not to be outdone, another businessman built an opulent Greek Revival mansion across the street. It was once owned by Bangor's mayor and is now home to the **Bangor Historical Society Museum.** Downstairs a number of eclectic displays include locally made furnishings and 19th-century portraits by Jeremiah Hardy.

1 PORTLAND

Maine's largest city strikes an inviting balance between urban complex and coastal village. In the lively **Old Port Exchange** district, narrow streets wind past brick warehouses and commercial buildings transformed into quaint boutiques, restaurants, and artisans' shops. From here ferryboats depart for cruises on Casco Bay, past Cape Elizabeth's **Portland Head Light**, commissioned by George Washington and still in use.

Details of Portland's past live on in many of its carefully preserved buildings. The **Wadsworth-Longfellow House,** boyhood home of poet Henry Wadsworth Longfellow, was the city's first brick residence. Filled with family furnishings and mementos, it includes an 18th-century kitchen. Reformer Neal Dow carved a place in local and national history, and his 1829 mansion, the **Neal Dow Memorial,** was a meetinghouse of the temperance, abolition, and women's rights movements. On Danforth Street, amid the manifold Federal-style houses, rises **Victoria Mansion,** a stone villa complete with a Tuscan tower.

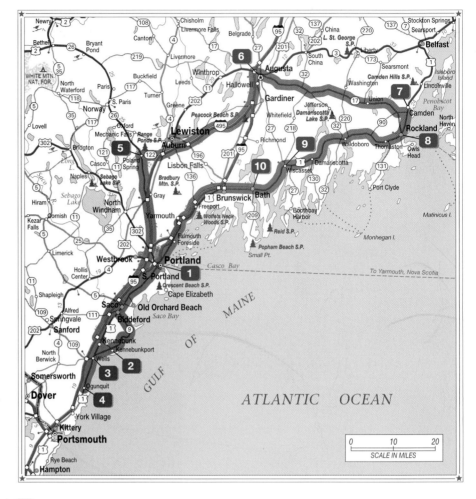

A veritable feast of lobster is offered in Kennebunkport and other nearby villages.

2 KENNEBUNKPORT

Summer folk flock to Kennebunkport, a haven for artists and writers and former President George Bush, whose vacation retreat overlooks a picturesque rocky inlet. Art galleries abound, and the **Kennebunkport Historical Society** offers tours of the historic district.

At the **Seashore Trolley Museum,** trolley cars from around the world have been collected and lovingly restored. A vintage car ferries visitors into the past on a scenic 2½-mile tour.

3 WELLS

Formerly a fishing village, Wells, with seven miles of wide, white sand beach, was fated to become a popular seaside resort. It is also a shopper's paradise, with outlet stores and boutiques featuring locally made wares. But tourists aren't the only ones to visit the Wells area. Migrating birds, such as the Canada goose and black duck, take rest in the **Rachel Carson National Wildlife Refuge.** Gulls, terns, and songbirds call

the preserve home, and can be glimpsed from tranquil walking trails.

If your tastes run more to the manmade, consider a visit to the **Wells Auto Museum,** where some 80 antique cars gleam amid vintage nickelodeons, arcade games, and toys.

4 OGUNQUIT

Ogunquit is known for having one of the finest beaches on the Atlantic coast. To the south, sheer-faced **Bald Head Cliff** looms large, sending a dramatic spray of salty surf back to the sea. **Marginal Way,** a mile-long footpath, wends its way to a drawbridge leading to Perkins Cove, where quaint shops and restaurants serving the sea's magnificent bounty await discovery.

▶ *Inexpensive all-day parking is available at the municipal lot behind the town hall and also at Footbridge Beach. You can board a trolley from either location to any place in Ogunquit, in season.*

At the **Ogunquit Museum of American Art,** visitors can examine the works of such artists as Charles Burchfield, Marsden Hartley, and Rockwell Kent. An outdoor sculpture garden offers stunning views of the cove and the ocean beyond.

5 POLAND SPRING

The last remaining active Shaker community in America, **Shaker Village,** near Poland Spring, is a living relic. Here such traditional activities as herb farming and the making of rosewater continue. Seventeen buildings epitomize the simple, functional beauty of the Shaker esthetic. Several, including the ministry shop and the meeting-house, can be seen on guided tours from Memorial Day to Columbus Day. The Shaker Museum showcases designs in furniture, textiles, and farm tools, many of which are still copied today.

6 AUGUSTA

The copper dome of the **State House,** designed by Charles Bulfinch, rises grandly above Augusta. Though the massive granite building has been many times remodeled, the original portico remains. While in town, tour the Federal-style governor's mansion, known as the **Blaine House,** and the **State Museum,** which chronicles Maine's social and natural history. Here you'll see gems and minerals, archeological artifacts, one of the oldest American-made locomotives, and a variety of objects made in Maine.

7 CAMDEN

This natural harbor sheltered by the Camden Hills is the home port of a fleet of passenger schooners that ply the Maine coast, and cruise boats offering shorter tours of Penobscot Bay. **Conway House** is a restored frame farmhouse dating from about 1770. A brick oven, blacksmith shop, herb garden, and barn containing carriages and farm implements are on view. Stop in the **Mary Meeker Cramer Museum,** located on the grounds, to see its ship models, quilts, and period costumes.

Just north on Rte 1, **Camden Hills State Park** spreads across 5,000 acres. Here hikers to the top of Mt. Battie are rewarded with panoramic views of the bay, though there's a paved road to the summit for the less ambitious.

8 ROCKLAND

Rockland, host of the annual Maine Lobster Festival in the first week of August, is also home to the **Farnsworth Art Museum,** with 18th-, 19th-, and 20th-century American art as well as European and Oriental pieces. Seascapes painted by the likes of Andrew Wyeth and Winslow Homer find a fitting home here, along with landscapes and other paintings. Next door is the **Farnsworth Homestead,** one of

American music boxes, player pianos, and mechanical instruments. Take the guided tour to hear demonstrations of these orchestras-in-a-box. Before leaving the area, stop by **Fort Edgecomb State Historic Site.** The blockhouse here was built to protect Wiscasset during the War of 1812, but today the serene site offers a prime picnic spot where idlers provide an audience for harbor seals at play.

▶ *Rail/Sail offers scenic train rides out of Wiscasset, with views of wildlife including deer, eagles, and ospreys. Catch the fall foliage special.*

Picturesque Camden, nestled beneath the Camden Hills, beckons to vacationers. Regattas draw competitive sailors here, while yachting lures the private boater.

Maine's great Greek Revival mansions, filled with things Victorian.

9 WISCASSET

The self-proclaimed Prettiest Village in Maine, Wiscasset is lined with grand old mansions built by sea captains and shipping merchants. Don't miss the **Nickels-Sortwell House,** restored after serving as an inn and a private home. Its elaborately carved elliptical stairway rises three stories high. In the historic waterfront district, the decaying hulks of two four-masted merchant schooners rest on display in the harbor, moored there since 1932.

The **Musical Wonder House** offers a fanciful collection of European and

10 BATH

The city of Bath boasts a long and venerable shipbuilding history. In 1607 English settlers crafted Bath's first ship from local timbers, and today Bath Iron Works produces enormous steel vessels. But the wooden ship still reigned as king when the largest six-masted schooner built in America, the *Wyoming,* was given form at the Percy & Small Shipyard. Today several restored shipyard buildings are part of the **Maine Maritime Museum.** Exhibits range from marine art and nautical memorabilia to the labor of lobstermen. In the Apprenticeshop, shipwrights demonstrate the time-honored techniques of wooden-ship building.

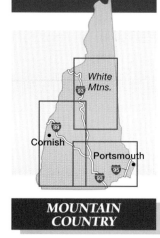

New Hampshire

New Hampshire is a seamless marriage of spectacular granite vistas, rocky seacoasts, covered wooden bridges, and steepled churches rising through the crests of tall white pines.

MOUNTAIN COUNTRY

1 WHITE MOUNTAINS

Three unmistakable profiles distinguish New Hampshire's White Mountains: **Mount Washington**'s weather-beaten peak, the granite-chinned Old Man of the Mountain, and the antlered visage of the ubiquitous moose. To get the lay of the land, start at the town of **Bretton Woods**, at the foot of Mount Washington. At 6,288 feet, Mount Washington is the highest mountain in the Northeastern United States; the greatest wind speed ever clocked in a surface weather station—a whopping 231 m.p.h.—was measured on its summit. Bretton Woods has been a popular destination since the 19th century, in large part because of the breathtaking passenger-train ride to the mountain summit, a trip once described by P. T. Barnum as "the second greatest show on earth." Since 1869 the **Mount Washington Cog Railway** has safely chugalugged up and down the mountain's steep face.

The region's annual early-summer Moose Mania Weekend pays homage to the shaggy brown monarch of the 773,000-acre **White Mountain National Forest.** For information on area festivities, contact the Berlin Chamber of Commerce. A string of mountain ranges provides a dramatic backdrop for moose-watching, as well as for stellar hiking, white-water rafting, and downhill and cross-country skiing.

▶ *For those drivers faint of heart, guided van tours are available to carry visitors to the summit of Mount Washington and back.*

2 GLEN

Witness a speech by George Washington himself in a simulated journey through the past at **Heritage New Hampshire.** Utilizing life-size theatrical sets and high-tech audiovisuals to bring to life more than 300 years of New Hampshire history, a Heritage tour takes you from a 1634 English street to the ripping finale—a train ride through

The Cog Railway has toted passengers up and down Mount Washington since 1869.

the rugged Crawford Notch.

If the family bus is sound of wind, limb, and brake, then take a detour to Pinkham Notch, on Rte. 16, to steer to the top of the **Mount Washington Auto Road.** At an average grade of 12 percent and replete with the same giddy curves it had when it opened in 1861, the eight-mile corkscrew road is an attraction in itself and takes 30 minutes each way. At the peak are a glassed-in viewing area and museums.

3 MOUNT WASHINGTON VALLEY

The rumble of iron wheels calls rail buffs to North Conway, where an 1874 depot is the starting point of the **Conway Scenic Railway**, an 11-mile rail ride. The tour is conducted in period coaches pulled by either an antique steam or a diesel-electric locomotive. Guests traveling first class ride in original Pullman Parlor Cars.

As you pass through Conway on Highway 16, you may want to take a side trip straight through the White Mountains on the **Kancamagus Highway** (Route 112). Spanning the 34 miles between the towns of Conway

The White Mountains cast an azure reflection on Beaver Pond in the Great Gulf Wilderness.

and Lincoln, the Kancamagus slices through the Rocky Gorge Scenic Area, passes near Sabbaday Falls, and traverses Kancamagus Pass. South of Conway is the hamlet of Albany, where you can cross the Swift River on the 136-foot **Albany Covered Bridge**, a horse-and-buggy span opened in 1859.

4 WOLFEBORO

Founded in 1759, this popular summer-resort region began drawing tourists in the 1830's. By the 1850's, thousands flocked to the shores of the slate-blue Winnipesaukee, the state's largest lake. Today visitors can enjoy the lake and soak up a bit of the past at the **Gov. John Wentworth Historic Site.** The only remaining evidence of the house is its massive stone foundations, but a trip to the Wolfeboro Historical Society will supply many details on the palatial summer home of New Hampshire's last Colonial governor. The tidy old town of Wolfeboro, on the lakefront, retains a traditional New England look while serving as a sports center for fishing, diving, biking, and cross-country skiing. Tour the 71-square-mile lake on the cruise boat M.S. *Mount Washington*.

5 MOULTONBOROUGH

A multimillionaire shoe magnate built a remarkable home nearly a hundred years ago on a mountaintop plateau above Lake Winnipesaukee. Today visitors can tour the lavish interiors of the **Castle in the Clouds,** an architectural pastiche of extraordinary quality and charm. The stone mansion has spectacular 360° views. The vast estate can be toured on foot or on horseback, along 85 miles of trails in the sylvan forests of the Ossipee Mountains. The shoe magnate did not fare so well: he invested in Soviet bonds in the thirties and in 1941 died penniless.

6 HOLDERNESS

A 200-acre sanctuary for New Hampshire's native creatures and flora, the **Science Center of New Hampshire** is prettily situated near the shores of ethereal Squam Lake (the setting for the movie *On Golden Pond*). The science center features indoor and outdoor ex-

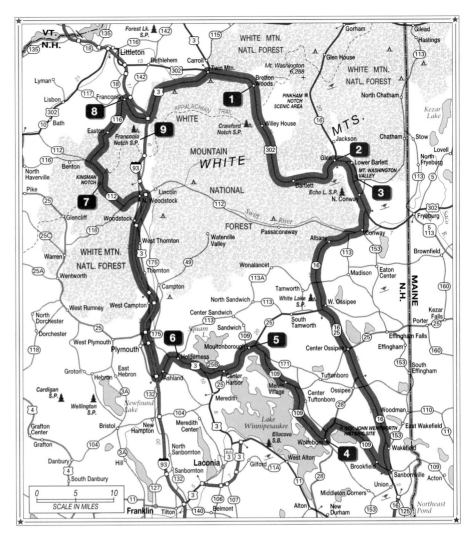

hibits along a three-quarter-mile nature trail, where visitors may encounter animals of all kinds: deer, owls, eagles, wildcats, muskrats—even bears.

▶ *Tours in small boats, leaving from Holderness, are an excellent way to see Squam Lake.*

7 KINSMAN NOTCH

Ancient geological disturbances have given the modern-day New Hampshire landscape many dramatic bumps and turns, among them the glacier-sculpted **Lost River Gorge.** The river tumbles over waterfalls, through caves formed by fallen boulders, and into potholes. Take the self-guided tour of the gorge over walkways and bridges.

8 FRANCONIA

Robert Frost spent five productive years in a white clapboard farmhouse overlooking the Franconia Valley. It was

here, from 1915 to 1920, that he composed such classic poems as "Mending Wall." Two rooms in the **Frost Place** display signed first editions and personal items. Outside, a yard of wildflowers and sugar maples leads to the Poetry Trail, a half-mile nature trek posted with lines from Frost's poems.

9 FRANCONIA NOTCH

Franconia Notch State Park spreads its 6,500 acres under the gaze of the **Old Man of the Mountain.** This 40-foot-high granite face was hewn from mountain cliffs above glistening Profile Lake, known as the Old Man's Wash Bowl. Take the eight-minute cable-car ride on the **Cannon Mountain Aerial Tramway;** when it reaches the 4,180-foot summit, the views extend into four states and Canada. Nearby, boardwalk strollers are treated to waterfalls and covered bridges along the **Flume,** a spectacular granite-walled chasm.

1 CORNISH

Artists put this modest village on the map in the early 1900's when they flocked here in the wake of Augustus Saint-Gaudens, one of America's most celebrated sculptors, who lived in a hilltop estate beside the Connecticut River. Today at the **Saint-Gaudens National Historic Site** the house appears as it did nearly a century ago, when the creator of such popular works as the "Shaw Memorial" in Boston and "General Sherman" in New York renovated a Federal-style country tavern called Huggins' Folly—with a little help from his friend, the noted architect Stanford White. Here Saint-Gaudens entertained members of the star-studded Cornish

The longest covered bridge in the country, the Cornish-Windsor Bridge is a fine example of the state's treasured covered spans. This 470-foot-long wooden bridge, built in 1866, links Cornish, New Hampshire, and Windsor, Vermont.

art colony. But the sculptor's most important legacy may be in his studios and gardens. Many of his greatest works are on permanent display here. Take the woodland walks; in the summer, outdoor music concerts are held on the grounds.

In a state justifiably known as a treasury of covered bridges, the **Cornish-Windsor Bridge** is, at 470 feet, the longest covered bridge in the entire United States. The wooden bridge has spanned the Connecticut River, in the shadow of Vermont's Mount Ascutney, since 1866 and links Cornish to Windsor, Vermont.

2 HANOVER

The **Hood Museum of Art**, at **Dartmouth College**, is home to one of the finest university art collections in the United States. Ancient art, old masters, American art, American Indian art, African art, Chinese bronzes and ceramics, and silver are among the collections on display. Artists represented include Winslow Homer, Pablo Picasso, and Paul Revere.

► *Hanover, home to Dartmouth College, is not the only classic New England college town with a lovely countenance. Visit picturesque New London, the site of Colby Sawyer College, near Lake Sunapee.*

In fact, the entire Dartmouth campus is impressive enough to be called a work of art. Laid out in the heart of this quintessential New England town, the Ivy League university was founded in 1769 and named for an English benefactor, the earl of Dartmouth. Classes are still held in the 1829 **Wentworth Hall.** The handsome Georgian and Federal structures of **Dartmouth Row** form the core of the campus.

3 GRAFTON

Rich mineral deposits have been unearthed from **Ruggles Mine** since it was opened in 1803 by local landowner Sam Ruggles. Today the old mine, with its yawning pits and giant arched tunnels, is open to visitors, who pay to dig to their heart's content. Underfoot are more than 150 minerals, from beryl to feldspar to zircon, to excavate and take home. In the old days the mine's vast supply of mica was the stuff of bonanzas: it was used in making stove windows and lamp chimneys.

4 GROTON

One of the more remarkable examples of the varied geological landscape of New Hampshire is **Sculptured Rocks,** where over the ages rushing water has carved a capricious gallery of odd shapes among the stones. Picnic spots are sprinkled throughout the area, located two miles west of Groton.

5 FRANKLIN

A simple two-room farmhouse of dark-stained weatherboard marks the **Daniel Webster Birthplace,** where one of the great national political figures of his era was born in 1782. Much of the little house standing today is believed to be original and is filled with period furnishings from the time of Webster's birth and early years. His father, a farmer and patriot, had served in the French and Indian and Revolutionary wars. Sickly as a youth, little Daniel grew up to attend Dartmouth College. He became a lawyer, a U.S. congressman, and a senator and served as secretary of state under three presidents.

6 WARNER

The **Mt. Kearsage Indian Museum** exhibits of American Indian art, artifacts, and philosophy are supplemented by the written and taped testimony of many noted American Indians. Guides lead tours through rooms of Indian basketwork, beadwork, weaving, quillwork, and fishing equipment. Visit the forested two-acre Medicine Woods, where plants used by Indians for dye, food, and medicine are grown.

7 HILLSBOROUGH

The 14th president of the United States (and the only one to come from New Hampshire), Franklin Pierce was born in a handsome Federal-style home in Hillsborough in 1804. The elegant, 15-room house at the **Franklin Pierce Homestead Historic Site** reflects the family's affluence, with polished archi-

Pink-and-white rhododendrons blanket the Monadnock mountain region every July.

tectural flourishes and even a ballroom. Restored in late-1830's period furnishings, the house is open for tours in the summer. As president of the United States from 1853 to 1857, Pierce strove in vain to reconcile a nation already headed inexorably toward division.

You'll pass through two classic New England villages, both straight out of a Hollywood set, on the scenic route to Rhododendron State Park: **Hancock** and **Fitzwilliam**. Hancock's main thoroughfare is lined with Colonial homes and picket fences. The 18th-century **John Hancock Inn** is the oldest continually operating inn in New England and boasts Primitive murals. On the serene Fitzwilliam green is the **Fitzwilliam Meeting House**, built in 1817.

8 RHODODENDRON STATE PARK

More at home in the Southern Smokies and the Alleghenies, *Rhododendron maximum* nevertheless thrives in this corner of New Hampshire's Monadnock mountain region. An extraordinary 16-acre concentration bursts into pink-and-white blooms every mid-July. A mile-long trail that winds up Little Monadnock Mountain provides excellent views of the rhododendron and assorted wildflowers.

9 KEENE

Wyman Tavern, a Colonial tavern built by Capt. Isaac Wyman in 1762, has been restored as a period house and museum, with many of its original furnishings intact. Located on Main Street, the inn has had several brushes with

history. The founders of Dartmouth College held their first meeting here, in 1770, the same year that classes began on the new campus in Hanover. Five years later, Captain Wyman himself led Keene's militiamen off to Massachusetts to fight in the Revolution.

▶ *Take a detour onto scenic state Rte. 101 from Peterborough to Keene to see brilliant fall foliage. You'll pass Dublin Lake and get a splendid view of Mount Monadnock.*

10 CHESTERFIELD GORGE

The fast-running Wilde Brook has carved its way through bedrock for thousands of years to create Chesterfield Gorge, a shaded, steep-walled sanctuary that is the top attraction of the **Chesterfield Gorge Natural Area**.

A three-quarter-mile trail follows the brook through the gorge, past cool stands of oak, pine, and hemlock.

11 CHARLESTOWN

Old Fort Number Four is a reconstruction of the 1744 fortified village of Charlestown. It's also a living-history museum, where costumed interpreters reveal the fort's volatile past and demonstrate Colonial craftsmanship. A stockade and watchtower were built at Charlestown to protect isolated settlers from attacks by the French and the Indians. By 1747 the wisdom of erecting Old Fort Number Four at this site became clear, as settlers were able to successfully defend themselves against numerous heavy assaults. Today visitors can witness reenactments of militia musters and encampments.

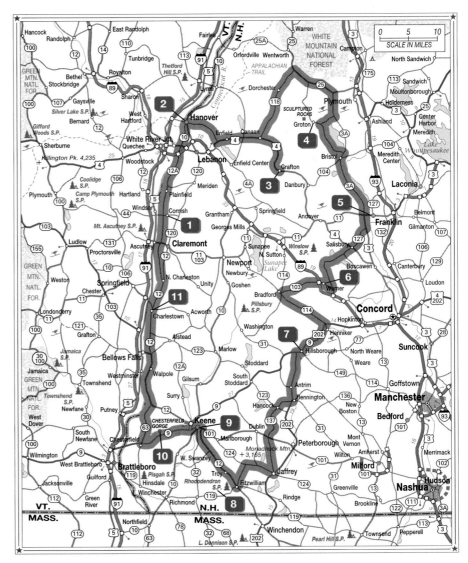

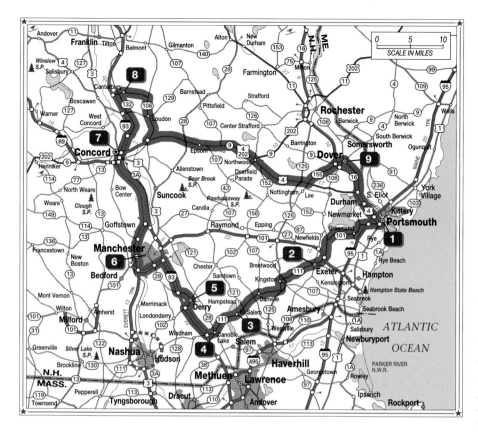

Another of Portsmouth's architectural gems is the **Wentworth-Coolidge Mansion,** a 42-room waterfront structure whose oldest section may date back as far as 1695. Much of the existing house is original, right down to its pre–Revolutionary War wallpaper.

Harbor cruises are a great way to appreciate the scenic sweep of this old port city. Cruises are also offered to an offshore archipelago called the **Isles of Shoals,** a summer resort with stone churches and weather-beaten cottages.

Just east of Portsmouth, in the harbor on Great Island, **New Castle** has a decidedly Colonial flavor, evidenced in the narrow streets lined with charming period homes. First settled in 1623, this old-time fishing village has been safeguarded for more than 350 years by two fortifications. The ruins of fort walls are all that remain of **Fort Constitution,** a British stronghold that was captured by colonists in 1774. Spectacular ocean views unfold at the other New Castle stronghold, **Fort Stark,** situated on 10 acres overlooking Little Harbor. The fort was on active duty from the Revolutionary War through World War II.

▶ *Take the walking trail from Fort Constitution to the town for a close-up view of the 18th-century homes.*

2 EXETER

The state's capital of Revolutionary dissent is now a charming, peaceful vil-

PORTSMOUTH TO DOVER

1 PORTSMOUTH

New Hampshire is more than granite mountains, pellucid lakes, and small, tidy farms. It is also home to the quintessential New England rocky coast. True, New Hampshire's share of the Atlantic's edge is only 18 miles long, but that's enough to harbor Portsmouth, one of the nation's oldest and most fascinating seaports, first settled in the 1620's. Located at the mouth of the Piscataqua River, Portsmouth and its wealth of historic buildings, beautifully preserved and maintained, creates an old-time seaport atmosphere.

One of Portsmouth's oldest neighborhoods, the 10-acre **Strawbery Banke** —named for the wild berries that once blanketed the riverbanks—is today a virtual museum of New England architecture, crafts, and gardens. More than 40 historic structures line the streets, from the 1695 **Sherburne House** to such 18th- and 19th-century structures as the **Wheelwright House,** which has period food-preparation demonstra-

tions; the **Pitt Tavern,** a gathering place for Revolutionary patriots; the **Goodwin Mansion,** a governor's home; the **Drisco House,** which illustrates three centuries of change in the same house; and the **Nutter House,** the boyhood home of a popular Victorian author, Thomas Bailey Aldrich. You'll witness craftsmen building boats and artisans coopering and potting. Gardens replicating those from the past three centuries transport visitors across the years.

Lovely Strawbery Banke is one of the oldest neighborhoods in Portsmouth and a living museum of Colonial architecture. This view is from the garden at the 1850's Goodwin Mansion; it faces the red-shingled 1790 Jones House.

lage, home of a celebrated preparatory school and many architectural relics. The formal Georgian exterior of the **Gilman Garrison House** gives visitors little indication of its massive log interior from the 1600's. The sawmiller John Gilman built his house much like a fortified garrison, outfitting it with a portcullis, an iron grating that could be lowered to block the entryway.

The **American Independence Museum** is housed in the national historic landmark Ladd-Gilman House, in downtown Exeter. Built in 1721, the house was the location for New Hampshire's treasury during the Revolution. Rare documents, militaria, and period furnishings are exhibited.

3 NORTH SALEM

America's Stonehenge is the name given a huge megalithic site in the North Salem woods that has intrigued archeologists, historians, and astronomers for years. A 25-acre tract of walls, chambers, and large standing stone slabs, the place once known as Mystery Hill Caves may have been used to determine solar and lunar events. Some believe it served as the site for rituals. Stone and bone artifacts have been found, and in 1970 a radiocarbon test indicated that the artifacts are 4,000 years old. But there is yet no conclusive answer to the mystery of America's Stonehenge.

4 CANOBIE LAKE

In an era of glitzy high-tech theme parks, a traditional family amusement park has a nostalgic, uncluttered appeal. In operation since 1902, **Canobie Lake Park** retains such classic touches as an antique carousel, a steam train, and a paddle-wheel riverboat. But the modern age, too, has inspired many of the park's newer rides, such as the Corkscrew roller coaster and the popular wooden coaster Yankee Cannonball.

5 DERRY

The **Robert Frost Farm** is in most respects a typical New England farmhouse of the 1880's. But while farming was not Frost's forte, the poet enjoyed great success from the writing he completed during his residence here, from 1900 to 1909. The two-story white clapboard house has been restored to its appearance during Frost's occupancy and is filled with period furnishings.

▶ *Share Frost's inspiration by walking the half-mile nature trail past Hyla Brook and the stone wall made famous in the poet's works.*

6 MANCHESTER

The **Currier Gallery of Art** is a noted repository of paintings and sculptures by American and European masters, spanning the 14th to 20th centuries. The Beaux Arts structure holds impressive decorative-arts exhibits as well, in-

The federal eagle on the wooden tavern sign from Concord's 1815 Eagle Hotel was a widely used symbol for the new republic.

cluding collections of New England furniture, pewter, and silver. A museum highlight is the **Zimmerman House**, a 1950 structure that was designed by Frank Lloyd Wright in his "Usonian" style—the architect's term for buildings that are functional and uniform.

7 CONCORD

Be the captain of your own simulated space flight at the **Christa McAuliffe Planetarium**, a memorial to the young New Hampshire teacher who died in 1986 aboard the space shuttle *Challenger*. Each seat in the planetarium is equipped with controls that allow visitors to map their own three-dimensional spaceflight on the star-filled, 40-foot domed screen above.

New Hampshire's colorful past is traced in thousands of artifacts at the **Museum of New Hampshire History,** founded in 1823. A red-and-yellow Concord coach and a large wooden eagle from New Hampshire's State House dome are on display. The museum also features a fine-arts collection of 19th-century paintings of the White Mountains. The museum was designed in 1911 by Guy Lowell, the architect of the Museum of Fine Arts in Boston.

8 CANTERBURY

In the rolling Canterbury Hills, the Shaker religious sect—dedicated to spiritual perfection, order, and the stripping away of excess—established a community in the late 18th century. Here, the industrious sect built one of its most important villages. Some two dozen spare, white-clapboard structures remain in today's museum community of homes, shops, meetinghouses, and a schoolhouse. Note the fine workmanship in the Shakers' architecture, furniture, and inventions—such as the flat broom, still crafted on-site.

▶ *Taste authentic Shaker cooking at the Creamery Restaurant, in the heart of the village, where fresh-churned butter, maple baked beans, and rosewater apple pie are among the house specialties.*

9 DOVER

Dover is New Hampshire's oldest permanent settlement, founded in 1623. A three-structure complex underscores the town's antiquity. At the hand-hewn **Damm Garrison House,** built in 1675, much of the structure's original form remains, as do gun portholes from the house's service as a fortified garrison. Colonial utensils and furniture are displayed. The **Hale House,** built in 1813, was the home of the abolitionist senator John P. Hale from 1840 to 1873 and contains period furniture, paintings, and one of the first Chickering pianos. (Trivia note: John Hale's daughter, Lucy, was the girlfriend of John Wilkes Booth.) The **Woodman House,** constructed in 1818, is a natural-history museum with an extensive Indian-artifact collection.

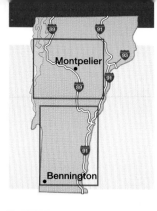

Vermont

Nowhere is the foliage of autumn so fiery as in the rolling Vermont countryside, with its picturesque patchwork of farms and villages, rich in history and sweet with the finest maple syrup.

THE GREEN MOUNTAINS

1 BENNINGTON

Grandma Moses lived near this mountain-flanked city, and Robert Frost is buried in its oldest cemetery. Today Bennington still attracts as many artists, poets, and writers as it always has.

Their first stop is often the **Bennington Museum** in downtown Bennington, a renowned repository of 18th- through 20th-century paintings, glasswork, and Chippendale furniture. More Grandma Moses works are exhibited here than in any other public collection. Even the schoolhouse she attended has been moved to the museum site.

Nearby stands another gem of Bennington's historic district: the **Bennington Battle Monument**, a 306-foot-tall obelisk commemorating a 1777 battle in which Vermont's Green Mountain Boys defeated British troops.

▶ *Telephone the Vermont Hotline (802-828-3239) from early September through late October for tips on when fall foliage will be at its peak.*

2 ARLINGTON

America's most beloved illustrator called this scenic town home from 1939 to 1953. You'll see why when you visit the **Norman Rockwell Exhibition,** housed in an 1875 church, with several hundred of Rockwell's *Saturday Evening Post* covers and other works. Your hosts will be people Rockwell used as his models—older now, but still the same friends he painted holding Thanksgiving turkeys, praying in church, and tucking their children into bed at night.

3 MANCHESTER

With tree-lined streets and nearby skiing, this small residential enclave has

been one of New England's most popular resorts for more than a century.

Just outside of town, amid 400 acres of tranquil trails and magnificent formal gardens, sits **Hildene**, a 24-room Georgian Revival mansion with gorgeous views of the Battenkill Valley and the Green Mountains beyond. From its completion in 1904 until 1926, the mansion served as a summer home for Abraham Lincoln's son, Robert Todd Lincoln, and still contains many original furnishings.

Just south of Manchester, the 5.2-mile **Sky Line Drive** twists and turns its way toward the peak of 3,852-foot Mount Equinox. The summit affords stunning views of the mountains below.

▶ *If you visit Hildene in winter, catch one of three evenings of romantic candlelight tours between Christmas and New Year's Day.*

4 PROCTOR

Marble prevails in Proctor, where the public buildings and even the sidewalks are made of the "sparkling stone." The **Vermont Marble Exhibit,** housed in the Vermont Marble Company, lets visitors observe firsthand the sculpting and finishing of this revered material. The

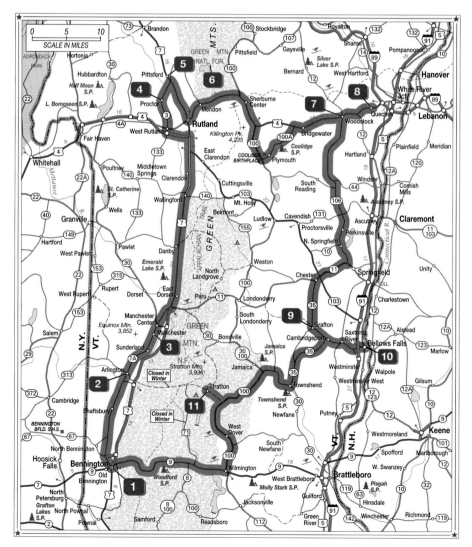

Calvin Coolidge became president in the house of his birth (right), with the oath of office administered by his own father, a notary public.

Hall of Presidents features exquisite white marble bas-relief carvings of all our chief executives.

Just south of the village, **Wilson Castle** stands ready to transport you into a realm of fabulous wealth. A mid-19th-century architectural masterpiece, this 32-room mansion includes 13 fireplaces and 84 stained-glass windows.

5 PITTSFORD

The **New England Maple Museum** tells what they call The Sweetest Story Ever Told. Dioramas and antique sugaring tools look back to the days when American Indians taught settlers to make maple syrup by placing hot rocks in hollowed logs brimming with sap. You'll find old wooden buckets and horse-drawn sleds used to cart the thick sap down the mountain. Visitors can observe demonstrations of syrup making and, best of all, savor a taste of the final product.

6 GREEN MOUNTAIN NATIONAL FOREST

The intersection of Routes 4 and 100 offers a good starting place for a drive through the tree-filled expanse that straddles what some call the Spine of Vermont. Running for nearly two-thirds the length of the state, the forest is a 350,000-acre home for bears, moose, wild turkeys, and deer. For people, it offers campgrounds, picnic areas, and 500 miles of walking trails that wind through the pristine wilderness.

Farther south, in Plymouth, summer visitors can see the birthplace of Calvin Coolidge at **Plymouth Notch**, where he was sworn in as president of the United States by the light of a kerosene lamp. Also here is the one-room schoolhouse Coolidge attended, the dance hall used as the 1924 summer White House, and the still-operating cheese factory owned by Coolidge's son.

7 WOODSTOCK

This peaceful New England village, featuring a host of 19th-century structures, is home to the **Billings Farm and Museum,** a working farm demonstrating cheese making, ice cutting, maple sugaring, and other period farm tasks. There is also a re-created kitchen, workshop, and country store. You can even try your hand at churning butter.

Also in Woodstock, the 1807 **Dana House,** home of the Woodstock Historical Society, exhibits 18th- and 19th-century furniture, engravings, silver, dolls, toys, and paintings.

8 QUECHEE GORGE

You don't have to be able to pronounce the Ottauquechee River to enjoy its beauty. Trails and picnic areas overlook the mile-long Quechee Gorge, Vermont's Little Grand Canyon, where the river cuts into a stunning glacier-carved chasm. In the village of Quechee, a 162-foot-high bridge spans the gorge, offering a dramatic view.

9 HISTORIC GRAFTON VILLAGE

Imagine staying at an inn that was established back in 1801, not long after memories of the Revolutionary War had begun to fade. You can do just that at **The Old Tavern** in this beautifully restored 19th-century village, where gravel paths wend through town and sheep graze in nearby fields. When Rudyard Kipling stayed at the inn, he sat on the porch and listened to the **Grafton Cornet Band,** which still plays on the village green on Sundays in summer.

10 BELLOWS FALLS

In Bellows Falls, hop on the "Flyer" and turn back the clock. Named after a railroad that ran from the 1930's through the 1950's, the **Green Mountain Flyer** travels 26 miles along a bed that has served as an Indian trail, pioneer path, and stagecoach route. Riding in one of eight vintage coaches, you'll enjoy an ever-changing display of waterfalls, covered bridges, and farms that dot the postcard-perfect landscape.

11 STRATTON

Skiers flock to Stratton Mountain in the winter, but others visit in autumn to view the breathtaking foliage by way of a gondola ride to the summit. From mid-September to mid-October you can catch the celebrated **Stratton Arts Festival,** where cheek by jowl with exhibits of painting and sculpture are ceramics, toys, quilts, and glassware.

Autumn falls on Quechee Gorge, *where scenic glen-side picnic spots abound.*

1 MONTPELIER

Dominated by what may be the nation's most charming statehouse, this smallest of America's capital cities mocks the saying that bigger means better.

Granite columns buttress the main portico of the 1859 **Capitol.** High above, perched atop a gold-leaf dome, a statue of Ceres, goddess of agriculture, gazes out at the mountains nearby.

A short walk away, the Vermont Historical Society's **Vermont Museum** displays the last panther shot in Vermont and other local relics.

▶ *Quilters won't want to miss the Vermont Quilt Festival, held in nearby Northfield each July. Contact the Central Vermont Chamber of Commerce in Barre for dates.*

2 WATERBURY

Northwest of Montpelier, a hot spot for lovers of Heath Bar Crunch and New York Super Fudge Chunk awaits. Visitors to **Ben and Jerry's Ice Cream Factory** get to watch creamy confections being made on a live production line. Free samples are offered, and a gift shop is open all year.

In nearby Waterbury Center, the **Cold Hollow Cider Mill** presses sweet juice from crisp apples year-round. Sharing space with the mill in an old rustic barn is a huge country gift shop. Apple goodies abound: strudels, cobblers, and apple butter.

3 MIDDLEBURY

He outran the best quarter horses, outpulled the best draft horses, and seemed never to get tired. He was Justin Morgan, a Vermont horse whose offspring gave rise to America's first light horse breed: the Morgan. Just outside Middlebury the **University of Vermont Morgan Horse Farm** breeds and trains some 70 stallions and mares. Visitors can tour the large Victorian barn and watch workout sessions.

In town the white stone buildings of **Middlebury College** form the core of this quaint village, chartered in 1761. Guides lead visitors through the handsome 1829 **Sheldon Museum,** a columned mansion filled with 19th-century furnishings, decorative arts, farming tools, and more.

The nearby **John Strong Mansion,** west of town, features two hidey-holes. One was built into the house when it was constructed in the 1790's, possibly as a place to hide during Indian attacks. It can hold as many as 40 people.

4 BASIN HARBOR

To gaze out at Lake Champlain is to sense how Vermont's Inland Sea influenced life here in the past, and still does. In October 1776, during the American Revolution, Benedict Arnold ran five ships aground on the lakeshore and set them on fire to keep them from the British. Paddle-wheel steamers plied Champlain's waters after the Revolution, carrying logs, livestock, and goods

***These 19th-century dolls** are but two of more than 1,000 at the Shelburne Museum.*

to canal boats heading for New York City and Canada. These distant days are commemorated at the **Lake Champlain Maritime Museum,** where visitors can pore over nautical prints, examine a full-size working replica of Benedict Arnold's gunboat, the *Philadelphia,* and visit a workshop with vessels made by local residents over the past 150 years.

5 CHARLOTTE

They splash all the pathways around you with color—violets in spring, black-eyed Susans in summer, purple asters when days grow short. Wildflowers abound at the **Vermont Wildflower Farm,** a six-acre site with flowering fields and forest glades. Interpretive plaques identify the flowers and explain their herbal and medicinal uses. In the gift shop browsers are tempted by nature jewelry, pressed flowers, and china with floral designs.

▶ *If you'd like to create your own color-filled meadow, you can purchase wildflower seeds here. Horticulturalists are on hand to help you choose.*

6 SHELBURNE

You'll need at least a day to sample the riches of one of Vermont's most popular attractions: the **Shelburne Museum,** a sprawling complex of 37 exhibit buildings and historic homes. You might start your tour at the huge, horseshoe-shaped barn, used to shelter a collection of more than 200 carriages and sleighs. Lovers of ships will enjoy the *Ticonderoga,* a 220-foot side-wheeler that carried passengers across Lake Champlain in the early 20th century. Other attractions include a working carousel, a delightful collection of weathervanes, and a 500-foot-long miniature circus.

At nearby **Shelburne Farms,** you'll find that one man's humble cottage is another's imperial mansion. For railroad magnate William Seward Webb, this 110-room manor house was merely a cozy retreat. Set on 1,000 stunning acres overlooking Lake Champlain, the turn-of-the-century estate now serves as an elegant inn during warm-weather months. Tours of the farm include its five-story barn, which covers a full two acres and houses a bakery, furniture store, and exhibits. There's also a working dairy, where cows produce milk for Cheddar cheese that visitors can buy.

7 BURLINGTON

With its rough-cut boards and open hearth, the restored **Ethan Allen Homestead** features much of its original materials. That's impressive, since

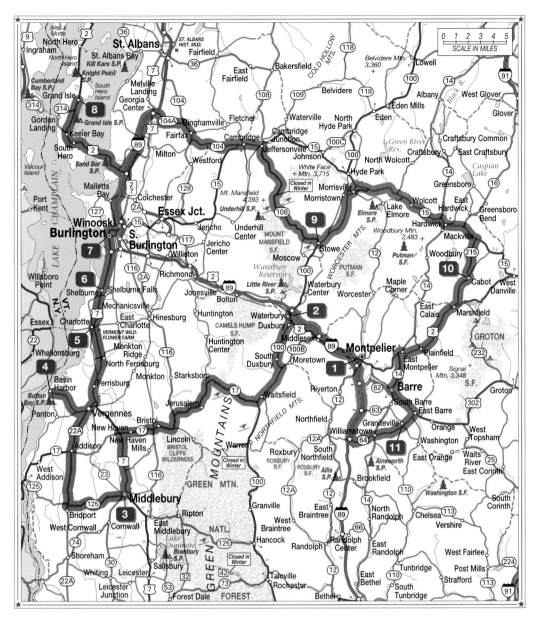

Stowe's alpine array of ski lodges and shops. In summer you can take the winding 4½-mile auto toll road to the summit, where walkways offer views that can stretch 60 miles over parts of three states and Quebec.

▶ *If you prefer to leave the car behind, the Gondola Skyride will shuttle you up the mountain and back.*

Thrill seekers will want to ride the **Stowe Alpine Slide**. During summer, take the Alpine Chairlift at Spruce Peak to the slide's starting gate.

10 CABOT

Back in 1919, farmers seeking to join the fledgling **Cabot Cooperative Creamery** could do so by pledging $5 a cow and a cord of firewood for the boiler. A few things have changed: today's creamery is a multimillion-dollar business, processing as many as 330 million gallons of milk each year.

During your visit, you'll watch naturally aged Cheddar cheeses—said to be among the finest in America—being made, along with a variety of other dairy products. You can sample them in the well-stocked gift shop, where the creamery's goods are sold.

11 GRANITEVILLE

Here shuttle buses skirt the lip of the gaping 475-foot-deep **Rock of Ages Granite Quarry**. The ride offers a rare, close-up look at how miners do daily battle with nature. At the Manufacturing Division, an observation deck overlooking the production floor allows you to watch through a haze of rock dust as workers carve and polish granite slabs. Visitors are welcome to weigh down their pockets with shiny samples from the scrap pile.

the farmhouse was occupied by Vermont's most famous Revolutionary hero two centuries ago.

A host of exhibits at the homestead's visitor center lets you peer into details of Ethan Allen's colorful life. But the site's most charming aspect may well be its location on the banks of the Winooski River. With picturesque walking trails that wind along the water, it's a beautiful place for a stroll or a picnic.

8 LAKE CHAMPLAIN ISLANDS

Via bridge and causeway, you can drive for some 30 miles through this tranquil cluster of islands, glimpsing small dairy farms, scenic apple orchards, and rustic lakeside retreats. Grand Isle boasts what is thought to be the oldest log cabin in

America: the 1783 **Hyde Log Cabin**, its sturdy hand-hewn cedar beams held together by a mixture of clay and straw.

If you have extra time, continue north to **Isle la Motte**, where a large granite statue commemorates the island's discovery by Samuel de Champlain in 1609. Also there is the **St. Anne Shrine**, dedicated to Vermont's first French settlement, Fort Sainte-Anne, established back in the 17th century.

9 STOWE

Stowe is Mount Mansfield, and Mount Mansfield is Stowe. The village and mountain have been linked in the minds of vacationers for more than a century. Mount Mansfield juts 4,393 feet above sea level and towers over

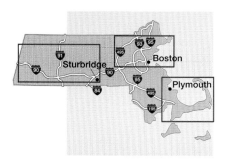

Massachusetts

The rumblings of a new nation began here, on salt-sprayed wooden ships, on rugged coastlines rimmed by churning gray seas, on cool green hillsides wearing the scent of musket fire.

HISTORIC BOSTON

1 BOSTON

Boston is a walker's paradise. To savor the city's rich past, take the three-mile marked **Freedom Trail**, which links 16 sites, starting at the **Boston Common**, the oldest park in the country. Next, stop at the "new" **State House**, whose cornerstone was laid by Samuel Adams in 1795. Several blocks away is the **Old State House**, built in 1712, which overlooks the scene of the 1770 Boston Massacre, when frightened British soldiers fired into a mob of angry colonists, killing five Bostonians. Nearby **Faneuil** (pronounced FAN-yul) **Hall**, given to the city by the merchant Peter Faneuil in 1742, once resounded with the cries of Revolutionary firebrands. Today Faneuil Hall is skirted by an indoor and outdoor marketplace. Street performers and colorful pushcarts give the area a merry hum of activity. To the east is the 19th-century **Quincy Market**, with its stately granite porticoes, now a shopping/food complex.

Only minutes away is Charlestown harbor, home of the **U.S.S. *Constitution***, the world's oldest commissioned warship afloat. Known as Old Ironsides, the *Constitution* was launched in 1797 and won two fierce battles against British ships in the War of 1812. Onboard, youngsters learn to tie nautical knots, lie in a ship's hammock, and daydream about life in the age of sail.

The Boston waterfront is a bustling pastiche of fishing piers, hotels, and shops, but its hottest attraction may be the **New England Aquarium**. Trade stares with a tankful of sharks and barracudas as you descend a spiral walkway. Then trek to the lively North End to see the oldest structure in Boston, Paul Revere's home, circa 1680.

Skyline of contrasts: Boston's Customs Tower soars above the 1825 Quincy Market.

2 BROOKLINE

John F. Kennedy was born in a handsome three-story house on Beals Street, now the **John Fitzgerald Kennedy National Historic Site**. Here America's 35th president spent his first four years. Restored to its early-20th-century appearance, the eight-room structure contains many original furnishings, including the bassinet used by four of the Kennedy children. A taped narrative by the president's mother, Rose Kennedy, accompanies the house tours.

3 CAMBRIDGE

Of the 100-odd seats of higher learning in the Boston region, perhaps the most prestigious is **Harvard University**. Its libraries and museums alone would be the pride of any community. The **Widener Library** has a Gutenberg Bible and a Shakespeare First Folio from 1623. Harvard's nine superb museums have collections ranging from pre-Columbian artifacts to contemporary paintings.

▶ *Free tours of Harvard Yard can be arranged at the university information office at Holyoke Center.*

Old Cambridge is an easy walk from Harvard Square. The **Common** was once reserved for grazing farm animals but is now peppered with a steady stream of students. Visitors can tour the nearby **Hooper-Lee-Nichols House**, whose oldest section dates back to 1683, and the 1761 **Christ Church**, Cambridge's oldest house of worship.

A few blocks away is the poet Henry Wadsworth Longfellow's 1759 Georgian mansion. Its original furniture includes Longfellow's desk and a chair made from a "spreading chestnut tree," evoking a line from his poem "The Village Blacksmith." Longfellow died here in 1882.

4 LEXINGTON

On April 19, 1775, in the gray early-morning mist on the town green, the first shots of the Revolution were exchanged between British troops and Capt. John Parker and his Minutemen, who were alerted during the night to the British raid by Paul Revere riding horseback through the countryside.

Three structures from the time of the skirmish are among several standing today. **Buckman Tavern** displays period furniture and weapons and a door that still shows a bullet hole. The **Hancock-Clarke House**, built in 1698, exhibits the drum used to rally the Minutemen onto the green. The tiny 1695 **Munroe Tavern** served as a British headquarters during the fighting at Lexington. A bullet hole in its ceiling is a grim reminder of that tumultuous time.

5 CONCORD

Here on the North Bridge is where the real commitment to war began, where "with ... Droms and fifes agoing," a corps of plucky Minutemen—farmers,

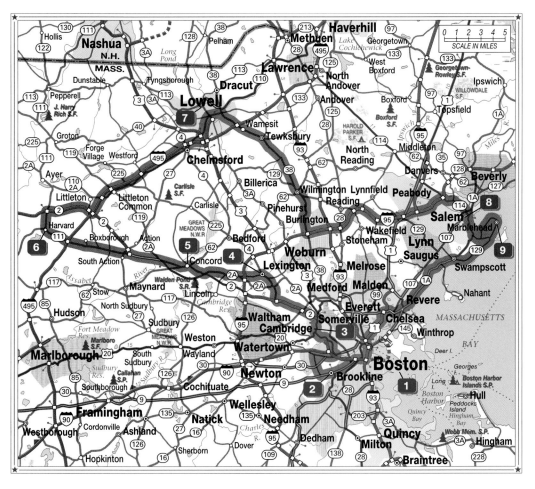

utopian commune founded by the transcendentalist Bronson Alcott, father of Louisa May. Exhibits in the **Fruitlands Farmhouse** trace this movement, which espoused self-sufficiency and asceticism. The **Picture Gallery** displays Hudson River School art, while the c.1790 **Shaker Museum** contains examples of sturdy Shaker furniture and handicrafts. View Henry Thoreau's arrowhead collection at the **American Indian Museum.** Museums are open from spring into October.

7 LOWELL

This 1826 mill town is often called the Cradle of the American Industrial Revolution. At the **Lowell National Historical Park,** the preserved brick and granite relics of factory life are a monument to the immigrants who flooded the area to work in one of the nation's largest cloth-manufacturing centers. This it remained until the 1920's, when cheap labor in the South lured mill owners to relocate.

Women ran the power looms; evidence of their grim, regimented lives is on display in the restored boarding-house near the **Boott Cotton Mills Museum.** Afterward, you can take a boat ride on the old canals.

The **Whistler House Museum of Art** was the birthplace of the celebrated painter James Abbott McNeill Whistler. The 1823 house contains several of Whistler's etchings and many fine 19th- and 20th-century American paintings.

8 SALEM

This city isn't shy about admitting to the hysteria that gripped its citizenry in 1692. A sound-and-light show at the **Salem Witch Museum** tells the sorry tale of the witch-hunts that resulted in the deaths of 20 people.

Fortunately, Salem's past is much more than witchcraft, and its pedigree

---

blacksmiths, and storekeepers from neighboring towns—first fought back against the British. Angered by the raid on Lexington, the Minutemen forced panicking British soldiers to flee to Boston. The 750 wooded acres of the **Minute Man National Historical Park** commemorate the events of April 18 and 19, 1775.

Concord was also home to many important figures of 19th-century literature. The nation's largest collection of Henry Thoreau artifacts can be found at the **Concord Museum.** The writer's bare-bones lifestyle is reflected in the furniture that he crafted by hand, on exhibit in the museum.

The **Ralph Waldo Emerson House** was the poet and essayist's home from 1835 till his death. Many of the items on display are original, right down to the hat jauntily placed on a newel post.

▶ *The visitor center is open seven days a week, year-round. Self-guided walking-tour maps are available for the 10-minute stroll to the North Bridge.*

6 HARVARD

Spread out on a mossy hillside are the four structures known collectively as the **Fruitlands Museums**, once a

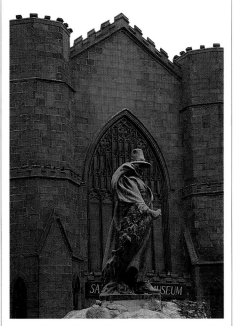

"Witch City" founder Roger Conant guards the portals of the Salem Witch Museum.

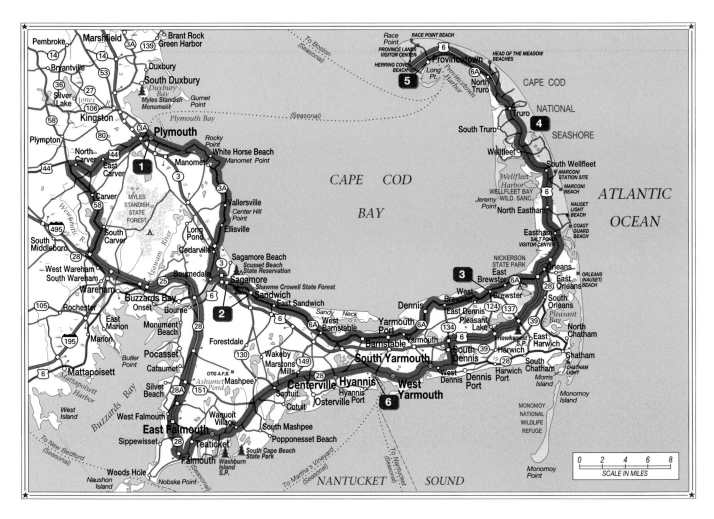

as a vital seaport is underscored at the **Salem Maritime National Historic Site,** where the **Custom House**—crowned by a splendid gilded eagle—once numbered Nathaniel Hawthorne among its employees. His office looks much as it did in the 1840's.

The 1762 **Derby House** is a typical example of a prosperous merchant's home. Elias Derby's belongings here include an ornate ivory fan from China. Nearby stands the spellbinding **House of the Seven Gables,** a dark, romantic structure that inspired the Hawthorne novel of the same name.

9 MARBLEHEAD

This lovely cobblestoned seaport, founded by fishermen and shipbuilders in 1629, has a harbor much revered by yachtsmen. From **Chandler Hovey Park,** you can get splendid views of the shoreline, with fleets of sailboats in constant liquid motion. Visit the 1768 **Jeremiah Lee Mansion,** in the city's historic district. It's one of the nation's

finest pre-Revolutionary homes, with 16 rooms of elegant furnishings.

▶ *Don't miss Marblehead's annual Christmas Walk, the first weekend in December, when Santa arrives by lobster boat and the city celebrates with tree lightings, music, and free trolley service.*

CAPE COD

1 PLYMOUTH

The Cape Cod peninsula, a gently curved half-circle shaped by wind and water, is a beloved vacation spot for visitors and natives alike. Although Plymouth is technically north of the Cape, as a place of beginnings it's a proper starting point. In fact, the site of one of the first permanent European settlements in America was not even the Pilgrims' original landfall of choice. They first scouted Provincetown, on Novem-

ber 13, 1620—stopping to wash clothes—but, seeking a more protected harbor, chose Plymouth, in December of 1620. Whether the colonists' first steps into the New World were actually upon the great boulder on the shore is the stuff of legends, but the reality was a grim one: most of the settlers remained on the *Mayflower* until shelters could be built; before winter's end half had died from the cold or disease. A visible reminder of the colonists' determination and tenacity amid harsh conditions, **Plymouth Rock** is enshrined on the shore, canopied by a palatial McKim, Mead & White granite portico.

Today Plymouth is a lovely seaside town whose economy is driven by tourism, fishing, and cranberry farming. You could spend a day at **Plimouth Plantation,** a remarkable re-creation of the original Pilgrim village, where guides in period costumes offer a detailed look at such day-to-day Colonial activities as bread baking, sheep shearing, fish salting, and musket drills.

2 SAGAMORE/SANDWICH

This part of the Cape was once home to a thriving glass industry, and collectors the world over still pay handsomely for antique handblown relics. View first-hand the craft practiced in Sagamore at **Pairpoint Crystal**, where master glass-blowers use mouth pipes to create colorful, ornamental lead crystal, just as artisans did in centuries past.

Incorporated in 1639, the town of Sandwich is world-renowned for its glassware. Many beautiful examples of handblown crystal have been preserved in the **Sandwich Glass Museum**, on Main Street.

▶ *Route 6A, called the King's Highway, is more a country lane than a highway. Along the tree-lined route, 18th-century homes, stone walls, and rock gardens are graceful reminders of simpler times.*

Sandwich is also a lovely town for strolling, complete with clapboard churches and centuries-old homes. For an intimate look at Colonial New England, visit Sandwich's **Hoxie House.** Built around 1637, this classic saltbox of thick, hand-hewn timbers is the oldest house on Cape Cod and is furnished with period furniture. Set on a grassy knoll that stretches toward tranquil Shawme Pond, the Hoxie area is also a delightful place for leisurely walking. Stop in next door at **Dexter's Grist Mill**, a 17th-century mill where corn is still ground for demonstration and sale.

3 BREWSTER

Good fortune on the high seas brought prosperity to the charming town of Brewster in the early 19th century. Visit the rows of elegant sea captains' homes that reflect those times. If you are traveling in the spring, be sure to stop by the **Herring Run.** The shimmering waters of Herring Brook are so crowded with fish heading up the run's concrete ladders that you can reach right in and scoop them up.

Plan a visit to the **Cape Cod Museum of Natural History.** Dedicated to preserving the Cape's fragile environment, this sanctuary and educational center offers exhibits and nature walks through miles of scenic trails.

4 CAPE COD NATIONAL SEASHORE

This magnificent area covers nearly 30,000 acres and features high cliffs, rolling dunes, broad beaches, miles of walking trails that wind through marshes, cedar swamps, and grasslands, and an astonishing range of wildlife. Visit the **Salt Pond Visitor Center,** where films and exhibits interpret the fragile ecological system of the barrier peninsula. Or stop in at the visitor center in Eastham to pick up maps of the area and view the exhibits.

5 PROVINCETOWN

A thriving fishing port and artists' retreat, Provincetown lies at the tip of the Cape's curl and has some of the most spectacular scenery on the east coast.

Summer beachgoers can explore the 1897 Old Harbor Lifesaving Station in Provincetown.

On the narrow main thoroughfare, 18th- and 19th-century shingled houses sit alongside galleries and trinket shops. Stop in at the Chamber of Commerce for walking-tour maps.

For a superb view of the Cape, climb **Pilgrim Monument**, a 252-foot granite tower. Hike or bike the trails that twist through the town's wind-sculpted sand dunes or opt for the narrated dune-buggy tours.

6 HYANNIS

The urban center of the Cape, Hyannis is often bypassed by visitors shuttling off to other Cape destinations. But this lively village has much to offer. Be sure to catch a show or a concert at the **Cape Cod Melody Tent.** For some 40 seasons the raising of the massive striped tent has announced the arrival of summer on the Cape.

Stroll down Main Street, past one of the oldest buildings in the area, the **Hyannis Public Library.** The former town hall, nearby, houses the **Kennedy Museum.** Here you can linger over family photographs and personal documents, which help to paint a vivid picture of the life and times of the country's 35th president.

Speaking of Kennedys, many visitors steer for nearby **Hyannis Port,** hoping to catch a glimpse of a member of the famous family. One of the loveliest villages on the Cape, Hyannis Port is also one of the most private—with no shops, restaurants, inns, public beaches, or parking spaces. If you are determined, nonetheless, to spot the **Kennedy Compound,** board a sight-seeing boat at Hyannis Port harbor. You'll have an unobstructed view of a former Summer White House.

From Hyannis, drive west to **Woods Hole,** a quaint seaside village that is home to the **Woods Hole Oceanographic Institution,** the largest independent oceanographic laboratory in the world. Its deep-sea sub, *Alvin,* was used to explore the undersea wreckage of the *Titanic.*

It's only a ferry ride from Hyannis to **Nantucket** or **Martha's Vineyard**, whose handsome historic homes complement the islands' lush natural beauty. A ferry to Martha's Vineyard runs from the town of Woods Hole as well, and in the summer season, an inter-island ferry carries passengers to and from the two islands.

Nantucket's cobblestone streets, lined with charming saltboxes trimmed in rose-covered picket fences, are more conducive to strollers than to cars. The island's elegant homes reflect the prosperity of its 19th-century whaling heritage. The Nantucket Historical Association maintains 11 properties that visitors can tour, including the **Old Mill**, fashioned in part from shipwreck wood in 1746, and the **Whaling Museum.**

A sunny hideaway for the rich and famous, lovely Martha's Vineyard is New England's largest island. Catch the late-summer **Grand Illumination**, in Oak Bluff, when Victorian gingerbread cottages are wreathed in gossamer paper lanterns and strollers are entertained by bandstand musicians.

▶ *The Cape Cod Scenic Railroad in Hyannis offers relaxing tours of little-seen parts of the Cape. You'll glide past sand dunes, cranberry bogs, and unspoiled areas unreachable by car or on foot.*

STURBRIDGE & BERKSHIRES

1 OLD STURBRIDGE VILLAGE

The time is circa 1830, the setting a rural New England community so evocative of life in a bygone America that you would swear Andrew Jackson still occupied the White House. On a 200-acre tract of rolling fields and woodland, more than 40 period buildings from other New England sites have been faithfully assembled and restored. Many function as they did more than 150 years ago. Sheep graze by the **Center Meeting House** on the village common, tended by a shepherd in a tall straw hat; their wool will be spun into

yarn on a period loom. Fine wood-frame buildings rim the common, with costumed interpreters on hand to show visitors around. An old-time general store stocks goods made by Old Sturbridge artisans: potters, coopers, blacksmiths, and tinsmiths clad in period garb. Dirt paths wind their way to a picturesque water-powered sawmill, a gristmill, and to the **Pliny Freeman Farm**, where field hands raise animals, harvest vegetables, press cider, and mend fences using the tools and methods of the early 19th century.

▶ *The village's roads are like those of the 1830's and are likely to be dusty or even muddy. Choose sturdy walking shoes for your tour.*

A stalwart pair of oxen hauls hay on a country road in Old Sturbridge Village.

2 SPRINGFIELD

From its early days as a farming community, Springfield has grown to become the largest city in western Massachusetts. Its fame rests on two remarkable inventions: the Springfield rifle, standard issue to American infantrymen up through World War I, and the game of basketball, devised by James Naismith in 1891. You can see the rifles and other weapons of local make at a museum in the old **Springfield Armory**, which supplied the nation with shoulder arms from the late 18th century until 1968. The **Basket-**

ball Hall of Fame celebrates Naismith's brainchild with memorabilia, movies, and interactive displays.

3 TYRINGHAM

The wildly fanciful **Gingerbread House** resembles nothing so much as a gnome's cottage blown up to adult size. It served as a studio for Sir Henry Kitson, the sculptor who fashioned the Minuteman statue at Lexington. Kitson constructed a three-story work space, erected stone pillars with grottoes in between, and topped it all with an 80-ton beam-and-shingle roof designed to simulate the rolling contours of the Berkshire hills. Gingerbread House is now a local art gallery.

4 STOCKBRIDGE

A fashionable enclave of artists and the like, the quaint village of Stockbridge is home to the outstanding **Norman Rockwell Museum**, with a sizable collection of original art by this master of apple-pie American life.

Nearby **Chesterwood**, the summer estate of sculptor Daniel Chester French, provides formal gardens, woodland walks, antique furnishings from Europe and America, and the plaster casts for one of French's most famous works: the immense Lincoln Memorial statue in Washington, D.C.

5 LENOX

A summer resort area of patrician families from New York and Boston, Lenox is filled with country estates from the late 19th and early 20th centuries. Most notable among them is **The Mount**, a sprawling American classical mansion that was the home of Edith Wharton, the first woman to win a Pulitzer Prize; it stands amid formal Italian gardens designed by the author herself.

▶ *Guided walking tours of Lenox and Stockbridge are offered by the Berkshire Tour Company, by appointment.*

Tanglewood, nestled in the hills west of Lenox, is the picturesque summer home of the Boston Symphony Orchestra. Music lovers converge here by the thousands with blankets and picnic baskets in hand.

6 HANCOCK SHAKER VILLAGE

One of America's oldest and best-preserved Shaker sites, **Hancock Shaker Village** was founded in 1790 by the breakaway Protestant sect known for celibacy, spiritual fervor, and extraordinary craftsmanship. "Hands to work, hearts to God" was the sect's motto. Evidences of Shaker skill and ingenuity abound here in the clean, spare lines of Hancock's 21 buildings, in the neat symmetry of its herb gardens, and in the straight-back chairs hung on wall pegs in the **Brick Dwelling House** (with its separate entrances for men and women). In the 1826 **Round Stone Barn,** a single worker could pitch hay to 52 cows from a circular walkway in the barn's center.

In nearby Pittsfield sits **Arrowhead,** the rustic 18th-century farmhouse where Herman Melville lived with his family while he wrote his great sea novel, *Moby Dick,* in 1850.

7 HISTORIC DEERFIELD

A tomahawk scar still visible on the doorway of the Old Indian House at the **Memorial Hall Museum** marks Deerfield's most grimly dramatic moment:

Shaker handiwork, refined to the essentials of form and function, is artful in its simplicity. Sunshine paints a room at Hancock Shaker Village, where a prominent washstand calls ever to mind the virtues of cleanliness.

a bloody attack by French and Indian warriors in 1704 that virtually wiped out the original settlement and all of its inhabitants. Since then little has happened to mar the town's gentle tranquillity. Along a tree-lined, mile-long stretch known simply as **The Street** rises a host of handsome Colonial and Federal houses. Inside the homes you'll find unrivaled collections of furnishings, paintings, textiles, silver, pewter, ceramics, and other artifacts from the 18th and 19th centuries.

8 NORTHAMPTON

With handsome buildings, tree-shaded streets, interesting boutiques, and an oddly bohemian air, Northampton is best known as the home of **Smith College,** founded in 1871. Visit the **Smith College Museum of Art** for its fine collection of 19th- and 20th-century European and American art.

9 AMHERST

The Connecticut River valley, broad and richly fertile, has long been a region of higher learning. Graduates of **Amherst College,** founded back in 1821, include abolitionist clergyman Henry Ward Beecher and President Calvin Coolidge. The college's **Pratt Museum of Geology** displays an interesting collection of meteorites, fossils, and American Indian artifacts.

The town of Amherst was also home to Emily Dickinson, one of America's greatest poets. She was born in the Federal-style **Dickinson Homestead** in 1830 and died there, a spinster and recluse, in 1886. The visionary poems on which her reputation rests are thought to have been discovered here in a chest. The Homestead, now faculty housing, can be visited by appointment.

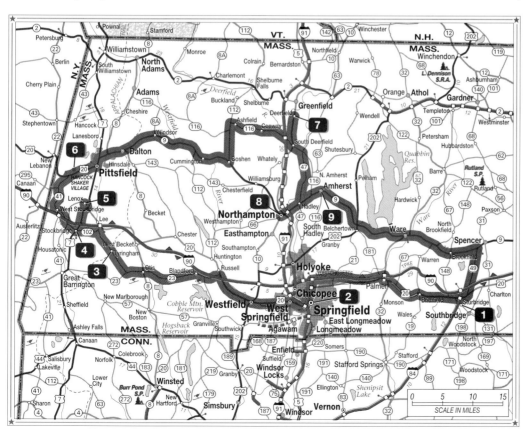

Newport

Rhode Island

With lavish mansions, unspoiled islands, and even a winery or two, the smallest state in the nation is packed with history, authentic New England flavor, and an allure all its own.

RHODE ISLAND COAST

1 NEWPORT

Virtually all of America's prominent families—from the Astors to the Kennedys—have summered in this gracious city by the sea. Six of their spectacular vacation homes are open for viewing on mansion tours offered by the Preservation Society. The most extravagant among them, **The Breakers**,

The Cliff Walk, offering views of the palatial Newport mansions on one side and the slate-colored sea on the other, was once a path used by fishermen in pursuit of a day's work.

features 70 rooms and took some 2,000 workers two years to complete. After seeing these incredible palatial estates, it's hard to believe that former owners, such as railroad king Cornelius Vanderbilt II, blithely referred to them as "summer cottages."

▶ *Newport can be chaotic during its summer music festivals. To avoid the crowds, visit in spring or fall, or wait until December and see the mansions "dressed" in their holiday best.*

Not on the tour but worth a visit are **Belcourt Castle**, a Louis XIII–style

grandiosity with the owners in residence; **Hammersmith Farm**, reception venue for the wedding of John F. Kennedy to Jacqueline Bouvier, filled with family photos and memorabilia; and **The Astors' Beechwood Mansion**, former home of Caroline Astor, who devised the Four Hundred list of America's social elite. (Conveniently, 400 was also the number of guests that could be entertained in her ballroom.) Here actors dressed as servants, so-

cialites, and friends of "The Mrs. Astor" re-create the spirit of Newport's Gilded Age. Stroll the three-mile Cliff Walk along the coast for a different view of these ornate seaside jewels. (Watch your footing—portions of the walk are narrow and rocky.)

Touro Synagogue, America's oldest Jewish house of worship, stands in sharp contrast to the gold and marble excesses of the mansions. Built in 1763, it is considered a masterpiece of simple Georgian architecture.

Occasional site of the America's Cup yacht race and former site of the tennis tournament now known as the U.S.

Open, Newport is the home of the **Museum of Yachting** and the **International Tennis Hall of Fame**. For a look at Newport's seafaring heritage, visit the **Naval War College Museum**. End the day with a ride along Narragansett Bay on the **Star Clipper Dinner Train**.

2 JAMESTOWN

Across the bridge from Newport lies this peaceful community, the only settlement on mile-wide Conanicut Island. After strolling by some of the town's historic homes, head to **Beavertail Lighthouse and State Park**, on the craggy southern tip of the island. A three-mile walking trail offers stunning views of the Rhode Island coastline and winds its way to Beavertail Lighthouse. The original lighthouse was burned, along with the rest of Jamestown, by the British in 1775. The present tower, built in 1856, is still in use.

3 SAUNDERSTOWN

Gilbert Stuart, one of America's most celebrated portrait artists, famous for his renderings of George Washington, was born in a gambrel-roof house here in 1755. The **Gilbert Stuart Birthplace** is now a Colonial museum, filled with period furnishings. Adjacent to the home, America's first water-powered snuff mill, built by Stuart's father, is still in operation.

4 NARRAGANSETT PIER

Once a Victorian resort, this town retains much of the charm that brought vacationing families here more than 100 years ago. A real gem is **Sand Hill Cove**, a quiet beach with calm surf, perfect for swimming.

One section remains of the **Narragansett Pier Casino**, once the hub of the Narragansett summer scene. Called the Towers, the turreted structure now houses a visitor center.

The **South County Museum** at Canonchet Farm is a faithfully restored 19th-century working farm. The 174-acre park offers nature trails, picnic areas, and a working print shop.

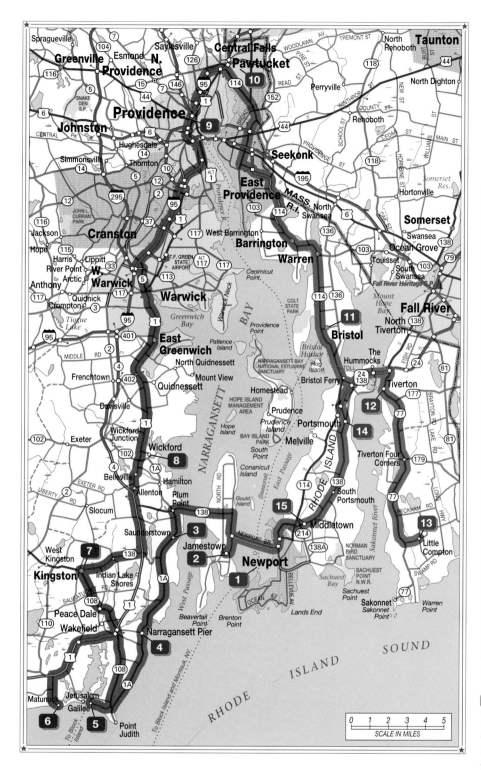

The Southeast Light, poised against an azure sky, overlooks a bluff on Block Island.

Beach, on the east coast. Hearty walkers can continue north to the **Clayhead Nature Trail.** Known as The Maze, the trail consists of 11 miles of manicured paths leading to breathtaking cliffside views of the Atlantic and, eventually, to **Settlers' Rock,** on the north shore, marking the spot where the island's first settlers landed.

Block Island Cemetery, a traditional New England graveyard dating from the 17th century, stands near the center of the island. On the south end, **Mohegan Bluffs** rise above the rocky shoreline. From this natural grandstand it's easy to see why many people compare the shores of Block Island with the rugged coasts of Ireland and Scotland.

6 MATUNUCK

For an unusual treat, take in a summer stock performance at **Theatre-by-the-Sea,** a restored barn theater that's listed in the National Register of Historic Places. Matinee and evening performances of Broadway shows run May through October. The nearby **East Matunuck State Beach** is one of the finest on the east coast.

7 KINGSTON

In the village of Kingston, with a collection of 18th- and early-19th-century homes, you'll find the **Fayerweather**

5 GALILEE/BLOCK ISLAND

The quaint fishing village of Galilee, on Point Judith, is the departure point for the year-round ferry to windswept Block Island, one of Rhode Island's most spectacular attractions. Just 11 square miles in size, the unspoiled island packs in plenty of colorful history. Before it became a resort popular with artists, it was a favorite haunt of 18th-century smugglers, robbers, and pirates. Locals still tell tales of buried treasure and pirate ghosts who walk the island at night. Other sometime inhabitants include more than 150 species of migrating birds.

The ferry arrives in the **Old Harbor,** a quaint area brimming with interesting shops and restaurants. From here it's a short stroll to picturesque **Crescent**

Craft Center. Built in 1820, it was once the home of George Fayerweather, an African-American blacksmith, and his American Indian wife and their 12 children. Today visitors come here in the summertime to watch weekly demonstrations of crafts, from Brazilian embroidery to basket weaving, and to purchase the one-of-a-kind wares of the Fayerweather Craft Guild.

8 WICKFORD

Wickford is like a storybook example of the perfect New England town, with quaint shops, boutiques, and art galleries. **Smith's Castle,** a mile north of the business district, is a rather grand name for the simple two-story 17th-century plantation house built in 1678 by Richard Smith at the trading post that had once been owned by Rhode Island colony founder Roger Williams. Guests included Benjamin Franklin and Lafayette. Today costumed interpreters lead tours of the house, furnished with 18th-century antiques; a tour of the grounds includes a mass grave of Colonial soldiers and an 18th-century-style flower and herb garden.

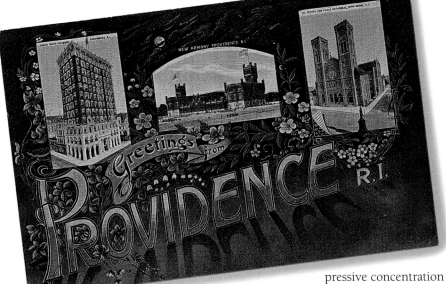

From here you can take a quick inland detour to the town of Exeter to visit the **Dovecrest Trading Post & Museum,** a living history museum of early Rhode Island Indian life.

9 PROVIDENCE

Rhode Island was founded as a haven for those seeking religious freedom, and it's no wonder that the capital, once a shipping center, is today a friendly place with a progressive state of mind carried over from its earliest days. A host of colleges and universities keeps the town young and vibrant.

As you wander through the ivy-covered campus of Brown University, take time to visit the **John Carter Brown Library,** with an outstanding store of Americana as well as historical maps and documents. On the streets surrounding the campus, you'll find everything from preppy clothing shops to underground bookstores. The **Museum of Art** is located on the Rhode Island School of Design campus. It offers a fine collection of Latin American, European, and American painting, furniture, and decorative arts, but its highlight is without a doubt a remarkable 12th-century Japanese Buddha.

Pick up a map at the Providence Preservation Society office, then walk the city's Mile of History down **Benefit Street,** with cobblestone sidewalks, old-fashioned streetlamps, and an impressive concentration of well-preserved Colonial homes. Nearby is the **John Brown Mansion,** a three-story Georgian residence described by John Quincy Adams as "the most magnificent and elegant mansion that I have ever seen on this continent."

For shopping, head to the **Arcade,** said to be America's oldest indoor shopping center. A National Historic Landmark, it is interesting for its Greek Revival architecture as well as its vast assortment of stores.

The **State Capitol,** modeled after the nation's Capitol, features one of the largest self-supported marble domes in the world. The Capitol's art collection includes a full-length portrait of George Washington by Rhode Island's own Gilbert Stuart.

► *If you're looking to savor a local treat, head to the neighborhood of Fox Point and pick up a loaf of mouth-watering Portuguese sweet bread.*

After roaming the streets of Providence, take a break at **Roger Williams Park.** Parents and kids will have a ball at the Zoo, Museum of Natural History, and Planetarium. Also in the park, Carousel Village features rides, amusements, and a wonderful restored Victorian carousel. Those seeking quieter pursuits will be content to stroll through acres of flower gardens and tropical greenhouses.

When hunger strikes, head for **Federal Hill,** the city's Little Italy, filled with plain and fancy family-run Italian restaurants and cafés.

10 PAWTUCKET

Pawtucket (the Algonquian word for "place by a waterfall") was home to America's first water-powered textile mill, now the **Slater Mill Historic Site.** The mill has been described as the birthplace of the American Industrial Revolution. Here you can see traditional hand-spinning and textile-weaving demonstrations, an authentic 19th-century machine shop, and the eight-ton waterwheel that powers the shop.

11 BRISTOL

Stately mansions, expansive gardens, and a historic harbor are highlights of this Narragansett Bay town. Like Newport, Bristol experienced its glory days at the turn of the century, when firearms maker Samuel P. Colt owned a home here. Colt's former estate is now **Colt State Park,** with 460 coastal acres where visitors can picnic, enjoy saltwater fishing, or visit **Coggeshall Farm Museum,** which features a working farm and blacksmith shop.

One hundred years ago, no yachtsman worth his salt owned anything but a Bristol-built Herreshoff craft. **Herreshoff Marine Museum** traces the history of the company that designed and built six successful America's Cup defenders between 1893 and 1920. A number of classic sailing and power yachts are on view. Members of the family are occasionally on hand to meet and talk with visitors.

When Pennsylvania coal magnate Augustus Van Wickle bought his wife a yacht (a Herreshoff, of course), he searched for the perfect mooring site, and found it in Bristol. Overlooking the bay, **Blithewold Mansion and Gardens** was the Van Wickles' summer home. Tour the 45-room mansion, built to resemble a 17th-century English manor, then stroll the 33 acres of beautifully landscaped grounds. The arboretum is truly innovative, with more than 50,000 flowering bulbs, a Japanese water garden, and a 90-foot-tall giant sequoia—the largest east of the Rockies—among its plantings.

► *Plan to visit Blithewold in the morning, when it's less crowded, and then see the Herreshoff Marine Museum, which is open only in the afternoon.*

Those with a penchant for archeology or an interest in North American Indians will want to visit the **Haffenreffer Museum of Anthropology,** run by Brown University. Set in 375 acres of woodland, it is near the site where Indian chief King Philip was ambushed and killed in 1676, ending King Philip's War. A fascinating collection of art and artifacts is on display.

12 TIVERTON

Climb the hill to the spot where **Fort Barton** once stood, and you'll be rewarded with a panoramic view of the Sakonnet River, Narragansett Bay, and Rhode Island Sound. The fort, built in 1777, was an American stronghold during the Revolutionary War. Nature trails wind through the grounds, and a printed guide explains the area's importance to Colonial strategists.

Ruecker Wildlife Refuge offers 48 acres of woodland, meadow, marsh,

A carefully tended paradise surrounds Blithewold Mansion, a stone's throw from the bay.

and open water. Ospreys and herons are among the birds that fly overhead.

13 LITTLE COMPTON

Wilbor House, built in 1680 and continuously occupied by eight generations of Wilbors, is the high point of this bucolic town and home of the Little Compton Historical Society. Restored rooms represent three centuries, from the Colonial Great Room to the 18th-century bedroom with its embroidered bed curtains and the 19th-century bedroom with a beautiful burled wood bed. Fascinating furnishings and trinkets abound. An adjoining barn contains historical farm equipment, carriages, sleighs, and other vehicles.

Wine lovers will want to sample a glass of America's Cup White at **Sakonnet Vineyards,** the oldest vineyard in the state. Tours of the winery are offered in season, and the tasting rooms are open year-round.

14 PORTSMOUTH

In 1778 Portsmouth was the site of the only major Revolutionary War land battle fought in the state. The remains of **Butts Hill Fort** and the **Memorial to Black Soldiers** commemorate the Battle of Rhode Island.

Since then, life has been relatively peaceful here, and the town's major sites are of a pastoral or spiritual nature. Picturesque **Portsmouth Abbey and School** is a Benedictine religious center and preparatory school. Its Church of

St. Gregory the Great houses an unusual wire sculpture by Richard Lippold.

Green Animals Topiary Gardens is a delight for young and old. Eighty animals and geometric figures sculpted from trees and shrubs dot the colorful Victorian garden. Stop in the main house for a look at the small Victorian toy museum.

► *Combination tickets are available for Green Animals Topiary Gardens and the Newport mansions.*

15 MIDDLETOWN

The 1812 windmill at **Prescott Farm** still grinds cornmeal from Rhode Island flint corn. It's the focal point of this restored Colonial farm where British General Richard Prescott was captured during the Revolutionary War. Another Englishman, Bishop George Berkeley, arrived here by mistake in 1729 while sailing to Bermuda. His antique-filled home is now **Whitehall Museum House.**

The Ocean State boasts beautiful beaches, and Middletown's **Second Beach** is one of the area's finest, where you can walk for miles on the long, wide expanse of white sand. Nature lovers will want to explore the nearby 450-acre **Norman Bird Sanctuary,** where eight miles of walking trails wind through verdant woodlands and past salt marshes and grassy cliff overlooks. A museum contains mounted birds and other natural history exhibits.

Connecticut

The state that defines the Yankee spirit is steeped in history, from the maritime heritage of Mystic to the carefully preserved villages that pepper the countryside with New England charm.

1 HARTFORD

In the 19th century Connecticut's capital was home to a vibrant community of writers and political thinkers. They congregated at **Nook Farm**, a shady enclave west of downtown, where both Mark Twain and Harriet Beecher Stowe built homes. The **Mark Twain House** is an ornate Victorian fantasy, decorated with whimsical brick mosaics and an expansive porch resembling a deck on a Mississippi riverboat. The **Harriet Beecher Stowe** house is a quiet cottage, where the author of *Uncle Tom's Cabin* spent much of her time gardening and sharing horticulture tips with friends.

Don't miss the **Wadsworth Atheneum**, a cultural gem in the heart of downtown. Though it's located in this most traditional of cities, and is one of the country's oldest public art museums, it is known for its innovative exhibits, including surrealist paintings by René Magritte. Also displayed are works by Thomas Cole and other Hudson River School painters, and an exquisite European porcelain collection.

2 WEST HARTFORD

Father of the dictionary and author of the classic *Blue-Backed Speller*, Noah Webster was born in West Hartford in 1758. Costumed guides lead tours of the **Noah Webster House**, a simple farmhouse filled with Webster memorabilia and period furnishings. Some first editions of the lexicographer's early works are on view.

3 FARMINGTON

Affectionately known as Charmington, this inviting town brims with fine historic homes. Many of the graceful clapboard buildings belong to **Miss Porter's School**, a 150-year-old private girls' school that counts Jacqueline Onassis among its alumnae. Near the town center is the **Stanley-Whitman House**, built around 1720. An excellent example of early New England architecture, it features period furnishings along with a restored 18th-century herb and flower garden.

▶ *Twice a year, in June and September, Farmington hosts an Antiques Weekend, attended by hundreds of dealers from all over the country. Collectors will want to book hotel accommodations well in advance.*

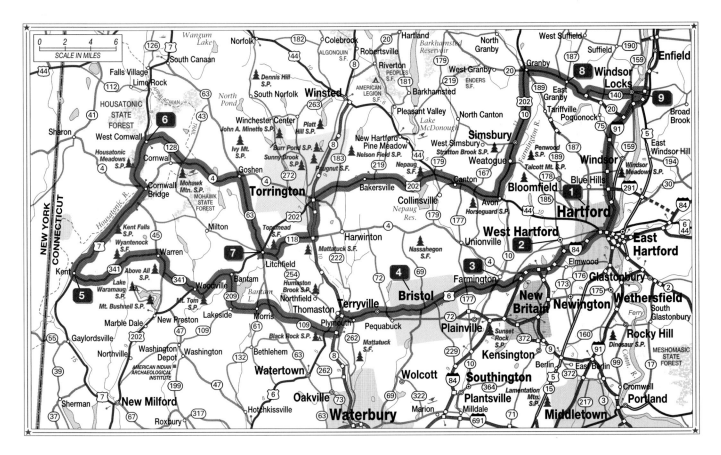

Farmington's highlight is **Hill-Stead Museum**, once the home of industrialist Alfred A. Pope. It was designed by his daughter Theodate Pope Riddle, one of the country's first female architects and a friend of Impressionist painter Mary Cassatt. The furnishings and grounds are lovely, but the museum is most remarkable for its paintings by Whistler, Cassatt, Monet, Manet, and Degas. As stipulated in the daughter's will, the Hill-Stead collection never travels; to see these works, you must visit them here.

4 BRISTOL

Celebrate everyday things at the **American Clock & Watch Museum** in Bristol and the **Lock Museum of America** in neighboring Terryville. The clock museum features more than 3,000 timepieces in a 19th-century house. At the lock museum some 22,000 locks, keys, and pieces of ornate hardware are on display.

There's nowhere else quite like the **New England Carousel Museum**, which houses a delightful collection of antique hand-carved carousel horses. Best of all, visitors can watch painters and carvers carefully restoring old pieces to their former glory.

5 KENT

Travelers in search of New England charm often find themselves in Kent, where antique shops and art galleries abound. Also here is **Bull's Bridge**, a covered bridge once used by George Washington and still open today.

Folks with a taste for American history will enjoy the **Sloane-Stanley Museum**. A collection of early American tools was donated by artist-writer Eric Sloane, famous for his distinctive illustrated books about early America. The museum also features a re-creation of Sloane's studio.

6 WEST CORNWALL

Have your camera handy as you approach West Cornwall, home of the **Cornwall Bridge**. One of Connecticut's three remaining covered bridges, it has been in continuous service since 1837. Stop in the quaint village here to explore the shops.

7 LITCHFIELD

This well-preserved village has long been home to famous figures: Ethan Allen, Henry Ward Beecher, and his sister Harriet Beecher Stowe were born here. Today actors, writers, and artists gravitate to this rural hideaway.

Surrounding the town green are the grand Colonial Revival homes of the **Litchfield Historical District**, built in

First Congregational Church of Litchfield graces the town green with classic charm.

the 18th and 19th centuries and later remodeled. Also here and open to the public is the **Tapping Reeve House and Law School**, America's first law school, founded in 1784. Aaron Burr was Reeve's first student.

▶ *To see the homes in the historical district, join the open-house tour in mid-July or the holiday tour, complete with music, in mid-December.*

Bird-watchers flock to the rolling woodlands of **White Memorial Foundation**, a 4,000-acre wildlife sanctuary bordering Bantam Lake. Wine lovers will want to take a relaxing stroll through beautiful **Haight Vineyard**. Tours and free tastings are offered year-round. And gardeners won't want to miss **White Flower Farm**, a nationally known nursery with 10 acres of display gardens and 30 acres of growing fields.

8 EAST GRANBY

The **Old New-Gate Prison and Copper Mine** is one of the strangest Colonial sites you're likely to encounter. During the Revolutionary War, Tories and British prisoners were shackled underground in the working copper mine. Visitors can venture into the tunnels and see how the shackles were bolted to the rocks. Later, New-Gate became the first state prison in the U.S. Inmates continued to work the mines until they rebelled, using their mining tools as weapons. Years later they were put to the more manageable task of making shoes in aboveground shops.

▶ *Watch your step in the mine tunnels, which are dimly lit, and be sure to wear sturdy walking shoes.*

9 WINDSOR LOCKS

The net-covered fields that dot this region, known as Tobacco Valley, are planted with tobacco, most of which is used for the outer wrappers of cigars.

One of the world's great collections of aircraft awaits aviation buffs at the **New England Air Museum** at Bradley International Airport. Here more than 75 historic flying machines appear ready for takeoff. If you prefer earthbound travel, visit the **Connecticut Trolley Museum**, where you ride an antique trolley or steam train into the past.

CONNECTICUT SHORELINE

1 MYSTIC

Some of the fastest clipper ships in the country were built in this pretty riverside village. Visitors can relive Mystic's maritime heritage at the **Mystic Seaport Museum** (exit 90 on I-95), where wooden sailing ships bob in the harbor, and ship carvers and sailmakers carry on the bygone ways of waterfront life. Costumed interpreters and more than 40 salt-worn buildings re-create the ambience of a 19th-century seafaring town. Berthed here is the *Charles W. Morgan,* the last of America's great whaling vessels, which you can board.

At **Mystic Marinelife Aquarium,** highlights include the ever-popular outdoor penguin pavilion, Seal Island, and indoor shows starring playful dolphins, whales, and sea lions.

▶ *Mystic is one of Connecticut's most-visited tourist destinations, and it can be crowded in summer. If possible, visit on a weekday or during the school year.*

A special lantern-lit tour of the seaport takes place near Christmas, with re-enactments of holiday scenes from the late 19th century that visitors take part in. Tickets go on sale during the first week of October, and you must act fast to get them—this is a treat worth planning ahead for.

2 GROTON

Much of the action in this shoreline town, a U.S. submarine base, takes place underwater. The **U.S.S. *Nautilus,*** the first nuclear-powered submarine, is now a fascinating museum. Tours include a look at the control room and working periscopes.

Take time to admire the view from **Fort Griswold State Park.** Remains of the Revolutionary War fort, where Col. William Ledyard was murdered after surrendering to the British, presides over the Thames River, which locals pronounce just as it's spelled. Climb the granite obelisk of Groton Monument for an even better view.

3 NEW LONDON

During the Revolutionary War Benedict Arnold raided New London and burned nearly all of the buildings. Happily, a few were spared. Among them are the **Joshua Hempsted House,** the oldest remaining house in the city, and the adjacent **Nathaniel Hempsted House.** Both contain furnishings and artifacts tracing several generations of one of New London's early families.

The stone **Shaw-Perkins Mansion** is a grander affair, built in 1756. It was once the home of Capt. Nathaniel Shaw and served as Connecticut's Revolutionary War naval headquarters. Nearby, the restored **Nathan Hale Schoolhouse** is where Connecticut's beloved patriot taught before enlisting. Finally, visit the

The Mystic Seaport Museum keeps America's great maritime heritage alive.

Monte Cristo Cottage, boyhood home of playwright Eugene O'Neill and setting for his plays *Ah, Wilderness!* and *Long Day's Journey Into Night.*

New London is best known as the home of the **U.S. Coast Guard Academy,** and a self-guided tour of the Academy grounds is a high point of any visit. On Fridays in spring and fall, visitors can observe formal dress parades, and on weekends the tall ship *Eagle* can be boarded when in port. Just north of the Academy, the **Connecticut College Arboretum** offers lovely walking trails and more than 300 varieties of native trees, shrubs, and plants.

A redcoat fife-and-drum corps recalls the British burning of New London in 1781.

4 MADISON

Hammonasset Beach State Park is Connecticut's largest waterfront park, with two miles of white sand beach, pretty picnic areas, campgrounds, and hiking trails. Swimmers, boaters, fishermen, and scuba divers congregate here.

Madison is not without its taste of history, of course. The 1785 **Allis-Bushnell House** features period rooms with corner fireplaces and original paneling, along with antique china, kitchenware,

and clothing including hats, gloves, shoes, and stickpins from the 1800's.

5 GUILFORD

When Rev. Henry Whitfield's house was built in 1639, it was built to last. The home's 30-inch-thick stone walls —unusual for Colonial construction— may have been intended to make the structure impenetrable so that villagers could gather here if the town fell under attack. Today the **Henry Whitfield State Museum** is New England's oldest stone residence. Restored in 1904, the museum houses a fascinating collection of early American antiques.

The **Hyland House** illustrates more typical Colonial saltbox construction. It features original furnishings, along with several walk-in fireplaces and an assortment of 17th-century cooking utensils.

Off the coast of Guilford are the tiny **Thimble Islands,** where the pirate Captain Kidd once romped. Today celebrities take cover here. Visitors can tour the islands, peppered with pirate legends, on summer cruises.

6 NEW HAVEN

In many ways New Haven, the first planned city in America, is Connecticut's most interesting urban center. **Yale University** is the pride of the city. Though located in the heart of downtown, the Gothic Ivy League campus maintains a mood of academic serenity. Of particular interest: **Yale University Art Gallery,** with a vast collection of 13th- through 20th-century art; **Beinecke Rare Book Library,** including medieval manuscripts and a Gutenberg Bible; and the **Yale Collection of Musical Instruments,** with some 800 pieces from the 16th to 20th centuries.

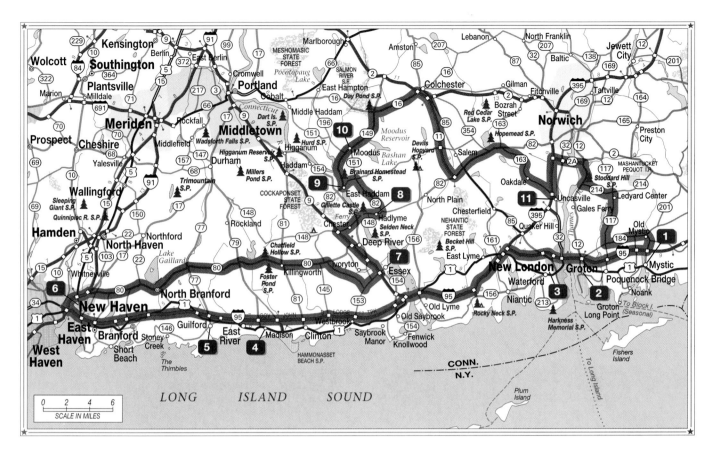

Adjacent to Yale is the **New Haven Green**, 16 acres of lawn that remain as plotted in the 1600's. Here sit three beautiful 19th-century churches. On the far side of the campus is **Grove Street Cemetery**, where Charles Goodyear, Noah Webster, and Eli Whitney are buried.

Near New Haven Harbor, visit **Black Rock Fort** and **Fort Nathan Hale** for their spectacular views and **Pardee-Morris House**, an 18th-century farmhouse, for its American primitive furnishings and pretty gardens.

Lovers of Italian food shouldn't miss **Wooster Street**, heart of New Haven's Little Italy. Debates rage over which restaurant serves the best pizza. Try white clam pizza, a local specialty.

▶ *Most of the family-owned restaurants serve delicious meals, but if you want pizza, go early. At dinnertime, especially when Yale students are in town, the wait can be interminable.*

7 ESSEX

Essex is the essence of authentic New England flavor, filled with quaint shops and cafés. Main Street, lined with sea captains' houses, leads to the **Connecticut River Museum** on the river's edge. Here you can view exhibits on the river's history, including a full-size reproduction of America's first submarine.

No visit is complete without a journey on the steam-powered **Valley Railroad**. The nine-mile trip along the river is most breathtaking when the fiery leaves of autumn are at their peak. Return by train or board a riverboat for a scenic cruise back to Essex.

8 HADLYME

Actor William Gillette gained fame in the 1900's portraying Sherlock Holmes on Broadway, and one can almost imagine his character living in the actor's home, **Gillette Castle**. Built between 1914 and 1919, the castle, complete with stone bastions and parapets, features a room devoted to the fictional detective. Surrounding the home is a state park, which offers a commanding view of the Connecticut River.

9 EAST HADDAM

Stop in East Haddam for a look at the restored **Goodspeed Opera House**, a splendid Victorian theater, which stages musicals from April to December. Aficionados of the genre will be fascinated by the Library of Musical Theatre, open by appointment. Don't miss the view of the Opera House from across the Connecticut River in Haddam.

10 MOODUS

The strange rumblings heard here on occasion are not caused by evil spirits, as the American Indians believed, but probably by seismic activity—though no one knows for sure.

Three generations of family furnishings and artifacts fill the 1816 **Amasa Day House**. Original stenciled designs still mark the floors in two rooms. A museum of local history is housed in a barn on the grounds.

11 UNCASVILLE

This town was named for Mohegan Indian chief Uncas, whose descendants founded the **Tantaquidgeon Indian Museum.** Here you'll find crafts, ritual objects, ceremonial clothing, and artifacts of Mohegan and other New England American Indians. A Mohegan Wigwam Powwow is held the third weekend in August.

MID-ATLANTIC

*T*ogether, the small towns and great cities of the five states that lie between the Appalachian Mountains and the Atlantic Ocean create one magnificent museum, alive with America's history, culture, and beauty. The driving tours that follow on the next 42 pages—through New York, Pennsylvania, New Jersey, Maryland, and Delaware—take you to the places where our nation took form: Independence Hall, the "invention factory" of Thomas Edison, the bustle of Manhattan, and the gleaming marble halls of Washington, D.C.

Choose a peaceful drive through the idyllic towns of the Pennsylvania Dutch country, the waterfalls and pristine creeks of the Delaware Water Gap, or the splendid solitude of the Adirondack Mountains. Or tour the grandest of houses: the opulent estate known as Winterthur and the Frank Lloyd Wright masterpiece called Fallingwater.

Nature, too, is dazzling here. See the waterfowl of Chesapeake Bay, the wild ponies of Chincotegue Island, the raptors of Hawk Mountain. Twenty tours of the highlights of the towns, the cities, and the countyside of this vast and beautiful treasury of Americana are at your fingertips—giving you a brand new look at our glorious national past.

Adirondack Park

Oswego

Buffalo   Syracuse

Albany

Erie

Scranton   Southampton

Manhattan

Pittsburgh   Columbia   Elmont

Harrisburg   Sandy Hook

Philadelphia

Wilmington

Baltimore   Atlantic City

Washington

Cambridge

Pennsylvania Dutch Country

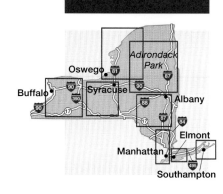

New York

You can have it all in the Empire State: the dazzle of Manhattan, the pure mountain air of the Adirondacks, the romance of Niagara Falls, the verdant farmland that fueled a fledgling nation.

MANHATTAN & THE HUDSON VALLEY

1 MANHATTAN

New York truly is a wonderful town. No other city in America can match it in sheer scale—it's bigger than life. The country's original melting pot is a vibrant modern city in a living-museum tableau: a place where sleek skyscrapers rise high above cobblestone streets and minimalist cafés sit beside centuries-old buildings. Its energetic population is hungry with ambition; for here the rewards can be as grand as the dreams.

► *As in any city at rush hour, public transportation can be crowded and cabs difficult to find. But New York is one of the world's great walking cities, so hoof it!*

The **Empire State Building**, in the heart of midtown, is no longer the tallest skyscraper on the globe, but it remains one of the classiest. Go for the view from the 102nd floor and the gorgeous Art Deco lobby.

Shoppers combing Fifth Avenue stores can rest their weary feet behind the **New York Public Library** in the cool environs of beautiful **Bryant Park.** Farther uptown is the world-famous **Plaza Hotel.** You can stroll through its sumptuous lobby; a painting of Eloise, the fictional heroine of children's books who lived at the Plaza, hangs here.

Upper Fifth Avenue bordering Central Park is known as Museum Mile. The intimate **Frick Collection** was once the pre–World War I mansion of the industrialist Henry Clay Frick; masterpieces by Vermeer, Rembrandt, and Renoir hang in beautifully appointed rooms.

You can spend days in the **Metropolitan Museum of Art.** Ever popular is the 2,000-year-old Temple of Dendur,

transplanted from Egypt and ringed by a marble moat, or the sunny Impressionists in the 19th-century gallery. On warm weekend evenings, have a glass of wine and watch the moon rise over a spectacular city skyline in the museum's Roof Garden. Look to the west, and you'll spot **Cleopatra's Needle,**

an ancient Egyptian obelisk, peering through the park's treeline.

Farther uptown are the **Guggenheim Museum**—its singular spiral design is by Frank Lloyd Wright—and the **Cooper-Hewitt Museum,** a former private mansion now featuring design and decorative-art exhibits. See the **American Museum of Natural History,** west of Central Park, for the dinosaur skeletons and the **Hayden Planetarium.**

Central Park is one of the world's great urban parks. The park's **Loeb Boathouse** is a hidden gem. After museum hopping, relax here with a cold drink or take a rowboat ride. **Bethesda Fountain,** a splendid Italianate struc-

ture, gives the scene a European flavor. The view of the city skyline from Central Park's moss-green **Sheep Meadow** is one of the best-kept secrets in New York; in the summer, sunbathers and joggers abound here.

Downtown in the financial district, ride the ear-popping elevator 107 stories up to the **World Trade Center** observation deck. Or take a stroll on the expansive waterfront square of the **World Financial Center** and watch yachts maneuver into the docks. In **Chinatown,** the influx of innovative

An oasis in the Big Apple, *Bethesda Fountain in Central Park is a popular rendezvous site.*

Hong Kong chefs has revitalized the restaurant scene. Dine in one of the gleaming new eateries and then stroll to nearby **Little Italy** for cappuccino and an Italian pastry at a sidewalk café.

Take the ferries to the **Statue of Liberty** and **Ellis Island** at **Battery Park.** Or take a less crowded, less costly ride on the **Staten Island Ferry,** past the many monuments in New York Harbor.

The tranquil stone structures of the **Cloisters,** in upper Manhattan, are built from the actual ruins of French monasteries. Encircling them are carefully replicated medieval gardens. The collection's famous Unicorn tapestries are one of only two sets in the world.

2 MONROE

Take the splendid **George Washington Bridge** over the Hudson River to the **Palisades Interstate Parkway,** a scenic roadway that skims the river and its steep woodland palisades. Detour off the parkway for the scenic overlooks of the Hudson and Manhattan. Farther north, you'll glimpse deer or other wildlife as you drive through beautiful **Bear Mountain State Park.** Boating, hiking, fishing, and picnicking facilities are available.

In Monroe, visit **Museum Village,** a lively 19th-century re-creation of a preindustrial American village. On-site artisans include cobblers, blacksmiths, potters, and harness makers. You can see butter being churned and horseshoes being hammered out.

3 GOSHEN

The **Trotting Horse Museum,** home of the Hall of Fame of the Trotter, is a former stable that now houses harness-racing memorabilia. Don't miss the Hall of Fame statues and the display of sulkies in the loft. Out back is the **Historic Track,** the oldest track for trotters in the country.

From Goshen, detour to **Pine Island,** a hamlet within the town of Warwick that is known for its rich black dirt and fields of onions. These sweet-tasting, world-famous onions are among the wide range of produce sold at roadside farmstands that represent some 14,000 acres of local vegetable farms.

4 WASHINGTONVILLE

Founded in 1839, **Brotherhood Winery** is the oldest winery in the United States. Tour the landscaped vineyards and vast cellars, the largest in the country, and then enjoy the complimentary wine tasting. Open year-round, Brotherhood holds regular autumn grape stompings at harvest time.

5 MOUNTAINVILLE

Don't miss the **Storm King Art Center.** Named for nearby Storm King Mountain, the 400-acre park is an enormous outdoor sculpture garden filled with a permanent collection of works by such contemporary artists as Alexander Calder and Louise Nevelson, comple-

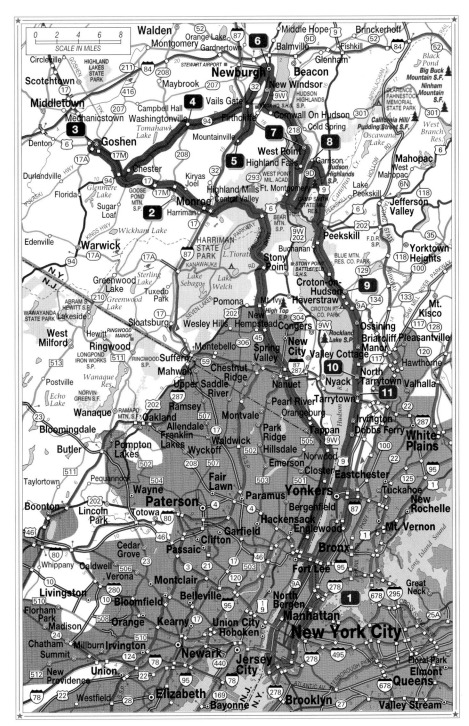

mented by sculpture exhibitions that are rotated annually. The views alone are worth the price of admission.

6 NEWBURGH

Here George Washington awaited word on peace negotiations that would end the Revolutionary War. Within the **Washington Headquarters State Historic Site** are the **Jonathan Hasbrouck House** (the structure that served as the headquarters building) and a small mu-

seum. The general had his troops standing by in nearby Vails Gate at **New Windsor Cantonment.** Today guides reenact military drills and daily life at the camp, which once housed 7,000 soldiers and their families.

▶ *You'll get an exhilarating taste of the hairpin Highlands on Storm King Highway (Rte. 218) into West Point—the road follows the black stone river cliffs in a supremely scenic drive.*

7 WEST POINT

The monumental stone structure built on the cliffs overlooking the Hudson River houses the **United States Military Academy,** the renowned training ground for U.S. Army officers. The **West Point Museum** has a large collection of historic militaria (a Civil War surgeon's instruments are particularly sobering). Take a guided bus tour of the campus or pick up a map at the visitor center and strike out on your own.

At Trophy Point, overlooking the Hudson, you can still see some of the 114-pound links of a chain barrier that was suspended across the river to prevent enemy ships from passing during the Revolutionary War. Behind you is the parade ground, overseen by statues of generals Washington, Eisenhower, and MacArthur. **Constitution Island,** where the Great Chain was anchored, can be visited on guided boat trips.

8 GARRISON

Cross the Hudson by way of the **Bear Mountain Bridge,** a graceful span seemingly suspended in midair amid soft green hills. Built in 1924, the bridge is less crowded than its counterparts downriver, and the view is terrific. You'll have to backtrack north about five miles to reach Garrison, with its stunning view across the river of West Point. Garrison's waterside landing, complete with latticed gazebo, is straight out of a movie set—in fact, *Hello Dolly!* was filmed here. It's also a favored setting for weddings and picnics. The old train depot is now a theater, and the **Garrison Art Center** is located in a turn-of-the-century structure on the Hudson.

On a bluff north of town is **Boscobel,** a Federal-style manor built by States Morris Dyckman 20 years after the Revolutionary War. Filled with English antiques, the mansion has views of the Hudson that rival those in a classic Hudson River School painting.

Don't miss **Cold Spring,** a 19th-century gem just north of Garrison, with quaint inns, antique shops, and tree-lined streets. Watch the sun set across the Hudson River, where glittering trains coil around the black hills of the lower Adirondacks.

9 CROTON-ON-HUDSON

This town was once part of a massive Dutch Colonial estate belonging to the Van Cortlandt family. In the 1920's it served as a rural salon for such Greenwich Village intellectuals as John Reed and Edna St. Vincent Millay. **Van Cortlandt Manor,** the family mansion, overlooks the Hudson and Croton rivers and contains original furnishings. Stroll

Hats off: Graduating West Point cadets toss their caps in the air, a time-honored tradition.

through the manor's restored 18th-century flower and vegetable gardens.

10 NORTH TARRYTOWN

Philipsburg Manor was the 18th-century country home of a Dutch Colonial family. The estate encompasses a sturdy stone house, a gristmill, and an active farm. Two miles and two centuries away is **Kykuit,** a 40-room mansion built on an 87-acre estate by John D.

Rockefeller and later lived in by his grandson, Gov. Nelson A. Rockefeller. The reservation-only tours start at the Philipsburg Manor visitor center and sell out months in advance.

One block away is the lovely 1849 **Sleepy Hollow Cemetery,** the site of the grave of Washington Irving, the author of *The Legend of Sleepy Hollow* and *Rip Van Winkle*. A map at the cemetery office provides directions to his plot.

11 TARRYTOWN

Washington Irving built a charming home, **Sunnyside,** where he lived for 25 years until his death. The estate grounds are perfect for a warm-weather picnic, when the gabled Dutch cottage is cloaked in violet wisteria. Less than a mile away is the considerably grander **Lyndhurst,** former home of the railroad tycoon Jay Gould. Set on a riverside bluff, the Gothic Revival structure is filled with assorted Victoriana.

WESTERN LONG ISLAND

1 ELMONT

Horse lovers flock to the lush turf at **Belmont Park,** the historic horse-racing venue and third leg of thoroughbred racing's Triple Crown. Founded in 1895 by the Westchester Racing Association and its leader, August Belmont II, the racetrack park was opened on May 4, 1905, before 40,000 fans. Over the years the park has hosted the great horses in racing, from Citation in 1948 to Secretariat in 1973.

▶ *Take the Breakfast at Belmont tour: enjoy breakfast at a trackside table while horses are given their morning workouts. Then take a guided tram tour of the stable and paddock areas.*

2 OLD WESTBURY

Don't be surprised if the ravishing redbrick Georgian mansion at **Old Westbury Gardens** looks familiar. Westbury House's exterior has appeared in many Hollywood films, including *Love Story* and *North by Northwest*. Home to John

An ornamental entry to Westbury Gardens, the elegant turn-of-the-century gardens and mansion in Old Westbury, speaks of an era long past. The gardens were featured in the 1993 movie The Age of Innocence.

and Margarita Phipps almost a century ago, Westbury House has more than its share of treasures: paintings by Thomas Gainsborough and John Singer Sargent, gilded mirrors, crystal chandeliers. The estate's sumptuous formal gardens alone are worth a visit. Don't miss the Cottage Garden, with its thatched cottage playhouse.

3 OYSTER BAY

This historic town was named by Dutch settlers in 1639 who reported finding an abundance of "fine oysters" in the waters here. Local legend has it that

Oyster Bay has two main streets instead of one because of disagreements between the Dutch and the English over directions in town planning. During the Revolutionary War, the town was the home of Robert Townsend, a spy for George Washington. The Townsend family home, the 1738 **Raynham Hall**, is a museum containing Colonial and Victorian furnishings.

Theodore Roosevelt's **Sagamore Hill** is a sprawling, cheerful mansion that was the summer White House during Roosevelt's terms as the 26th president of the United States. The house is as

colorful as the man himself, filled with big-game trophies and bold Victorian furnishings. The graves of Roosevelt and his wife, Edith, are located nearby, at **Youngs Memorial Cemetery.**

Finally, don't miss **Planting Fields Arboretum,** more than 400 acres of beautifully cultivated gardens and natural woodlands. The British financier William Robertson Coe deeded the estate to New York State as a nature center. **Coe Hall,** his 65-room Tudor Revival mansion on the arboretum grounds, is open for guided tours April through September. Visit the grounds for unsurpassed flora in the spring and summer; in winter you'll find the greenhouses filled with a glorious profusion of multicolored camellias on even the darkest, chilliest days.

► *Oysters—raw, fried, or stewed—are front and center at the Oyster Festival, Long Island's largest street festival, held here annually the first weekend after Columbus Day.*

4 COLD SPRING HARBOR

Long Island is a region of great contrasts—amid miles of suburban sprawl there will suddenly appear a pastoral oasis. Cold Spring Harbor, a picturesque former 19th-century whaling village, is such a place. The town's nautical heritage is celebrated at the **Whaling Museum.** On display is a fully equipped whaleboat and an outstanding collection of scrimshaw—intricate whalebone or whale ivory carvings made by sailors during long days at sea. Just down the street is the DNA Learning Center, part of the **Cold Spring Harbor Laboratory.** Exhibits emphasize genetics and biotechnology—the focus of the lab's Nobel Prize–winning research.

Just across the street is the **Cold Spring Harbor Fish Hatchery and Aquarium.** Since 1883 the hatchery has raised fish—mainly

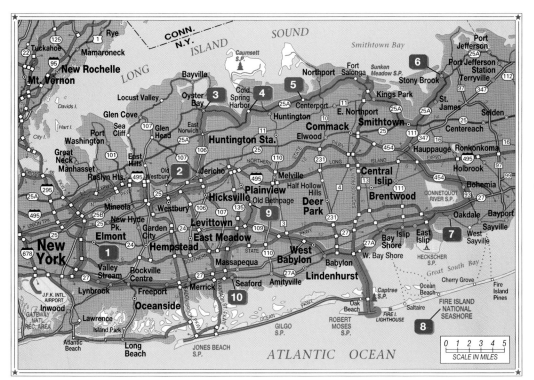

New York • 73

freshwater trout—to stock private ponds and streams. The aquarium features freshwater fish native to New York State.

5 CENTERPORT

The North Shore is historically where Long Island's "old money" resides. The **Suffolk County Vanderbilt Museum** is the former mansion home of William K. Vanderbilt II, great-grandson of the railroad king Cornelius Vanderbilt. When he died in 1944, William Vanderbilt left this estate and a trust fund for its maintenance to Suffolk County. The 24-room Spanish Revival–style mansion—complete with gold-plated bath fixtures and a Napoleonic Empire master bedroom suite—features museum wings that appear much as they did when Vanderbilt built and filled them with natural-history artifacts for his own private pleasure. On the grounds is one of the largest and most sophisticated planetariums in the country.

Elegance inside and out: *A c.1850 Bavarian state coach is one of the 80 historic carriages on display at the Dorothy and Ward Melville Carriage House, in Stony Brook.*

6 STONY BROOK

This pleasant town, settled by Boston colonists in the 17th century, is a wonderful place for strolling and viewing historic homes and the fine harbor view. Maps for self-guided walking tours of the town center are available in most Village Center shops. From there it's an easy trek to the **Museums at Stony Brook,** a museum complex with period buildings that house a variety of collections. The centerpiece is the **Dorothy and Ward Melville Carriage House,** containing some 80 historic horse-drawn vehicles restored to their original splendor. In the **History Museum** take some time to inspect the period rooms re-created in perfect miniature. The **Art Museum** features the works of William Sidney Mount, a local 19th-century genre painter.

7 OAKDALE

The **Bayard Cutting Arboretum** is a lovely park on the former estate of William Bayard Cutting. It features a collection of domestic and imported evergreens. Azaleas, rhododendrons, and wildflowers are among the park's specialties. The Cutting family's 68-room Tudor mansion houses a small natural-history museum.

8 FIRE ISLAND

This narrow, 32-mile-long barrier island is home to some of the East Coast's prettiest beaches. There are 17 island communities, each with a distinct personality, from family-oriented **Sailors Haven** and **Saltaire** to lively **Kismet** and **Ocean Beach.**

Cars are prohibited on most of the island, so you can either drive across Great South Bay to **Robert Moses State Park** and walk over or you can take a passenger ferry from the mainland at Bay Shore or Sayville. Many of the island roads have been supplanted by boardwalks—where bikes with baskets are the popular mode of transportation and residents tote baggage to and from the ferry landing on gaily painted children's wagons.

Fire Island is a nature lover's paradise, with eight miles of preserved wilderness for hiking and a sunken forest—a nature preserve located below sea level. Fishing is always reliable in Great South Bay, where hefty bluefish and striped bass abound. Visit the 1858 **Fire Island Lighthouse,** with a keepers' quarters, a visitor center, and a museum.

▶ *Tours are given of the 182-step lighthouse tower in the summer season. Self-guided-tour maps are also available at the visitor center.*

9 OLD BETHPAGE

The **Old Bethpage Village Restoration** is a vibrant living-history site that recreates the lives of farm villagers in the 18th and 19th centuries. The place looks so authentic that you might be surprised to learn that the village never actually existed but is made up of bits and pieces of historic Long Island buildings, transplanted here to be restored and preserved. Costumed interpreters demonstrate traditional crafts, cooking, and occupations. Old Bethpage Village is open year-round, and each month features different events, from 19th-century lawn games in summer to candlelight tours at Christmas.

10 SEAFORD

Continue south to the **Tackapausha Museum and Preserve.** Here you'll see what Long Island must have looked like centuries ago, when its sole inhabitants were American Indians and assorted fauna. This small museum is devoted to ecology and wildlife and serves as an introduction to the 80-acre nature preserve. Pick up a trail guide at the museum and take a self-guided walk through the preserve.

1 SOUTHAMPTON

Welcome to the Hamptons, Long Island's toniest beach communities. In summer, New York City high society establishes its headquarters here. It's a good bet you'll be rubbing elbows with the rich and the famous on your trips to the market or walks on the beach. For it is the glorious beaches, after all, that remain the region's top draw.

The Hamptons *beaches are some of the country's finest and cleanest. This Southampton locale protects its fragile dunes from the often raw Atlantic Ocean elements with a zigzagged erosion fence and clumps of sturdy sea oats.*

▶ *Taking the train is a smart alternative to driving to the Hamptons from New York City on summer weekends and at rush hours. Slightly pricier are Hampton "jitneys"—big, comfortable buses that require reservations.*

The village of Southampton is dotted with clipped green lawns and shingled estates. Many of the local shops along the quaint main street are actually satellites of Manhattan's exclusive Fifth Avenue emporiums. Settled by Pilgrims in 1640, Southampton is one of the oldest towns on Long Island. Considered to be the oldest frame house in the state, the 1648 **Halsey Homestead** is a shingled cottage that can be toured in the sum-

mer. Visit the **Southampton Historical Museum,** housed in a white 1843 Greek Revival mansion. Museum items range from 19th-century costumes, furniture, and china to American Indian artifacts. Also part of the museum complex are several restored wooden buildings lining brick paths that make up **The Village Street 1887.** Included are a country store, a one-room schoolhouse, and a cobbler's shop. Nearby is the **Parrish Art Museum,** with a highly regarded collection of 19th- and 20th-century American art and an inviting arboretum and sculpture garden. Movie lovers, take note: the grave of Gary Cooper is located at **Sacred Hearts of Jesus and Mary Cemetery.**

2 RIVERHEAD

Located in a rich agricultural county, the town of Riverhead is rimmed by pastoral farmland that produces potatoes, corn, grapes, and strawberries. The region's long-standing farm heritage comes to life at the **Hallockville Museum Farm.** The barn dates back to the original homesite, built by a Revolutionary War soldier around 1765. The farm's evolution over 200 years is reflected in the homestead's hodgepodge of architectural styles and additions. The historical emphasis is on the farm's most productive years, from 1880 to 1910, when, among other things, it grew hay for all the horses in New York City.

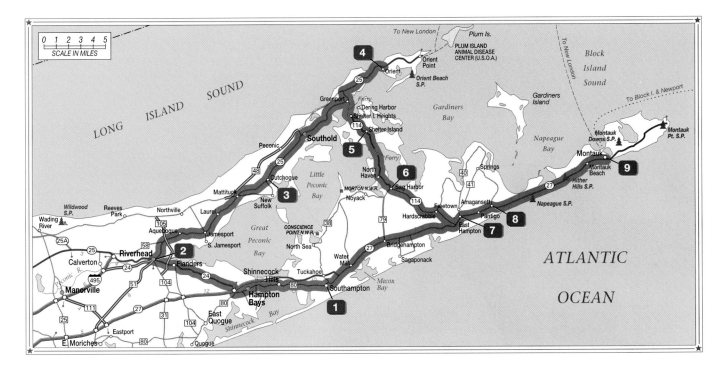

The **Suffolk County Historical Society Museum** stands on the banks of the Peconic River and features local art and artifacts, including early photographs and pre-Colonial Indian tools.

▶ *See the town and its environs from the decks of the* Peconic River Lady *paddle wheeler, which offers dancing and theme cruises.*

3 CUTCHOGUE

The lush land once known primarily for its vast potato farms is now Long Island's wine country. Although the oldest winery in the area, **Hargrave Vineyard**, was established as recently as 1973, local wines have already rated awards and high praise. Take the marked **Wine Trail**, along Routes 25 and 48, where many wineries offer tasting tours. Roadside farm stands and pick-your-own farms are abundant.

Among the several historic structures on the Village Green is the 1649 English Colonial **Old House**. The structure contains original leaded-glass windows and a fluted chimney.

4 ORIENT

The rich maritime heritage of Orient, an old seafaring village on Gardiners Bay, is relived in the museum of the **Oysterponds Historical Society**, a grouping of restored 18th- and 19th-century buildings containing period-room settings and regional artwork. Visit the popular 459-acre **Orient Beach State Park** for great beach views, shelling, and bird-watching.

A sunny summer bounty greets visitors to the popular Amagansett Farmer's Market.

5 SHELTER ISLAND

Another hideaway for the rich and famous, lovely Shelter Island possesses a New England reserve that sets it apart from the jazzier Hamptons. This is due in part to its relative remoteness: although cars are permitted, the island can only be reached by ferry. A third of the island is devoted to **Mashomack Preserve**, a 2,039-acre nature preserve. **Shelter Island Heights**, with Victorian homes perched atop seaside cliffs, was recently designated a national historic district. Self-guided-tour maps are available at most retail stores or at the office of the *Shelter Island Reporter*.

The original structure of the **Havens House** dates to 1743. Open for tours in the summer, the restored farmhouse has period furniture and a fully equipped barn.

6 SAG HARBOR

Once among the busiest whaling ports in the country, much of Sag Harbor has the look of a 19th-century seaport village, with grand old Colonial houses and a harbor brimming with sails. You can see artifacts from the town's whaling past at the **Sag Harbor Whaling Museum**. The exterior roof trim of the Greek Revival structure is in the shape of harpoons and blubber spades.

7 EAST HAMPTON

This lovely seaside town, with neat picket fences lacing elm-shaded streets, remains unmarred by tall buildings or glitzy resorts. It's a moneyed community nonetheless, with sumptuous mansions and celebrities sporting baubles as big as the Ritz. The center of town is lined with 18th-century homes. Visit John Howard Payne's childhood home, the 1650 **Home Sweet Home**, a charming saltbox that inspired Payne to write the now famous song ("Be it ever so humble…"). It's now a museum with period furnishings. **Hook Mill**, one of the many historic windmills dotting the landscape, is open to tourists in summer. Literary-history buffs fascinated with the American expatriates who lived abroad in the 1920's may want to check out the **South End Cemetery**, overlooking the Town Pond; F. Scott Fitzgerald cronies Gerald and Sara Murphy are buried here, alongside East Hamptonites from the 17th century.

8 AMAGANSETT

Amagansett has quiet, tree-shrouded streets, weathered saltbox homes, and a broad beach. Its lack of pomp doesn't deter urban fast-trackers, who flock here for the unhurried pace. Founded in 1650, Amagansett is home to the **East Hampton Town Marine Museum**, which features exhibits and dioramas detailing the town's whaling heritage. The 1725 **Miss Amelia Cottage Museum** is a Cape Cod house outfitted with period furniture made by the Dominy family, local furniture and

The Montauk Lighthouse has guarded Long Island's rocky easternmost point since 1796.

clock makers. Don't miss the **Amagansett Farmer's Market**, open seasonally, with farm-fresh local produce and gourmet exotica.

▶ *Take a bike ride on Bluff Road, the five-mile back road between East Hampton and Amagansett. This old Montaukett Indian route passes gnarled oaks and palatial estates.*

9 MONTAUK

Located at the tip of Long Island, Montauk has a raw, windswept beauty. In the 1930's it was slated to be the Miami of the North by developer Carl Fisher, who built a village center and a luxury hotel. But fate, in the guise of the Great Depression, intervened, and it took Montauk until the 1980's for another boom to arrive: tourism. Today, handsome resorts are surrounded by large tracts of pristine parkland.

George Washington commissioned the building of the 1796 **Montauk Lighthouse**. In its base is a small museum. From the top—137 steps—you can appreciate how isolated Long Island's easternmost point is.

ALBANY & THE CATSKILLS

1 ALBANY

It's not the Taj Mahal, but the **Governor Nelson A. Rockefeller Empire State Plaza** does set a high standard in marble. Acres of pure white stone characterize this half-mile pedestrian concourse in the heart of New York's capital city. Along its 12-block length are high-rise marble office towers, displays of modern art, and a unique egg-shaped performing arts center.

Ironically, the 1960's-era concourse deposits pedestrians at the 19th-century **State Capitol**, a gem of diverse architectural styles where Edwardian opulence reigns. Nearby are the cavernous exhibition halls of the **New York State Museum**, covering topics from Ice Age New York to the Big Apple.

Two other attractions lure lovers of local history: the **Albany Institute of**

History and Art, a smallish treasury of furnishings, Hudson River School paintings, and more; and the **Schuyler Mansion State Historic Site**, a Georgian mansion built for a Revolutionary War general and visited by Benjamin Franklin and George Washington.

2 CAIRO

Feed a zebra. Pet a deer. Ogle lions and tigers. As game farms go, the **Catskill**

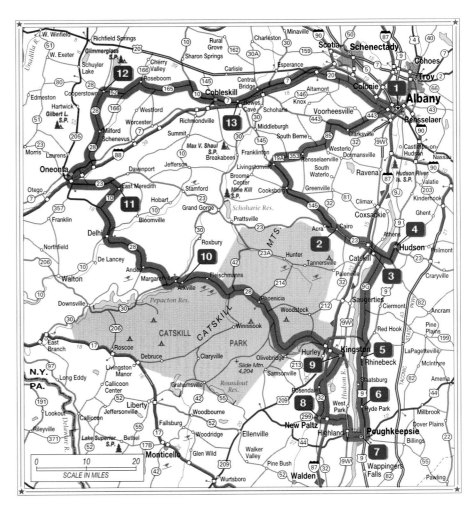

Game Farm is a granddaddy of sorts, one of the oldest and best known in the country. More than 2,000 animals from around the world serve as the main attraction. Children delight in touching the docile creatures in the farm's large contact area and in visiting the nursery for newborn animals.

3 CATSKILL

If you don't fancy trout streams, hiking trails, and cool mountains, keep driving toward flatter environs. But if you do

crave the outdoors, stay awhile in the verdant recesses of **Catskill Forest Preserve**, a 278,000-acre park near the 150-year-old town of Catskill.

Signs at clearly marked trailheads note walking distances to peaks ranging in altitude from 2,500 to 4,000 feet. For sportsmen, the Beaver Kill River and Willowemoc Creek offer angling on streams where the venerable sport of fly fishing first caught on.

4 HUDSON

Dutch explorer Henry Hudson dropped anchor here in 1609. Nearly four centuries later, out-of-towners are still compelled to stop in Hudson. The **American Museum of Fire Fighting** contains a wealth of fire-fighting equipment dating back as far as 1725. Set on 250 acres, the **Olana State Historic Site**, a Persian-Gothic mansion, was once the home of celebrated Hudson River School painter Frederic Edwin Church. Set atop a hill, it commands scenic views of the Hudson River and the river valley, framed by its large picture windows.

5 RHINEBECK

It's one thing to discover a museum filled with antique airplanes dating from 1908 to 1937. It's another to be able to see the planes take flight—and to fly around in them. On weekends at the **Old Rhinebeck Aerodrome,** pilots reenact World War I dogfights. And, for a fee, they'll take willing adventurers on a 15-minute barnstorming flight in an open-cockpit biplane.

Rhinebeck, with a charming business district, is also the site of the biggest county fair in New York, held in August, and the 1766 **Beekman Arms,** said to be the oldest inn in America.

6 HYDE PARK

The **Home of Franklin D. Roosevelt National Historic Site** offers visitors not only a history lesson but a chance to peer into the private life of a great man. America's 32nd president grew up on this 300-acre estate, and later his wife, Eleanor, and their children thought of it as a second home. After touring the home and grounds, visitors can peruse presidential memorabilia at the **Franklin D. Roosevelt Library and Museum** next door.

▶ *Plan your trip to Hyde Park around lunch at the celebrated Culinary Institute of America—but don't forget to make reservations.*

Two miles away is another immensely popular attraction: the fieldstone cottage at the **Eleanor Roosevelt National Historic Site,** where the first lady lived from 1945, when her husband died, until her own death in 1962. Nearby is the Gilded Age **Vanderbilt Mansion National Historic Site,** with original French and Italian furnishings.

7 POUGHKEEPSIE

With a few dots and dashes, Samuel Morse tapped out, "What hath God wrought!" The year was 1844, and the inventor of Morse code had just transmitted his now-famous telegraph message. In 1847 Morse purchased a

World War I triplanes play weekend war games high above the trees in Rhinebeck.

Victorian mansion overlooking the Hudson. Today the **Young-Morse Historic Site** is filled with period furnishings, fine china, Morse memorabilia, and a model of his original telegraph.

8 NEW PALTZ

Settled by French Huguenots back in 1678, New Paltz is made famous by **Huguenot Street.** A narrow thoroughfare past trendy shops and modern landmarks leads to six stone structures, built between 1692 and 1720, that constitute what is said to be the oldest street in America with its original houses. Guided tours allow visitors inside each home.

9 KINGSTON

The historic village of Kingston was New York's first capital. The state's first senators met at a merchant's home, now the **Senate House State Historic Site,** with rooms furnished as they would have been in 1777 and paintings by Hudson Valley artists. Also in Kingston is the **Trolley Museum of New York,** offering rides along the Hudson River in antique trolleys.

10 ARKVILLE

No matter what season you choose for your ride through the Catskills on the **Delaware and Ulster Rail Ride,** expect

a breathtaking journey. Spring bathes the hillsides in pale yellow-green. In summer the lush slopes seem as dense as the tropics. Autumn ushers in a crimson landscape. You'll view the scenery from a vintage railcar, just as vacationers here did in the early 1900's. Special events include train "robberies" and chicken barbecues.

11 EAST MEREDITH

Niagara Falls it isn't, but Kortright Creek packs enough power to run the mill at **Hanford Mills Museum,** which opened as a sawmill in 1820. They still cut wood here, thanks to a cumbersome but functional alignment of wheels, belts, and pulleys that transfers power from a 10-foot-high waterwheel to a circular saw that whines through pine boards with ease. The sawmill, gristmill, and woodworking shop feature exhibits and demonstrations.

12 COOPERSTOWN

Founded by the father of author James Fenimore Cooper, Cooperstown is a rural gem. Artisans at the **Farmers' Museum** revive blacksmithing, horseshoeing, and other forgotten skills. The nearby **Fenimore House** contains James Fenimore Cooper memorabilia as well as folk art and paintings.

In the village center the **National Baseball Hall of Fame and Museum** is filled with bats, gloves, and other mementos from the greatest ballplayers on earth. This shrine to America's national pastime chronicles the history of baseball through photos, audiovisual displays, and a room where the plaques of inductees give true fans goose bumps.

▶ *Combination tickets are available to all three Cooperstown attractions.*

13 HOWES CAVE

Caverns may not typically inspire thoughts of romance, but 160 feet below ground, some 300 couples have tied the knot at the **Howe Caverns** bridal altar, a softly lighted alcove along the banks of a subterranean stream. Guides lead visitors along a 1.5-mile labyrinth of walkways, bridges, and dripping cave walls, and tours include a boat ride on an underground lake.

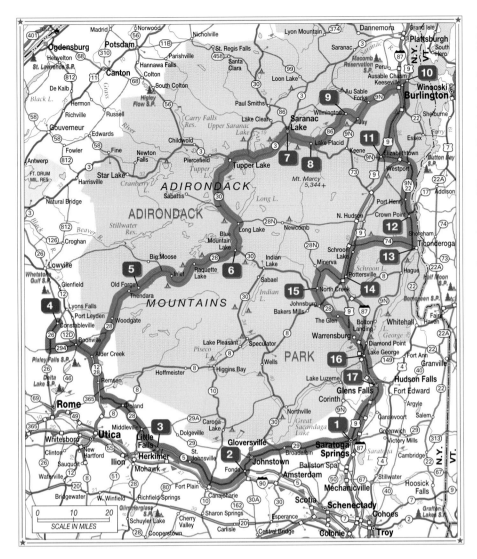

photos, memorabilia, and video clips of inductees to its Hall of Fame.

A short drive south of town on Rte. 9-P is **Saratoga National Historical Park**, where the musket fire of an important Revolutionary War battle rang out. Reconstructed earthwork defenses and a nine-mile auto tour with interpretive markers recount the bloody event.

2 FONDA

In a Mohawk village just outside present-day Fonda, an Indian maiden began her journey toward sainthood. Here in 1676 Kateri Tekakwitha was baptized by French missionaries. Persecuted by her people, she fled to Canada, where she took a vow of chastity. She died at age 24 of a high fever. Today Franciscan friars maintain the **National Shrine of Blessed Kateri Tekakwitha.** On the grounds is the only fully excavated Iroquois village, where the outlines of 12 longhouses and a stockade are marked. Artifacts dug from the site—and from all the Americas—are on display in the Native American Exhibit on the ground floor of the shrine.

3 LITTLE FALLS

During the summer of 1777, the Mohawk Valley was in danger of being lost to the British. Nicholas Herkimer, a wealthy businessman and brigadier general, rallied troops to fend off the attack. Herkimer was seriously wounded in the battle and died not long thereafter, a hero. Today his restored brick home, **Herkimer Home State Historic Site,** transports visitors to the Revolutionary War era with period furnishings and many of Herkimer's personal belongings. Guides dressed in period garb demonstrate colonial handicrafts and farm chores. During the "sugaring off" in early spring, visitors can watch as maple sap is transformed into syrup.

4 CONSTABLEVILLE

Few of his far-flung neighbors in the early 1800's had seen anything like the new home of William Constable, Jr. Imagine their amazement as limestone arrived by ox and artisans from points distant came to fashion the interior woodwork for the 10-room Georgian mansion, now **Constable Hall.** Com-

---

SARATOGA & THE ADIRONDACKS

1 SARATOGA SPRINGS

A century ago, a bubbling spring turned this erstwhile pastoral village into a playground for the social elite. The sick gathered here to drink in the supposed curative powers of the spring waters, and the rich stayed on to revel in horse racing and gamble their winnings in elegant casinos. Today visitors can still drink of the fabled waters and enjoy a mineral bath at **Saratoga Spa State Park,** with mineral springs, bathhouses, footpaths, golf courses, swimming pools, and picnic areas. Also within the park is the **Saratoga Performing Arts Center,** summer home of the Philadelphia Orchestra, New York City Opera, and New York City Ballet.

Only in August can you take in the thoroughbred races at the Saratoga Race Course, but the **National Museum of Racing and Hall of Fame** celebrates the sport year-round. Not far away, the **National Museum of Dance** offers

Lithe dancers from the New York City Ballet lure summer visitors to Saratoga.

pleted in 1819, it features such innovations as a fireproof office and two wine cellars. Family furnishings and artwork remain, and the formal flower garden, in the shape of the Irish flag, still blooms with descendants of the original plantings. An embroidered deerskin coat, a gift from the local Indians, hangs in the coatroom.

5 OLD FORGE

Gateway to countless lakes, rushing streams, and thousands of acres of lush forest, this is a wilderness lovers' paradise. Canoe trips through the eight-lake Fulton chain begin here, and lake cruises ply the placid waters. In summer at **McCauley Mountain** ski area, you can pack a lunch and glide to the summit by way of chairlift for a panoramic picnic.

Just south of Old Forge, in Thendara, the **Adirondack Centennial Railroad's** vintage passenger train offers a stunning nine-mile ride.

6 BLUE MOUNTAIN LAKE

The twenty-odd buildings of the **Adirondack Museum** recall the elaborate Adirondack camps owned by the likes of J.P. Morgan and Alfred G. Vanderbilt, millionaires who took to the mountains during the 19th and early 20th centuries to escape the city and commune with nature. Exhibits reveal how early residents here braved the rugged wilderness, with displays on logging, hunting, trapping, and transportation. You'll also find examples of Adirondack furniture, early canoes and guideboats, a trolley car turned diner, and a log hotel.

7 SARANAC LAKE

Saranac Lake was a village of lumberjacks and mountain guides when Dr. Edward Livingston Trudeau arrived in 1876. Attributing the improvement of his tuberculosis to the clean mountain air, Trudeau founded the area's first sanatorium and research facility. Soon other sanatoriums and "cure cottages" sprang up. One of these, the **Robert Louis Stevenson Cottage,** was used by the writer during the winter of 1887–88. Today it houses a sizable collection of Stevenson memorabilia.

Surrounded by lakes, the village is the perfect setting-off point for boaters, hikers, and fishermen. In February it hosts the Winter Carnival, with delicate ice sculptures and a grand ice palace.

8 LAKE PLACID

Lake Placid conjures up images of barreling skiers and the 1980 Winter Olympics, but by summer, after the snow has melted, a warm-weather playground emerges. Tour boats leave from the marina to explore the lake's shores. Take the Olympic Site Tour to see the

Winter stillness descends like a blanket over an Adirondack campsite.

snow-stripped bobsled and luge runs and ride to the top of the 90-meter ski jump. You can even ice-skate in front of imaginary crowds at the Olympic Arena rink. In July two horse shows thrill equestrians.

▶ *To avoid the summer traffic, board a trolleybus making tours of Lake Placid from July 4th to Labor Day.*

Famed abolitionist John Brown made his home at Lake Placid during an effort to help blacks establish a self-sufficient farming community. Today the **John Brown Farm State Historic Site** contains his restored farmhouse and a graveyard in which Brown and some of his followers are buried.

9 WILMINGTON

Wilmington is the entrance to the **Whiteface Mountain Veterans Memorial Highway.** Completed in 1935, this five-mile toll road offers breathtaking vistas as it climbs toward the 4,867-foot pine-covered summit of **Whiteface Mountain** and ends just 276 feet short of the peak at Whiteface Castle. To reach the top, you can climb a stone stairway or ride an elevator cut into the heart of the mountain. On a clear day the view extends into Canada and Vermont. If you'd rather leave the car behind, you can ride the chairlift to the mountain's lower, 3,600-foot peak. Back at the base, a network of bridges and paths lets you explore the dramatic **High Falls Gorge.**

10 AUSABLE CHASM

Here sheer walls of rock rise some 200 feet above the rushing waters of the Ausable River. A tour of the chasm includes a ¾-mile hike on dangling suspension bridges and winding walkways, past plunging waterfalls and raging rapids, culminating in a boat ride through the swirling waters.

11 ELIZABETHTOWN

Picture how the Adirondacks' first settlers conquered the seemingly impenetrable woods and braved the bitter winter cold. The **Adirondack Center Museum** offers a fascinating snapshot of their lives. Exhibits here re-create aspects of the pioneer existence, which was not without frills: antique dolls, toys, and costumes take their place beside tools and spinning wheels. The Colonial Garden includes a wildflower walk and a maple-sugar house.

12 CROWN POINT

At the **Crown Point State Historic Site** are the carefully preserved ruins of a stone fort, built in 1734 by the French to gain control of the ship traffic through the narrows of Lake Champlain. The well-placed stronghold was later taken by the British and then by the Green Mountain Boys. Exhibits at the visitor center and museum include artifacts uncovered at the site.

A few miles away, the **Penfield Homestead Museum** features a num-

An old-fashioned paddle wheeler at Lake George ferries passengers into the past.

ber of restored 19th-century buildings, including the Crown Point Iron Co., believed to be the first industrial company to use electricity in its operations.

13 TICONDEROGA

Built as a French fortification in 1755, **Fort Ticonderoga** on Lake Champlain fell into British and then American hands before it was abandoned in 1777. Today, restored according to the original French plans, the fort houses weapons and artifacts of the Colonial and Revolutionary periods. In summer, "recruits" engage in period drills, fife-and-drum concerts, and cannon firings.

14 POTTERSVILLE

Like a tangled ball of yarn, rushing streams thread their way through and around rock formations at the **Natural Stone Bridge and Caves.** Follow the walking trail into the various caves for a firsthand view of waterfalls, pools teeming with trout, and "mermaids"—swimmers who navigate the underground waterways. At the rock and mineral shop, you can select a sample and have it custom cut and polished.

15 NORTH CREEK

Gore Mountain in North Creek is a well-known ski area; but for gemologists, there is more than just snow here. When the powder melts, visitors can tour a gaping open-pit mine just 800 feet from the mountain's summit, part of **Gore Mountain Garnet Mine.** One

of the largest garnet mines in the world, it operated from 1878 to 1983.

16 LAKE GEORGE

Lake George village, lined with motels, miniature golf courses, and amusement parks, offers an innocent 1950's feel amid the many shops that spin taffy and sell souvenirs. But the real lure is the 32-mile lake itself, hosting campers, boaters, and

water-skiers. Hundreds of islands dot the water's landscape, many with campsites. To see the lake in all its grandeur, set sail on one of several excursion boats, or drive the **Prospect Mountain Veterans Memorial Highway** at the southern tip of the lake. The view from the summit is said to span 100 miles.

The area's historic significance can be traced to the 1750's, when the British

constructed **Fort William Henry** to protect the lake, which was part of the water route to Canada. Events at the fort became the basis for James Fenimore Cooper's *The Last of the Mohicans.* Today the reconstructed fort offers artifacts, cannon firings, and screenings of the original movie version of the book.

▶ *During the summer, consider staying in other lakefront villages, such as Diamond Point or Bolton Landing, to avoid the crowds. Either is a short drive from the area's attractions.*

17 GLENS FALLS

Named for the power-producing falls on the Hudson River, the town of Glens Falls grew to be an important industrial center of the 19th century. Fortunately for today's visitors, industry was kind to two families who would become important benefactors of art. The **Chapman Historical Museum** occupies the De-Long family house, which has been restored to its Victorian elegance. In addition to period furnishings, costumes, and textiles, the museum contains a one-of-a-kind collection of 7,000 photographs by noted artist and writer Seneca Ray Stoddard.

The town's highlight is undoubtedly the **Hyde Collection.** Housed in a Florentine villa, it represents the finest in 15th- through 20th-century art, amassed by a prominent Glens Falls couple with the intent of making the works accessible to the public. Among the masters represented are Rubens, Rembrandt, and Degas.

1 SYRACUSE

Once the capital of the Iroquois Confederacy, Syracuse is now a major business center and home to the famous Syracuse China. Fittingly, the **Everson Museum of Art** features a comprehensive ceramics collection along with American paintings from the 18th through 20th centuries.

At the **Discovery Center of Science and Technology,** kids and adults can learn a thing or two about gravity, magnetism, and other mysteries through hands-on exhibits. Also worth a visit is the **Erie Canal Museum,** housed in a former canal-boat weigh station, where visitors board a reconstructed canal boat to tour the exhibits.

2 CORTLAND

This modest college town, home to the New York State College at Cortland, boasts a Victorian gem, the **1890 House Museum,** the high point of Cortland's Historic District. The four-story limestone mansion belonged to a window-screen manufacturer with the wonderfully Dickensian name of Chester Wickwire. An excellent example of turn-of-the-century craftsmanship, the house features finely carved oak and cherry woodwork, ornate wall stencils, and stained-glass windows.

3 ITHACA

Nestled in the heart of the Finger Lakes region, Ithaca, at the southern tip of Cayuga Lake, is undeniably the area's most beautiful city, with scenic gorges and breathtaking waterfalls at every turn. Both **Buttermilk Falls State Park** and **Taughannock Falls State Park,** in nearby Trumansburg, are camera-worthy spots for a picnic.

Cornell University is the city's cornerstone. Bracketed by Fall Creek and Cascadilla gorges, the campus is unforgettable. Head to the top of the **Herbert F. Johnson Museum of Art** for a bird's-eye view of Cayuga Lake. **Cornell Plantations** offers acres of woodlands, botanical gardens, and greenhouses, and bird-watchers can stroll four miles of sanctuary trails at **Sapsucker Woods,** home of the Cornell Laboratory of Ornithology.

▶ *For a head-spinning view of Fall Creek Gorge, venture onto Cornell's 138-foot-high suspension bridge.*

4 WATKINS GLEN

Car-racing enthusiasts already know about this village, home of the Watkins Glen International racetrack. But others will want to discover the scenic beauty of **Watkins Glen State Park.** Here 300-foot cliffs rise above the 1½-mile-long glen, punctuated by 18 waterfalls. The gorge is illuminated nightly by a sound-and-light show, in season.

5 CORNING

Home of the Corning Glass Company, Corning also produces materials used in fiber optics and other advanced technologies. It's all explained at the **Corning Glass Center,** where you can see precious glass objects, fiddle with interactive displays, and watch Steuben Glass Factory craftspeople turn bubbles of molten glass into works of art.

Downtown, the **Rockwell Museum** displays Western art by Frederic Remington and others, Indian artifacts, antique toys, and more Steuben glass.

6 HAMMONDSPORT

Hammondsport, bordering Keuka Lake, is the heart of New York's wine country. Follow the **Keuka Lake Winery Route** to sample the fruits of the region. **Taylor Wine Cellars** is the area's largest, with a 35,000-gallon wine tank that is now used as a theater. Also fun are the smaller, family-owned vineyards. Visit **Heron Hill** for its lovely setting. At **Bully Hill Vineyards,** owned by a renegade member of the Taylor wine-making family, you'll taste wines with such curious names as Space Shuttle White and Love My Goat Red. For true connoisseurs, the adjacent **Wine Museum of Greyton H. Taylor** contains historical and technical exhibits on wine making.

At the center of town is the **Glenn H. Curtiss Museum of Local History,** named for the famous naval aviation pioneer and Hammondsport native.

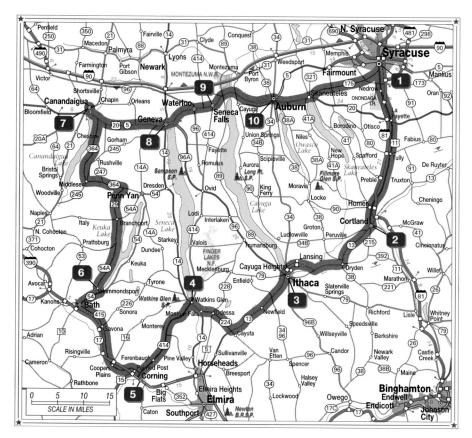

Threadlike Rainbow Falls meets the tumbling cascades of Glen Creek at Watkins Glen Gorge, one of the most stunning spectacles in the eastern United States. A well-hidden network of stone paths and bridges winds along the length of the narrow chasm, past caverns and grottoes and hardy shrubs that cling to the cliffs.

Displays include a replica of Curtiss's famed plane, the *June Bug*.

▶ *To tour the lake, board the Keuka Maid for a lunch, dinner, or all-day cruise, in season.*

7 CANANDAIGUA

The pride of this town, on the shore of Canandaigua Lake, is the 50-acre **Sonnenberg Gardens** estate, where magnificent theme gardens—Italian Renaissance, rose, Japanese, and others—surround a Victorian stone mansion like Elysian fields. Visitors can tour the mansion's period rooms. Nearby is the **Granger Homestead**, a Federal-style house featuring 19th-century decorative arts and a carriage museum.

8 GENEVA

The Federal-style **Prouty-Chew House**, with period rooms and an impressive costume collection, is the highlight of the South Main Street Historic District. Just outside town is **Rose Hill Mansion**, called one of America's greatest Greek Revival homes. It overlooks Seneca Lake, the largest of the Finger Lakes, and is decorated with museum-quality pieces in Empire style.

9 SENECA FALLS

Here Elizabeth Cady Stanton and other suffragettes held the first Women's Rights Convention in 1848, at which Stanton read a declaration stating that "all men and women are created equal." Stanton's home is the main attraction at **Women's Rights National Historical Park.** Nearby, the **National Women's Hall of Fame** celebrates outstanding women in all fields of endeavor.

10 AUBURN

This rather ordinary city was home to two extraordinary people. William H. Seward was Lincoln's Secretary of State, governor of New York, engineer of the Alaska Purchase, and one of the best-connected men of his time. Throughout the Victorian **Seward House** are relics from his fascinating life.

A staunch abolitionist, Seward sold a small house in town to Harriet Tubman, an escaped slave who led hundreds to freedom by way of the Underground Railroad. The white clapboard **Tubman House** is open to visitors by appointment. Before leaving town, stop by **Willard Memorial Chapel**, designed entirely by Louis Comfort Tiffany of Tiffany-lamp fame.

1 OSWEGO

The superior strategic position of this port city made it a much-fought-over site during America's formative years. Overlooking Oswego Harbor, **Fort Ontario State Historic Site**, dating back to the French and Indian Wars, remained active through the 1940's. Today Fort Ontario has been restored to its 1868–72 appearance. In the summer, to the roar of cannons and the rolling sound of fifes and drums, troops dressed in period costume perform military drills. View the recently excavated stone fort and shards of 18th-century porcelain from earlier occupations. The barracks and fortifications can be explored using the park's self-guided-tour brochure.

2 SACKETS HARBOR

On July 19, 1812, British ships attacked the harbor of this Lake Ontario shipbuilding town, and here what is believed to be the first American cannon shot of the War of 1812 was fired. As the war progressed, the Sackets Harbor naval base became a staging ground for a planned invasion of Canada, and a major battle was fought here in May 1813. Today the **Sackets Harbor Battlefield State Historic Site** chronicles the pivotal events of the war. The restored 1817 **Union Hotel**, now a visitor center, offers local-history displays. Each July a sea of colorful tents springs up on the battlefield as costumed participants prepare for the annual battle reenactment.

Take a self-guided walking tour of Sackets Harbor, called the Williamsburg of the North, past the town's wealth of early-19th-century homes. Walking-tour guides are available at the Sacket Mansion.

3 CLAYTON

The lovely Thousand Islands have attracted people to their shores since the turn of the century. Throughout the years the riverfront town of Clayton has served as the region's hub for services,

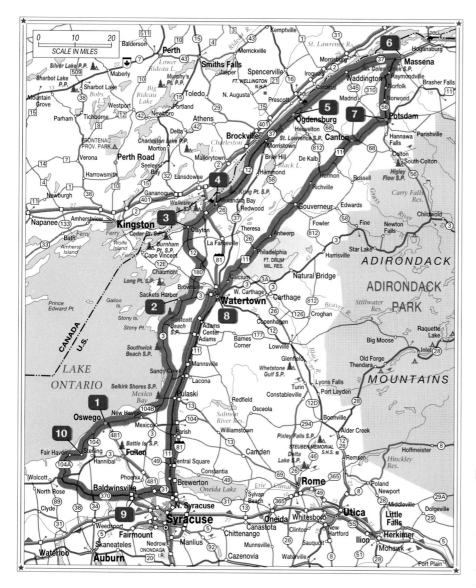

lanes in the world, links the Midwest to the Atlantic Ocean. Big cargo ships glide along the Seaway under the slender **Thousand Islands International Bridge,** built between Alexandria Bay and Clayton in 1938; it is the longest international bridge linking Canada and the United States. Between the spans is the 400-foot **Skydeck** observation tower, with panoramic views of the Seaway.

Those who prefer a tent or cabin to a motel room should make an early reservation for one of the popular waterfront campsites at the **Dewolf State Park** on pretty **Wellesley Island,** home of scores of Victorian houses.

5 OGDENSBURG

The noted American-frontier artist Frederic Remington grew up in this town, the oldest settlement in the region. Today the **Frederic Remington Art Museum** houses the most extensive collection of his works, including a recreation of his studio. Among the more than 200 works are oil paintings, watercolors, and bronzes.

6 MASSENA

In Massena things happen in a big way. Because of a precipitous drop in the St. Lawrence River here, the **Dwight D. Eisenhower Lock** was built during the Seaway construction to accommodate the passage of deep-draft vessels. Twenty-two million gallons of water raise or lower huge cargo ships 40 feet in 10 minutes. Adjacent viewing decks and a visitor center offer close-up looks at the awesome ships passing through, as well as interpretive displays.

▶ *To be sure to see the lock in operation, phone ahead for a schedule of the day's ship passages.*

One hundred and fifty million gallons of water a minute pass through the **Moses-Saunders Power Dam,** one of the largest hydroelectric dams in the United States. Among the exhibits in the visitor center is a hand-carved 16th-century wooden map. Both the lock and the power dam can be reached and viewed from **Robert Moses State Park,** where camping is available amid 2,300 acres of recreational land.

transportation, and culture. Many of the old buildings are preserved; the **Clayton Historic Walking Tour** showcases architectural highlights. Don't miss the 1897 **Thousand Islands Inn**—where the famous Thousand Islands salad dressing was created when the inn was known as the Heard Hotel—and the 1904 **Town Hall/Opera House.** Pick up free walking-tour maps at the Clayton Chamber of Commerce. Or explore the beauty of the river and islands on daily boat tours, leaving from the Riverside Drive dock.

The craft on display in the **Antique Boat Museum** include birchbark canoes, launches used by presidents, and millionaires' pleasure boats. Each August the museum hosts an antique boat show, and boat-building classes are available from May to October.

4 ALEXANDRIA BAY

"The Bay," the Thousand Islands's other major port town, offers a lively range of family activities, from superb fishing to hot-air ballooning to old-fashioned horse-and-buggy carriage tours. Excursion boats leave daily on sightseeing, dinner, and cabaret cruises. A popular destination is **Heart Island,** where **Boldt Castle** rises formidably above the trees. Constructed as a summer home by the hotel magnate George C. Boldt for the love of his life, wife Louise, the stone mansion was left uncompleted following her sudden death.

The town fronts the **St. Lawrence Seaway,** a deep-channel passageway that runs from Cape Vincent to Massena and was excavated from the river bottom in the 1950's. The Seaway, now one of the busiest commercial shipping

7 POTSDAM

Founded in 1803, Potsdam is a diverse community whose historic business district is lined with landmark structures dating from the 1820's to the 1930's. Much of the 19th-century architecture was constructed with the prized local red sandstone. Take the self-guided 3.5-mile walking tour using maps distributed at the **Potsdam Public Museum.** Housed in a former church, the museum has a collection of fine English ceramics from the 18th and 19th centuries. The story behind the discovery of the stained-glass Merritt Memorial Window, missing and presumed lost for years, is alone worth the trip.

▶ *Be on the lookout for the slow-moving horse-drawn carriages of the Amish who live in the region.*

8 WATERTOWN

First settled in 1800, this bustling retail center is home to **John C. Thompson Park,** created by the Central Park designer Frederick Law Olmsted. It's also the site of the **Sci-Tech Center,** where visitors can play hands-on scientist.

Watertown is surrounded by the silos and pasturelands of northern farm country. The area's rural heritage is relived at the **Agricultural Historical Museum,** in Stone Mills. A farm kitchen, a turn-of-the-century cheese factory, and sewing machines are among the exhibits. Volunteers demonstrate old-time farm activities.

9 BALDWINSVILLE

Each spring the **Beaver Lake Nature Center** serves as host to 20,000 migrating geese on their southern stopover. In the warm months hikers can enjoy 10 miles of bark-covered hiking trails; in winter the region's average 120-inch annual snowfall makes for fine cross-country skiing and snowshoe hikes.

10 STERLING

The spirit of Merry Olde England comes alive at the **Sterling Renaissance Festival,** held on July and August weekends in a re-created 1585 village within Sterling. With more than 600 performers on staff, the festival presents a raucous street celebration, with spontaneous minstrel and magic shows, juggling, and other slices of Renaissance life. Don't miss the appearance of Queen Elizabeth I on her summer sojourn into the countryside.

A jouster gets his man at the Renaissance Festival, held on July and August weekends in a re-created Elizabethan village in Sterling. Jousting tournaments, puppet shows, and crafts demonstrations are among the daily entertainments. Street performers representing all walks of Renaissance life— lords, ladies, jugglers, artisans, and dancers—interact with their modern-day guests.

1 BUFFALO

There are no buffalo here—and there never were. But the city of Buffalo does boast a fine collection of 19th- and 20th-century structures. In **Allentown,** one of the country's largest historic preservations, many Victorian houses now serve as restaurants, antique shops, and art galleries.

▶ *While in Buffalo, be sure to sample authentic Buffalo wings, which are actually spicy chicken wings. The Anchor Bar on Main Street serves the original recipe.*

Elsewhere in town, the **Albright-Knox Art Gallery,** a handsome Greek Revival structure, contains sculptures from 3000 B.C. to the present. Most notable is its collection of contemporary art by Jackson Pollock and Frank Stella, alongside traditional works by Gilbert Stuart and George Bellows.

The **Theodore Roosevelt Inaugural National Historic Site** served as an army post and was later the scene for the swearing in of our nation's 26th president. Noted for one of the best collections of period clothing in the country, this Greek Revival structure also displays relics from Roosevelt's inauguration and the assassination of his predecessor, William McKinley— including the handkerchief the assassin used to conceal his gun.

On a less morbid note, the **Buffalo Zoological Gardens** highlights a Diversity of Life exhibit, with creatures from poison arrow frogs to burr-eating spiders. Lowland gorillas prowl through a rain forest, and prehensile-tailed porcupines and other animal oddities occupy a Small Mammal House. Outdoors are a rare white tiger and a one-horned rhino, one of the few living in captivity.

At the **Buffalo and Erie County Botanical Gardens,** 12 greenhouses with three glass domes dating from the 1890's hold a vast collection of plants. An entire greenhouse is devoted to cacti; rare cycad trees are also cultivated.

Bring a sandwich when you visit the **Tifft Nature Preserve**. This 264-acre expanse of wildflowers, marsh, and wildlife encourages picnicking and even fishing. A visitor center displays mounted animals and birds, and guided walks are offered on Sundays.

2 NIAGARA FALLS

Few natural spectacles rival the staggering beauty of **Niagara Falls,** long a mecca for honeymooners. Napoleon's nephew and his bride started the trend back in 1803.

Goat Island separates the American and Canadian falls, and provides up-close views. For a dramatic perspective, follow the **Cave of the Winds** walkway to the base of the American falls. Slickers and footwear are provided. While you're still dripping, board the *Maid of the Mist* at Prospect Point for a heart-pounding ride to the base of the thundering Canadian falls, called Horseshoe Falls. **Prospect Point Observation Tower** offers the best panoramic view

from the American side. Two elevators descend to near the foot of the falls for a closer look.

As you can imagine, the Niagara River is a mighty source of power. Exhibits at the **Niagara Power Project** explain how the hydroelectric energy is produced and harnessed, and a mural by Thomas Hart Benton depicts the awe of one of the first Europeans to view the falling waters.

▶ *For the best panoramic view of the falls, cross over to Canada. U.S. citizens don't need a passport.*

3 LEWISTON

Skirting the Niagara River farther north is the unique **Earl W. Brydges Artpark**—part park, part visual and performing arts center. There are nature trails, fishing docks, and scenic picnic spots to be sure—but art workshops and theatrical performances are the real draw. At night concerts and plays take place in the park's theater.

4 YOUNGSTOWN

Battle reenactments and fife-and-drum corps re-create life at **Old Fort Niagara,** once of great strategic importance to several nations. Begun by the French in 1679, it was captured by the British in 1759 and then taken over by the Americans after the Revolutionary War.

Today the restored stronghold, part of Fort Niagara State Park, includes cut stone battlements, blockhouses, and a drawbridge, as well as a 1726 fortified French "castle." Cool breezes off Lake Ontario fan picnickers and hikers here.

5 MEDINA

From the historic village of Medina, you can drift down the Erie Canal on the *Miss Apple Grove,* a mule-drawn replica of an early-20th-century packet boat that operates May through October. The two-hour trip includes a narrated description of canal life in the 1840's.

6 ROCHESTER

Birthplace of amateur photography, Rochester is best known as the home of George Eastman, who gave us the first Kodak camera. Eastman's 50-room Colonial Revival mansion today houses the **International Museum of Photography and Film,** with a massive collection of photographic art, from daguerreotypes to images by modern masters. Interactive exhibits explore the history of photography, and some 11,000 cameras are on display.

This is a museum lovers' town. For a sampling of 5,000 years of art, visit the **Memorial Art Gallery** of the University of Rochester. Strengths of the collection include medieval and 17th-century art, 19th- and early-20th-century American and French paintings, American folk art, and American and European prints and drawings. The **Rochester Museum and Science Center** offers a

Horseshoe Falls *explodes in a sea of foam and mist as the* Maid of the Mist *tour boat approaches (right). Yellow-slickered adventure seekers approach the base of the American falls on foot via the Cave of the Winds walkway (below).*

planetarium, nature center, and natural- science and anthropology exhibits.

▶ *Flower lovers take note: Highland Park features a Lilac Festival each May, with some 500 varieties.*

Two historic homes are well worth a visit: the **Campbell-Whittlesey House,** a beautiful Greek Revival structure built in 1835, and the **Stone-Tolan House,** a Federal-style frame farmhouse turned tavern with a 1792 kitchen.

At the **Margaret Woodbury Strong Museum,** thousands of items of Americana, from furniture to toys, document the social and cultural developments of the 19th and early 20th centuries. More than 20,000 antique dolls are on display. Another 19th-century relic worth a visit is the **Susan B. Anthony House,** which contains buttons, posters, photos, and other memorabilia from the woman suffrage movement. The movement's founder made her home here from 1866 until her death in 1906, and was arrested here in 1872 for the crime of voting.

7 MUMFORD

Rural 19th-century America lives on at the **Genesee Country Village and Museum,** where more than 55 period buildings have been assembled. Among the highlights are the 1820 Jones Farm, with its stenciled interior walls, and the 1870 Octagon House, which combines Gothic Revival and Italianate effects. Costumed interpreters spin yarn, dye wool, and weave delicate handicrafts. A carriage museum contains an ornate beer wagon and more than 40 other horse-drawn vehicles, and a gallery features a sizable collection of wildlife art.

8 GENESEO

Geneseo draws aviation buffs who come to marvel at the collection of fighters, bombers, and other World War II aircraft at the **National Warplane Museum.** A British Spitfire, a German ME-109 Messerschmitt, and a B-17 Flying Fortress in flying condition are on display. Annual events include a Fly-In Breakfast in June, and the 1941 Wings of Eagles, an August air show featuring more than 100 aircraft.

9 LETCHWORTH STATE PARK

Sheer cliffs soar as high as 600 feet along 17 miles of the **Genesee River Gorge,** often called the Grand Canyon of the East. Three roaring waterfalls include 107-foot Middle Falls, a stunning spectacle when lighted on summer nights. A paved road winds through the park, offering superb vistas. For hikers, there are nearly 100 miles of foot trails. Stop by the park's **William Pryor Letchworth Museum** to view exhibits on the early history of the area.

10 ARCADE

The **Arcade & Attica Railroad** takes train lovers back to the age of steam. You'll ride in open-window turn-of-the-century steel cars through 15 miles of some of New York's prettiest farmland. Grover Cleveland's 1886 private honeymoon car is on display at the railroad's headquarters.

Don't leave town without visiting the 1902 Queen Anne–style **Gibby House,** with its curious fish-scale-and-board exterior and interior oak woodwork.

11 SALAMANCA

Salamanca, formerly a railroad center, may well be the only city in the nation located on an Indian reservation. Local Indian history is remembered at the **Seneca-Iroquois National Museum,** where artifacts, crafts, and mounted wild animals are on display.

The **Salamanca Rail Museum,** housed in a restored 1912 depot, exhibits objects from early-20th-century railroading. There is an authentically furnished ticket office, and two cabooses and other cars await visitors outside.

12 JAMESTOWN

Edging the southern tip of Chautauqua Lake, Jamestown celebrates a rich Swedish heritage. Swedish and Italian period rooms are among the exhibits at the **Fenton Historical Center,** a handsome Italianate-Victorian mansion built for a New York governor in 1863. Set off on a self-guided walking tour to explore the town's remarkably varied architectural styles, ranging from Gothic Revival to Art Deco. Maps are available at the chamber of commerce.

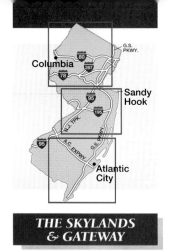

New Jersey

The Garden State is full of surprises—from the wild Pine Barrens to the appealing Delaware River towns, from windswept ocean parks to the remains of a rich Colonial past.

THE SKYLANDS & GATEWAY

1 COLUMBIA

Like a snake wriggling along the valley floor, the broad, meandering Delaware River threads its way through 40 miles of thickly forested rises of the Kittatinny Ridge, cutting a dramatic gap in the mountains. At the **Delaware Water Gap National Recreation Area,** you'll find 70,000 acres of parkland flush with pristine creeks and falls, countless species of wildlife and native flora, and striking vistas at every turn.

In addition to exploring the natural wonders—many of the 60 hiking trails are no more than a half-mile—you can visit such attractions as **Peter's Valley Craft Center,** where resident artisans demonstrate their skills and sell pottery, woodwork, and gold and silver jewelry.

Another favorite stop is **Millbrook Village,** a re-creation of a 19th-century farming community that grew up around a gristmill. More than 20 re-

The "invention factory" of Thomas Edison displays rows of gadgets that were created here.

stored and reconstructed buildings— from a simple log cabin to a cider mill to a smokehouse—portray a typical river-valley settlement. You can walk through Millbrook Village at any time of year, but summertime is best: costumed interpreters practice their chores on the weekends. You may want to pack a picnic lunch, since no food is served in the village.

▶ *For the most scenic drive—and the best chance to spot wildlife at dawn and dusk—follow the 40-mile-long Old Mine Road along the river.*

2 HIGH POINT STATE PARK

From the 1,800-foot summit of the tallest peak in New Jersey, the rugged landscape falls away in a mosaic of slopes and ridges, glens and ravines. Here, along the crest of the Kittatinnies, **High Point State Park** preserves some 15,000 acres of unblemished woodlands and meadows dotted with tumbling streams and a cedar bog of eerie, primeval beauty. For a panoramic view of the countryside, climb the 291 interior steps of the **High Point Monument,** the 220-foot granite structure on the mountain's peak. Then strike out on one of the shorter hiking trails for a close-up look at wildlife and wildflowers, including such insect eaters as pitcher plants and sundews, on display in the growing season.

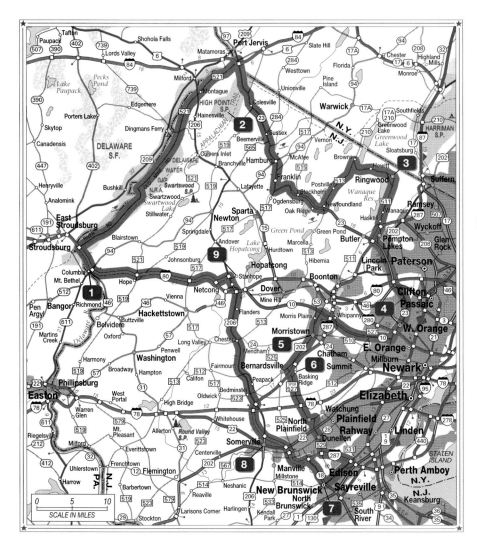

3 RINGWOOD

Ringwood Manor, in Ringwood State Park, overlooks the rolling, iron-rich Ramapo Mountains, where a furnace established in 1740 provided five ambitious ironmasters with their fortunes. The last to reign at Ringwood was the wealthy Abram S. Hewitt, who built a baronial 51-room château around the original home and filled it with family heirlooms and art, including eight works from the Hudson River School of painters. Mrs. Hewitt developed the extensive formal gardens, which were adorned with European statuary and a fountain believed to be from the gardens at Versailles.

Also in the park is the **New Jersey State Botanical Garden,** at Skylands. Surrounding a 1920's English Jacobean mansion is a handsome restored estate garden, where you can amble from dawn to dusk amid 96 glorious acres of annuals and perennials, magnolias, azaleas, and heathers.

4 WEST ORANGE

Delve into the mind of a genius at the **Edison National Historic Site.** Here you'll find one of Thomas Edison's greatest innovations—the research center itself. Some 500 patented items were developed at his "invention factory" between 1887 and 1931 by the hardworking staff affectionately called muckers—Edison, of course, being the chief mucker. Edison once boasted that the lab could create anything from a "lady's watch to a locomotive."

After touring the labs, workshops, and library, you can screen one of Edison's early films in a replica of his studio, the Black Maria, and take a tour of **Glenmont,** his luxurious 23-room estate. Even at his home, which is filled with original furnishings and mementos, Edison was hard at work. The second-floor sitting room was his "thought lab," where, surrounded by bookshelves and ensconced in a plush armchair, Edison fueled his imagination.

▶ *To tour Glenmont, pick up passes early from the visitor center in the laboratory at Main Street and Lakeside Avenue—only a limited number are available each day.*

5 MORRISTOWN

The Continental Army twice encamped here west of the Watchung Mountains—in 1777 and 1779–80—near the iron forges that produced their munitions. At the 1,700-acre **Morristown National Historical Park,** you'll see reconstructions of the rough-hewn huts, where soldiers shivered through the winter, and the elegant **Ford Mansion,** where Washington was headquartered.

Another mansion, the 1912 home of the lawyer Peter Frelinghuysen, now houses the **Morris Museum,** with collections of art, ethnography, and natural history. The 127-acre estate of his aunt Mathilda has become the **Frelinghuysen Arboretum,** renowned for its exquisite roses, lilacs, and fruit trees.

6 BASKING RIDGE

Wooded swamps, grasslands, and cool marshes rippling with cattails provide a

wilderness habitat for hundreds of plant and animal species at the **Great Swamp National Wildlife Refuge.** Wander down the boardwalk to an observation blind or along the nearly nine miles of trails at this 7,300-acre preserve to see a living encyclopedia of the natural world. There's a wide variety here—from giant shagbark hickories to dainty violets, from graceful blue-winged teals to twittering marsh wrens, from fun-loving river otters to rare blue-spotted salamanders. The background music you hear might be birdsong, frog peeps, or a red fox furtively rustling through the dense underbrush.

▶ *Warm-weather trekkers should take tick and mosquito repellent. The trails are often muddy, so wear rugged, sturdy footgear.*

7 NEW BRUNSWICK

A college town since 1771, New Brunswick offers a number of sights clustered around the campus of Rutgers University. **Rutgers Gardens,** open year-round, is a beautiful 20-acre horticultural laboratory with flower displays and the world's largest collection of American hollies. Also at Rutgers you'll find geology and art museums and the **New Jersey Museum of Agriculture,** with exhibits on farming from the pre-Colonial period to the present.

New Brunswick, which boasts the largest Hungarian population in America, is the site of the **Hungarian Heritage Center.** Permanent and rotating exhibits feature fine and folk art, as well as historic coins and manuscripts.

Moonlight casts a pale glow on the snow-covered Morristown Civil War Monument, unveiled to great fanfare in 1871. The first monument to be raised in the city was welcomed by a thousand marching soldiers. It faces the 1893 First Presbyterian Church.

8 SOMERVILLE

Evidence of the once-thriving Dutch settlement in New Jersey is the **Old Dutch Parsonage State Historic Site.** The parsonage was built in 1751 of bricks brought from Holland, and it housed the first seminary in the New World for the Dutch Reformed Church. Period furnishings and historic local and Colonial memorabilia are on display. The minister at the parsonage befriended General George Washington during his stay at the nearby **Wallace House Historic Site** in 1778–79. Built for a prosperous tea merchant, the Georgian home has been restored to its elegant 18th-century appearance.

9 STANHOPE

Formerly a bustling ironmaking community and canal port, the village of Waterloo was rescued from oblivion after World War II by two designers who turned a ghost town into a picture-perfect living-history museum. Spanning the Colonial to the Victorian eras, **Waterloo Village** has some 30 sites, including a gristmill, an apothecary, and gardens. Traditional trades, such as broom making and candle dipping, are demonstrated by costumed craftsmen.

In the summertime Waterloo is alive with the sounds of music. It's the host of weekend music concerts at the annual **Waterloo Festival for the Arts.**

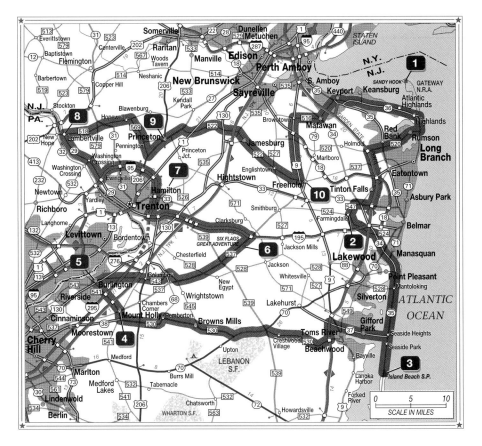

THE PIEDMONT

1 SANDY HOOK

Sited on an ever-shifting spit of sand jutting into New York Bay, the Sandy Hook Unit of the **Gateway National Recreation Area** is a natural and historic treasure. At its northern end lies the 1764 **Sandy Hook Lighthouse**—the oldest operating lighthouse in the country—and **Fort Hancock,** a turn-of-the-century military complex used until the 1970's for coastal defense. Toward the southern end is the **Spermaceti Cove Visitor Center,** where you'll find an array of curious apparatus once used by "surfmen"—the rescuers from the local U.S. Lifesaving Service established here in the 1870's.

In between are miles of short walking trails over shrub-covered dunes, tidal marshes, and mudflats. There are also six miles of bathing beaches—from quiet **North Beach** to crowded **Area D,** complete with a food and drink bar. There's even an old holly forest, the

trees oddly stunted by the salt air. Bird lovers keep their eyes trained on the skies and wetlands for glimpses of herons, horned owls, plovers, and some 300 other species that flock to this barrier peninsula.

▶ *For a breathtaking view of ships cruising into New York harbor—and a choice swimming beach—head to North Beach, on the northern tip of the park. Parking fees are in effect from Memorial Day to Labor Day.*

2 FARMINGDALE

The towering brick beehive stack of the Howell Works went "out of blast" in 1846, but the self-sufficient company town that surrounded the iron furnace has come back to life as **Allaire Village.** Part of **Allaire State Park,** an unspoiled 3,000-acre enclave just minutes from the bustling Jersey shore, the village has a remarkable number of original 19th-century structures still standing. In all, some 20 sites—including the carriage house, carpenter shop, and general store—line a curving gravel road and recall the days when iron spurred the young nation's growth.

Stroll the park's woodland trails, hop an old-fashioned buggy for a ride down a bridle path, or board the narrow-gauge Pine Creek Railroad for a steam excursion along a scenic route.

3 ISLAND BEACH STATE PARK

In a state distinguished by a 127-mile-long seacoast strewn with inviting beaches, **Island Beach State Park** stands out for its superlative natural beauty. Ten miles of fine white sand stretch along the Atlantic side of the barrier peninsula, littered only with gnarled knots of driftwood, encrusted seashells, and the occasional starfish or seahorse washed up by the waves. As a backdrop to the beach, there is a chain of grass-dotted dunes, which give way to expanses of scrubby beach plum, heather, and bayberry bushes. The southern bay side of the park has been designated as a wildlife refuge, where more than 200 species of birds have been spotted.

▶ *Visit Island Beach in September and October, when migrating monarch butterflies cling to the branches of goldenrod in cloudbursts of color.*

4 MOUNT HOLLY

This charming Quaker town, with an 18th-century Friends meetinghouse still standing in the central historic district, features a sobering sight: the **Burlington County Prison Museum.** Within the masonry walls of this 1810 structure, designed by Robert Mills, the architect of the Washington Monument, you'll see a massive front door, interior vaulted ceilings, austere cells with fireplaces, and a reputedly haunted "dungeon," with an iron ring in the center of the floor. Handcuffs, leg irons, and other devices used in 150 years of law enforcement are also on display.

In a park east of town is the home of the eccentric inventor and entrepreneur Hezekiah B. Smith, who campaigned for Congress in 1878 in a carriage drawn by a moose named February. **Smithville Mansion,** his 1840 Greek Revival house, is decorated with period furnishings and landscaped with a boxwood-maze garden. The old schoolhouse next door displays artifacts from Smith's life and career, including one of his company's high-wheeled Star bicycles. An 1881 ad campaign featured a famous athlete pedaling a Star down the steps of the Capitol.

5 BURLINGTON

Settled by Quakers in 1677, this riverside city presents a string of historic homes along its central High Street. The handsome brick **Bard-How House,** built in 1743, is outfitted with 18th-century antiques and decorative arts, including a tall-case clock built by a prominent local clockmaker. The **Captain James Lawrence House** is filled with objects from the War of 1812, in which the naval hero lost his life. Next door is the **James Fenimore Cooper House,** where the author of the Leatherstocking tales was born in 1789. Four rooms display Cooper memorabilia, as well as furnishings that belonged to Joseph Bonaparte, who emigrated nearby in 1817 after brother Napoleon was defeated at Waterloo.

6 SIX FLAGS GREAT ADVENTURE

Just the clatter of the Great American Scream Machine hurtling over its steel tracks is enough to make your heart pound at **Six Flags Great Adventure,** a mammoth theme park with 100 thrill rides on land and water, nightly fireworks shows, and live entertainment. There are classic amusements to enjoy as well, straight from a country carnival, such as the old-fashioned 19th-century carousel. You may find all the adventure you need at the adjoining drive-through safari (allow 45 to 90 minutes, depending on your speed), where 1,500 wild animals from all the continents roam freely over 350 acres of natural habitats.

***The Gothic-style chapel** at Princeton University towers over the tree-shaded campus.*

7 HAMILTON

The **Kuser Farm Mansion** was built in 1892 as the country home for a remarkable family that, among sundry other pursuits, helped found what would become 20th Century Fox, manufactured the prestigious Mercer car, and even counted top-ranked tennis players in their number. German craftsmen fashioned the ornate fireplaces and the rich oak paneling that grace the rambling 22-room dwelling. In the dining room, guests at Sunday buffets sat at the carved mahogany table to watch prerelease feature films on a giant curved CinemaScope screen. Outdoors, formal gardens, clay tennis courts, and a tennis pavilion evoke the warm summer weekends when the Kusers would host the leading lights in American society.

▶ *Father Christmas makes an appearance at the mansion in December for a Victorian Holiday Open House, with 19th-century decorations, holiday music, and a tree lighting.*

8 LAMBERTVILLE

This enchanting little town beside the Delaware River, once a ferry stop and busy canal port, is now a browser's paradise. You can while away a weekend here strolling among antique shops, flea markets, and art galleries and then stopping for a repast in a cozy café.

Just downriver is the **Howell Living History Farm,** a restoration of a typical turn-of-the-century Delaware Valley homestead. The 126-acre site, with gardens, an apple orchard, grain fields, a sheep barn, and an ice house, is still worked completely by hand. Depending on the season, you may see horse-drawn plows tilling the cropland or workers shearing sheep, husking corn, or pressing cider. On many Saturdays throughout the year, special events are held, including hayrides and a winter ice harvest. Call in advance to check.

9 PRINCETON

Venerable **Princeton University,** whose handsome main campus sprawls over 160 acres of this pleasant community, was originally quartered at **Nassau Hall.** The 1756 sandstone building, its facade laced with ivy, also served as a barracks for soldiers during the Revolutionary War and as the site of the Continental Congress in 1783. In contrast to this stately structure is the **John B. Putnam Memorial Collection**—a remarkable outdoor assemblage of 20th-century sculpture by such modern masters as Pablo Picasso, Alexander Calder, and Henry Moore, located throughout the campus.

Just outside the town Princeton Battlefield State Park surrounds the **Thomas Clarke House.** This Quaker farmstead, which stood in the thick of the 1777 Battle of Princeton, contains period furnishings and weaponry.

10 FREEHOLD

In the intense afternoon heat of June 28, 1778, Mary Hays carried canteens of water to revive Continental gun crews engaged in a fierce artillery duel in the Battle of Monmouth, then took over her husband's post at the cannon. "Molly Pitcher" became an honorary officer for her bravery, and the spring from which she drew water has been commemorated at **Monmouth Battlefield State Park.** The hour-by-hour action of the troops who fought here, in the longest battle of the Revolution, are traced on an electric map at the visitor center, which also features weaponry, munitions, and archeological exhibits.

Stop by **Battleview Orchards,** which adjoins the Monmouth Battlefield State Park, and pick your own strawberries, blueberries, peaches, apples, or even pumpkins—in season, of course.

JERSEY SHORE & PINE BARRENS

1 ATLANTIC CITY

As you're chauffeured down the boardwalk in a wicker rolling chair—the traditional way to travel here—the charms of this seaside city seem as abundant as beach sand. The steel-blue surf is pounding on one side, dazzling casinos are pulsing on the other, and saltwater taffy beckons from concession stands.

To learn how the Queen of Resorts earned her crown, head for the **Atlantic City Historical Museum,** where memorabilia give a nostalgic patina to the people, places, and publicity stunts that have played a role in this century-old playground. Another look back in time is offered by **Lucy the Elephant,** a can't-miss National Historic Landmark south of the city, in Margate. To see the museum in her belly, climb up inside the leg of this six-story-tall, tin-skinned pachyderm, built in 1881 to draw visitors to the area; then survey the shoreline from the howdah on her back.

Escape the crowded gambling mecca by heading to the **Forsythe National Wildlife Refuge, Brigantine Division,** a tranquil sanctuary for 257 bird

A parade of glorious Victorian homes lines Beach Drive, the seaside boulevard of Cape May. Many of these 19th-century gems have been restored as B&B's.

species that spreads over 33,000 acres of woodlands and wetlands. Take the eight-mile self-guiding Wildlife Drive through the refuge, open till sunset.

2 OCEAN CITY

As cozy as Atlantic City is glitzy, **Ocean City** has remained true to its roots as a family retreat. The boardwalk, eight-mile-long beach, and water are clean and safe, and the amusements are just plain good fun. No nightclub clutter here: the town has been dry since its beginnings 100 years ago as a Methodist retreat. But Ocean City is far from dull—there's a year-round calendar of whimsical events, from the Hermit Crab Race to the Night in Venice, in July, when fancifully decorated pleasure boats parade on the bay.

▶ *Like many Jersey Shore towns, Ocean City requires that each summer visitor over 12 buy a badge to gain entry to the beach. Buy them at booths on the boardwalk or beach.*

You can duck out of the sun at the **Ocean City Historical Museum,** where Victorian artifacts and relics from the *Sindia,* a four-masted bark that was shipwrecked in 1901, are on view.

3 SWAINTON

At **Leaming's Run Gardens,** consistently named one of the most beautiful gardens in America, you never know what you'll find at the end of a woodland path. It might be a cottage garden abundant with blooms, a flower bed ablaze in 70 variations of yellow, or a

sylvan pond laced with water lilies. In all, 26 gardens are hidden among the 30 acres, attracting hundreds of flittering hummingbirds each August.

The biggest surprise awaits in the woods, where a log-cabin replica of a Colonial farmhouse has been built. Nearby is a 1730's barn, where the original property owner, a prosperous whaler named Thomas Leaming, made barrels for whale oil.

4 CAPE MAY

Out of the ashes of the disastrous fire that destroyed this town in 1878 grew a handsome resort distinguished by some 600 examples of the extravagant architecture fashionable in the Victorian age. A walking tour of **Cape May**—or a ride on a trolley or horse-drawn carriage—takes you into neighborhoods of grand gingerbread homes, painted in a riot of colors. Don't miss the elegant **Mainstay Inn;** the **Emlen Physick Estate,** which houses a museum of Victoriana; and **Congress Hall,** site of Benjamin Harrison's summer White House.

▶ *Buy your tickets to the popular Gaslight Tour of Cape May mansions a few days in advance. Tours are held every Wednesday night in summer.*

Two miles west, the scene changes from built-up resort to beach refuge. **Cape May Point State Park** preserves 190 acres of shoreline, dunes, and wetlands. You can view the local songbirds from blinds or observation decks, or climb to the top of the 1859 **Cape May Point Lighthouse** for a bird's-eye view.

5 BRIDGETON

This small city boasts the largest historic district in New Jersey, with more than 2,200 buildings from the 1700's and 1800's. An even earlier chapter in local history is documented at the **George J. Woodruff Museum of Indian Artifacts,** where you'll find 20,000 American Indian objects. The **New Sweden Farmstead Museum,** in City Park, is a reproduction typical of the 17th-century settlements built here by Swedes and Finns. Its log house, stable, and sauna are all outfitted with period Scandinavian furnishings.

6 MILLVILLE

A bubble of molten glass, ashimmer with inner fire, jiggles at the end of a blowpipe. Given a puff of breath, it may bloom into a vase, a paperweight, a bottle, or a pitcher. This bit of alchemy is performed daily by the artisans of **Wheaton Village,** a re-creation of the 19th-century glassmaking community here that rivaled Pittsburgh in glass production. There are a general store, a train depot, and a pharmacy—complete with an old-time ice-cream parlor. The **Museum of American Glass** sparkles with wares, from Mason jars to Tiffany lamps.

7 EGG HARBOR CITY

Long famous for its produce, South Jersey has also earned a reputation for notable wines. Tucked among the truck farms of the Garden State are acres of vineyards, originally established by European vintners in the mid-1800's. One of the oldest wine-making operations in America is **Renault Winery,** founded in 1864 and noted for its sparkling wines. A guided tour leads you through a wine cellar and a museum of wineglasses dating back to the 1200's.

▶ *If your feet were made for stomping, visit the winery for the Labor Day harvest festival and stomping contest.*

8 BATSTO

The colonists who believed that the sandy, pine-studded wilderness blanketing this region was barren could not have been more mistaken. The **Pine Barrens,** a unique ecosystem stretching over a quarter of the state, is among the richest habitats in America, where wild orchids and cranberry bogs cozy up to blue herons and rare tree frogs.

In the heart of the Pine Barrens is the 109,000-acre **Wharton State Forest,** New Jersey's largest state forest, with miles of hiking trails, camping areas, and sand roads. It is also the site of **Batsto Historic Village,** a restoration of an ironworks that flourished from 1766 to 1855. Iron ore for the Batsto furnaces was mined from the bottom of local bogs and streambeds and proved invaluable in the making of Revolutionary War weaponry. The settlement includes a mill, a general store, workers' cottages, and an exquisite 36-room ironmaster's mansion.

9 BARNEGAT LIGHT

Since 1858 the 172-foot-tall **Barnegat Lighthouse,** on Long Beach Island, has been a welcome sight—originally for sailors, who relied on Old Barney to guide them through the treacherous channel, and now for visitors, who ascend its 217 steps to take in the seascape. Surrounding the landmark is **Barnegat Lighthouse State Park,** a picturesque 36 acres where you can watch boats cruising the inlet, enjoy shorebirds playing tag with the tide, and walk the expansive beach. You may find a relic from the more than 200 ships that have wrecked on the Barnegat Shoals.

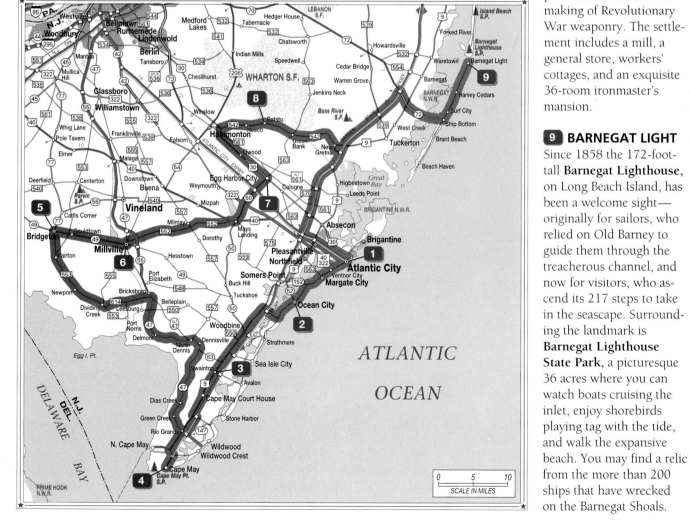

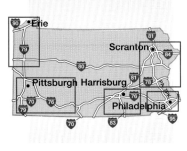

Pennsylvania

Lovely wooded countryside, meandering rivers, and serene Amish farmlands belie the hardscrabble immigrant roots and mighty industrial core that give this state its spirit and steel.

PHILADELPHIA COUNTRYSIDE

1 PHILADELPHIA

Philadelphia was founded in 1682 by William Penn, a Quaker who envisioned a "greene Countrie Towne" with freedom and tolerance for all. It's no wonder that the city became the birthplace of democracy, where sylvan parks flourished.

Early democratic milestones played out in 1776 at **Independence Hall**—the focus of the 45-acre **Independence National Historical Park**—where today you'll find the inkstand used by signers of the Declaration of Independence and artifacts from the Constitutional Convention. Across the mall is the glass pavilion sheltering the Liberty Bell, on view 24 hours a day.

▶ *Parking garages are readily accessible in the historic area. Maps of city neighborhoods and walking-tour guides are free at the visitor center.*

Penn's "greene Towne" is home to the largest landscaped urban park in the world. **Fairmount Park** has 9,000 acres of parkland, with scenic drives, bicycle paths, and horse-riding trails tracing both sides of the Schuylkill River. The park is the home of seven handsomely restored 18th- and 19th-century mansions and **Boathouse Row,** a cluster of gingerbread boathouses, illuminated in the evenings with strings of soft white lights. Boathouse Row houses local rowing clubs, whose sculls can still be seen slicing gracefully through the water, as they have here since the 1830's.

At the park's southern tip lie two cultural treasures: the **Philadelphia Museum of Art,** with its cache of American, European, and Asian art; and the **Rodin Museum,** the largest collection of the

esteemed sculptor's work outside Paris. A few blocks beyond is the **Franklin Institute**, a hands-on science and technology museum whose top attraction is a walk-through model heart.

2 VALLEY FORGE

A tribute to the hardships suffered by the Continental Army during the relentless winter of 1777–78, **Valley Forge National Historical Park** spreads over 3,000 acres of tranquil countryside just 20 miles from Philadelphia. You can tramp the **Grand Parade**, where 12,000 untrained volunteers were converted into disciplined soldiers. Washington's headquarters, in a gristmiller's house, is open to the public, and artifacts relating to the encampment are on view at the **Valley Forge Historical Society Museum.** Don't miss the carillon concerts at the **Washington Memorial Chapel** on Sunday afternoons from Memorial Day to Labor Day.

3 MEDIA

A noted purveyor of collectible and decorative wares, the **Franklin Mint** also boasts a handsome museum showcasing many of the objects the mint has created since its founding in 1964.

There are coins and medals in precious metal, leather-bound books, dolls, and figurines in porcelain, crystal, and bronze. Among the museum's treasures are a porcelain bowl by Andrew Wyeth, statuary by Norman Rockwell, and bejeweled eggs by Igor Carl Fabergé.

4 CHADDS FORD

Little more than a country crossroads tucked beside Brandywine Creek, the

Rowers cross the shimmering Schuylkill River in Philadelphia in slender sculls. Since the 1830's rowing clubs have been housed in Boathouse Row, Victorian gingerbread boathouses strung along the city's riverfront.

village of Chadds Ford boasts an exceptional art museum. The **Brandywine River Museum** occupies a renovated Civil War–era gristmill, whose rough-hewn beams and plank floors create a handsome stage for the museum's collection of 19th-century landscapes, still lifes, and illustrations. Included are works by Chadds Ford's own: N.C., Andrew, and Jamie Wyeth.

5 LONGWOOD

With more than 1,000 acres of outdoor gardens and four acres of glass-enclosed conservatories, **Longwood Gardens** is one of the country's premier horticultural parks. The former estate of the industrialist Pierre S. du Pont, the gardens are open year-round and display some 11,000 plant species, from 400-year-old bonsai trees to hula hoop–size water lilies. Just as spectacular are the fountains, which perform to a play of colored lights and music on warm summer nights.

6 ELVERSON

Like a ring of fire amid the farmlands, the furnaces of Pennsylvania turned out ton upon ton of iron in the 1700's and 1800's, casting cannon for the Continental Army and kettles for housewives. An entire plantation was built up around one of the largest furnaces, Hopewell, in 1771. At the **Hopewell Furnace National Historic Site,** along French Creek, the early-19th-century industrial complex and workers' village—including an ironmaster's mansion and a company store—have been restored. Exhibits trace the technology of ironmaking, from the charcoal hearth to the cast house, where iron was molded into a finished form.

7 CENTER POINT

All notions of how the interior of a Colonial-era home should look are dispelled at the **Peter Wentz Farmstead.** Surrounded by a barn and gardens, the stately 1758 fieldstone house seems typical of local period homes. But surprises await: the woodwork is painted in salmon, turquoise, and gold, and the walls are splashed with flamboyant curlicues and squiggles—all original colors and patterns uncovered during restoration. The house was twice used in 1777 as headquarters by George Washington; a second-floor sitting room is set up as his office.

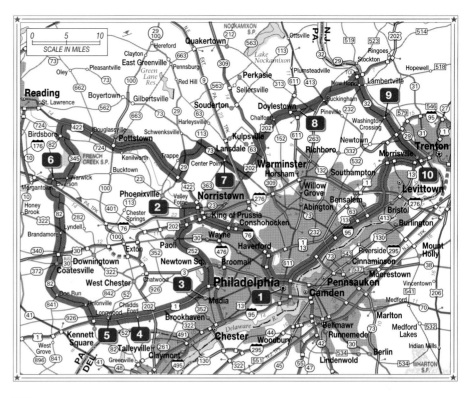

Every day is a topiary tea party at the Alice's Wonderland display at Longwood.

8 DOYLESTOWN

In the heart of bucolic Bucks County, this charming town has long been home to a diverse creative community. One author gave his hometown a museum: the **James A. Michener Art Museum,** housed in an 1884 jail, showcases a permanent collection of Bucks County art and many of Michener's personal items, including his desk and typewriter.

The town's most enigmatic native, scholar-archeologist Henry Mercer, amassed tools, handicrafts, and other everyday objects of preindustrial America, fearing their ultimate loss to the Machine Age. Today 50,000 such relics are stacked chockablock in the **Mercer Museum,** the bizarre castlelike repository he built in 1912. Equally exotic is Mercer's home, **Fonthill,** where 44 rooms are plastered with tiles produced at the **Moravian Pottery and Tile Works,** the still-operating ceramics factory he founded next door.

9 WASHINGTON CROSSING

A Christmas Day highlight in this riverside village is the annual reenactment of George Washington's crossing of the Delaware River in 1776—a bewigged lookalike for the general leads a flotilla of Durham boats across the icy river.

The festivities are part of **Washington Crossing Historic Park,** which preserves such local landmarks as the **McConkey Ferry Inn**—site of General Washington's last meal before he embarked for Trenton—and the **Thompson-Neely House,** used as an officers' headquarters. Nearby is the 110-foot-tall **Bowman's Hill Tower,** which affords eye-popping vistas of the surrounding countryside.

▶ *Another good time to visit the park is in late April or early May, when meadow wildflowers are in bloom at Bowman's Hill Wildflower Preserve, an 80-acre enclave of native plants.*

10 MORRISVILLE

The Delaware River rolls gently past the site William Penn selected for his home, **Pennsbury Manor,** in 1683. The state's founding father built a sprawling estate here that had all but disappeared into the underbrush by the 1930's, when it was painstakingly reconstructed on the foundations of the original building. The grounds have been planted with many of the same horticultural specimens that Penn himself grew. Even the barnyard is stocked with livestock raised in Penn's day, from guinea fowl to Red Devon cattle.

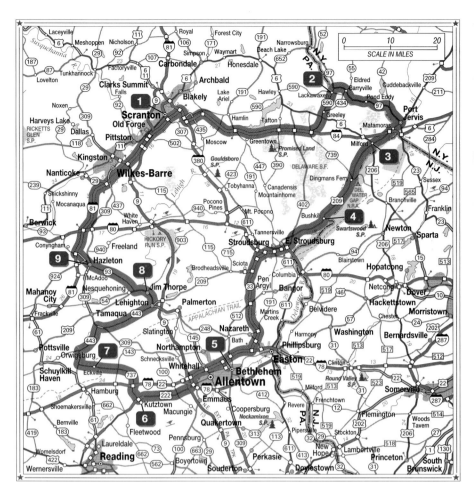

THE POCONOS

1 SCRANTON

Scranton lies in coal country, atop a vast basin of the hard, hot-burning anthracite that fueled the state's industrial might in the 1800's. The role coal has played in the region—not only in commerce but in immigration and every aspect of community life—is the focus of the **Pennsylvania Anthracite Heritage Museum**. Here you'll see tools, miners' personal effects, photographs, and even a re-created kitchen.

▶ *Hard hats and jackets are provided at the Lackawanna Coal Mine Tour, but visitors should dress warmly and comfortably for underground sightseeing.*

Next door, the **Lackawanna Coal Mine Tour** offers a fascinating experience—a chance to walk in the foot-steps of a miner. You'll descend 300 feet via an enclosed cable car into the old Slope 190 Mine and, with a former miner at your side, trek through coal veins that were once the subterranean workplaces for thousands of miners.

Closely linked to the coal industry was the railroad, whose past is honored at the 40-acre **Steamtown National Historic Site** with a collection of more than 100 locomotives and railcars from the 1850's to the 1950's. A favorite is the Union Pacific's Big Boy, a gargantuan 500-ton engine built in 1941 to haul heavy freight between Cheyenne and the Wasatch Mountains of Utah.

2 LACKAWAXEN

Some of the most popular tales ever spun about the American West were written by a former dentist living in this remote village overlooking the upper Delaware River. Zane Grey abandoned his dental career in 1905 and went on to compose such classics as *Riders of the Purple Sage* and *The Lone Star Ranger* from an office in a rambling clapboard house, now the **Zane Grey Museum**. Mementos spanning his careers and interests are on view, including dental equipment, sports gear from his university days, his desk, and a well-worn Morris chair with a lapboard where Grey often worked.

3 MILFORD

It was in the scenic woodlands of the Pocono Mountains that Gifford Pinchot was inspired to pursue forestry; the two-time state governor would go on to become America's first leader in environmental conservation. Pinchot's home was **Grey Towers**, a 42-room mansion completed in 1887, which overlooks Milford and the Delaware River valley and is now a national historic landmark. Reminiscent of a French château, the estate sprawls over 102 acres and boasts exquisite gardens, terraces, and such unusual features as the Finger Bowl—a stone table for al-fresco dining with a pool of water at its center. Inside the opulent mansion are artworks, photographs, original furnishings, and family memorabilia.

4 BUSHKILL

As you near **Bushkill Falls**, the crunch of fragrant evergreen needles underfoot is gradually drowned out by the pounding of water over the jagged ledges and verdant ravines of the Pocono Mountains. With a drop of 300 feet, Main Falls is the largest of several waterfalls in the region, shaped eons ago by glacial activity. To follow the course of the frothy creeks that spill over in a series of eight cascades, walk over rustic wooden bridges and observation decks and along trails that wind beneath a canopy of hemlock, pine, and maple.

▶ *You can reach a lookout for the Main Falls after an easy 15-minute walk from the parking area.*

5 BETHLEHEM

Often cited for its steel manufacturing, Bethlehem is also home to the oldest Moravian community in America, who founded this small city in 1741. The self-sufficient European Protestant sect prospered along the banks of Monocacy Creek. There the group built a thriving industrial complex, which has been restored and rebuilt to include a tannery, gristmill, and waterworks. In town the historic district is clustered around the city's oldest building, Gemeinhaus, now the **Moravian Museum of Bethlehem**—a five-story log building where decorative arts and musical instruments used in the sect's worship services are exhibited. Nearby is the **Central Moravian Church**, which at Christmastime displays a Putz, an elaborate crèche that originated with the Moravians.

6 KUTZTOWN

Imagine dancing deep beneath the earth, in a torch-lit chamber whose walls glisten like sheets of ice. Nearly a century ago square dancers did just that, in the cool, spacious Crystal Ballroom, one of many wonders in **Crystal Cave**. Discovered in 1871, the limestone cavern runs to 125 feet below the surface; you can explore 500 feet of it via railed, concrete walkways. A guide leads you past such sculptural curiosities as the Prairie Dogs, a stalagmite mound that resembles a group of animals peeking comically from their burrows; the Totem Pole, a rippled column of "faces"; and the Bridal Veil, a white, lacy formation.

▶ Temperatures in the cavern usually hover around 55 degrees, so take along a sweater or a jacket. Shoes with sturdy treads are also advisable, as moist conditions sometimes make the cave floor slippery.

7 ECKVILLE

Soaring and spiraling over the **Hawk Mountain Sanctuary** each autumn come some 20,000 raptors—hawks, eagles, falcons, turkey vultures, and other birds of prey—using the ridge's updrafts to conserve energy for their southward migration. It's a spectacular sight, best observed from two rock promontories (one just a comfortable three-minute stroll from the parking area) at this 2,200-acre preserve in the Appalachian mountains. Begun in 1934 in response to the local slaughtering of thousands of hawks, Hawk Mountain Sanctuary was the first refuge in the world created to protect birds of prey and offers interpretive programs on the weekends and nature workshops. The sanctuary is also one of the foremost natural lookouts in the country. You can rent binoculars at the visitor center to get a close-up glimpse of migrating birds—more than a million so far have been sighted at the preserve.

8 JIM THORPE

The landscape around this idyllic Lehigh River town, in the Pocono foothills, seems transplanted from an Alpine valley. Indeed, the region was known as the Switzerland of America when men descended here in the late 19th century and became millionaires, building mansion upon mansion on the town's main street—appropriately nicknamed **Millionaire's Row**.

Asa Packer, a coal-boom millionaire, spared no expense in constructing his hilltop estate in 1860. Open to the public, the 20-room brick Victorian **Asa Packer Mansion** is outfitted in mahogany, marble, and the intricately carved furniture that was the height of mid-19th-century fashion.

The **HO-Scale Model Train Display**, in a restored building in the business district, is a train buff's paradise. Thirteen miniature trains whiz around some 1,000 feet of track, over 100 bridges, and past 200 tiny buildings.

And, yes, the town itself—originally called Mauch Chunk—was renamed after the gold-medal-winning star of the 1912 Olympic Games. Although Thorpe never lived here, the town paid the athlete high tribute by changing its name to his; Thorpe's mausoleum lies just outside of town.

9 HAZLETON

In its heyday in the 1870's, Eckley, nine miles east of Hazleton, was home to more than 1,000 laborers who worked the anthracite coalfields. The mines have closed, but the town has been preserved as **Eckley Miners' Village**, a 100-acre living example of a privately owned mining, or "patch," town. Patch towns sprang up around individual mining stakes; the resulting topography often resembled a patchwork quilt.

Your immersion in the culture of coal begins at the visitor center. On exhibit are photographs, maps, and personal possessions belonging to the old mining families. Then walk or drive down the main street, where 70 original homes stand. While some are still occupied by retired miners, you can tour a doctor's office and an 1890 two-family home furnished to reveal the living conditions of the immigrant miners.

Russet hills frame the Victorian downtown of Jim Thorpe, named for the Olympic hero.

1 HARRISBURG

Overshadowed by the splashier cities to the east and west, the capital city of Harrisburg is an undiscovered treasure with an unhurried pace. For a look at the culture of the Commonwealth, start at the **State Museum of Pennsylvania,** which features exhibits on archeology, politics, technology, and art.

Across the street you'll see the 272-foot-tall dome of the **State Capitol** towering over the horizon. The elegant Italian Renaissance–style marble capitol was dedicated in 1906 and is filled with notable artworks. After craning your neck to view the paintings around the rotunda, glance underfoot: the floor is paved with about 400 mosaic-tile scenes that create a graphic narrative of early state life.

A wealth of parks adds to Harrisburg's allure. Running for five miles along the east bank of the Susquehanna is **Riverfront Park,** a scenic spot for a leisurely stroll or a picnic lunch. **Reservoir Park,** northeast of downtown, is a 90-

A common sight in Pennsylvania's scenic Amish country is an old-fashioned horse-drawn buggy. The religion of the Plain People forbids them to drive cars.

acre site with gardens, fountains, and an arts colony, where artists in residence produce and display their wares.

▶ *Stop by the amphitheater in Reservoir Park for free concerts on Saturday afternoons in July and August.*

2 HERSHEY

This is the town that chocolate built—or, more precisely, that Milton S. Hershey built—in 1903. Even the streetlights will make your mouth water: they're shaped like giant chocolate Kisses. Chocoholics flock to **Hershey's Chocolate World** for a 10-minute tour of the chocolate-manufacturing process, from the harvesting of cocoa beans to the packaging of the candy. At the 23-acre **Hershey Gardens,** you'll see thousands of colorful tulips, roses, and mums in season. Wafting through the air at all times is the pervasive aroma of chocolate—or, to be more exact, cocoa-hull mulch.

3 LITITZ

Among the sects to immigrate to the New World was a group of German descendants from Moravia, who founded Lititz in 1756. The Moravians' legacy is enshrined along Main Street, where the **Moravian Church** and the communal **Brothers' House** and **Sisters' House** still stand. Nearby is the 1792 **Johannes Mueller House,** which contains period furnishings and artifacts from the town's Moravian past.

Along with their faith, the German settlers brought a tasty knotted yeast bread that has become the unofficial local mascot: the pretzel. Julius Sturgis became America's first commercial pretzel baker in 1861, and the **Sturgis Pretzel House** still turns out, in 200-year-old ovens, traditional soft pretzels (best slathered with spicy mustard). Try your hand at twisting a rope of dough into the familiar knot—it's not as easy as it looks.

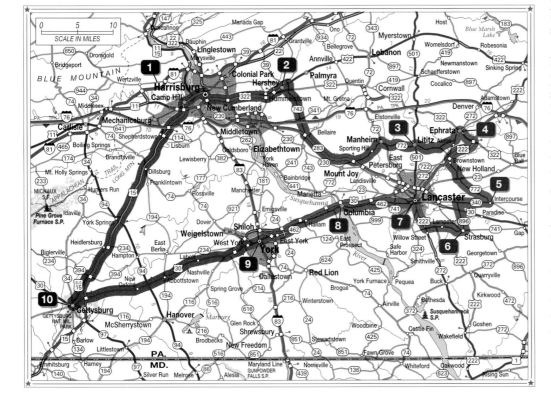

4 EPHRATA

Like Lititz, Ephrata was settled by German sectarians, but these radical Christians believed in a life of austerity. At the superbly restored **Ephrata Cloister**, a medieval-style monastic village begun in 1732, you'll see the plank benches and wooden pillows used in the sleeping cells. Be sure to duck your head under the low doorways—just as the pietists had to do in an unavoidable gesture of humility.

Denied material comforts, the cloister's inhabitants were nonetheless industrious. Besides establishing a printing press and composing hymns, they produced incomparable hand-illuminated manuscripts, or *Frakturschriften,* now on display in the chapel.

5 INTERCOURSE

The world of the Plain People is examined at **The People's Place** interpretation center, in the heart of lovely Pennsylvania Dutch country. These sects—the Amish, Mennonites, and Hutterites—are made up of religious separatists who live lives of austerity and simplicity based on a conservative interpretation of the Bible. Here a feature film, a slide show, and exhibits explain their ways of life. Across the street, the **People's Place Quilt Museum** exhibits 19th- and 20th-century Amish quilts. More than mere bed coverings, the beautifully crafted quilts, recognizable by their bright colors and geometric patterns, are today a highly regarded form of folk art.

▶ *For religious reasons, the Amish do not allow themselves to be photographed; point your cameras toward the lovely landscape instead.*

6 STRASBURG

You'll see plenty of Amish horse-drawn buggies around town—the religion of the Plain People prohibits them from driving cars—but Strasburg celebrates two other modes of travel as well. At the **Gast Classic Motorcars Exhibit** it's easy to fancy yourself behind the wheel of any one of more than 50 vintage and exotic vehicles, from a 1911 Maxwell to a rare 1948 Tucker to a sleek 1981 Lamborghini Countach.

The **Railroad Museum of Pennsylvania** chronicles the state's preeminence in rail transportation through a collection of locomotives and rail mementos. Hop aboard the country's oldest short line at the adjoining Strasburg Rail Road and take a round-trip steam excursion aboard 19th-century wooden coaches to the nearby town of Paradise.

7 LANCASTER

The state capital from 1799 until 1812, Lancaster is today the center of the Pennsylvania Dutch community. At the **Amish Homestead** and the **Amish Farm and House** you'll discover a way of life little changed since the Plain People began to settle here in the 1720's. The fertile fields are tilled with horsepower, and the tidy, simply furnished homes are operated without electricity or other modern amenities.

▶ *Avoid the crowded main routes by striking off on back roads for a more peaceful trip and an unobscured look at Amish farmsteads.*

For an overview of the agricultural heritage of the region, head north on the Oregon Pike to the **Landis Valley Museum.** Visitors to this complex can see exhibits that include a tavern, several farmsteads, a country store, and a transportation display with Conestoga wagons and antique sleighs.

The only president born in Pennsylvania was James Buchanan, whose elegant Federal mansion, **Wheatland,** reflects his ownership from 1848 to 1868. It was from this house that Buchanan successfully waged his presidential campaign. Wheatland is beautifully decorated for the annual Christmas candlelight tours.

8 COLUMBIA

Punch a 1920's time clock for admission to the **Watch and Clock Museum,** the largest of its kind in the United States. Lest you think clocks do no more than ticktock, here you'll be serenaded with a symphony of timepieces that melodiously ring, clang, and fife in the hour. You'll see everything from a 1750 pocket sundial to an ultra-slim Curvex wristwatch from the 1940's.

9 YORK

This small city played a large role in history: it hosted the Continental Congress during the adoption of the Articles of Confederation in 1777 and served as the nation's capital while British troops occupied Philadelphia during the Revolutionary War. Its 18th-century heritage is documented in a central historic district that includes a reconstruction of the **York County Colonial Court House,** where the Congress convened until 1778.

10 GETTYSBURG

For three days in July 1863, the fiercest conflict of the Civil War raged on here; today the serenity of these fields belie the battleground carnage. The 3,500-acre **Gettysburg National Military Park** is a memorial to that battle. Start at the visitor center, where an electric map traces troop movements via colored lights. The nearby **Cyclorama Center** houses a huge circular 1884 painting detailing the battle's climax.

Within the park is the **Gettysburg National Cemetery.** This is where Abraham Lincoln delivered his memorable dedication address. Adjacent to the park is the **Eisenhower National Historic Site,** the farm the Eisenhowers used as a country getaway. Inside are family furnishings, mementos, and Ike's oil paintings—one of which is a portrait of his two eldest grandchildren. In the yard is his personal putting green, complete with sand trap.

1878 Apostolic Clock at the Hershey Museum.

1 PITTSBURGH

The once gritty Iron City has ceded to a glittering urban center with a world-class skyline. Nevertheless, Pittsburgh's hardworking heritage of smokestacks, steel mills, and shrewd-minded tycoons is here to be discovered, at scores of attractions throughout the city.

You can start at the open-air museum at **The Riverwalk at Station Square,** where mammoth industrial artifacts, like the abandoned toys of giants, are displayed. Situated at the principal station of the former Pittsburgh & Lake Erie Railroad, the museum boasts such formidable-sounding equipment as a 10-ton Bessemer converter and a large ingot mold.

The cultural complex known as the **Carnegie** is as impressive as the empire amassed by its founder, the wealthy steel magnate and philanthropist Andrew Carnegie. Comprised of an art museum rich in Impressionist paintings and decorative arts from Europe and America, the Carnegie also includes a renowned natural-history museum and a science center with a planetarium.

Andrew Carnegie's business colleagues also left their marks on the city. Henry Clay Frick lived at **Clayton,** a magnificent French château–style estate whose family heirlooms offer a glimpse into the privileged life of a Victorian-era millionaire. View the art collection belonging to Frick's daughter Helen, at the nearby **Frick Art Museum,** where works from the 15th through the 18th centuries are exhibited.

Another Carnegie crony, Henry Phipps, bestowed the lovely **Phipps Conservatory** to the public in 1893. Displays of palms, cacti, orchids, and seasonal plants thrive under two acres of shimmering glass greenhouses.

2 JOHNSTOWN

Johnstown, nestled in a lovely mountain landscape at the confluence of the Conemaugh River and Stony Creek, has long been beleaguered by floods. The **Johnstown Flood National Memorial**

marks the starting point of the disaster of May 31, 1889, when 20 million tons of water spilled over the storm-eroded earthen banks of the South Fork Dam, sweeping a wall of water and debris— said to tower between 30 and 40 feet high—through Johnstown. A museum at the visitor center recalls the scene through a film, a model of the dam, and exhibits. At the **Johnstown Flood Museum,** artifacts, photographs, newspaper reports, and a lighted relief map vividly chronicle Johnstown's waterlogged past and its reemergence from catastrophe. Be sure to see the Academy

The steel magnate Andrew Carnegie, as painted by Andy Warhol, realized his dream of a world-class art museum in Pittsburgh.

Award–winning film, *The Johnstown Flood,* shown in the museum at regular intervals daily.

To get the lay of the landscape, take a seat on the **Inclined Plane Railway.** Built in 1891 and ascending 505¾ feet at a grade of 71 percent, this is one of the oldest and steepest cable railways in the world—and a remarkably quick evacuation route to higher ground.

3 CRESSON

Delivering goods and settlers westward, canals were a major mode of transportation in the country in the early 19th century. From 1834 to the mid-1800's, the **Allegheny Portage Railroad** provided an ingenious solution to the Herculean task of transporting over mountains: this 36-mile-long rail line,

linking the eastern and western branches of the Pennsylvania Canal system, was used to piggyback packet boats up and down a steep rise (1,398 feet up one side; 1,172 feet down the other) via a series of 10 inclined planes. Few traces of the line remain, but a visitor center evokes this marvel of technology with a film, a full-scale model locomotive, and rail relics. At the summit is the **Lemon House,** a restored 1832 tavern.

4 BEDFORD

Cross the covered bridge at **Old Bedford Village** and you're delivered into the preindustrial past of the rural Allegheny Mountain region. Here, at this replica of a 1790's pioneer settlement, you can tour some 40 structures, from a potter's shop to a tavern to a log residence. Some of the buildings were moved from their original locations in the region and have been rebuilt at this 72-acre living-history museum. Costumed interpreters throughout the village demonstrate traditional handicrafts and domestic arts, such as hearth cooking, tinsmithing, and weaving.

5 SOMERSET

The region's rich rural past, from the 18th-century pioneer days to the 20th-century industrial era, is explored at the **Somerset Historical Center.** A modestly furnished log house and smokehouse recall the arduous lives led by settlers who braved the formidable Allegheny Front. A circa-1876 general store and a mechanical corn husker reflect the progress wrought by railroads and automation in isolated mountain communities. And, to savor the sweet process of turning sap to syrup, don't miss the restored maple-sugar camp.

▶ *The maple trees around Somerset that are tapped for syrup making from mid-February to March present a spectacular foliage show in fall.*

6 OHIOPYLE

Of all of Frank Lloyd Wright's triumphs, **Fallingwater** is arguably his most acclaimed architectural work. Built in 1939 as a retreat for the Pittsburgh merchant Edgar J. Kaufmann, Sr., this sandstone-and-concrete house

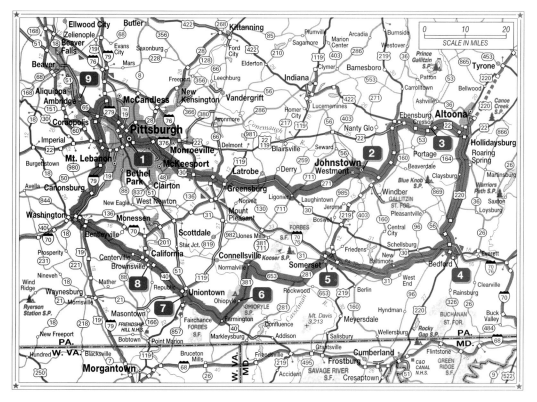

1754, with replicas of the stockade, entrenchments, and storehouse.

Overlooking the fort is **Mount Washington Tavern,** an 11-room brick inn built around 1827 on the first federally funded turnpike, the National Road. This restored stagecoach station evokes the days when waves of westbound settlers washed over this route into the Ohio Valley.

8 BROWNSVILLE

Buried within the 22-room brick structure called **Nemacolin Castle** is a simple stone trading post from 1789. The post was built on a migration route for pioneers that was hewn from the wilderness by the Cresap expedition, guided in the mid-1700's by Nemacolin, a Brandywine Delaware tribal chief. The structure would be enlarged and embellished by its prosperous owner until it reached its present size in 1847. Original and period furnishings—from the rough-and-tumble frontier times to the more ornamental Victorian epoch—are represented in Nemacolin Castle. Of note are a rosewood Louis XIV–style bed, an 18th-century rocking horse, and a Victorian breakfront brimming with period china.

9 AMBRIDGE

William Penn planned his colony of Pennsylvania as a "holy experiment" in religious toleration, a haven for persecuted sects from Europe seeking freedom of worship. Among them was the Harmony Society, a group of industrious Germans who established the utopian community of Economy here in 1824. Their agricultural and manufacturing center has been preserved as **Old Economy Village,** where 17 expertly restored buildings reveal the Harmonists' communal way of life. You'll see the 22-room home of the sect's founder, the Feast Hall, members' living quarters, and such commercial enterprises as a tailor's shop.

is dramatically poised atop the cascading waterfalls of Bear Run. Inside are the family's original furnishings, including Tiffany glassware and pieces designed by Wright. Outdoors you can stroll through the sculpture collection and follow 20 miles of marked trails into a woodland landscape.

Take a leisurely drive through the scenic **Laurel Highlands,** whose forests are carpeted in swaths of mountain laurel in summer and bathed in russet and gold in fall.

7 UNIONTOWN

It was near Fort Necessity, in Jumonville Glen, during the opening salvos of the French and Indian War, that 22-year-old George Washington's mettle as a military leader was first tested. To prepare for battle, the future first president had this palisaded fort hastily erected in 1754, referring to it in a scribbled journal entry as his "fort of necessity." **Fort Necessity National Battlefield** commemorates the rain-soaked, daylong skirmish of July 3,

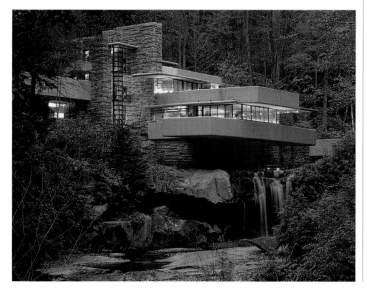

Frank Lloyd Wright designed Fallingwater to blend with the natural terrain of rock outcroppings and waterfalls. The house, built for the Pittsburgh merchant Edgar J. Kaufmann, Sr., in 1939, has been called the "union of powerful art and powerful nature."

1 ERIE

First laid out in 1795, the city of Erie is the state's only port on the Great Lakes. Like an arm embracing the city, the Presque Isle peninsula curls into Lake Erie and forms a gentle bay. The 3,200-acre spit of land has been turned into a popular state park with a wealth of recreational facilities, offering everything from swimming off its sandy beaches to bird-watching along its hiking trails. A visitor center, information kiosks, and pontoon-boat tours of the lagoon will help you appreciate this unique preserve, home to countless wildlife and plant species.

▶ *Autumn is a prime time to visit Presque Isle State Park: the foliage and wildflowers are particularly striking, and the migrations of waterfowl are just beginning.*

Docked across the bay is the **U.S. Brig Niagara,** a reconstruction of the flagship commanded by Lieutenant Oliver Hazard Perry when American forces won the Battle of Lake Erie in 1813. The battle was memorable not only for its decisive U.S. victory but also for Perry's immortal line: "We have met the enemy and they are ours."

The 123-foot-long vessel, whose double masts reach more than 100 feet skyward, has been outfitted with four

Migratory waterfowl, *such as this drake mallard, flock to Presque Isle in the autumn.*

A blue finger of water trails through marsh grass at Presque Isle, which has the only surf-swimming beaches in the state.

reproduction carronades—32-pound guns for close-range combat. Ready for inspection below deck are hammocks and lockers in the sailors' quarters, officers' cabins, and the wardroom.

2 WATERFORD

Historic Waterford was once on the front line of the struggle between the French, the English, and the American Indians for control of the continent's interior. At the **Fort Le Boeuf Museum,** you'll see Waterford's past laid out in minutely detailed models of an Iroquois village and the fort the French built here in 1753, as well as in displays of artifacts uncovered in an ongoing archeological dig across the street, behind the landmark 1826 **Eagle Hotel.**

▶ *To arrange a tour of the museum, contact the museum director at the Department of Sociology/Anthropology/Social Work at the Edinboro University of Pennsylvania.*

Waterford was also the site of George Washington's first diplomatic mission as an officer. The town's historical complex has the only known statue of Washington dressed in a British uniform. He is shown delivering his order

from the British that the French abandon their Ohio Valley possessions.

The **Amos Judson House,** a Federal Greek Revival home built by a prosperous merchant and cabinetmaker in 1820, is filled with original furnishings and period artifacts. A mahogany secretary crafted by Judson himself stands beneath his portrait. The Chickering pianoforte in the living room was only the second such instrument to be carted over the Alleghenies.

3 TITUSVILLE

A glassy coat of oil on the surface of a creek lured Edwin Drake here in 1857. The former railroad conductor was called to Titusville on behalf of the Seneca Oil Company to improve the yield of the company-owned oil spring. It was Drake's brainstorm to drive a pipe down to bedrock and drill inside it. Striking a gusher, he thus launched an oil boom that forever altered America. The **Drake Well Museum** pays tribute to the birth of the petroleum industry with a detailed replica of Drake's derrick and engine house, along with an oil-tank railcar, a pipeline station, and an 1868 fire engine. Period photographs documenting the era of oil discovery are displayed in the main museum building.

The **Oil Creek & Titusville Railroad** travels a 13-mile route through the old oil fields, passing vestiges of villages and wells that sprang up during the oil fever. The train departs from an 1892 freight house in Titusville, where the mansions of oil barons still stand.

4 GROVE CITY

The ancient art of metalsmithing is kept alive at **Wendell August Forge,** which was founded in 1923 and is the oldest operating forge in the United States. A self-guided tour through the forge gives a smith's-eye view of the remarkable transformation wrought by hammer and anvil, fire and imagination. Working in bronze, pewter, copper, and sterling silver, artisans handcraft jewelry and a range of decorative pieces. Stop in the showroom and gift shop for a display of the forge's wares, from serving pieces to jewelry to shimmering Christmas ornaments.

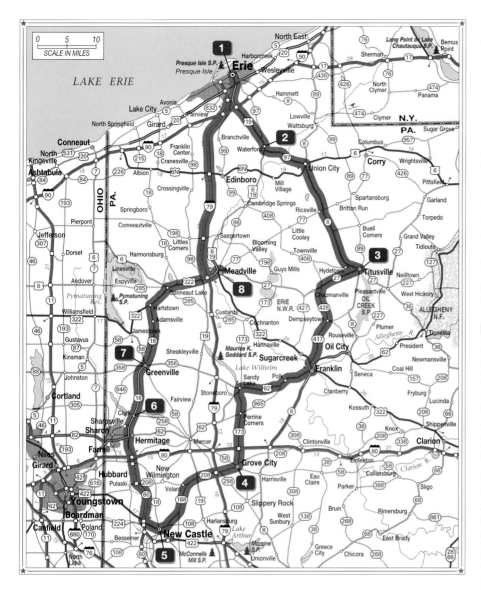

appropriately named **Tara.** Built by a wealthy landowner in 1854, the Greek Revival structure was renovated in the 1920's to emulate the antebellum mansions of the South and completely refurbished in the 1980's as a romantic country inn and museum. Follow the swirling hoop skirts of costumed guides into room after room of Remington bronzes, Civil War–era weapons, and top-quality antique furnishings—such as President Buchanan's dining table and a Meissen porcelain chandelier. Of course, there's plenty of memorabilia from the 1939 Academy Award–winning film, including a playbook, autographed photographs of the stars, and a bed jacket worn by Vivien Leigh.

7 GREENVILLE

A hulking behemoth of iron and steel, all connecting rods and driving wheels, Engine No. 604 is the only surviving example of the largest switch locomotive ever built. The 322-ton steam workhorse, which hauled iron ore in Minnesota until 1960, is now at the **Greenville Railroad Museum,** a choice assembly of mid-20th-century rail equipment clustered outdoors around replicas of two railroad buildings from the 1920's. Don't miss the Empire touring car at the Railway Express office; the sturdy five-seater—advertised as The Little Aristocrat—was one of only 500 manufactured in Greenville between 1913 and 1914.

8 MEADVILLE

An exceptionally refined residence for the rugged mid-19th-century Allegheny Plateau, the **Baldwin-Reynolds House** was built in the 1840's by the Supreme Court Justice Henry Baldwin and completed one year before his death. The three-story estate house has parquet floors, marble fireplaces, and woodwork in now-rare curly maple. In addition to original and locally crafted furnishings, the house features historical displays of militaria, currency, and souvenir spoons. Also on the property is a doctor's office from the early 1900's, outfitted with all of the necessities of a rural medical practice: an eye chart, a skeleton, a pharmacy, and, of course, a doctor's fee schedule.

5 NEW CASTLE

Among the wealth of Victorian gems situated in the fashionable North Hill section of town are two early-20th-century mansions belonging to two siblings who lived side by side. The houses have been reinvented as the **Hoyt Institute of Fine Arts.** The 25-room **Hoyt East** hosts rotating exhibitions of paintings, sculpture, and crafts by local artists. **Hoyt West** has been restored as a house museum, where silk wall coverings, walnut paneling, and other sumptuous appointments recall a life of privilege. Of special interest are the "modern" household conveniences (used by servants, of course), such as a central vacuuming system and a stove-heated clothes dryer, and the German suit of armor poised at the top of an ornate staircase. The Institute is surrounded by four acres of lush formal gardens, including the original rose beds of Hoyt West, known in its original incarnation as Rosewall.

Take a detour 10 miles north of downtown New Castle to lovely Amish country. You'll pass scenic farmland and reach the towns of **New Wilmington** and **Volant.** In Volant an old gristmill has been converted into shops; in New Wilmington you can buy local cheese and Amish crafts.

▶ *Guided motor-coach tours through the Amish country operate out of Volant and Hermitage.*

6 CLARK

You'll think you've stepped onto the set of *Gone With the Wind* when you visit this massive colonnaded mansion,

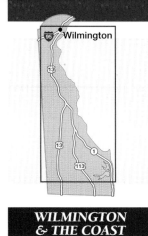

Delaware

With the gorgeous shores of Rehoboth Beach, a cluster of cultural gems in Wilmington, and acre upon acre of rich farmland, it's no big surprise that Delaware is nicknamed the Small Wonder.

WILMINGTON & THE COAST

1 WILMINGTON

The largest city in the second-smallest state, Wilmington is a key industrial center but is equally proud of its Colonial past. Settled by Swedes in 1638, it later served as a campground for George Washington's army en route to the Battle of Brandywine.

The **Delaware Art Museum** is renowned for its pre-Raphaelite paintings and illustrations by artists such as Howard Pyle and N.C. Wyeth. Other galleries highlight American painters, from Winslow Homer to Maxfield Parrish. Built in the 1850's in rural Gothic style, **Rockwood Museum** looks like a scene out of *Wuthering Heights*. Its 14 display rooms, filled with original furnishings, reveal how masters and servants lived at the turn of the century.

Hagley Museum is the 240-acre enclave of the du Ponts, built by Eleuthère Irénée du Pont, who made his fortune in black powder. His riverside mill, shops, and workers' community depict American industry in its infancy. Eleutherian Mills, du Pont's impressive Georgian home, displays furniture, art, and antiques owned by five generations of du Ponts.

Two more du Pont bastions await visitors. **Nemours Mansion,** named for the du Ponts' hometown in France, is filled with French furnishings. A stroll through this Louis XVI–style château, with its extraordinary tapestries, paintings by Old Masters, and elaborate gardens, is an invitation to fantasize about the lifestyles of the fabulously rich.

▶ *Tours of Nemours Mansion are often booked well in advance, and reservations are necessary. Note that visitors must be at least 16 years of age.*

No trip to Wilmington is complete without a visit to the **Winterthur Museum**, a sprawling mansion owned by yet another du Pont, housing what is arguably the world's finest collection of American furniture and decorative arts. Winterthur's 175 period rooms contain

The Chinese Parlor at Winterthur boasts American pieces in Chinese Chippendale style.

gleaming gem after gem—Duncan Phyfe chairs, elegant Chippendale tables, plenitudes of Shaker furnishings.

2 NEW CASTLE

A Colonial village reminiscent of Williamsburg, New Castle is delightfully different because it's a living town. The streets are sprinkled with quaint shops, restaurants, and inns and surround the New Castle Green, laid out by William Penn in 1683. On the green is the **New Castle Court House,** Delaware's capitol before the Revolutionary War. Here you can pick up a map of a five-block historic walking tour. Just off the green are two of New Castle's oldest buildings. The precipi-

tously sloped roof and deep eaves of the **Dutch House** recall the town's 17th-century beginnings; inside you'll find a 16th-century Dutch Bible and a courting bench. The **Amstel House,** completed in 1738, is a Georgian beauty where George Washington reputedly attended a wedding.

A stroll across the common leads you to another treasure, the **George Read II House and Garden,** begun in 1797 by the son of one of the signers of the Declaration of Independence. This dignified 14-room Federal mansion, with its intricate plasterwork, taproom, and exterior kitchen, is considered one of the finest historic homes in America.

3 FORT DELAWARE STATE PARK

Reached by a boat that steams out of Delaware City, this park centers around an imposing pentagon-shaped granite fort that occupies much of Pea Patch Island. Surrounded by a moat, the garrison served as a prison during the Civil War. The fort's museum is a repository for a host of Civil War memorabilia, and a section of its massive ramparts provides views of herons nesting in the marshes below.

4 BOMBAY HOOK NATIONAL WILDLIFE REFUGE

From early November through March, Canada geese swoop down in veritable hordes on this 12,000-acre preserve nestled in the tidal swamps and marshes of Delaware. But year-round its walking trails, 12-mile driving loop, and observation towers provide views of other kinds of wildlife as well— whistling swans, woodpeckers, river otters, and even vultures.

5 JOHN DICKINSON PLANTATION

John Dickinson, a gentleman farmer famed for his articulate protests against England's Colonial tax policy, lived in a grand brick Georgian mansion, built by his father around 1740. Together with a restored smokehouse, granary, barn, and slave quarters, it recalls life here in the Revolutionary War era.

6 LEWES

Enchanting Lewes (pronounced "Lewis") is the gateway to Delaware beach country, and the terminus of the Cape May ferry. The town is a haven for fishermen, bicyclists, and history buffs; but its narrow streets, restored homes, and historic waterfront belie a sad history. Shortly after Lewes was founded by a band of Dutch whaling men, Indians killed all of its residents.

Still, the Dutch returned to the place they called Zwaanendael—or Valley of the Swans. Today the **Lewes Historical Complex** includes a country store, doctor's office, and maritime museum. The **Zwaanendael Museum** is housed in an adaptation of a Dutch town hall. Inside, local history displays include artifacts from a sunken British warship.

▶ *To tour the harbor, take a sunset cruise, leaving Fisherman's Wharf in summer. Dolphin- and whale-watching cruises are also offered.*

7 REHOBOTH BEACH

Sun, sand, and surf are the order of a summer day at Rehoboth Beach, the undisputed capital of Delaware's 25-mile strip of beaches. The parade of tourists on the beach and the restaurant-lined main drag slows down in the

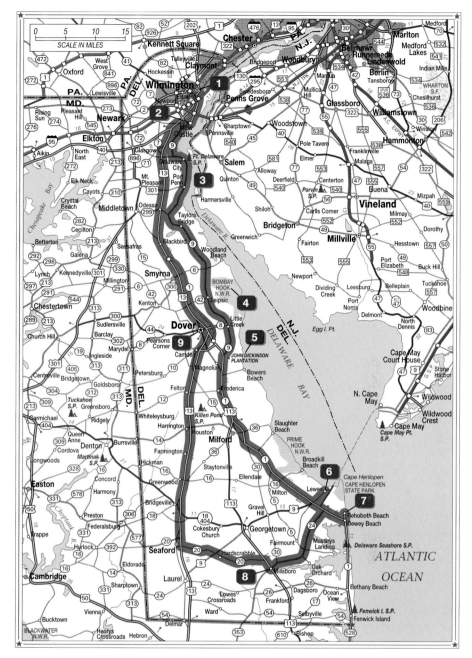

off-season, creating a quiet getaway for bird-watchers and beachcombers.

8 MILLSBORO

Once a dominant tribe on the Delmarva Peninsula, only a few hundred Nanticokes remain today. Six miles east of town the **Nanticoke Indian Museum** preserves a part of their past with a rich collection of spears, baskets, and regalia. In September nearby Oak Orchard is the site of a colorful powwow.

9 DOVER

In 1683 William Penn ordered the layout of what would become Delaware's capital city. Its wide, well-manicured green is the site of the gambrel-roofed **Old State House.** In a nearby tavern, state legislators were the first to ratify the U.S. Constitution. Clustered around the green is a collection of handsome l8th- and 19th-century homes and the nostalgic **Johnson Victrola Museum.** Dover Heritage Trail, Inc., offers guided walking tours of the historic green and Victorian Dover.

Finally, the **Delaware Agricultural Museum and Village** gives visitors a taste of farm life on the Delmarva Peninsula, from the arrival of the first settlers to the mid 20th century.

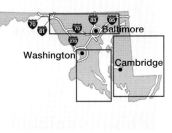

Maryland

From the marble stoops of its row houses to the saltwater byways and rural flatlands of the Chesapeake, Maryland offers an appealing mix of historic sites and placid coastal towns.

BALTIMORE & THE NORTH

1 BALTIMORE

A thoroughbred among American cities, this venerable old port has never looked better now that its **Inner Harbor** has been magnificently rebuilt. Shopping pavilions, lush parks, inviting restaurants, and modern office buildings mingle with historic sites along Baltimore's age-old waterfront.

The city's star attraction is the **National Aquarium in Baltimore**, home to more than 5,000 marine creatures in a variety of briny habitats. Fish of astonishing beauty and size swim in vast tanks, inches from the rapt gaze of visitors. Dolphins frolic in the Marine Mammal Pavilion.

Moored nearby is a far older attraction: the **U.S. Frigate *Constellation***, a priceless naval relic and the oldest warship continuously afloat. Tours of the restored vessel are offered. A few blocks down the harbor, in the restored neighborhood of **Fells Point**, is a collection of some 350 well-preserved Federal buildings. Guarding the harbor's entrance is **Fort McHenry**, above which Francis Scott Key saw, by "the rockets' red glare," the Star-Spangled Banner still waving after an 1814 British attack.

▶ *Baltimore's city markets are good, inexpensive places to lunch. Stands at the Broadway Market at Fells Point sell everything from deli items to seafood delicacies to flowers.*

Baltimore also boasts a wealth of museums, including **Walters Art Gallery**, with a Renaissance treasure-house of fine art. Among its most interesting pieces is the mysterious Rubens Vase, carved from one piece of agate around A.D. 400. Owners have included Byzan-

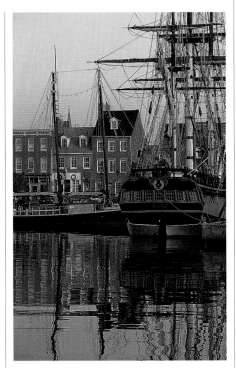

***Fells Point**, once an enclave of sailors and sea captains, savors its maritime past.*

tine emperors, French kings, and the painter Rubens; yet it has disappeared for centuries at a time. Today it is worth millions of dollars.

The **Babe Ruth Birthplace**, in the row house where Ruth was born, traces the exploits of the Babe, the Baltimore Orioles, and other Maryland big-timers. Nearby, the **B&O Railroad Museum**, site of the nation's first passenger train station, delights rail fans with its collection of antique cars and locomotives.

The **Maryland Historical Society**, housed in an elegant 1846 mansion, displays collections from four centuries of Maryland life, including its treasured jewel, the original "Star-Spangled Banner" manuscript. You can also tour **Carroll Mansion**, home of Charles Carroll, one of the signers of the Declaration of Independence, and **Homewood**, where his son lived. Also of note is Benjamin

Latrobe's **Basilica of the Assumption**, the country's first Roman Catholic cathedral, dedicated in 1821.

2 ELLICOTT CITY

Thirteen miles west of the B&O Railroad Museum in Baltimore is a second monument to early railroad history. Ellicott City was the destination of *Tom Thumb*, America's first steam engine, which first puffed from Baltimore in 1830. The terminal is now the **B&O Railroad Station Museum**, with a restored waiting room, ticket office, and model railroad display. Many of the stone buildings in town are home to antique shops and restaurants.

3 FREDERICK

This handsome city, laid out in 1745, has played host to a number of important episodes in American history. But the incident for which it is best known—a woman's bold defiance of Confederate general Stonewall Jackson, remembered wistfully in "Barbara Frietchie," John Greenleaf Whittier's poem—may be mostly myth. The house from which the 95-year-old patriot was said to have waved a Union flag as Confederate troops marched past has been rebuilt as the **Barbara Fritchie House and Museum**. Frederick also has many impressive period structures; among them is **Schifferstadt**, a stone farmhouse built in 1756 in Colonial German style.

4 SHARPSBURG

One mile north of Sharpsburg at Antietam Creek, the 41,000-man Confederate army under Gen. Robert E. Lee, fresh from victory at Manassas, met head-on the 87,000-strong Union forces of Gen. George B. McClellan. The result was the bloodiest day of the Civil War, with some 23,000 soldiers killed or wounded. More than 4,000 men fell along a road that would forever be known as Bloody Lane. At **Antietam National Battlefield**, maps, interpretive signs, and monuments document the immortal battle.

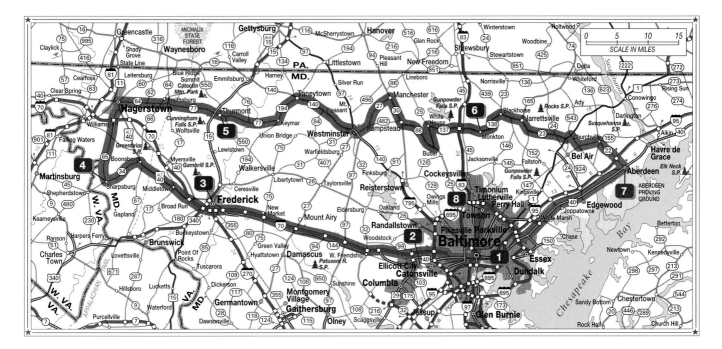

▶ Civil War buffs may want to continue a few miles south to visit another historic site, Harpers Ferry National Historical Park, in West Virginia.

5 THURMONT

Near this mountain gateway are the trail-laced forests of **Catoctin Mountain Park** and **Cunningham Falls State Park.** The 1856 **Roddy Road Covered Bridge** spans past and present as it crosses Owens Creek. Peach and apple orchards, berry gardens, and markets dot the landscape, with fruit for picking or purchasing.

6 MONKTON

The eclectic tastes of the late Harvey Ladew—landscape designer, foxhunter, collector—live on at his lavish 22-acre estate, now **Ladew Topiary Gardens.** From a farmhouse Ladew created an elegant manor, with 15 well-tended theme gardens and dozens of topiary figures. The Oval Library interior is considered a masterpiece.

7 ABERDEEN

At the Aberdeen Proving Ground, military hardware buffs will have a field day at the **U.S. Army Ordnance Museum.** Here are gathered the massive leftovers of America's armed conflicts. Tanks, artillery, body armor, a German V-2 rocket, even the German "Anzio Annie" railroad cannon, rest peacefully here.

8 TOWSON

Beckoning visitors to Towson is the **Hampton National Historic Site.** In its time, this extraordinary Georgian mansion, begun in 1783, was one of America's great private homes. Set on 60 manicured acres and topped by a grandiose cupola, the house was occupied by the Ridgely family until 1948. Many original furnishings and artworks remain, most notably a rare complete set of elaborate Baltimore painted furniture. Magnificent formal gardens grace the grounds, and a handful of outbuildings includes intact slave quarters.

A silent cannon at Antietam recalls a tragic chapter of the Civil War.

1 WASHINGTON, D.C.

Capital of the United States, center of international influence, treasury of monuments and museums, Washington, D.C., is one of the world's most diverse cities. It was Pierre L'Enfant's challenge, in 1791, to design a city that would be a magnificent symbol for the burgeoning nation. A French-born engineer, L'Enfant devised a street plan after culling ideas from maps of various European cities, most notably Versailles: broad avenues running diagonally, like the spokes of a wheel, across a grid of irregular rectangular blocks. This created circles, triangles, and squares at intersections where monuments and fountains could be placed.

Today the city's handsome skyline remains free of high rises and is softened by the tens of thousands of trees planted in the 1870's and early 1900's. It's a particularly glorious place in the spring, when sprays of pink and white cherry blossoms seem to temper the edges of this high-powered city.

Most of Washington's attractions within walking distance of one another are near the panoramic greens of the **Mall,** one of the oldest federal parks in the country. To many Americans, the

Mall is sacred ground, leading to such famous landmarks as the Jefferson, Lincoln, and Vietnam Veterans memorials, the **Washington Monument,** and the **White House.** The **U.S. Capitol**'s tumultuous past reflects the country's own: burned by the British in 1814, it was rebuilt and later capped by a 335-foot-high dome during the Civil War.

A good bet if you're pressed for time is the **Smithsonian Institution,** the world's largest museum complex, where you can easily walk from one attraction to the next. Visit the **National Air and Space Museum** to see the Wright brothers' *Flyer* and Charles

Warner Theatre, an exquisite Roaring Twenties movie palace with a marble and gold-leaf grand lobby. The **U.S. Holocaust Memorial Museum** honors the victims of World War II Nazi atrocities. And don't forget the **National Archives,** where original copies of the Declaration of Independence and the U.S. Constitution are displayed.

▶ *Think of the U.S. Capitol as the center of a compass, from which 90-degree segments extend to form the designations NW, NE, SE, and SW. Lettered streets run east–west and numbered streets north–south.*

whose chapel houses Tiffany windows and the crypt of the American Revolutionary War naval hero John Paul Jones.

Back from the harbor stand the elegant mansions of early American nabobs. Tour the 1765 **William Paca House,** a Georgian masterpiece whose restoration led to the discovery of original Prussian blue walls, or the 1774 **Hammond-Harwood House,** designed by the architect William Buckland. African-American culture is the theme at the **Banneker-Douglass Museum,** situated in a former Victorian Gothic church and named for two prominent Maryland-born black leaders.

3 CALVERT CLIFFS STATE PARK

Embedded in 100-foot-high clay cliffs along Chesapeake Bay are marine fossils from the Miocene epoch, a pre–Ice Age period when the region was bathed by a vast, shallow ocean. Fossil hunters may scavenge—but not dig for—the relics that come to rest on the shoreline. Shark's teeth are among the finds. The park has 13 miles of nature trails.

4 SOLOMONS

Maryland's maritime heritage is documented in the **Calvert Marine Museum,** which sits prettily beside a restored 1883 lighthouse at the confluence of the Patuxent River and the Chesapeake Bay. Exhibits include a re-creation of an offshore seabed. In the Discovery Room, you may dig to your heart's delight through a pile of Chesapeake shore sand in quest of sharks' teeth.

5 ST. MARYS CITY

A living-history museum is being built from the ghostly remnants of the first capital of Colonial Maryland. Founded in 1634, the largely Catholic colony of St. Marys thrived until the capital was moved to Annapolis in 1694. The town gradually disappeared into rural underbrush. Today, St. Marys City is being reconstructed from foundations and artifacts unearthed in an ongoing archeological excavation. The most exciting and significant findings have been the three lead coffins unearthed from beneath the site of the **Great Brick Chapel.** They contain the 300-year-old

The nation's capital celebrates America's birthday in high style with an explosion of fireworks over the Washington Monument and the Lincoln Memorial. In the background is the Capitol, whose 335-foot-high cast-iron dome, painted white to resemble marble, was constructed during the bleakest days of the War Between the States.

Lindbergh's *Spirit of St. Louis.* The national museums of **American History** and **Natural History** have an eclectic range of exhibits, from the original Star-Spangled Banner to the Hope Diamond.

There's no categorizing some of the city's other notable attractions. The **Library of Congress,** open to everyone, has among its 30 million books an original Gutenberg Bible, from 1450. Visit the basement museum in **Ford's Theatre,** where the gun used to assassinate Lincoln is on exhibit. See a show at the

2 ANNAPOLIS

This is how a mid-Atlantic seaport *should* look: a bustling harbor ringed by a colorful hodgepodge of historic buildings—spanning more than three centuries—lining narrow, crooked streets. Once dubbed the Athens of the New World, Annapolis is Maryland's capital city. The **State House,** whose octagonal dome and cupola were completed in 1794, is America's oldest state house in continuous use. Just north of the State House is the **U.S. Naval Academy,**

remains of a man, a woman, and a young child in a remarkable state of preservation. The man's long red hair was intact, as were the sprinklings of rosemary, said to be a 17th-century herb of remembrance. Scientists have determined that the three are members of the founding family of Maryland, the Calverts. Today the village—with a tobacco plantation, a reconstructed state house, and a replica of a 1630's square-rigged sailing ship—is alive with activity, as costumed interpreters reenact Colonial life. Visitors can play at being archeologists during the **Tide Water Archaeology Dig**, held the last weekend in July; digging tools are provided.

6 PORT TOBACCO

Local Indians had already settled this pleasant spot by the time English colonists arrived in 1634. The village the natives called Potobac became Port Tobacco, a major shipping port for the exportation of its gold leaf namesake. Several structures on the town square recall those days, including the reconstructed **Port Tobacco Courthouse**. Inside, the **Charles County Museum** exhibits detail the region's rich past.

7 WALDORF

The **Dr. Samuel A. Mudd House Museum** marks one of the stops that John Wilkes Booth made in his night flight after the assassination of President Lincoln. Booth and an accomplice fled on horseback to Dr. Mudd's farmhouse at four in the morning for treatment of Booth's leg, broken in his leap onto the Ford's Theatre stage. The doctor would later claim that the men presented false names and wore disguises, but he was sentenced to life imprisonment nonetheless. A presidential pardon freed Dr. Mudd four years later. The home holds family furnishings.

8 CLINTON

Considered a "safe house" for Confederate sympathizers during the Civil War, the restored **Surratt House and Tavern** was another stopover for Booth and his accomplice after the flight from Ford's Theatre. The 1852 tavern belonged to Mary Surratt, who was later convicted of harboring a fugitive and hanged.

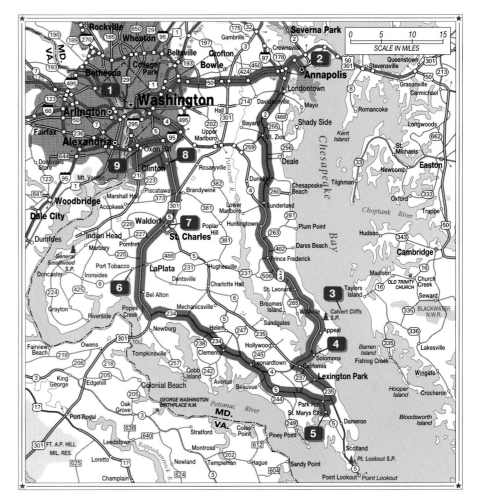

▶ *The Surratt Society offers those on its mailing list full-day spring and fall tours of the route John Wilkes Booth took in his flight from Ford's Theatre. Write the Surratt Society at P.O. Box 427, Clinton, MD 20735.*

9 OXON HILL

An early-19th-century masonry fort is the centerpiece of **Fort Washington Park**, which stretches over 341 acres just south of Washington, D.C. George Washington chose this Potomac River bluff as the site for a fortification to protect the new capital. The original fort was destroyed in 1814 and rebuilt in 1824. Costumed interpreters lecture on 19th-century life. Reserve a spot to see the vintage military drills by torchlight.

Lend a hand with farm chores done the old-fashioned way at the 485-acre **Oxon Hill Farm**, operated by the National Park Service. Sheepshearing is but one of the seasonal chores carried out using turn-of-the-century methods. A Fall Festival is held each October.

1 CAMBRIDGE

One of the Eastern Shore's largest towns, Cambridge presents a handsome countenance. Encircling a sheltered harbor beside the broad Choptank River, the town has a longtime maritime heritage as a deepwater port. Fanciers of historic architecture should stroll down brick-paved High Street, lined with stately 18th- and 19th-century buildings. Walking-tour maps are available at most shops and restaurants.

▶ *Tour High Street in the spring, when the blooms of the Bradford pear trees show it off at its best.*

After three centuries, the **Old Trinity Church**, located eight miles southwest of Cambridge, is still holding regular services. The church was constructed in

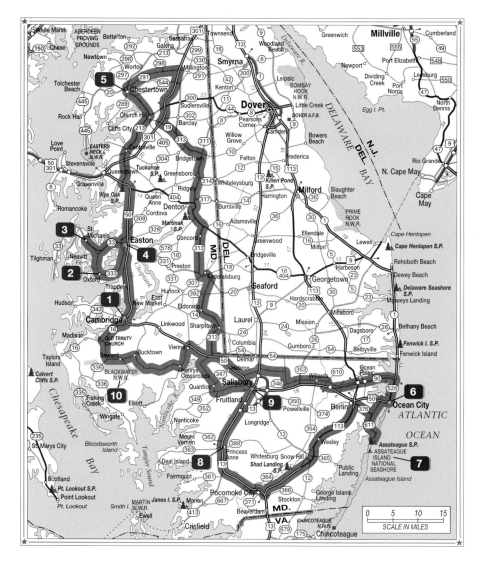

The 1879 **Hooper Strait Lighthouse** is a white six-sided structure on iron pilings. Screwed into the muddy bay floor, the pilings were used to stabilize the lighthouse against peripatetic ice floes.

▶ *Cruise the Chesapeake on the An-napolitan II, which takes summer excursions into St. Michaels from Annapolis. The Maritime Museum offers waterfowl cruises in the crisp late-fall months.*

4 EASTON

A village of sophisticated tastes and culture, Easton has its roots in the 17th century. The wide, shady streets guard such relics as the **Third Haven Friends Meeting House** of 1682, one of America's oldest frame houses of worship. Quakers from all over boated to church here; among them, it is said, was William Penn. The Georgian **Talbot County Courthouse** has anchored the town square since 1794. Pick up a walking-tour map at the Talbot County Historical Society headquarters, a restored 19th-century shop.

Visit Easton in April for the **Mid-Atlantic Maritime Festival.** The three-day celebration of nautical craftsworks features model ships, photography exhibits, and live music. In November an annual three-day **Waterfowl Festival** honors the region's bountiful wildlife.

5 CHESTERTOWN

A handsome panorama greets visitors driving in from the south: the mansions of Water Street reflected on the Chester River under a cool canopy of trees. It's a scene that has remained unaltered for more than 200 years. Founded in 1706 as a trading center, the town itself has changed little since the days when it was a prosperous port. It even had its own version of the Boston Tea Party: in 1774 residents boarded a docked brigantine and dumped a cargo of highly taxed tea into the bay.

A stroll through the neat, compact streets is the best way to enjoy Chestertown's centuries-old architecture. You can tour the elegant **Geddes-Piper House,** headquarters of the Historical Society of Kent County. Portions of the house were built in the late 1700's.

1675, and its adjoining cemetery contains the 19th-century grave of Anna Ella Carroll—a feminist before the word was coined—who many claimed played a major role in determining Union strategy during the Civil War.

2 OXFORD

Settled since the 1660's, Oxford thrived for nearly a century as an important port. Today the town is a pleasing mix of vintage watermen's homes and elegant Colonial mansions. Stroll or drive by the immaculately restored homes along Morris Street. Shops and boutiques now occupy the stores that once supplied sailors and commercial fishermen. From a nearby dock, the **Oxford-Bellevue Ferry,** which takes automobiles, has crossed the mile-wide Tred Avon River since 1683.

Oxford and St. Michaels are linked by the ferry and a lovely rural road. Rent

bikes in either town for the six-mile trek on **Bellevue Road,** which meanders past old homes and green fields.

3 ST. MICHAELS

Many travelers find St. Michaels to be the ultimate Eastern Shore town. A fleet of sailboats and fishing boats still plies the local bay waters. St. Michaels' popularity has created a lively shopping area in the historic downtown district, but the village remains simply that—a small town with an unhurried pace, and not a stoplight in sight.

The **Chesapeake Bay Maritime Museum** is set in the heart of town on 18 waterfront acres. Moored at the docks are classic specimens of the sail-powered workboats once crafted here, like the *Edna Lockwood,* a restored 1889 two-masted bugeye, and the 1955 *Rosie Parks,* one of the last of the skipjacks—as oyster-dredging boats were called.

6 OCEAN CITY

Maryland's popular resort town sprawls along 10 miles of barrier-island beach; in summer the permanent population of 7,000 swells to more than 250,000 people a week. At its heart is a bustling old-time boardwalk, crammed with saltwater-taffy shops, wax museums, and pizzerias. Catch the sights from a nifty boardwalk tram or simply stroll—choose your own tempo.

History buffs may want to inspect the early lifesaving equipment and vintage bathing suits, from bloomers to woollies, at the **Ocean City Life Saving Station Museum**, opened in 1979 in an 1891 lifesaving station.

Operating out of easy-to-reach marinas, charter boats rumble eastward to the Gulf Stream to snag such deep-sea quarry as tuna and wahoo. Eating Eastern Shore style can be as much fun as the fishing. Simply do as the natives do: gather some friends, spread newspapers about, pick up a mallet, and crack open a dozen or two of the region's world-renowned steamed blue crabs.

7 ASSATEAGUE ISLAND

The modern world has never tamed this 37-mile-long island on the Eastern Shore of Maryland and Virginia. A dynamic landscape of constantly shifting sands, Assateague Island today remains as pristine as it appeared when the first settlers arrived. And undeveloped it will

stay: the National Park Service is its chief landlord; the state of Maryland operates a park and campground. There are reams of simple pleasures here—swimming or fishing the broad Atlantic beaches, nature walks through the dunes and thickets, clamming and crabbing. You can get lessons on the latter from NPS naturalists, who offer interpretive programs in the summer.

Catch a glimpse of the Chincoteague ponies, the famous herds of wild ponies that romp on the island's dunes. You're assured a seabird sighting at the **Chincoteague National Wildlife Refuge**, at Assateague's southern end, established in 1943 as a resting and feeding ground for migrating birds.

▶ *Sample oysters in their natural state or gussied-up at the annual Oyster Festival, held on neighboring Chincoteague Island on Columbus Day weekend; buy tickets in advance from the Chincoteague Chamber.*

8 PRINCESS ANNE

This small town was laid out in 1733; much of its Colonial architecture is intact and spruced up annually for **Old Princess Anne Days**, a house and garden tour held every October. Tour the impressive **Teackle Mansion**, built by Littleton Teackle, who supplied lumber for the U.S. Capitol during the Jefferson administration. The brick house is filled

with ornate period furnishings. Stroll from the mansion past picket fences and boxwood gardens to **St. Andrew's Episcopal Churchyard**, where the Teackles are buried, and then on to the **Washington Hotel**, built in 1744; it features separate staircases for men and women, a Colonial preference.

9 SALISBURY

The largest city on the Eastern Shore, Salisbury hums with a harbor full of pleasure craft and commercial boats. One out of every eight of the 95,000 residents of this food-processing industrial town works for the poultry industry. Salisbury is home to birds of a different feather as well: decorative and antique decoys and wildlife paintings in the **Ward Museum of Wildfowl Art**, opened in 1992. Nearby, you can see the live versions of these birds at the **Salisbury Zoo**, often cited as one of the finest small zoos in the country.

Salisbury's **Newtown Historic District** is largely Victorian; its Colonial structures were destroyed in two late-19th-century fires. The Federal **Poplar Hill Mansion** is an exception; it survived as a fine example of transitional Georgian architecture. Homes in the Newtown Historic District are open to the public during the **Newtown Festival**, held the first Saturday in October.

10 BLACKWATER NATIONAL WILDLIFE REFUGE

Stretching beneath the Atlantic flyway, this sanctuary of tidal marsh, freshwater ponds, and woodlands has a five-mile-long wildlife drive open to cars, bikers, and hikers. The length of the drive includes a bike path; a ride takes about 90 minutes. Rent bicycles in nearby Oxford or Easton.

▶ *Avoid the refuge in the summer months: flies and mosquitoes are plentiful and ravenous.*

You're guaranteed sightings of some form of wildlife and perhaps even a glimpse of a bald eagle or a peregrine falcon, both endangered species. Waterfowl by the thousands have been sighted here during prime migration season, from October through December.

An 1879 lighthouse *is one of the bayside exhibits at the Chesapeake Bay Maritime Museum.*

SOUTHEAST

Florida Everglades

*T*he magnolia-and-honeysuckle South of yore has seen great upheavals; it is now one of the fastest-growing regions in the country. Everyone seems to be heading for points southward for a taste of a gentler lifestyle, a warmer clime, and the famous Southern hospitality. The region's languid pace continues to charm, but progress has imparted a joyous vitality: the place is humming.

The following 29 tours take you to a South both old and new. Journey to the sites of America's infancy: Jamestown, the first permanent English settlement in the New World, and to Roanoke Island, where a 16th-century colony vanished without a trace. Visit the South of colonnaded plantation homes along the River Road in Mississippi and Louisiana and spy a colt testing his legs on the bluegrass fields of Kentucky. Make a pilgrimage to Tennessee's music capitals, Memphis and Nashville. Savor the spicy cultural mix of Miami, dine royally in New Orleans, and marvel at the ultimate New South city, Atlanta. Home of the old and the new, the Southeastern U.S.—from West Virginia to the Gulf Coast—remains a vibrant part of our national character.

The next 60 pages show you why, as you drive through these 11 colorful states.

Wheeling · Harpers Ferry · Charleston · Louisville · Charleston · Arlingto · Richmond · Lexington · Lynchburg · Edenton · Nashville · Knoxville · Chapel Hill · Memphis · Charlotte · Chattanooga · Oxford · Atlanta · Birmingham · Charleston · Vicksburg · Savannah · Alexandria · New Orleans · Mobile · Jacksonville · Tallahassee · Orlando · Tampa · Miami

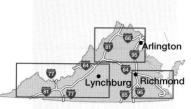

Virginia

In Virginia, where the majestic Blue Ridge Mountains reign, the seeds of American history were sown in turn by the Jamestown colonists, George Washington, and Thomas Jefferson.

NORTHERN VIRGINIA

1 ARLINGTON

Arlington, rising augustly above the Potomac, is linked to the heart of Washington, D.C., by Memorial Bridge. Originally part of the District of Columbia, it was returned to Virginia in 1847.

Dominating the hill at the end of the bridge is the massive Greek Revival mansion where Robert E. Lee lived for

changing of the guard—every half hour in summer and every hour from October to April—is an impressive ritual. Nearby, the massive bronze **Marine Corps Memorial**, depicting the raising of the American flag at Iwo Jima, is a sobering sight.

▶ *To save yourself a lot of walking when you visit Arlington National Cemetery, board the Tourmobile, leaving from the visitor center.*

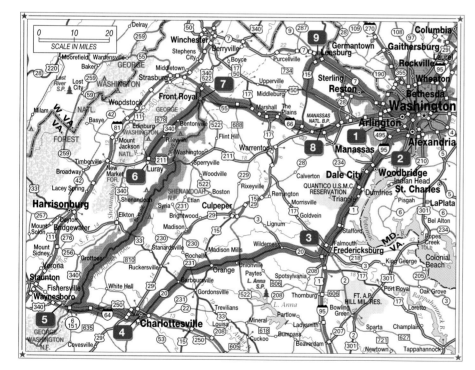

many years. Stately **Arlington House**, now restored, features original furnishings. It sits on the grounds of **Arlington National Cemetery**, the final resting place of many distinguished Americans. Among them: Presidents John F. Kennedy and William Howard Taft, Generals John J. Pershing and George C. Marshall, Chief Justice Oliver Wendell Holmes, and Joe Louis. At the Tomb of the Unknowns, the regular

A sprawling symbol of American martial strength, the **Pentagon** is one of the world's largest office buildings, occupying 29 acres. Visitors may venture within on a 90-minute tour that includes a look at the military art collections.

2 ALEXANDRIA

Once home to George Washington, Alexandria is said to have the nation's largest collection of original 18th- and

early-19th-century structures. **Old Town** is a charming collection of brick townhouses, bow-windowed shops, and early warehouses. Visitors can tour **Gadsby's Tavern Museum**, where George and Martha danced; the **Stabler-Leadbeater Apothecary Shop**, one of the nation's oldest; the **Old Presbyterian Meeting House**, where Washington's funeral was held; the **Boyhood Home of Robert E. Lee,** a Georgian townhouse; and **Christ Church**, where Washington worshiped. A handy source of information, including walking tour maps, is the **Ramsay House Visitors Center,** housed in a gambrel-roofed home, the oldest residence in town.

Alexandria's restored waterfront features the notable **Torpedo Factory Art Center,** where scores of artists create and display works.

Finally, nine miles to the south, standing serenely by the Potomac, is legendary **Mount Vernon**, Washington's beloved plantation estate, with many original furnishings and relics.

3 FREDERICKSBURG

George Washington spent much of his youth in Fredericksburg, later the center of Civil War battles. The 40-block National Historic District preserves such 18th-century classics as the **Rising Sun Tavern**, scene of pre-Revolutionary rallies, and the **Hugh Mercer Apothecary Shop**, which Washington used as an office during his visits. Three other sites have close Washington ties: elegant **Kenmore**, home of Washington's sister Betty (tours include samples of gingerbread made from her mother's recipe); the **Mary Washington House**, home of the first president's mother; and the **George Washington Masonic Museum**, where he was initiated as a Freemason in 1752.

James Monroe's law office is now the **James Monroe Museum and Memorial Library**. Mrs. Monroe's gowns and gems are on display. Noted painter Gari Melchers is honored at **Belmont**, his former home and studio. The **Fredericksburg Area Museum and Cultural**

The Shenandoah Valley's dimpled blue-green splendor, framed by the Blue Ridge and Allegheny mountains and soaked with Civil War history, is a perfect haven for cyclists—and curious cows.

Center, housed in the 1816 Town Hall, contains interesting bits of local history.

▶ *The visitor center provides free parking passes for any city street. The center also offers tour tickets that save up to 33 percent on admission prices to certain Fredericksburg sites.*

Civil War buffs should not miss **Fredericksburg and Spotsylvania National Military Park,** encompassing Fredericksburg Battlefield and three other battle sites. The park has its own visitor center in Fredericksburg, where you can plan a self-guided tour.

4 CHARLOTTESVILLE

The original campus of the **University of Virginia,** Thomas Jefferson's "academical village," remains as he designed it, the Rotunda flanked by classical pavilions in a composition cited among the world's architectural masterpieces.

Monticello, the home that Jefferson designed, built, and then redesigned, enjoys equal rank. Set on a glorious mountaintop, it offers a host of artifacts that reveal Jefferson the Renaissance man. On the road to Monticello, **Historic Michie Tavern** sits on land once owned by Patrick Henry's father. Formerly a rest stop for weary travelers, it is now a museum and restaurant. About two miles distant in these Blue Ridge foothills is **Ash Lawn–Highland,** the simple farmhouse James Monroe called home, where peacocks still strut in the boxwood gardens.

5 WAYNESBORO

Waynesboro, nestled in the beautiful Shenandoah Valley, enjoys a strategic position near the intersection of the **Blue Ridge Parkway** and the **Skyline Drive.** To the south the parkway rambles along the crest of the Blue Ridge Mountains all the way to the Great Smokies. To the north snakes the magnificent Skyline Drive. This 105-mile ribbon of road runs the length of **Shenandoah National Park,** a 300-square-mile woodland paradise. From lofty summits of the Blue Ridge Mountains along the way, a series of spectacular views of the Shenandoah Valley spreads before you.

▶ *Views from the Skyline Drive are best in winter, spring, and late fall; as summer progresses, a haze diminishes visibility. Most park facilities are closed November through March.*

6 LURAY

One of the most beautiful caves in the world, **Luray Caverns** boasts elaborate, colorful rock formations and the only "stalacpipe" organ in existence. This one-of-a-kind underground instrument makes music when stalactites hanging from the cave's ceiling are struck.

7 FRONT ROYAL

A northern gateway to Shenandoah National Park and the Skyline Drive, this town edging the Shenandoah River is where you'll find **Skyline Caverns,** featuring a profusion of delicate white crystalline formations called anthodites.

Front Royal was also the home of Confederate spy Belle Boyd, and the site of a surprise attack on a Federal garrison by Stonewall Jackson's men. The battle resonates dramatically in the **Warren Rifles Confederate Museum.**

8 MANASSAS NATIONAL BATTLEFIELD PARK

One of the most historic places on American soil remains much as it was when two important Confederate victories were won here. Self-guided walking and driving tours include such history-drenched settings as Henry Hill, where Thomas J. "Stonewall" Jackson won his nickname by "standing like a stone wall" and refusing to yield.

9 LEESBURG

This handsome old town is the seat of Loudoun County, which stretches from near Washington to the Blue Ridge Mountains. The **Loudoun Museum** spotlights the area's history and is the starting point for walking tours of the town's 19th-century historic district.

Leesburg is horse country, and **Morven Park** is an important venue for steeplechase racing. Its imposing columned mansion is open for tours, along with a carriage museum and a fox-hunting museum. Six miles south, another great estate, **Oatlands,** stages equestrian events and can be toured.

The Book Room at Monticello housed one of the largest private libraries in the nation.

1 RICHMOND

Rising high above the sparkling James River, Virginia's capital may seem at first too new for a city with such a past. But amid the shiny skyscrapers many vintage landmarks remain as emblems of an early greatness.

If a visitor sees only one, it should be the 1788 **Capitol,** designed by Thomas Jefferson. The building was the Confederate Capitol in the 1860's, an era vividly recalled at the nearby **Museum and White House of the Confederacy** and at the **Richmond National Battlefield Park.** Reaching further back in time, Revolutionary words echo on Church

Daily life during the Revolutionary War is evoked by costumed reenactors at the Yorktown Victory Center. At a Continental Army encampment, stews made with dried meat and potatoes simmer over open fires.

Hill, where in the white-frame **St. John's Episcopal Church** Patrick Henry delivered his "Liberty or Death" speech in 1775.

Treasured artifacts at the **Virginia Historical Society** range from Princess Pocahontas's gold buttons to Jeb Stuart's bloodstained sash, while the special province of the **Valentine Museum** is Richmond history. The **Edgar Allan Poe Museum** honors the author of "The Raven," and the **Virginia Museum of Fine Arts** displays world-class art from ancient to modern times.

2 WILLIAMSBURG

Virginia's 18th-century capital was awakened from a long slumber by a colossal restoration funded by John D. Rockefeller, Jr. Today the handsome little city's 173-acre historic district is an incomparable collection of more than 500 buildings, most of them Georgian, from an authentic woodshed to the Governor's Palace. Almost 90 structures are original. Some 50 18th-century houses, shops, and public buildings are open to visitors, and hundreds of costumed craftsmen and interpreters practice scores of Colonial trades.

On the outskirts of town, **Busch Gardens** theme park offers rides and attractions with Old World motifs in five re-created European villages.

▶ The Williamsburg Historic Area must be toured on foot, but a shuttle bus from the visitor center will bring you to the edge of town and back.

Eight miles southeast is **Carter's Grove,** a red-brick Georgian gem dating back to 1750. Set on an 800-acre plantation, it has been called the most beautiful house in America.

3 JAMESTOWN

Only the foundations remain of the original village of Jamestown, the New World's first permanent English settlement. But you can walk among the ruins where Capt. John Smith and Pocahontas lived at **Colonial National Historical Park,** which offers a visitor center and a museum.

Next door at the **Jamestown Settlement,** interpreters dressed as hardy settlers make tools and armor and answer questions in a replicated fort. You can also take a gander at replicas of the three small ships that brought the 104 original colonists to Jamestown.

4 YORKTOWN

The surrender of Lord Cornwallis, which effectively ended the Revolutionary War, still seems like recent history at the **Yorktown Battlefield.** Self-guided tours of the battlefield, part of **Colonial National Historical Park,** include encampments and fortifications. At the visitor center, George Washington's original field tent stands pitched for battle. At the adjacent **Yorktown Victory Center,** a Continental Army encampment is manned by costumed interpreters, and exhibits about the Revolution thrill history buffs.

In the town proper stands the historic **Moore House,** where the terms of surrender were negotiated. Here too is the restored **Nelson House,** whose owner, a commander of the Virginia militia, ordered it bombarded when he came home to find it behind enemy lines.

5 NEWPORT NEWS

Named for Capt. Christopher Newport, who brought supplies and news from England, Newport News boasts one of the world's great maritime collections at the **Mariners Museum.** Here an assortment of relics—figureheads, paintings, ship models, arms, decorative art, rare artifacts, and boats from around the world—pay tribute to the area's long seafaring heritage.

Nearby, the **War Memorial Museum of Virginia** tells the American military saga through thousands of artifacts. From **Waterman's Wharf,** cruise boats sail forth in the historic harbor of Hampton Roads, where the ironclads *Monitor* and *Merrimack* (called the *Virginia* by the Confederates) did battle.

6 HAMPTON

Hampton is the oldest continuously inhabited English-speaking settlement in the United States. It is also where the U.S. space program got its start. The **Virginia Air and Space Center** is a monument to high-flying technology, with exhibits of aircraft and spacecraft, space suits, and even a lunar rock.

A Roman merchant ship is one of 16 miniature ships at the Mariners Museum.

Close by is **Fort Monroe,** a star-shaped, moat-encircled masonry fortress completed in 1834 and still on active duty. Its **Casemate Museum** includes the cell where Confederate President Jefferson Davis was imprisoned.

7 VIRGINIA BEACH

One of America's major resort cities, The Beach, as it is known to Virginians, boasts almost 30 miles of sandy seashore and a 2-mile-long boardwalk. There are quiet spots as well: the vast marshes and woodlands of **Back Bay National Wildlife Refuge** and the beautiful walking trails and superb beaches of **Seashore State Park.**

Old Cape Henry Lighthouse is a fine 1791 relic, and the **Adam Thoroughgood House,** a small brick cottage, is older still, dating back to the 1600's. The **Life-Saving Museum of Virginia,** on the boardwalk, displays thrilling tales of shipwreck and rescue. And the **Virginia Marine Science Museum** introduces visitors to live denizens of the state's waterways.

8 NORFOLK

Virginia's premier port city is more than just a pretty waterfront, although **The Waterside** is indeed a pleasant place to shop, eat, and stroll.

The **Chrysler Museum** ranks among the nation's finest, with particular strength in French Academy and Italian Baroque paintings and an 8,000-piece glass collection. Tribute is paid to a notable American war hero at the **Gen. Douglas MacArthur Memorial,** where the general is entombed. The 1792 Georgian **Moses Myers House** is not only beautiful but filled with family furnishings from five generations.

The **Hermitage Foundation,** a Tudor mansion with a lovely river view, contains a superb collection of Oriental art. At the **Norfolk Botanical Gardens,** canal boats and 12 miles of footpaths lead through 150 acres of native plants. Yet Norfolk is linked first and foremost with the enormous **Norfolk Naval Base,** the largest in the world. Buses tour the base, April through October.

9 PORTSMOUTH

Sometimes overlooked in the broad shadow of Norfolk, this historic seaport offers plenty of attractions all its own. The **Portsmouth Naval Shipyard Museum** traces the naval history of the area. Visitors can step aboard the adjacent **Lightship Museum,** once a floating lighthouse, for insights into a vanished era. Among the restored 18th- and 19th-century residences of charming **Olde Towne** is the 1846 courthouse, now a fine arts center and children's museum.

▶ *Although most of the historic homes are closed to the public, they may be viewed from the outside via a trolley tour that runs between Olde Towne and the waterfront.*

10 PETERSBURG

An important rail and road junction and Union objective during the Civil War, Petersburg was a polished, prosperous little city whose residents suffered during a 10-month-long siege.

In the antebellum **Old Towne,** Petersburg's wartime history unfolds at the **Siege Museum,** housed in a magnificent 1839 Greek Revival building that was once the city's grain exchange. An antique vault and a money-printing machine at the 1817 **Farmers Bank** recall simpler times.

Downtown the beautiful **Centre Hill Mansion** is filled with Victorian antiques, and a block-long brick tunnel connects the house to the river docks. **Old Blandford Church,** graced with Tiffany stained-glass windows, stands as a Confederate memorial. Locals claim that the sight of a group of schoolgirls placing flowers on some of the graves in the adjacent cemetery was the inspiration for Memorial Day.

On the outskirts of town, **Petersburg National Battlefield** preserves trenches and earthen forts where the fighting raged, including the famous Battle of the Crater, which Grant called "the saddest affair I have witnessed in the war."

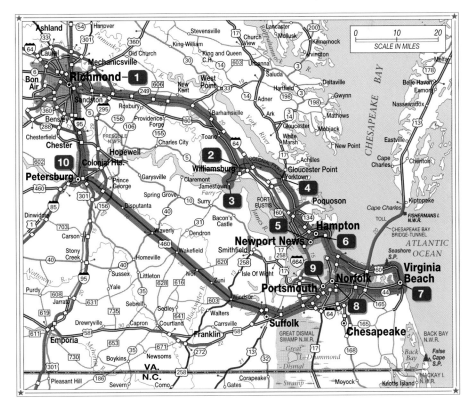

1 LYNCHBURG

Founded at a ferry crossing in the 1750's, Lynchburg is nestled in the foothills of the Blue Ridge Mountains. It became a bustling river port, shipping tobacco down the James River on fleets of pole-powered bateaux. The area's history is recounted in a building that saw much of it, the 1855 **Old Court House.** Another landmark, **Point of Honor,** is a handsome Federal mansion built in 1815 by Patrick Henry's physician on the site of a duel.

In nearby Bedford County sits **Poplar Forest,** the private retreat of Thomas Jefferson. One of the first octagonal homes in America, it was designed and built by Jefferson for those times when the crush of guests at Monticello became overwhelming. The house, currently being restored, is open for tours.

2 BOOKER T. WASHINGTON NATIONAL MONUMENT

The great educator and founder of the Tuskegee Institute in Alabama was born near present-day Burnt Chimney, as a slave, in 1856. The 224-acre site, where

At Mabry Mill off the Blue Ridge Parkway, corn is still ground into meal during regular demonstrations. Scattered around the mill are mountain-industry relics: an old-time corn liquor still, a lumber-drying rack, and a corn planter.

you'll find restored buildings and a reconstructed log cabin, re-creates the environment of Washington's boyhood. Costumed interpreters demonstrate open-hearth cooking and the making of lye soap, and tend crops and farm animals appropriate to the period.

3 ROANOKE

Mountain-locked Roanoke is set in one of the most beautiful locations of any American city, a convenient place from which to enter the Blue Ridge Parkway. The city itself offers a wealth of recreational and cultural activities. An extraordinary heart-of-town cluster called Center in the Square includes the

Roanoke Museum of Fine Arts, the **Roanoke Valley Historical Society and Museum,** and the **Mill Mountain Theatre.** Also in the square is one of the nation's oldest farmers' markets. Mill Mountain, with a zoo and park on its crest, rises a few blocks away.

▶ *Look for signs for the Blue Ridge Parkway at the entrance to Mill Mountain Zoo.*

Long an important railroad center, Roanoke is home to the **Virginia Museum of Transportation,** featuring a large collection of locomotives and cars, many built here during the steam era.

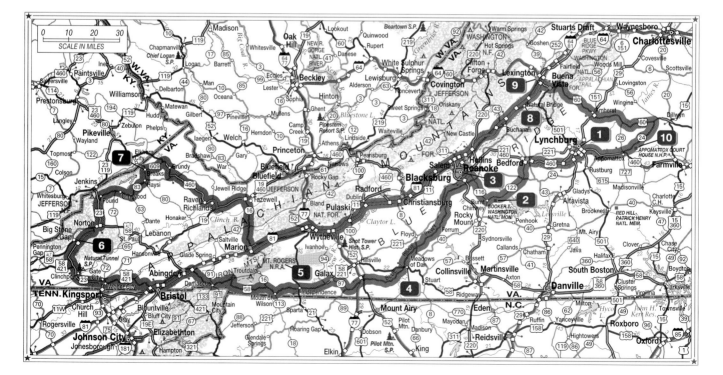

4 MEADOWS OF DAN

About 60 miles south of Roanoke, along the Blue Ridge Parkway, the traveler encounters one of the state's most photographed sites: a water-powered gristmill so perfectly picturesque that it might have come from a movie set. **Mabry Mill,** just north of Meadows of Dan, is the real thing, however. The turn-of-the-century waterwheel still spins in homage to the mill's commercially active years, when it ground out cornmeal and buckwheat flour. Also here is a blacksmith shop and a sorghum press. In summer interpreters demonstrate period skills ranging from wood carving to weaving.

5 MOUNT ROGERS

Virginia's highest point at 5,729 feet, soaring Mount Rogers lends its name to this vast 117,000-acre segment of Jefferson National Forest, **Mount Rogers National Recreation Area.** A network of hiking and horseback-riding trails includes more than 60 miles of the Appalachian Trail, as well as the Virginia Highlands Horse Trail. Campers, hunters, and fishermen will find no finer playground.

6 BIG STONE GAP

Around the turn of the century, novelist John Fox, Jr., lived and worked in this rugged mountain country, drawing on his surroundings for inspiration for such bestsellers as *The Trail of the Lonesome Pine.* Today that story is retold each summer in an outdoor musical drama at the **June Tolliver Playhouse.**

The 1890's home of the novel's heroine is now an arts and crafts center, the **June Tolliver House,** while Fox's 20-room home, dating from 1889, is the **John Fox, Jr. Museum.**

Still another notable site, the **Southwest Virginia Museum,** relates local history in a massive four-story stone mansion dating from the 1880's. Here you'll find pioneer and American Indian artifacts, miniature log houses, a quilt collection, and Civil War firearms.

► *The only motels with restaurants near Big Stone Gap are 9 miles north, in the town of Norton, and 12 miles south, in Duffield.*

7 BREAKS

A fork of the Big Sandy River cuts through the rugged Cumberland Mountains at the Virginia-Kentucky border, creating the Breaks of the Cumberland, a natural wonder sometimes called the Grand Canyon of the South. The two states teamed up to create 4,600-acre **Breaks Interstate Park.** A drive to the canyon rim reveals breathtaking views.

8 NATURAL BRIDGE

About 15 miles south of Lexington, the Natural Bridge is billed as one of the Seven Natural Wonders of the World. George Washington thought it impressive enough to carve his initials high up on one rocky wall. Thomas Jefferson bought the bridge and 157 acres for 20 shillings, built a log cabin, and welcomed guests. Soaring 215 feet above Cedar Creek, with a span of 90 feet, the limestone formation is a breathtaking sight, viewed from the banks of the determined little stream that sculpted it.

9 LEXINGTON

Center of higher learning, civic monument of the Scotch-Irish, Valhalla of the Confederacy—Lexington, practically unchanged since the 19th century, is all these things. Its educational roots date back to 1749, when a small academy was founded here. Now called **Washington and Lee University,** it was endowed by George Washington. Robert E. Lee became its president after the Civil War. The white-columned hilltop façade is one of the country's most notable campus settings. **Lee Chapel and Museum,** where the general is buried, contains a white marble recumbent

statue and preserves Lee's office exactly as it was when he died in 1870.

Stonewall Jackson and George C. Marshall head the pantheon at the adjoining **Virginia Military Institute.** A professor at VMI before the Civil War, Jackson is remembered at the **VMI Museum,** where many of his personal possessions are displayed. Just down the parade ground, the **George C. Marshall Museum and Library** honors the World War II leader, a VMI alumnus.

The **Stonewall Jackson House,** in the heart of town near the visitor center, contains original Jackson furnishings. Jackson is buried in the town cemetery, his grave marked by a striking statue.

► *From April though October you can see historic downtown Lexington via a narrated horse-drawn carriage ride, which begins near the visitor center.*

10 APPOMATTOX COURT HOUSE

Wilmer McLean's northern Virginia farm was too close to the Civil War battleground at Manassas for comfort; so he moved his family to the remote village of Appomattox Court House. But in April 1865 destiny led Generals Grant and Lee to his parlor, where they sat down to declare an end to the fighting. Today the reconstructed house, with its accurately furnished surrender room, is one of 27 buildings in **Appomattox Court House National Historical Park.** Museum exhibits and an audiovisual program detail the final campaign. Around the tiny town, on the hills and fields of this farming region, markers point out the positions of Lee's and Grant's armies.

Stonewall Jackson guards the entrance to the Virginia Military Institute barracks. The bronze statue depicts Jackson on the battlefield at Chancellorsville, where he received his mortal wound. He was shot by his own men, who mistook him for a Union soldier.

West Virginia

Ancient peaks and deep green valleys make the Mountain State one of the most beautiful in the nation. Here wild whitewater streams rush while time itself slips peaceably by.

THE NORTHERN MOUNTAINS

1 WHEELING

During the 1850's Wheeling was an important trading post. Its three R's—river, roads, and railroad—made it one of America's wealthiest cities. Roughly 80 percent of the town was built before 1910, creating a repository of outstanding Victorian architecture.

The **L.S. Good House,** one of several open for tours, offers 22 noteworthy stained-glass pieces as well as intricate interior woodwork. Mr. and Mrs. Good were the donors of Oglebay Park's **Good Children's Zoo**—named not for the young visitors' conduct but for the Goods' son. The park, now a recreational resort, was the Oglebay family's gift to the city. Their summer home, the **Mansion Museum,** also in the park, features eight period rooms.

The park and the rest of the city are wired for the **Festival of Lights/City of Lights,** held from November through January. Downtown displays include 250 giant snowflakes. In the park more than a million colored lights twinkle. The **Wheeling Suspension Bridge,**

The Wheeling Suspension Bridge, *built in 1849, is one of the oldest of its kind.*

once the world's longest single-span suspension, is illuminated year-round but is especially dramatic against the festival's sparkling backdrop.

▶ *Highlights of the festival can easily be seen by car. In the park follow the signs to the nearly 50 displays. Stop at the visitor center or any hotel for a map of the downtown attractions.*

2 MOUNDSVILLE

Step back in time some 2,000 years at **Grave Creek Mound State Park** and imagine the effort it took to move some 60,000 tons of dirt by the basketful to build the largest conical burial mound in the Americas. The Adena mound, erected in stages from about 250 to 150 B.C., measures 69 feet high and 295 feet in diameter at its base.

Take the short, easy walk to the mound summit before viewing excavated artifacts at the park's **Delf Norona Museum.** Here you'll see pottery vessels and an extraordinary collection of personal ornaments, evidence of the Adena culture's extensive trading: beaten copper from the western Great Lakes, glassy mica from the Carolinas, and necklaces made of shells from the Gulf of Mexico. Stone gorgets unearthed in the mound are thought to have been worn as armor to protect the throat but may have served simply as ornamentation. You'll also ponder some details still unexplained, such as the meaning of an inscribed sandstone tablet uncovered at the mound.

3 MORGANTOWN

The rapid-transit system at **West Virginia University,** with its elevated computer-driven cars, looks like something from Disneyland but is actually part of a federal research project, providing transportation for students and townspeople. You can stop at the museum at the **College of Mineral and Energy Resources** to see tools, models, and photographs relating to coal mining and drilling for oil and gas. You'll even get a free sample of bituminous

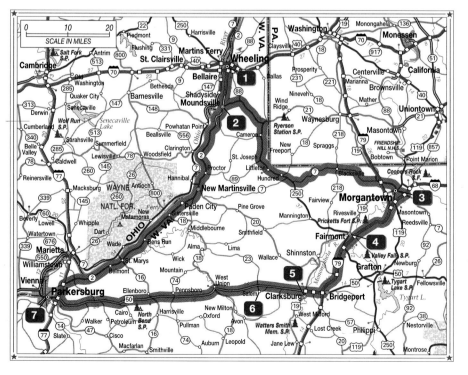

The massive mound at Grave Creek can be climbed via stone steps, visible as a diagonal slash near the top of the hill.

coal. The **Cook-Hayman Pharmacy Museum**, also on the train line, displays artifacts from a 19th-century pharmacy, including pill molds and capsule-making machines.

Nine hiking trails crisscross the university's **Core Arboretum**, noted for its native trees, shrubs, and plants.

4 FAIRMONT

In 1774, seeking safety from raiding Cherokees, Shawnees, Senecas, and Mingos, Jacob Prickett and his neighbors built a log refuge fort on a small rise overlooking the Monongahela River. For the next 20 years between 80 and 100 families found sanctuary here during Indian attacks; their stays ranged from a few days to a terrifying seven weeks. The compound, including Spartan cabins, bastions, and a meetinghouse, has been reconstructed at **Pricketts Fort State Park**. Artisans are on hand to demonstrate period skills, from rifle making to hearth cooking.

Jacob's great-grandson Job built the adjacent **Job Prickett House**, a two-story brick farmhouse, 60 years after the fort was dismantled. Its civilized touches—wood floors, glass windows, items ordered from catalogs—reveal how quickly the frontier was tamed. During July the outdoor drama *Pricketts Fort: An American Frontier Musical*, looks back on the fort's saga.

Perched on a hilltop, Fairmont was named by the Indians for its commanding location—a fair mount—and once overlooked the town of Valley Falls. According to legend, Cherokees called the plunging water there Evil Spirits Fall,

and sure enough, the town suffered the scourge of raging, wind-whipped fire, followed three years later by a flood that effectively ended its existence. Nature now reigns supreme at **Valley Falls State Park**, where kayakers experience the thrill of precipitous drops, boulder-lined chutes, and intricate rapids. On sunny afternoons the rocky promontories overlooking the falls become a rookery of sunbathers.

5 CLARKSBURG

Clarksburg, birthplace of Stonewall Jackson, boasts one of the state's most architecturally and historically intact downtown business districts. Among its stately houses is **Waldomore**, an 1839 Classical Revival mansion, now a small repository of West Virginia history and culture. Downstairs rooms are furnished with fine Victorian furniture; the dining room holds a banquet table that belonged to Stonewall Jackson's mother. Upstairs a genealogical library helps West Virginians trace their family trees.

The **Stealey-Goff-Vance House**, once owned by the mother of former Secretary of State Cyrus Vance, is a charming two-story structure built by Jacob Stealey, a tanner, in 1807. Now the home of the Harrison County Historical Society Museum and furnished with Victorian pieces gathered from Central West Virginia, it is open to visitors on Friday afternoons from May through September.

In front of the courthouse, a poignant sculpture remembers the Indians, pioneers, and European immigrants who settled this part of the state. Every Labor Day weekend, descendants of one

such group join with visitors to celebrate at the **West Virginia Italian Heritage Festival.**

6 SALEM

Twenty pioneer-era log structures gathered from the surrounding countryside make up **Fort New Salem** on the Salem–Teikyo University campus. An outdoor living-history center, the recreated Appalachian frontier community includes a blockhouse, tin shop, kitchen, and meetinghouse. In the wood shop, a craftsman reproduces old farm tools and Early American furnishings. In the apothecary shop, medicinal herbs from the garden hang to dry.

7 PARKERSBURG

Even Hollywood could not improve on the dramatic tale associated with the opulent Blennerhassett Island home of Harman and Margaret Blennerhassett. Aaron Burr's visit here nearly 200 years ago ended their idyllic existence when the two men were arrested for treason after plotting to establish an empire in the Southwest. Not long after, the loveliest private estate in the Ohio Valley burned to the ground.

▶ *For a special treat, take a horse-drawn wagon ride around the island.*

Reconstructed on its original site, the mansion is again beautifully furnished as part of **Blennerhassett Island Historical State Park**. A video introduction is given at the **Blennerhassett Museum** near Point Park, the departure point for stern-wheelers carrying visitors to the island.

An air of luxury surrounds the reconstructed Blennerhassett mansion, the lavish island home of a wealthy Irishman. Built in 1800, the original house was destroyed by fire 11 years later.

1 HARPERS FERRY

The picturesque hillside town of Harpers Ferry, at the confluence of the Potomac and Shenandoah rivers, was the scene of a fateful episode that helped ignite the Civil War. On October 16, 1859, abolitionist John Brown and a band of his men seized the federal arsenal here in an attempt to arm the slaves for rebellion. Captured by U.S. Marines under Robert E. Lee, Brown was later hanged for treason.

A strategic objective for the Confederates during the Civil War, today Harpers Ferry is home to **Harpers Ferry National Historical Park**, largely restored to its 19th-century appearance. Buildings open to the public include a blacksmith shop, tavern, and dry-goods store. **Harper House**, built by the town's founder and furnished in period style, and **John Brown's Fort**, the fire station where Brown staged his last stand, can also be toured.

▶ *Park at the visitor center off Rte. 340. There you can board a shuttle bus to the lower town district, where you'll find the museums and historic exhibits. Parking is scarce in town.*

Hand-hewn stone steps in the park lead to a river overlook that Thomas Jefferson considered to be "worth a voyage across the Atlantic." On the way up you'll pass the 1830 **Saint Peter's Catholic Church**, which survived the war by flying both the Union and Confederate flags.

In summer park guides dressed in 19th-century garb conduct tours and demonstrations. During **Old Tyme Christmas**, you can see the park by way of a romantic candlelight walk complete with caroling. June and September bring the popular **Mountain Heritage Arts and Crafts Festival,** which takes place just outside town.

2 ROMNEY

The road west out of Harpers Ferry crosses the lush Shenandoah Valley and

A rolling vista unfolds from Canyon Rim overlook in Blackwater Falls State Park.

winds through mountain foothills to Romney, a town that changed hands more than 50 times during the Civil War. The **Davis History House**, used as a meeting place by the Confederates, and **Literary Hall**, filled with period furnishings, are among the sites you can tour during September's **Hampshire Heritage Days**, when the town opens its historic homes and re-creates Civil War encampments.

Black bears like this sleepy cub roam the wooded wilderness of the highlands.

Bald-eagle sightings are all but guaranteed on the ***Potomac Eagle***, a turn-of-the-century train that cuts through a mountain pass favored by nesting birds.

3 SMOKE HOLE CAVERNS

Indians once used these caverns to smoke venison; billowing clouds of smoke escaping from the cave's natural chimneys could be seen for miles. Later both Union and Confederate troops hid ammunition, gold bars, and coins here. Settlers found the cave's seclusion ideal for operating moonshine stills, one of which remains. Today visitors come to see the world's longest ribbon stalactite and Crystal Pool, where rainbow and golden rainbow trout swim.

4 SPRUCE KNOB– SENECA ROCKS

Within **Spruce Knob-Seneca Rocks National Recreation Area,** Seneca Rocks, a sheer spine of Tuscarora sandstone jutting nearly 900 feet above the North Fork Valley, is considered by rock climbers one of the best vertical climbs in the East. Legend has it that an Indian princess chose to marry the warrior who could follow her to the top. For the nonclimber there's a 1.3-mile trail, complete with rest stops, leading to a stunning overlook. Watching ant-like figures make their way to the crest from the visitor center at the base is less taxing but still rewarding.

A detour south on Rte. 33 takes in **Seneca Caverns**, where underground tours are offered. Just past the Seneca Caverns turnoff, a partially paved road climbs 12 miles to the summit of West Virginia's highest peak, 4,862-foot **Spruce Knob**. At the top **Whispering Spruce Trail** winds for half a mile along the base of an observation tower, with views of the distant Alleghenies. Popular with anglers in spring and summer, the area is especially beautiful in fall, when the rolling countryside parades its brilliant palette of colors.

5 BLACKWATER FALLS

The 20-mile-long Blackwater River is the centerpiece of this heavily forested state park. With it comes one of West Virginia's best-known attractions: a dramatic umber-colored waterfall that tumbles five stories. The dark waters are colored by acid from fallen spruce and hemlock needles. Stairways and boardwalks provide up-close views.

The park offers a nature and recreation program for hikers, horseback riders, and lovers of wildflowers. Stouthearted walkers can join naturalists from Canaan Valley and Blackwater Falls state parks in May and October for a hike between the two (about eight miles) and a mountaintop cookout.

6 CANAAN VALLEY RESORT

At 3,200 feet above sea level, this highland valley (pronounced "Kuh-*nayn*") is

across the state border, may look like a modern metropolis. But its past has not been forgotten. The **Chesapeake and Ohio Canal National Historical Park**, stretching from Georgetown in Washington, D.C., to Cumberland, recalls the days when the waterway was an important conduit for coal, flour, grain, and lumber. The length of the towpath—most of which is now dry—is open for hiking, biking, and picnicking. Exhibits at the visitor center in Cumberland tell the story of the canal's short-lived heyday.

Trains also played an important role in Cumberland. These days the steam-

road scenes, a 1900 schoolroom, and a medical room complete with a foot-operated dentist's drill. A carriage house even has a surrey with a fringe on top.

8 BERKELEY SPRINGS

En route to Berkeley Springs, you'll follow a winding road through Paw Paw, where C&O Canal builders tunneled a mile through sheer rock. Just outside Berkeley Springs, the **Prospect Peak** overlook provides a view of the Potomac River that has been called one of the best vistas in America.

American Indians discovered the mineral springs here, but not until George Washington became a frequent visitor did this become the nation's first spa. Visitors can soak in the sweet waters at **Berkeley Springs State Park**, with warm springs, bathhouses, and swimming. Overlooking the park is the 1889 stone-turreted **Berkeley Castle**, built by Col. Samuel Taylor Suit to win a lady's hand.

Columbus Day weekend brings the **Apple Butter Festival**, when kettles of the concoction can be seen simmering over open fires. Year-round, collectors can shop in two downtown malls with nearly 100 antique dealers.

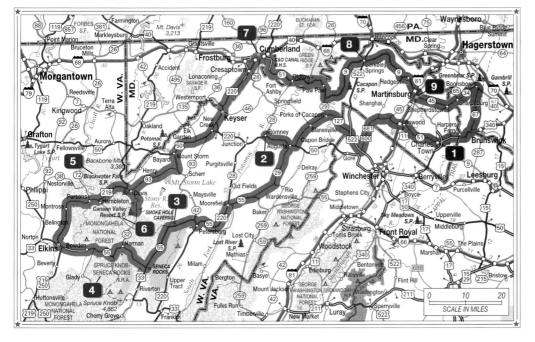

surrounded by grand peaks rising yet another 1,000 feet. In winter **Canaan Valley Resort State Park** becomes a popular downhill and cross-country ski destination. The ski lifts run year-round and provide gorgeous views.

Around the park's luxury lodge roam wildlife from deer to wild turkeys to black bears. There are also cabins, an indoor pool and spa, tennis courts, and an 18-hole championship golf course. Hikers and fishermen can make the most of the woods and streams nearby.

7 CUMBERLAND

After driving through a succession of small towns that seem straight out of the 1950's, Cumberland, Maryland, just

powered **Western Maryland Scenic Railroad** chugs between Cumberland and neighboring Frostburg.

▶ *Follow the signs on Interstate 68 for the tourist information center downtown, a good place to pick up maps and begin your tour.*

In the **Washington Street Historical District**, homes and mansions built in the 1800's by coal and rail barons span architectural styles from Federal through Georgian Revival. **History House**, a three-story townhouse once owned by the C&O Canal president, contains Victorian furnishings, B&O Railroad china glazed with historic rail-

9 MARTINSBURG

Orchards occupy much of the countryside around Martinsburg, part of the first settled area in the state. In fall the sharp smell of apples fills the air. Visitors can take an orchard tour during the **Mountain State Apple Harvest Festival** in mid-October.

An important railroad hub, Martinsburg was coveted by both sides during the Civil War. A brick B&O Railroad roundhouse was rebuilt after the war, and the **Triple Brick Museum** was constructed in 1874 to house railroad workers. The famous Confederate spy Belle Boyd grew up in this town and lived in the Greek Revival **Belle Boyd House** for several years.

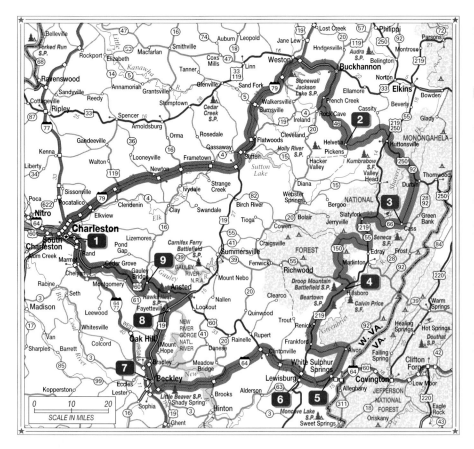

1 CHARLESTON

Straddling the great Kanawha River, West Virginia's handsome capital climbs toward the low-lying hills on the horizon. The lavish **State Capitol Complex** includes the handsome Georgian Colonial **Governor's Mansion** and the gold-domed **State Capitol.** Designed by Cass Gilbert, the capitol features a two-ton cut-crystal chandelier. The adjacent **Cultural Center** showcases West Virginia arts and history.

The **Vandalia Gathering** celebrates the state's traditional cultures each Memorial Day weekend on the grounds of the capitol. Hailing the region's riverboat heritage is the **Charleston Sternwheel Regatta,** a 10-day affair that winds up on Labor Day weekend. The **P.A. Denny** stern-wheeler plies the river waters in spring, summer, and fall.

2 HELVETIA

As you travel into a wild southwest corner of Randolph County in search of Helvetia, imagine how Swiss city folk must have felt in 1869 when they arrived in a wilderness they had been promised was a thriving Swiss community. They quickly mastered the necessary survival skills, however, and turned the forest into farmland. You'll still hear traces of a Swiss-German accent in the speech of the handful of descendants that remains today.

Stop at **The Hütte** for authentic Swiss fare, and at the **Beekeeper Inn,** formerly a beekeeper's house. A small log museum displays artifacts belonging to the original settlers, and **Helvetia Commu-**

nity Hall offers an extraordinary collection of glass-plate photographs dating from the turn of the century.

3 CASS

In the early 1900's Cass was the site of a mountain logging town. Today visitors can stay in logging-camp houses at **Cass Scenic Railroad State Park.** Here the world's largest collection of geared Shay steam locomotives, which once hauled virgin timber, now takes sightseers up Bald Knob, the state's second-highest point, from Memorial Day through October. The enormous **Cass Country Store** houses a souvenir emporium, soda fountain, and restaurant.

In nearby Green Bank, stop at the **National Radio Astronomy Observatory,** where scientists study pulsars and other outer-space phenomena through gigantic radio telescopes.

The spectacularly scenic route from Cass to Hillsboro takes you through the Monongahela National Forest along Rte. 150, the 22-mile parkway section of the two-lane **Highland Scenic Highway.** Four overlooks offer views of the Allegheny Highlands. Stop at the Cranberry Mountain visitor center outside Hillsboro for information on the area.

▶ *Note that the parkway is not maintained for winter travel and is usually closed from December to March.*

4 HILLSBORO

In the farm community of Hillsboro you'll find the stately white pillared **Pearl S. Buck Birthplace,** where the Nobel and Pulitzer Prize–winning author was born in 1892. Inside are fami-

*The elegant **Greenbrier** sits near a spring whose legendary waters were once said to cure every ailment "except chewing, smoking, spitting, and swearing." Today visitors still come to relax in the hotel's spa and soak their cares away.*

ly artifacts, from dishes to an organ, and furnishings including the bed in which Buck was born. Also on display are clothing and shoes from China, where she lived for many years.

Nearby **Droop Mountain Battlefield State Park** was the scene of the 1863 Civil War battle that wrested the Greenbrier Valley from Confederate control and settled the future of the new state of West Virginia. Today the park offers picnic areas, hiking trails, and an observation tower. Battle reenactments take place the second weekend in October, and tours are given year-round.

South of Hillsboro a massive eroded rock formation, part of **Beartown State Park**, is a favorite haunt of naturalists. Its immense boulders are cracked along regular fault lines that make the whole configuration resemble streets and passages in a silent sandstone city.

▶ *Always bring a jacket to Beartown. Even in summer, temperatures can dip down to 40°F.*

5 WHITE SULPHUR SPRINGS

Southern gateway to the **Monongahela National Forest**, White Sulphur Springs is almost synonymous with **The Greenbrier**, a world-famous resort that owes its existence to the clear but acrid waters that have attracted leisure-seekers since 1778. The resort, which served as a hospital during the Civil War, has been the choice of 22 presidents and notables from around the world since the first resident cottages were built in 1834. Today a modern spa pipes in the famed waters from the spring on the grounds.

6 LEWISBURG

This genteel farming town lies at the intersection of the Kanawha and Seneca trails, now U.S. highways. Here dozens of shops and galleries inhabit more than 60 well-maintained buildings from the 18th and 19th centuries. The 1796 **Old Stone Church**, with its original slave balcony, and the 1820 **North House Museum**, with artifacts from local history, serve as indexes to the region's past. Lewisburg's own **Carnegie Hall**, built by the famous philanthropist in 1902, is new by comparison.

For a change of pace, head underground to **Lost World Caverns**, whose main room measures a whopping 185 feet long, 85 feet wide, and 60 feet high. Packed with hundreds of stalactites and stalagmites, it is one of America's most richly decorated caves.

7 BECKLEY

For years fortunes were hauled out of the mountains here in the form of coal. Today this historic coal-mining hub presents the **Exhibition Coal Mine** in New River Park, employing real miners to lead tours of the turn-of-the-century operation. Visitors are shuttled through underground passageways for a glimpse of the heyday of man-and-mule mining. The neighboring **Youth Museum of**

Southern West Virginia caters to kids, with a planetarium, changing exhibits relating to science and the arts, and hands-on science stations. At the adjacent **Mountain Homestead**, visitors can immerse themselves in regional 19th-century history. There is a period log house, a one-room school, a blacksmith shop, and a traditional garden, as well as craft demonstrations.

Some 10 miles east is the **Cliffside Amphitheater**, where summer entertainment includes the musical *Hatfields and McCoys,* which brings to life the famous family feud. There are also hiking trails and rhododendron gardens.

8 FAYETTEVILLE

Fayetteville, listed in the National Register of Historic Places, delights white-

water sports enthusiasts drawn to the area by the New and Gauley rivers. Close by rises the 3,030-foot-long **New River Gorge Bridge**, the world's longest steel arch span. Look on as parachutists jump and rappellers dangle from the bridge on Bridge Day, the third Saturday in October.

Stretching from the New River Gorge Bridge to Hinton is the **New River Gorge National River**, encompassing 53 miles of stunning scenery and some of America's best whitewater recreation. The park centers around the New River, which, ironically, geologists estimate to be around 65 million years old. The Canyon Rim visitor center at the north end of the bridge offers exhibits on the river's history.

The thrill of whitewater lures serious sportsmen to West Virginia. On the New River, rafters shoot the raging rapids. Those who prefer land can simply enjoy the scenery.

▶ *Anglers will want to bring their fishing rods; this section of the New River offers excellent fishing, especially for smallmouth bass.*

9 GAULEY BRIDGE

Where the New and Gauley rivers combine to form the Kanawha River, the crumbling stone piers of **Gauley Bridge**, destroyed during an 1861 Confederate retreat, remind visitors that this was once a strategic Union stronghold.

Two spectacular overlooks at **Hawks Nest State Park** in nearby Ansted take in the bridge and the New River Gorge. An aerial tramway runs from the park's lodge to the riverbank, and a lake at the bottom of the gorge offers excellent fishing. A museum displays Civil War and American Indian artifacts.

Louisville
Lexington

Kentucky

The state of coonskin caps, Daniel Boone, and lacy dogwood trees, Kentucky is best known for its bluegrass, which springs from the rich soil that breeds champion stallions and smooth bourbon.

THE BLUEGRASS HEARTLAND

1 LEXINGTON

This is the heart of Thoroughbred country. Rich limestone deposits in the soil are said to provide the minerals that build the strong bones of the racing steeds bred here, on the rippling fields of blue-budded grass. Get an equine education at the **Kentucky Horse Park,** just minutes north of downtown. Amble through this working horse farm and visit the grave of Man o' War. Ride across the huge park on horseback, in a covered wagon pulled by draft horses, or, when snow covers the gentle hills, in a horse-drawn sleigh.

Put your newfound horse sense to the test at **Keeneland Race Course,** where meets are held each April and October. Louisville's Churchill Downs, of Kentucky Derby fame, may be more renowned, but Keeneland, founded in 1936, has a genteel, Old World grace. In place of a blaring loudspeaker, discreet tote boards silently convey race results. Daily workouts can be viewed from dawn to 10 A.M. at no charge.

Lexington has its share of extravagant antebellum houses to tour. Snow-white dogwoods soften the classical lines of **Ashland,** the reconstructed home of the Great Compromiser, the statesman Henry Clay. Most of Ashland's furnishings are original to the house, just two miles from downtown. One of the finest Federal homes in Kentucky is situated in the heart of town. The 1814 **Hunt-Morgan House** was built by the state's first millionaire, John W. Hunt.

Sports lovers may want to take in a game at **Rupp Arena,** where the University of Kentucky Wildcats carry on a winning hoops tradition. Those immune to basketball fever can take a stroll on lanes flanked by fuchsia red-

Thoroughbred estate: *Calumet Farm, in Lexington, has produced eight Derby winners.*

buds, pink dogwoods, and silvery ponds at the **Lexington Cemetery,** a jewel from the garden-cemetery era of the mid 1800's. If you're shopping in nearby **Victorian Square,** you'll uncover another window on the past: the 100-year-old **Hutchinson Drug Store,** where old-fashioned chocolate sodas are still served at the six-stool counter.

2 NATURAL BRIDGE

Soak up the ancient wonders of the Appalachian foothills at **Natural Bridge State Resort Park,** deep within the

Daniel Boone National Forest. The main attraction is Natural Bridge, a huge sandstone arch with a yawning 80-foot base—only 10 feet smaller than Virginia's Natural Bridge. The 1,900-acre park has miles of hiking trails lined with dogwood trees. For overnight stays, the state park system offers cozy lodges, log cabins, and campgrounds.

▶ *You can pick up a map at the Hemlock Lodge for the 36-mile drive through Red River Gorge, one of the oldest natural gorges in the country.*

3 BYBEE

The drive from Natural Bridge Park winds through pretty hill country to the town of Bybee, home of **Bybee Pottery.** Founded in 1845, the company produces simple, elegant stoneware washed in colorful glazes with names like Bluegrass Green and Bybee Blue.

4 BEREA

Wooden dulcimers and homespun weaves are among the items handcrafted in Berea, dubbed the Folk Arts and Crafts Capital of Kentucky. The works of local artisans fill downtown shops. At the **Berea College Appalachian Museum,** exhibits give you a view of the traditional southern highlands culture.

Berea College was founded in 1855 as the South's first interracial college. Its **Draper Building** is modeled after Philadelphia's Independence Hall. Tours of the campus leave from historic **Boone Tavern.**

Amid a thunderous crashing *of hooves, jockeys maneuver for position at Keeneland Race Course, the sister course to Louisville's Churchill Downs.*

5 RENFRO VALLEY

Nestled between the hills just off the interstate, Renfro Valley is a town that preserves one aspect of old-time mountain culture: the **Barn Dance.** In its heyday in the 1940's, the town was host to many famous country acts, including country-music legend Red Foley and the comedy team Homer and Jethro. Although the dancing has been relegated to the stage, this quaint reconstructed village still hosts live country-music shows, in two barns, every weekend, March through December.

▶ *For the best seats, call 800-765-SING. You can reserve months in advance, but the payment need not be made until you arrive.*

6 DANVILLE

Founded in 1775, Danville boasts one of the largest concentrations of antebellum and Victorian architecture in the South. Don't miss the **McDowell House & Apothecary Shop,** where, on Christmas Day, 1809, Dr. Ephraim McDowell became the Father of Abdominal Surgery when he performed the world's first successful abdominal operation—without anesthetic, to boot. Now a museum, the shop has an extensive collection of apothecary wares.

The **Pioneer Playhouse** is a summer-stock dinner theater whose outdoor stage has launched the career of many stars. Even the ticket office has been touched by fame: it was featured as the depot in the 1956 film *Raintree County.*

Centre College was founded in 1819. You can tour the 1820 **Old Centre,** the oldest college building still in active use west of the Alleghenies.

▶ *Cool your touring heels in Boyle Pharmacy, where a nickel will still buy you a steaming cup of coffee.*

7 HARRODSBURG

Thick wooden bulwarks surround the grounds of **Old Fort Harrod State Park,** marking the first permanent English settlement west of the Alleghenies and now a living-history museum to pioneer life. The homesteaders who settled here honed the art of salt-curing and hickory-smoking hams. The result was the sublime country ham that Kentucky is known for. Try the 1845 **Beaumont Inn** version, aged for two years until the ham turns a deep mahogany.

8 PLEASANT HILL

More than 30 original buildings grace the **Shaker Village of Pleasant Hill,** a 2,700-acre restored Shaker community from the 19th century. The Shakers were a communal sect whose industrious members believed in pacifism and

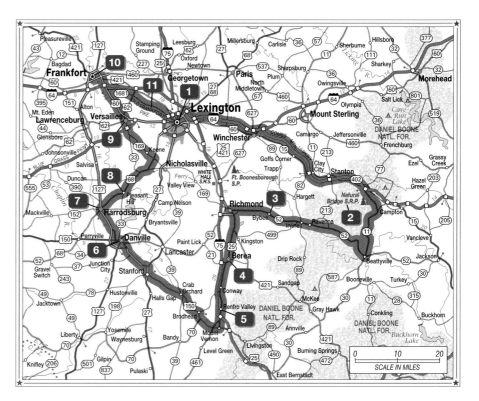

celibacy. Today the village presents demonstrations of Shaker craftsmanship, and the **Centre Family Dwelling** is a museum furnished with Shaker pieces. The village's dining room serves regional specialties like Shaker lemon pie—made with the whole lemon, sliced thin as communion wafers.

9 VERSAILLES

Forget your French primer—around here they pronounce it VUR-sales. Downtown are two blocks of 18th- and 19th-century buildings. This is the home of the **Bluegrass Scenic Railroad,** which takes visitors on a gently rocking tour of the countryside, through fields of bluegrass and past river bluffs, in a 1940's passenger car.

10 FRANKFORT

The government buildings in this state capital are a glorious valentine to democracy. The **State Capitol** features intricate Ionic columns and is considered one of the most beautiful statehouses in the country. On the grounds you can admire the riot of colors in **Kentucky's Floral Clock.** Visit the **Old State Capitol,** with its circular stairway.

And though democracy is the official form of government in Kentucky, bourbon is still king. To get an education in the art of bourbon making, tour **Leestown Company,** one of the oldest distilleries in the state.

11 OLD FRANKFORT PIKE

This is the scenic route in your drive back to Lexington. The winding two-lane road is flanked by solid stone fences built more than a century ago. Ancient trees form a bower over the roadway, which is lined with handsome horse farms, such as **Three Chimneys,** home of Triple Crown winner Seattle Slew. Five miles outside of Lexington is the **Headley-Whitney Museum,** a repository for somewhat idiosyncratic bejeweled trinkets called bibelots and a collection of fine Oriental porcelain.

1 LOUISVILLE

The name Louisville conjures up visions of icy mint juleps and nimble chestnut mares with lustrous coats. Yet this vibrant city alongside the Ohio River also boasts a sleek urban skyline, high culture, and a wealth of historic districts, all set in a sylvan landscape: the Greater Louisville area has more parkland than any other region of its size in the United States.

No visitor can leave Louisville without a trip to **Churchill Downs**, since 1875 the site of horse racing's greatest spectacle, the **Kentucky Derby,** held here the first Saturday in May. The first jewel in racing's Triple Crown is generally over in two minutes, but the people-watching is an all-day affair. Racing seasons run from late April through June and during the month of November. The **Kentucky Derby Museum** includes a tour of the famous racetrack.

▶ *Children are allowed into areas where betting occurs but must be accompanied by adults.*

Start your trek through Louisville at the **Belvedere,** the riverside park whose sumptuous views often extend to the **Falls of the Ohio,** an ancient fossil bed and park preserve. Belvedere provides prime front-row viewing of the **Louisville Falls Fountain,** the world's tallest computerized fountain, which floats in the Ohio River, the border between Kentucky and Indiana. From spring through autumn, the fountain blasts a rainbow of colors into the night sky. You can also view this high-tech wonder in old-fashioned style from the decks of the *Belle of Louisville*—the oldest operating stern-wheel steamboat on the Mississippi River system—or from the red-leather seats of a horse-drawn carriage.

Stroll past the grand Victorian mansions and townhouses in Old Louisville's **St. James Court** and **Belgravia** neighborhoods. Visit in October, when the **St. James Art Fair** is held. The old storefronts on **Main Street** are dressed in the country's second-largest collection of cast-iron façades. On the other end of the spectrum is **Butchertown,** where working-class meat packers resided in modest homes called shotgun cottages in the mid-1800's. Nineteen-year-old Thomas Edison lived in one of the cottages and walked to work at Western Union every day. His stay in Louisville ended after only a year when the relentless experimenter spilled sulfuric acid on his boss's desk—and was summarily fired. The cottage he lived in is now restored as a museum.

Three presidents have been guests at lovely **Locust Grove,** a 1790 plantation home set amid flowering dogwood trees five miles from town.

Culturally, Louisville is on a fast track. The renowned **Actors Theatre** is a Tony Award–winning repertory theater. The **Louisville Ballet** and the **Louisville Orchestra** offer performances and concerts year-round at the **Kentucky Center for the Arts.** The **Kentucky Shakespeare Festival** is held alfresco in Louisville's Central Park every summer; admission is free. Next door to the **University of Louisville** is the **J.B. Speed Art Museum,** which counts among its collection works by Rembrandt, Picasso, and Monet. End the day with a leisurely stroll by the duck pond at **Cave Hill Cemetery,** a 144-year-old woodlands graveyard.

2 BARDSTOWN

The town where the outlaw Jesse James was born and Stephen Foster found inspiration is now best known as the capital of bourbon whiskey distilling. Indeed, barrels of whiskey seem to be aging on every corner. **Heaven Hill** is made here, **Jim Beam** comes from nearby Clermont, and **Maker's Mark** is distilled in Loretto at a national historic landmark facility. Most of the distilleries provide tours or exhibits. Stop in at the **Oscar Getz Museum of Whiskey History** and see antique-bottle and distilling-equipment displays.

Bardstown teems with historic structures, best seen on the old-fashioned carriage rides that operate from Courthouse Square. Visit **My Old Kentucky Home State Park,** site of the 1818

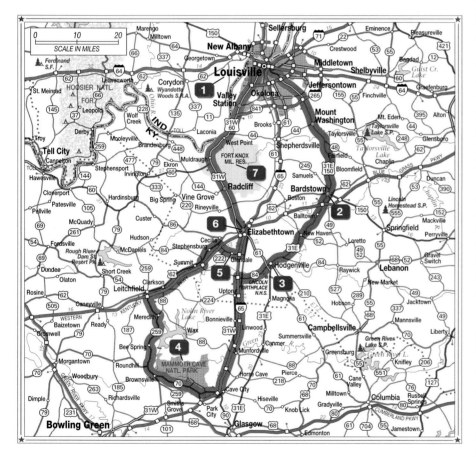

Into the deep go visitors to Mammoth Cave National Park, whose Historic Cave Tour ventures into massive subterranean passageways, carved from water filtering through limestone deposits.

Federal-style mansion that inspired Stephen Foster to write "My Old Kentucky Home." In honor of the 13 colonies, the house has 13 front windows, 13 steps on each stairway to the second and third floors, and 13-foot ceilings. Gleaming poplar floors frame rare period and original furnishings. **Old Talbott Tavern**, a former stagecoach stop whose guests have included Abraham Lincoln and Daniel Boone, is the oldest stagecoach stop and inn west of the Alleghenies. And don't miss what many visitors consider to be the best-kept secret in Kentucky: the 1819 **St. Joseph's Proto-Cathedral**, with 34-inch native-limestone walls, 40-foot yellow poplar columns, and 16th- and 17th-century paintings often attributed to Rubens and Van Dyck.

3 HODGENVILLE

Of all of Kentucky's memorable frontier figures—from Daniel Boone on—Abraham Lincoln is the one of whom most residents are proudest. Tucked into the state's trademark beautiful rolling woodlands is the 116-acre **Abraham Lincoln Birthplace National Historic Site**. This memorial marks the spot where the 16th president was born in 1809 and includes the cabin where his family lived until he was two years old.

▶ *The site is open every day; admission is free. To avoid crowds, visit anytime but July or August.*

About 10 miles away is **Abraham Lincoln's Boyhood Home**, a log-cabin reproduction of the house Lincoln lived in until he was eight years old. In downtown Hodgenville the **Lincoln Museum** features wax figures representing 12 periods in Lincoln's life.

4 MAMMOTH CAVE

The same process of water filtering through limestone deposits that is said to make Kentucky Thoroughbreds grow strong bones has carved out the world's most extensive cave system. At **Mammoth Cave National Park** hundreds of miles of passages snake below the earth; so far, only 335 miles have been charted and explored. Wondrous underground rivers and lakes are among the attractions on one of the cave tours, which winds through subterranean passages and past prehistoric artifacts from a civilization that existed here about 2,500 years ago.

Close by are sundry spelunking attractions. **Crystal Onyx Cave** and **Mammoth Onyx Cave** hold remarkable onyx formations. The **Jesse James Cave** was said to be a hideout for the outlaw and his gang and contains an ancient Indian burial ground as well.

▶ *Daily ranger-led tours of Mammoth Cave include one for the disabled.*

5 GLENDALE

Much of this tranquil community has been included on the National Register of Historic Places. Its downtown section, which resembles a thriving frontier trading post, is straight out of another era. Crammed with antique stores, craft shops, and even an old-time country store, this former railroad town often resounds with the clip-clop of horse-drawn carriages as nearby Amish residents pass through the 19th-century streets.

6 ELIZABETHTOWN

This lakeside town welcomes visitors with costumed walking tours conducted by the likes of P. T. Barnum, Carry Nation, Col. George A. Custer, and Sarah Bush Lincoln, the president's stepmother. The **Lincoln Heritage House** features stairways and mantels handcrafted by the president's father.

Perhaps the quirkiest exhibit in town is the **Schmidt's Museum of Coca-Cola Memorabilia**, located at the Coca-Cola Bottling Company of Elizabethtown. The museum houses the world's largest private collection of artifacts relating to the soft drink. See a century's worth of promotional material, from trays to calendars to toys to playing cards dating back to 1886.

7 FORT KNOX

While Fort Knox's most noted fixture—a hefty portion of the nation's gold reserves—is closed to the public, you can view exhibits on the history of the fort and on the Gold Bullion Depository at the **Patton Museum of Cavalry and Armor**, located next door. The museum specializes in the history of armored, mechanized warfare. One display includes personal items used by Gen. George S. Patton, Jr., including his ivory-handled pistols. Tanks and other army vehicles dot the landscape of **Keyes Park**, where the museum stands.

Cola, anyone? This c.1912 poster is among the artifacts on exhibit at Schmidt's Museum of Coca-Cola Memorabilia.

Tennessee

Bounded by the mighty Mississippi River, the Volunteer State is a versatile playground, luring visitors with blue-misted mountains, colorful cities, a rough-hewn heritage, and Southern geniality.

KNOXVILLE & THE MOUNTAINS

1 KNOXVILLE

Sitting in the shadow of the Great Smoky Mountains, Knoxville is a scenic charmer with a spruced-up urban center. The largest city in East Tennessee perches prettily on a hill overlooking the Tennessee River. For a panoramic view, ride to the top of the golden glass globe known as the **Sunsphere** (the Knoxville Visitors Information Center), the former centerpiece of the 1982 World's Fair. For a leisurely look about, hop aboard the *Star of Knoxville*, a 500-passenger riverboat that offers sightseeing and dinner cruises.

Tennessee's frontier past can be glimpsed at the **Blount Mansion**, dating from 1792. The stately frame dwelling—considered a mansion in pioneer days—was the home of William Blount, one of the signers of the U.S. Constitution, and the site of the drafting of the state constitution.

Not far away is the **James White Fort**, a re-creation of the home of the city founder, Gen. James White. The fort dates from 1786, when White became the first settler to make his home on this Indian-dominated frontier. Here you can tour seven fully furnished log buildings and a stockade.

The **University of Tennessee**, just west of downtown, grew out of little Blount College, founded in 1794. Today, in an annual fall ritual, hundreds tailgate from boats at the university's riverside football stadium.

2 GATLINBURG/PIGEON FORGE

These twin cities are popular gateways to the Great Smoky Mountains. Pigeon Forge resembles a giant amusement park, fairly overflowing with miniature golf courses, water parks, and souvenir shops. You could spend a whole day at **Dollywood**, Dolly Parton's theme park, which offers rides, music, and a regional-crafts market. An oasis of serenity in the heart of town is the **Old Mill**, an 1830 wooden grain mill that still produces stone-ground flour and grits.

Gatlinburg, nestled against a scenic mountain backdrop, has its share of resort attractions, including the **Guinness World Records Museum** and an aerial tram leading up to **Ober Gatlinburg**, a recreation park with an ice arena, a chairlift, and an alpine slide. In the chilly months the skies of the city come alive with dancing lights in honor of the **Winterfest Celebration.**

▶ *Parking is at a premium in Gatlinburg; from April to November smart visitors park on the edge of town and take the fast trolley in.*

The **Great Smoky Arts & Crafts Community** is a collection of more than 80 handicraft shops just outside town; visit in April when the artisans put on a spring show. To savor the region's natural beauty, trek the three-mile trail to **Grotto Falls**, in the Great Smokies. The path meanders past a virgin hemlock forest and behind the falls.

3 GREAT SMOKY MOUNTAINS

This is the most visited national park in the country. The wondrous Smokies get their name from the blue haze that hovers over mossy mountain peaks. Highlights of this 800-square-mile jewel include a 70-mile section of the **Appalachian Trail**; the observation tower atop 6,643-foot **Clingmans Dome**; and **Cades Cove,** where an 11-mile loop drive passes many of the restored structures of this isolated mountain community, founded in 1819.

4 OAK RIDGE

This was just another rural Southern community until 1943, when the government's top-secret Manhattan Project

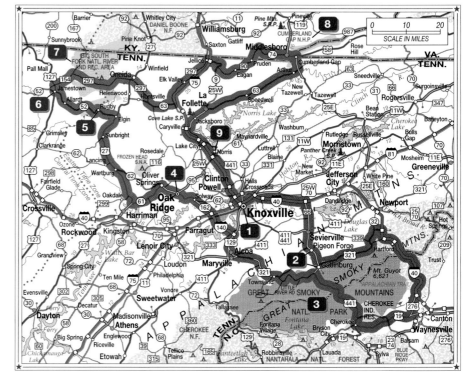

A heavenly light pierces a chasm at the top of Mount LeConte, a rugged 6,593-foot peak set among the soft green hills of Great Smoky Mountains National Park.

transformed it into a hornet's nest of activity. Approximately 3,000 people were given a mere few months to relocate. The goal? To search for ways to extract plutonium from uranium and cook up an atomic bomb. Scientists succeeded, creating the bomb that effectively ended World War II.

These days the buzz of activity is at the **American Museum of Science and Energy,** which features interactive displays, demonstrations on energy, and an exhibit on the Manhattan Project.

Learn more about the town's nuclear heritage by taking the 38-mile **Oak Ridge Self-Guided Motor Tour,** which begins at the visitor center. The tour includes the now decommissioned **Graphite Reactor,** the world's first nuclear reactor to operate at full power.

5 RUGBY

A Utopian colony founded in 1880 by Thomas Hughes, author of *Tom Brown's School Days,* the village of Rugby was created for the younger sons of English gentry, who by law could not inherit property and who were left with few socially acceptable professional options back in England. Hughes wrote that the British gentry "would rather see their sons starve like gentlemen than thrive in a trade or profession that is beneath them." Hughes envisioned Rugby as a place for the boys to make a living using practical skills.

Today many of the restored 19th-century structures are open to the public, including the 1887 **Christ Church, Episcopal,** with English hanging lamps

and German stained glass, and **Kingstone Lisle,** a house built for Hughes in 1884. The **Thomas Hughes Free Public Library** contains what many consider to be one of the finest collections of Victorian literature in America.

▶ *Watch highway signs between Rugby and Allardt for Colditz Cove State Natural Area, a wilderness area with a miniature falls and rare plants.*

6 JAMESTOWN

Local hero Sgt. Alvin C. York was once touted by Gen. John J. Pershing as "the greatest soldier of the war." The war was World War I, and the man who would win the Medal of Honor and see Gary Cooper portray him in the 1941 film *Sergeant York* lived 10 miles north of town. **Alvin York's Farm and Gristmill** is open daily. Forty-five minutes northeast of the farm are the natural caves of **Pickett State Rustic Park.**

7 BIG SOUTH FORK

The **Big South Fork National River and Recreation Area** is a relatively undiscovered gem of a park that features sandstone bluffs towering over 500-foot gorges carved by the Big South Fork of the Cumberland River. Don't miss 113-foot **Yahoo Falls,** the **Twin Arches** (the largest double sandstone arches east of the Mississippi), or (also within the park) the restored coal-mining community of **Blue Heron,** just over the state line in Kentucky. Visitors can glean a sense of what life was like when coal was king from listening to the tape-recorded stories of the miners who worked here when the mine was active, from 1938 to 1962. View the park's rugged grandeur aboard the cozy **Big South Fork Scenic Railway.**

8 CUMBERLAND GAP

Cumberland Gap National Historical Park spills over three state borders into Tennessee, Kentucky, and Virginia. It was through the Cumberland Gap, on a trail blazed in part by Daniel Boone, that the settlers of this region crossed into the frontier after the Revolutionary War. You can still see parts of this road in the park, which also offers superb views at the top, earthen Civil War fortifications, and the ruins of an old iron furnace.

9 NORRIS

The **Museum of Appalachia,** on the outskirts of town, shows off the most complete collection of artifacts of Appalachian culture in the world. This 65-acre outdoor museum displays some 25

Mountain music sets this dancer's toes tapping at the 150-year-old Peters Homestead House, one of several log buildings on exhibit at the Museum of Appalachia, near Norris.

log buildings, including a leather shop and a loom house. Mountain memorabilia—from a banjo fashioned from a fruitcake tin to a cage for a coal-mine canary—fills every nook of the on-site **Appalachian Hall of Fame.** In early October hundreds of area craftspeople gather for the five-day annual **Fall Homecoming,** where mountain skills and folkways are demonstrated and the fiddle-and-banjo twang of bluegrass music fills the air.

The town of Norris was established in the 1930's as a New Deal model town; the **Norris Dam** here was the first TVA dam built in the valley.

PLATEAUS & VALLEYS

1 CHATTANOOGA

At the foot of Lookout Mountain, in the elbow of the Tennessee River, Chattanooga's impressive vistas earn it the title Scenic Center of the South. The city's strategic location, in the geographic center of the Tennessee Valley, has over the years made it a much-coveted prize. Chattanooga is the site of battlefields and the **Chattanooga Choo-Choo.** This 30-acre complex marks the site of the first post–Civil War rail link between North and South and is now a popular attraction where visitors can dine in old railroad cars, stroll through a Victorian garden, or take a trolley ride. The town's newest jewel is the **Tennessee Aquarium,** the only aquarium in the country whose main focus is on freshwater rather than saltwater marine life. You'll see live alligators, river otters, and sharks in natural habitat exhibits in this shimmering 12-story glass-and-chrome structure, built in 1992.

Chickamauga-Chattanooga National Military Park, just outside town, is the nation's largest and oldest military park. During a two-month series of Civil War battles here in 1863, Union forces, though starving and surrounded, overwhelmed a defiant Rebel army and retook fog-shrouded Lookout Mountain. "The battle of Lookout Mountain is one of the romances of the war…it is all poetry," wrote Ulysses S. Grant.

Hang gliders hover above the cloud-covered hills of western Lookout Mountain. On the mountain's eastern face is **Lookout Mountain Incline Railway,** the steepest passenger railway in the world, with a 72.7 percent grade near the top. **Signal Mountain** overlooks the Tennessee River Gorge, often called the Grand Canyon of the Tennessee River.

▶ *For a stellar view of the city and its heavenly mountain environs, visit the Point Park visitor center on Lookout Mountain.*

***Amazon River dwellers** thrive in a replicated flooded forest at the Tennessee Aquarium.*

Rock City Gardens, on Lookout Mountain, offers 10 acres of unusual rock formations, gardens, and overlooks—including a view of seven states from Lover's Leap—all made famous by the See Rock City signs painted on old barns all over the region. Within Lookout Mountain Caverns is **Ruby Falls,** a 145-foot natural waterfall flowing 1,120 feet below the surface of the mountain.

2 SEWANEE

The little town of **Sewanee** is the site of the University of the South, which is commonly called by the town's name. With its neo-Gothic buildings tucked deep into the forest, the small campus looks like Oxford University transplanted to the Old South. The majestic bell tower, patterned after Oxford's, and the stained-glass chapel, with a 5,000-pipe organ, were built by the Episcopal Church. Professors and honor students wear academic robes even today.

Nearby, in the resort town of Monteagle, you can tour the award-winning **Monteagle Wine Cellars,** whose grapes are grown on the soaring hills of the Cumberland Plateau.

3 McMINNVILLE

Cumberland Caverns is the site of saltpeter mines from Civil War times. One-and-a-half-hour tours of this registered historic landmark include a sound-and-light show in the Hall of the Mountain King, the largest cavern room in the eastern United States. A highlight is the magnificent crystal chandelier, which originally adorned the Lowe's Metropolitan Theatre in Brooklyn, New York, and is now hung from the ceiling of the cave and lighted for special events.

4 SMITHVILLE

You'll find Appalachian treasures to take home at the **Joe L. Evins Appalachian Center for Crafts,** which both exhibits and sells fine crafts and artworks of wood, fiber, glass, metal, and clay. The center also offers regional-crafts workshops, arranged through Elderhostel, where such traditional skills as rag-rug making, quilting, and split-oak basketry are taught.

▶ *Bring your dancing shoes to town on July Fourth, when the National Fiddlers Jamboree competition is held.*

Between Sparta and Crossville, stop to stretch your legs at the **Virgin Falls Pocket Wilderness,** one of the last virgin timber woodlands in the country. Hiking stalwarts can trek to the falls.

5 CROSSVILLE

Often referred to as the Showplace of the New Deal, the octagonal **Homestead Tower Museum,** built in 1937–38, served as the headquarters for the Cumberland Homesteads Project—a planned community of stone houses launched during President

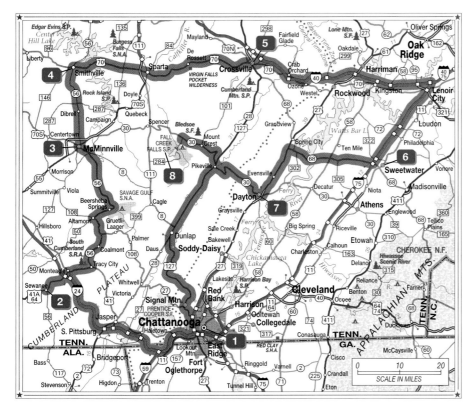

as the Scopes Monkey Trial. The restored second-floor courtroom of the **Rhea County Courthouse** is where the celebrated lawyer Clarence Darrow and the equally celebrated orator and prosecutor William Jennings Bryan dueled over the antievolution statute passed earlier that year by the state legislature. Bryan's silver tongue won the jury over; ironically, he died from a heart attack five days later, and the conviction was ultimately overturned.

It seems that evolution was not foremost on the minds of the local businessmen who had persuaded a young teacher to challenge the law simply as a way to boost Dayton's economy. The strategy worked: in the basement museum, open only during courthouse hours, exhibits reveal how 10,000 people a day poured into town to hear the compelling testimony. Residents profited by selling truckloads of souvenirs, and a local drugstore concocted a drink in honor of the occasion and dubbed it the Monkey Fizz.

8 FALL CREEK FALLS

The centerpiece of **Fall Creek Falls State Park** near Pikeville is 256-foot **Fall Creek Falls**, the highest waterfall east of the Rockies. The 16,000-acre woodlands, one of the first of Franklin Roosevelt's New Deal state parks, is relatively unspoiled and boasts virgin wilderness, dramatic gorges, fine hiking trails, and plenty of modern amenities, including one of the top-rated public golf courses in the United States.

Franklin Roosevelt's New Deal era. Most of the original homes are still standing and can be seen from the top of the museum's 80-foot tower, where you'll also get a view of the Cumberland Plateau hills. At the museum you can examine photographs, documents, and artifacts from the Roosevelt era.

Crossville is also home to the celebrated **Cumberland County Playhouse,** one of the largest professional theaters in rural America. The theater, operated by the family that opened it in the 1960's, features major American musicals as well as productions with an Appalachian theme.

6 SWEETWATER

From cockfights and clandestine moonshining stills to a saltpeter mining operation run by Confederate soldiers, the underground lake and caverns known today as the **Lost Sea** have seen lots of activity. The 4½-acre lake, stocked with hefty rainbow trout, has been dubbed by the *Guinness Book of World Records* as the largest underground lake in the United States. You can get a close-up view of its thriving aquatic life by taking a glass-bottom-boat ride. The caverns are famous for their large collection of anthodites, rare crystalline

cave formations commonly referred to as cave flowers. The fossil of a six-foot-long Pleistocene-epoch jaguar was excavated from the caverns in 1939.

▶ *The Lost Sea trout are lovely to look at but off-limits to fishermen—so leave your rod and reel at home.*

7 DAYTON

In 1925 this little town played host to one of the most riveting courtroom dramas the country has ever witnessed— the creation vs. evolution debate known

High above this rocky creek basin tumbles Fall Creek Falls, the scenic showstopper of Fall Creek Falls State Park. Fall Creek is ringed by pristine wilderness that was set aside as state parkland in the 1930's.

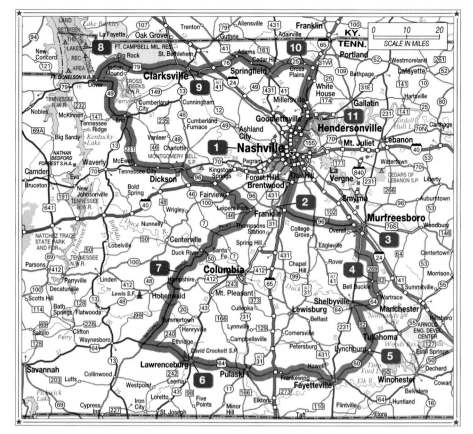

1 NASHVILLE

From the street upon street of country-music honky-tonks to the cool elegance of Vanderbilt University, Nashville is a city of many facets. Dubbed Music City USA, this congenial town is also Tennessee's capital and a Southern financial center. Indeed, the campuses of Nashville's myriad centers of higher learning are a mere two-step away from country music's **Music Row,** the eight-square-block recording district where hit songs are mined like gold.

Vanderbilt University was born of a million-dollar gift from Cornelius Vanderbilt in 1873; view the impressive on-campus architecture of Kirkland Hall (1905) and the Fine Arts Building (1880). The **State Capitol** was built in the 1850's in a modified Greek Revival style that has often been duplicated since. You may blink twice when you see the replica of the **Parthenon**—built to scale—in **Centennial Park.** Inside is the largest indoor statue in the Western world, the 42-foot-high goddess Athena. The structure was raised in 1896 to celebrate the state's centennial and to capitalize on the city's nickname, the Athens of the South. At Riverfront Park, amid 20th-century high-rises, is **Fort Nashborough,** a reconstruction of the fortification built there in the 18th century, which would ultimately grow into the city of Nashville.

But it is as the world's capital of country music that Nashville lets down its hair. The town is catnip for songwriters and musicians, who swagger into town in cowboy boots and ten-gallon hats. The **Country Music Hall of Fame** exhibits the sequined costumes of those who reached stardom. The Hall of Fame also oversees RCA's historic **Studio B,** where Elvis Presley did most of his Nashville recording. Traveling downtown, you can make a pilgrimage to the newly refurbished **Ryman Auditorium,** where the original **Grand Old Opry**—whose radio show has been staged before a live audience since 1925—performed from 1943 to 1974.

Opryland, nine miles northeast, includes the current Grand Ole Opry, a splashy theme park, and the headquarters for The Nashville Network (TNN).

The antebellum South is alive at **Belle Meade Plantation,** called the Queen of Tennessee Plantations. Seven miles from downtown, this 19th-century Greek Revival structure is supported by stately limestone columns. The 1890's carriage house and stable hold a collection of antique carriages.

The **Hermitage,** the home of America's seventh president, is 20 miles from downtown. Andrew Jackson and his wife, Rachel, built this elegant plantation, ringed by a classic English garden. Just after Jackson's first election, Rachel died. Upon serving two terms, Jackson retired here in 1837; it is said that every day of the last eight years of his life he would visit Rachel's tomb at sunset.

2 FRANKLIN

Travel back in time in the village of Franklin, where 19th-century houses with grillwork porches line the street. Franklin was a prosperous farming community until 1864, when more than 1,750 Confederate soldiers lost their lives at the Battle of Franklin. You can still see the bloodstains of dead and wounded Rebel soldiers on the elegant wood floors of the 1826 **Historic Carnton Plantation.** The house was used as a makeshift hospital after the battle. The buildings of the 1830 **Carter House,** built by slaves using sun-dried bricks, bear bullet holes from the battle.

3 MURFREESBORO

Oaklands's early-19th-century origins were modest. Additions to the simple two-room house over the years, however, reflect the growing prosperity of its owners. Today it is a showcase of antebellum architecture; tour year-round.

The **Stones River National Battlefield** is the 400-acre site of one of the bloodiest Civil War battles west of the Appalachians. Take the self-guided driving tour of the battlefield using maps available at the visitor center.

4 BELL BUCKLE

This village of fewer than 500 people comes as a charming back-roads discovery. Nestled in green hills that blaze yellow and rust in autumn, Bell Buckle has converted the rustic turn-of-the-century red brick buildings of its old town center, Railroad Square, into shops chock-full of country crafts, antiques, and traditional quilts.

▶ After crossing the tracks at Railroad Square, take a spin on Highway 82 northeast through forested hills that rival New England's for fall color.

Legend has it that Bell Buckle got its name when Cherokees slaughtered a cow and hung its bell and buckle on a tree to warn white settlers to stay away. The bell and buckle were also used by scouts to direct homesteaders to fertile pastureland. Today the emerald-green fields that surround the town are ringed by white fences and grazed by sleek Tennessee walking horses.

Close by is **Shelbyville,** known as the Walking Horse Capital of the World and the site of the national Tennessee Walking Horse Celebration.

5 LYNCHBURG

This small town is one of the most popular destinations in Tennessee, owing in no small part to the presence of the **Jack Daniel's Distillery,** where sour-mash whiskey is made. A 90-minute guided tour—led by good ol' country boys straight out of central casting—shows how it's done. But no tasting or buying till you're beyond the city limits, please: Lynchburg is dry.

After your tour, pay a lunchtime visit to **Miss Bobo's Boardinghouse,** whose renowned family-style, midday country meals are booked ahead for months.

6 LAWRENCEBURG

One block south of the town square, the **Davy Crockett Museum** was built on the site where the famous frontiersman lived from 1817 to 1822. A life-size bronze statue of Crockett, who died at the Alamo at the age of 49, was dedicated in the public square here on September 14, 1922.

7 NATCHEZ TRACE PARKWAY

Follow the historic **Natchez Trace** on a lovely parkway begun by the National Park Service in the late 1930's. Some 300 segments of the old Trace have been preserved. The 445-mile **Natchez Trace Parkway** closely traces the route through woodlands and alongside fertile farm country; the road has few intersections and no commercial activity.

8 LAND BETWEEN THE LAKES

The 170,000-acre **Land Between the Lakes** is a national recreation area built by the TVA between Kentucky Lake and Lake Barkley. Among its treasures are a buffalo herd, a 19th-century living-history farm, and 200 miles of trails and waterways.

The first major Union victory and the battle that confirmed Ulysses S. Grant's mettle as a commander occurred nearby in February 1862. Modern-day visitors to **Fort Donelson National Battlefield** can take a leisurely automobile tour through the battlefield on 10 miles of marked roadway.

▶ During hunting season, hikers, bikers, and horseback riders visiting the Land Between the Lakes recreation area are advised to wear blaze-orange safety clothing and a small bell.

9 CLARKSVILLE

This city of 90,000 is an architectural gold mine: 15 acres of 19th-century design are on display in the downtown historic district. Take a stroll on the **Cumberland RiverWalk,** along the riverfront promenade, or take the self-guided walking tour using maps from the Tourist Commission. Visit the 1792 **Sevier Station,** the oldest standing structure in the county, and the **Smith-Trahern Mansion,** an 1859 mansion with a stunning winding stairway.

10 CROSS PLAINS

Cozy up to an egg cream in a cushy black-and-chrome Art Deco booth and travel back in time at **Historic Thomas Drugs,** built in 1915. Try the old-fashioned phosphates or salty lemonades at the soda fountain as one of the store's original ceiling fans lazily whirs above your head. Showcases of burnished oak and beveled glass—one still retaining its 1915 shipping tag—line the walls and countertops.

11 HENDERSONVILLE

One of the oldest masonry homes in Tennessee, **Rock Castle** is built on seven levels and combines Georgian and Federal styles. Five generations of the same family occupied this home from the late 18th century to the 1930's.

Hendersonville is a popular stop for country-music lovers. Visit the **House of Cash,** a museum dedicated to singer, songwriter, and country-music legend Johnny Cash. The town was also the home of Conway Twitty, the late singer whose stage name was conceived when he spread a map before him, closed his eyes, and pointed to Conway, Arkansas, and Twitty, Texas.

Bluegrass legend Bill Monroe (left) is one of the many stars to have headlined at the Opry.

1 MEMPHIS

Built on the bluff where Hernando de Soto discovered the mighty Mississippi River, colorful, festive Memphis is where W. C. Handy birthed the blues, Elvis Presley gave away Cadillacs, and ducks learned to live the fat, easy life in a grand Southern hotel.

The Memphis skyline reflects the city's growth as a thriving modern commercial center. But the waterfront retains the romance of its riverboat past, reinforced by the horse-drawn carriages that clip-clop down waterside streets and the leisurely cruises on the **Memphis Queen Line.** Don't miss the riverfront **Pyramid,** a shiny 32-story tower of steel whose base is large enough to cover six football fields. Inspired by the Egyptian pyramids in ancient Memphis, the Pyramid is a year-round sports and entertainment complex.

On Front Street, board the sleek monorails that take visitors to **Mud Island,** a 52-acre river park dedicated to life on the Mississippi. Get your feet wet, literally, at the **RiverWalk,** a five-block-long miniature model of the river. Ninety information panels track the Mississippi's twisting 900-mile journey from Illinois to the Gulf of Mexico.

Crowds gather at the **Peabody Hotel** for one of the best shows in town—the parade of the resident ducks. The elevator opens at 11 A.M., and five mallards make a mad dash for the lobby fountain, where they while away the day. At 5 P.M. the duckmaster leads them back to the elevator for the ride to the roof, where they turn in for the evening.

Two blocks south is the **Beale Street Historic District,** home of the blues. Here are blues clubs, restaurants, and the house where W. C. Handy, the composer of "St. Louis Blues," lived. Handy was widely credited with fusing black folk music and ragtime, utilizing the "blue" note, the slightly flattened third and seventh notes on the scale. In nearby **Handy Park,** beneath a statue of the composer, musicians perform impromptu concerts.

The **National Civil Rights Museum,** located at the Lorraine Motel downtown, is a shrine to the civil rights movement and an educational facility. It was at this motel that Dr. Martin Luther King, Jr., was slain as he stood on the balcony outside Room 306-7. Today the room remains just as it was on the night when the civil rights leader closed the door to leave for dinner.

Music legend Elvis Presley's white-columned paean to domestic life, **Graceland,** is also something of a shrine; fans come by the thousands to tour the mansion, lay flowers on the

A rock 'n' rolling neon Elvis—the old Heartbreak Hotel Restaurant sign—greets visitors in its new home at Graceland.

grave, and gape at the Elvis look-alikes who pour into town as if rolling off an assembly line. Located 10 miles from downtown, Graceland features gold records and bejeweled jumpsuits. About the only thing you won't see here is Elvis himself—perhaps.

▶ *Early birds arriving around 7 A.M., before the tours begin, are allowed free walk-up visits to the Graceland grave sites.*

The **Memphis in May International Festival** is a monthlong fete honoring a different country and its culture every year. More than 100 events blend the music, dance, theater, visual arts, and food of the chosen country, including the **Beale Street Music Festival** and the **World Championship Barbecue Cooking Contest.** The month ends with the **Sunset Symphony,** a sundown concert on the banks of the river.

2 HENNING

Alex Haley, the prize-winning author of *Roots,* grew up in this small town (pop. 635), where he lived in a two-story house built by his grandfather in 1918. As a child, Haley sat on the porch, listening to his grandmother and her five snuff-dipping sisters rock and tell the stories of their slave ancestors. There was Kunta Kinte, who was sold into slavery at 16, and Chicken George, who brought the family here from North Carolina. The stories inspired Haley to write the novel that won him a Pulitzer Prize in 1977 and spurred millions to dig for their own roots. The writer's grave lies on the front lawn of the restored **Alex Haley House Museum,** and Chicken George and other Haley family members are buried in nearby **Bethlehem Cemetery.**

3 REELFOOT LAKE

Just outside Tiptonville lies one of nature's loveliest creations. **Reelfoot Lake** was formed by the New Madrid earthquakes in the winter of 1811–12, when the Mississippi River reversed its flow. **Reelfoot Lake State Resort Park** is one of the state's most unusual animal and nature habitats. The spectral shadows of submerged forests lie beneath the lake surface. Its shallow waters are studded with cypress trees and lily pads. Between December and mid-March about 200 American bald eagles winter on the lake. Daily eagle-viewing tours are led by park rangers; advance reservations for the tours are advised.

4 TRENTON

On permanent display in **City Hall** is the world's largest collection of teapots. Not your standard enamel pots by any means, these rare porcelain *veilleuse-théières* (pronounced VAY-uhz tay-air), or "night-light teapots," were collected over 40 years by Dr. Frederick Freed. The teapots originated in the 18th century, when European ceramists developed a warming dish for medicines in sickrooms and nurseries that rested on a pedestal filled with oil. When lit, the flame shone through the translucent porcelain, like a night-light. Many have unusual shapes—a spout shaped like a bobbin in a woman's hand, a pedestal in the form of a dolphin. Three of the pots bear the Napoleonic crest and the letter *N*. The exhibit is free and open daily; a festival in May includes a teapot-lighting church service.

5 HUMBOLDT

The world's largest strawberry shortcake, roughly 10 feet in diameter, is served at the opening ceremony of the **West Tennessee Strawberry Festival**. In actuality, the big cake is thousands of minicakes, carefully arranged, slathered with whipped cream, and crowned with fresh, ripe strawberries. The festival, held every first full week in May, dates back to 1934, when citizens were seeking ways to rescue a dwindling strawberry crop. Although the

A "night-light" teapot with a Napoleonic crest is on display at City Hall in Trenton.

berry has been largely supplanted in today's local economy, the festival is bigger than ever—50,000 to 70,000 people have been in attendance in recent years, and each leaves with a mini strawberry shortcake of his or her own.

6 JACKSON

The **Casey Jones Home & Railroad Museum** is the house of the legendary railroad engineer, John Luther Jones,

better known as Casey. The grounds include a replica of a steam engine. Museum displays are designed to flesh out the story of Casey's last ride, on April 30, 1900, from Memphis to Vaughn, when a caboose and three rail cars were stuck on the track ahead. Casey shut down the throttle and threw on the brakes, but the trains crashed, the locomotive left the tracks, and the engineer was killed. A friend and fellow railroader, Wallace Saunders, composed the ballad that brought Casey immortality.

7 PINSON MOUNDS

The **Pinson Mounds State Archaeological Area** is a collection of 12 American Indian ceremonial mounds, spread out over 1,162 acres, that date from A.D. 500. Among them is Sauls Mound, the second-tallest Indian-built mound in the country. Designed to resemble an Indian mound, the on-site museum houses a theater and exhibits. Six miles of trails provide access to the mounds and include a nature walk. Several of the trails are open for biking.

▶ *Fish lovers shouldn't miss the tasty local catfish served—with or without bones—in many area restaurants.*

8 SHILOH NATIONAL MILITARY PARK

One of the bloodiest battles of the Civil War was fought here, on the west bank of the Tennessee River, on April 6 and 7, 1862. The 4,000-acre park is a memorial to the 23,746 casualties from the Union and Confederate armies. A 9.5-mile self-guided auto tour follows the course of the battle. The park contains a visitor center, picnic sites, a hiking trail, a national cemetery, a library, and a shop filled with memorabilia.

9 GRAND JUNCTION

One hour east of Memphis lies a town where hunting dogs are forever immortalized. At the **National Bird Dog Museum** the front yard features a bronze sculpture of a dog handler, a pointer, a setter, and 22 game birds on the rise. Inside are portraits, trophies, and all the trappings of the bird-dog world. The national field trials are held on the nearby **Ames Plantation**.

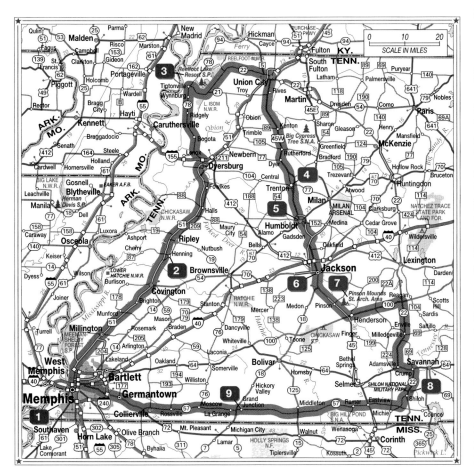

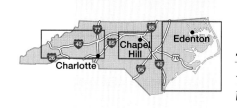

North Carolina

The Tarheel State has some of the most varied landscapes in the country, from the mighty western peaks to the ivied halls of the Piedmont to the shimmering necklace of barrier beaches.

THE COASTAL PLAIN

1 EDENTON

What is often touted as "the South's prettiest town" at one time held a loftier position. Incorporated in 1722, Edenton was a prosperous port in pre-Revolutionary America and later a crucial commercial hub for the newly formed nation. Nestled on the mossy banks of Edenton Bay, the town is filled with spectacular 18th-century architecture. The 1758 **Cupola House** has a Chinese Chippendale staircase and is one of the oldest houses in town. The 1767 **Chowan County Courthouse** contains the best-preserved 18th-century courtroom in America. Daily guided walking tours leave from the visitor center.

2 MERCHANTS MILLPOND

Swamplands generally suffer an unsavory reputation, but at **Merchants Millpond State Park** the swamp is a place of ethereal beauty. Visitors can glide in canoes under bald cypresses curtained with gauzy Spanish moss and see an untamed landscape. Take a hike on the nine miles of trails or canoe along the millpond, where the varied forms of wildlife happily coexist: white egrets, noisy swamp warblers, and sun-worshiping pond turtles, called cooters.

▶ *In summer, wear insect repellent, pants, and socks to ward off ticks.*

3 KILL DEVIL HILLS

The broken necklace of barrier islands known as the Outer Banks is one of the most popular salt-air playgrounds in the country. Credit the area's wind-swept beauty and pounding surf to geography: the 120-mile-long strip of land juts far out into the Atlantic and so is vulnerable to the whims of weather.

In 1903, Orville Wright rode against the brisk island winds in a homemade airplane for 120 feet. You can see the Wright brothers' reconstructed camp, replicas of the original Wright *Flyer* and their 1902 glider, and a granite marker at the takeoff spot of that first powered flight, at the **Wright Brothers National Memorial**, in Kill Devil Hills.

Travel on the beach road to **Nags Head.** Seaward are the Unpainted Aristocracy—the grand old wooden cottages that have withstood the elements since the late 1800's. Many of the cottages have been placed on rollers and

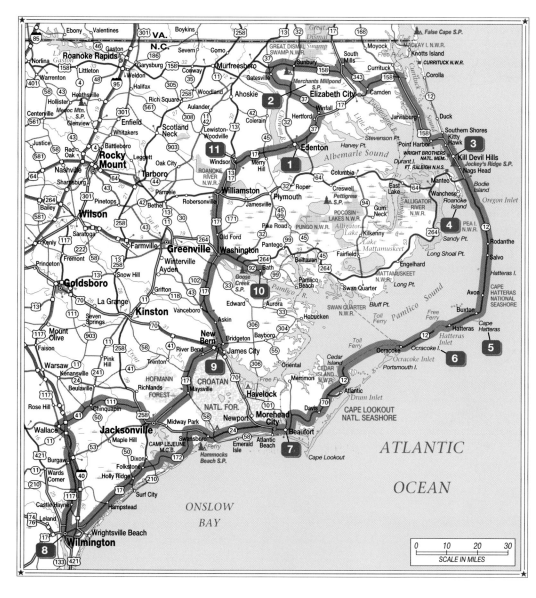

It's an angler's paradise in the roiling blue surf at the Cape Hatteras National Seashore.

moved back from the beach regularly to protect them from the encroaching sea; at low tide the old house pilings often make a ghostly emergence.

▶ *There are only two main routes to and from the Banks. Avoid peak travel times, particularly weekends, when weekly rentals begin and end.*

4 ROANOKE ISLAND

About 35 years before Plymouth Rock, the first attempted settlement by English colonists in what is now the United States was in these dense woodlands. The colony was doomed, however: The 116 men, women, and children vanished, with only the word CROATOAN carved into a palisade post. It's a mystery that continues to grip the public's imagination. At the **Fort Raleigh National Historic Site,** you can see the reconstructed earthen fort and colonial artifacts. Adjacent to the park is the lush 16th-century-style **Elizabethan Gardens,** built in 1951 to memorialize those first colonists. Since 1937, summer visitors have flocked next door to see *The Lost Colony,* an outdoor dramatization of the ill-fated settlement.

Drive into town or cruise in and tie your dinghy to a waterfront slip, but don't bypass the village of **Manteo.** It's Mayberry R.F.D. on the water: You may hear the squeals of children crabbing on a dock or see a sopping retriever emerging happily from a swim in the marsh. It's no wonder Andy Griffith calls Roanoke Island home. It's also the home of the *Elizabeth II,* a replica of

the first colonists' 16th-century wooden sailing vessel.

5 CAPE HATTERAS

Preserved for eternity in the **Cape Hatteras National Seashore** are 70 miles of pristine shoreline, held fast by sea oats and tawny dunes. To get there, you'll cross the **Herbert C. Bonner Bridge,** a spectacular span arching over the turquoise waters of **Oregon Inlet.** The spits of sand under the bridge are prime fishing areas, promising ice chests of hefty puppy drum and flounder. Offshore fishermen charter boats out of the **Oregon Inlet Fishing Center** to hunt for blue marlin—giant sailfish that shimmy on the ends of their tails to shake a hook. Once off the bridge, bird-watch from one of the raised platforms at the **Pea Island National Wildlife Refuge.** In Rodanthe, visit the gray-shingled **Chicamacomico U.S. Lifesaving Service Station,** built in 1910, where old-time lifesaving drills are reenacted in the summer. Lifesavers of old were kept busy plucking mariners from the Graveyard of the Atlantic, so named because of the shifting **Diamond Shoals** and rough currents. More than 600 ships have been snagged here. Often visible at Beach Access Ramp No. 27, south of Salvo, is the hull of the *G. A. Kohler,* a four-masted schooner wrecked in 1933.

The towering candy-striped **Cape Hatteras Lighthouse** comes into view on the approach to Buxton. The 208-foot lighthouse is the tallest in the country; its beam can be seen 20 miles

offshore. At the **Point,** the warm Gulf Stream and the frigid Labrador Current visibly collide from opposite directions, in a spectacular clashing of sea foam.

6 OCRACOKE ISLAND

A 40-minute free ferry ride from Hatteras Island brings you to this gem of an island, the place where the pirate Blackbeard lived and lost his head. Stop for a swim at glorious **Ocracoke Beach.** Wainscoted seafood shanties and a fleet of sailboats encircle **Silver Lake.** Six miles from the Hatteras ferry landing are the **Ocracoke Pony Pens,** home of the wild horses descended from Spanish mustangs said to have been shipwrecked here more than 400 years ago.

Take a picnic lunch and a bottle of wine for the 2½-hour car-ferry ride south to **Cedar Island.** The ferry travels over the liquid expanse of the Pamlico Sound, often ushered by shrimp boats and dancing porpoises.

▶ *In the summer, it's essential to make advance ferry reservations.*

7 BEAUFORT

This charming waterside town, founded in 1709, is full of 200-year-old homes. The **Beaufort Historic Site** consists of nine historic buildings, including an apothecary shop and a jail. The **Hammock House,** built in the early 1700's, is the oldest house in town. Local lore has it that Blackbeard hanged one of his wives from a front-yard tree. Cross **Taylor's Creek** by boat to watch the wild ponies cavort on **Carrot Island.**

From Beaufort, travel to the quaint fishing village of **Swansboro.** Five miles south is **Hammocks Beach State Park,** an island that can be reached only by seasonal ferry or private boat. It's worth a trip: you may have this beautiful island—and the scores of snowy sand dollars underfoot—all to yourself.

8 WILMINGTON

Dubbed Hollywood East for the numerous big-budget films that are made here, Wilmington is a bustling port city tempered by gracious antebellum architecture and small-town cordiality. House tours through one of the state's largest historic districts depart daily from the foot of Market Street. Nearby **Thalian Hall** is a restored 1850's theater. Tour the **U.S.S. *North Carolina,*** docked in the Cape Fear River. At the time of her commissioning in 1941, the battleship was considered the world's most powerful sea weapon. The lush gardens of **Orton Plantation Gardens,** 15 miles south on Rte. 133, were planted in 1910 on rice-plantation grounds.

9 NEW BERN

The riverfront town where the pharmacist C. D. Bradham invented Brad's Drink—now known as Pepsi-Cola—in the 1890's, New Bern was the original state capital. **Tryon Palace,** the state's first capitol, was built in 1770 and was called "the most beautiful building in the Colonial Americas." Much of the palace burned in 1798; the remaining structures languished for 150 years until the estate's restoration in the 1950's. It is now a Colonial showcase, with period furnishings and formal gardens. To study the town's wealth of 18th- and 19th-century architecture, pick up a walking-tour map at the visitor center on Pollock Street.

10 BATH

The oldest town in North Carolina is also one of its tiniest: just over 200 residents and a town acreage of six blocks, perched in a scenic setting on Bath Creek. Its appeal lies in its rich cache of 18th-century architecture. Tour the 1751 **Palmer-Marsh House,** which features massive double chimneys, or the 1734 **St. Thomas Church,** the oldest church in use in the state.

11 WINDSOR

Painted a pale butterscotch, **Hope Plantation** sits regally on a landscaped lawn. Until the 1970's, this four-chimneyed mansion, amid peanut farmland five miles from Windsor, was in a state of near ruin. Today, thousands come yearly to see the beautifully restored house, the home of Governor David Stone, who built it in 1803. Still visible are the words scrawled by the grief-stricken governor on his private library wall after the death of his wife: "O for the past gone days when I could gase [sic] on my wife."

A peach of a crop is readied for market in the foothills town of West End, near Pinehurst. The early-summer bounty of ripe peaches is one of North Carolina's top fruit crops.

THE PIEDMONT

1 CHAPEL HILL

They call it Blue Heaven, in reference to both the robin's-egg skies and the ubiquitous university colors. A state-of-the-art college town, Chapel Hill is the site of the **University of North Carolina,** the oldest state university in the country, opened in 1795. The first university building, **Old East,** was completed in 1795 and still functions as a simple, unadorned residence on the edge of **McCorkle Place,** a beautiful, shady commons area filled with squirrels, brooding graduate students, and fly-by Frisbees. The Greek Revival **Playmakers Theatre** is a working theater built in 1851. View the celestial light show at the **Morehead Planetarium,** where the first NASA astronauts contemplated the heavens. Then snuggle into an old wooden booth at the classic collegiate eatery **Carolina Coffee Shop,** open since 1922.

▶ *Take a self-guided campus tour with audiotapes and brochures offered at the university visitor center.*

2 BYNUM

Some locals call it the world's largest stump and root zoo. Others call it brilliant folk art. See what the fuss is about by ambling over to Clyde Jones's yard on Thompson's Recreation Road. You can't miss Jones's outdoor artworks; amid the simple wood-frame houses of this old mill town is a mind-boggling menagerie of his creations—elephants, pigs, dolphins, and more—all miraculously carved with a chainsaw from the homeliest stumps and roots. Jones will be either at home or at **Tuck's Country Store**—which takes his messages—or driving his riding lawn mower through town accompanied by his dog, Speck. Leave your wallet at home, however: though many a limousine has called with a trunkful of cash, Jones rarely sells his work, preferring to give it away to local children.

3 PINEHURST

As you approach Pinehurst, the countryside changes from North Carolina's characteristic green fields of tobacco to a landscape of simply greens—golf greens, that is. This is golf country, and residents raise not tobacco but post-links drinks. Here you'll discover at least 10 world-class golf courses.

You'll also discover scenic horse country, notably in and around **Southern Pines.** Take in a horse race at the **Pinehurst Harness Track,** a historic 1916 racetrack.

4 SEAGROVE

One resource the South has always had plenty of is clay. In Seagrove, making pottery has been the order of business since the 1700's. You'll want to visit several of the more than 50 pottery studios in the area, where pots are spun and fired almost every day. **Jugtown,** set in a complex of rustic old buildings, is particularly popular. Most local retail stores offer a map of area studios.

5 LEVEL CROSS

The man stock-car racing fans defer to as "King Richard" has his own museum. The **Richard Petty Museum**, adjacent to the family racing complex, is filled with wall-to-wall memorabilia devoted to the former race-car driver's triumphs behind the wheel. Inside, you can watch a short film on Petty's life in the fast lane and view an enormous portrait of King Richard himself.

6 GREENSBORO

In 1960, four black students at North Carolina A&T were denied service at a whites-only lunch counter at the former **F. W. Woolworth** store. The students refused to leave and thus put into motion one of the state's landmark civil-rights sit-ins. The site is marked by a plaque and the former students' footprints preserved in the sidewalk.

The **Greensboro Historical Museum** displays memorabilia belonging to the celebrated short-story writer William Henry Porter, better known as O. Henry, who lived here until he was 19.

7 HILLSBOROUGH

An endearing aspect of this pastoral prerevolutionary former state capital is its size. You need only minutes to meander through the quiet, green historic district. These days the old houses are inhabited by writers, artists, and professors from the area universities. Stroll by some 40 historic sites using a self-guided-tour map, available at the **Hillsborough Historical Society.**

8 DURHAM

Although signs label Durham as the City of Medicine, U.S.A., and patients flock to **Duke Medical Center** to shed poundage on the famous Rice Diet, this is a tobacco town, whose name is a part of one of its products—Bull Durham. Even now, in these reformist times, the air often fills with the irresistibly rich odor of dry-cured tobacco. Visit the **Duke Homestead State Historic Site and Tobacco Museum,** to see where the tobacco industry and its first tycoon, James B. Duke, got their start. Included is the original two-story factory. If you prefer to sniff at even sweeter vegetation, swing by the **Sarah P. Duke**

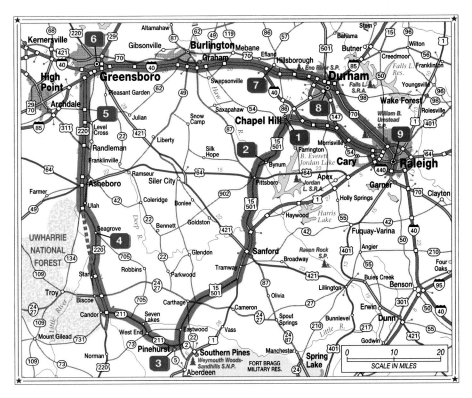

Gardens, an intoxicating sprawl of fields and flowers. The gardens border the beautiful grounds of **Duke University,** where campus aficionados should make two stops: the soaring neo-Gothic **Duke Chapel,** built in 1930–32 and designed after the original Canterbury

The old Durham Bulls stadium sign, immortalized in the baseball film Bull Durham, *rewards homers with flashing eyes and snorts of steam.*

Cathedral, and **Cameron Indoor Stadium,** a classic 1939 basketball gymnasium, where the hardwood floors, still in use, wear a copper patina of age.

▶ *Preview a Broadway show before it hits the Great White Way when "Broadway at Duke" kicks off its season in September.*

9 RALEIGH

Raleigh completes the tri-city **Research Triangle** (Durham and Chapel Hill are the other points), an area where three world-class universities, two teaching hospitals, and a nest of high-tech laboratories are all located within a 25-mile radius. Raleigh is a pleasant, unassuming state capital, appropriate to a state that proudly claims to be a valley of humility between two mountains of conceit (Virginia and South Carolina). To savor the essence of the region, spend time at the **Raleigh Farmers Market,** open every day except Sunday, year-round. The staggering array of produce includes such seasonal delicacies as butter beans and collard greens.

If you prefer paintings to collard greens, don't miss the 6,000-piece collection at the **North Carolina Museum of Art.** The museum itself is a work of art, with a glass elevator that overlooks a landscape of billowing green trees. Head downtown to inspect the Cherokee County marble and Carolina hardwoods that went into building the **Governor's Mansion,** a gabled Victorian. Then follow the stream of government office workers to the booths at **Clyde Cooper's Barbecue,** serving genuine North Carolina barbecue and truckloads of iced tea since 1938.

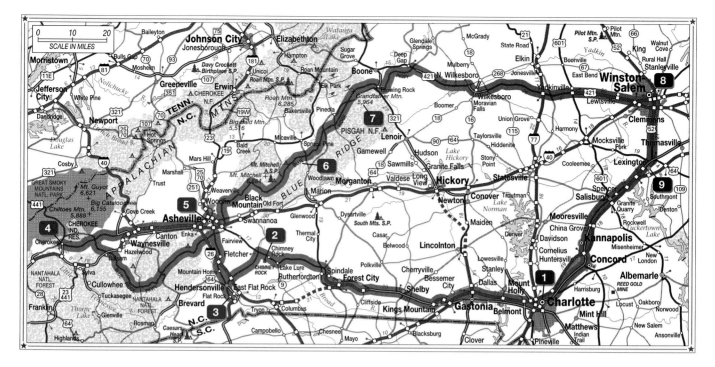

1 CHARLOTTE

This glittering New South city has gained a reputation of late as an international banking center. But the panning for gold began for real in these foothills in the late 1700's. That's when the nation's first gold rush occurred after a local farmer, John Reed, unearthed a 17-pound nugget, which he promptly sold for $3.50. At the **Reed Gold Mine,** 20 miles east of the city, you can pan for your own gold near the spot Reed discovered his.

In Charlotte proper, the **Mint Museum** offers a fine collection of American paintings, including works by Thomas Eakins and Andrew Wyeth. The **Discovery Place,** a hands-on science and technology center, features a tropical rain forest with waterfalls. In season, the hottest ticket in this basketball-crazed region is a seat at the **Charlotte Coliseum** to see the Charlotte Hornets, the teal-clad NBA basketball team.

2 CHIMNEY ROCK

Suspended in the clouds above the entrance to Hickory Nut Gorge, this circular stone bluff provides a spectacular view of nearby **Lake Lure,** as well as the **Blue Ridge Mountains** to the west. **Chimney Rock Park** was the setting for the 1993 film *The Last of the Mohicans;* you'll find costumes and stills from the movie in a glass-enclosed shop at the summit. To get there, you can climb up one of three moderate to strenuous well-marked trails, two of which take you past 404-foot **Hickory Nut Falls.** All promise breathtaking vistas. If you prefer a gentler ascent, ride the elevator in a 26-story shaft blasted inside the rock. Be on the watch for ghosts, as several 19th-century newspaper accounts

Jugtown pottery made in the 1930's and '40's is on permanent display at the Mint Museum in Charlotte.

reported sightings of a spectral cavalry battle in the rock's vicinity. The apparition was later traced to the otherworldly wisps of blue clouds and vapors that swirl about the peaks at twilight.

3 FLAT ROCK

In 1945, at the age of 67, the Pulitzer Prize–winning poet Carl Sandburg and his wife, Lilian, became enamored of the rolling Blue Ridge woodlands and bought this handsome 240-acre farm and home, built in 1838. Today **Connemara** is maintained by the National Park Service, which offers interpretive tours and summertime poetry readings in Sandburg's garage. In the house it's as if the Sandburgs had just stepped out of the room: a calendar from 1967, with hair appointments penciled in, hangs in the dining room. Walls are lined top to bottom with books, many of which are stuffed with Sandburg's white markers, denoting favorite passages. The living room features original Edward Steichen photographs of the Sandburgs as young marrieds. In the **Goat Barn** you'll be gently nuzzled by the affectionate resident goats, the same breeds that Mrs. Sandburg raised. Sandburg died here in 1967 at the age of 89.

▶ *An easy 30-minute hike from the Goat Barn leads up a winding woodlands path to a favorite Sandburg scenic vista atop Glassy Mountain.*

The entire town of Flat Rock is a national historic site, having been settled as a mountain retreat in the 1830's by wealthy Lowcountry planters. Built in that era as a private chapel, the **Church of St. John in the Wilderness** is today a lovely example of early-19th-century Renaissance-style architecture.

4 CHEROKEE

In 1838, 14,000 Cherokees were rounded up in this region by federal troops and marched to Oklahoma on the Trail of Tears. A thousand or so escaped into the Great Smoky Mountains, where they lived until 1866, when they finally secured the right to come back and lay claim to their own land. Their heritage is honored at the **Museum of the Cherokee Indian,** which houses a comprehensive collection of artifacts and Cherokee writings. Next door is the **Oconaluftee Indian Village,** where you can witness demonstrations of Cherokee life prior to the arrival of English settlers. Cherokee also serves as a gateway to the **Great Smoky Mountains National Park,** a majestic preserve of 500,000 acres, one of the country's most-visited national parks.

5 ASHEVILLE

Framed by a heavenly Blue Ridge backdrop, Asheville is both a gracious, slow-tempo Southern city and a hot tourist destination. A taste of the former is the novelist Thomas Wolfe's home, the white-frame Old Kentucky Home boardinghouse, at the **Thomas Wolfe Memorial.** The house is furnished as the Wolfes left it in the 1920's and contains the author's typewriter and personal effects.

Somewhat more commodious is the **Biltmore Estate,** the largest private home in the United States. This monumental 250-room mansion on an 8,000-acre property was built for George Vanderbilt. Opened to guests on Christmas Eve, 1895, the estate is a dazzling amalgam of man-made pomp and incomparable natural surroundings. You can stand on the South Terrace and gaze out on sweeping Blue Ridge countryside and sumptuous grounds designed by the Central Park designer Frederick Law Olmsted. Visit when the **Rose Garden** and the **Azalea Garden** are in bloom. Many rooms can be toured; among them, a palm-fringed winter garden that crops up in Hollywood movies, and a medieval-style banquet hall with 72-foot ceilings and 16th-century Flemish tapestries. Visit from mid-November to New Year's Eve, when the house is dressed in holiday

The Biltmore Estate, in autumn colors, casts an imperial reflection on the lagoon.

finery and dried roses from the vast rose gardens decorate the estate-cut evergreens adorning each room. Tasting tours are held daily at the award-winning **Biltmore Winery,** ensconced in the estate's old dairy.

6 THE BLUE RIDGE PARKWAY

The **Blue Ridge Parkway** weaves through the North Carolina and Virginia mountains for almost 500 scenic miles. This is a highway built expressly for meandering. Consider leaving the parkway temporarily to visit and hike in such areas of natural beauty as the **Pisgah National Forest,** a wilderness of waterfalls and trout-filled streams; **Mount Mitchell,** the highest point east of the Mississippi River; and **Linville Gorge,** a rugged canyon of great depth and raw beauty.

▶ *Allow plenty of driving time for the twisting mountain roads and the parkway's 45-m.p.h. speed limit.*

7 GRANDFATHER MOUNTAIN

If your idea of fun is blowing about in the wind atop a 218-foot-long, mile-high swinging bridge, by all means stop for a spell at this private park, dominated by 5,964-foot **Grandfather Mountain.** On the second weekend of July, join the largest gathering of Scottish clans in the eastern United States in the **Scottish Highlands Games,** a celebration of sheep-herding, caber-tossing, and kilt-wearing.

8 WINSTON-SALEM

A city that tobacco built, Winston-Salem is a handsome, moneyed center for the arts. It's also the home of **Old Salem.** Founded in 1766 by a Protestant sect known as the Moravians, Old Salem is a living museum that preserves the buildings and crafts of these peaceful settlers. Costumed guides often cook in a large fireplace or play the 1797 organ. Notice the clean, austere lines of the **Single Brothers House.** Moravians were buried according to gender and marital status, as evidenced by the adjacent cemetery, **God's Acre.**

9 LEXINGTON

The great debate presses on in the barbecue wars between the states. Aficionados consider the western North Carolina version—wood-smoked pork tossed in a vinegar and tomato sauce—hard to beat. Lexington is a nationally recognized barbecue mecca, with more than a dozen restaurants competing to serve the best barbecue in the state, if not the world. Ask for yours slathered with coleslaw on a warm bun. The Parade of Pigs launches the annual **Barbecue Festival** here in October.

A young lass relishes a Highland fling at the Scottish clans reunion and Highlands Games on Grandfather Mountain.

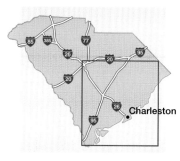

South Carolina

The Old South lives on in this lovely, languid region, where sweet magnolias flower under a buttery hot sun, plantation ruins line dusty back roads, and a fierce ancestral pride lingers.

Charleston

LOWCOUNTRY & THE PIEDMONT

1 CHARLESTON

Earthquakes, fires, war, and hurricanes: Charleston has taken quite a beating in its 300 years of existence and withstood such insults in grand fashion. Its unsurpassed antebellum architecture has been preserved intact: post–Civil War economic hardships ensured that few could refurbish in the latest Victorian mode. "Too poor to paint; too proud to whitewash," trumpeted the locals.

A good introduction to the feisty city psyche is the award-winning film *Dear Charleston*, shown in rotating venues around the city; check for times and places at the **Charleston Visitor Center.** Then stroll the cobblestoned streets or reserve a seat on a horse-drawn bug-

Battery. Tour boats to the fort operate year-round from the town of Mount Pleasant. The harbor view is grand from the porches of the Greek Revival **Edmondston-Alston House.** The **Nathaniel Russell House** (c. 1808) features a dazzling free-standing staircase. The late-17th-century **Elizabeth O'Neill Verner House** was the intimate home of the beloved local artist.

St. Michael's 186-foot-high ivory steeple is a Charleston landmark. The 1761 church is the city's oldest. Buy a freshly woven sweetgrass basket from the local artisans in the open-air stalls of the **Old City Market.**

▶ *Charleston is a city built for walking. But if you must drive, be sure to note the street signs at every corner— many of the town's 18th-century streets are narrow and one-way.*

side restaurant. Or drive to **Boone Hall Plantation,** three miles northeast of town. The sweeping avenue of oaks is said to be the inspiration for the one Hollywood depicted in the movie *Gone With the Wind;* you can tour the pecan groves and nine original slave houses. Drive on to **Sullivan's Island,** a summer retreat for Charlestonians. Many of the island's distinctive gingerbread cottages were built in the early 1900's.

2 PLANTATION COUNTRY

Drayton Hall, nine miles west of Charleston, was the only mansion along the west side of the Ashley River left unscathed by Union troops. Legend has it that the 1738 Georgian Palladian structure was rescued from sure annihilation when Dr. Drayton had the house posted as a smallpox hospital.

At **Magnolia Plantation and Gardens,** the camellias are so old and thick they've grown into trees. Built in the 1680's, one mile from Drayton Hall, the gardens include magnificent azaleas and hand-carved footbridges.

America's oldest formal gardens, laid out in 1741, are still grandly tended at **Middleton Place,** four miles north of Magnolia Plantation. Grassy terraces lead to the Ashley River. The plantation's surviving building is now a museum, displaying family furnishings.

3 BEAUFORT

Time seems to stand still in this classic Southern seaport, where gracious houses date from as long ago as 1717. Many movies—including *The Big Chill* and *Prince of Tides*—have utilized its picture-perfect small-town tableau. The 1712 **St. Helena's Episcopal Church** served as a hospital during the Civil War. Tombstones were pressed into service as operating tables.

4 HILTON HEAD ISLAND

A resort of world renown, this smartly developed island hosts celebrated tennis and golf tournaments and offers fine white-sand beaches. Visit the **Pinckney Island National Wildlife Refuge,**

Elegance reigns in Charleston on the Battery, where grand antebellum homes front an oak-filled park and Charleston Harbor. The lacy verandas admit welcome sea breezes during the hot summers.

gy from one of the several carriage companies in town. Start at the **Battery,** a formerly fortified seawall, where the verandas of pastel mansions look out onto a peacock-blue sea. **Fort Sumter,** the Federal stronghold where the first shots of the Civil War rang out, fronts the

The Charleston peninsula is ringed by sea islands with white-sand beaches and broad-leaved palmetto trees. Take the lofty 150-foot-high **Cooper River Bridge** to **Mount Pleasant,** where shrimp boats chug in and out of Shem Creek. Sample she-crab soup at a creek-

where you can hike through tropical foliage and swim. Or take a sightseeing boat to **Daufuskie Island,** where many of the old traditions of Gullah—a freed-slave culture with a unique language—have been preserved. In *The Water Is Wide,* Pat Conroy wrote of his life in 1969 as the lone teacher on the island.

5 ORANGEBURG

The region's fertile farmland and long growing season assure **Edisto Memorial Gardens** of flowering foliage much of the year. Alongside the black waters of the North Edisto River, the gardens spill over with azaleas, dogwoods, and camellias. As the official test garden of All-American Rose Selection, Inc., Edisto has more than 9,500 roses on view.

6 COLUMBIA

A reporter wrote of General Sherman's torching of this capital city in 1864: "There is not a rail upon any of the roads within twenty miles of Columbia

Golfer's paradise: Hilton Head Island features top-flight courses in palm-studded settings.

but will be twisted into corkscrews before the sun sets." The city was razed, but Sherman's esthetics ruled when he saw the **State House.** It survived and today is considered one of the country's most beautiful state capitols.

Nearby is the tree-lined campus of the **University of South Carolina.** Visit the **Mann-Simons Cottage–Museum of African-American Culture,** the

c.1850 home of a Charleston slave who purchased her freedom and walked 150 miles to Columbia. Just outside of town is the **Riverbanks Zoo,** one of the first zoos in the country to replace cages with open habitats.

7 SUMTER

This historic city was settled in 1740. Its **Swan Lake Iris Gardens** swell with Japanese iris. Black and white swans glide in lakes encircled with lilies. The **Sumter Opera House** is a European-style castle with a 100-foot clock tower.

8 MYRTLE BEACH

The wild and woolly Grand Strand, a 60-mile strip of white-sand beach and a popular family resort area, centers around **Myrtle Beach,** which overflows with amusement parks, golf courses, and fireworks stands. Four miles south of the old fishing village of Murrells Inlet is the first public sculpture garden in America. **Brookgreen Gardens** was laid out on the grounds of an 18th-century rice plantation and includes a live-oak allée. Southward, at the pretty, under-stated beach towns of **Litchfield Beach** and **Pawleys Island,** the crowds thin. Rock yourself to sleep in one of the famous Pawleys Island rope hammocks.

9 GEORGETOWN

This deepwater port city dates from 1526 and retains many prerevolutionary and antebellum structures. Several grand private estates are open to the public during the two-day **Plantations Tours** in spring. The restored **Hopsewee Plantation** (c.1740), 12 miles south, is open March through October.

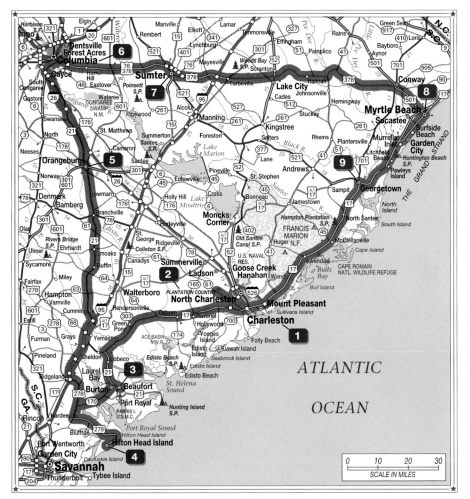

Georgia

From Atlanta to the romantic Sea Islands, the belle of the South is a mosaic of mirrored skyscrapers, white-sand beaches, pine-scented mountains, down-home food, and friendly folk.

ATLANTA & THE SOUTH

1 ATLANTA

Atlanta's Southern heart beats to a cosmopolitan pulse. A shining city built on the red-clay foothills of the Appalachians, Atlanta has come a long way since its tattered Reconstruction days, when Georgians named it state capital and the phoenix its symbol. Today the city offers a mix of sophistication and down-home tradition: on the one hand, you can shop and dine in the chic part of town, **Buckhead**, or take in the **Atlanta Opera**; on the other, you can cheer on the Braves and Falcons, raft the **Chattahoochee River**, or seek out the perfect barbecue shack.

For a taste of Old Atlanta, tour the 1840's **Tullie Smith House**, on the grounds of the Atlanta Historical Society. The simple wood-frame house is one of the few antebellum structures to survive General Sherman's fiery 1864 March to the Sea, in which the Union army cut a 300-mile trail of devastation through Georgia. On the same site, the society maintains the 1920's **Swan House**, a Palladian masterwork with a swirl of free-standing stairs. Tours of the **Fox Theater**, the last of the city's grand Depression-era theaters, are given three days a week by the Atlanta Preservation Center. The center offers seasonal tours of historic neighborhoods, including **Druid Hills**, whose gracious homes formed the backdrop for the movie *Driving Miss Daisy*. More movie lore can be traced to the Victorian **Oakland Cemetery**, where the author of *Gone With the Wind*, Margaret Mitchell, is buried. Downtown is the **Martin Luther King, Jr., Center**, where you'll see the civil rights leader's marble tomb with an eternal flame. Nearby, King's boyhood home is open for tours.

Set among woodland gardens, the Carter Presidential Center has a full-scale reproduction of the Oval Office.

Spend some time at the **High Museum**, with its collection of 19th-century American landscape paintings. At **The World of Coca-Cola**, track the evolution of Coke since an Atlanta druggist concocted the soft drink in 1886. Fill 'er up at a futuristic soda fountain, which sends a stream of cola 10 feet through the air neatly into a cup.

▶ *Driving through the maze of Atlanta streets can be tricky. Use a detailed city map, and remember that 32 streets are named some variation of Peachtree. Or simply opt for the fine bus and rapid rail (MARTA) system.*

Sixteen miles from downtown is the Mount Rushmore of the South, **Stone Mountain Park**, where three Confederate leaders on horseback—Lee, Davis, and Jackson—are etched on a granite mountainside. On summer nights a laser show illuminates the three so stirringly that they all but gallop off the mountain. The 3,200-acre park's steam trains pass an antebellum plantation.

2 MACON

In its time it was called the finest house in the South. The 1850's **Hay House** was outfitted with such cutting-edge technology as an intercom system, an elevator, and central heating. The elaborately adorned Italianate structure features stained-glass windows and trompe l'oeil marbleized walls.

3 ANDERSONVILLE

Roughly a third of the Federal prisoners at the Confederacy's largest military prison died here from lack of food and water. At the **Andersonville National Historic Site** you'll see two of the more than 60 escape tunnels within the compound. The tragedy is underlined by the relentless line of graves at the **National Cemetery**, where Clara Barton was aided by a prisoner named Dorence Atwater, who kept the list of names of the 13,000 Union casualties.

The opulent Fox, a Moorish-style 1920's theater in Atlanta, was originally built as a Shriners headquarters. Today the restored movie palace is host to Broadway musicals and concerts.

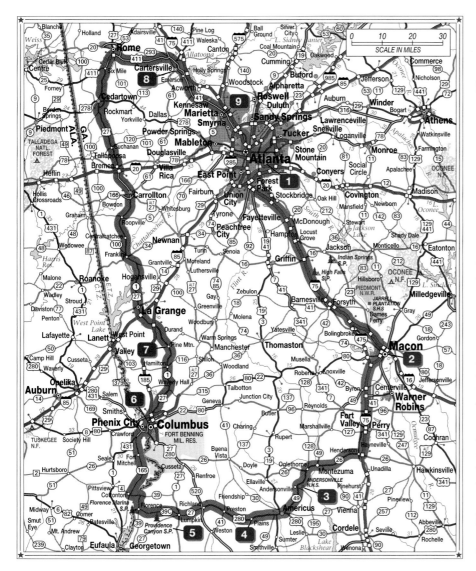

the treasures in nearby Fort Benning's **National Infantry Museum** is General Grant's traveling liquor chest.

7 PINE MOUNTAIN

In the 1930's industrialist Cason Callaway began revitalizing the region's spent, abandoned cotton fields. At **Callaway Gardens**, completed in 1952, the magnificent environs Callaway created compete only with the top-notch recreational options—from canoeing to golf to tennis. The **John A. Sibley Horticultural Center** is one of the finest greenhouses in the world, a place where footpaths trail beneath a 22-foot waterfall. In the **Cecil B. Day Butterfly Center,** nearly 1,000 species of butterflies flit around a crystal conservatory, often alighting on visitors' shoulders.

Franklin D. Roosevelt sought the therapeutic waters of **Warm Springs**, a mountain resort 20 miles east of Pine Mountain, to soothe his legs, crippled by polio years before. It was at the **Little White House** in 1945 that the 32nd president died while posing for a portrait. The unfinished painting, the partly burned logs in the fireplace, and his leather chair remain as he left them.

8 CARTERSVILLE

Coca-Cola's first wall sign was painted in 1894 on the side of the **Young Brothers Pharmacy** on Main Street. Four miles west on Rte. 113/61 is **Etowah Indian Mounds State Historic Site,** where an advanced tribe of Indians lived and farmed from about A.D. 1000 to 1500. A museum displays some 400 artifacts excavated from the site.

9 MARIETTA

The commandeering in 1862 of the Rebel locomotive *General* by James J. Andrews and his band of Union soldiers captured the country's imagination and inspired Buster Keaton's 1926 film *The General.* You can see the famous locomotive at **Big Shanty Museum,** housed in an authentic cotton-gin mill. Just North is the 3,000-acre **Kennesaw Mountain National Battlefield Park,** scene of a Civil War skirmish in 1864. The park has Confederate trenches and 16 miles of foot trails through woodlands and open meadows.

4 PLAINS

Jimmy Carter is a man steeped in his environment. In Plains, a small town set down in peanut country, everyone has a story to tell about the 39th president. The ambience is down-home at the **Jimmy Carter National Historic Site** visitor center, in an 1888 train depot, where even the on-site video, narrated by Jimmy and Rosalynn Carter themselves, has a home-movie quality.

▶ *Escorted van tours of Carter's boyhood haunts depart from 9:15 to 5:00 daily from Plain Peanuts, which distributes free peanut and peanut-brittle samples with the ride.*

5 PROVIDENCE CANYON

Some 170 years ago settlers cleared these steep wooded hillsides for farmland. Shallow ditches carved by water flowing unimpeded through plowed fields were transformed over time into 16 gaping "canyons"—deeply hued erosion gulleys where wildflowers now proliferate. The 1,100-acre **Providence Canyon State Conservation Park**— the Little Grand Canyon—is 150 feet deep and half a mile long in places. An interpretive center offers maps for the easy three-mile loop trail around the canyon rim.

6 COLUMBUS

Remnants of pre–Civil War ironworks, gristmills, and cotton warehouses make up Columbus's **National Historic Landmark Industrial District.** Cannons for the Southern cause were forged here. Visit the **Confederate Naval Museum,** where you'll see salvaged remains of the Confederate ironclads *Jackson* and *Chattahoochee.* Among

1 SAVANNAH

In 1733 an idealistic Colonial pioneer named James Oglethorpe envisioned a city built around 24 green squares. He created a plan so logical that, three centuries later, visitors marvel at its brilliance. Today these shaded squares form the foundations for one of the largest urban historic-landmark districts in the country.

This port city, on the Savannah River and minutes from the Atlantic, blossomed as a 19th-century center of cotton trade. The bustling waterfront row market, **Factor's Walk,** once hummed with the dealings of cotton brokers. It now shelters the **Riverfront Plaza,** with hotels, restaurants, and a maritime museum. From the waterfront, thoroughfares lead south to Oglethorpe's cool green squares, where historic homes drowse under dense live oaks and Spanish moss brushes the sidewalks.

Savannahians salvaged their handsome environs in large part by surrendering to General Sherman during his March to the Sea. "I beg to present to you as a Christmas gift," Sherman wrote to Lincoln in December 1864, "the City of Savannah." The town's post-Reconstruction blues were not lifted until 1955, when concerned citizens formed the Historic Savannah Foundation to oppose the imminent demolition of one of Savannah's oldest homes. Thus was the 1820 **Isaiah Davenport House** rescued—by a hairbreadth—from the wrecking ball. Today the Federal-style brick home, built up high to catch the breezes, welcomes thousands of visitors each year. The 1819 **Owens-Thomas House** is considered the finest example of English Regency architecture in America. The founder of the Girl Scouts was born in 1860 in the 1820 **Juliette Gordon Low Birthplace;** many of the Gordon family possessions are on display. Each of the houses can be toured year-round. Private homes are opened up to the public for the annual house tours in March.

A restoration award-winner, the 1896

King-Tiddell Cottage serves as a museum of African-American culture. The pretty Victorian house is neatly skirted by a latticed gingerbread porch. Van tours along the **Negro Heritage Trail** leave from here.

2 BRUNSWICK

Gateway to the semitropical barrier islands known as the **Golden Isles,** Brunswick is a shrimping port with a moss-drenched historic district. Among the sights is an oak tree that is said to have inspired the poet Sidney Lanier to write "The Marshes of Glynn." These same salt marshes, the heart of the region's ecosystem, wind lushly between Brunswick and the islands.

▶ Bridges from Brunswick to St. Simons Island, Jekyll Island, and Sea Island provide car access to the Golden Isles. Cumberland Island can be reached by passenger ferry from St. Marys.

On the land side, eight miles north of town, is the **Hofwyl-Broadfield Plantation,** where rice was farmed from 1807 to 1915. You can spend a day here, among scented magnolias and live oaks that shade nature trails and a camellia garden. The simple plantation house (c.1860) contains family heirlooms.

3 ST. SIMONS ISLAND

Traces of the African culture established when slaves found refuge on these white-sand shores endure on the Golden Isles, where the old plantation days saw an economy driven by rice, indigo, and Sea Island cotton crops. Today, on the largest of the Golden Isles, the economy revolves around tourism. But vestiges of the past linger. Sturdy live oaks ring the site of the English settlement, **Fort Frederica,** founded, like Savannah, by James Oglethorpe. The fort was a key bastion against the Spanish when the coast was disputed territory.

Croquet is but one of the many leisurely pursuits at the elegant Jekyll Island Club Hotel, formerly the Victorian clubhouse for the Gilded Age millionaires who owned the island.

On the road to Frederica is the **Old Christ Church**, an 1884 Gothic structure painted ivory and veiled in Spanish moss. The church was built on the site where the English clergymen John and Charles Wesley held services in 1736. Study the history of the island at the **Museum of Coastal History**, in the old lighthouse keeper's dwelling next to the 1872 **St. Simons Lighthouse**. St. Simons connects by causeway to **Sea Island**, northernmost of the isles and site of some of the region's ritziest resorts, including the historic **Cloisters**.

4 JEKYLL ISLAND

America's Gilded Age, in the late 19th century, saw nine-mile-long Jekyll Island become a favored playground for America's richest families. A select group—among them, the Morgans, Rockefellers, and Pulitzers—bought the island in 1886 and built grand "cottages" clustered around the **Jekyll Island Club**. The state bought the island in 1947, and the millionaires' Victorian clubhouse is now a resort hotel, complete with croquet lawn. Three of the old mansions can be viewed on guided tram tours through the **Jekyll Island Club Historic District**. Tours leave hourly from the orientation center.

5 ST. MARYS

This fishing port is known for its locally harvested rock shrimp, a sweet-tasting crustacean encased in a hard shell. At the **Orange Hall Welcome Center**, a mansion completed in 1833, you'll find pamphlets detailing the 38 sites of the St. Marys historic district. Armadillos began migrating to the area from Florida 50 years ago and thrive in nearby

Crooked River State Park, where hiking paths trail past a salt marsh. Picnic beside Crooked River or dip a shrimp net into the waters off the dock.

6 CUMBERLAND ISLAND

Pristine Atlantic beaches. Ghostly ruins of mansions in forests of live oak. Far-off lightning storms that shimmer like fireworks in the night sky. These are but a few of the treasures of **Cumberland Island National Seashore**, one of the last of America's unspoiled barrier islands. The National Park Service provides tour guides and hiking maps. The island serenity is ensured by the strict limits on the number of people visiting each day—300. Other than campsites, the island's only lodging is the nine-guestroom **Greyfield Inn**, a plantation-style house built in 1901.

▶ *Mosquito and tick repellent is a must in the summer. Park rangers recommend that hikers spray boots and socks, tuck long pants under socks, and secure with a rubber band.*

7 WAYCROSS

Waycross is best known as the portal to the swamplands with the tongue-tickling Seminole name: **Okefenokee**, or "land of the trembling earth." The home of the comic-strip possum, Pogo, this national wildlife refuge covers 500,000 Georgia acres. Underlaid by a vast peat bog, Okefenokee is rich with herons and gangly bald cypresses. A convenient entrance is eight miles south of town at **Okefenokee Swamp Park**. Here you can stroll a boardwalk deep into the swamp to a 90-foot observation tower or take a 20-minute guided motorboat tour.

8 JESUP

Jesup is known for the mighty tower clock in its 1903 red-brick courthouse and numerous handsome century-old homes. Sportsmen know it for another reason: proximity to the excellent freshwater fishing in the vast watershed of the **Altamaha River**, with almost 40 miles of frontage in Wayne County and five public landings.

Swamp flora: Golden club, an aquatic plant whose yellow spikes are covered with tiny flowers, thrives in the lush habitat of the Okefenokee Swamp Park, near Waycross.

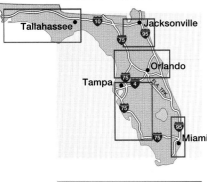

Florida

Beautiful beaches, leisurely boat rides, ornate mansions, glimpses of pelicans, parrots, and palms—there's much to see in this state, from exotic Miami to the friendly Florida Panhandle.

1 MIAMI

A lively multinational metropolis with a tropical flavor, Miami is famous for its lush parks and exotic gardens, impressive architecture, spirited nightlife, and international cuisine.

To delve into the city's past, drive through the shady streets of Coconut Grove to the **Vizcaya Museum and Gardens**. Ten acres of elegant formal gardens and splashing fountains spread from this Italian Renaissance–style villa overlooking Biscayne Bay. Inside, dazzling European works of art decorate 34 of the mansion's 70 rooms.

Vizcaya is at its most romantic when seen on the moonlight tours, held on nights of the full moon in October and November and from January to April. Make reservations well in advance.

At the nearby **Museum of Science and Space Transit Planetarium**, more than 150 hands-on exhibits, rare natural history specimens, live demonstrations, and multimedia laser shows give you an intriguing look at the past and the future. Fix your eyes on the stars at the observatory and stroll through a Florida aviary at the wildlife center.

▶ *Miami addresses are not hard to find. From downtown, the city is divided into quadrants—northeast, northwest, southeast, and southwest—and most addresses include quadrant letters.*

2 CORAL GABLES

Lush vegetation, plazas, and fountains adorn this Mediterranean-style Miami neighborhood dating from the 1920's. Tiled roofs top Spanish-style homes of "coral rock." The quarry that supplied this native limestone was transformed into the country's most distinctive pub-lic swimming spot, the **Venetian Pool**, adorned with vines, flowers, palms, waterfalls, loggias, towers, and a bridge.

More rarefied flora blooms at the **Fairchild Tropical Garden**, the largest tropical botanical garden in the conti-

A walk on Ocean Drive in Miami Beach makes visitors feel they've entered a 1930's movie.

nental United States. You can walk the 1½-mile path or take a tram tour to such highlights as the Rare Plant House, a rain forest, and a sunken garden.

The **Miami Metrozoo** sprawls over 290 tropical acres without a cage in sight. Moats keep the animals in environments designed to duplicate their natural habitats. There are more than 240 species here, including rare white Bengal tigers. A comfortable—and free—air-conditioned monorail gives you a bird's-eye view of the zoo.

3 BISCAYNE NATIONAL PARK

A haven for marine life, this relatively undiscovered park lies 96 percent underwater. Venture into its sunken realm for excellent boating, fishing, snorkeling, scuba diving, and birding.

In the warm waters of Biscayne Bay, lobsters, manatees, and sea turtles swim. A glass-bottom boat will ferry you to the living coral reefs 14 miles offshore, where rainbow-hued tropical fish meander among the brain coral and undulating sea fans in exceptionally clear waters. You might see green eels, angelfish, electric-blue parrot fish, even porpoises. Bald eagles, herons, and egrets fly overhead, and forests of mangroves dot the mainland.

4 EVERGLADES NATIONAL PARK

The largest subtropical wilderness in the United States, the Everglades is renowned for the extraordinary wildlife and flora of its delicate ecosystems. More than a million acres of grasslands and shallow waters are punctuated by tree-covered islands, inhabited by some 400 species of land and water birds.

Turn off the park's main road into the **Royal Palm Visitor Center** and follow the paved path and boardwalk of the **Anhinga Trail**—one of five major nature trails—into a world of vivid birds, darting fish, and ponderous alligators. Continue on the main road to **Flamingo,** at the southern tip of the park, where you'll find fishing, boat tours, canoe rentals, canoe trails, a tram ride, and lodging. At **Shark Valley,** near the park's northern entrance on Rte. 41, a two-hour tram ride carries you to an observation tower for sweeping views of the "river of grass," only inches deep.

▶ *Visit in winter or early spring for good weather, fewer mosquitoes, and the best chance to see wildlife. Bring insect repellent no matter what the season, and reserve lodging well in advance.*

5 PALM BEACH

An enclave of elegance and wealth since the turn of the century, Palm Beach still glitters. Approaching the town on **Ocean Boulevard,** you'll see some of the country's most opulent mansions, each gazing out to sea.

Step into the Gilded Age at the **Henry Morrison Flagler Museum,** built in 1901 by oil and railroad magnate Henry Flagler. Superbly refurbished, the lavish marble palace has period rooms with original furnishings, paintings, silver, porcelain, costumes, and for amusement, a 1,200-pipe organ. Other exhibits illustrate local history, such as the construction of the railway that put Florida on the map. Outside, climb aboard Flagler's railroad coach, fully restored down to the original carpet pattern and a copper-lined shower.

On **Worth Avenue** you'll find some of the world's finest—and most expensive—baubles, clothes, art, and antiques. Well-known international names embellish many of the 250 shops —but there's no charge for browsing. A bubbling fountain provides the centerpiece for the **Esplanade,** a two-tiered cluster of shops surrounding a tiled courtyard brimming with flowers.

6 DELRAY BEACH

Within the serene oasis of a 150-acre pine forest preserve is **Morikami Museum and Japanese Gardens,** where colorful koi fish splash through the water as you feed them. Enter the museum, built in Japanese style with a meditation garden in the center, to explore exhibits

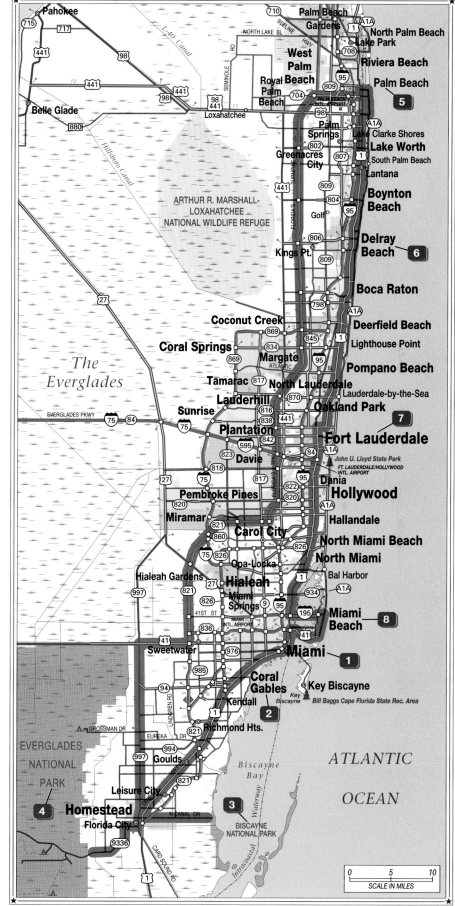

on the tea ceremony, Japanese baths, and the art of origami. You'll also see pottery, toys, furniture, musical instruments, and a forest of bonsai trees.

7 FORT LAUDERDALE

Known as the Venice of America, this city has a labyrinth of waterways that wind through hundreds of miles. Flotillas of yachts bob in marinas or linger in front of palatial waterfront homes.

Even the creatures of the deep are on view. At **Ocean World** dolphins and sea lions cavort in daily shows. Sea turtles and sharks slide through huge tanks, and you can feed the dolphins.

For a tranquil interlude in the city, tour the historic **Bonnet House**. Here you can ramble through orchid-filled grounds, listen to the parrots, and watch swans gliding on a pond. Completing the menagerie is a whimsical collection of carved wooden animals.

Also not to be missed is the city's **Museum of Art**, home to an impressive collection of American Indian, Oceanic, West African, and pre-Columbian art.

▶ *The best way to feel the nautical spirit of Fort Lauderdale is to hail an inexpensive water taxi to cruise to shops, cafés, and other attractions. Flag one down at virtually any dock or seawall.*

8 MIAMI BEACH

Tons of sand have been carted in to expand the beautiful 10-mile-long beachfront as once-quiet **South Beach** buzzes with new activity: artists, writers, and fashion photographers have made it their neighborhood of choice. As a result, more than 1,000 candy-colored architectural treasures in the **Art Deco District**—including the small hotels that front Ocean Drive—have come to life as never before, with international restaurants, sidewalk cafés, nightclubs, and innovative boutiques and galleries. Complete with etched glass and neon, the buildings date from the 1920's through the 1950's, and now form America's largest national historic-preservation district.

▶ *Architectural tours of the Art Deco District are held on weekends by the Miami Design Preservation League.*

1 TAMPA

A booming business center in the heart of Florida's "sun coast," Tampa is home to **Busch Gardens**, counterpart to the Busch Gardens in Virginia, and the most popular attraction in the state after Disney World. This family theme park with a turn-of-the-century African twist fits Timbuktu, the Congo, and the Serengeti Plain onto 300 acres.

▶ *Most people bear right when they enter the park. To avoid the crowds, get there early and visit the attractions in reverse order.*

On an open-air skyride, you soar above free-roaming lions, giraffes, rhinos, elephants, and zebras. You can also watch African craftsmen at work, see snake charmers in a sultan's tent, and wander among exotic birds in a free-flight aviary. Heart-pounding adventure rides satisfy thrill-seekers.

Back on this continent, the **Tampa Museum of Art** exhibits works highlighted by classical Greek and Roman sculpture and artifacts. Near the museum, stroll on cobblestone streets past colorfully tiled storefronts in Tampa's Latin quarter, **Ybor City**, where Cuban artisans still hand-roll cigars the way their grandparents did.

At the **Museum of Science and Industry (MOSI),** you'll find a butterfly garden, fossil gallery, ham radio station, and Challenger Center featuring simulated spaceflights.

2 WINTER HAVEN

Situated in the midst of some of Florida's finest citrus groves, Winter Haven is best known as the site of **Cypress**

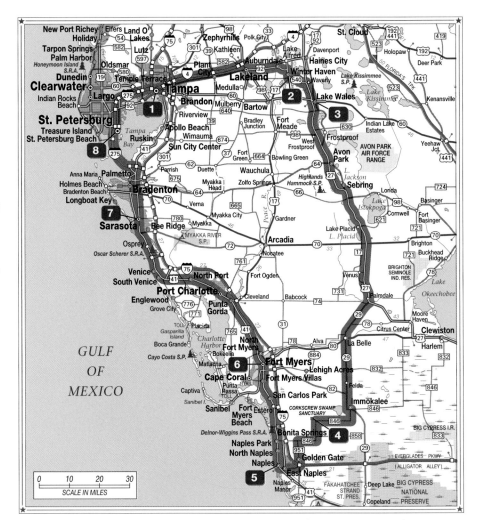

High-flying water-ski shows at Cypress Gardens dazzle visitors with dramatic stunts.

Gardens. Here lush formal subtropical gardens featuring more than 8,000 varieties of plants from 75 countries stretch over 233 acres. The flora competes with lovely Southern belle hostesses sporting enormous pastel hoopskirts. For a splendid overview, head for the mushroom-shaped Island in the Sky, a revolving platform affording views from 16 stories above the park.

There's plenty more to see at Cypress Gardens beyond the gardens themselves. You can listen to vintage recordings at the radio museum, where scores of antique sets and memorabilia recall the early wireless era. A minutely detailed model railroad exhibit is among the country's most elaborate. Aerial acts, water-ski shows, the Feathered Follies bird show, and the colorful butterfly conservatory may also strike your fancy. Conclude your visit with a quiet boat ride beneath shady stands of ancient cypress trees.

3 LAKE WALES

Bok Tower Gardens draws visitors here with leafy, shaded paths that meander through 128 acres planted with enormous live oaks, magnolias, azaleas, and Oriental species. Rising above this serene sanctuary, a carillon atop a stately 200-foot tower built of coquina rings out at regular intervals. Swans glide silently over the surface of a slender pool that reflects the tower's image.

4 CORKSCREW SWAMP SANCTUARY

Escape to the swampy wilderness that reigned in Florida before the waves of development hit by exploring the 11,000 unspoiled acres of this National Audubon Society preserve. Look high in the branches of 500-year-old bald cypress trees and you may sight nesting wood storks. Closer to water level you'll find a variety of ferns, orchids, wading birds, and alligators.

▶ *To discover more than meets the eye, be sure to bring binoculars to this and other wilderness areas.*

5 NAPLES

Once a quiet fishing village, Naples has transformed itself into a sophisticated city, lush with tropical vegetation and abounding in superb public beaches, elegant shops, and fine restaurants.

Some 2,000 furry playthings from around the world inhabit the **Teddy Bear Museum.** Whimsical displays include bears attending business meetings, taking tea, and riding in hot-air balloons. Real wildlife can be found at **Jungle Larry's Zoological Park and Caribbean Gardens.** A tram leads through the 52-acre jungle teeming with exotic creatures. Kids love the Wild Animal Show, Tropical Bird Circus, and elephant rides.

6 FORT MEYERS

The main residential street of Fort Meyers, dubbed the City of Palms, is lined with royal palms, many planted by Thomas Edison, who built a winter estate here. At **Thomas A. Edison's Winter Home** you'll find the inventor's laboratory, beautiful botanical gardens,

and a museum of Edison's inventions. Also on the grounds is the **Henry Ford Winter Home,** known as Mangoes, the winter retreat of Edison's longtime friend. The home is decorated and furnished in 1920's style.

For shell seekers, the tides washing **Sanibel and Captiva islands,** connected to the mainland by a mile-long causeway, carry a glistening gold mine. On Sanibel Island, the **J. N. "Ding" Darling National Wildlife Refuge** is a favorite among bird lovers, hosting 290 avian species. You can wend your way through the tranquil retreat by car, bike, foot, or boat to catch glimpses of blue herons, black anhingas, roseate spoonbills, and brown pelicans.

7 SARASOTA

Sarasota, with more than its share of performing arts centers and theaters and even its own opera company, is considered the cultural center of Florida. It is also known as Circus City. Endless days of sunshine lured circus king John Ringling and his troupe here for the winters. Today his prized collections of Baroque and decorative arts are displayed at the **John and Mable Ringling Museum of Art,** part of the **Ringling Museum Complex.** Bristling with

At Corkscrew Swamp Sanctuary, the anhinga (above) spreads its wings to help its feathers dry. The swamp-loving alligator (left) is often confused with its far more aggressive cousin, the crocodile.

columns and towers, his ornate mansion, **Ca' d'Zan** (House of John), is modeled after a Venetian palace. Brightly painted wagons, glittering costumes, posters, and other circus memorabilia evoke the excitement of the ring at the **Circus Galleries.**

8 ST. PETERSBURG

Surrounded by 28 miles of sandy beaches, St. Petersburg is one of the top vacation spots on Florida's west coast. Its focal point is **The Pier,** an inverted pyramid that extends a quarter of a mile into Tampa Bay and houses shops, restaurants, and an observation deck offering views of the bay and the city.

Step into the surreal world of melting watches and other bizarre imagery at the **Salvador Dali Museum,** where more than 1,000 works testify to the vivid and eerie vision of the Spanish artist. Equally thought-provoking are the hands-on displays at **Great Explorations!,** where kids of all ages can make neon tubes glow in wild colors, crawl though an endless pitch-black Touch Tunnel, and ponder brain-tickling puzzles and games.

ORLANDO & CENTRAL

1 ORLANDO

Counted among the most popular tourist destinations in the world, Orlando lies at the hub of central Florida's lake country. One of the area's biggest attractions after Walt Disney World is **Sea World,** a sprawling marine life park that entertains while it educates. As the star of the show, enormous Shamu, the killer whale, defies his size by soaring through the air, spinning, twisting, twirling, and splashing.

▶ *In peak season, arrive as much as 45 minutes early for the Shamu show to get a seat. You can watch the whales swim while you wait.*

Throughout the park, multimedia presentations and interactive displays draw you into the lives of the denizens of wa-

Goofy, Mickey, and Pluto *welcome visitors to Walt Disney World's Fantasyland, "the happiest land of all," home of the storybook Cinderella Castle. At It's a Small World, boats float past tuneful tots from many nations, first seen at the 1964–65 World's Fair. For more grown-up thrills, head to Frontierland or Adventureland. For a break, visit the air-conditioned Main Street Cinema, where classic Disney cartoons play continuously.*

tery worlds, including endangered manatees, ferocious sharks, writhing eels, acrobatic dolphins, sleepy sea lions, and stealthy stingrays. Don't miss the Penguin Encounter, where you can watch the curious birds swim and frolic through a glass tank. Aboard the Bermuda Triangle ride, visitors go on a simulated deep-sea dive and get jolted by an underwater earthquake.

Universal Studios Florida puts you in pictures with rides and attractions featuring mind-boggling special effects. You can take an action-packed ride "back to the future" and bicycle across the sky with E.T. You'll also go behind the scenes of this working movie and television studio for the inside scoop on how cartoons, monster makeup, audio recording, television taping, and filmmaking are done. You can even edit an episode of *Murder, She Wrote.*

In a city of replicas and re-creations, **Church Street Station** is housed in the real thing. This entertainment, shopping, and dining complex fills a downtown block of turn-of-the-century edifices—including a vintage train depot—with 20 live shows nightly. The interiors are richly appointed, their themes ranging from European to aviation to Western. When you're in need of a quiet, natural retreat, take in the

Leu Botanical Gardens, where old roses, camellias, and orchids bloom beneath shady oaks circling a lake.

At the **Charles Hosmer Morse Museum of American Art** in nearby Winter Park, you enter a glowing realm of jewellike stained-glass windows, blown glass, and Tiffany lamps. Jewelry, pottery, and paintings from the 19th and 20th centuries round out the collection.

2 WALT DISNEY WORLD

Undoubtedly the world's best-known amusement phenomenon, Walt Disney World is a self-contained land of enchantment, offering sprawling theme parks, resorts, and campgrounds.

Live performances, animated figures, parades, and fireworks enliven the **Magic Kingdom,** home of the Cinderella Castle in Fantasyland, one of seven theme areas. Roaring through Frontierland, the Big Thunder Mountain Railroad takes you on a heart-stopping roller-coaster ride. At Liberty Square, the Haunted Mansion is home to waltzing holograms, flying objects, and talking portraits. Tomorrowland's Space Mountain ride rushes you through 180-foot drops and devious spins.

Epcot honors Disney's vision of an Experimental Prototype Community of Tomorrow. The park is divided into

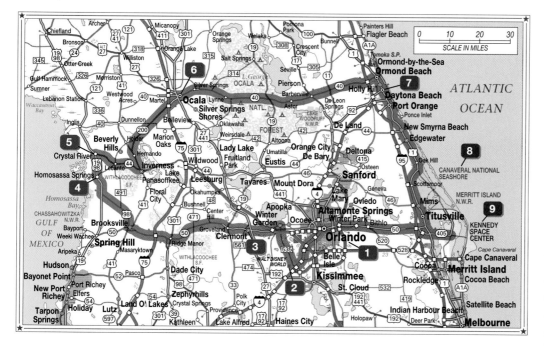

lands and woodlands and to live snake and alligator exhibits. Enjoy a quiet picnic in the landscaped Garden of the Springs, where a pavilion overlooks the Homosassa River.

5 CRYSTAL RIVER

American Indian temple and burial grounds dating as far back as 200 B.C. have been unearthed at the **Crystal River State Archeological Site.** Pottery, arrowheads, and relics indicating an advanced astronomical calendar are on display. Climb one of the earthen mounds for pretty river views.

In and around the **Crystal River National Wildlife Refuge,** accessible only by water, manatees gather in winter. Visitors can watch and even swim with the curious sea cows. Stop by the chamber of commerce for a list of dive shops offering boat tours and rentals.

6 OCALA

The scent of pine pervades much of **Ocala National Forest,** where springs, lakes, rivers, and hiking trails among cypress and hardwood trees lure nature lovers. In Ocala, the marble and granite **Appleton Museum of Art** houses a collection of more than 6,000 pieces of pre-Columbian, Oriental, African, and 19th-century decorative and fine arts.

The village of **Silver Springs** boasts what is very likely the largest limestone artesian spring in the world. The clear waters and abundant wildlife here inspired the invention of the glass-bottom boat. Board one to view the underwater wonders of the spring, or take a jungle cruise to spot giraffes, llamas, and ostrich. It's no wonder Tarzan movies and the television series *Sea Hunt* were filmed here.

7 DAYTONA BEACH

You can walk for miles along the shoreline here—but you can also drive your car along 18 miles of Daytona's 23-mile stretch of hard-packed sand. Speed records were set on this strip as early as

two sections. Future World showcases science and the imagination with attractions like the Spaceship Earth ride, scripted by science fiction writer Ray Bradbury. The flight simulator–style Body Wars takes you on an exciting voyage through the human bloodstream, while Cranium Command looks inside the mind of a typical 12-year-old boy. The imposing Living Seas offers a ride around a 5.6-million-gallon tank with up-close views of some 4,000 salt-water creatures.

Surrounding a 40-acre lagoon is the other half of Epcot, World Showcase. Here you can step into a re-created corner of 11 nations, including Japan, France, Morocco, China, and Norway. Architecture, exhibitions, food, and shops showcase each culture while native musicians, dancers, and actors add to the authentic ambience.

▶ *Most people tour Future World first. To beat the crowds, go early and start with World Showcase. If you plan to have dinner at one of the restaurants in World Showcase, go to Earth Station in the morning to make reservations.*

Take a backstage tram tour at **Disney-MGM Studios Theme Park** through actual television, film, and animation production studios. Or get into films yourself on The Great Movie Ride, which puts you in the middle of some

of Hollywood's most famous scenes. Other showstoppers are the Indiana Jones Epic Stunt Spectacular and *Jim Henson's Muppet Vision 3D Movie.*

3 CLERMONT

For a panoramic view of miles of citrus groves and surrounding lakes, visit the 226-foot **Florida Citrus Tower.** A tram tour takes visitors for a closer look. In Clermont you can also tour something you may not expect to find in Florida—a winery. Founded in 1989, the **Lakeridge Winery and Vineyards** offers free tours and tastings.

4 HOMOSASSA SPRINGS

In an underwater glass observatory, you stand at eye level with scores of fresh- and salt-water fish and other marine life that inhabit the Spring of 10,000 Fish at **Homosassa Springs State Wildlife Park.** Winding trails lead through wet-

Manatees *thrive in the warm, clear waters of the spring-fed Crystal River.*

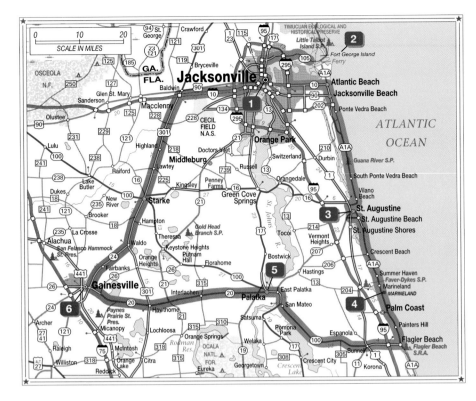

1902, and racing continues at full tilt today at the **Daytona International Speedway.** A van tour offers a close-up look at the World Center of Racing.

▶ *To avoid the spring break crowds, don't visit in mid- to late March.*

Second-highest in the country, the 1887 **Ponce de Leon Lighthouse** is open to the public, offering sweeping views of the beach and the sparkling waters of the Atlantic. Get another perspective aboard the *Dixie Queen* **Riverboat,** which cruises the Halifax River.

8 CANAVERAL NATIONAL SEASHORE

The last stretch of undeveloped beach in eastern Florida, this refuge of natural shoreline, dunes, and shallow lagoons was preserved by Congress in 1975. Within its wilds you might spy any of 300 species of birds and animals, including brown pelicans, turtles, manatees, and, of course, gators. The area was not always uninhabited, however. **Turtle Mound,** a 31-foot-high stack of oyster shells, was left by the Surreque Indians perhaps as long ago as A.D. 600. From May to August at **Playalinda Beach,** giant sea turtles gather by the hundreds to lay their eggs.

9 KENNEDY SPACE CENTER

The first man to walk on the moon blasted off here in 1969. Begin your tour of the **John F. Kennedy Space Center** at the visitor center complex called **Spaceport USA.** You'll feel as if you're floating in space at **Galaxy Center,** where films containing footage taken by astronauts in space are projected onto a 5½-story screen. Stroll through the **Rocket Garden,** with rockets from each stage of the space program.

Two separate bus tours carry you to sites otherwise off-limits, including the 52-story Vehicle Assembly Building, a lunar module, the space shuttle launch pad, the original site of Mission Control, and the Air Force Space Museum.

JACKSONVILLE & THE NORTHEAST

1 JACKSONVILLE

In terms of area, Jacksonville is the largest city in the continental U.S., centered on a sparkling blue waterfront and surrounded by wilderness. Stroll the 1.2-mile **Riverwalk** boardwalk, on the south bank of the St. Johns River, as it winds its way through town. It is bordered by restaurants, shops, hotels, and the Friendship Fountain, a flowing spectacle of stunning proportions.

Nestled among formal gardens replete with reflecting pools, azaleas, and Italianate statuary, the **Cummer Gallery of Art** offers an outstanding selection of American 18th- and 19th-century paintings, including works by Thomas Eakins, Gilbert Stuart, and Winslow Homer. A gleaming collection of Meissen porcelain is among the largest in the world, and delicate Japanese netsuke carvings of ivory, wood, and jade will delight lovers of Asian crafts.

For wilderness, wildlife, and history, head out to the replicated **Fort Caroline National Memorial,** where a French settlement lasted briefly in the 16th century. The adjoining 600 acres make up the maritime woodlands and marshes of the **Theodore Roosevelt Area.** As you hike the two-mile trail, keep an eye out for pelicans, wood storks, and wildflowers.

2 FORT GEORGE ISLAND

Bought by slave trader Zephaniah Kingsley, the circa 1800 **Kingsley Plantation State Historic Site** is thought to be the oldest existing plantation in Florida. On the grounds of the modest riverfront house where Kingsley and his West African wife lived are the remains of several slave cabins and exhibits detailing the era.

3 ST. AUGUSTINE

Founded half a century before the Pilgrims came ashore at Plymouth Rock, St. Augustine is the oldest permanently settled city in the United States. Ponce de Leon landed here in 1513 in his misguided quest for the Fountain of Youth.

The 14-foot-thick walls of **Castillo de San Marcos National Monument,** erected to protect Spanish settlers from the British, stand watch over Matanzas Bay. You enter this 17th-century fortress by crossing a double drawbridge spanning a 17-foot-wide moat. Around the courtyard, garrison rooms are furnished in period style or as museums of military history. Climb the stairway to ramparts overlooking the bay, the Old City Gate, and the charming Colonial section of town.

► *Train and trolley tours circle the historic city, stopping at all the major attractions. Purchase a discounted three-day pass at the visitor information center.*

On a site occupied since the early 1600's stands the **Oldest House.** The coquina-shell walls and hand-hewn cedar beams of the present structure, also called the González-Álvarez House, date from the early 18th century. Inside are furnishings from several periods, including a Spanish brazier that was used not only for cooking but also to smoke mosquitoes out of the house. Outdoors, ornamental gardens reflect plants grown by American Indian, Spanish, and British owners.

You stroll into a Victorian village on the first floor of the **Lightner Museum,** housed in the former Alcazar Hotel,

At the Lightner Museum, *Victorian treasures, such as this mid-19th-century English clock, fill the former Alcazar Hotel, a Spanish Renaissance –style gem from America's Gilded Age. Of note is the collection of American Brilliant Period cut glass.*

built in 1888 by Henry Flagler, the railroad magnate whose vision was to develop Florida into an American Riviera. Three floors overflow with massive furniture, Oriental art, European porcelain, natural history specimens, and Art Nouveau. A Victorian science and industry room displays a dinosaur egg, an Egyptian mummy, and a stuffed lion that belonged to Winston Churchill. To delight your ears, a display of mechanical musical instruments includes an

1874 German orchestrion that mimics an entire orchestra, and an automated violin. An antiques mall occupies what was once the hotel's indoor pool.

Near the center of town on St. George Street sits a re-created Colonial village evocative of mid-18th-century times. This is St. Augustine's **Restored Spanish Quarter,** where people in period costume demonstrate period skills, including the fine arts of lace-making and cabinetmaking.

Nearby is the **Oldest Store Museum,** a refurbished general store that operated from 1835 until 1960. Of the 100,000 items on display, most hark back to the 19th century. You'll find high-button shoes, butter churns, and red flannel underwear. There are "new-fangled" gadgets, too: Victrolas, sewing machines, and a 1927 Model T Ford.

4 MARINELAND

Created in 1938, this oceanfront park was Florida's first marine life attraction. Here dolphins delight audiences with their aquatic feats in an amphitheater overlooking the Atlantic, while sea lions dive, bark, and glide. In a 450,000-gallon oceanarium swim 125 species of sea life, including giant turtles and stingrays. Watch through portholes as divers feed sharks by hand. The bubbling 35,000-gallon Wonders of the

Spring teems with largemouth bass, crappie, and sunfish. A shell museum offers some 6,000 specimens.

5 PALATKA

Nature trails and walkways thread through 85 acres of azaleas that bloom in February and March at **Ravine State Gardens.** Palms, jasmine, mimosa, and banana trees sprout above thick mosses and leafy ferns. Dip into one of three ravines for a cool refuge or a picnic embellished with butterflies and birdsong.

6 GAINESVILLE

The cobblestone plazas of this college town are sprinkled with sidewalk cafés where you can soak up sun and slip into the leisurely pace of the region. On the campus of the University of Florida, the **Florida Museum of Natural History** offers an excellent collection of rare seashells and an aviary of mounted birds. You can explore a reproduction of a north Florida cave, marvel at the majesty of frescoes inside the likeness of a Mayan temple, and examine a recreation of a Timucuan household.

An unusual collection is exhibited at the **Fred Bear Museum,** assembled by Mr. Bear from his bow-hunting exploits around the globe. Tracing the history of archery back to the Stone Age, the displays encompass American Indian, Eskimo, and African implements, crafts, tools, and weapons. Stuffed game, including a Kodiak bear, a moose, and a buffalo, loom silently above.

For a look at natural history in progress, venture down into one of Florida's famous sinkholes at **Devil's Millhopper State Geological Site.** Spanning five acres and descending to a depth of 120 feet, the sinkhole was formed about 10,000 years ago, when an underground cavern collapsed. Fossilized sharks' teeth and other paleontological finds confirmed that the state was once covered by the ocean. Walking trails wend past aromatic pines and giant ferns to a scenic waterfall.

Gardens of every variety abound at **Kanapaha Botanical Gardens.** Wildflower, rock, bamboo, and butterfly gardens spread throughout 62 acres bristling with vines and palm trees and alive with hummingbirds.

1 TALLAHASSEE

With rolling green hills and enormous oaks draped in Spanish moss, the state capital belongs more to the Deep South than to the subtropical zones of the rest of Florida. To discover its charms, drive one of five **Canopy Roads**, narrow lanes lined with ancient arbors and antebellum plantation homes.

▶ *For maps and information on the Canopy Roads, go to the visitor information center in the New Capitol.*

Begun in 1923 by a New York financier, the magnificent **Maclay State Gardens** surround a restored mansion that served as his winter retreat. Like a 300-acre living quilt, the property is adorned with more than 200 varieties of flowers; 28 acres are devoted to camellias and azaleas. Quiet nature trails wind past lakes, woodlands, and reflecting pools where you can swim, boat, picnic, and fish.

For a panoramic vista stretching to the Gulf of Mexico, ascend to the observatory of the **New Capitol.** Dating from 1845, the strikingly restored **Old Capitol** is known for its fine dome, white columns, turn-of-the-century furnishings, and bright red and white awnings.

Bordering one of the top bass-fishing spots in the country, the **Lake Jackson Mounds State Archeological Site** is an 18-acre excavation of an American Indian ceremonial complex that flourished about A.D. 1200. Six earthen temple mounds and one burial mound remain. To see ongoing excavations, visit the **San Luis Archaeological and Historic Site,** where guided tours take you through a former 17th-century Spanish mission and Apalachee Indian townsite.

2 ST. MARKS NATIONAL WILDLIFE REFUGE

Salt marshes, cypress swamps, hardwood forests, and magnolia groves here harbor a wide variety of wildlife, from black bears to whitetail deer to wild turkeys. You can picnic, fish, or observe some 250 species of birds, including

Giant cypress trees *soar in the wetlands of Apalachicola National Forest. A swollen base, or buttress, helps anchor the tree in the soft, wet soil. The forest has the largest population of red-cockaded woodpeckers in the world. Look for them in live pine trees.*

nesting bald eagles during the winter months. The **St. Marks Lighthouse,** built in 1831 with stone from an old fort, is still operating today.

3 APALACHICOLA

The elegant Southern homes and colorful fleet of this fishing and oystering village are postcard-perfect. Honoring the physician who devised an early form of air conditioning, the **John Gorrie State Museum** displays a replica of his early-19th-century invention, along with other local history exhibits. Some feel the cooling contraption is what made the development of Florida possible. For natural cooling, seek shade under a pine or hardwood tree in **Apalachicola National Forest,** where rivers and springs offer fishing, swimming, and wildlife watching.

4 GRAYTON BEACH STATE RECREATION AREA

Long stretches of white sand within this 400-acre park make up one of the most beautiful and unspoiled beaches in the continental U.S. Beyond the aquamarine waters you'll discover tall dunes, pine forests, and a picturesque lake. Walk the mile-long nature trail for up-close views. Swimming, fishing, picnicking, and camping are available.

5 DESTIN

Once a sleepy fishing village, Destin is now a resort town that draws anglers who fish for record-breaking red snapper, blue marlin, and other catches.

▶ *Visit in October to catch the Destin Deep-sea Fishing Rodeo, a month-long fishing tournament.*

To explore the ocean's floor without getting wet, wade into the dry aquarium at the **Destin Fishing Museum.** Lighting and sound effects give you the feeling of being underwater as you explore a sandy bottom covered with sea fans, turtles, sponges, and coral.

Crowd pleasers at the **Museum of the Sea and Indian** include mounted sharks and alligators, a stuffed killer whale, and a preserved mola. Tomahawks, beadwork clothing, and a dugout canoe are among the vast assortment of American Indian artifacts.

6 FORT WALTON BEACH

Fort Walton Beach and neighboring Destin, with their ivory-colored sands and jewel-toned waters, are part of a region aptly called the Emerald Coast.

The **Indian Temple Mound Museum,** with more than 6,000 pieces, has the world's largest collection of prehistoric southeastern American Indian ceramics. Weapons and funerary masks are also part of exhibits tracing the life of four tribes back 10,000 years. The adjacent 600-year-old mound is one of the largest ever discovered.

You'll see some 5,000 examples of more recent military equipment from World War I to the present at the **Air Force Armament Museum,** adjacent to Eglin Air Force Base, the largest in the Western Hemisphere. Rockets, bombs,

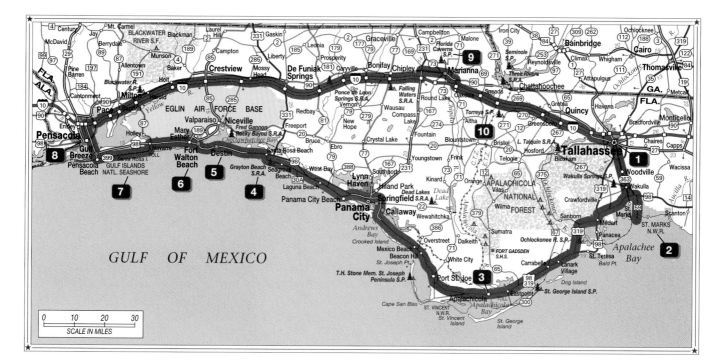

engines, and aircraft are displayed here, including an SR-71 Blackbird spy plane and a Russian MiG-21.

7 GULF ISLANDS NATIONAL SEASHORE

Stretching 150 miles from Destin to Gulfport, Mississippi, this 135,000-acre preserve encompasses some of the world's most pristine beaches. Its coastal shores and barrier islands are a haven for hundreds of species of birds and a sandy retreat for swimming, boating, fishing, scuba diving, and camping.

8 PENSACOLA

Reflecting its Spanish, British, and French heritage, Pensacola contains three historic districts, where magnolias and live oaks spread their branches above cobblestone streets illuminated by gaslight streetlamps and lined with handsome homes trimmed with wrought-iron balconies.

In the **Seville Historic District,** some of Florida's oldest homes mingle with restaurants and boutiques. Within the district, at Historic Pensacola Village, costumed "townspeople" are often on hand, performing chores and demonstrating 18th- and 19th-century crafts amid museums and restored homes and shops. **Palafox Historic District** was once the commercial hub of old Pensacola. Finally, drive through an en-

cyclopedia of historic architecture in the **North Hill Preservation District,** but keep in mind that the Queen Anne, Tudor, Art Moderne, Neoclassical, and Mediterranean Revival homes are all private residences.

Established in 1914, Pensacola's **Naval Air Station,** the world's oldest, is headquarters for the Blue Angels precision flying team and is open to the public. On the grounds the **National Museum of Naval Aviation** has more than 100 aircraft tracing naval air history from the 1911 Curtis A-1 Triad. A 1919 NC-4 Flying Boat, the first plane to cross the Atlantic, is displayed along with an F-14 Tomcat fighter jet. Visitors can scramble through a re-created aircraft carrier flight deck or take the controls of a jet trainer.

9 FLORIDA CAVERNS

Rangers lead visitors through a dry limestone cavern to marvel at the eerie formations of stalactites and stalagmites and the "waterfalls" of rock at **Florida Caverns State Park** near Marianna. Aboveground trails meander through a magnolia forest to swimming, fishing, and camping sites.

10 TORREYA STATE PARK

Situated on 150-foot-high bluffs near Greensboro, this preserve affords spectacular views of the Apalachicola River and is home to the rare tree for which the park is named. You can picnic, hike a seven-mile loop trail that crosses deep ravines, and visit an 1849 Greek Revival plantation house decorated with 19th-century antiques.

Sailboats are for rent in Destin, where white sands and emerald waters lure beach lovers. Deep-sea fishing boats and party boats are also available, as is scuba diving instruction.

Alabama

Site of the first Confederate capital and yet a cradle of the civil rights struggle, this is stirring country indeed, from the foothills of the northeast to the sugar-white beaches of the Gulf coast.

NORTHERN & CENTRAL ALABAMA

1 BIRMINGHAM

Birmingham was the scene of wrenching civil rights protests in 1963, the same year Rev. Martin Luther King, Jr., wrote his "Letter From a Birmingham Jail." Today the city pays moving homage to that turbulent time with a six-block Civil Rights District. Visitors can tour the **Birmingham Civil Rights Institute,** which houses exhibits that depict the landmarks in the struggle for equality from World War II to the present. Other sites in the district are **Kelly Ingram Park,** the focus of grassroots resistance in the city; the **Alabama Jazz Hall of Fame;** the **Sixteenth Street Baptist Church,** where four black children attending Sunday school were killed by a bomb; and the **Fourth Avenue Business District.**

Birmingham has changed in another way as well: it is no longer the iron and steel town whose foundries lit the sky with an orange-red glow for nearly a century. But it still carries a few vivid reminders of its former status as the Pittsburgh of the South. Among them is the 55-foot-high cast-iron statue of **Vulcan,** Roman god of the forge, who, from his pedestal atop Red Mountain, rules over the city with an iron fist.

Below Red Mountain stands the imposing **Sloss Furnaces National Historic Landmark.** Here visitors can see boilers, ovens, and casting sheds that once resounded with the terrifying, deafening sounds of molten iron pouring from bucket to mold like lava. Greek Revival **Arlington,** Birmingham's only remaining antebellum mansion, displays a life portrait of Seminole chieftain Osceola and a fine collection of Old Paris porcelain, popular with planters in the South.

2 TUSKEGEE

Booker T. Washington founded the Normal School for Colored Teachers, now Tuskegee University, in 1881 as a trade school for blacks. Many of its graduates fanned out across the South to teach other blacks. At the **Tuskegee Institute National Historic Site** you can visit the original buildings, constructed by the first students, who also farmed the surrounding fields. Washington's campus home, **The Oaks,** was built by students from bricks they made themselves and contains original family furnishings. Also here is the **George Washington Carver Museum,** devoted to the life and work of the teacher and botanist who developed some 300 products from peanuts, including a milk substitute and soap.

3 MONTGOMERY

Two men separated by oceans of time and political intent are remembered in Montgomery: Jefferson Davis and Martin Luther King, Jr. A bronze star on the west portico of the white-domed **Alabama State Capitol** marks the spot where

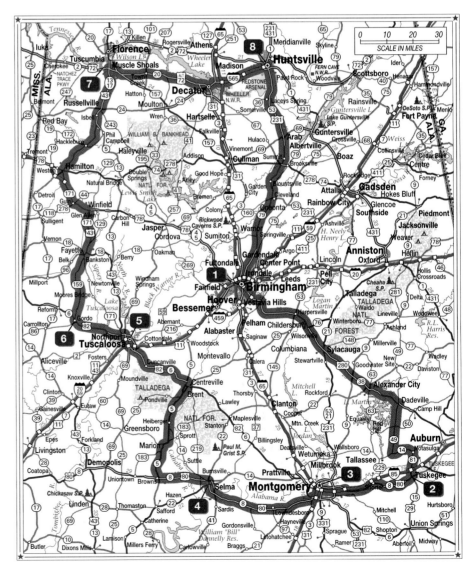

Davis was sworn in as president of the Confederacy in 1861. Across the street is the **First White House of the Confederacy,** where Davis lived with his family during the three months that Montgomery served as the Confederate capital. The elegant house, built in 1835, contains Confederate artifacts and Davis family relics, from rosary beads made by Mrs. Davis with her daughter's hair to Mr. Davis's eyeglasses and smoking jacket.

Nearly a century after the Civil War, Martin Luther King, Jr., helped lead the 1955 Montgomery bus boycott from the pulpit of the **Dexter Avenue King Memorial Baptist Church,** where he preached. A mural in the basement traces his role in the civil rights movement. But perhaps the most obvious monument to King and countless other protesters is the city's integrated bus system, now available to anyone with exact change.

The dramatic **Civil Rights Memorial,** designed by Maya Lin, the architect of the Vietnam War Memorial, features the names of 40 heroes who died in the civil rights struggle engraved in its smooth granite surface.

4 SELMA

Here in the heart of the Alabama Black Belt—so called for the color of its rich topsoil—Selma was a favored community for cotton planters and traders during the antebellum era. In 1865 a Confederate arsenal here and much of the city were looted by Union troops. But you can catch a whiff of Selma's gone-with-the-wind epoch at **Sturdivant Hall,** the finest surviving pre–Civil War residence in town. Built by Thomas Helm Lee, cousin of Robert E. Lee, the mansion contains a rare George Washington commemorative clock, dating from 1807.

▶ *Visit in late March to join the annual Historic Selma Pilgrimage, which goes to Sturdivant as well as private antebellum and Victorian homes not otherwise open to the public.*

Before you leave Selma you might want to stroll across the **Edmund Pettus Bridge,** a quiet monument to the civil rights marchers who clashed there with local law enforcement officers on what would be known as Bloody Sunday, March 7, 1965, and whose subsequent march on Montgomery led to the passage of the Voting Rights Act five months later.

5 TUSCALOOSA

Home of the University of Alabama, Tuscaloosa contains several stately buildings that survived the fire set by Union troops who captured the town in 1865. Among them is the University's 1829 **Gorgas House,** now a museum

At the Civil Rights Memorial, a film of water flows over the names of 40 men, women, and children—activists, martyrs, and random victims of the civil rights struggle. The words on the wall, often quoted by Martin Luther King, Jr., are paraphrased from the Bible.

displaying an impressive collection of antique furniture and silver. The eloquent wife of the school's president talked the soldiers out of burning down her home, the **President's Mansion,** an 1841 Greek Revival structure with an elegant double winding staircase leading to a second-story entrance.

Some wags over the years have expressed their desire that the university become an institution the football team could be proud of. This may be less a criticism of the school than an indication of just how dominant Alabama football has been over the last several decades, an impression that will be confirmed by a visit to the **Paul "Bear" Bryant Museum.** Here fans can see memorabilia relating to the legendary football coach, including a Waterford crystal replica of one of his distinctive houndstooth hats.

6 GORDO

Tucked deep into the piney country outside Gordo is one of the most surprising institutions in the state: **Ma 'Cille's Museum of Miscellanea.** It was started circa 1962 by Lucile House, a resident who felt the local children should have access to a museum. (The name 'Cile was misspelled 'Cille on the museum sign and has become permanent.) The museum offers an astounding and idiosyncratic array of exhibits. There is a brick building full of dolls, a country store, a furnished log cabin, and outbuildings overflowing with bottles, photographs, furniture, and animals stuffed by Lucile herself.

▶ *To find the museum, turn off Rte. 82 onto Rte. 86, and look for the sign.*

7 TUSCUMBIA

Just south of the Tennessee River city of Florence, Alabama, sits the small town of Tuscumbia, where Helen Keller was born in 1880. **Ivy Green** is the modest frame cottage where Keller was raised and where she studied with her teacher, Anne Sullivan, who remained with her for 49 years. The house contains 19th-century furnishings and mementos of Keller's early life, including toys, clothing, a Braille typewriter, and a Braille wristwatch and alarm clock. On the grounds is the original pump where Keller learned her first word: *water.*

8 HUNTSVILLE

Northern Alabama—and Huntsville in particular—has always been a little out of step with the rest of the state. During the Civil War, many of its residents favored secession from the Confederacy in order to set up the pro-Union state of Nickajack.

These days local sentiment favors leaving the planet altogether, for Huntsville is home to the massive **U.S. Space & Rocket Center,** which has one of the world's largest collections of

The space shuttle Pathfinder looms large at the U.S. Space & Rocket Center.

space rockets and missiles. Visitors can work the controls of an Apollo capsule replica and ride a motion simulator to Jupiter, then stroll outside to the Rocket Park and gaze up at the Saturn V, a 363-foot rocket that boosted Americans to the moon. It was developed at NASA's adjacent Marshall Space Flight Center, where some of America's first spacecraft were built and tested, and where work continues on the Space Station. A bus tour of the NASA center is included in the price of admission to the Space & Rocket Center.

Huntsville's historic Twickenham District boasts a superb collection of antebellum homes, including the 1814 **Leroy Pope House,** possibly the oldest brick residence in the state. Walking tour maps of the area are available at the visitor center.

MOBILE & THE GULF COAST

1 MOBILE

Adorned in spring with blooming azaleas and shaded by ancient, moss-draped oaks, Mobile is the grande dame of Alabama's cities. Founded nearly 300 years ago by the French, the city remains an elegant combination of European culture and Southern charm.

Start your tour at **Fort Condé,** a reconstructed 1711 French fortress that also serves as the city's welcome center. Here costumed guides usher visitors back in time to French-ruled Mobile, before the important port settlement was taken by the English, then the Spanish, and finally by American troops during the War of 1812.

Much of that history can be discovered near the fort at the **Museum of the City of Mobile,** located in the 1872 Bernstein-Bush House. The museum's collections include artifacts from the European periods as well as the Confederate years, and the glittering gowns of former Mardi Gras queens, mementos of the Mardi Gras celebration first held here in 1830—about 20 years before the New Orleans fete.

More recent history floats on Mobile Bay just east of downtown. The battleship U.S.S. *Alabama* was saved from the scrap pile in 1964, with the help of thousands of schoolchildren who donated their nickels, dimes, and quarters to bring the World War II veteran home. Now the ship serves as the centerpiece of the **U.S.S.** *Alabama* **Battleship Memorial Park,** with more than 20 restored military aircraft, artillery pieces, and the submarine U.S.S. *Drum.*

▶ *The upper deck of the U.S.S.* Alabama *can be steamy, especially in summer. Wear cool clothing, and expect to do a lot of stair climbing.*

Mobile's most colorful claim to fame is celebrated each spring during the **Azalea Festival.** In March and April, visitors can follow the Azalea Trail past more than 27 miles of streets lined with the planted pastels.

Venture to the Oakleigh Garden District, one of several historic districts in the city, to tour **Oakleigh,** a grand Greek Revival structure named for the venerable live oaks that surround it. Built by a cotton broker in the 1830's, the house contains period furnishings, including an English supper table carved from one piece of wood, antique kitchen utensils and tools, and party favors from early Mardi Gras balls.

2 HISTORIC BLAKELEY PARK

There is plenty to delight history buffs in this park near the town of Spanish Fort. Occupied by American Indians some 4,000 years ago, it was the site of the 19th-century waterfront boomtown of Blakeley, then larger than Mobile. Much of the town was wiped out by the yellow fever epidemics of 1828 and 1830. In April of 1865, Union troops routed a Confederate force here during a battle fought on the day Lee surrendered to Grant.

Today the park preserves American Indian mounds, town ruins, and Civil War fortifications, including earthen forts, rifle pits, and battery sites. Guides paint a picture of life here before and during the skirmish.

3 POINT CLEAR

Visitors have been coming to this bayside community near Fairhope since 1847, when the **Grand Hotel** first opened its doors. Two other structures have occupied the site of the original hotel since then, but the Grand is still known for its elegance and Southern hospitality. Set on an azalea-and-oak–planted point of Mobile Bay, the hotel features three restaurants, a 36-hole championship golf course, tennis courts, a marina, and one of the South's largest swimming pools.

In summer the eastern shore of Mobile Bay is the place to be to reap the bounty of the sea. When a naturally occurring lack of oxygen sends bottom-dwelling sea life swimming for shore, flounder, shrimp, and crab are easy catches. Locals call this event a jubilee, and at the first report of one—usually in the wee hours of the morning—they come running with washtubs, buckets, and cooking pots to collect the harvest.

gan to the island's eastern tip. The site of a French outpost in the early 1700's, Dauphin Island has withstood nearly three centuries of hurricanes, naval attacks, and land developers. Today it is a quiet haven for bird-watchers and those seeking a respite from the summertime beach crowds.

▶ *The Mobile Bay Ferry trip takes 30 minutes. Bring a bag of bread crumbs along to feed the flocks of seagulls that follow the ferry, and binoculars to see the families of dolphins that often swim alongside.*

At the eastern tip of the island, Fort Morgan's sister stronghold, **Fort Gaines,** houses a museum that traces the histories of the two Mobile Bay garrisons, with artifacts including an anchor from Admiral Farragut's flagship.

7 BELLINGRATH GARDENS

A popular soft drink provided the financial base for these stunning public gardens, officially **Bellingrath Gardens and Home,** near Theodore. Coca-Cola bottling magnate Walter Bellingrath and his wife, Bessie, bought the site for a fishing camp in 1918. Later, inspired by gardens they saw in Europe, they turned it into a horticulturalist's dream.

More than 250,000 azaleas flower between late February and April. Starting in February, thousands of daffodils, tulips, and hyacinths spring into bloom. Some 3,000 hybrid tea rose bushes fill the gardens with color from April to December, and chrysanthemums dazzle visitors in late autumn. More than 200 Boehm porcelain birds and flowers are exhibited in a gallery on the grounds.

4 FOLEY

Alabama beachgoers have learned to leave a day free for shopping at the **Riviera Centre** in Foley, a complex of more than 100 outlet stores that feature everything from menswear to housewares. Clothes from top designers rub shoulders with lesser brands. And a food court offers almost any kind of food you're hungry for.

▶ *Shoppers engulf the center in summer, but don't be afraid of the crowds. Designed as an Old World–style marketplace, the Riviera has wide, easily traveled walkways that link the shops.*

5 GULF SHORES

With miles of snow-white beaches, this Gulf coast resort town has long been a popular summer vacation spot. But in recent years such attractions as **Gulf State Park** have made it a year-round destination. The park offers pristine beaches, the state's longest fishing pier, and trails that wind through coastal backwaters, marshes, and wetlands.

A Civil War chapter in American naval history unfolded 20 miles west of Gulf Shores at **Fort Morgan.** Built in

the early 1800's to guard the entrance to Mobile Bay, the fort gained fame when it was attacked by a Union fleet commanded by Adm. David Farragut on August 5, 1864. Farragut's fleet faltered as one of his ships hit an underwater mine known as a "torpedo." According to legend, the determined admiral won the battle, and entered history, when he gave the order, "Damn the torpedoes! Full speed ahead!"

6 DAUPHIN ISLAND

Alabama's only barrier island is linked to the mainland by a bridge to its northern edge and by the Mobile Bay Ferry, which runs daily from Fort Mor-

Bursts of color bestowed by flowering kale and bright red azaleas grace the Rustic Bridge Rockery at Bellingrath Gardens. The pretty wooden bridge, draped with ivy geraniums, spans Mirror Lake.

Alabama • 163

Mississippi

This romantic region of vast Delta plantations and softly scented woodlands sings with a new song of progress. Come for the fine museums, top-notch recreation, and sizzling-hot blues.

SOUTHERN MISSISSIPPI

1 VICKSBURG

When Vicksburg fell to Union troops in 1863, so fell the hopes, say historians, of Dixie. The loss of the "Gibraltar of the Confederacy" in a bloody 47-day siege spelled the loss of control of the Mississippi River. The past literally reverberates at the **Vicksburg National Military Park**—particularly in the summer, when the living-history program includes a barrage of musket and cannon firings twice a day. You can

Rolling on: The Delta Queen, a historic paddle wheeler built in 1926, carries passengers up and down the Mississippi in the tradition of the great "floating wedding cakes" of the steamboat era.

spend an entire day at the 1,800-acre park, which includes a visitor center, the **National Cemetery**, and the Union ironclad **U.S.S. Cairo,** salvaged 100 years after it sank in the Yazoo River in 1862. For an extra fee, licensed guides will lead two-hour tours.

The month-and-a-half-long siege was chronicled in a remarkable diary kept by Emma Balfour, who, from her perch

in her elegant three-story home, reported "mortars…passing entirely over the house." The **Balfour House,** a magnificent 1835 Greek Revival mansion, is open daily for tours. Mrs. Balfour's diary is on permanent display at the Mississippi Department of Archives, in Jackson.

Many other antebellum mansions survived the shelling. Stop by the Vicksburg Convention and Visitors Bureau for a walking-tour map of the downtown historic district. Or visit during the annual **Vicksburg Spring Pilgrimage**, from late March to early April, when several private 19th-century buildings are open to the public.

The focal point of downtown is the monumental **Old Court House Museum,** an 1858 Greek Revival structure with 30-foot Ionic columns. Union efforts to destroy the courthouse halted when Rebels converted it into a prison for captured Federal soldiers.

The principal testing and research facility of the Army Corps of Engineers,

the **Waterways Experiment Station** exhibits scale models of many of America's waterways. Afterward, view the real thing by taking a sightseeing tour of the Mississippi. For the adventurous, there's an hour-long hydrofoil tour of the river region offered by **Mississippi River Adventures,** located at the city waterfront.

▶ *Reservations are a must for the overnight cruises on the* Delta Queen *or the* Mississippi Queen, *the luxury paddle wheelers that ply Old Man River. Climb aboard in Vicksburg, Natchez, or Greenville.*

2 JACKSON

They called it Chimneyville during the Civil War: so bombarded was Mississippi's state capital by Union fire that the city skyline became a ghostly visage of burned-out homes and lone chimneys. Only a handful of Jackson's antebellum buildings remained. Luckily, among the survivors were the stately **City Hall,** with its statue of Andrew Jackson in front, and the **Old Capitol,** which now houses the **Mississippi State Historical Museum.** Both structures can be toured, as can the opulent 1903 **New State Capitol Building,** patterned after the national capitol and crowned with a golden eagle.

Nearby is the restored 1842 **Governor's Mansion,** whose snow-white portico is modeled after an Athenian monument. The second-oldest executive mansion still in use in the country is open for morning tours from Tuesdays to Fridays.

Head over to the **Jackson Zoological Park,** a 75-year-old zoo that was revamped in the late 1980's to create natural habitats for more than 500 animals. Stroll the boardwalk through the open-air **Rain Forest,** where monkeys hang from spindly tree branches.

Time-travel to the rural South of the 1920's at the **Mississippi Agriculture and Forestry Museum.** This exhibit of an old-time farm village and a crossroads town is composed of authentic structures transplanted from around the state. Seasonally, the cotton mill and the cane mill are cranked up; during the November harvest festival, sugarcane syrup made on-site is sold.

At the end of the day, relax in the serene environs of **Mynelle Gardens,** three miles from downtown. You can perch yourself on one of several cast-iron settees or rock gently in a porch swing in a gazebo. Seven acres of perennials and annuals adorn the botanical park, open daily year-round.

3 WOODVILLE

It has been said—by experts at Harvard University, no less—that this small town is the truest remnant of the Old South in America. Shady live oaks surround the 1855 courthouse square and its yellow-brick colonnaded courthouse. Just down the square are the stately offices of the **Old West Feliciana Railroad**—the first standard-gauge railroad in America. Walking

Old South splendor: No expense was spared in the construction of Stanton Hall in 1858.

tours of the historic district are provided by the Woodville Civic Club.

Woodville's most hallowed site lies just outside of town. **Rosemont,** built

in 1810, was the childhood home of the president of the Confederacy, Jefferson Davis. Teardrops of moss and lacy ivy wreathe the handsome red-brick house, open from March through December. Many of Davis's mother's rosebushes still bloom alongside the porch.

4 NATCHEZ

"To see Natchez under the moonlight," someone once said, "*that* is what it's all about." The town's more than 500 antebellum structures, softened by moss-draped oaks, certainly catch the eye, by either sun or moon. The most extravagant, **Longwood,** is but a façade: the mansion's interior was never finished, because of the Civil War. An octagonal confection with a Moorish cupola, the house still holds workers' tools from when construction was halted in 1861. Visit the white-columned grandeur of 1858 **Stanton Hall** in the springtime, when the house is framed by crimson azaleas underfoot and a spidery crown of oak branches.

Many of Natchez's mansions sprang up during an early-19th-century economic boom, when the city hummed as a center of Mississippi River trade. **Natchez-Under-the-Hill** was a raucous rivermen's hangout, referred to as the Barbary Coast of the Mississippi. There's little chance of being shanghaied today, as the area is chockablock with shops, restaurants, and bars—many with great views of the river.

From Natchez to Vicksburg you'll be traveling on the **Great River Road** (Rte. 61), a scenic trail of riverfront plantations and small towns. You will branch off briefly when you hook up to the **Natchez Trace,** an 8,000-year-old Indian trail, at the parkway entrance north of Natchez. A modern roadway more than 400 miles long follows the trail, amid cypress swamps, abandoned towns, and ancient Indian mounds.

▶ *No commercial vehicles are allowed on the Trace, and the 50-m.p.h. speed limit is strictly enforced.*

Stop in Lorman on your way to Port Gibson. The **Old Country Store,** on Rte. 61, is the genuine article, little changed since 1890 and open seven

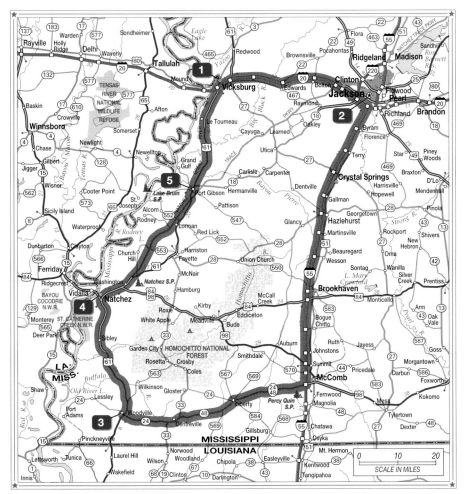

days a week year-round. Locally made cheese is sliced on an old-fashioned cheese cutter, and fresh coffee is always brewing. There is also an on-premises museum of plantation life.

5 PORT GIBSON

In a lush wooded setting 12 miles southwest of Port Gibson on Rte. 552, 23 Corinthian columns rise mutely against the sky. They mark the ruins of **Windsor Mansion,** a once-magnificent Greek Revival home built in 1861. Before the mansion burned down during a party in 1890, Confederate soldiers used the mansion's roof as an observation deck.

Ulysses S. Grant proclaimed the town of Port Gibson "too beautiful to burn" during the Civil War. With its wealth of

Remnants of the past: The ruins of once-grand Windsor Mansion lie near Port Gibson.

19th-century homes and churches, the town is still a showstopper. Stop in at the 1805 **Samuel Gibson House,** the town's oldest home and site of its tourist board, and pick up a touring map. Or simply follow the green markers of the **Port Gibson Tour** past the town's 19th-century jewels. Scan the skyline for the **First Presbyterian Church,** built in 1859. A golden hand with one finger pointing heavenward tops the steeple.

NORTHERN MISSISSIPPI

1 OXFORD

It is in the tales of William Faulkner that this lovely, sleepy college town makes the leap from the ordinary to the legendary. Faulkner's white-columned house, **Rowan Oak,** built in 1840, was where the winner of the Nobel and Pulitzer prizes cast about for inspiration for his imaginary Yoknapatawpha County tales. The home appears much as it did when Faulkner lived there and is open to visitors six days a week year-round. Look closely and you'll see an outline of his novel *A Fable,* written in pencil on the study wall. Faulkner is buried in **St. Peter's Cemetery,** on the other side of town.

Faulkner is not the only writer to have found Oxford inspiring: John Grisham, Barry Hannah, and Larry Brown are among the authors who live and work there. It's a good bet that they've spent some time deep in the stacks at **Square Books,** whose extensive collection of Southern literature is housed in a turn-of-the-century drugstore.

The **University of Mississippi**—Ole Miss, to most—spreads out over 640 gently sloping acres. Among its antebellum buildings are the 1848 **Lyceum** and the 1853 **Old Chapel.** There are lively on-campus museums to tour as well. The **Center for the Study of Southern Culture,** in the 1857 Barnard Observatory building, features rotating displays on Southern culture.

2 HOLLY SPRINGS

Stately pillared mansions rim the quiet streets of Holly Springs. Virginia farmers migrated to this region about 1832, clearing land and building extravagant homes. During the Civil War, control of the town changed hands a total of 59 times. Local lore has it that the city was spared a fiery end thanks to the special attention paid the Union soldiers by a few of the townswomen.

Start your tour at **Courthouse Square,** where more than a hundred 19th-century structures stand. Maps of the area are available at the chamber of commerce. **Montrose,** with its grand colonnaded portico and plantation-made bricks, now houses the Holly Springs Garden Club; visit by appointment only. The Gothic Revival houses **Airliewood** and **Cedarhurst** are often included in the town's annual Spring Pilgrimage tour of homes.

3 TUPELO

You may not see Elvis Presley's ghost in Tupelo, but you can't miss the two-room frame house where he was born in 1935. The **Elvis Presley Birthplace** and the **Elvis Presley Memorial Chapel** can be found at 306 Elvis Presley Drive and are part of the **Elvis Presley Park.** Here you can picnic, swim, play tennis, or simply get the lowdown on other Elvis hot spots in town.

4 COLUMBUS

Founded in 1821, Columbus has retained a goodly share of antebellum mansions, as the town was spared the Union fire that disfigured so many other Southern cities. Tickets for daily rotating tours of six historic houses can be purchased at the door or by mail from the Columbus Historic Foundation. Among them, **Amzi Love** is a charming 1848 cottage where tours are given by the eighth-generation owner of the house. The palatial 1835 **Rosewood Manor** reigns on a hill surrounded by a spectacular rose garden in bloom from February to November. The 1857 **White Arches** displays account ledgers from the original plantation and is said to be haunted by a resident ghost.

The rectory of **St. Paul's Episcopal Church** was the boyhood home of the playwright Tennessee Williams and now serves as an official state **Welcome Center.** The church itself, built in 1860, boasts a glorious Tiffany window.

Six miles from the city is **Waverley Plantation,** a spectacular restored estate, open daily. The house's octagonal core is a great open rotunda rimmed by two spiral staircases on the inside and topped by a cupola on the outside.

For two weeks in April, the city hosts its annual **Pilgrimage,** when costumed guides lead visitors through 13 historic houses. "Pilgrimage" tours were born in Mississippi in 1932, when frost de-

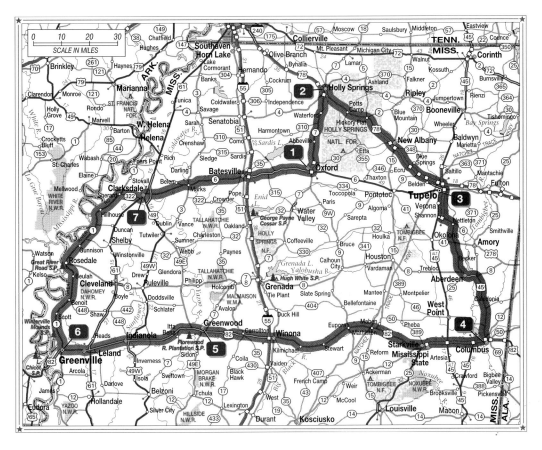

6 GREENVILLE

Greenville is a city on the move—literally. Floods, fire, and more floods have forced the city to pick up and rebuild three separate times—but never far from its original site alongside the Mississippi River. In 1935 a series of levees was built to keep the river at bay, and Greenville now nestles on the banks of **Lake Ferguson.** A drive along the levee to the river will give you a firsthand look at just how vulnerable the low-lying Delta is. Get a secondhand look at the region's history of floods at the **Greenville Flood Museum.**

Winterville Mounds State Park, three miles north, contains one of the largest groups of Indian mounds in the Mississippi Valley. A museum exhibits artifacts from the mounds, a ceremonial site for the early Mississippian culture.

From Greenville to Clarksdale you'll be traveling along the Mississippi on the **Great River Road,** a scenic trail of plantations and small Southern towns.

7 CLARKSDALE

For anyone in thrall to blues and rock and roll, here, say purists, lie the roots. It was at the crossroads of Rte. 49 and Rte. 61 that Mississippi native son Robert Johnson is said to have sold his soul to the devil in order to be the best blues player of all time. The guitarist and songwriter died young in 1938, but he proved to have a profound influence on 1960's musicians, who consider this crossroads sacred ground. The **Delta Blues Museum** honors the region's music heritage with memorabilia and rare recordings. On exhibit is the Muddywood guitar, constructed from a cypress log taken from blues legend Muddy Waters's birthplace nearby.

Listen to old-time blues and have a little trimmed off the sides in the bargain at **Wade's Barbershop.** Wade, a fount of blues trivia, performs between trims.

---

stroyed a Natchez garden tour, and the idea of opening up mansions to visitors was hatched. Today, elaborate spring pilgrimages are held in more than 20 Mississippi towns. Call or write the State of Mississippi for information.

5 GREENWOOD

The Delta spreads out in flat green marshland and tendrils of snaky rivulets from here to the Mississippi River. It was here that cotton was king. To find out why, stop alongside the highway and scoop up a fistful of the country's richest soil, thanks to years of constant flooding. Note the balmy air, testament to the extravagant nine-month growing season. Then, to learn more about the Delta's cotton heritage, visit **Cottonlandia.** The museum houses everything from fossilized whale bones from the area's sea-bottom past to pre-Columbian artifacts from the region's Indian occupations. For more cotton lore, make a beeline for the town's **Cotton Row**—one of nine spot cotton markets in the nation. Guides are available to show you around.

Two miles from town, the **Florewood River Plantation** is a replica of a typical Delta plantation house. Stretch your legs on the two miles of trails at the **Malmaison Wildlife Management Area,** 10 miles northeast of town, the former estate of Greenwood Leflore—a Choctaw chieftain and a state legislator for whom the town is named.

▶ *The trails at Malmaison meander through gully country—ideal snake habitats. There's little danger, however, if you stay on the trails and don't poke about in the foliage.*

The legendary heritage of the blues is celebrated at Clarksdale's Delta Blues Museum.

Louisiana

Journey down the Great River Road beneath sun-washed magnolias to the Delta bayous, where native folk let the good times roll to a peppery mix of festivals, fun, and fabulous food.

NEW ORLEANS &
CAJUN COUNTRY

1 NEW ORLEANS

Raucous, seductive, elegant: the New Orleans character is as changeable and elusive as the morning fog over the great Mississippi bend that gave the Crescent City its original nickname. Today a pleasure-driven, languorous tempo earns it the moniker the Big Easy. Call it what you will, New Orleans is an American original.

Much of the city is best seen on foot. A downtown neighborhood that is particularly conducive to walking is one that has changed little since French army engineers laid it out in 1721. The **French Quarter**, or Vieux Carré (pronounced view-kah-ray), is a 90-block section bordered by the river. The neighborhood's well-preserved French- and Spanish-flavored historic architecture is trimmed in arabesques of fanciful ironwork in the form of flowers, grapevines, and fauna.

The heart of the French Quarter lies in the parade ground the French called the Place d'Armes, now **Jackson Square.** Carriage-tour companies operate from this location. The square is graced by **St. Louis Cathedral,** one of the oldest cathedrals in the United States, and the two principal structures of the city's Spanish colonial period, the **Cabildo** (the 1795 capitol) and the **Presbytère** (priest's house), both now part of the Louisiana State Museum. Two blocks away you can snag homemade hot pepper sauce and gumbo-to-go at the centuries-old **French Market,** a 24-hour farmers' market and shopping bazaar.

You can tour many of the neighborhood's fine house museums. On the eastern end of the Quarter, the 1857 **Gallier House Museum,** home of the famed architect James Gallier, Jr., displays a superb period interior and a

A giant voodoo doll *is made ready for its unveiling at a Mardi Gras party in New Orleans.*

garden in the rear. Nearby is the romantic 1826 **Beauregard-Keyes House,** the home of Gen. P.G.T. Beauregard, later restored by the novelist Frances Parkinson Keyes. The 1831 Georgian **Hermann-Grima House,** at the west end of the Quarter, retains its courtyard, slave quarters, and stable.

▶ *Light sleepers may want to search for lodgings away from the commercial districts of the French Quarter or avoid rooms overlooking the noisiest thoroughfares.*

The city's **Mardi Gras** festivities, held in the period preceding Lent, are legendary. Depending on your appetite for mass congregation, Mardi Gras is both a world-class fete of stupendous color and costume—and human gridlock. **Royal Street** is one of the finest thoroughfares for antiques in the world yet is only one block away from **Bourbon Street,** a gaudy, tumultuous center of music and T-shirt emporiums. Just off Bourbon is legendary **Preservation Hall,** where you can hear traditional Dixieland jazz performed for pocket change. The acoustics of this modest music hall, its interior little more than wooden benches and peeling paint, are said to be nearly perfect.

A refurbished riverfront lined with malls, markets, and promenades now offers the gleaming new **Aquarium of**

A French Quarter morning: The city wakens to the smells of chicory coffee and warm beignets. Here the morning dew freshens the balcony flora at the Pontalba Apartments, built in 1851 by a wealthy baroness, whose initials are visible in the elaborate ironwork.

the Americas, where myriad forms of aquatic life—from Mississippi Gulf waters, the Amazon rain forest, and coral reefs—frolic in a 16-acre complex.

For a glimpse at unfettered wildlife, take a guided swamp tour in bayou flatboats mere minutes from downtown. Van transportation to and from the swamp is often included; reserve at least 24 hours ahead. On **Louisiana Swamp Tours**, Cajun guides will take you deep into the fragrant bayou, where alligator sightings are common.

shimmer beneath a cool overhang of Spanish moss, and bike trails ring old plantation grounds. Behind the park is the **Audubon Zoo**, consistently named one of the top zoos in the country. Stop in to see the rare white alligators and Suri, the resident white tiger.

A star attraction in itself is New Orleans cuisine, where two schools of cooking reign: Creole was a New World concoction, conceived from a multitude of traditions and refined over time into a sophisticated cuisine. Cajun recipes

You'll find traditional New Orleans dishes at **Galatoire's**, whose Sunday brunch of smooth Sazerac cocktails and Creole bistro food is a famous local tradition. Before dinner, though, rub elbows with the natives over a dozen plump, briny oysters at the marble oyster bar at **Acme Oyster House**.

2 DESTREHAN

Said to be the oldest intact plantation house along the lower Mississippi Valley, **Destrehan** dates from the 1780's. Despite some remodeling during the Greek Revival era, the house, capped by a West Indies hip roof, retains an aura of the Louisiana Colonial period from the time of its ownership by prominent French settlers. Local lore has it that the famous smuggler Jean Laffite was a guest at the house.

3 HOUMA

Houma is the convergence point of seven waterways that lace the region; hence the need for more than 50 bridges and the town's lofty nickname of the Venice of America. This fertile Cajun country was dubbed *terrebonne*—the "good earth"—by early French settlers. It is also a Cajun-country center for guided tours and fishing expeditions deep into the Louisiana swamp; a good

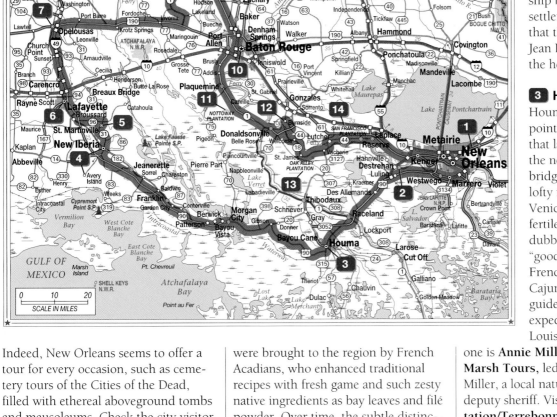

Indeed, New Orleans seems to offer a tour for every occasion, such as cemetery tours of the Cities of the Dead, filled with ethereal aboveground tombs and mausoleums. Check the city visitor guide for details.

A different world lies uptown, across Canal Street and the Central Business District. Still served by the popular St. Charles Avenue Streetcar, the **Garden District** is a treasury of antebellum homes and gardens, where bougainvillea pours over pastel walls. At the upper end of the Garden District is the 385-acre **Audubon Park**. Here lagoons

were brought to the region by French Acadians, who enhanced traditional recipes with fresh game and such zesty native ingredients as bay leaves and filé powder. Over time, the subtle distinctions between the two schools have blurred; many chefs simply refer to it as southern Louisiana cuisine.

▶ *Get a quick fix on cooking New Orleans style at the New Orleans School of Cooking, whose three-hour culinary demonstrations, held daily except Sunday, end with a full meal, complemented by iced tea and beer.*

one is **Annie Miller's Swamp & Marsh Tours**, led by Alligator Annie Miller, a local naturalist and a former deputy sheriff. Visit **Southdown Plantation/Terrebonne Museum**, where you can view rotating exhibits on Acadian culture.

4 NEW IBERIA/AVERY ISLAND

Claiming both Acadian and Spanish roots, New Iberia is home to one of the most famous plantation mansions of the Old South. The white-columned **Shadows-on-the-Teche**, dating from 1834, is today a property of the National

Trust for Historic Preservation. Named for the great oaks' play of shadows on the lawn, the house was the setting for D. W. Griffith's 1923 film *The White Rose* and contains period furnishings and 1861 watercolors of the plantation.

Nearby Avery Island is where the McIlhenny Company has been concocting Tabasco sauce, a Cajun staple, for 130 years. Tour the Tabasco factory, where you'll learn that the pepper mash used to make the sauce must be fermented for three years and that the company's very first batch was poured into 350 cologne bottles. Founder Edmund McIlhenny's son, Ned, cultivated the 200-acre **Jungle Gardens,** where lush camellias and azaleas grow and **Bird City** is a sanctuary for waterbirds.

A crawfish boil makes for choice eating at this family gathering in Basile. Common throughout Louisiana, these freshwater crustaceans are prepared in gumbos and étouffées, but "pinching tails" is a community affair.

5 ST. MARTINVILLE

This town is at the heart of the legend surrounding *Evangeline,* Henry Wadsworth Longfellow's poem of star-crossed love. St. Martinville welcomed both the Acadians from Nova Scotia and transatlantic refugees from the French Revolution in the 18th century. The **Longfellow-Evangeline State Commemorative Area,**

with its 1830's plantation, interprets aspects of the local culture. In the town's historic district, the cemetery of old **St. Martin de Tours Catholic Church** is celebrated as the gravesite of the woman who inspired *Evangeline.* A still-standing oak tree by Bayou Teche is said to be where she met her lover.

6 LAFAYETTE

The "capital" of French Louisiana is famous for its festivals, food, and distinctive Gallic dialect. Although Lafayette is a commercial and industrial center, the old heritage that began with the arrival of the Acadians in the 1760's endures in such annual events as the **Festivals Acadiens,** in September. The **Lafayette Museum** is situated in a handsome 1800 townhouse. Among its displays are costumes from Lafayette's own **Mardi Gras,**

a celebration that matches New Orleans's in color and spectacle but with a distinct emphasis on Cajun—from such regional dishes as crawfish étouffée and jambalaya to the spicy Cajun folk music known as zydeco. Bring your dancing shoes to **Vermilionville,** a living-history museum that offers live Cajun music in the afternoons and on weekends.

The complex of real and replicated structures reveals two centuries of Cajun and Creole life.

A detour to Henderson, east on Interstate 10 at Exit 115, will deliver you to Levee Road, where you can take two swamp tours operated by **McGee's Landing** and **Angelle's Atchafalaya Basin Tours.**

▶ *Because swamp tours are popular with groups, use directory assistance to call in advance to make reservations; both tour companies will add another boat to accommodate you and your party.*

7 OPELOUSAS

The third-oldest city in the state, Opelousas was once the home of the frontier hero Jim Bowie. Today's visitors can find a museum of Bowie memorabilia as well as **Le Vieux Village of Opelousas,** a historic district of early structures. **Main Street Revived** dances are held every Friday night in the warm months. Residents welcome visitors to swing to the street music, generally of the toe-tapping Cajun variety.

8 ST. FRANCISVILLE

A small town of antebellum charm on the east bank of the Mississippi, St. Francisville is the centerpiece for the beautiful parishes of **East** and **West Feliciana** (Spanish for "happy land"). The Felicianas are high and rolling, vastly different geographically from most of Louisiana and a center of English—not French—settlement. Many of the 150 historic buildings in St. Francisville are noted in the self-guided-tour map, available at the **West Feliciana Historical Society Museum.** Annually, on the third weekend of March, a pilgrimage to historic houses, gardens, and churches—a different selection of homes every year—gives visitors a close-up view of life in the small-town antebellum South.

Two miles east of St. Francisville is **Rosedown Plantation,** built in 1835. An allée of live oaks frames the mansion's impressive Georgian façade. Inside are 19th-century pastel wallpaper and a swirling mahogany staircase. John James Audubon once lived and painted at **Oakley Plantation,** now part of the **Audubon State Commemorative Area,** a 100-acre wildlife sanctuary. View the painter's tiny room, where he thrilled at the surrounding "...rich magnolias covered with fragrant blossoms, the holly, the beech, the tall yellow poplar...." Ten miles west is **Greenwood,** a templelike 1820's mansion that was destroyed by lightning in 1960 and rebuilt from 1968 to 1984. The 28-columned house has starred in many films, including the TV miniseries *North and South.*

On the west side of the river is **Parlange Plantation,** 20 miles from town, near New Roads. To reach this handsome 1750 French Colonial, cross on the St. Francisville–New Roads ferry and then drive five miles south.

9 PORT HUDSON

Although it is not well known, Port Hudson was the site of one of the longest sieges in American military history. This key Confederate stronghold was defended for 48 days in 1863 by a Rebel force of 6,800 against a Union army of about 30,000. The exhausted defenders finally surrendered on hearing the news that Vicksburg, 150 miles to the north, had been captured. The **Port Hudson State Commemorative Area** includes living-history programs and six miles of trails through trenches and redoubts.

10 BATON ROUGE

The handsome state capital is dominated by wide, extravagant avenues and a 34-story white marble Art Deco skyscraper that is America's tallest statehouse, with an observation deck from which to view the Mississippi. This **Capitol** was part of the legacy bequeathed by Gov. Huey P. Long, as well as the site of his assassination, in 1935. Bullet scars still pock the marble in the corridor where Long was gunned down. A few blocks away, on the banks of the river, stands Louisiana's **Old State Capitol.** Built in 1850 in the Gothic Revival style and expanded in 1882, it was recently restored and now serves as the state's Center of Political and Governmental History. Baton Rouge also has multiple governors' mansions: Huey Long's 1930's Georgian

Parlange Plantation, *near New Roads, was built in 1750 among live oaks and magnolias.*

house is open on weekends for self-guided tours, and the present plantation-style mansion can be seen weekdays by appointment only. The oldest plantation house in Baton Rouge is **Magnolia Mound,** a 1790's Creole structure lived in by an aide-de-camp to General Lafayette during the American Revolution. A even wider view of early Louisiana life can be found at the **Louisiana State University Rural Life Museum,** which includes an entire community of 19th-century buildings moved to the site from around the state.

11 NOTTOWAY PLANTATION

The highways that wind lazily along the Mississippi's banks between Baton Rouge and New Orleans are known collectively by a singular term: the **River Road,** or Great River Road. Along this 77-mile stretch of Louisiana there once existed a plantation culture of enormous wealth and luxury. The passage of time and the demands of a modern economy have industrialized much of the region, but fascinating traces, like time capsules, remain from the antebellum years. Among the more magnificent is the 1859 **Nottoway Plantation,** an ornate Italianate and Greek Revival–style mansion sometimes referred to as White Castle. Legend has it that the massive 64-room house was saved from sure annihilation during the Civil War by the intercession of a Union officer who had once been a guest of the owner, John Hampden Randolph. Randolph's own rosewood master suite is on display, as is the re-creation of the room of his daughter, Cornelia, who in 1903 wrote a thinly disguised novel of her experiences at Nottoway, called *The White Castle of Louisiana.* Today Nottoway is operated as a house museum and historic inn.

12 BURNSIDE

The pleasures of driving the River Road include hopping the frequent ferries and bridges that span the broad, churning Mississippi. One such link is the **Sunshine Bridge,** named in honor of a little town called Sunshine that formerly stood nearby.

▶ *In crossing the banks of the Mississippi along the River Road, remember that ferries going west to east depart at the hour and half-hour, and ferries going east to west depart at the quarter-hour and three-quarter hour.*

Driving downstream from Nottoway, the traveler can cross to the east bank on Rte. 70 to Burnside and see two of the finest survivors of the antebellum era. **Houmas House,** dating from 1840 and once the center of a 20,000-acre sugar plantation, is an ivory-colonnaded vision staffed by costumed guides. The Bette Davis film *Hush, Hush, Sweet Charlotte* was filmed here. The mansion, protected by a 20-foot dirt and grass levee, hugs the river. Nearby **Tezcuco Plantation,** a wrought-ironed Greek Revival house, was built in 1855 and features a life-size dollhouse. You can stay in cabins on the grounds.

13 OAK ALLEY PLANTATION

Take the Sunshine Bridge back to the west bank of the river, where one of the most soul-stirring sights on the lower Mississippi appears. Three miles west of the old French settlement of Vacherie, the Greek Revival façade of **Oak Alley** crowns the end of a quarter-mile allée of ancient live oaks. The gnarled trees—some with trunks eight feet thick—were planted long before the present house was built in the late 1830's. The broad fields of the rural landscape are planted, as they have been for centuries, in spiky sugarcane. Oak Alley is now an inn and restaurant.

14 SAN FRANCISCO PLANTATION

The Lutcher–Vacherie Ferry will carry you back to the east bank of the Mississippi. Five miles east on Rte. 44 is one of the more ornate residences ever built in the United States. **San Francisco Plantation** is an 1856 mansion whose peach and blue Steamboat Gothic gingerbread trim crowns a deep front gallery supported by Corinthian columns. Inside the house, the high-spirited decor features decorative ceilings and velvet Brussels carpeting.

NORTHERN LOUISIANA

1 ALEXANDRIA

The oldest standing structure in central Louisiana, **Kent House** reflects the romance of frontier life in a Creole colony. Built by a French planter between 1796 and 1800—just about the time that Alexandria was founded as a trading outpost on the Red River—Kent House is a central cottage flanked by two pavilions, all raised on brick piers and connected by graceful verandas. Authentic structures from other plantations were moved to Kent House and include slave quarters, a detached kitchen, and the only functioning open-kettle sugar mill in the state.

In early spring take a stroll along the **Wild Azalea Trail** in nearby **Kisatchie National Forest**. The trail, Louisiana's longest, wanders 31 miles through piney woods and hardwood bottoms. From mid-March till mid-April the woods are brilliant with the delicate pink blossoms of azalea and the snow-white petals of dogwood.

Haunting columns of cypress are a hallmark of the Kisatchie Forest lowlands terrain.

2 HODGES GARDENS

Sweet olive, magnolia, and wisteria scent the air in this 4,700-acre park, nestled among rolling pine woods. Founded by A. J. Hodges in 1956, the gardens have one of the largest collections of antique roses in America. Take the 10-mile paved drive around the lake by bicycle or car or on foot. Stroll the 60-acre formal gardens, where streams weave through beds of seasonally changing flowers. A conservatory and greenhouse is filled with orchids and palms.

3 FORT JESUP

Lt. (and future President) Zachary Taylor established this frontier outpost on the **San Antonio Road** to protect settlers from Indians and to put down slave rebellions on neighboring plantations. In 1845, Fort Jesup was a staging area for troops preparing to enter Texas at the beginning of the Mexican War.

At the **Fort Jesup State Commemorative Area,** all

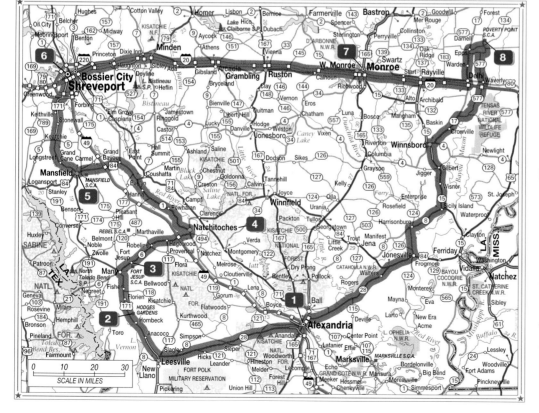

that remains of the once sprawling complex is a kitchen of squared timbers and an immense fireplace. A museum in the reconstructed officers' quarters tells the fort's story through maps, papers, and a diorama.

4 NATCHITOCHES

Four years before New Orleans was founded, Natchitoches was an incorporated town. Locals refer to the oldest permanent settlement in the Louisiana Purchase Territory as NAK-a-tush and revel in showing off its 60-block historic district, the perfect Deep South setting for such films as *Steel Magnolias*. You can savor the days when cotton was king as you stroll past old mercantile buildings with filigreed cast-iron grillwork and graceful townhouses, once home to prosperous river planters.

Take a cruise on **Cane River Lake,** a 32-mile-long dammed lake that was once part of the Red River. Boat excursions leave from the lake banks near the quaint **Roque House,** a restored 1803 structure built in the Bousillage style; the walls are made of riverbank clay, moss, and animal hair and covered with cypress or plaster. On the first Saturday in December, thousands of people journey to Natchitoches for the **Christmas Festival of Lights,** a holiday tradition that dates back to 1927. A fireworks display is capped by the glorious illumination of scores of wire sculptures along the waterway banks.

▶ *Reserve a room before summer if you plan to attend the Festival of Lights; up to 150,000 people converge on the town during the celebration.*

The lake runs through the center of town to the **Cane River Plantation Area.** To visit the old Creole plantations, drive south on Rte. 494, which weaves through cotton farms and pecan groves, following the course of the lake. Of the seven plantations in the valley, **Melrose** is one of the most interesting. It was owned by Marie Therese Coincoin, a freed slave born in 1742, who with her sons managed a prosperous plantation business. So prosperous, in fact, that Coincoin was able to purchase the freedom of several of her sons and

at least one grandchild. Melrose features the **Big House,** a traditional Louisiana plantation structure built in 1833, and the **Yucca House,** the original main building, constructed of virgin cypress. The **African House** served as a storehouse and—legend has it—a jail for rebellious slaves. In the early 20th century, the plantation became a salon for celebrated writers and artists. Look for the primitive artist Clementine Hunter's richly hued murals on the upper story of the African House.

The **Kate Chopin Home Bayou Folk Museum** lies at the southern end of Cane River Lake in Cloutierville. The museum, once the home of the novelist Kate Chopin, is a two-story structure built by slaves between 1806 and 1813. Chopin's novel *The Awakening,* published in 1899, was considered shocking because it described a woman's desire for self-fulfillment. Today it is regarded as an American masterpiece.

5 MANSFIELD

One of the bloodiest and most important battles of the Civil War was fought just to the south of this little Southern town, noted for its shady, tree-lined streets and antebellum mansions. It was there that in 1864 a Confederate unit led by Gen. Richard Taylor defeated a Union army twice its size. An interpretive trail winds through the 176-acre **Mansfield State Commemorative Area,** which features a yearly reenactment of the battle; a museum brings the battle vividly to life with Civil War weapons and personal diaries.

The African House, *on Melrose Plantation, has been both a jailhouse and a storehouse.*

6 SHREVEPORT

This inland port was named for Henry Shreve, the man who managed to unblock a 160-mile-long logjam that had made the Red River unnavigable above Natchitoches. Shreveport is now a heavily industrialized city, but it has its charms. The **R. W. Norton Art Gallery** has a surprisingly strong collection of European and American masters, including works by Auguste Rodin, Charles Russell, and Frederic Remington. In the spring thousands of azaleas on the museum's 40 acres compete for your attention.

Just west of Shreveport is the **American Rose Center,** America's largest park dedicated to the national flower. Twenty thousand roses—from heirloom to thornless to celebrity—are planted among the 44 acres of gardens.

7 MONROE

Bibles spill from every nook of the **Emy-Lou Biedenharn Foundation,** whose **Bible Museum** numbers among its treasures three Bibles brought to America by early English settlers. The **Biedenharn Home,** built by Emy-Lou's father, Joseph, the first bottler of Coca-Cola, is a magnificent mansion with a fountain in the reception hall. In back is the **ELsong Garden,** Emy-Lou's theme garden, where laser beams trigger melodies appropriate to particular areas along the winding pathways.

More than 700 exotic animals live in natural habitats at the **Louisiana Purchase Gardens and Zoo.** Here also are formal gardens, moss-laden live oak trees, and a miniature train ride.

8 POVERTY POINT

At **Poverty Point State Commemorative Area** is one of the most important and mysterious archeological discoveries ever made in this country. Twelve centuries before Christ, American Indians built a city on a series of six concentric earth ridges overlooking the Mississippi floodplain. The concentric rings remain, as well as four ceremonial and burial mounds. The largest mound is shaped like a great bird and is 72 feet high. In the warm months, guided tram tours will take you for a close-up view of the mounds.

MIDWEST

An Iowa cornfield

*T*he Midwestern states *are indeed the heartland of America—a place where rippling fields of grain and tidy small towns give us the comforting sense that all is well. Artists and writers have long celebrated the Midwest character: Longfellow sang of the lake shores of Minnesota, Sandburg of Chicago's big shoulders, and Mark Twain of the Mississippi. On canvas, Grant Wood and Thomas Hart Benton brought the region's sturdy people to life.*

Many of the 19 driving tours on the following pages—through Michigan, Ohio, Indiana, Arkansas, Missouri, Iowa, Wisconsin, Illinois, and Minnesota—evoke a sweet nostalgia. You'll relive the early days of the automobile at the Henry Ford Museum in Michigan, conjure up visions of Tom Sawyer in Missouri, and journey to the town where Abe Lincoln lived in Illinois. Farther north you'll savor the sharp tang of Wisconsin Cheddar and explore the shores and islands of the Great Lakes. The charms of the Midwest are legion, from the Ozarks of Arkansas to the glittering Twin Cities of Minnesota, from the fertile farms of Iowa to the architectural wonders of the Windy City. The next 38 pages take you there to see for yourself.

Michigan

From the mighty city that gave us the automobile to a quaint Victorian island where no cars are allowed, Michigan is a state of contrasts, colored by cherry blossoms and sparkling lakeshores.

SOUTHERN MICHIGAN

1 DETROIT

As you drive around the Motor City, thank Henry Ford. In 1896 he started America's love affair with the automobile when he cruised in his motorized quadricycle from Detroit to Dearborn, the most important nine miles ever driven. In 1914, when Ford offered people $5 a day to work on his invention, the moving assembly line, thousands of tenant farmers and sharecroppers resettled in Detroit. The city, and the world, have never been the same.

Today visitors can tour the opulent homes of several auto barons. The 1927 **Lawrence Fisher Mansion,** built by a founder of Fisher Body Company and president of Cadillac Motors, is one of the most lavish, with walnut pillars, gold-leaf ceilings, and original artwork from Asia and India.

At the **Detroit Institute of Arts,** one of the country's top collections traces man's artistic creations from prehistory to the present day. Gaze at Diego Rivera's powerful 27-panel mural "Detroit Industry," and hunt for the artist's self-portrait hidden in the work.

In the 1960's, led by Berry Gordy, Jr., black musicians in Detroit gave the world the Motown Sound, named for the motor town where it all began. The **Motown Historical Museum,** where the first hits were recorded, is located in a brick house known as Hitsville USA. Exhibits include one of Michael Jackson's costumes from The Jackson Five.

▶ *To travel within the downtown business district, ride the People Mover. This elevated light rail travels a three-mile loop making 13 stops, including Greektown, the place to go for authentic Greek fare.*

2 DEARBORN

On the University of Michigan campus at Dearborn, the 1914 **Henry Ford Estate** was one of the best mechanically equipped homes of its day. A six-level powerhouse designed by Ford and

Icons of America's past *are preserved for posterity at the Henry Ford Museum.*

Thomas Edison still supplies the electricity, heat, and light. Bathroom faucets marked "Air" served as early blow-dryers. Paths wind through the extensive gardens on the grounds.

Despite saying "History is more or less bunk," Ford set out to save as much Americana as he could at the **Henry Ford Museum & Greenfield Village.** Today the museum contains everything, including the kitchen sink: the fixtures

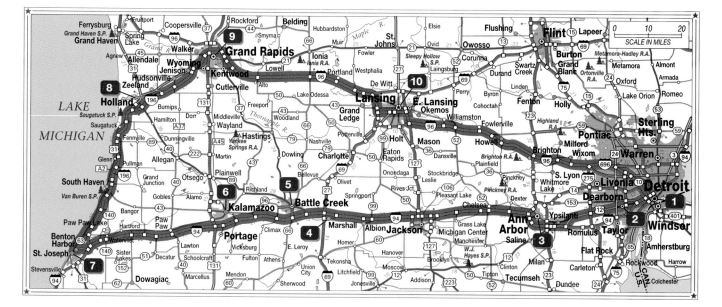

pass overhead on a conveyer belt in a $6-million multimedia presentation, "Made in America." There are priceless objects, such as the rocker in which Lincoln was shot in Ford's Theater, and more than 100 historic cars, including the limousine John F. Kennedy rode in on the day of his death. Among the structures moved from around the country to Greenfield Village are the Wright brothers' home and bicycle shop, Thomas Edison's Menlo Park laboratory, and the farmhouse where Henry Ford was born, along with operating sawmills and an early machine shop.

▶ *You must purchase separate tickets to the Henry Ford Museum and Greenfield Village. Or, to save money, buy a combination ticket and your second day is free.*

3 ANN ARBOR

Ann Arbor, whose streets are lined with restaurants, boutiques, and art galleries, is the home of the highly regarded **University of Michigan.** The name of the city honors the wives of its founders, both named Ann, and its trees. Enjoy their colorful foliage on a crisp fall Saturday when the Wolverines battle for the Big Ten championship. Or visit in late July to catch the **Ann Arbor Art Fairs,** three simultaneous events that combine to make one of the biggest fairs in the country.

4 MARSHALL

In the 1830's, when Marshall was vying to be the state capital, one optimistic resident built the still-standing Greek Revival **Governor's Mansion.** When the town lost out to Lansing by one vote, "progress" passed it by. Today it is a Victorian gem, with a rich array of 19th-century architecture. The eccentric **Honolulu House** was built in 1860 by Abner Pratt, former U.S. consul to Hawaii, to remind him of his island home. Here you can pick up a list of Marshall's other historic houses.

The **American Museum of Magic,** open by appointment, amuses sleight-of-hand fans with posters, lithographs, and apparatus used by famous magicians, including a giant padlocked milk can from which Houdini escaped.

5 BATTLE CREEK

In the mid-1800's, Battle Creek was the headquarters of the lacto-vegetarian Seventh-Day Adventists. Church member Dr. John Kellogg, interested in the nutritional benefits of grains, believed that "you are what you eat." He and his brother Will and another resident, C.W. Post, made Battle Creek the Cereal Capital of the World. During the **Cereal City Festival** in June, the world's longest breakfast table is set up downtown and free cereal is served to more than 50,000 people.

An abolitionist stronghold, Battle Creek was home to the abolitionist, evangelist, and former slave Sojourner Truth from 1856 to 1883; she is buried in **Oak Hill Cemetery.**

6 KALAMAZOO

The city whose name has inspired many a verse and lyric sits in the middle of one of Michigan's wine regions, where more than 200 varieties of wine are bottled. You can tour local vineyards, stomp grapes, and sample wines the first weekend after Labor Day during the **Wine and Harvest Festival.**

Car and plane buffs will have a roaring time in Kalamazoo. Rare World War II aircraft, such as the P-40 Warhawk and the Grumman Hellcat, are highlights of the **Kalamazoo Aviation History Museum.** At the **Gilmore Classic Car Club Museum,** historic Michigan barns house some 130 antique autos, including a 1948 Tucker driven only 19 miles.

7 ST. JOSEPH/BENTON HARBOR

These twin cities on opposite banks of the St. Joseph River sit amidst a bountiful fruit-growing region. Dozens of roadside markets and pick-your-own farms supply apples, peaches, pumpkin pies, and more. Several wineries in the surrounding area offer tours and tastings. In May some 30 communities gather for the **Blossomtime Festival** in St. Joseph, which features a Blossomtime Ball and a Grand Floral Parade.

8 HOLLAND

In May, during the **Tulip Time Festival,** millions of hybrid tulips bloom in Holland, Michigan, settled in 1847 by Dutch immigrants. Year-round you can watch craftsmen make wooden shoes

A children's parade stars in the Tulip Time Festival in Holland. The festival is kicked off by a true Dutch street scrubbing, carried out by thousands of costumed residents armed with buckets of water and brooms.

and paint traditional blue-and-white delftware at the **DeKlomp Wooden Shoe and Delft Factory.** A working 1780's windmill, brought over from the Netherlands, turns in the breeze at **Windmill Island.** The working mill produces flour that visitors can buy.

9 GRAND RAPIDS

A center of fine furniture making, Grand Rapids was home to early lumber barons, who built fabulous homes in the **Heritage Hill Historic District.** This is also the site of several Frank Lloyd Wright–designed residences.

▶ *Some of the homes open their doors to visitors during the Heritage Hill Home Tour in October.*

The **Public Museum of Grand Rapids** tips its hat to furniture making with Mission Style pieces by Gustave Stickley and works by George Nelson, the Father of Modernism. Also in the museum are natural history exhibits and a re-created 1890's street. The **Grand Rapids Art Museum** displays Renaissance, German Expressionist, and American paintings.

In addition to furniture, Grand Rapids produced a president: Gerald Ford. At the **Gerald R. Ford Museum,** a replica of the Oval Office during his administration lets you envision him in the seat of power. Other exhibits recount Ford's personal life and career.

10 LANSING

With one log cabin and a sawmill, Lansing seemed an unlikely spot for the state capital but was nonetheless given the honor in the mid-1800's. The restored Victorian **State Capitol,** dedicated in 1879, is dominated by an elongated Welsh tin dome. Inside are lighted glass floor tiles in the rotunda, chandeliers designed by Tiffany, floors of white marble and black slate, and historic memorabilia. More history can be found two blocks away in the **Michigan Historical Museum,** which offers a walk-through copper mine and a replica of a 1957 Detroit auto show, complete with a vintage red Corvette.

The Lansing factory of Ransom E. Olds was once the nation's largest car producer, and Oldsmobiles are still made here today. The **R.E. Olds Museum** displays the first Oldsmobile, along with the Reo, Star, and Durant.

The Grand Hotel on Mackinac Island is a bastion of old-fashioned elegance.

NORTHERN MICHIGAN

1 TRAVERSE CITY

The resort town of Traverse City, center of one of the world's largest cherry-growing regions, sits on a two-pronged extension of Lake Michigan called Grand Traverse Bay. The bay's convoluted perimeter provides Traverse City and its environs with some 250 miles of shoreline, where wide beaches and endless sand dunes beckon.

Venture north along orchard-lined Rte. 37, through Old Mission Peninsula. The drive is most beautiful in mid-May, when the cherry trees are in bloom. At the tip of the peninsula

stands the **Old Mission Lighthouse,** one of the oldest on the Great Lakes.

Back in Traverse City a true treat awaits. The tall ship *Malabar,* a two-masted schooner, is just right for a day trip, a sunset cruise, or an overnight stay in one of eight staterooms.

2 SLEEPING BEAR DUNES NATIONAL LAKESHORE

There's no need to travel to the Sahara to see truly massive sand dunes. On this 33-mile strip of Lake Michigan shoreline, mountainlike dunes—among the world's largest—loom over the water. Bike or drive the 7.1-mile **Pierce Stocking Scenic Drive** for excellent views of the dunes and the lake.

Imagine entire forests being buried by blowing sand, only to be uncovered years later as the migrating sands move away. Such "ghost forests," resembling giant matchsticks jutting from the sand, are Sleeping Bear's trademark.

To experience Lake Michigan's nautical heritage, take the 90-minute ferry ride from the mainland village of Leland to **South Manitou Island.** Looking down from the island's dunes, you can see shipwrecks strewn in the shallows. A hike to the Valley of the Giants brings you to some of the largest white cedar trees in existence. Jeep tours explore abandoned 19th-century apple orchards and farms. The ferry also serves **North Manitou Island,** where visitors can hike and camp among 15,000 acres of forested wilderness.

3 MACKINAC ISLAND

Bicycles and horse-drawn carriages rule the roads of this timeless resort island, where no cars are allowed. Reached by ferries from St. Ignace and Mackinaw City, the island, pronounced MAK-i-naw, is edged with high cliffs and sprinkled with strange rock formations.

Perched on a bluff overlooking the harbor is **Fort Mackinac,** built by the British in 1780. Costumed guides lead visitors through the fort's 14 original buildings. Artillery and musketry drills echo the sounds of the past.

The island's air of 19th-century gentility is epitomized by the graceful, sprawling **Grand Hotel,** open since 1887. A magnificent 660-foot-long ve-

The Grand Sable Dunes at Pictured Rocks National Lakeshore sit atop 300-foot banks created by glacial meltwater deposits. Reach them via the beautiful Ghost Forest Trail, accessible from Grand Sable Falls.

randa, supported by 40 three-story pillars, overlooks the Straits of Mackinac.

▶ *In summer an easy way to see the island is by a carriage tour, which stops at all the major attractions. Bicycles can be rented on Main Street.*

The eight-mile-long **Lake Shore Road,** which circles the island and can

north, was on the rise back in the 1860's, the forests that supplied charcoal for the smelters had been depleted. Meanwhile, coke-fired furnaces in Ohio began churning out better-quality iron, and by 1891 Fayette had become a ghost town. Today in **Fayette State Park,** visitors can tour the old town hall, a hotel, and six other buildings, as well as blast-furnace ruins.

through mid-October from Munising on the southern shore of Lake Superior.

The colorful cliffs give way to equally beautiful inland splendors. Maps available at information centers in Munising Falls and Grand Marais point the way to 60-foot-high **Munising Falls,** pristine **Twelvemile Beach,** and the shifting sands of **Grand Sable Dunes.**

6 TAHQUAMENON FALLS

When the Chippewa camped here, on the banks of the Tahquamenon River, they fished for walleye, hunted deer, and enjoyed two striking waterfalls that thunder nearby. Within **Tahquamenon Falls State Park,** just west of Paradise, the Tahquamenon Falls is the scene of the legend of Hiawatha. The Upper Falls, 200 feet wide, with a 50-foot vertical drop, is one of the largest east of the Mississippi. The Lower Falls roars in cascades that drop 22 feet.

7 GAYLORD

Far from the Alps, this village boasts what may be the nation's only Swiss-style taco fast-food restaurant. The Alpine motif is part of a town-wide makeover that has seen Gaylord, sister city to Pontresina, Switzerland, transform itself into The Alpine Village. There is even an authentic glockenspiel (carillon) on Main Street, complete with 23 bells and two moving figures dressed in Alpine garb. During **Alpenfest,** in July, Gaylord folk don lederhosen and dirndls for a colorful parade.

8 GRAYLING

Set amid stands of pungent jack pine, Grayling is home to a rare songbird called the Kirtland's warbler. Only about 1,000 exist in the world, all in this area. Mid-May through early July, the U.S. Fish and Wildlife Service offers tours of the birds' nesting grounds.

▶ *The free tours depart from the Holiday Inn in Grayling, which offers a special package deal for birders.*

Seven miles northeast of town, **Hartwick Pines State Park** boasts a 49-acre grove of giant white pines, including the 350-year-old Monarch, which stands 155 feet tall.

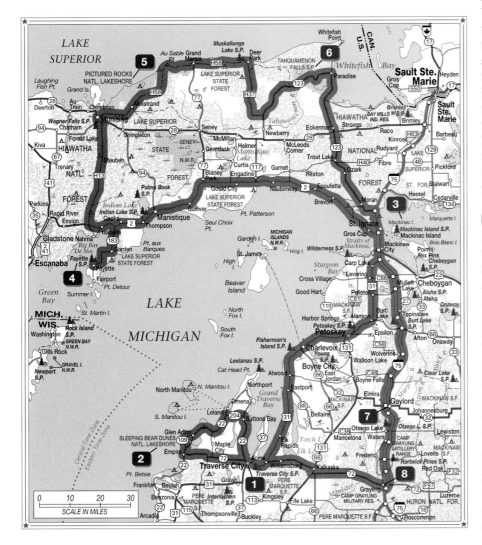

be pedaled in about two hours, boasts an impressive claim to fame: it may be the only state highway in the nation upon which an accident involving a motorized vehicle has never occurred.

4 FAYETTE STATE PARK

Over a century ago, the iron-smelting boomtown of Fayette, on the shores of Lake Michigan's Big Bay de Noc, went bust. Although the demand for pig iron, smelted from ore mined 75 miles to the

5 PICTURED ROCKS NATIONAL LAKESHORE

Nature as primeval sculptor displays some of her finest work along this 43-mile stretch bordering Lake Superior. Multihued sandstone cliffs rise 200 feet, carved by wind, waves, and ice into myriad shapes, and "painted" orange, black, green, and white by minerals seeping from the rocks. A good way to view the spectacle is on a three-hour excursion boat tour, departing late May

Ohio

Ohio has more than its share of bustling cities, but slows its pace on the lovely islands of Lake Erie and in Holmes County, where the largest Amish settlement in the world prospers.

CLEVELAND & THE NORTH

1 CLEVELAND

In 1796, Moses Cleaveland led the Connecticut Land Company's first surveying party into the wilds south of Lake Erie. Unfortunately, he never returned to insist that his namesake settlement spell his name correctly.

Even misspelled, Ohio's second-largest city is an industrious and ethnically diverse town that in recent years has systematically pulled itself up from its Rust Belt nadir. In **The Flats,** on both banks of the Cuyahoga River, revelers pack the docks lined with lively restaurants and nightclubs housed in former warehouses.

More serious-minded are the attractions within **University Circle,** a walkable square mile of world-class museums, gardens, and music and other cultural institutions. **The Cleveland Museum of Art** is a connoisseur's jewel box, as rich in Asian art as in Western. **The Western Reserve Historical Society** shows off its high-Victorian decorative arts in the 1911 Hay mansion. The admission fee also covers the **Crawford Auto-Aviation Museum,** where antique planes join an automobile collection that features cars from 1897 to the present, including the Cleveland car industry's first vehicle, an 1898 Winton, through its last, a 1932 Peerless.

▶ *For a panoramic view of the city, head for the observation deck of the 52-story Terminal Tower, built atop a former railroad station.*

Across town from University Circle, rockets stand in ranks at the **NASA Lewis Research Center.** An Apollo space capsule and models of satellites and space shuttles are also displayed.

2 AKRON

A Tudor Revival treasure, **Stan Hywet Hall and Gardens** was the home of Franklin Seiberling, cofounder of Goodyear Tire and Rubber, and his family. Ohio's largest private house, it was completed in 1915, and is furnished with a combination of venerable European pieces and the best of American craftsmanship. You'll find 16th-century Flemish tapestries, linenfold paneling, and a Sheffield candelabra. One thing you aren't likely to spot is a telephone; such modern contraptions are tastefully hidden. The 70-acre garden, from lagoon to conservatory to teahouse, is more impressive still.

3 CANTON

Football fans can pick up the phone and eavesdrop on Red Grange's visit with President Coolidge or relive Tom Dempsey's record-setting 63-yard field goal at the **Pro Football Hall of Fame.** To marvel at the Immaculate Reception during the 1972 Steelers-Raiders game, just touch the "Fantastic Finishes" video. And be sure to see the Hall's oldest pigskin, an 1890's football shaped like an ostrich egg.

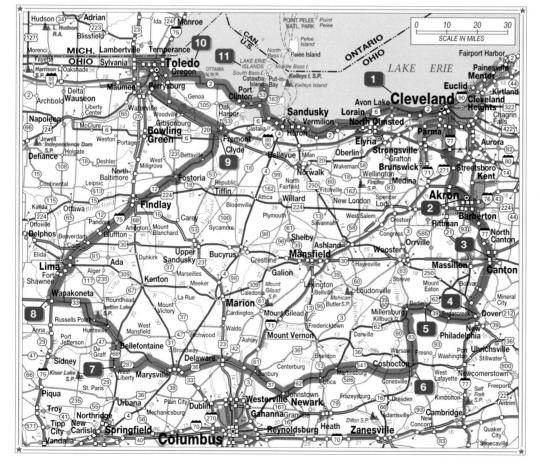

A garden court at the Cleveland Museum of Art offers visitors a verdant oasis. Below, a Chinese serving pedestal, inlaid with blue, green, and red pigment, dates from about 500 B.C.

4 DOVER

One look inside the **Warther Museum** proves that the inspired hands of Ernest and Freida Warther were rarely idle. Warther carved in his spare time for more than 50 years, chronicling the evolution of the steam train in ebony, ivory, walnut, and pearl. His wife, Freida, collected and mounted more than 73,000 buttons. Rooms bulging, the Warthers opened the museum, and today a third generation shows off grandfather's handiwork and sells the hand-honed cutlery he developed.

5 BERLIN

It is here in Holmes County—not in Lancaster, Pennsylvania—that you'll find the world's largest concentration of Amish. Pastoral Berlin, where trademark horse-drawn buggies travel narrow country roads, is the perfect spot to sample Amish cheese and mouthwatering baked goods, shop for rolltop desks, and sleep under hand-stitched quilts. The Mennonite Information Center helps visitors respectfully explore the Amish and Mennonite ways of life. A giant cyclorama depicts their European persecution and subsequent flight to America.

▶ *October is the busiest tourist month in Holmes County; visit April though June to avoid the crowds. When in any Amish community, drive with extra caution and watch for slower-moving horse-drawn buggies.*

6 COSHOCTON

Pulled along at four miles an hour aboard the *Monticello III*, visitors glide back in time to the canal revolution of the 1830's and 40's. **Roscoe Village** on the Ohio & Erie Canal was just one of thousands of towns along the watery trenches that linked America's vast terrain. The restored living-history settlement bustles again with a blacksmith's shop, a general store, a one-room schoolhouse, and a craftsman's house where a weaver demonstrates his trade. All are contained in a walkable district of Greek Revival buildings, brick sidewalks, and wrought-iron lampposts.

7 WEST LIBERTY

When you spot turrets towering above the cornstalks here, you may think it's a mirage. But two castles do indeed rise like Brigadoon from the fields of West Liberty. After seven years of painstaking crafting, a former Civil War general, Abram Piatt, completed his Norman-style castle, **Mac-A-Cheek,** in 1871 and filled it with family antiques collected over several generations. Ten years later his brother Donn completed his Flemish-style home, **Mac-O-Chee,** now filled with treasures from Asia and Europe. Both castle names are variations on the Shawnee for "smiling valley."

8 WAPAKONETA

At the **Neil Armstrong Air and Space Museum,** an old black-and-white bike seems out of place alongside the solid-gold model of a lunar module, the *Gemini 8* spacecraft, and the glinting moon rocks. But the bike, suspended from the rafters, may be the most telling of all the Armstrong memorabilia in his hometown museum. The lad who became the first man to walk on the moon earned his pilot's license before his driver's license—and he needed some way to get to the airport.

9 FREMONT

Behind wrought-iron gates brought from the White House itself, the **Rutherford B. Hayes Presidential Center,** known as Spiegel Grove, was the nation's first presidential library. After his 1877– 81 term, Hayes and his wife, Lucy, returned to the red-brick mansion here, where many heirloom furnishings remain. Gilded Age style is also on parade in the adjacent museum, which features a White House carriage, daughter Fanny's dollhouse, and Lucy's wedding and inaugural gowns.

10 TOLEDO

Toledo has been known since the turn of the century as a glass-manufacturing center, so it's fitting that the **Toledo Museum of Art** glitters among the world's glass collections. Alongside ancient Egyptian art, African sculpture, and paintings by such masters as Rubens and Rembrandt, priceless glass may be found. On display is a magnificent lamp, gilded and enameled, from a 14th-century Egyptian mosque, and a punch bowl and cup set, blown and cut to gargantuan proportions for the 1904 Louisiana Purchase Exposition.

11 LAKE ERIE ISLANDS

An island-hopping cruise from Sandusky to Kelleys Island and South Bass Island may be the best way to tour the remote and beautiful Lake Erie Islands, where visitors dine on lake-fresh perch, sip locally made wines, and travel leisurely by golf cart.

South Bass Island's **Put-in-Bay** is a quaint village where charming inns, restaurants, and boutiques rival fishing as the main attraction. Head for the 352-foot-high observation deck of **Perry's Victory and International Peace Memorial** for a stunning view of the is-

The Perry Memorial at Put-in-Bay is said to be the largest Doric column in the world.

lands, which might be Canadian today if Commodore Oliver Hazard Perry hadn't defeated the British Royal Navy here in 1813.

Serene **Kelleys Island,** a national historic district, is a naturalist's retreat, with a rare Lake Erie sand beach and massive spring migrations of warblers. At **Glacial Grooves State Memorial,** scars raked in limestone by a great ice sheet 30,000 years ago are still visible.

CINCINNATI & THE SOUTH

1 CINCINNATI

This venerable Ohio River town was remembered by Longfellow as Queen of the West. Today its glittering downtown district around **Fountain Square Plaza** is interconnected by one of the nation's first skywalk systems.

The river's edge may be the best place to begin your visit. The **Bicentennial Commons** at Sawyer Point includes a four-mile Riverwalk heritage trail and the dramatic Cincinnati Gateway Sculpture, which is topped by flying pigs raising their cloven hooves in civic salute to memorialize the city's pork-processing heyday.

Mount Adams rises from the river basin, a trendy neighborhood of skinny shotgun houses, Victorian taverns, coffeehouses, and chic galleries. On sum-

mer evenings, locals turn out in force for dinner or a nightcap served up with sweeping city views.

▶ *While in Cincinnati, try the chili. The chili parlors keep their recipes secret, but chocolate and cinnamon are thought to contribute to the taste.*

Mount Adams flows out into **Eden Park,** where gardens and a picturesque lake surround the exotic plantings of the **Krohn Conservatory.** The park's crowning glory is the **Cincinnati Art Museum.** The Romanesque interior of the 1886 museum was recently restored, a fitting showcase for one of the country's best general collections.

The city's other main museums are located in **Union Terminal,** itself a National Historic Landmark. The half-domed behemoth houses the **Cincinnati Museum of Natural History,** with a shivery Ice Age exhibit, and the **Cincinnati Historical Society Museum,** with a step-aboard steamboat.

A hidden gem is the **Taft Museum,** housed in an 1820 Federal-style residence. Chinese porcelains, Flemish tapestries, and works by Turner and Whistler are on view.

Take an exotic side trip through the steamy miasma of Jungle Trails, a rain forest habitat at the **Cincinnati Zoo and Botanical Garden.** Already world-famous for its white tigers, lowland gorillas, and Komodo dragons, the zoo has created a realm of fog-shrouded vines and synthesized jungle cries for a host of fascinating Asian and African rain forest animals, many endangered.

2 LEBANON

While visiting Lebanon in 1842, Charles Dickens grumbled that the town's signature inn, **The Golden Lamb,** served only nonalcoholic libations. But instead of holding a grudge, Ohio's oldest inn named a guest room after him. If Dickens himself materialized today, he would find the tall red-brick building much as it was 150 years ago, and the pillows fluffed and inviting in the Dickens Room, which features a massive Victorian bedroom suite. The inn also boasts a large collection of Shaker furnishings.

3 DAYTON

While not as mystifying as the Stonehenge monoliths, the towering pole in the center of **SunWatch Village,** on the outskirts of town, served its prehistoric people just as well. One set of angled shadows signaled the time of planting and harvesting, another time of hunting, trapping, and winter fishing. Today the rhythm of 13th-century daily life for the Fort Ancient Indians pulsates again within a circle of some 25 houses, several of which have been excavated and rebuilt.

Dayton, hometown of Orville and Wilbur Wright, is a fitting location for the world's oldest and largest military aviation museum, the **United States Air Force Museum.** On the grounds of Wright-Patterson Air Force Base, it covers the entire history of military aviation, from an original Wright *Flyer* to *Bockscar,* the B-29 that dropped the atomic bomb on Nagasaki, to an F-117A from Operation Desert Storm.

The Art Deco Union Terminal in Cincinnati opened as a passenger train station in 1933 and now houses the Museum Center. Its rotunda is filled with murals and details from the Art Deco era.

such geological curiosities as Devil's Bathtub, a giant pothole formed by swirling sand and gravel. Ash Cave, the largest of its kind in the state, was named for the mounds of ashes, thought to be remnants of ancient American Indian campfires, discovered by the pioneers. Large enough to seat hundreds of people, it was used as a meeting place in the 19th century. A 90-foot waterfall plunges to the valley floor below.

▶ *Beginning hikers may want to walk the paved path to Ash Cave, or the gentle gorge trail (as opposed to the rugged rim trail) through beautiful Conkle's Hollow.*

4 WILBERFORCE

Named for British abolitionist William Wilberforce, this town is home to what is now called Wilberforce University, the first black university in the country, founded for escaped and freed slaves.

At the **National Afro-American Museum and Cultural Center,** a permanent gallery celebrates "Victory to Freedom: Afro-American Life in the '50's." Music, photographs, and videotapes pay tribute to the Civil Rights era, covering World War II through the passage of the Voting Rights Act in 1965.

5 YELLOW SPRINGS

Weekend shoppers flock to the village of Yellow Springs, where leaders of the 1960's counterculture are among those who retail crystals, pottery, and Birkenstock sandals behind their own shop counters. Beyond its business district, the 1820's spa town has retained dozens of 19th-century Federal, Greek Revival, and Italianate homes.

Walk or bike the **Little Miami Scenic Trail,** which skirts the edge of **Glen Helen.** This 1,000-acre nature preserve belongs to Antioch University and is crossed by the Little Miami River. At its raptor center, visitors can see some 13 species of hawks and owls.

6 COLUMBUS

Birthplace of author James Thurber, Ohio's well-kept capital is perched on the cutting edge of science and technology, an exemplary home for **COSI, Ohio's Center of Science & Industry.** In the center's outdoor Science Park, visitors can ride a high-wire cycle and lift a car with the help of a giant lever. Inside, you can direct and tape your own newscast or music video.

A pealing schoolbell and clanging blacksmith hammer are among the sights and sounds in the re-created **Ohio Village.** A composite of small Buckeye towns from the 1860's, it has the obligatory town hall, one-room schoolhouse, and hotel-tavern, and such commercial necessities as the harnessmaker, blacksmith, and general store. Costumed living-history artisans are ready to discuss the finer points of a coverlet weave or a gunstock's finish.

7 HOCKING HILLS

With unimaginable force, glacial meltwaters gouged out the sandstone here with the ease of children filling beach buckets. Tens of thousands of years later, the ferocity stands petrified as **Hocking Hills State Park,** where waterfalls flow into a gorge studded with

8 RIO GRANDE

Nestled in the Appalachian foothills, Rio Grande sits amidst a region of rich farmlands, tobacco fields, and grazing cattle. Farm trucks used to follow the oinking pigs to **Bob Evans Farm.** Today the only porkers here may be two Vietnamese potbellied pigs hogging their share of attention at the petting barnyard. The original farm of sausage magnate Bob Evans is now a living-history center devoted to the crafts, farming, and people of the area. Sign up for a wagon tour, canoe trip, or horseback ride, or strike out through the woods on carefully tended trails.

9 SERPENT MOUND

An observation tower at **Serpent Mound State Memorial** overlooks one of the world's most magnificent prehistoric effigy mounds. It is attributed to the Adena people, though recent archeological findings may point elsewhere. Built of stone and yellow clay as early as 1000 B.C., the five- to eight-foot-high mound slithers for nearly a quarter-mile from tail to gaping jaws. The reason for the shape of the mound remains a mystery, though it is believed to have religious significance. A museum displays archeological exhibits and artifacts.

Indiana

This industrious heartland state has plenty of treasures: gentle hills dusted with wildflowers, cornfields studded with wooden windmills, and scenic railways crisscrossing Hoosier forestland.

SOUTHERN INDIANA

1 INDIANAPOLIS

A wealth of cultural activities compete for the savvy traveler's attention in Indiana's capital and largest city. But what more appropriate place to start your driving tour than at the **Indianapolis Motor Speedway,** home of the Indianapolis 500? This world-famous car race is held here every year on the Sunday before Memorial Day. A bus tour will take you for a lap around the 2½-mile track.

▶ *Get your racing fix and avoid the crowds to boot by attending the Indy practice and qualifying trials on the three weekends before the big race.*

At the **Hall of Fame Museum,** you can see several race-winning cars as well as beautifully restored antiques,

Hands-on archeologists: *Kids dig for "dinosaur" fossils at the Children's Museum.*

including Stutzes and Duesenbergs.

Racing is not the only game in town. Basketball roots run deep in Indiana. Big-time hoops events are held in the 60,500-seat **Hoosier Dome** downtown. The dome is an attraction in itself, with an eight-acre Teflon-coated roof. Also downtown is **Union Station,** an 1888 Romanesque train terminal, with shops, eateries, and nightclubs.

Hoosiers do not live by sports alone. The **Indianapolis Museum of Art,** which sits in a 152-acre park, is a gem. Here you'll find Renaissance and Old Master paintings. The park is also home to the **Lilly Pavilion of Decorative Arts,** once the château-style home of J. K. Lilly, Jr., and now a showcase of furniture, porcelains, silver, and gold. The monumental **Indiana War Memorial** contains a museum of war memorabilia. The hands-on exhibits at the world's largest children's museum, the **Children's Museum of Indianapolis,** include a role-playing area, where kids can dress up as letter carriers or grocers; a nature center, with a simulated limestone cave to explore; and a colorful wooden carousel.

2 NOBLESVILLE

A dramatic living-history re-creation of an 1836 pioneer settlement, the **Conner Prairie Museum** features more than a dozen restored log cabins, workshops, a general store, and houses—each manned by costumed guides who interact with visitors while engaging in day-to-day frontier activities.

3 METAMORA

Restored to its heyday as a bustling 19th-century canal town, Metamora has more than 100 shops, each with frontier wood-and-fieldstone storefronts. The **Whitewater Canal State Historic Site** preserves 15 miles of tree-lined

Speedway thrills *are shared by thousands at the annual Indianapolis 500 car race.*

waterway. In summer take the 25-minute cruise on the *Ben Franklin III,* a 19th-century canalboat pulled by draft horses. The 1845 **Metamora Grist Mill** still grinds wheat and corn; the flour is sold in the gift shop. The canals are illuminated by candlelight on three weekends before Christmas during the **Old Fashioned Christmas Walk.**

Paddlers can arrange a canoe trip—through churning white water or gently rippling streams—at **Whitewater Valley Canoe Rental, Inc.,** eight miles east in Brookville, which offers 17 different warm-weather options.

4 AURORA

A transplanted Scotsman, Thomas Gaff, made his fortune here in the 1800's distilling whiskey and brewing beer. Gaff also owned a fleet of riverboats and built a mansion home along the fanciful lines of a steamboat. **Hillforest** rests on a scenic bluff overlooking the Ohio River. This national historic landmark house features elaborate moldings and *trompe l'oeil* decorations.

5 MADISON

The winding road southward to this port city is the **Chief White Eye Trail,** which slashes through sylvan valleys and crosses glistening streams. Three miles northeast of Canaan, set back among spruce trees, is the grave marker

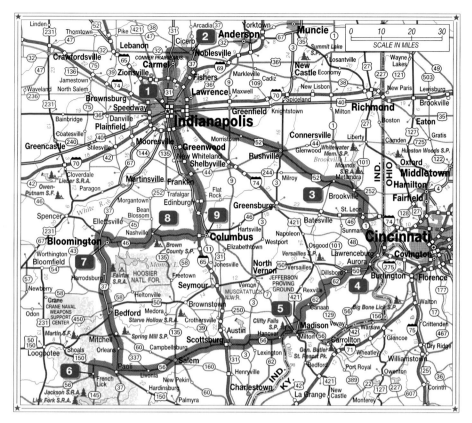

of the Wyandotte Indian chief killed near here in 1812. The descent into Madison is rimmed with rocky cliffs, where 19th-century homes overlook the Ohio River valley. The town itself looks like something out of the steamboat age and has more than 130 blocks of historic architecture. Visit the **James Lanier State Historic Site,** a handsome antebellum mansion adorned with an octagonal cupola.

One mile west of Madison is the 1,360-acre **Clifty Falls State Park.** Its cliffside waterfalls and rocky gorge are accessible by 10 hiking trails.

6 FRENCH LICK

A salt lick lured animals—and subsequently French hunters and trappers—to these scenic hillsides in the late 1600's and gave French Lick its unusual name. The reputed curative powers of three artesian springs transformed the town into a bustling spa. The 1901 **French Lick Springs Resort** was once a gambling mecca for bigwigs and Hollywood types. You can tour the restored hotel and admire its creamy-white pillars and crystal chandeliers. Stroll the garden and get a cool drink from the marble-topped Pluto artesian spring.

One mile north in the little town of West Baden Springs, you will be able to spy the massive unsupported dome of the **West Baden Springs Hotel** looming above the treetops. The now-closed hotel was considered one of the wonders of the world at the time of its construction in 1901.

▶ *From April through November, the French Lick Scenic Railway takes visitors from an old railroad depot in French Lick through forestlands.*

Twenty miles north is Mitchell and **Spring Mill State Park.** This recreational park features a working 19th-century gristmill, powered by cave water. The pioneer village that grew up around it has been restored; you can tour a blacksmith shop and an apothecary. The park has seven hiking trails, from half a mile to 2½ miles long. In the spring the hilly trails are framed by tufts of violets; in the summer rosy milkweed and dark blue lobelia line the paths. Trail Five circles the shallow lake, where you can rent paddleboats. Cruise the park's cave system on the 15-minute **Twin Caves Boat Ride.**

7 BLOOMINGTON

This laid-back college town recalls an earlier era—albeit a relatively recent one. The celebrated music and arts curriculum at **Indiana University** has long attracted artists and bohemians. Art galleries, vegetarian restaurants, and book and music shops give the downtown a loose, freewheeling style reminiscent of the 1960's. Visit the **Indiana University Art Museum,** designed by I. M. Pei. Stop in to see the **Thomas Hart Benton Murals,** in the IU Auditorium entry hall. Here are many of Benton's colorful populist murals of Indiana culture.

8 NASHVILLE

The densely forested curves and rises of Rte. 46 into this bucolic town retain the natural beauty that lured artists to the Indiana hill country in the early 1900's. You can savor the crisp, fresh air, the

A gristmill of old continues to grind cornmeal at Spring Mill State Park. The 1817 structure is part of a restored pioneer village that thrived as a 19th-century mill town.

profusion of redbud and dogwood trees in the spring, and the fruits of local artisans' labors at the **Brown County Art Guild.** And until you've tried the fried biscuits with apple butter—standard fare at most local restaurants—you simply haven't arrived. Five miles north is the little town of **Bean Blossom,** where Bill Monroe, the father of bluegrass music, stages his **Bluegrass Festival** twice a year, in June and September.

9 COLUMBUS

I. M. Pei and Robert A. M. Stern are among the world-class architects who have created stunning landmarks for this small city of 33,000 people. The path was set for America's Architectural Showplace in the 1950's, when a local philanthropic foundation began putting up the fees for contemporary architects to design some 30 buildings. Today more than 50 striking structures grace Columbus, giving the city a high-culture sheen. You can arrange a guided architectural tour or pick up maps for self-guided walking tours at the **Columbus Visitors Center.** Afterward, savor a double chocolate malted at the marble-and-mahogany soda fountain at **Zaharako's,** circa 1900.

Windmills in a cornfield, *like this one near Goshen, are a typical farmland sight.*

NORTHERN INDIANA

1 SOUTH BEND

The five Studebaker brothers opened a blacksmith shop here in 1852 and by the Civil War were building army wagons. From 1902 to 1964, Studebaker was one of the giants of the automotive industry. The **Studebaker National Museum** collection ranges from Conestoga wagons to the carriage that took Abraham Lincoln to Ford's Theatre on the night of his assassination.

The town is home to the **University of Notre Dame,** founded in 1842. Guided tours of the tree-shaded campus and into the massive Golden Dome can be arranged through the Department of Public Relations.

The only man-made white-water waterway in the country is the **East Race Waterway,** which offers public rafting and kayaking on a 2,000-foot-long course downtown. Stretch out on a grassy knoll under the stars during the **Firefly Festival of the Performing Arts,** a music and theater festival held all summer long at the outdoor amphitheater in St. Patrick's Park.

2 ELKHART

The gateway to Amish country sits astride the Big Elkhart and Little Elkhart rivers. Legend has it that local Indians named the town after the resemblance between an offshore river island and the heart of an elk. You'll find maps for strolling the waterside parks and footbridges at the **Elkhart County Convention and Visitors Bureau.**

Famous for the manufacture of quality band instruments, Elkhart is becoming equally well-known for its **Miles/ Elkhart Jazz Festival,** held annually in mid-July. Thousands attend the three-day fete, where big-name performers play in the 70-year-old restored Elco Theatre and other downtown sites.

► *Festival attendees reserve hotel and motel lodging months in advance. Those who reserve late should contact the Convention and Visitors Bureau for bed-and-breakfast listings.*

Quilting *is a community effort in northern Indiana, where weekly gatherings like this one near Thayer produce beautifully crafted quilts.*

Eight miles away, stop in **Goshen,** called Maple City for its abundance of maple trees. The historic district boasts a charming town square and a 1920's soda shop. The September **Michiana Mennonite Relief Sale** raises funds for worldwide relief efforts and is famous for its one-day auction of handmade quilts and whopping breakfasts of all-you-can-eat pancakes and sausages.

3 SHIPSHEWANA

It's been called the number one tourist attraction in the state. From April to October the weekly **Auction and Flea Market** runs the gamut in offerings— from antique signs to homemade popcorn. In the summer 1,000 vendors travel weekly to this picturesque town from as far away as Chicago and Lansing, Michigan, to hawk their wares.

Shipshewana is located in the heart of the third-largest Amish community in the country. The story of their voyage to America is vividly told at **Menno-Hof Mennonite-Amish Visitors Center.** Squeeze into a cramped "hold" recalling comfortless voyages on 17th-century sailing ships; kids can climb into a loft stocked with storybooks and toys.

4 FORT WAYNE

Within the angular glass skyscrapers of a revitalized downtown is an oasis of plump banana plants, tumbling waterfalls, and tall palms. The **Foellinger-Freimann Botanical Conservatory** is

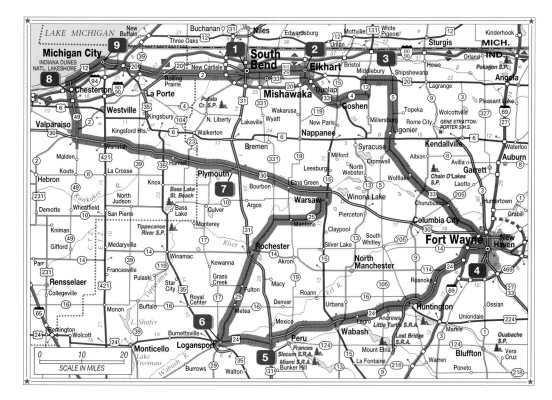

only. In **Riverside Park** hop on **The Carousel**, a wooden 1892 model. Grab the brass ring to win a free ride.

En route to Plymouth you'll be crossing Indiana's lake district. Stop in **Warsaw**, where three lakes—Winona, Center, and Pike—offer prime swimming and fishing.

7 PLYMOUTH

This is blueberry country, full of pick-your-own berry farms. On the Labor Day weekend, 600,000 visitors flock to the **Marshall County Blueberry Festival**. It features the Blueberry Stomp, where runners squish through berries to reach the finish.

one of the Midwest's largest passive-solar conservatories, with a Sonoran desert, a rain forest, and floral displays.

Visit the **Lincoln Museum**, which has the largest collection of Lincoln memorabilia in the world. And pay your respects to the 19th-century folk hero who sowed apple orchards throughout the Midwest. The grave of John Chapman—better known as Johnny Appleseed—is in **Johnny Appleseed Park.**

5 PERU

This city has sawdust in its veins. Peru's life under the big top began when a local livery stable owner acquired a small wild-animal show and built it into the Hagenbeck-Wallace Circus. Eventually, the city was the winter headquarters for 10 major circuses. Peru honors its big-top heritage at the **Circus City Festival Museum.** The **International Circus Hall of Fame** honors circus stars of long ago. In July the magic returns with **Circus City Festival**, where local children perform in a three-ring circus.

6 LOGANSPORT

More than 80 trains a day once rumbled through this historic rail hub. The tracks are quiet now, but rail buffs will find their appetite sated at the **Iron Horse Museum**, an old depot full of rail memorabilia; visit by appointment

8 CHESTERTON

Scrambling up and down dunes, exploring trails, and swimming are hot pursuits at **Indiana Dunes National Lakeshore**. This park has a pretty Lake Michigan beach—and **Mount Baldy**, a traveling sand dune, towering 135 feet above the lake. Mount Baldy moves southward at a rate of about four feet a year. In town, check out the snow globes and tiny edible Munchkin houses at the **Yellow Brick Road** shop and fantasy museum of *The Wizard of Oz* relics. The **Wizard of Oz Festival**, held in September, draws an amazing number of costumed Munchkins and scarecrows to town. The three-day festival is free and is attended by original movie Munchkins and approximately 70,000 other people.

9 MICHIGAN CITY

The show has indeed been the thing at the **Canterbury Summer Theatre** for 25 years. The theater has a resident troupe that performs musicals and comedies in a restored 1867 church.

Gleaming with marble and polished rare woods, the **Barker Mansion** is a turn-of-the-century jewel. The 38-room house was built by the industrialist John H. Barker in 1857.

Ducks in a row: This family of ducks finds the living quiet and easy in a lily-pad pond off Rte. 13 near Middlebury.

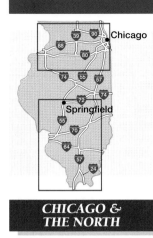

Illinois

Chicago pulses with life, while tiny river towns along the Mississippi take it slow. Springfield, in the middle of it all, remembers an honest country lawyer named Abe, who changed our nation.

1 CHICAGO

Chicago's suburbs still sprout up in the cornfields, but the Windy City is no longer the "toddlin' town" it was once dubbed. Now it is a big-shouldered giant, with a dense collection of modern architectural treasures and some of the finest museums in the country.

According to legend, Mrs. O'Leary's cow kicked Chicago into the modern age by starting the Great Fire in 1871.

Frank Lloyd Wright's *distinctive furniture adorns his Oak Park dining room.*

The city that rose phoenixlike from the flames invented the skyscraper and later the Prairie style of architecture. Look around—and up—to see some of the most memorable landmarks: the 110-story **Sears Tower**, the world's tallest building (visit the Skydeck on the 103rd floor); Louis Sullivan's **Carson Pirie Scott** building, with elaborate cast-iron ornamentation; Mies van der

Rohe's glass-and-steel **Federal Center Plaza**; and a local favorite, the white terra-cotta **Wrigley Building**. The Frank Lloyd Wright–designed **Robie House**, in the residential neighborhood of Hyde Park, perfects the Prairie style. In the suburb of Oak Park is the famous **Frank Lloyd Wright Home and Studio**, which Wright designed when he was 22 years old and remodeled as his family grew and his ideas developed.

▶ *The Chicago Architecture Foundation offers walking tours as well as a boat tour along the Chicago River. Stop in one of the Visitor Information Centers for a list of companies offering sightseeing cruises on Lake Michigan.*

Don't miss one of Chicago's biggest draws: the **Museum of Science and Industry**. Highlights range from a working coal mine to a German sub captured during World War II to a pulsating 16-foot model of a human heart.

At the **Field Museum** the largest mounted dinosaur in the world leads the way to an astounding array of natural history exhibits, including an underground Egyptian tomb site complete with 23 mummies. Across the street the **John G. Shedd Aquarium** has the world's largest indoor oceanarium.

The Art Institute of Chicago displays Grant Wood's "American Gothic," and the best of French Impressionism and Postimpressionism, including Seurat's "Sunday Afternoon on the Island of La Grande Jatte." Perhaps locals like Seurat's painting because it reminds them of their 29 miles of parkland along Lake Michigan, where city folk gather on sunny afternoons. A host of parks and beaches lie within walking distance of the downtown district, called the Loop, and the **Magnificent Mile** to the north, a stretch of Michigan

Avenue where posh shops lure big spenders and window-shoppers alike. If your feet tire out, cruise along Lake Shore Drive for pretty water views.

2 LOCKPORT

Nature laid out a system of connecting waterways between Lake Michigan and the Gulf of Mexico, providing excellent inland transportation—with a few gaps. The young state of Illinois remedied this problem in the 1800's by digging the 96-mile Illinois & Michigan Canal, connecting the Great Lakes to the Mississippi River and making Chicago the nation's largest inland port. Today the **Illinois & Michigan Canal National Heritage Corridor** transports the mind's eye to the 19th century with old locks, restored towpaths, and historic canal buildings, while scenic state parks along the way provide quiet retreats.

Lockport, once the canal headquarters, is one of the most historic canal towns. Stop in the **I&M Canal Visitors Center** for information. Adjacent is a 2½-mile hiking and biking trail that connects to the **I&M Canal State Trail**, stretching from Joliet to LaSalle-Peru. At the **Illinois and Michigan Canal Museum**, housed in the original canal commissioner's office, artifacts and exhibits tell the story of the waterway, and a reconstructed pioneer settlement helps bring back the canal era.

At the **Isle à la Cache Museum** in Romeoville, north of Lockport on Rte. 55, guides dressed as French fur traders recall life here some two centuries before the canal was built.

▶ *Lockport celebrates Old Canal Days the third weekend in June, with craft demonstrations, wagon rides, walking tours, and entertainment.*

3 BISHOP HILL

Tucked amidst pungent pig farms and rustling cornfields is the former Swedish utopian colony of Bishop Hill, which existed from 1846 to 1861. Many original buildings at **Bishop Hill State Historic Site** have been restored

Chicago sprawls mighty and wide, an architectural Athens and model of city planning, designed by Daniel H. Burnham to "outrival Paris."

to their 1860's appearance. The Greek Revival **Steeple Building** is topped by a one-handed clock. Paintings by Olof Krans, one of America's great folk artists, are displayed in the **State of Illinois Historical Museum.**

4 GALESBURG

Carl Sandburg's father was among the immigrants who came to work the railroads here. The Sandburgs' three-room, sparsely furnished home is now the **Carl Sandburg State Historic Site.** Behind the cottage is Remembrance Rock, where the poet's ashes are buried.

In 1858 at the Old Main building at **Knox College,** Abraham Lincoln debat-ed Stephen Douglas before an estimated crowd of 20,000. As Lincoln stepped through a window onto the platform, he is said to have joked, "At last I've been through college."

5 MOLINE AND ROCK ISLAND

Moline and Rock Island, along with Bettendorf and Davenport, Iowa, make up what are called the Quad Cities. In Moline, past and present meet head-on at the **Deere & Company Administrative Center.** Antique plows and agricultural memorabilia are housed in a stark glass-and-steel building, designed by Eero Saarinen, that is considered a modern architectural masterpiece.

In the middle of the Mississippi, Arsenal Island was the site of a military prison during the Civil War, when some 12,000 Confederate troops were imprisoned here. About 2,000 Confederate soldiers are buried in the **Confederate Cemetery,** and some 15,000 soldiers from all of America's armed conflicts lie at rest in the **Rock Island Arsenal National Cemetery.** The **Rock Island Arsenal Museum** houses a large collection of firearms.

The **Black Hawk State Historic Site,** in the city of Rock Island, was home to the Sauk Indians—including the famed warrior Black Hawk—for nearly a century. On display in the **Hauberg Indian Museum** are such priceless artifacts as a dugout canoe more than 200 years old and a stunning necklace made with 20 grizzly bear claws interspersed with glass trade beads.

6 GREAT RIVER ROAD

A beautiful section of the Great River Road, a National Scenic and Recreational Highway following the entire course of the Mississippi, runs from Rock Island to Galena. Along the way **Mississippi Palisades State Park,** north of Savanna, and the **Long Hollow Scenic Overlook,** west of Elizabeth, offer spectacular views. From Savanna to Galena, deep ravines to the east are set against lime-

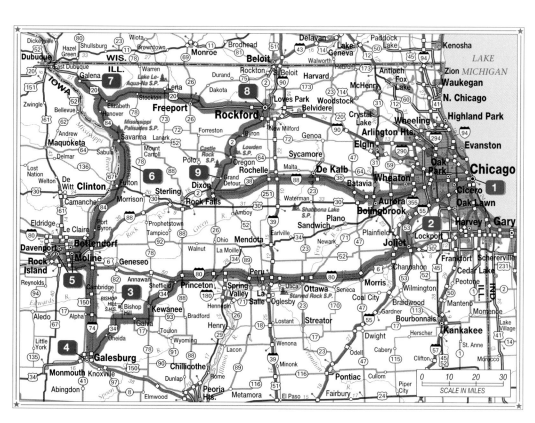

stone bluffs thick with hardwood trees, where bald eagles often winter. To the west the Big Muddy wanders, its serenity interrupted only by the occasional barge or "floating wedding cake"—an old-fashioned paddle wheeler carrying tourists from St. Paul to New Orleans.

7 GALENA

The richest city in Illinois in the 1830's, this was the hub of the world's largest lead-mining center. When the ore ran out, a bonanza of fine architecture remained. Eighty-five percent of the buildings in Galena, called one of the finest antiquing towns of the Midwest, are listed in the National Register of Historic Places. The 1860 **Ulysses S. Grant Home State Historic Site** was a gift from Galena citizens to Grant on his return home from the Civil War. Most of the original furnishings remain.

▶ *Visitors throng to Galena during the spring and fall home tours, the second weekend in June and the last full weekend in September. Make hotel reservations well in advance.*

8 ROCKFORD

The place where the Rock River was forded in the 1800's became Illinois's second-largest city: Rockford. A highlight is the **Time Museum**, where water clocks, sundials, and jewel-encrusted watches chronicle the history of time measurement. A satellite signal display gives the most accurate time known.

9 GRAND DETOUR

Driving through the rich black farmlands of northern Illinois, one wonders how farmers here managed before John Deere invented the steel plow that broke the prairies and changed America forever. At the **John Deere Historic Site**, you can tour his homestead, containing furnishings from the 1830's, and a reconstructed blacksmith shop.

Neighboring Dixon was home to another man who made history. Born in Tampico, Ronald Reagan once reminisced: "Everyone has a place to come home to. For me, Dixon is that place." **Ronald Reagan's Boyhood Home**, a white frame structure, is furnished to look as it did when Reagan lived here.

1 SPRINGFIELD

Strolling through Springfield, it's easy to imagine that Abraham Lincoln, the tall, rawboned country lawyer, still practices here. Desks at the **Lincoln-Herndon Law Offices** are strewn with documents, as though the attorneys had just stepped out to lunch. Lincoln's stovepipe hat hangs in the Quaker-brown **Lincoln Home National Historic Site**, the only home he ever

Lincoln sold most of his things before he moved to Washington, but many were recovered and again grace the Lincoln Home.

owned, where he lived with his family for 17 years. His words echo through the **Lincoln Depot**, from which, worry etching his face, he left to assume the awesome burdens of the presidency.

▶ *Admission is free to the Lincoln Home, but you do need a ticket. In spring and summer there may be a wait. To avoid waiting and guarantee getting a tour, pick up a ticket in the morning for a specific tour time.*

At the **Old State Capitol**, where Lincoln made his famous "House Divided" speech, costumed guides lead tours of the splendid Greek Revival building on Fridays. At the **Lincoln Tomb State Historic Site**, the president rests beneath the inscription "Now He Belongs to the Ages."

Also making his presence felt in Springfield was architect Frank Lloyd Wright. The **Dana-Thomas House** is the best-preserved and most complete of Wright's early Prairie-style houses. It contains original Wright-designed white oak furniture and art-glass doors, windows, and light panels.

North of town, near Petersburg, **Lincoln's New Salem State Historic Site** re-creates the village where young Abe, the community's postmaster, studied law in a cooper's shop by the light of a fire fueled by wood shavings. The reconstructed buildings include two stores that he owned and clerked in.

2 VANDALIA

For an old-fashioned ham-and-bean supper on the lawn of the **Vandalia Statehouse**, visit in mid-June during the **Grand Levee** festival, featuring music, 19th-century arts and crafts demonstrations, and a candlelight tour of the building. The statehouse, which served as the seat of Illinois government from 1820 to 1839, saw Abraham Lincoln cut his political teeth as a freshman state representative. His famous foe, Stephen Douglas, also served here. Built by the townspeople in 1836, the building houses some original furnishings and many period pieces.

3 MOUNT VERNON

View works by artists such as John Singer Sargent, take a class in pottery or weaving, explore a nature trail, or enjoy a sculpture park at **Cedarhurst**, a cultural center set on 85 acres of wildflower-carpeted woodland. There are chamber music concerts, a bird sanctuary, and the Mitchell Museum, which houses an impressive collection of late-19th- and early-20th-century paintings by American artists, including Thomas Eakins and Mary Cassatt.

4 METROPOLIS

Dominating the courthouse square in Metropolis is a statue of this city's adopted son: Superman. Visitors can step into a red-and-blue phone booth to call the man from Krypton, pick up a copy of the local newspaper, the *Daily Planet,* or visit the **Super Museum,** packed with superhero memorabilia. The second weekend in June, a four-day festival honors the Man of Steel.

5 CAIRO

Magnolias bloom in Illinois's southernmost city, whose lavish public and private buildings were built from Civil War spoils. Once a strategic Union stronghold with latent Southern loyalties, Cairo bristles with history. At **Mound City National Cemetery** are the graves of fallen soldiers from the Civil War and every war since. Gen. U. S. Grant, who made his headquarters at Cairo, later stayed at **Magnolia Manor,** an 1869 brick Italianate home, one of several on Millionaires Row.

6 CARBONDALE

Ten miles south of Carbondale, **Giant City State Park** gets its name from "streets" created by massive sandstone formations. The handsome sandstone-and-white-oak lodge here was built in the 1930's by the Civilian Conservation Corps. Fishing, hunting, hiking, and camping are available.

Nearby, nestled in the Shawnee National Forest, is the 3,200-acre **Touch of Nature Environmental Center,** a haven for hikers, bikers, bird lovers, and canoeists. It offers rustic accommodations, camping, and family outdoor adventure programs.

7 CHESTER

The French fleur-de-lis once flew over this scenic region of the central Mississippi Valley. Its Gallic roots are evident in the 1802 **Pierre Menard Home,** a first-rate example of Southern French Colonial architecture, furnished with aristocratic 19th-century pieces.

Nearby, the battlements of **Fort Kaskaskia State Historic Site** overlook Kaskaskia Island, site of the first state capital and the only community in Illinois west of the Mississippi. The now sparsely populated island is home to a 650-pound church bell cast in France in 1741, which, complete with a crack, is called the Liberty Bell of the West.

8 COLLINSVILLE

The Pyramids, the Taj Mahal, and deep in America's heartland, the **Cahokia Mounds**—all three are recognized as United Nations World Heritage Sites. At Cahokia Mounds are the ruins of the largest prehistoric city north of Mexico,

dating from A.D. 800. At its height it had 20,000 residents. Still standing are 75 earthen mounds, including the largest in the New World, and a series of wooden sun calendars, dubbed Woodhenge because of their functional similarity to Stonehenge. An interpretive center offers exhibits and an audio-visual history of life in the ancient city.

9 ELSAH

This tiny river town, listed in the National Register of Historic Places, is nestled amid limestone bluffs near the confluence of the Mississippi and Illinois rivers. Its winding, flower-lined streets are sprinkled with quaint stone

cottages and a small handful of charming inns. Picturesque apple and peach orchards abound in the surrounding area, and cyclists who follow the scenic **Great River Road Trail,** which stretches from Alton to Grafton along the Mississippi, are likely to spot bald eagles perched ever-watchful on the bluffs from December through March.

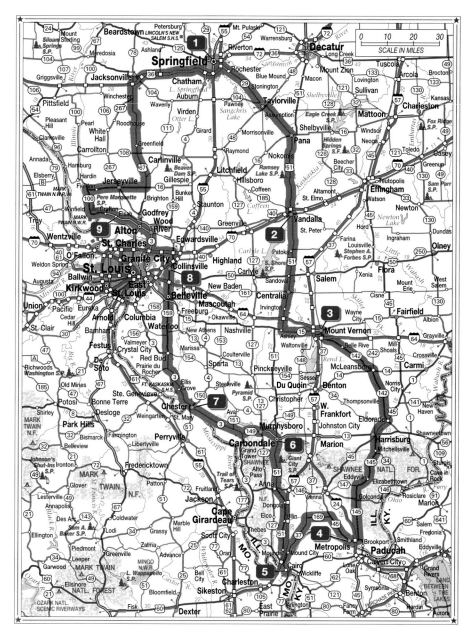

Arkansas

This scrappy frontier state is a scenic wonder, full of sparkling lakes nestled in the creases of ancient mountains, and vibrant modern cities brimming with hope and a proud heritage.

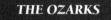

THE OZARKS

1 CONWAY

This burgeoning central Arkansas town boasts three colleges and plenty of frontier history. Every April, Conway residents celebrate their pioneer roots with the **Toad Suck Daze** festival, which takes its name from a former ferry crossing where rivermen drank whiskey at a tavern "till they swell[ed] up like toads." To the strains of mountain music, you'll be treated to platefuls of locally caught fish and the sight of trained toads on tricycles.

Early travelers patronized the **Daniel Greathouse Home**, an inn on the Butterfield Overland Mail route in the mid-1800's. Moved to the county courthouse grounds in 1966, the two-room house, made of massive cypress timber, is considered one of the finest examples of log workmanship in the country. Tours are by appointment only.

Five miles west of Conway atop Arkansas River bluffs, **Cadron Settlement Park** was a stopping place for the Cherokee Nation on its march along the Trail of Tears. A national historic site, Cadron Settlement includes a Trail of Tears memorial. Bordering the park is **Cadron Creek**, a canoeing stream.

2 PETIT JEAN

Legend has it a French mademoiselle, miserable over the departure of her beau to the New World, posed as a cab-in boy aboard his ship. The vessel traveled up the Arkansas River to trade with Indians, and her secret was discovered when she became ill. After she died in her lover's arms, grieving sailors and Indians buried her body at the top of the mountain at what is now **Petit Jean Point.** This is Arkansas's first state park, carved out of the wilderness by the Depression-era Civilian Conservation Corps. Petit Jean has a lodge, a restaurant, and 20 miles of hiking trails.

3 MOUNT NEBO

Majestic Mount Nebo rises 1,800 feet above the Arkansas River valley, overlooking 34,000-acre **Lake Dardanelle** and assorted mountain ridges. Once an antebellum resort for the wealthy, Mount Nebo is now a state park, offering cozy, fully furnished cabins for rent and 14 miles of hiking trails. Bicycles can be rented at the visitor center.

Sunsets are revered on these peaks, and for good reason: they're spectacular. A twilight hayride to **Sunset Point** picks up passengers from cabins and campgrounds on summer weekends. On the other end of the mountaintop, pilgrimages are made to **Sunrise Point** for its equally spectacular sunrise show.

▶ *The zigzag climb to the summit of Mount Nebo includes 13 hairpin turns. RV's over 20 feet should not attempt the drive. To avoid overheating, put the car in low gear and turn off the air conditioning.*

Between Ozark and Fayetteville you'll cross the rugged **Boston Mountains** along the **Pig Trail**, so named for its two curlicue lanes and the migrations of University of Arkansas Razorbacks who swarm the scenic roadway on weekend jaunts.

4 FAYETTEVILLE

The newly restored **Old Main** stands atop one of the city's highest hills. Boasting twin red-brick towers and a slate-gray mansard roof, it's an impressive gateway to the 1871 **University of**

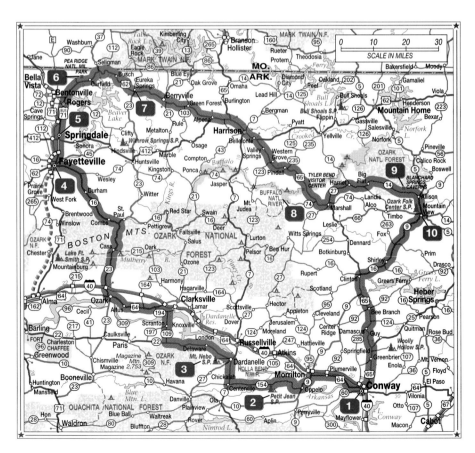

Arkansas and the oldest building at this land-grant university. The picture-perfect campus—afire with brilliant scarlet and rust foliage during football season—is lined with sidewalks bearing the name of every graduate since the school's beginnings in the 1870's.

The city's **Walton Arts Center** has rotating art exhibits, opera productions, and music concerts. In the center of the pretty town square is the 1906 **Old Post Office**, the town's original post office, now a restaurant. The square is ringed by an immense flower bed, dogwoods, and a seasonal farmers' market offering such local delicacies as purple hull peas, okra, and turnip greens.

River reverie: Canoeists pause to admire the scenery in their passage along the Buffalo National River. Cavernous limestone bluffs and glassy waterfalls line the river route.

5 SPRINGDALE

Springdale is at the epicenter of the state's rags-to-riches business successes: this is a region that spawned Tyson Foods, Wal-Mart, and J. B. Hunt. Despite the area's fame as corporate headquarters for those and other national firms, the northwest Arkansas cities retain their town-square charm.

Springdale is the originating point for the **Scenic Ozark Railway Journey**, a daylong, 134-mile round-trip diesel locomotive trip aboard elegantly restored turn-of-the-century railroad cars. The train travels up and over the top of the Ozark Mountains, through the Winslow Tunnel, on trestles above treetops, and into valleys along meandering streams. There's a three-hour lunch stopover in picturesque downtown **Van Buren**, where Victorian-era storefronts swell with antique and craft shops; *Biloxi Blues* was filmed here.

In the first four days of July the **Rodeo of the Ozarks** is celebrated; preludes to the main event include a country-music street dance and Stagecoach Inn days, with barbecue and fried chicken served in an open-air pavilion.

The 45-minute scenic drive from Springdale to Eureka Springs takes you on winding roads through flowering dogwood stands and lush forests.

6 PEA RIDGE

The biggest Civil War battle fought west of the Mississippi is relived in tours and exhibits at the **Pea Ridge National Military Park**, just north of

Rogers. The 1862 battle between Union troops and a Rebel force that included local Cherokees prevented the Confederates from invading Missouri and capturing St. Louis. Parklands abound here: the Lost Bridge Park is 8 miles away; Prairie Creek Park, 10 miles.

Just south is **Beaver Lake**, where the crystal-clear waters and sunsets are legendary. It's no wonder that Bill Clinton selected Beaver Lake as the spot to spend the first vacation of his presidency. The 30,000-acre lake teems with striped and largemouth bass.

7 EUREKA SPRINGS

The "Switzerland of the Ozarks" is a treasury of Victorian mansions and cottages perched on rocky ledges. Tour the

Autumn in the Ozarks makes for fine mountain scenery and scores of craft shows.

Rosalie House, a gingerbread confection built in 1889, and the three-story Victorian **Queen Anne Mansion**, with stained glass and cherry woodwork. Eureka Springs is a thriving artists' colony, where potters, jewelers, and weavers sell their wares in quaint shops in the town's historic district.

The mountain serenity was said to have moved renowned architect E. Fay Jones to create **Thorncrown Chapel**, a breathtaking Frank Lloyd Wright–inspired glass sanctuary, open daily.

▶ *Couples come from all over the world to marry in the chapel. Only specific hours are allowed for weddings, so be sure to book at least six months in advance.*

Eureka Springs Gardens was developed around Blue Spring, a watering hole frequented by prehistoric Indians some 10,000 years ago. Cherokees who passed here on their journey along the Trail of Tears rested beneath overhanging bluffs nearby. Paths take visitors past the spring and through 33 acres of gardens and pine-studded forest.

8 BUFFALO RIVER

The **Buffalo National River**, the country's first river to be protected by Congress as a free-flowing stream, glides through 132 miles of superb Arkansas Ozark highlands scenery. Limestone bluffs soar 500 feet or more above the water, amid massive boulders, mirror pools, and lofty waterfalls. You can rent canoes without guides or flat-bottom johnboats with guides from any number of commercial outlets along the course, or check in at the **Tyler Bend Visitor Center** for a good place to view the river from shore. Out of the park and into the **Ozark National Forest**, you can reach **Twin Falls** by a rugged one-mile hike from **Richland Creek Campground**, but nearby **Falling Water Falls** affords equally breathtaking scenery without a long hike.

9 BLANCHARD SPRINGS

Blanchard Springs Caverns, called by many the cave find of the century, echo with the constant dripping of calcium-rich water, which over the years has built mighty stalagmites and "soda straw" stalactites. Take a cave tour through huge underground rooms of sparkling flowstone and towering columns. The half-mile **Dripstone Trail**, through two mammoth rooms of flowstone, is the shorter of two trail tours. The more strenuous **Discovery Trail**, through water-carved passageways, has nearly 700 stair steps.

▶ *Make your reservations in advance; cave tours are limited to 30 people.*

Outdoors, a paved trail leads visitors to the spot where Blanchard Springs becomes a tumbling waterfall. Have a picnic under the pines at **Sandfield Bluff**, or dip into the cool waters of the **North Sylamore Creek**.

10 MOUNTAIN VIEW

The endless folds of hills and hollows that make up the ancient mountain range known as the Ozarks often ring with the sounds of mountain music. During the **Arkansas Folk Festival**, which draws thousands every spring, the mellow twang of fiddles, dulcimers, and banjos echoes through the streets of this unspoiled center of Ozark music and culture. All year, local crafters sell whittled art, quilts, and woodwork from their front porches and from the **Arkansas Craft Guild**. Just north of town on Rte. 9, the **Ozark Folk Center** is a living museum that preserves the culture of the Ozarks's earliest settlers, with on-site demonstrations of candle-making, weaving, and blacksmithing.

1 LITTLE ROCK

Perched on the bluffs overlooking the Arkansas River, Little Rock is home to three state capitols. The original is included in the **Arkansas Territorial Restoration**, a collection of pioneer-era buildings with rotating historical exhibits. The handsome white-pillared classic on the banks of the Arkansas River, now the **Old State House Museum**, housed the state's first legislature. The current capitol is a gold-domed one-quarter-scale replica of the nation's Capitol, much of it built of Arkansas white marble. Free tours take visitors into hushed elevated galleries to view the Senate and House chambers.

Downtown's **Quapaw Quarter** neighborhood is filled with classic Victorian houses. The 1881 Italianate **Villa Marre**, featured in the opening scenes of television's *Designing Women*, is open for tours. The stately brick and granite façade of **Central High School**, site of a 1957 school integration crisis, is now a national historic site.

2 ARKADELPHIA

The beauty of this charming town is enhanced by the Caddo River, which skims the city. Take scenic Rte. 7 north to **DeGray Lake Resort and State Park**, a 1,000-acre park offering swimming along the 13,800-acre lake, tennis, and hiking. Along the lakeshore is an 18-hole championship public golf course. Lake bass and catfish are plentiful and scrappy. A 132-slip marina rents all manner of boats, from flat-bottom skiffs to fully equipped houseboats.

3 HOPE

Before President Bill Clinton put "a place called Hope" on the national map, this town of some 10,000 residents was best known for its gargantuan watermelons—some weighing more than 200 pounds—and the town's annual **Watermelon Festival**, in August. Today watermelon decor takes a back seat to Clinton memorabilia. The 42nd president was known as Billy Blythe when he lived in the two-story white house just south of the railroad tracks and attended Miss Marie Purkin's School for Little Folks. A new visitor center is located in the town's railroad depot, chock-full of Clintoniana.

4 WASHINGTON

When Union soldiers marched into Little Rock in 1863, the state's Confederates fled southwest and established a Rebel government in this cotton town, a rest stop for weary westbound travelers. When the railroad passed the town by in 1874, so did modern times. A restoration foundation was created in 1958 to preserve the town's historic structures. The **Old Washington Historic State Park** includes 15 historic structures set amid a 19th-century landscape of 150-year-old catalpa trees.

A thermal bath at one of Hot Springs's sumptuous Gilded Age bathhouses (left) may include a soothing body wrap (above).

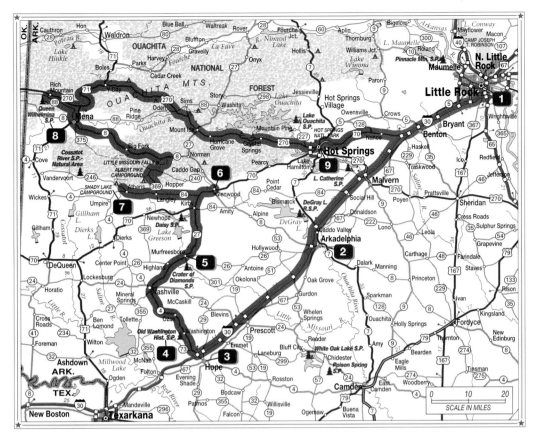

(pronounced WASH-i-taw) is one of the nation's oldest and largest national forests.

Perched atop the mountain is the **Queen Wilhelmina State Park and Lodge**, known as Arkansas's Castle in the Sky. Built in 1897 as a resort retreat for rail passengers and financed largely by Dutch interests, the resort was named for the Dutch queen.

Southward is **Cossatot River State Park–Natural Area**, featuring prime white water for kayaking and two churning waterfalls: **Cossatot Falls** and **Devil's Hollow Falls**. Translated roughly, *cossatot* is French for "skull crusher"; it's not for beginners. Novices should catch the action from the shore.

5 MURFREESBORO

John Huddleston found a diamond in a field two miles southeast of this small town in 1906. Today the **Crater of Diamonds State Park**, the only public diamond mine in North America, is a state park that lets visitors dig to their hearts' content and keep what they find. Genuine diamonds are the chief attraction, but other semiprecious gems and minerals—such as amethyst, jasper, and quartz—can be found. The park includes 888 pine-scented acres on the banks of the Little Missouri and has campgrounds and picnic areas.

▶ *Diamonds have an oily outer surface that dirt and mud do not stick to, making them easier to spot after a rain. Look for a small, well-rounded crystal—a diamond of several carats may be no larger than a marble.*

6 GLENWOOD

Both novice and experienced canoeists will thrill to the scenic cliffs, swoops and shoals, and serene pools of the **Caddo River**, which flows by Glenwood. Day-trippers include fishermen vying for smallmouth bass and catfish.

7 SHADY LAKE

Fed by mountain streams and tucked up against the **Caney Creek Wilderness Area**, the **Shady Lake Recreation Area** offers top-notch facilities, a 1930's-style bathhouse, and a jewellike 25-acre lake with a grassy beach. American Indians lived here 5,000 years ago and carved arrowheads from the novaculite rock. Just northeast, the Little Missouri River slashes through the **Albert Pike Campground**, which offers prime fishing and white-water canoeing. Follow the Forest Service Road out of the campground to reach **Little Missouri Falls**, carved from novaculite rock.

8 QUEEN WILHELMINA STATE PARK

On your drive from Mena to **Rich Mountain**, nearly 3,000 feet above sea level in **Ouachita National Forest**, you'll be taking in the heights on the spectacular **Talimena Scenic Drive**. Ouachita National Forest has some of the most beautiful scenery in the state of Arkansas, as well as excellent camping, hiking, and touring options. From an old Indian word meaning "good hunting grounds," Ouachita

9 HOT SPRINGS

The steamy mineral waters at this cosmopolitan resort have been a sizzling hot spot since long before their discovery in the 16th century. Nestled in the Ouachita Mountains, Hot Springs has another claim to fame: it is the boyhood hometown of Bill Clinton. See his hangouts on a **Clinton Hometown Van Tour**, offered by several local guides.

Many come for the soothing waters of **Hot Springs National Park**, which threads through the city. Don't miss the restored Gilded Age **Bathhouse Row**. A half-dozen baths offer the traditional Hot Springs thermal bath, which includes a leisurely soak in 100-degree waters and a rapturous "needle shower"—fine streams of warm water.

▶ *Most bathhouses do not accept reservations, but call ahead to make sure you won't have to wait in line.*

The park visitor center, the elegantly restored **Fordyce Bathhouse**, is also a museum. Follow your bath with a real treat: the saucy ribs at **McClard's Bar-B-Que**—one of Mr. Clinton's favorite culinary haunts.

Missouri

This heartland state is as all-American as apple pie. Travel the ragtime route up the Mississippi to St. Louis or beat a trail to jazzy Kansas City, where fountains spring up on shady boulevards.

ST. LOUIS & THE OZARKS

1 ST. LOUIS

Founded by fur traders in 1764 on a bluff overlooking the Mississippi River, St. Louis thrived as a bustling center of commerce into the 20th century. Suburban sprawl forced an inner-city decline, but the St. Louis blues were lifted when **Busch Stadium**, home of the baseball Cardinals, opened in 1963 and the gleaming **Gateway Arch** was dedicated two years later on a grassy esplanade by the river. Today you can ride a tram to the top for views of the

A man-made lake within the 1894 St. Louis Union Station train shed is the setting for paddleboat rentals and music concerts year-round.

mighty river. The revitalization of the city included the restoration of handsome Victorian homes around **Lafayette Square,** one of the city's first public parks. The turreted **St. Louis Union Station,** at its opening in 1894 the largest railway facility in America, has been transformed into an elegant shopping, hotel, and food complex. Beneath the vaulted steel-beam roof of the former train shed, you can glide along a man-made lake in a rented paddleboat.

Today the metropolitan area's 2.5 million residents have much to crow about. The Grammy Award–winning **Saint Louis Symphony Orchestra,** founded in 1880, performs on National Public Radio 52 weeks a year. Visitors come from miles away to view the exquisite Byzantine-style mosaics at the **New Cathedral** and to relax in the heavenly environs of the 79-acre **Missouri Botanical Garden,** a public garden since 1859.

Forest Park, the site of the 1904 world's fair, has a wealth of attractions. The elegant **Saint Louis Art Museum,** built for the fair, has fine pre-Columbian and German Expressionist collections. The animals at the **St. Louis Zoo** live in replications of their natural habitats. The new **St. Louis Science Center** has dazzling celestial shows and a 76-foot wraparound domed movie screen. The Art Deco **Jewel Box,** fronted by water-lily ponds, blossoms with hothouse flora. The **Muny** produces Broadway hits under summer-night skies; it's the oldest and largest outdoor musical theater in the

country. See live entertainment year-round amid the lavish interiors of the **Fox Theatre,** a restored Moorish-style movie palace that opened to great fanfare in 1929.

▶ *The Muny gives away a little over one-tenth of its 12,000 seats nightly on a first-come, first-served basis, beginning at 6:30 P.M.*

The city's heritage as a mecca for jazz music, imported by showboats traveling upriver from New Orleans, lives on today on the cobblestoned streets of **Laclede's Landing,** site of the city's original settlement. Here 19th-century riverfront levees and warehouses, restored as restaurants, shops, bars, and offices, resound with music year-round.

2 STE. GENEVIEVE

The first settlers who came to the Mississippi Valley were French. They left their mark on this charming town, the oldest permanent settlement in the state, with more French Colonial vertical log homes than anywhere else on the continent. Established about 1735, Ste. Genevieve was in the 18th century as big and as brassy as its river-trading rival to the north.

Visit the **Memorial Cemetery,** circa 1787. Lining the hillsides are weathered headstones, often inscribed in French, marking the graves of early residents.

But it is the houses that are the French settlers' most treasured legacy. The elegantly furnished 1780's **Maison Guibourd-Valle House** has hand-hewn oak beams and a formal old-world garden. The 1818 **Felix Valle House State Historic Site,** built of limestone in the Federal style, holds a French Christmas by candlelight in early December. The 1770 **Bolduc House** has been called the most authentically restored Creole house in the nation. The 1770 **Amoureaux House** is believed to be the oldest structure in the state. All of the homes can be toured; the Amoureaux House is open for pre-arranged group tours only.

The Jewel Box, in St. Louis's Forest Park, has an Art Deco façade and a plant-filled interior.

3 IRONTON

At 1,772 feet above sea level in the rugged St. Francois Mountains, **Taum Sauk Mountain,** nine miles from Ironton, is Missouri's tallest peak. Among the points of interest are the three waterfalls that make up **Mina Sauk Falls** and the narrow passageway called **Devil's Toll Gate.** You can hike a portion of the **Ozark Trail,** through rocky glades studded with prairie grass.

One end of the 17-mile **Taum Sauk Trail** begins at Johnson's Shut-ins State Park, 20 miles from Ironton on the rolling **Black River.** Here are canyon-like gorges and fine swimming holes.

Nearby are the ancient red granite boulders of **Elephant Rocks State Park.** The largest—27 feet high—is named Dumbo. A self-guided Braille trail follows a softly sloping paved path past the enormous, rounded rocks.

4 PARK HILLS

These mine openings once produced nearly 80 percent of the nation's lead. At the **Missouri Mines State Historic Site** the powerhouse of the St. Joseph Lead Company's Federal Mill No. 3 has been converted into a museum of minerals and Missouri mining history.

At **St. Francois State Park,** seven miles north, near Bonne Terre, you can drop a canoe into the slow-moving Big River and leisurely drift the day away. The 2,735-acre park has several hiking and equestrian trails; try the **Swimming Deer Trail,** a slightly strenuous 2.7-mile hike over hilly terrain that dazzles with a crayon box of wildflowers in the warm months. The road follows the river, where picnic sites are plentiful.

5 SULLIVAN

Four miles east of town, **Meramec State Park** is a pastoral 6,789-acre river park, where you can rent canoes or inner tubes to traverse the spring-fed Meramec River or camp out on the scenic riverside. Take the 90-minute tour into **Fisher Cave,** a natural cavern.

▶ *Even during the summer, the cave temperature stays a constant 60°F; bring a sweater or jacket.*

The 70-million-year-old caves at **Meramec Caverns,** five miles northeast in Stanton, were used as a hideout by Jesse James and his gang in the aftermath of an 1874 train robbery. Today 80-minute guided tours along well-lighted walkways equipped with handrails show off underground wonders like the colossal Stage Curtain—a limestone formation that stands 72 feet tall and is 40 feet thick—and the Wine Table, a limestone-and-iron "table" standing on three legs.

6 AUGUSTA

Scenic alpine hillsides and a citizenry boasting a rich German heritage give this area the nickname the Missouri Rhineland. Augusta was founded by German immigrants in the early 1830's. It is now a flourishing wine center. At **Mount Pleasant Winery** you'll very likely be serenaded by guitar and mandolin music while you sample wine on the terrace; in winter you can sip indoors in front of a welcoming fire.

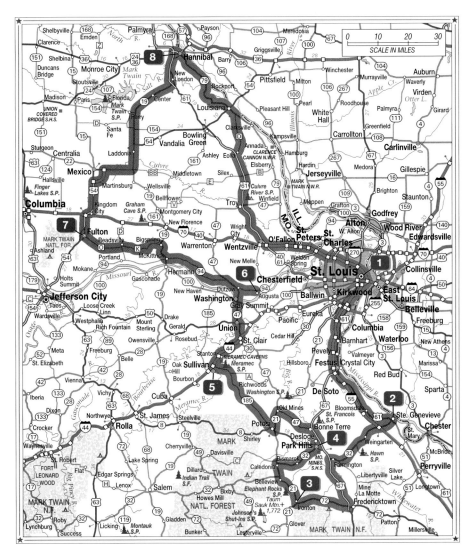

To the northwest, in Dutzow, the sounds of oompah music and the heady scent of grilled bratwurst will draw you to **Blumenhof Winery.** Tasting tours are held in the Swiss chalet–style building. A short stroll away you can pick up the **Katy Trail,** a hiking and biking path that follows an old railroad corridor for more than 200 Missouri miles.

7 FULTON

The **Winston Churchill Memorial and Library** is a reconstruction of the historic Christopher Wren church of St. Mary Aldermanbury, which suffered severe damage in World War II. In 1965 the church remains were dismantled and the 7,000 stones were numbered, scrubbed clean of London soot, and shipped across the ocean. Craftsmen duplicated the church's interior, now a library. Among the treasures are five paintings by Churchill. Just west of the memorial is a sculpture by Churchill's granddaughter Edwina Sandys. Dedicated in 1991, the sculpture is composed of eight sections of the Berlin Wall, the largest continuous section of the wall on display in America.

8 HANNIBAL

In Mark Twain's *The Adventures of Tom Sawyer,* the writer's hometown is immortalized as St. Petersburg, the quaint river hamlet where Tom and Huck found endless adventure. Today Hannibal—a place the writer once described as a "white town drowsing in the sunshine of a summer's morning"—retains its small-town magic. Mark Twain grew up as Samuel L. Clemens in a white clapboard 1843 house. In the five-building complex that makes up **Mark Twain's Boyhood Home and Museum** are a freshly painted picket fence and Norman Rockwell's famous illustrations of Huck and Tom.

You can tour two rooms of the nearby **Becky Thatcher House,** home of Twain's childhood sweetheart, Laura Hawkins, fictionalized as Becky Thatcher, Tom Sawyer's first love. The one-hour guided **Mark Twain Cave Tour** leads into the subterranean setting that swallowed up Tom and Becky. Or hop aboard the **Mark Twain** riverboat for a one-hour cruise on the Mississippi.

1 KANSAS CITY

No cowtown this, Kansas City has been called one of the most beautiful cities on earth. Urban planning has provided for tree-shaded boulevards, handsome architecture, and scores of shimmering fountains. Indeed, you'll find fountains everywhere, even at the Kansas City Royals' Kauffman Stadium. Some of the most elaborate adorn elegant **Country Club Plaza,** one of the oldest shopping centers in the country. It was built in the style of a Spanish alfresco marketplace. A map of the Plaza's collection of fountains and European and American artwork is available from the Plaza Merchants Association. See the city's attractions aboard the **Kansas City Trolley,** which provides service between the Plaza, downtown, and the entertainment-retail complex known as **Crown Center,** where the **Hallmark Visitors Center** traces the history of the world's largest greeting-card company—and lets you push a button to create a perfect Hallmark ribbon bow.

In midtown the city's splendid archi-

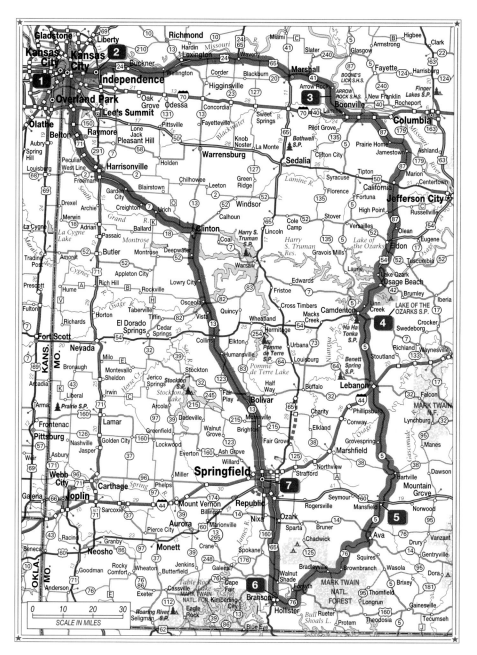

tecture is pillowed in urban parkland. The 1914 Beaux Arts **Union Station** was at one time one of the largest railway depots in the country. Here, in June 1933, Pretty Boy Floyd and his gangster friends shot their way out of the station, killing four G-men.

The trolley also loops around to one of the city's unburied treasures: the *Arabia* **Steamboat Museum.** The *Arabia* sank in the Missouri River in 1856 and challenged treasure hunters for decades. In 1988 the steamboat was raised; inside was a remarkably well-preserved cargo—gilt-edged china, buttons, and preserved fruits.

Afterward, head to **Arthur Bryant's** famous barbecue restaurant for a heaping plate of the unequaled pork ribs, marinated in a sauce of tomato purée and highly classified secret ingredients.

2 INDEPENDENCE

The hometown of Harry S. Truman, Missouri's only president, is also known as the Queen City of the Trails. It was a jumping-off point for pioneers hitching their wagons to the westward trails. They are commemorated at the **National Frontier Trails Center,** where, among other things, you can peek inside diaries kept by pioneer mothers.

The **Harry S. Truman Library** features a reproduction of Truman's Oval Office, right down to the famous The Buck Stops Here sign. Nearby, the handsome Victorian home of Truman and his wife, Bess, still looks the same, with all its original furnishings intact.

3 ARROW ROCK

A preserved frontier village that captures life in the days of the covered wagon, the **Arrow Rock State Historic Site** lies where the Santa Fe Trail crossed the Missouri River. You can stroll the canopied boardwalk past charming 19th-century architecture. Guided tours of restored buildings—such as a one-room jail and an 1834 tavern—can be arranged by contacting the Friends of Arrow Rock, whose number can be obtained by calling the local directory assistance. In the summer, don't miss a performance at the **Lyceum Theater,** Missouri's oldest professional theater.

4 LAKE OF THE OZARKS

One of the largest man-made lakes in the world, the **Lake of the Ozarks** spreads out over 86 square miles; its vast shoreline runs some 1,150 miles. **Bagnell Dam,** the massive structure that harnessed billions of gallons of water to form the recreational lake, was constructed in 1931 from bedrock and rises 148 feet. Tours of Bagnell Dam and the **Osage Hydroelectric Power Plant** are available to visitors year-round; call in advance for times.

At **Lake of the Ozarks State Park,** Missouri's largest state park, you can rent a pleasure boat and cruise the lake or hire a guide to direct you to the best fishing spot. Call in advance to reserve one of the eight charming but primitive log cabins. Each of the cabins sleeps up to six people.

Near Camdenton, **Ha Ha Tonka State Park** overlooks the Lake of the Ozarks from atop a beautiful bluff. You can scout the ruins of a European-style castle or traipse through fields of buttery-yellow coneflowers.

5 MANSFIELD

Visit the **Laura Ingalls Wilder–Rose Wilder Lane Home and Museum** to see where the writer lived while she wrote the popular *Little House* children's books on pioneer life in the 1870's. Here are Pa's fiddle, Almanzo's tools, and many other inspirations for Laura Ingalls Wilder's tales.

6 BRANSON

This once-sleepy town has metamorphosed into the Nashville of the Ozarks. Five million visitors flock to Branson yearly to see nonstop family entertainment and live music acts in theaters along the burgeoning Strip.

▶ *With Branson's popularity has come gridlock. Pick up an alternative-routes map at the local chamber of commerce and avoid driving before and after show times.*

Headliners flock to Branson, a scenic Ozark village that has transformed itself into the host for more musical acts per square mile than any other place in the country.

Off the Strip, Branson's small-town charms emerge amid the region's natural beauty. Nature lovers make a beeline for **Table Rock Lake,** which has prime bass fishing and scuba rentals. Nine miles west on Rte. 76, the **Silver Dollar City** theme park showcases pioneer crafts. Carvers, quilters, and weavers work in a 1890's mountain hamlet.

7 SPRINGFIELD

A Missouri nickname—the Cave State—is underscored at **Fantastic Caverns,** billed as America's only drive-through cave. On the one-hour, one-mile tour, you'll ride in bright red Jeep-drawn trams through an underground landscape of stalactites and stalagmites, formed by centuries of water trickling deep beneath the Ozark peaks. Although sunlight never penetrates the cave, many rare species of animals—like the grotto salamander—can be seen scuttling about the cavern walls.

Iowa

Endless golden cornfields and neat grids of fertile farmland spread across the vast plains of Iowa, where small river towns join Dutch and Danish settlements that retain their Old World charm.

1 DES MOINES

Situated at the confluence of the Des Moines and Raccoon rivers, Iowa's capital city is both a modern metropolis and a sleepy prairie town. Founded in the 1840's as a military outpost, the city's

and 20th-century European and American art and a collection of modern sculpture housed in a wing designed by I.M. Pei. At the **State Historical Building**, Iowa artifacts include Indian beads and folk art from the Amish and the Amana Colonies.

Several historic homes recall the success of early Des Moines businessmen.

The old-time general store *at Living History Farms, fully stocked, doubles as a post office.*

fortunes have risen and fallen with the waters, and the great flood of 1993— when residents went nearly a month without drinkable water—made Des Moines the object of national attention. The floodwaters have receded, but the message they sent remains: life on the prairie is still a rugged affair.

▶ *To get a sense of the flood's magnitude, visit the Court Avenue District, a historic area of shops and coffeehouses. Some of the stores display photographs of the flood.*

Internationally acclaimed for its design is the **Des Moines Art Center**, with a large permanent display of 19th-

In the turn-of-the-century Sherman Hill Historic District is **Hoyt Sherman Place**, a restored Victorian mansion built in 1877. **Salisbury House**, a 42-room English Tudor mansion set on nine wooded acres, houses art and furnishings dating back to the 15th century. **Terrace Hill**, known as the Palace of the Prairie when it was built in 1869, is now the governor's mansion; it is notable for its intricate glasswork, which includes a 13-foot stained-glass window framed by a double staircase.

Experience farm life on the plains at **Living History Farms**, just west of town in Urbandale, where "pioneers" carry out farming tasks the 19th-century way. You'll find replicas of the oval

bark lodges from an Ioway Indian village, and a 19th-century town with a doctor's office, bank, and general store.

2 ELK HORN

The largest rural Danish settlement in the country, Elk Horn is so authentically Danish that it has its own **Danish Windmill**, built in Denmark in 1848 and transplanted here in 1976. The massive blades turn by day to grind flour, which is sold in the millhouse museum. Nearby, **Bedstemor's House** (grandmother's house, in Danish) is decorated as it was in the early 1900's and shows the craftsmanship of the Danish carpenters who settled the area.

3 COUNCIL BLUFFS

In a journal entry dated August 3, 1804, explorers Meriwether Lewis and William Clark recorded their now historic meeting with American Indians at the "council bluff" above the Missouri River. The name stuck, and Council Bluffs grew into a prosperous rail-and-river town. **RailsWest Railroad Museum**, housed in an 1898 depot, honors the town's railroad beginnings with a scale-model display, an antique handcar, and other memorabilia.

The lavish Victorian **Historic General Dodge House** was built by Civil War general Grenville M. Dodge, a railroad builder and banker. Its 14 rooms, beautifully restored and furnished, testify to the prosperity of the times.

Those with a taste for the macabre will marvel at the **Squirrel Cage Jail**, which offers a chilling look at the rough mechanisms of frontier justice. In use from 1885 to 1969, the jail housed prisoners in a three-story metal drum divided into 10 pie-shaped sections on each level; rotating the drum allowed one cell to be opened at a time.

4 MISSOURI VALLEY

The night after their meeting on the council bluff, Lewis and Clark camped five miles upstream at what is now the **DeSoto Bend National Wildlife Refuge**, near the town of Missouri Valley. The prehistoric floodplain offers refuge to migratory waterfowl, bald eagles, and other birds. As many as 500,000 snow geese and blue geese fly here each year, and in fall the duck population numbers 30,000. Stop at the visitor center for excellent views, or take a 12-mile drive through the refuge's woods, prairie, and wetlands.

▶ *Autumn is the best time to visit, though you may be asked to stay in your car so as not to disturb the birds. During the Fall Auto Tour, numbered stops are discussed in a brochure explaining the migration.*

Missouri Valley is the starting point for a trip through the beautiful Loess Hills. By turns lush and desolate, these ancient hills teem with variety: deep canyons, dense woodland, pristine prairies, and micro-deserts scorched by sun and wind. Charming towns nestle in the hollows, and recreational oppor-

tunities for the amateur naturalist and hiker abound. Drive one of several well-marked scenic routes for the best views; maps are available at the Harrison County Museum and Welcome Center located on Rte. 30.

5 SIOUX CITY

Sioux City sits at a wide bend in the Missouri, and its civic and cultural life centers around the busy waterfront. For a bit of history, visit the **Sergeant Floyd Riverboat Museum**, named for the only fatality on the Lewis and Clark Expedition. (Floyd's burial place, two miles downstream, is marked with a 100-foot white stone obelisk.) The museum chronicles the history of river transportation on the Upper Missouri with rare photos and artifacts.

Local history is the focus of the **Sioux City Public Museum**, housed in an unexpectedly massive Gothic mansion of gray stone. It is overshadowed only by the **Woodbury County Courthouse**,

the largest public Prairie-style building in the United States.

6 ORANGE CITY

What Elk Horn is to the Danish, Orange City is to the Dutch. During the Tulip Festival on the third weekend in May, Orange City transforms itself into a 19th-century Dutch village, but Dutch flavor abounds year-round. **Vogel Windmill** is a full-size working replica, complete with authentically furnished miller's quarters, and the **Dutch Miller's Home** re-creates domestic life in 19th-century Holland. You can even buy wooden shoes there. The **Century Home**, built in 1900 by Orange City's first mayor, has period furnishings and a 1903 handmade pump organ. Call for an appointment.

7 OKOBOJI

The town of Okoboji, gateway to Iowa's Great Lakes, practically floats in the middle of a freshwater ocean. The lakes —West Okoboji, East Okoboji, and Spirit—were dug by the same glacier that turned Minnesota into a water-sports paradise. They are surrounded by resorts, parks, campgrounds, and honky-tonk pleasures, such as **Arnolds Park Amusement Park.** Here you can board the *Queen II*, a replica of an 18th-century steamboat, for a cruise of West Okoboji Lake, nicknamed Big Blue for its remarkably clear, deep-blue waters. On the park grounds the **Iowa Great Lakes Maritime Museum** chronicles the history of the area with photographs and a fine wooden boat collection.

In Okoboji proper the **Lakes Art Center** offers exhibits including works by Grandma Moses and the Wyeths. Long at peace now, the **Abbie Gardner Sharp Cabin** was the only dwelling to survive the Spirit Lake Massacre, a

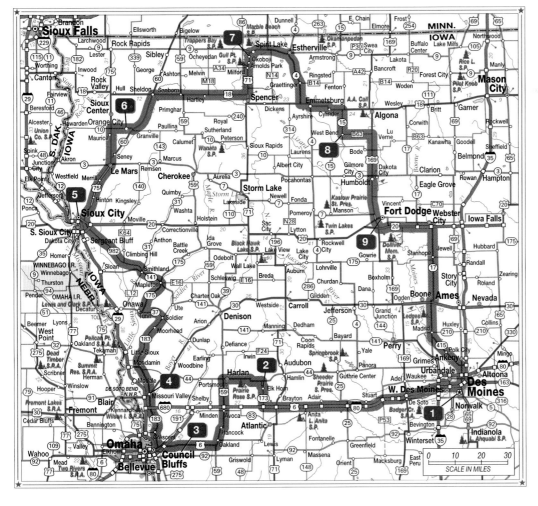

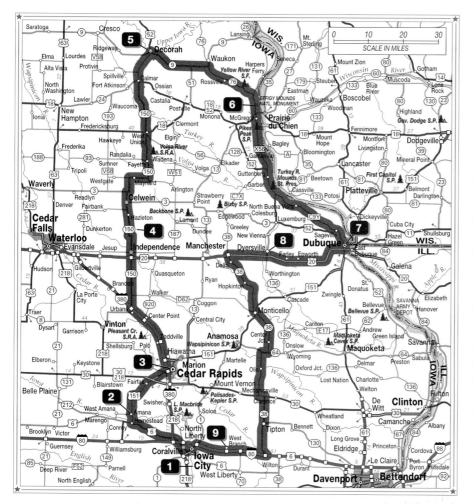

1 IOWA CITY

This city served as Iowa's first state capital until Des Moines assumed the honor in 1857. Disgruntled locals were given an impressive consolation prize, however—the University of Iowa, now renowned for its programs in space science and medicine, and the Writers' Workshop, once attended by Flannery O'Connor and John Irving.

The **Old Capitol**, a Greek Revival masterpiece crowned with a gleaming gold dome, towers above the campus. You can tour the fine collection of 20th-century American and European art at the university's **Museum of Art** or catch a performance by world-famous artists on one of the university's stages.

▶ *For a real taste of small-town Iowa, ask for directions to the Sutliff Bridge, an 1898 wood-plank truss bridge 18 miles north. Locals pick up fried catfish at the nearby tavern and dine at a picnic table on the bridge.*

bloody 1856 uprising of a band of Sioux against local white settlers.

8 WEST BEND

Touted by Iowans as the Eighth Wonder of the World, the **Grotto of the Redemption** startles visitors with a kaleidoscopic landscape of gems and minerals, valued at more than $2.5 million. The grotto is actually nine separate grottoes covering an entire city block, each portraying a scene from the life of Christ. A replica of Michelangelo's *Pietà* sits atop a 40-foot mountain of semi-precious stones.

A few blocks away, visitors can see the last traditional sod house in Iowa. Next to the **Sod House** is a restored one-room schoolhouse and an 1885 country church, now a museum of pioneer and American Indian life.

9 FORT DODGE

A visit to the **Fort Museum** in Fort Dodge will dispel any notion of time's passage. The museum and its frontier

village, with a general store, jail, log chapel, and other period buildings, recall the city's origins as an isolated military post on the vast prairie. A collection of pioneer and American Indian artifacts is housed in a reconstructed Civil War fort that was built and manned by local residents to protect themselves from the Sioux.

2 AMANA COLONIES

In 1855 a German religious group called the Community of True Inspiration established a communal society in these seven villages—Amana, South, West, High, Middle, East, and Homestead. Faced with financial problems and restless young people, the community switched in 1932 to individual

In Iowa, farms cover 93 percent of the state. More corn is grown here than in any other part of the country, and while much of it feeds the nation, farmers feed half of it to their hogs.

stock ownership in the Amana Society, which still runs many of the farms and local businesses of the Amana Colonies.

▶ *You'll need to drive from village to village. Go first to the Welcome Center in Amana to pick up a brochure, watch a film, and plan your visit.*

Prosperity endures throughout the meticulously tended villages, with their trim brick houses and neat flower gardens. Sample rhubarb or dandelion wine at any of 10 wineries, watch furniture being crafted at one of three factories, tour the **Amana Woolen Mill,** which has been in operation since the colonies were founded, or visit any of five museums, including the **Communal Kitchen Museum** and the **Museum of Amana History**. If it seems a lot of rooms are painted blue, it's because, as legend has it, the only color allowed was one that would remind people of heaven. Try one of the local restaurants for family-style German meals from which no one walks away hungry.

3 CEDAR RAPIDS

Painter Grant Wood lived most of his life in and around Cedar Rapids, a leading industrial center since the mid 19th century. The largest permanent collection of Wood's work found anywhere is on display at the **Cedar Rapids Museum of Art,** a dramatic building with a soaring glass Winter Garden.

To the east, at **Palisades-Kepler State Park,** it's the limestone palisades that soar—75 feet above the Cedar River. You can hike cliff-top trails, fish in the river, or picnic under towering trees.

4 HIGHWAY 150

The drive from Cedar Rapids to Decorah is a picture postcard of Iowa's rural charm: rolling fields planted with corn and soybeans, interrupted periodically by a smart farmhouse with red-painted barns, a well-kept kitchen garden, and chickens strutting in the yard. Small towns along the way are friendly places to stretch your legs or have a bite to eat.

5 DECORAH

Decorah was the gateway to the west for many Norwegian immigrants in the 1850's, some of whom put down roots in this charming town and gave it its unique flavor. You can trace their hard road from the old country at **Vesterheim, the Norwegian-American Museum**. Its collection includes an immigrant's log cabin, a stone-and-frame mill that was a gathering place for Norwegian farmers, a small sailboat

Grant Wood's stark portrayals of the people of Iowa are Cedar Rapids treasures.

that made the arduous voyage across the Atlantic, intricately carved furnishings and altarpieces, and folk art.

Homesick composer Antonin Dvorak spent the summer of 1893 in nearby Spillville, settled by Czechs. The building where he stayed now houses the **Bily Clock Museum,** with elaborate musical clocks carved by farmers Frank and Joseph Bily. The highlight is surely the Apostle Clock, from which the 12 apostles parade every hour.

6 EFFIGY MOUNDS NATIONAL MONUMENT

With basketful after basketful of earth, along nearly 1,500 acres of high bluffs overlooking the Mississippi, American Indians built this exceptionally large group of burial mounds from about 500 B.C. to A.D. 1300. Most of the 196 mounds are conical or linear in design, but some resemble enormous bears and birds, including the Great Bear Mound, 137 feet long. An interpretive trail with river views traverses the mounds. At the visitor center, artifacts and a short film on the mound builders offer clues to their mystical beliefs.

7 DUBUQUE

From Effigy Mounds, the Great River Road winds over the bluffs rising above the Mississippi to Dubuque, Iowa's oldest city. Prospering 19th-century lumber barons, riverboat captains, and lead miners built her substantial public buildings, verdant parks, and the majestic mansions that top the bluffs overlooking downtown. In those days the well-heeled took the **Fenelon Place Elevator,** the world's steepest and shortest cable railway, home to these palaces. On a clear day the view from the top takes in parts of three states.

Don't miss the **Mississippi River Museums,** a complex of six buildings featuring exhibits of river lore and artifacts, including one of the last steam-powered side-wheelers.

8 DYERSVILLE

Soaring twin spires visible long before you reach Dyersville signal that this is not a typical Iowa farming town. The **Basilica of St. Francis Xavier** is a Gothic wonder, with 64 stained-glass windows and elaborately painted religious scenes. Another curiosity sits in a cornfield just outside town: a well-groomed baseball diamond created for the movie *Field of Dreams*. Visitors come to sit on the bleachers or play a pickup game, just as in the movie.

9 WEST BRANCH

Herbert C. Hoover was born in a two-room cottage here in 1874 and was buried on a nearby hillside in 1964. In between, he made a fortune in mining, distinguished himself as a humanitarian and statesman, and served as the nation's 31st president. At the **Herbert Hoover National Historic Site,** you can tour the cottage and visit a replica of the blacksmith shop where Hoover's father worked. Also on the site is an 1853 schoolhouse, the Friends Meetinghouse where the Hoover family attended services, and the Presidential Library and Museum, a repository for manuscripts, photographs, and films that follow Hoover's career.

Wisconsin

Beyond the verdant dairy farms of Wisconsin lie the most picturesque of towns, the gently washed shores of Lake Superior, and an unusually beautiful landscape shaped by glaciers.

SOUTHERN WISCONSIN

1 MILWAUKEE

The marshland at the convergence of the Milwaukee, Menominee, and Kinnickinnic rivers blossomed from wilderness to boomtown in almost record time: from 1833, when a treaty was signed with the Indian tribes that lived there, to 1835, when white settlers and speculators poured in. From the beginning the city was populated by immigrants. By 1910 a full three-quarters of the people of Milwaukee either were from another country or had a parent who was foreign-born. Twenty percent were Germans, among them men named Pabst and Schlitz—who in the mid-19th century built the breweries that eventually made Milwaukee famous. Today the giant breweries are open for free tours. The **Pabst Brewery**

The Grand Avenue *retail center in the heart of Milwaukee spans four city blocks.*

is the oldest facility and boasts magnificent handwrought copper brew kettles. You can also tour the **Miller Brewing Company**; its intriguing Caves Museum was dug out of the bluffs by German and Welsh brewers to keep their aging beer cool.

▶ *A small skywalk system in Milwaukee links the Grand Avenue retail center with other downtown sites. Two walks cross the Milwaukee River.*

If you're staying overnight in Milwaukee, see what's on the evening bill at the **Pabst Theater**, a beautiful 1895 Victorian Baroque building with superb acoustics. And don't miss the sumptuous 37-room **Pabst Mansion** on elegant Wisconsin Avenue; a newly restored Ladies' Parlor boasts wall and drapery fabrics custom-woven in France. For a view of the past, visit the **Milwaukee County Historical Center**, housed in an imposing Beaux Arts former bank, with re-creations of a bank, a pharmacy, and a cooper's shop as they were at the turn of the century.

Mid-July is an ideal time to visit this city, if only to see the famous **Great Circus Parade**, featuring antique circus wagons that were once owned by Ringling Brothers. But any time of year you can see what are known by locals as "the domes" and officially named the **Mitchell Park Conservatory**. There are three domes here: a desert environment, a tropical one, and a third used for stunning seasonal floral displays.

2 EAGLE

The State Historical Society's 576-acre living-history museum, **Old World Wisconsin**, is a celebration of Wisconsin's European immigrant heritage. More than 50 historic buildings, including a church, a schoolhouse, and out-

houses, have been gathered from all across the state. Norwegian, Finnish, Danish, and German farmsteads have costumed interpreters who may even invite you to do a bit of gardening, 19th-century style; in August you can see a thresher powered by two horses on a treadmill.

3 FORT ATKINSON

At the **Hoard Historical Museum and Dairy Shrine,** you'll learn how W. D. Hoard began a campaign in favor of dairying as wheat farming began to wane. Wisconsin is, in a sense, his dairyland. The museum, housed in Hoard's 1860's mansion, also has exhibits on the Black Hawk War of 1836, pioneer quilts, and Indian prehistory. **Aztalan State Park**, 12 miles north, is the site of a Mississippian Indian village that thrived in the 12th century.

4 MOUNT HOREB

A quaint farming community and a shopper's paradise, Mount Horeb is also the home of the **Mustard Museum,** where more than 1,800 types of mustard are on display. The **Wisconsin Folk Museum** has exhibits of whittling, rosemaling—highly stylized Norwegian floral painting on wood—and quilts.

Three miles west on Rte. 18/51 is Little Norway, an 1856 farmstead built by immigrant Osten Olson Haugen. A costumed guide will show you a group of wonderfully carved trolls and several outbuildings, including a *stabbur,* an odd-shaped granary peculiar to the Norwegians. But the real wonder is the *stavekirke,* an intricately ornamented replica of a 12th-century wooden church. This one is comparatively young—it was built for Chicago's 1893 Columbian Exposition—but its blackened wood makes it look like something built in the days of the Vikings.

5 MINERAL POINT

In 1830 Mineral Point was a boomtown, thanks to the abundant deposits of lead and zinc in the hilly area around the town. Cornish miners came in 1832 and dug into the hills like badgers, living in hillside dugouts called "badger holes" so that they could work year-round—hence Wisconsin's nickname: the Badger State.

Pendarvis, on Shake Rag Street—named for the Cornish wives' habit of waving towels to call their husbands home from the hillside mines—is a collection of six Cornish miners' rock-and-log houses, full of mining memorabilia.

The town itself is now a charming artists' retreat. Here you can visit the studios of rug weavers, glassblowers, and jewelers for crafts demonstrations. Stop in at a restaurant for saffron cake or a pasty, a Cornish meat pie.

6 HOUSE ON THE ROCK

This extravagant architectural wonder nine miles south of Spring Green must be seen to be believed. It was built in the 1940's as a retreat, atop a 60-foot rock outcropping 450 feet over the Wyoming Valley, by an eccentric artist and entrepreneur named Alex Jordan, who is said to have carried materials up a rope ladder in baskets strapped to his back. The original stone "house" is built around trees and has massive fireplaces and waterfalls in the rooms. Jordan's retreat soon became a repository for his astonishing collections of dolls, cannons, music boxes, carousel animals, armor, and more. You'll need the better part of a day to see it all; the animated

Carvings on this circus wagon were disassembled in the 1920's to serve as decoration for a circus headquarters. Now restored, it is on view at Baraboo's Circus World Museum.

musical machines alone could furnish an entire museum. And don't miss the carousel, billed as the world's largest, replete with rabbits, fish, and mermen—but not a single horse.

7 SPRING GREEN

Taliesin, resting atop rolling hills in a peaceful Wisconsin River valley, was designed by Frank Lloyd Wright, and was his summer home. Wright was born in nearby Richland Center in 1867 but did not return to his native Wisconsin until 1902, when he built the Hillside Home School for two of his aunts: this building is now the home of the **Taliesin Fellowship**—a studio school for students of architecture. Wright started building Taliesin—the name, pronounced tal-ee-ESS-en, is Welsh for

"shining brow"—in 1911. He constantly tinkered with the design, letting students live on the site and become actively involved in the construction.

Three tours are available: of the school; of the school and the grounds; and, only recently, of the house, undergoing careful restoration.

Taliesin is one of seven of the state's 41 Wright-designed buildings that can be visited as part of the **Frank Lloyd Wright Wisconsin Heritage Tour.** Stop by the Spring Green Chamber of Commerce or the Frank Lloyd Wright visitor center for a tour map.

▶ *Visitors to Spring Green should stop in at some of the local cheese factories to sample the region's award-winning Wisconsin cheeses.*

8 BARABOO

The town of Baraboo was the birthplace in 1884 and winter quarters of the Ringling Brothers' circus until it merged in 1918 with the Barnum and Bailey Circus. The 75 circus wagons that are paraded through town every July come from Baraboo's **Circus World Museum.** There are live circus performances several times a day during the summer. As a bonus, the air is alive with the old-time sound of the calliope.

Nine miles northwest, on a secluded wooded site in **Mirror Lake State Park**

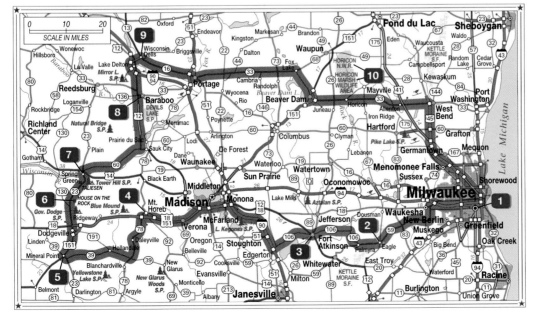

near the town of Lake Delton, is the only Frank Lloyd Wright–designed building in the world where you can stay overnight. The **Seth Peterson Cottage** is an intimate wood-and-glass marvel, whose restoration saved it from neglect and harsh Wisconsin winters.

▶ *Reservations for stays in the Seth Peterson Cottage should be made at least a year in advance. The house sleeps four.*

9 WISCONSIN DELLS

The rushing waters of the Wisconsin River long ago carved the surrounding sandstone into fantastic towers of rock for 15 miles along its banks. Called the **Wisconsin Dells,** the formations are best viewed from a boat. A cruise on the Upper or Lower Dells provides the most dramatic perspective on the rocks. Or you can take a rollicking ride on World War II amphibious "ducks."

The town nearest the Dells was named Kilbourn until 1931, when the city fathers changed it to Wisconsin Dells to draw tourists. Earlier, from 1865 to 1908, a local photographer named H. H. Bennett brought attention to the Dells with his dramatic stereoscopic and stop-action photographs—including one of a man jumping from one lofty rock tower to another. You can visit part of his studio at 215 Broadway to see the early photographs, and even purchase enlargements made from the original glass-plate negatives.

10 HORICON MARSH

This 32,000-acre freshwater cattail marsh, the largest in America, is an excellent spot for communing with nature—especially on spring or autumn afternoons, when flights of Canada geese fly overhead in honking wedges to and from their subarctic summer quarters. Paddle a pontoon boat into the inner marsh. Watch for great egrets, a threatened population in Wisconsin that nests successfully here. In the northern **Horicon Marsh National Wildlife Refuge,** take boardwalk trails across the wetlands for a close-up view of wild marsh fowl. Head to Quick's Point at the state-run **Horicon Marsh Wildlife Area** for the glorious sunsets.

DOOR COUNTY

1 STURGEON BAY

Visitors flock to Sturgeon Bay to enjoy this small town's pleasures—including two town districts on the National Register of Historic Places. The **Door County Maritime Museum**—with two locations on the peninsula—focuses on the history of the area's commercial fishing and shipbuilding industries.

▶ *The Door County Maritime Museum Festival, held the first full weekend in August, features a classic wooden boat show, boatbuilding contest, and other maritime activities.*

Shipbuilders still ply their trade in Sturgeon Bay. **Palmer Johnson, Inc.,** builder of sleek luxury craft and America's Cup winners, offers no tours—but leaves a door as big as a hangar's open in the summer so that visitors can watch the shipbuilders at work.

2 EGG HARBOR

All over the Door Peninsula the roadsides are strewn with white trillium each spring. Neat fields of apple trees and cherry trees float in pink and white blossoms. The vicinity of the tidy town of Egg Harbor is a prime place to take in the beauty. And if you crave a cherry pie, buy one of Wisconsin's best at the

Door County Market south of town. Or pick your own cherries at **Hyline Orchard,** one of many fruit and dairy farms dotting the peninsula.

3 FISH CREEK

You can cast for treasures in antique shops and art galleries in busy Fish Creek. Or walk down Main Street to the rocky shore of Green Bay for some serenity and a great view of the setting sun. Main Street passes in front of one of Door County's many bed-and-breakfasts, the **White Gull Inn,** famous for its fish boils—the county culinary treat that originated as 19th-century fast food for hardworking lumberjacks and fishermen. All fish boils involve much the same ingredients: whitefish, red potatoes, and white onions. Most are served with a locally made wine or beer, bread, butter, creamy coleslaw, and pie for dessert, made with Door

A fish boil is both a hearty meal and a Door County tradition. Here the savory blend of whitefish, red potatoes, and white onions is lifted from the fire, ready for the crowd to enjoy.

County tart Montmorency cherries. Fish Creek is also home to the **Orchard Country Winery,** where you can stop in for a taste.

Just north of Fish Creek, 3,700-acre **Peninsula State Park** is one of five state parks in Door County, which boasts more parks than any other county in the U.S. Sweethearts, families, and photographers all troop to the top of 75-foot-high **Eagle Tower** for a sweeping view of Green Bay and the setting sun. Another great park photo opportunity is **Eagle Bluff Lighthouse,** built in 1868 and open for tours each summer.

> *Eagle Bluff is the only Door Peninsula lighthouse that provides access to some of the living quarters. Climbing to the top is not allowed, however.*

4 EPHRAIM

With its classic white clapboard houses and pristine churches, Ephraim, whose name means "doubly fruitful," still retains the character of the early Norwegian Moravians who settled here in 1853. This picturesque village is a testament to Door County's nickname: the Cape Cod of the Midwest. Residents, however, claim that Cape Cod is the Door County of the East.

Ephraim, along with Sturgeon Bay and Fish Creek, helped start the tourist boom back in the 1890's, when Lake Michigan steamers arrived with vacationers from Milwaukee and Chicago. The old boathouse on the point where they landed in Ephraim, **Anderson Dock,** is one of the few places where unsolicited hand carvings on the walls—the calling cards of visitors—add to the ambience.

5 SISTER BAY

The startling sight of goats munching grass on the roof of **Al Johnson's Swedish Restaurant** in the tiny town of Sister Bay is a real traffic stopper, as well as a reminder that much of Door County was settled by people of Scandinavian descent.

Sister Bay is also the host for a joyous annual festival: **Fall Fest,** held every October on the weekend after Columbus Day and replete with bratwurst and brews. There's also a parade and an extensive arts and crafts exhibition.

> *Because great numbers of people flock to Fall Fest, you'll be wise to make hotel reservations a few months in advance.*

6 ELLISON BAY

In Ellison Bay, on "the Top-o'-the-Thumb"—the locals' name for the northernmost part of the Door Peninsula—the squeaking sound of the screen door slamming shut in the lovingly preserved, still-operating **Pioneer Store** recalls a time before air conditioners kept interiors cool in the summer. Inside, the old potbellied stove takes you back to another world.

The town has some fine bed-and-breakfasts, one with a gazebo and displays of works by local artists.

7 GILLS ROCK

A winding drive meanders to the tip of the island and the town of Gills Rock, which overlooks six-mile-wide Porte

***The Cana Island lighthouse** stands just off the peninsula near Baileys Harbor.*

des Morts Passage (French for "Death's Door"), a still-treacherous waterway filled with sunken ships. Two American Indian dugout canoes salvaged from the channel are the most valuable artifacts in the Gills Rock branch of the **Door County Maritime Museum.**

Death's Door hasn't intimidated local commercial fishers. Many still depart from Gills Rock and return to sell their catches direct to hungry visitors from their shanties and smokehouses overlooking the water.

8 WASHINGTON ISLAND

Ferries now safely transport vacationers all year long through Death's Door from the Northport and Gills Rock docks to Washington Island, one of dozens of islands off Door County and home to the oldest Icelandic community in the United States. Icelandic immigrant Chester Thordarson honored his homeland's architectural tradition by building the **Great Stone Hall**—not a residence but a community center—in neighboring **Rock Island State Park,** just north of Washington Island.

On your route southward to Baileys Harbor, stop at **Cana Island,** among the county's loveliest and smallest; its working 1869 lighthouse has long been a favorite of photographers.

▶ *The only access to Cana Island is by a rocky footpath, which is sometimes partially covered with water. Wear shoes you won't mind getting wet.*

9 BAILEYS HARBOR

When it comes to fishing, Baileys Harbor makes it possible for aficionados to brag endlessly: its waters yield perhaps the best aquatic bounty in the Midwest. In summer, you can charter a boat or bring your own to fish for pike, trout, walleye, salmon, bass, whitefish, and perch. In winter, you can join the locals for some invigorating ice fishing.

Ridges Sanctuary, more than 900 acres of ridged land deposited by the action of ancient ocean sand and later covered by vegetation, is home to rare flowers and frisky wildlife. Many orchids are native to Wisconsin. You'll spot beautiful mayflowers and delicate dwarf lake irises and such fauna as red foxes and white-tailed deer. Walk the level nature trails—from half a mile to five miles—for as long as you like.

South of Jacksonport, **Whitefish Dunes State Park** has some of the largest sand dunes on the lake—and one of the most scenic views. Within the park is **Cave Point County Park,** where towering limestone cliffs drop dramatically to Lake Michigan far below, and crashing waves splash water right up to where you're standing.

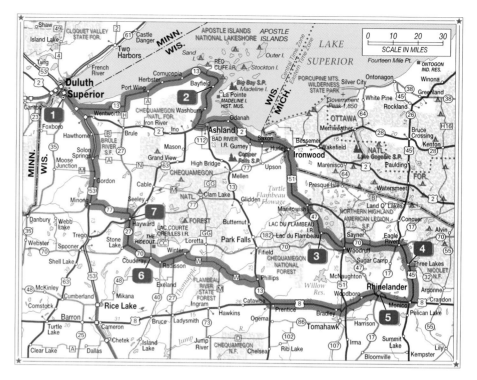

THE NORTH WOODS

1 SUPERIOR

The settlement of this port city situated on a large natural harbor began in 1665, when the Jesuit Claude-Jean Allouez built a mission there. A number of fur-trading posts later sprang up, and permanent settlers arrived in 1853. Today, with the city of Duluth, its port forms the western terminus of the St. Lawrence Seaway.

A fine example of Great Lakes Victorian elegance can be found at **Fairlawn Mansion and Museum,** built as the lavish 42-room home of Superior's second mayor. Tours of the entire house are held year-round.

Firehouse buffs will want to visit the restored **Old Firehouse and Police Museum** to see the last of the city's turn-of-the-century fire stations. The displays include a 1906 steam pumper.

2 BAYFIELD

This tiny town on the shore of Lake Superior has 50 buildings—many of them Victorian mansions—listed in the National Register of Historic Places. It also draws fishermen by the thousands. But the biggest attraction for tourists lies offshore: the Apostle Islands, standing like platforms in the water. Twenty of

The Freshwater Fishing Hall of Fame *in Hayward is a fish museum in the literal sense: its building is shaped like a giant muskellunge.*

them—all but Madeline Island and one more—are now part of the **Apostle Islands National Lakeshore.** Their name is the legacy of the first missionaries to arrive, who mistakenly counted 12. Nature has sculpted the islands into a beautiful world of red sandstone cliffs, inlets, bays, and sandy beaches. Sightseeing cruises from Bayfield give you a close-up view and let you land on some of the islands, where rangers will guide you on a nature walk.

Madeline Island can be reached by a car ferry that crosses between Bayfield and the island every 30 minutes during peak tourist season.

▶ *Arriving on Madeline Island in La Pointe, you can sign up for a bus tour if you left your car behind. You can also rent bicycles to tour the island.*

3 LAC DU FLAMBEAU

This town, in the heart of the Lac du Flambeau Band of **Lake Superior Ojibwa (Chippewa) Indian Reservation,** was named "lake of the torch" by the French explorers for the Chippewa custom of spearfishing by torchlight in the spring. The Ojibwa word for the custom that gave the town its name is **Waswagoning,** also the name given a walk-though American Indian village five miles east of town. Here is a museum of Ojibwa life, where the crafts of arrow making and canoe building are highlighted and dances and historical re-creations are often held. Overnighters can stay in cozy wigwams; it's advisable to reserve ahead. In the summer, powwows are held every Tuesday night in the adjacent **Indian Bowl,** where energetic native dancers, singers, and drummers participate.

4 THREE LAKES

Every year cranberry growers in Wisconsin and Massachusetts compete to be the nation's leading cranberry producer. Three Lakes is proof of Wisconsin's abundance. During **Cranberry Fest,** held the first weekend in October, a tour of crimson cranberry bogs leaves from Eagle River, 10 miles north of Three Lakes. The tour winds up at **Fruit of the Woods Wine Cellar,** where free 20-minute tours are offered

once an hour year-round. You can taste any of the fruit wines for which the winery is known—mostly cranberry but also strawberry, blackberry, apple, raspberry, and sometimes wild plum. There's also a shed where you can buy your own store of the tasty concoctions.

▶ *Demand is extremely high for the Bog and Winery Tour, held for only two days in mid-October. Call 800-359-6315 at least three months in advance to make your reservations.*

5 RHINELANDER

In **Pioneer Park** stands a fine logging museum and a one-room schoolhouse. But unusual even for the north woods is the park's fascinating **Civilian Conservation Corps Museum,** celebrating the men who built roads and parks and

planted trees here during the Depression. You'll see what they wore, how they were housed, and what they accomplished. Admission is free.

6 COUDERAY

A stone lodge six miles north of this small town, surrounded by outbuildings on a 45-acre estate, is called **The Hideout**—and better known as the retreat where Al Capone relaxed in the 1920's. The lodge itself is the main attraction, with its massive fireplace, custom-carved spiral staircases, and deer-antler light fixtures. Entering the main room is like being transported to the twenties. Outside are other curiosities. The garage, built to house Capone's eight black limousines, has

been turned into a restaurant, but the machine gun emplacement holes are still visible. There is also a room that is said to have been a grim holding cell for Capone's enemies. And you can peer into a few antique cars such as so-called wheelmen of the day might have driven. You may note a certain irony when you see that the gangster's lodge overlooks a beautiful lake—a scene that is the very picture of serenity.

7 HAYWARD

Fishing enthusiasts will love Hayward's **National Freshwater Fishing Hall of Fame,** a museum housed partly in a giant, four-story-high fiberglass replica of a muskellunge—a North American fish of the pike family. Believe it or not, an observation platform is located inside the muskie's mouth—and it's an excel-

Cranberries are harvested by flooding a bog, then stripping off the berries with a four-wheel-drive vehicle called a beater. Here, in Three Lakes, a worker pushes the floating berries onto a conveyor belt.

lent place to take pictures. Anglers will appreciate the outboard motor display and, perhaps, the exhibit of hooks removed from hapless fishermen; but everybody can appreciate the legend inscribed over one of the buildings: "Give a man a fish, feed him for a day; teach him to fish, feed him for life."

Logrolling, chopping, sawing, and shinnying up trunks are the chief attractions at the **Lumberjack World Championships,** held in Hayward every year in the last full weekend of July. Afterwards you can savor a lumberjack-size meal, especially on Rte. B at the popular **Historyland Cook Shanty,** where even before dinner is served, doughnuts as big as dinner plates are whisked to your table.

Minnesota

The lovely countryside of Minnesota has more lakes than any other state, set in scenery that ranges from refreshing pine forests in the north to fertile prairie farmland in the south.

1 MINNEAPOLIS/ST. PAUL

They're called the Twin Cities, but historically St. Paul and Minneapolis have been more fraternal than identical. Born in different decades, they spent their formative years growing up on opposite banks of the Mississippi. The more sedate older sibling, St. Paul, which once had the odd name Pig's Eye, has aged beautifully and is now graced with the state capitol, tree-lined streets, and elegant homes. The other twin, Minneapolis, boasts such a glittering skyline and vibrant arts scene that it's been nicknamed the Minne-Apple, the Upper Midwest's version of the Big Apple.

Over the years these rival siblings have grown closer. Between them their museums now sum up the North Star State's history. Start at the **Minnesota History Center** in St. Paul to see exhibits on everything typically Minnesotan: from A, for animals, like the bison, to Z, for below-zero weather. Other Minnesota mementos here include a Betty Crocker radio broadcast, Prince's costume from *Purple Rain*, a voyageur's canoe, and an actual 24-ton Soo Line boxcar.

Among the most imposing structures in St. Paul are the **Landmark Center,** built at the turn of the century to house the federal courts and now an arts and cultural center; the 1891 **James J. Hill House,** built by the railroad tycoon who linked St. Paul with Puget Sound; and the striking **Cathedral of St. Paul,** with a gleaming copper dome.

In Minneapolis the American Swedish Institute, built by an immigrant who started a Swedish-language newspaper in the late 19th century, is a wonderland of intricately carved wood and stained glass. The ornate porcelain-tile *kakelugnar* stoves are so beautiful that they can be viewed as works of art.

The **Walker Art Center** is the repository for 20th-century art running the gamut from Cubism to Minimalism. It would be hard to miss the whimsical sculpture in the museum's **Minneapolis Sculpture Garden,** just across the street. Entitled "Spoonbridge and Cherry," this huge representation of a silver spoon and a bright red cherry was created by Claes Oldenburg and his wife, Coosje van Bruggen.

The **Frederick R. Weisman Art Museum** is perhaps the most striking building in Minneapolis. Its collection of contemporary artworks is housed in a postmodern structure of sundry stainless steel shapes piled high.

▶ *Both cities have their own climate-controlled access to attractions: skyways. In St. Paul, 37 blocks are connected by 45 glassed-in, elevated walkways; in Minneapolis, 60 walkways connect 51 blocks.*

If you long to visit a mall, head straight for the country's largest: the **Mall of America,** a vast shopping and entertainment complex in the Minneapolis suburb of Bloomington. Many of the country's big-name stores are here, along with dozens of restaurants and nightclubs. Even the world's largest indoor amusement park is within the confines of this commercial extravaganza: **Knott's Camp Snoopy,** where the host is the lovable little canine himself.

Animal lovers will be surprised to find 8,000 acres of wilderness in the midst of this bustling city—the **Minnesota Valley National Wildlife Refuge,** containing a diverse wildlife population. Ten minutes south of the Mall of America is the **Minnesota Zoo,** where natural exhibits are home to 387 species.

2 TAYLORS FALLS

Like most frontier towns, Taylors Falls grew up along a highway of water, the St. Croix River, which separates Minnesota and Wisconsin. In the 1850's and 1860's, lumbermen built white

The twin cities of Minneapolis and St. Paul merge together as one shining metropolis.

You can tour the Mayo Clinic at 10 A.M. or 2 P.M. Monday through Friday; no admission is charged.

6 ROCHESTER

Late in the 19th century two young local country doctors joined their father in caring for the sick. The three eventually turned their small practice into a hospital—first called St. Mary's Hospital—that would eventually become one of the most famous in the world. The doctors were William Mayo and his sons William and Charles, and the hospital became the **Mayo Clinic.**

▶ *You can tour the Mayo Clinic at 10 A.M. or 2 P.M. Monday through Friday; no admission is charged.*

---

clapboard homes, like the Greek Revival **W.H.C. Folsom House,** in the **Angel's Hill Historic District,** to resemble their houses back east. These pristine homes still nestle high above the **St. Croix River**—now designated a National Wild and Scenic River but formerly a utilitarian way to transport millions of logs, cut from Minnesota's virgin forests, downstream.

3 STILLWATER

The birthplace of the Minnesota Territory in 1843, Stillwater, once the lumbering capital of the St. Croix River region, attracts day-trippers who admire its historic architecture, antique shops, and the quaint bed-and-breakfasts in lavish mid-19th-century homes.

A quarter-mile back from the St. Croix River is the **Falls Creek Scientific and Natural Area,** just north of Stillwater. This 135-acre natural area of old-growth white pines is one of 100 state nature preserves that protect rare and endangered plant and animal species in the state of Minnesota.

4 RED WING

With dozens of sites on the National Register of Historic Places and three national historic districts, Red Wing is arguably Minnesota's loveliest Mississippi River town. The grande dame 1875 **St. James Hotel** is resplendent in a town chock-a-block with stunning architecture. The intersection of Hill and Third streets, once called the most architecturally significant in Minnesota, presents an 1857 octagonal house, an 1867 French Second Empire house, and a 1913 Prairie Style home.

Watching the ornate re-created paddle wheelers and enormous flat barges ply the river as you're driving the **Great River Road** evokes a sweet nostalgia along this section of the Mississippi. Besides enjoying the magnificent scenery, travelers can fish; spy bald eagles, white swans, and egrets; and go hunting for agate rocks along the banks.

5 WABASHA

North of Wabasha, on the road from Red Wing, the Mississippi widens, creating sparkling blue **Lake Pepin.** Laura Ingalls Wilder, who grew up in several little houses on the prairie, lived for a year—1867—just across the lake, in the woods of Wisconsin.

In the town itself sits Minnesota's oldest hotel still in operation, the 1856 **Anderson House.** The famous old establishment is well-known for its unique bed warmers: purring cats lent free to overnight guests.

On your way west from Rochester to New Ulm, you may want to stop at the turn-of-the-century town of **Owatonna** to see what may be the most famous bank that the acclaimed Chicago architect Louis Sullivan designed: the 1907–08 Prairie Style **Norwest Bank.**

7 NEW ULM

Settled by Germans in the 1850's, the town of New Ulm still serves up the flavor of the old country in its food, architecture, and celebrations. A 45-foot freestanding glockenspiel dominates downtown, with bells that chime on the hour and animated figurines that play programmed pieces three times a day.

Because German Minnesotans are the state's largest single nationality group, you can expect quite a crowd at New Ulm's **Heritagefest,** held each year after the Fourth of July weekend. You'll hear the music of bands from Germany and Austria, feast on ethnic specialties, and shop for crafts.

8 REDWOOD FALLS

All around Redwood Falls are historic sites with ties to the 1862 Dakota Conflict, a tragic chapter in Minnesota history in which hundreds of people died. In that conflict 38 Dakota Indians were hanged in what is believed to be the largest mass execution ever carried out in the United States. Two historic sites tell the story—and from both sides. At **Fort Ridgely State Park,** 25 miles southeast of Redwood Falls, the one remaining fort building has been restored as a history center, with artifacts and 1860's soldiers' uniforms. A video at the center tells the story of the Dakota Conflict from the white soldiers' point of view. At the **Lower Sioux Interpretive Center,** seven miles east of Redwood Falls, the video that is presented gives you the story of the bloody conflict as the Dakotas saw it.

NORTHEASTERN MINNESOTA

1 DULUTH

The port of Duluth-Superior may be farther inland than any other port in the world—more than 2,000 miles from the sea. This western terminus of the St. Lawrence Seaway, located on Lake Superior at the mouth of the St. Louis River, handles more tonnage than any other city on the Great Lakes. A two-hour narrated cruise from Barker's Island on the *Vista Star* or *Vista King* will give you dramatic views of this vital port: you'll float under Duluth's 225-foot-high **Aerial Lift Bridge** and past

the world's biggest grain elevators. You'll also see the great ore docks that tower a hundred feet above the water; the imposing, now-silent docks are particularly impressive at night, when strings of lights form a glittering "necklace." Nighttime cruises, complete with dinner and dancing, are the best way to take in the view.

▶ *The boat tour of the harbor encounters heavy lake traffic from July through mid-August. The best time to take a cruise is late June or just before Labor Day.*

On **Barker's Island** is the **S.S. Meteor,** the last of the whaleback freighters that were launched by the dozen from a local shipyard at the turn of the century. Guided tours are given in summer. The odd-looking whalebacks were so named by a Great Lakes captain, who had a dream that led him to invent what he thought was the aerodynamic shape of the future.

A pleasant drive along Duluth's elegant Superior Street takes you past gracious mansions that bear witness to the city's boom years. Overlooking Lake Superior is **Glensheen,** a 39-room Jacobean manor house on a 22-acre estate completed in 1908 by Duluth millionaire Chester A. Congdon. The period furniture is lovely; included in a tour of

Glensheen is a look at the carriages and sleighs in the carriage house.

2 SAVANNA PORTAGE

Despite its rather miserable history, **Savanna Portage State Park** is an excellent spot for a picnic at the right time of year. This was one portage—a rough six miles through mosquito-infested swamps to reach Big Sandy Lake and the Mississippi River—that even the hardiest voyageur dreaded. Today more than 60,000 people a year visit the park to canoe, swim, and fish; but most know enough to stay off the six-mile portage trail in early summer and early fall. "Everything that bites lives here," says a ranger wryly. Autumn brings welcome relief. The land is ablaze with color, the temperature is crisp, and there's not an insect to be seen.

▶ *Mosquitoes and ticks are at their worst in early and mid summer. At those times use insect repellent and wear face netting.*

3 GRAND RAPIDS

Here Judy Garland was born Frances Gumm in 1922. In her stage debut, little Frances hammed it up so spectacularly during her parents' vaudeville show—when she ran onstage and interrupted her sisters' act—that Mr. Gumm had to forcibly escort his daughter offstage. The **Judy Garland Historical Center,** full of such memorabilia as scripts, sheet music, and early photographs, is located on the third floor (once the attic) of the former 1895 Central School building.

While you're at the center, treat yourself to some terrific homemade muffins in the restaurant on the first floor. Then grab a different kind of snack at the **Forest History Center,** where in two of the three living-history sites—a 1900 logging camp and a 1901 river wanigan, or logging-drive supply boat—costumed cooks will serve you up little samples of prunes and beans, along with other choice lumberjack chow.

4 HIBBING

There's much to see in Hibbing, Bob Dylan's hometown, and the surrounding Mesabi Range. You can start by slip-

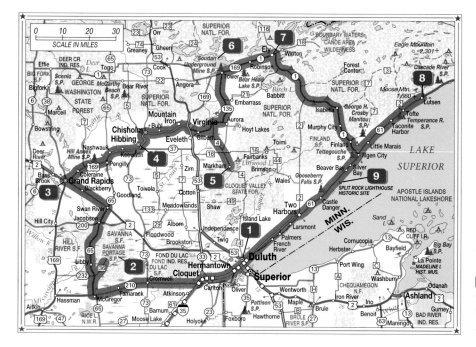

ping on a hard hat and plunging deep into the earth on the **Taconite Mine Tours.** Here you'll get a firsthand view as monstrous shovels extract taconite iron ore from the rich underground source. Note: Leave your own hard hat at home; the tour furnishes them, as well as safety glasses and earplugs. The guided tours are available at **Ironworld USA,** a theme park situated in a pastoral setting in nearby Chisholm.

5 MARKHAM

In a tribute to the contribution of Finnish immigrants to this part of the country, the St. Louis County Historical Society maintains the **Eli Wirtanen Homestead** amid gently rolling hills. The Finnish bachelor farmer lived here from 1904 until the 1950's. Wirtanen built most of the small structures himself, including the log house, privy, root cellar, barn—and of course the sauna. Life was hard, but there were compensations. From time to time Wirtanen had sauna parties in his little 10- by 12-foot structure, into which up to eight people could fit.

6 SOUDAN UNDERGROUND MINE

Soudan Underground Mine State Park is home to Minnesota's oldest, richest, and deepest underground mine, operated from the earliest days of the discovery of iron in the Vermilion Range. An hour-long guided tour begins with an elevator ride 2,341 feet down to a hard-rock world where the temperature is a constant 50°F.

▶ *Be aware that to reach the deepest part of the mine, you'll have to traverse a 32-step spiral staircase.*

You'll travel in an electric mining train down a 3,000-foot tunnel to a great cavity, where the last high-grade ore (65 percent iron) was pulled out of the earth in 1962. On the surface, you can doff your hard hat and enjoy the mining exhibits in the interpretive center.

7 ELY

Ely has for years been the traditional outfitting center for the million-acre **Boundary Waters Canoe Area**

Land of 10,000 Lakes may be Minnesota's moniker, but there are really some 15,000 of the sky-blue bodies of water here. The serene lakes of the vast Boundary Waters are heaven for canoeists and for fishermen partial to walleye.

Wilderness—one of America's great surviving wilderness areas. It's also the home of the **International Wolf Center**—appropriately located in a state with one of the most significant wolf populations outside Alaska—where visitors can join a wolf-tracking group and even take howling trips in the field; if your howl is right and your luck is good, a pack of wolves answers.

Also in Ely is the **Vermilion Interpretive Center,** where you will learn more about the American Indian cultures that were here first, and about mining, fur trading, and logging. The **Dorothy Molter Memorial Museum** consists of two cabins brought from faraway Knife Lake by dogsled and reassembled in Ely. For 56 years the beloved "lady of the wilderness," Dorothy Molter, a reg-

Wolves are occasionally seen prowling the North Woods. Minnesota has one of the largest wolf populations outside Alaska.

istered nurse and friend to world-famous explorers and Cub Scouts alike, lived 18 miles and six canoe portages from the nearest road. And even though she lived in a home that could hardly have been more remote, Dorothy Molter had a guest book containing thousands of visitors' signatures.

8 LUTSEN

If you want to get above it all, take the eight-minute **Lutsen Gondola** ride up to the summit of Moose Mountain, on which vantage point you can buy a light lunch and admire the view. On a clear day the visibility is 100 miles. For those in a hurry, there's the **Alpine Slide,** where you'll travel up Eagle Mountain on a chairlift and down on the slide—one sled per person, on a track, with brakes that will control your speed.

9 SPLIT ROCK LIGHTHOUSE

This historic site, set on a cliff that towers over Lake Superior, features the **Split Rock Lighthouse and History Center,** 54 feet tall and one of the state's best-known landmarks. Built in 1909–10, the lighthouse was at first manned seasonally by keeper Pete Young, who stayed from mid-April to mid-December. His wife, however, didn't care for eight months of isolation. So Young stayed alone. The quasi-bachelor's life must have agreed with Mr. Young: after 18 years, at age 70, he took retirement—and only because it was mandatory.

GREAT PLAINS
& MOUNTAINS

*N*owhere else in America does the landscape spread so vast and bold. Here the scenery is on an epic scale, from the lonely buttes, red spires, and painted pinnacles of Monument Valley to the Rocky Mountain peaks of Glacier National Park. The following 38 tours bring you the drama of the deserts and mountains and rustling prairie grasslands—places that still draw folk as hardy as the the pioneers who settled here.

Scattered among the 14 states are the very icons of America: the Grand Canyon, Mount Rushmore, and Yellowstone, where Old Faithful never disappoints. You'll revisit the Old West and tour ghost towns that whisper their past to passing tumbleweed. In Texas you'll stop in the Cowboy Capital of the World, where rodeos are a way of life. And in South Dakota you'll find that there really is a Little House on the Prairie. History, too, is ever-present, in the cliff dwellings and Spanish missions that dot the Southwest. On the next 76 pages, this part of America, from the fertile fields of the Great Plains to the magnificent mountains of the West, are yours to explore.

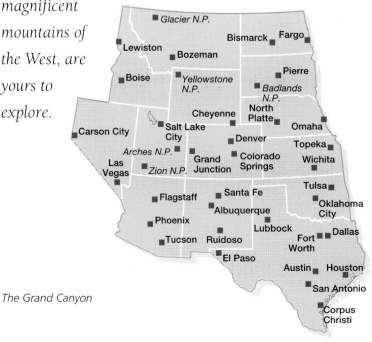

The Grand Canyon

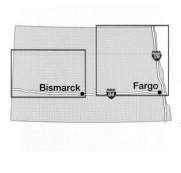

Bismarck   Fargo

North Dakota

Amid sweeping plains and lush Missouri River forests, this rough-riding country has a beauty all its own—raw, clean, and vast. Cross the Big Muddy and time-travel deep into the Old West.

THE WEST

1 BISMARCK

Chew the fat with North Dakotans, and they'll convince you that the Old West starts in the middle of the "Big Muddy," the mighty **Missouri River**, flanked by the capital city of Bismarck on the east and the town of Mandan on the west. "Here is where the map should fold," John Steinbeck once wrote. The striking contrasts between the east and west sides of the river were underscored in a Mandan Indian legend wherein the region was developed by two Creators, each with his own landscaping plan. The First Creator made the west side rich in woody draws, hills, and streams, and the Second Creator filled the east side with flatlands and ponds.

Bismarck was built on this flat eastern terrain. Its **State Capitol**, dubbed the Skyscraper of the Prairies, is an imposing presence, a clean-lined structure with a slick Art Deco interior of black-marble walls and wood paneling.

A sculpture of a buffalo pawing the lawn of the adjacent **North Dakota Heritage Center**'s museum is but one of the artifacts in the museum's eclectic collection. See the sinew-sewn buffalo-hide tepee and a mastodon skeleton.

▶ *Hotel and motel rooms are booked months in advance for the United Tribes Powwow, held the second weekend in September, when thousands witness native dancers and singers competing in full regalia.*

2 MANDAN

You've crossed the Big Muddy into the high-rolling Old West. Mandan's best-known residence, the **Fort Abraham Lincoln Home**, lies within **Fort Abraham Lincoln State Park**. It is a reconstruction of the house that Lt. Col. George A. Custer and his wife, Libbie, lived in from 1873 to 1876, when the cavalry complex alongside the Missouri was a center of trade. The Custers tried to impose a veneer of civilization on their simple frame house by adorning it with a harp and a piano and by holding balls at which Libbie Custer would sport a blond wig made from her husband's hair. But an untamed bobcat (now a stuffed model) inhabiting the basement was a forceful reminder of the omnipresent wilderness. The house was the last the couple would share. On May 17, 1876, Custer and the men of the 7th Cavalry left this post, never to return; they would lose their lives a month later in the ill-fated Battle of the Little Bighorn. The fort closed in 1891, and the house and the 80-odd wooden fort structures were dismantled and recycled on the lumber-scarce plains.

3 DICKINSON

The waving prairie grasses of the western Plains were thus described by Custer: "It does not require a very great stretch of the imagination… to picture these successive undulations as gigantic waves." Dickinson, which calls itself the Queen City of the Prairies, pays homage to its cattle-punching grassland heritage at the **Roughrider Days** Western festival in early July.

A sedate relative of Jurassic Park is the **Dakota Dinosaur Museum.** The 10 full-scale dinosaurs on exhibit are put together from casts, sculptures, and actual bones taken from dinosaur skeletons found in the Hell Creek Formation region of the badlands.

4 THE BADLANDS/MEDORA

Described as "hell with the fires out," the badlands initially seem inhospitable and barren. Look closer and discover a terrain blanketed with wildflowers and prairie grasses in the spring and sum-

Cowboys and cowgirls at heart thrill to the sweeping prairies and buttes of the Dakota badlands. Trail rides are offered by outfitters in Medora.

Sculpted over time: A rock is shaped by the elements in Theodore Roosevelt National Park.

mer. All provide sustenance for golden eagles, coyotes, bison, and wild horses said to be descended from Sitting Bull's war ponies. Washed by a fierce rainstorm or baked by the sun's rays, the rugged terra-cotta terrain of these badlands vibrates with life and energy.

Many have been energized by this still largely untamed land. In 1883 a French aristocrat, the marquis de Mores, founded the Old West town of Medora, named it after his beautiful American wife, and dreamed of boom times. Although de Mores's rollicking frontier town of saloons and hotels ultimately went bust, Medora (population under 100) today plays host to more visitors than any other site in the state. The 26-

room **Château de Mores**, a loving testament to high hopes, is a popular site.

Among those who visited in the 1880's was an Easterner turned rancher named Teddy Roosevelt. The once-puny asthmatic was enthralled and invigorated by this rugged countryside. "I never would have become president if it had not been for my experiences in North Dakota," he later wrote.

Don't miss the **Medora Musical**, a cheery song-and-dance tribute to Old Medora, held nightly at sunset at the Burning Hills Amphitheater. Or visit on Memorial Day weekend, when rough-and-ready cowpokes reveal their sensitive side at the annual **Dakota Cowboy Poetry Reading**.

▶ *Make a pit stop in the town of Beach before you head up Rte. 16, where you'll spot beautiful grasslands but few rest areas, gas stations, or stores.*

5 THEODORE ROOSEVELT NATIONAL PARK

This 110-square-mile park honors the conservationist president, whose environmental awareness was reinforced in North Dakota. In his two terms in the White House, from 1901 to 1909, Roosevelt secured congressional approval for no less than 5 national parks, 18

national monuments, 55 wildlife refuges, and 150 national forests.

Just inside the entrance to the park's **South Unit**, behind the visitor center, is Roosevelt's restored **Maltese Cross Ranch** cabin, where he lived periodically from 1883 to 1885. Seventy miles away, the even remoter **North Unit** has a 14-mile scenic drive offering sweeping vistas of bluffs streaked with color and herds of buffalo and longhorn cattle. Roosevelt's **Elkhorn Ranch** is midway between the two units.

6 FORT UNION/FORT BUFORD

As one of the major trading posts for the American Fur Company, **Fort Union** was quite an upscale structure for the early-19th-century Plains. Building it was a calculated move on capitalist John Jacob Astor's part: he simply wanted to impress and thus gain favor with the local Indians. Located at the confluence of the Missouri and Yellowstone rivers and surrounded by expansive prairies, the reconstructed fort has 18-foot-high palisades and appears much as it did when it served as the northern Great Plains' biggest shopping mall, where traders and Indians exchanged goods for furs.

The original Fort Union was torn down in 1867 when the army built **Fort Buford** a mile downstream to forcibly subdue the Sioux. Before it was abandoned in 1895, Buford was the imprisonment site of such Indian leaders as Nez Perce Chief Joseph and Sioux leader Sitting Bull.

Fifty miles east is the 460-acre **Lewis and Clark State Park**, on **Lake Sakakawea**, a prime recreation lake. At the visitor center pick up a self-guiding map for the half-mile **Prairie Nature Trail**, which slices through wooded ravines and past 60-million-year-old petrified stumps, old wagon ruts, and a fox den. Be on the lookout for clusters of prairie smoke, purple flowers that in vast numbers

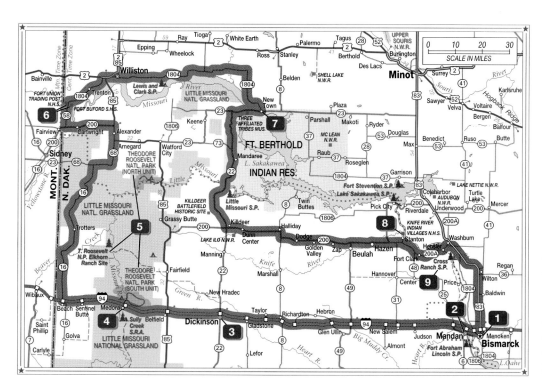

resemble clouds of smoke. Locals pluck the giant dandelions, known as Western salsify, and spritz them with hair spray to freeze the shape. At the top of the trail the view extends four miles.

7 NEW TOWN

The **Three Affiliated Tribes Museum,** four miles west of New Town on the **Fort Berthold Reservation,** displays arts, crafts, and historical items of the Mandan, Hidatsa, and Arikara tribes.

Southward from New Town you'll be traveling one of North Dakota's most scenic roads, **Rte. 22.** For some 60 miles this two-lane road winds through commercial-free badlands, passing rugged buttes and rolling prairies with nary a fast-food place in sight. Pull off at **Little Missouri State Park,** 17 miles north of Killdeer. Here is what locals consider the most beautiful section of the badlands—and the least worn from use. The park's **Badlands Trails Concessions** offers guided trail rides on horseback eight months of the year; you'll amble over grassy plains and past wild tiger lilies and a rattlesnake or two. But not to worry: trail interpreters match uneasy riders with the gentlest of mounts and can spot a rattler before the horses do.

▶ *These two-hour interpretive trail rides cross relatively virgin terrain. The trips are moderate to strenuous and often follow narrow pathways. Be sure to reserve ahead.*

8 KNIFE RIVER INDIAN VILLAGES

The Hidatsa culture that flourished for hundreds of years along these high Missouri River banks is memorialized at the **Knife River Indian Villages National Historic Site.** Walking tours pass the depressions left by 50 to 75 earth lodges, still revered by American Indians. In summer, turkey buzzards and golden eagles trace languid circles in the sky. Each fall the river's sandbars provide respite for migrating waterfowl.

9 CROSS RANCH STATE PARK

These grass prairies and river-bottom forests were discovered 200 years ago by Lewis and Clark and are now carefully preserved as **Cross Ranch State Park,** located along one of the last free-flowing undeveloped stretches of the Missouri River. Camp on your own "island"—spits of accreted land that jut out into the river—or hike on one of the trails in the **Cross Ranch Nature Preserve.** In the winter, cross-country skiers skim along these same trails.

VALLEYS, LAKES & PRAIRIES

1 FARGO

A century ago farmers called this place Eden. They still do today, tilling fertile black soil into checkerboard squares dense with wheat, sugar beets, and sunflowers. This is the **Red River Valley,** America's heartland. Fargo has served as an agricultural center since westbound settlers forded the river in carts.

Modern Fargo reflects that colorful past. On the city's outskirts a reconstructed pioneer village called **Bonan-**zaville boasts original buildings from around the state and carefully constructed replicas that give visitors a glimpse into turn-of-the-century life.

2 JAMESTOWN

Jamestown residents like to list its major attractions as "good food, green prairies, cool water, clean air, shady parks, fair prices, and friendly people." The myriad other reasons to visit include the world's largest buffalo, which towers over Interstate 94 on the edge of town. This three-story, 120,000-pound concrete statue most emphatically does not roam; it does, however, welcome visitors to **Frontier Village,** a restored prairie town with a schoolhouse, a drugstore, and a caboose. On the grounds is the **National Buffalo Museum,** filled with prairie artifacts.

At the 16,000-acre **Arrowwood National Wildlife Refuge,** 25 miles northwest of town, the James River meanders among marshes and lakes. A 5½-mile auto tour route offers views of duck broods in summer and migrating snow geese in fall.

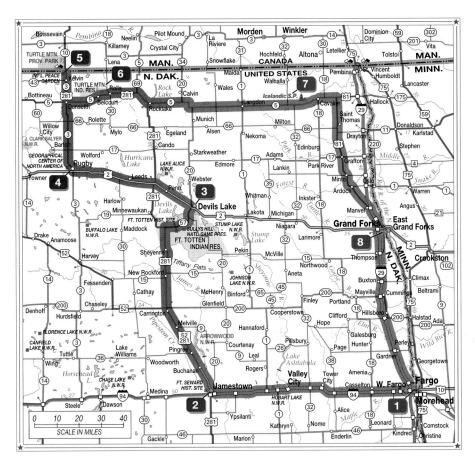

3 DEVILS LAKE

Drop a fishing line into Devils Lake or launch a boat along its 300 miles of shoreline. It's a prime swimming hole as well. Visitors to the lakeside city also named Devils Lake can take a self-guided walking tour of its turn-of-the-century historic district.

Twelve miles to the south stands one of the best-preserved military forts of the trans-Mississippi West. The U.S. Army began building **Fort Totten** in 1868. In addition to the fort, 16 other original structures remain; many are open to visitors.

For a different view of Fort Totten, climb the stepped overlook at the adjacent **Sullys Hill National Game Preserve**. Three hundred feet below, the fort and Devils Lake fall away toward the prairie horizon. A four-mile car route meanders past wallows frequented by herds of bison during the animals' grooming sessions. Bison grooming—when the beasts flop down and start rubbing their backs—often simply means a good back-scratch.

4 RUGBY

It's official: This town of 3,000 residents is the heart of a great continent. A fieldstone cairn at the intersection of Rtes. 2 and 3 marks the spot that a federal survey designated as North America's geographical center.

A short stroll away is the **Pioneer Village and Museum**. Its 27 restored pioneer buildings include a train depot, a log cabin, and a schoolhouse.

5 INTERNATIONAL PEACE GARDEN

What may have been the biggest traffic jam in North Dakota history took place here July 14, 1932. On this 2,300-acre parcel of rolling hill country 12 miles north of Dunseith on the Manitoba–North Dakota border, 50,000 people arrived for the dedication of the **International Peace Garden**. It's a sprawling floral showplace along the world's longest unfortified border, with one foot in Canada and the other in the United States. Take the self-guided auto tours through both countries into the beautiful garden, which has some 120,000 annuals. Here, too, are nature

United in color: On the Canadian border, the International Peace Garden commemorates the goodwill between the United States and Canada. Take the stone stairs into a formal garden (left), or view the annuals that enliven the Bulova Floral Clock (below).

trails bordering streams and lakes. A 120-foot-tall **Peace Tower** can be seen from either country.

▶ *Crossing the border into Canada is relatively hassle-free. But it's a good idea to call 701-825-6201 and request the pamphlet* Know Before You Go *for information on international border requirements.*

6 TURTLE MOUNTAIN RESERVATION

On your drive from the Peace Garden toward the small town of Rolla, you'll see an oasis amid the grasslands of the northern Great Plains. Forested hills rise up from the prairie and form an emerald island of trees. Named the **Turtle Mountains** 200 years ago by explorers, these lake-dotted hills have long been home to the Chippewa Indians. Just west, in Belcourt, the **Turtle Mountain Indian Reservation** houses the **Turtle Mountain Heritage Center**, where exhibits showcase Chippewa artwork and items from the fur-trade era. Two miles north of Belcourt, along a lovely lakeshore, is the **Anishinaubag Intercultural Center**, where visitors can tour a reconstructed Plains Indian village, step inside birch-bark and earthen dwellings, and rent canoes to paddle about on the lake.

7 ICELANDIC STATE PARK

Just west of Cavalier is a two-story frame homestead built by Icelandic immigrants between 1882 and 1890. The **Gunlogson Homestead and Nature Preserve** sheds light on a notable period of American history: the homesteading years, when immigrants settled land at the edge of the wilderness.

Located within **Icelandic State Park**, the Gunlogson Homestead is a focal point of the **Pioneer Heritage Center**, a complex whose exhibits trace the region's history through six time periods—from the early fur-trapping days to the era of such pioneers as the Gunlogsons. The 200-acre preserve has a three-quarter-mile nature trail, where woods and marshlands harbor wood ducks, kingfishers, and herons.

8 GRAND FORKS

Cream of Wheat was born in this Red River center for agricultural trade. The creamy white porridge owes its inception to Frank Amidon, the miller who invented it in 1893. Also born here was Thomas Campbell, who owned farm acreages so huge that he became known in the early 1900's as the Wheat King of America. Campbell's home, the **Campbell House**, shares space on the old family ranch with an original 1870's post office, a 1920's one-room schoolhouse, and the **Myra Museum**, which is filled with exhibits emphasizing the region's heritage.

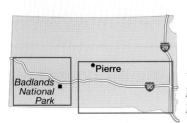

South Dakota

From the whispering ponderosa pines of the Black Hills to the blue-tinged prairies, South Dakota speaks in great pensive pauses, of thundering herds, old mining towns, and native ghosts.

Earthbound moonscape: *Badlands National Park has an otherworldly beauty.*

1 BADLANDS NATIONAL PARK

The desolate terrain of **Badlands National Park,** carved over the ages by natural forces, has a ravaged beauty. And with every gnawing wind, this isolated 366-square-mile geologic wonder gets even rawer. The stunning scenery, combined with guaranteed wildlife sightings—of bison, coyotes, and the occasional wandering poet—makes Badlands among the most popular national parks in the country. Motor the **Badlands Loop Drive** for terrific views of the jagged stone spires, or take an evening stroll on one of the ranger-guided **Night Prowls.** Information on all can be obtained at the park headquarters in **Cedar Pass.**

2 BUFFALO GAP

South Dakota's three national grasslands attest to the near reverence bestowed on the prairie in this Great Plains state. There's even a state grass: the western wheatgrass. The 596,000-acre **Buffalo Gap National Grassland** doesn't have much of a human population; instead it teems with such critters as antelopes, prairie dogs, and grouse. Rare Fairburn agates are found here.

3 PINE RIDGE RESERVATION

Home to the Oglala Sioux, the 1.7-million-acre **Pine Ridge Indian Reservation** is the most populous reservation in the state. Stop in at **Oglala Lakota College,** seven miles southwest of the town of Kyle, whose eagle-shaped main building was designed by an Arapaho architect, Dennis Sun Roads.

Thirty miles south is **Wounded Knee,** scene of the last major Indian-white conflict in the United States. There, on December 29, 1890, the 7th Cavalry killed some 150 Sioux men, women, and children and lost 25 troopers. The story is vividly told in Dee Brown's book *Bury My Heart at Wounded Knee.*

The **Oglala Sioux National Fair,** held in Pine Ridge in August, features traditional dancing and drumming. Exquisite native artwork—star quilts, beadwork, and quillwork—is sold at the **Red Cloud Heritage Center,** four miles northwest of Pine Ridge.

4 HOT SPRINGS

Mineral springs bubbling up from canyons made Hot Springs a health spa before the phrase was coined. Dip into the 87° F mineral waters at **Evans Plunge,** a huge, naturally heated indoor-outdoor swimming complex.

As many as 100 mammoths slipped to their death in a muddy sinkhole during

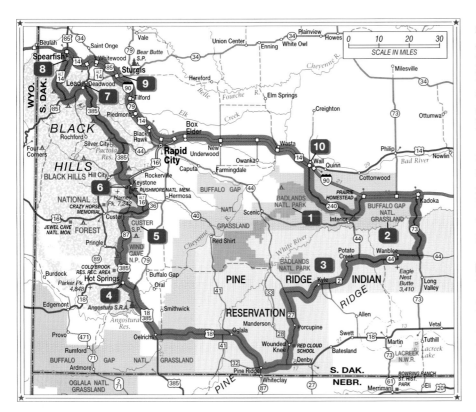

a period of time some 26,000 years ago. **Mammoth Site**, near downtown, has the largest fossil concentration of these Ice Age mammals found in their primary context—discovered in the place where they died—in the world. View the four complete mammoth skeletons unearthed in the ongoing excavation. Other Ice Age animals were found, from camels to giant short-faced bears.

The **Angostura State Recreation Area**, a freshwater reservoir rimmed by steep canyon walls 10 miles south of town, has miles of sandy beach.

5 CUSTER STATE PARK

This 73,000-acre park in the beautiful Black Hills is the habitat of thousands of animals. Tame "begging" burros can be approached without fear along **Iron Mountain Road**. Free-roaming bison graze along the roadside on the 18-mile **Wildlife Loop Road**. Take the **Buffalo Safari Jeep Tour**, an interpretive ride through the shallow canyonlands of the park's interior. Jeep tours originate at the **State Game Lodge**, the 1927 summer White House of Calvin Coolidge. Come in late September or early October for the annual **Buffalo Roundup**, where, to whoops and hollers, bison are herded by riders on horseback, in Jeeps, and in helicopters and led into buffalo corrals on the southeast end of the park. Later, at sales and auctions, the herd is reduced to numbers the range can comfortably manage.

▶ *View bison from inside the car, as these formidable animals can outrun a horse and may be dangerous.*

The soft, evergreen Black Hills can be toured on **Needles Highway**, a 14-mile scenic drive, where you'll slip through narrow stone tunnels. The park has 14 hiking trails; an easy hike is the one-mile trail that circles pretty **Sylvan Lake**. Buffalo often stop traffic in **Wind Cave National Park**, where the sixth-longest cave in the world can be explored in guided candlelight tours.

Much of the park is ringed by **Black Hills National Forest**, a rolling landscape of ponderosa pine. Signs bearing orange diamonds lead snowmobilers on the 300-mile network of groomed trails

from Custer to Spearfish. The two-hour trek to the top of 7,242-foot **Harney Peak** rewards hikers with a 60-mile view of the Black Hills.

6 MOUNT RUSHMORE

This is such an American icon that it's easy to assume the thrill will be diminished on seeing it up close. But no: the 60-foot-high heads of Washington, Jefferson, Teddy Roosevelt, and Lincoln, carved from the Black Hills just prior to World War II, continue to inspire awe.

Just 17 miles away, a fifth great figure

has joined the other four in the Black Hills. At the unfinished **Crazy Horse Memorial**, the Oglala Sioux leader sits astride a stallion; together they rise 56 stories high. The world's largest sculpture was begun in 1948. Hike the three miles to the memorial during the **Crazy Horse Volksmarch** in early June.

7 LEAD/DEADWOOD

These towns came alive in 1876 after George A. Custer confirmed the existence of gold in them thar—Black, that is—hills. Jewelry fashioned from Black Hills gold continues to be the hottest-selling item in the region.

Most folks gave up mining for riches the old-fashioned way long ago. Except for the **Homestake Mine**, still operating in Lead (pronounced leed), the only panning for gold is done by wrestling one-armed bandits in Deadwood's myriad gambling halls. Inside one, named after the old No. 10 Saloon, is a modest wooden chair that some would have

you believe Wild Bill Hickok was sitting in on the hot August night in 1876 when he was murdered playing poker. His cards? The "dead man's hand": pairs of black aces and eights. Hickok, Calamity Jane, and other colorful Wild West characters now turn up their toes in **Mount Moriah Cemetery**.

8 SPEARFISH

Limestone canyons thick with spruce tower over fast-moving **Spearfish Creek**, which crisscrosses the 19-mile **Spearfish Canyon National Forest**

Chief Crazy Horse is memorialized in this small-scale replica of the 563-foot image being carved into the granite of Crazy Horse Mountain. Watch the work progress from an observation point nearly a mile away.

Scenic Byway. Visit these forested hills in autumn, when the leaves of the aspen trees turn to gold.

▶ *The byway is a popular biking route. Exercise caution when driving these narrow, winding roads. If you're biking, wear a helmet.*

Cross-country skiers use the 20 miles of groomed trails on the **Big Hill Trail** network in Black Hills National Forest.

9 STURGIS

Warble "The Star-Spangled Banner" at **Fort Meade** and nary a head will turn: This is where, in 1892, the national anthem was first played officially. It has been played daily ever since. The fort was established as a U.S. cavalry post in 1878. Memorabilia of frontier life fill the **Old Fort Meade Cavalry Museum**, and the **Fort Meade Cavalry Cemetery** holds the remains of soldiers, wives, and Indian scouts.

Just east, **Bear Butte State Park** has a skyscraping mountain considered sacred ground by Plains Indians. Medicine bags and prayer ribbons lacing mountain trees are memorials left by Indian visitors.

The big-sky landscape was the perfect backdrop for the Old West army outpost in the movie *Dances With Wolves*. Guided van tours carry visitors to the film site, 25 miles east of Sturgis along the **Belle Fourche River**.

You'll see a dramatic change in topography when you cross Rte. 79 in **Rapid City**. Behind you to the west are the undulating Black Hills; ahead to the east lie vast prairie grasslands, pocked by ravines and streambeds.

10 WALL

This little town of 800 sits on a sun-baked plateau against the wall of the Badlands. Open prairies are still etched with ruts dug when covered wagons rolled westward. The economy centers on the state's biggest store, **Wall Drug**, a colossus that survived the Depression by giving away ice water. The goods run the gamut, from saddle spurs to an 80-foot dinosaur to miniature Mount Rushmores. Oh, yes—and you can still get a free cup of ice water.

GREAT LAKES & HERITAGE REGION

1 PIERRE

The state capital (pronounced peer) was christened in 1832 by a fur trader named Pierre Chouteau, Jr., who first sighted the spot from a steamship traversing the Missouri River. Begin your tour at the **Flaming Fountain**, on the **State Capitol** grounds, which burns year-round as a memorial to veterans. The 1908 Capitol is a Greek Revival showcase; inside are a colonnaded stairway, marble floors, and painted murals.

Three blocks away, at the **Cultural Heritage Center**, you'll find such historical artifacts as the lead plate that was buried by French explorers in 1743 on a bluff overlooking present-day Fort Pierre. The La Vérendrye Plate was acci-

dentally unearthed in 1913 by children at play on the hill. A national historic monument marks the site.

Most of *Dances With Wolves* was filmed only 25 miles north of the city, off Rte. 1806. The privately owned **Houck's Buffalo Ranch** welcomes gawkers to its spread, where a herd of 3,000 buffalo roam. It's recommended that you call ahead to reserve one of the 1½-hour Jeep tours.

▶ *If you're coming into Pierre from the west, set your watches ahead an hour to Central Standard Time. South Dakota lies in two time zones; the dividing line is roughly north-south down the middle of the state.*

A young Sioux dons traditional finery for a powwow at the Rosebud Reservation.

2 LOWER BRULE/CROW CREEK RESERVATIONS

Travel the **Native American Loop**, which winds through two major Indian reservations. From Fort Thompson you'll cross **Lake Sharpe**, an immense body of water created by the **Big Bend Dam** on the Missouri River. From here, drive through the **Lower Brule Sioux Reservation** and its 245,000-acre expanse of unbroken prairie. The only activity you'll encounter may be a loping antelope here, a buffalo there. In mid-August the **Annual Lower Brule Pow-wow** features high-spirited tribal dancing and singing and a rodeo.

The drive loops down to the small town of Chamberlain, where the **Akta Lakota Museum** houses a fine collection of Lakota Sioux art and artifacts. Just north is the **Great Plains Resource Center**. Here two hiking trails cut between prairies and woods before skirting the Missouri River. Looping up to Fort Thompson will carry you inside

the **Crow Creek Reservation**, which offers scenic river panoramas, game hunting, and native foods and crafts.

▶ *Maps and self-guided-tour cassette tapes of the Native American Loop are available by contacting the Chamberlain Chamber of Commerce.*

3 MITCHELL

In 1892, to celebrate the Corn Belt Exposition, the city built a massive exhibition hall whose façade was adorned with fantastic murals made entirely of locally grown grains. Thus the **Corn Palace** was born. Each year, thousands of bushels of corn are needed to reface the world-famous Moorish-style structure. The designs change annually and are colorfully accented by other grains and grasses grown by local farmers. The palace serves as a sports arena, convention hall, and performance auditorium.

4 DE SMET

There really *is* a Little House on the Prairie. Laura Ingalls Wilder moved into this modest frame house as a child in 1879. Decades later, she would draw on her experiences in this small town to write her world-famous series of pioneer adventure books. No fewer than 18 sites in present-day De Smet are immortalized in Wilder's *Little House* book series. In the summer guided tours take visitors through the shanty to which Laura's father, Charles Ingalls, first brought his family in 1879. Included is the two-story clapboard dwelling he built in 1887. The immense cottonwood trees shading the homes were mere saplings when Charles Ingalls planted them more than a century ago.

5 SIOUX FALLS

The most populous city in the Dakotas has also consistently been named one of the country's most livable places. To better understand what the "Sioux" in Sioux Falls means, visit the **Old Courthouse Museum**. This massive stone building was the county courthouse from 1890 to 1962. Today it holds exhibits that interpret the history of the Plains Indians and the region's first pioneer settlers.

The triple waterfalls that gave the city

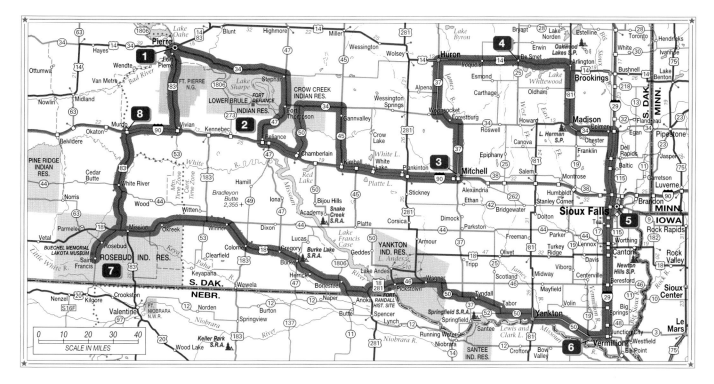

its name shower cascades of white water into the **Big Sioux River. Falls Park,** a mile from downtown, has walkways that afford fine vistas of the falls. Downhill skiers need drive only two miles from the city to **Great Bear Ski Valley** for prime powder.

6 VERMILLION

The South Dakota plains may seem an odd place to encounter a rare guitar made by Stradivari, antique music boxes, and a delicate ivory lute from Elizabethan times. Yet these are but a few of the musical artifacts at the **Shrine to Music Museum,** on the University of South Dakota campus.

Lewis and Clark spent time on this prairie. Curious about a cone-shaped mound the Sioux claimed was bewitched, the explorers ventured to the hill, the highest point in the county. From the top they saw "a most beautiful landscape" with "a sea of bufalow." To see **Spirit Mound** for yourself, take Rte. 19 eight miles north of town.

▶ *The road to Rosebud is the scenic Oyate Trail. The installation of signs marking Indian cultural sites along the way will be completed in 1996. Until then, contact the Vermillion Chamber of Commerce for information on the sites along the route.*

7 ROSEBUD RESERVATION

Sicangu Sioux Chief Spotted Tail selected this land for his people in 1877. He would be killed by a member of his own tribe in 1881. Today on the **Rosebud Reservation,** you can see Spotted Tail's gravesite, as well as a thundering herd of buffalo.

In **St. Francis,** southward on the reservation, stands the **St. Francis Mission.** Established among the Sioux in 1886, the Catholic mission was home to Father Eugene Buechel, who dedicated himself to chronicling the Sioux way of life. The **Buechel Memorial Lakota Museum,** at the mission, houses Father Buechel's collection of Sioux artifacts and the Lakota books he wrote.

8 MURDO

In 1954, A. J. Geisler decided he needed an attraction stronger than gasoline pumps to pull motorists into his service station. He rolled a 1913 Ford Peddler's Wagon into view. Now America's largest private collection of autos, the **Pioneer Auto Museum and Antique Town** displays 250 classic vehicles in 39 buildings. Among them is Elvis's personal motorcycle.

Corn-fed beauty:
A palace adorned with last year's crops remains one of America's most unusual sites. The Corn Palace, in Mitchell, is refurbished each year with fresh grains. The 1892 exposition hall is now used as an all-purpose entertainment center.

Nebraska

In Nebraska, cornfields ripple under clear skies, flocks of white cranes descend on the pristine Platte River, and visitors become acquainted with the most famous landmarks on the Oregon Trail.

OMAHA & THE EAST

1 OMAHA

The railroad helped build this town, and Omaha's residents haven't forgotten. Helping them remember is the **Western Heritage Museum,** an Art Deco structure once used as the city's main passenger terminal, Union Station. Sheathed in glazed terra-cotta, the old terminal has a restored waiting room that retains its original features: wood benches with heaters in the middle, stained-glass windows, murals, and chandeliers. Exhibits at the museum include a fully outfitted Conestoga wagon, a restored streetcar, and a collection of coins that date from 2,000 B.C. to the 1890's. Also on display are a replica of the 1911 *Vin Fiz* biplane that made America's first transcontinental flight.

Visit the pink marble **Joslyn Art Museum,** which houses a Western collection including works by Karl Bodmer,

George Catlin, and Frederic Remington. Or take in the **Henry Doorly Zoo,** a wonderland inhabited by polar bears and penguins and, in the world's largest indoor rain forest, animals from Asia, Africa, and South America. The 72,000-square-foot aquarium has a clear plastic underwater tunnel you can walk through to view sharks and 100 other species swimming against the background of a man-made coral reef.

▶ *The city is designed on a grid; streets running north and south are numbered, and streets running east and west have names. Dodge Street separates the city's north and south sides.*

2 NEBRASKA CITY

A wonderful idea took root in this old river town; it came to be called Arbor Day. Nebraska City resident J. Sterling Morton's resolution calling for a national tree-planting day was made a state law in 1872. Since then every state in

America and sundry foreign countries have come to recognize Arbor Day.

At **Arbor Lodge State Historical Park,** the Morton family's 52-room Neocolonial mansion is open for public inspection. The grounds around it include a rose garden, a prairie garden, and a half-mile tree-lined trail to a stand of American chestnut trees.

The mansion contains original furnishings and memorabilia. Its carriage house is filled with coaches, carriages, and other historical vehicles.

Just across the road, the **Arbor Day Farm** combines an 80-acre working apple orchard with public tours of apple-sorting and cider-making operations. Inside the farm's apple house, visitors have the rare opportunity of safely watching a working honeybee hive and sampling heirloom varieties of apples.

3 BROWNVILLE

This old steamboat town still pays homage to paddle wheelers past and present. Representing the past is the ***Captain Meriwether Lewis,*** a 1931 steam-powered side-wheeler the U.S. Army Corps of Engineers used until 1969 to dredge the Missouri River channel. Permanently docked at the

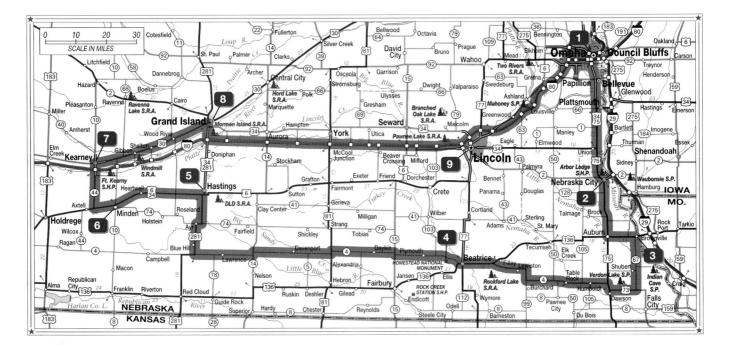

Fort Kearny was the first fort built to protect the hardy westward-bound pioneers who traveled the Oregon Trail. Its reconstructed blacksmith shop, shown here, was built with adobe bricks and a roof of brush.

Brownville landing, the boat now houses the **Steamboat Museum,** a collection of exhibits depicting the development of the river valley from prehistoric times to the present. Brownville's paddle wheeler of the present is the *Spirit of Brownville,* a 61-foot-long diesel-powered riverboat offering sightseeing and dinner cruises up the Missouri from late June through mid-August.

4 HOMESTEAD NATIONAL MONUMENT

If the prize were a large piece of land, free of charge, would you live in a sod house or a humble log cabin to get it? Thousands of settlers in the 1860's said yes as they filed claims for free government land under the newly passed Homestead Act of 1862.

One of the nation's first homesteaders, Daniel Freeman, lived here, on the banks of Cub Creek near present-day Beatrice. His original farm has been preserved as the **Homestead National Monument,** commemorating the homestead movement.

While no original Freeman buildings remain, a cabin built by homesteaders in 1867 has been relocated here from a nearby site. The tools and furnishings displayed were used by early pioneers.

5 HASTINGS

Dioramas of mounted crane specimens in natural settings at the **Hastings Museum** bring the migration spectacle to life. But another display attracts just as much attention: the origin of Kool-Aid. It pays homage to Edwin Perkins, the local man who invented the famous powdered drink in 1926.

Still another unusual feature in this small town is the **Lied IMAX Theatre,** which shows documentary films on science, nature, history, and space exploration every day on its huge screen, on the hour until 9:00 P.M.

6 MINDEN

It takes 26 buildings, many of which are historic structures transported to the site from throughout Nebraska, to contain the 50,000 historical objects displayed at **Harold Warp Pioneer Village.** They include three 19th-century locomotives, 350 antique automobiles, 20 historic flying machines, and 100 antique tractors. The oldest known steam-powered carousel, circa 1879, still charges but a nickel a ride. Buildings, including the 1860 Pony Express station and century-old Lowell Railroad Depot, evoke images of pioneer days.

Impressive collections on view include antique toys, china and glassware, model trains, and even antique washing machines. Among the washing machines is one from the 1890's whose power was generated by two German shepherds that took turns on a treadmill. Today the dog on the treadmill is made of wood, but visitors can punch a button to agitate the machine's wooden tank.

▶ *Free overnight passes are available at the Lowell Railroad Depot for visitors who aren't able to take in Pioneer Village's numerous sights in one day.*

7 KEARNEY

A fort near this town helped America push its way west. It was Fort Kearny, built in 1848 to protect pioneers probing lands that were not always friendly. Government records indicate that, between 1849 and 1850, some 30,000 people passed by the fort. They came with the gold rush or to work on the railroad or later to settle on prairie homesteads. Fort Kearny was the first in a series of military installations along the Oregon Trail built to make sure that pioneers could travel in safety.

Fort Kearny State Historical Park marks the spot where the fort was constructed. Shaded by two towering cottonwoods that were planted as seedlings, the fort's original parade grounds afford a look at a stockade and powder magazine from the old fort, as well as a sod-roofed replica of its blacksmith and carpenter shop.

8 GRAND ISLAND

Bird-watchers throughout the world know this town. It's the place where early spring finds 80 percent of the world's sandhill cranes—some 500,000 of the majestic, long-necked waders—convening on the nearby Platte River. Roosting on the river at night and feasting on waste corn in nearby fields during the day, the cranes create one of the world's most thrilling wildlife specta-

A mosaic medallion, "Ideals of the Future," *is one of many in the state capitol.*

cles. From late February through mid-April, birders head for Grand Island to observe them before they continue their northern migrations.

▶ *The Wings Over the Platte Festival, held the third weekend in March, offers visitors guided boat tours down the river to the crane fields.*

Located on an island in a man-made lake, Grand Island's **Stuhr Museum of the Prairie Pioneer** features a main building devoted to art and pioneer exhibits, and adjoins an 85-acre complex upon which a railroad town of the 1860's has been re-created. More than 60 buildings were moved to the museum and filled with period pieces.

9 LINCOLN

You won't have a problem locating the Nebraska **State Capitol** complex in Lincoln. Its spire is visible for 20 miles, towering more than 400 feet above the surrounding flatlands like a rocket ship ready for launch. Below it, one of America's most beautiful capitols has intricate marble mosaics on the inside domed ceiling and bas-relief sculptures of pioneer scenes on the outside.

Lincoln's **Museum of Nebraska History** also chronicles the history of Plains inhabitants, from prehistoric times through the mid-20th century. The emphasis is on natural science at the **University of Nebraska State Museum** in Morrill Hall, where you can see one of the world's five largest collections of fossil mammals, including the largest mounted mammoth skeleton; the Hall of Nebraska Wildlife, with 16 nature dioramas; and a brand-new dinosaur gallery with interactive exhibits.

Visitors strolling through Lincoln's **Historic Haymarket District,** a restored warehouse neighborhood, will find antiques by the hundreds. Dozens of boutiques, specialty shops, galleries, and restaurants keep streets in the Haymarket bustling year-round.

▶ *Be aware that a farmers' market draws crowds to the Haymarket on Saturday mornings from mid-May to mid-October. Choose to join the fun or visit on a quieter weekday.*

PLATTE RIVER & THE WEST

1 NORTH PLATTE

Where did the world's most renowned Wild West showman retreat when not on the road? Between seasons of his Wild West exhibition during the 1880's and 90's, William (Buffalo Bill) Cody came here to his Scout's Rest Ranch on the outskirts of North Platte. Part of Cody's 4,000-acre spread, including his home, a horse barn, and outbuildings, has been preserved as the **Buffalo Bill Ranch State Historical Park.**

Displays in the ranch house, set among period and original furnishings, chronicle Buffalo Bill's amazing life, from his days hunting buffalo to his stint as a world-famous performer.

▶ *Buffalo stew and cornbread are served at the Buffalo Bill Ranch on Wednesdays, Thursdays, and Fridays in July and early August at 6:00 P.M.*

North Platte's past revolved not only around Buffalo Bill but around the railroad. Founded in 1866 beside the tracks of America's first transcontinental Union Pacific route, the town pays tribute to its railroad heritage at two locations: **Cody Park** boasts the world's largest steam locomotive, *Challenger*

3977, standing outside an authentic old depot loaded with memorabilia. Nearby, the **Lincoln County Historical Society Museum** includes a re-created railroad town, with a depot, general store, church, and blacksmith shop.

2 OGALLALA

Listen hard enough here and you'll still hear the hooves of longhorns. Ogallala developed as an 1870's cattle town, where herds driven north from Texas were loaded onto trains bound for markets the railroad had created. Today, just north of town, **Lake McConaughy,** Nebraska's largest lake, provides picnicking, boating, and good fishing. Local events include the **Ogallala Round-up Rodeo** in August and the mid-September **Indian Summer Rendezvous**—a festival in downtown Ogallala featuring a rough-stock rodeo, a quilt show, and dancing. Summer visitors also can visit Ogallala's **Mansion on the Hill,** an imposing brick structure, built in the 1800's with 16-inch-thick walls. Furnished with antiques, the mansion features windows so tall they require three sets of shutters each.

3 CHIMNEY ROCK

Most Oregon Trail diaries mentioned it: a needle of rock towering 450 feet over the North Platte River. That spire is **Chimney Rock National Historic Site,** a world-famous landmark known for

Chimney Rock *told pioneers that they had 1,400 miles to go before reaching the Pacific.*

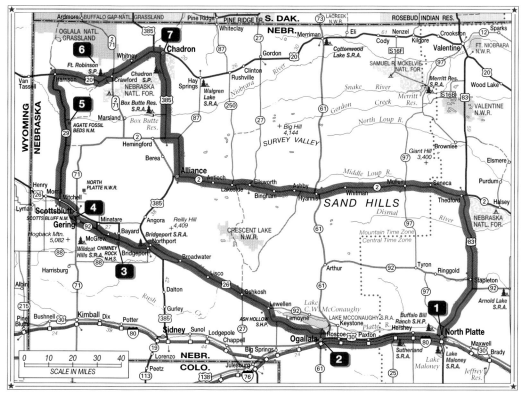

home base for America's Olympic equestrian team, and housed the World War II K-9 Corps.

Visitors can look into its past at 22,000-acre **Fort Robinson State Park,** where one museum interprets the park's geology and wildlife, and another recounts notable historical events. Accommodations include the **Fort Robinson Inn and Lodge,** a 1909 structure that originally housed enlisted men. Visitors also can tour the fort's original blacksmith, harness repair, and wheelwright shops, as well as reconstructed buildings.

Horseback riding, stagecoach rides, and guided nature walks show off the park's landscape of eroded buttes, prairie wildflowers, and stands of ponderosa pine. Nature lovers can rent one of the 31 former officers' quarters, now used as cabins, by calling the Fort Robinson Inn.

▶ *Cabins in the park, each with two to nine bedrooms, are in great demand. Reservations are available a year to the day in advance—so don't delay.*

7 CHADRON

Nebraska is flat for the most part, but there are topographic exceptions. The most striking may be the hill country around Chadron, where bluffs, broken ridges, and pine-covered buttes replace farm fields that normally roll on forever. Walking or driving to the scenic outlook at **Chadron State Park** entails climbing toward elevations of 5,000 feet. The summit view shows off a landscape that was once the domain of fur trappers and traders.

Trapping lore takes center stage at the **Museum of the Fur Trade,** just east of Chadron on Rte. 20. Here visitors can tour the reconstructed and fully stocked 1833 Bordeaux Trading Post, where Sioux Indians traded with fur companies, exchanging tanned buffalo robes for guns, kettles, blankets, and knives.

breaking the monotony of a 2,000-mile trek from Missouri to the Northwest. It also was a milepost for westbound travelers, indicating that nearly one-third of their trip lay behind them.

You can relive those days on the **Oregon Trail Wagon Train,** which leaves from Bayard, two miles south of the Platte River on Rte. 26. A three-hour trip in a covered wagon takes you to Chimney Rock; on 3- to 6-day tours you'll encounter old-time fur traders, Indians, and the Pony Express.

4 SCOTTS BLUFF

From the parking lot at **Scotts Bluff National Monument,** a paved footpath follows the original roadbed gouged by the wheels of westbound wagons long ago. Between 1841 and 1869, 350,000 travelers gazed in awe at the bluff's wind-sculpted face. The highest bluff, nearly 800 feet high, rises above the flatlands like the prow of a massive stone ship.

From the visitor center, both a 1½-mile paved road and a hiking trail of the same length climb to the windy summit of an escarpment. This lofty perch provides a panoramic view of the North Platte River valley and, to the east, Chimney Rock. Exhibits at the vis-itor center highlight Scotts Bluff's role as a landmark on the Oregon Trail

5 AGATE FOSSIL BEDS NATIONAL MONUMENT

Here, embedded in exposed layers of sedimentary rock underlying rolling grasslands 45 miles from Harrison, an extraordinary concentration of fossilized mammals provides a look at prehistoric two-horned rhinoceroses, beavers, and gigantic tusked pigs that stood seven feet tall at the shoulder.

From the monument's visitor center, a trail follows the Niobrara River toward fossil beds in the hills, where interpretive displays show what the animals looked like. At the monument's visitor center, browsers can view full-scale replicas of the animals whose bodies fossilized at the watering hole, as well as Lakota artifacts.

6 FORT ROBINSON

Few military installations in the nation boast so many varied chapters in their history as Fort Robinson, near the town of Crawford. Between its establishment in 1874 to protect settlers from Indian attacks and its closure in 1948, Fort Robinson witnessed the last tragic days of the Plains Indian Wars, served as

Topeka

Wichita

Kansas

There's no place like Kansas, nestled deep in America's heartland. Grain elevators punctuate the sunflower-sprinkled landscape, where buffalo roam and the last of the tall prairie grass sways.

TOPEKA & THE FLINT HILLS

1 TOPEKA

Topeka's name comes from the Omaha Indian expression for "a good place to dig potatoes" (meaning root vegetables they found here). The city came into being when Cyrus K. Holliday arrived with the intention of building a railroad. Topeka became not only the terminus for the Atchison, Topeka and Santa Fe but the state capital as well.

You'll find a steam locomotive bearing Holliday's name in the **Kansas Museum of History.** There are exhibits on the Bleeding Kansas period and the Civil War, and Plains Indian dwellings, including a buffalo-hide tepee and a grass lodge. A big hit is a display on popular culture from 1940 to 1980, featuring items from Beatles records to blenders.

Inside the French Renaissance–style **State Capitol,** a mural by John Steuart Curry depicts the Kansas clash between pro- and anti-slavery forces in the 1850's. It shows a wild-eyed John Brown brandishing a Bible in one hand and a rifle in the other. (A century later Kansas made history again when the landmark case *Brown* v. *Board of Education of Topeka* paved the way for desegregation.) Across the street the only full set of Tiffany stained-glass sanctuary windows west of the Mississippi graces the **First Presbyterian Church.**

Historic Ward-Meade Park centers on the 1870's Victorian mansion of one of Topeka's first families. In the park a turn-of-the-century village bustles, complete with a restored one-room schoolhouse, a livery stable, a general store, and a cabin where you can sit down to a hearth-cooked prairie meal.

A hay rake gathers loose hay into rows on the tallgrass prairie near Council Grove.

At the **Topeka Zoo,** in Gage Park, visitors come face to face with families of lowland gorillas by way of a glass tunnel that leads through their habitat.

The **Combat Air Museum** offers a lineup of vintage equipment from every 20th-century U.S. military conflict, including an EC-121 Super Constellation and a restored M.A.S.H. ambulance.

On the outskirts of town near Big Springs, visit **Serenata Farms,** where wagon ruts along the Oregon Trail are still visible. Wagon rides take visitors back to the 1850's, when wagon trains rolled across the prairie, covering 18 miles a day at most.

2 LAWRENCE

First settled in 1854, Lawrence was a center of the Free State Party in the midst of a proslavery stronghold. Between 1855 and 1859 it teetered on the verge of war as the two factions vied for power. The antislavery forces won out. Then, in 1863, the town was sacked and burned by William Clarke Quantrill and his Confederate raiders.

Today Lawrence boasts a tree-lined restored downtown, with art galleries, museums, and artists' studios. On the University of Kansas campus, don't

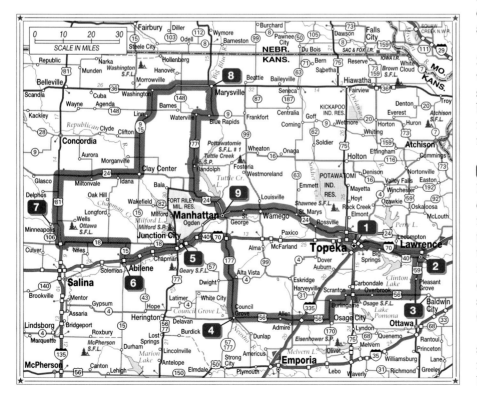

miss the **Dyche Museum of Natural History,** one of the largest in the country, and the highly regarded **Spencer Museum of Art.**

A handsome 1888 bank building houses the **Watkins Community Museum of History.** It displays relics of local history, an exhibit on Quantrill's raid, and an exhibit on James Naismith, the inventor of basketball, who was born here. Jabez Watkins, who built the building, owned 2.5 million acres of virgin pine forest in Louisiana, which helps explain why the third floor is decked with rare burley pine, ingrained with swirls, from floor to ceiling.

3 BALDWIN CITY

Legend has it that a shipment of maple trees was sent to Baldwin City by mistake and was planted here anyway. Today the colorful fall foliage is celebrated on the third weekend in October during the **Maple Leaf Festival.**

On the campus of Baker University, the **Old Castle Museum** is housed in a building that served as a landmark for travelers on the Santa Fe Trail. It contains American Indian artifacts, Santa Fe Trail relics, an old-time grocery store, and a collection of wedding dresses. Also of note is the **Quayle Rare Bible Collection** in Collins Library.

Don't miss the Train to Nowhere. The **Midland Railway** leaves from the historic Santa Fe Depot for a one-hour, 6½-mile ride through rolling farmland.

4 COUNCIL GROVE

Council Grove is cattle country, where ranchers still graze their herds on the vast grasslands. It is tucked in the heart of the **Flint Hills,** a region of stunning beauty, where rolling bluestem grass prairies, largely treeless, are interrupted by the dramatic limestone and flint outcroppings that prevented the land from being plowed. Today it is part of the largest remaining swath of tallgrass prairie in the Midwest. The drive from Council Grove to Junction City offers spectacular views.

A national historic landmark, Council Grove was the last outfitting stop on the Santa Fe Trail. By 1860 some 3,000 wagons, 7,000 people, and 60,000 mules had passed through town. Cara-

vans stopped at the **Last Chance Store** before continuing the long journey west. At the **Post Office Oak,** letters were left to be picked up by passing wagon trains. Only the trunk remains of another historic tree: **Custer's Elm Shrine,** the site of one of Custer's campsites. **The Old Calaboose** was one of the first jails on the Santa Fe Trail.

▶ *To see more of the Flint Hills in their full glory, drive south on Rte. 177 for all or part of the next 25 miles.*

The **Kaw Mission State Historic Site** was established by the Methodist Episcopal South Church as a school for American Indians. But the Kaws, doubtful about the curriculum of reading, writing, and farming, sent only orphans there. Later the school taught white settlers as well. Now a museum, it contains mission-period artifacts.

5 JUNCTION CITY

Upon entering Junction City, at the junction of the Republican and Smoky Hill rivers, you can easily see why one of the most important cavalry forts was

located here. **Fort Riley** was built to protect travelers on the Santa Fe Trail and was later the headquarters of the U.S. Cavalry. A marked tour includes the **U.S. Cavalry Museum;** the **Custer House,** similar to quarters General Custer lived in here; and the **First Territorial Capitol,** where a group of legislators chosen in a bogus election met for one day with the intention of making Kansas a slave state.

6 ABILENE

Abilene, at the end of the Chisholm Trail, was famed as one of the wildest cow towns in the West. Today the gunfights that erupt in the street at **Old Abilene Town** are staged, but the cattle-drive-era feel of the original and re-created buildings is real. The **Dickinson County Heritage Center Museum** offers exhibits on the Plains Indians and the cattle-drive period, and a 1901 carousel built by C. W. Parker.

Abilene was also the boyhood home of Dwight D. Eisenhower. The **Eisenhower Center** includes the house where he and his five brothers were raised, the Presidential Library, and the Museum.

7 MINNEAPOLIS

Stop by the chamber of commerce here to pick up **Red Post Tour** maps. The self-guided driving tours direct visitors past one-room schoolhouses, old churches, ghost towns, and even a buffalo herd. Red posts mark every turn.

To the southwest is one of the state's biggest surprises: some 200 sandstone spheres, formed underground and exposed by erosion, cluster at **Rock City.**

A bronze statue in Marysville honors the Pony Express, which ran day and night to move the mail from Missouri to California in 10 days. The daring mail runs ended two days after the transcontinental telegraph opened.

8 MARYSVILLE

This town was the first station on the Pony Express route. A bronze **Pony Express Rider** was dedicated here in 1985, on the 125th anniversary of the first cross-country mail rides. The **Pony Express Home Station Number One Museum** is the only home station still standing at its original location. Riders stayed here while awaiting mail from the other direction. On display is a sidesaddle that belonged to Robert E. Lee's daughter, and leather mittens worn by the Pony Express riders, with a trigger finger sewn in on each.

Hanover, 15 miles west, is the site of the **Hollenberg Pony Express Station.** Built in 1857, it is the only remaining unaltered relay station. The downstairs housed a grocery store, a tavern, and the family living quarters. Upstairs is a loft where Pony Express riders slept.

South of Marysville at **Alcove Spring,** limestone rocks bear messages left by travelers on the Oregon Trail. Gravestones mark the resting place of those whose journey ended here.

9 MANHATTAN

Far from the bustle of the Big Apple, the Little Apple was settled in 1857 by a group from the Cincinnati Company, who wanted to create a Manhattan in the Midwest. An enclave of Free Staters during the Bleeding Kansas period, it is

The wild and woolly days of the Old West come alive again on re-created Front Street in Dodge City. In summer mock shoot-outs, variety shows, and stagecoach rides kick up dust.

home to **Kansas State University,** one of the country's first land-grant colleges. Adjacent is the quaint stone **Isaac T. Goodnow House,** the home of a Free Stater who founded the college that became the university. The house features many original furnishings.

Head to Tuttle Creek Dam for views of **Tuttle Canyon,** carved by the 1993 flood. Here fossils and ancient rock layers as much as 290 million years old have been exposed. Five miles south is **Konza Prairie,** an 8,600-acre preserve of native tallgrass prairie. A nature trail skirts the northern edge.

THE SOUTH-CENTRAL PLAINS

1 WICHITA

This city at the fork of the Big Arkansas and Little Arkansas rivers began as a booming cow town on the Chisholm Trail. It went on to become the largest city in Kansas and a leading airplane manufacturing center. Its residents gather together for 10 days in May during the **Wichita River Festival.**

▶ *Trolley buses take visitors around downtown and to Old Town. Hail one anywhere on Douglas Street.*

A good place to enjoy the river is the **Wichita Boathouse and Arkansas River Museum,** which offers boat rides and rentals. A yacht that won the 1992 America's Cup is on display.

Don't miss **Old Town,** a recently redeveloped warehouse district with antique stores, restaurants, boutiques, and nightclubs. A weekend highlight here is the **Wichita Farm and Art Market.**

For a taste of the past, stroll through the **Old Cowtown Museum,** a collection of original and re-created buildings from 1865 to 1880. You'll find the city's first jail, a general store, a depot, a saloon, and the only fully restored wooden grain elevator in the country. The museum is one of 10 stops on the **Wichita Western Heritage Tour,** a self-guided auto tour. Maps are available at

---

the visitor center. Other stops include the Charles M. Russell Gallery at the **Wichita Art Museum;** the **Indian Center Museum,** brimming with American Indian art and artifacts; the **Wichita–Sedgwick County Historical Museum,** featuring an interesting Chisholm Trail exhibit; and **Botanica, the Wichita Gardens,** which offers native grasses, seasonal displays, and theme gardens.

The North American Prairie exhibit at the **Sedgwick County Zoo and Botanical Garden** offers a boat ride with views of frontier animals, such as grizzly bears, bison, eagles, and antelope.

2 BELLE PLAINE

Surrounded by farms, Belle Plaine is home to **Bartlett Arboretum.** In 1910 Dr. Walter Bartlett began pruning and nurturing this 20-acre haven for nature lovers. It includes beautiful formal gardens and an unusual variety of trees and shrubs. At Tulip Time in April, the whole town turns out to enjoy more than 30,000 blooms.

3 WINFIELD

Winfield is home to the **Walnut Valley Festival** in mid-September, which attracts thousands of bluegrass fans and includes the National Flatpicking Championships. There's also a replica of the Washington, D.C., **Vietnam War Memorial,** which bears the names of 777 Kansans who died in the war. But the highlight in this small town, even for grownups, is certainly a tour of the **Binney & Smith Crayola** factory.

▶ *The Crayola factory tours are immensely popular. Reservations are necessary and should be made as early as a year ahead.*

4 ARKANSAS CITY

Ark City, as it is called, on the banks of the Arkansas (pronounced Ar-KAN-sas) River, was one of five staging points for the Cherokee Strip Land Rush of 1893, when settlers drove their wagons at breakneck speeds to lay claim to land in what became part of Oklahoma. The **Cherokee Strip Land Rush Museum** offers thousands of artifacts, including claim certificates and a buckboard wagon loaded with household items.

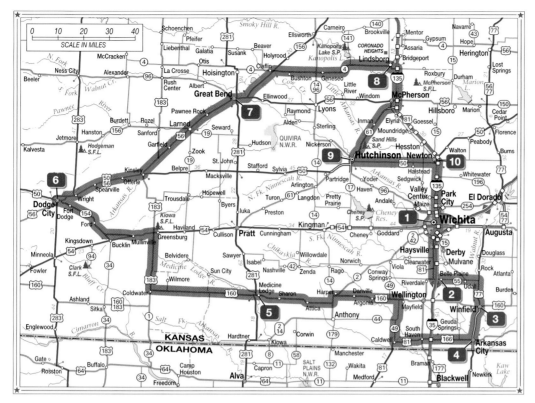

8 LINDSBORG

Lindsborg, founded by Swedish pioneers in 1869, has been host to the king of Sweden and countless others for the Easter performance of Handel's *Messiah* at Bethany College during the **Messiah Festival**. Swedish festivals take place throughout the year.

The **Birger Sandzen Memorial Gallery** honors the internationally known Swedish-American artist. Other working artists in the area open their studios to travelers.

The **Old Mill Museum and Pioneer Town** offers a host of Swedish pioneer artifacts in 12 historic buildings. A mill built in 1898 is still in working order. At the **REO Auto Museum**, antique autos are housed in a 1930 filling station.

9 HUTCHINSON

Grain elevators here stretch just a few feet short of half a mile long. The **Kansas State Fair** takes place the two weeks following Labor Day. But perhaps the biggest draw is the **Kansas Cosmosphere and Space Center**, where spacecraft from rockets to satellites are displayed. Some of the large-format films shown in the domed Cosmosphere rumble with special sound effects, giving you the feeling of traveling through space.

10 NEWTON

This is the center of one of the largest Mennonite settlements in the country. Bernhard Warkentin encouraged Mennonite migration to Kansas and promoted Turkey Red winter wheat, which made Kansas a major wheat producer. His Victorian home, **Warkentin House**, contains original furnishings. At Bethel College, the oldest Mennonite college in the nation, the **Kauffman Museum** has exhibits on the Mennonite migration and the people of the Plains.

5 MEDICINE LODGE

At Medicine Lodge the Red Hills and High Plains come together with buttes of red sandstone and mesas of shale. This was the site of a small medicine lodge used by the Plains tribes. In 1867, 15,000 representatives from five Plains tribes and 600 U.S. government officials negotiated a peace treaty here during the largest meeting of whites and American Indians in history.

▶ *Near Medicine Lodge are the beautiful Gypsum Hills. Follow the well-marked scenic drive on Rte. 160 for views of canyons carved by erosion and mesas capped by white gypsum.*

Medicine Lodge was also the home of the hatchet-swinging prohibitionist Carry Nation, who staged her first demonstration here. The **Carry A. Nation Home Memorial** contains a museum and many original furnishings.

The **Medicine Lodge Stockade** is a replica of an 1874 structure built to protect settlers from the Indians. Now a museum, it houses pioneer relics.

6 DODGE CITY

Anyone who watched *Gunsmoke* on television is familiar with Dodge City, once dubbed the Cowboy Capital of the World and the Wickedest Little City in America. A costumed Miss Kitty presides at the Long Branch Saloon on **Historic Front Street**, a re-creation of the main street as it looked in the 1870's. The **Boot Hill Museum** encompasses both Front Street and Boot Hill Cemetery, named for an unlucky gunman shot here and buried with his boots on.

The 1881 **Home of Stone**, a Victorian home with 2½-foot-thick limestone walls, features period furnishings and a room dedicated to pioneer mothers. Nine miles west is one of the best-preserved sections of the Santa Fe Trail.

7 GREAT BEND

Stroll on dusty roads back to the turn of the century at the **Barton County Historical Museum and Village**, complete with a pioneer rock home, a church, a depot, a barbershop, and a general store. Pioneer relics include a collection of period wedding gowns.

Cheyenne Bottoms Wildlife Area, a natural marsh, lies five miles northeast on Rte. 156. Situated on the migratory bird flyway, it is a bird-watcher's paradise. Some 30 miles southeast of Great Bend, more waterfowl take rest in the wetlands at **Quivira National Wildlife**

Oklahoma

Towns formed in frenzied land rushes dot the windswept plains of the Sooner State, where boundless fields of waving wheat surround cities rich in oil and American Indian history.

TULSA & THE NORTH

1 TULSA

Born beneath the branches of the sturdy **Creek Council Oak** at a bend in the Arkansas River, Tulsa was founded by the Lochapoka band of Creek Indians at the end of the devastating forced migration of the tribe. After oil was discovered here in 1901, Tulsa grew up fast, and began billing itself as the Oil Capital of the World.

The city has oil to thank for the **Philbrook Museum of Art,** housed in part in Villa Philbrook, the former home of oil baron Waite Phillips and his wife, Genevieve. The Italian Renaissance Revival mansion, complete with a lighted-glass dance floor and surrounded by 23 acres of gorgeous gardens, contains permanent collections that include Italian paintings and sculpture of the 14th to 17th century, American Indian works, African sculpture, and European and contemporary American art.

Another oilman, Thomas Gilcrease, of Creek Indian descent, helped finance the **Gilcrease Museum of Art.** It is one of the country's finest collections of the art and history of the American West, featuring pre-Columbian and American Indian works and the world's most comprehensive collection of paintings by Frederic Remington, Charles M. Russell, and George Catlin.

No tour of Tulsa is complete without a visit to the futuristic campus of **Oral Roberts University.** A visitor center in the Prayer Tower offers multimedia presentations and an observation deck with views of the Tulsa skyline.

2 CLAREMORE

A statue of actor, philosopher, and cowboy Will Rogers atop his favorite horse, Soapsuds, welcomes visitors to the **Will Rogers Memorial.** The museum houses many of Rogers's belongings from his family's ranch in Indian Territory—as Oklahoma was called before it was a state—and his days in Hollywood.

The **J. M. Davis Gun Museum** displays one of the world's largest gun collections; its more than 20,000 firearms span five centuries.

3 TAHLEQUAH

Set in the foothills of the Ozark Mountains beside the winding Illinois River, Tahlequah marked the end of the Trail of Tears, the forced march of some 16,000 Cherokees from the southeastern United States in 1838–39. The **Cherokee Heritage Center,** three miles south of the city, tells their tale. It includes the Adams Corner Rural Village, a reconstruction of an 1890-era crossroads community; the Tsa-La-Gi Ancient Village, which re-creates a 16th-century Cherokee settlement in authentic detail; and the *Trail of Tears,* an outdoor drama that comes alive with pageantry and dance.

4 MUSKOGEE

Fort Gibson Military Park, east of Muskogee, salutes Army life on the Indian Territory frontier. Built in 1824 as the first military post in what would become the state of Oklahoma, it contains 12 reconstructed log structures along with several original buildings and period rooms.

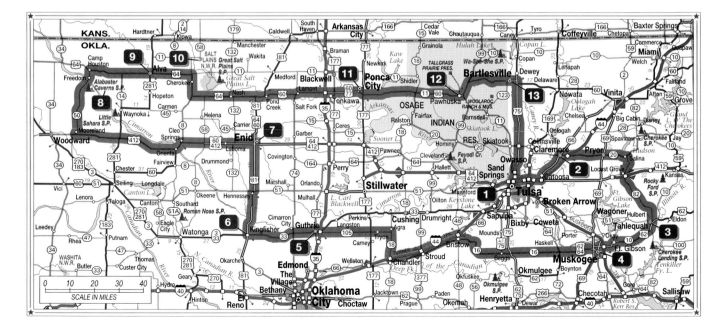

Overlooking **Honor Heights Park,** site of the annual Azalea Festival in April, is the **Five Civilized Tribes Museum.** Artifacts, books, jewelry, art, and photographs detail the history of the Cherokees, Chickasaws, Choctaws, Creeks, and Seminoles.

Near the port of Muskogee on the Arkansas River, visitors can board the city's most unusual attraction: the **U.S.S. Batfish.** The World War II submarine sank three enemy subs in less than four days.

5 GUTHRIE

Guthrie sprang up in a matter of hours during the 1889 Oklahoma land rush and was Oklahoma's first capital. When a bitter political dispute caused the capital to be moved to Oklahoma City, Guthrie became a sleepy little town. In fact, it slept through urban renewal. Most of its 19th-century buildings remain, and the 400-block downtown district is the largest urban area on the National Register of Historic Places. Museums include the **Oklahoma Territorial Museum** and the **Oklahoma Frontier Drugstore Museum.**

If you visit the week after Labor Day, catch the **Genuine and Original International Tom Mix Festival,** honoring that movie cowboy, who lived in Guthrie at the turn of the century.

6 KINGFISHER

Kingfisher was the home of Oklahoma's second territorial governor, Abraham Jefferson Seay. Seay hoped in vain that the town would become the territorial capital and that his lavish three-story brick home, **Seay Mansion,** would become the governor's mansion.

Across the street the **Chisholm Trail Museum** salutes the famed cattle trail across the no-man's-land of the Oklahoma Territory. A beaded game bag that belonged to Chief Sitting Bull and a deerskin tablecover from the family of Geronimo are on view. Outside is the log cabin where Adeline Dalton, mother of the infamous Dalton gang, lived.

7 ENID

Located on the Chisholm Trail, Enid sits amid the gently rolling wheat fields of northwestern Oklahoma. The city was founded on September 16, 1893—the same day that a pistol shot signaled the start of the Cherokee Strip land rush. The **Museum of the Cherokee Strip** traces the history of the 58-mile-wide strip from 1820, when it was set aside for the Cherokees as a route to the great hunting grounds of the West.

The **Railroad Museum of Oklahoma** displays a wide assortment of memora-

bilia. There are signal lanterns, step boxes, dining-car china, depot clocks, a mail car, and railroad paper money, used as currency before the days of government-printed greenbacks.

8 ALABASTER CAVERNS

Alabaster Caverns State Park boasts the world's largest gypsum cave open to the public. Along the three-quarter-mile trail through the cavern, visitors spot gleaming selenite crystals, pink alabaster, and most likely a few of the five species of bats that inhabit the cave.

An early explorer dubbed an area of shifting sand dunes north of the Cimarron River the Walking Hills. Winds whipping across the red-soil plains moved the dunes—some as tall as seven stories—up to 20 feet a year. Some 1,500 acres of dunes now make up **Little Sahara State Park,** 46 miles southeast of Alabaster Caverns. Visitors can call ahead for dune buggy tours.

9 ALVA

Ranches and farmlands surround Alva, home to the **Cherokee Strip Museum.**

Pioneer-era artifacts include an organ and a wooden telephone brought in during the land rush. A medical room contains a tonsil chair, in which patients had their tonsils removed. In the Indian Room are wooden hand-carved Indian heads from 12 different tribes.

The **Northwestern Oklahoma State University Natural History Museum** features fossils, American Indian relics,

***Philbrook Museum of Art** in Tulsa brims with American Indian works. Baskets like the one below, woven of willow, redbud, and fern, can take a year to make.*

and one of the finest mounted bird collections in the country.

10 SALT PLAINS NATIONAL WILDLIFE REFUGE

In the 19th century, Osage Indians collected salt from the Great Salt Plains to preserve their meat and other foods. The thin layer of salt that covers the land here was left by an ancient ocean. Today tourists dig for selenite crystals, which form just below the surface in the gypsum-rich soil. Whooping cranes, interior least terns, and bald and golden eagles are among the 250 species of native birds.

▶ *Digging for selenite crystals is a highlight of any visit to the refuge, but you must bring your own equipment. You'll need a hand trowel or spade, some cloths, and a bag or egg carton for carrying away your treasures.*

11 PONCA CITY

The Italian Renaissance mansion built by oil baron and philanthropist E. W. Marland is the pride of Ponca City.

Modeled after the Davanzatti Palace in Florence, Italy, **Marland Mansion and Estate,** built between 1925 and 1928 at a cost of $5.5 million, features gold-leaf vaulted ceilings, hand-carved wood paneling, and period furniture. At the foot of the hill leading to the mansion is a 17-foot-tall bronze **Pioneer Woman Statue,** by Bryant Baker, and the **Pioneer Woman Museum,** which salutes family life on the frontier.

Marland's first showplace home, built in 1916, now houses the **Ponca City Cultural Center and Indian Museum.** It contains memorabilia from the famous Miller Brothers Ranch and Wild West Show, American Indian art and artifacts, and Bryant Baker's studio.

12 PAWHUSKA

When oil was discovered in Pawhuska, the Osage became the wealthiest Indian tribe in America. The **Osage Tribal Museum,** the oldest tribal museum in the country, exhibits beautiful clothing, arts, and crafts.

Oil financed downtown Pawhuska's fine architecture, which includes a host of buildings in the National Register of Historic Places. The Santa Fe Depot houses the **Osage County Historical Museum,** which contains Old West artifacts and a display on the first Boy Scout troop in America.

About 18 miles north, the Nature Conservancy's **Tallgrass Prairie Preserve** is home to more than 500 varieties of plants, 300 species of birds, and 80 different mammals. A self-guided walking tour explores the forces behind the area's ecological diversity. Efforts continue to re-create a functioning tallgrass prairie ecosystem. A herd of 300 buffalo was reintroduced in 1993, and more will follow.

13 BARTLESVILLE

When the owner of a pipeline company here wanted to build a new office building, he asked around for a good architect—and hired Frank Lloyd Wright. The result is the spectacular 19-story **Price Tower,** the only skyscraper of Wright's ever completed.

Oilman Frank Phillips built the lavish **Frank Phillips Home,** which features beautiful mahogany woodwork, gold-

plated bath fixtures, and exquisite decorative arts. Simpler is the rustic retreat where he played host to future presidents and other notables, at the **Woolaroc Ranch and Museum.** The cabin is surrounded by a 3,500-acre wildlife preserve, where herds of buffalo and longhorn cattle roam. A museum displays Plains Indian artifacts, Colt firearms, and Western art, including paintings by Frederic Remington.

▶ *If a buffalo burger sounds tasty, Woolaroc is the place to try one.*

1 OKLAHOMA CITY

On April 22, 1889, thousands of land-hungry pioneers turned a stretch of open prairie into a full-fledged city. The discovery of oil in 1928 fueled greater growth. Today there is even a producing oil well on the grounds of the **Capitol.** Inside the building hang murals by Gilbert White, commissioned by oil baron Frank Phillips. Also on the grounds is the **State Museum of History,** which contains a fine collection of American Indian artifacts.

Chock-full of everything from saddles to a Montana sheepherder's wagon to John Wayne's movie memorabilia and personal art collection, the **National Cowboy Hall of Fame** reflects the culture of 17 Western states. The muse-

um's galleries hold paintings by Frederic Remington and Charles M. Russell as well as contemporary works.

At the **Kirkpatrick Center Museum Complex,** you can see the Grand Canyon in the world's largest photographic mural, fly with the Red Baron in the Air Space Museum, discover faraway galaxies in the planetarium, and encounter a two-story dinosaur in the Omniplex Science Museum.

The seven-story, 224-foot-long Crystal Bridge Tropical Conservatory is the crown jewel of the **Myriad Botanical**

The Crystal Bridge Tropical Conservatory at Myriad Botanical Gardens is lush with exotic plants from around the world. A skywalk makes it easy to peer into the treetops, where hidden plants grow.

Gardens. An urban oasis of walkways, ponds, waterfalls, fountains, native plants, and sculpture, the gardens are nestled on 17 acres of rolling hills surrounding a spring-fed lake.

▶ *The city's business district virtually shuts down at the end of the workday. For dinner, go to nearby Bricktown, a restored warehouse district filled with restaurants and shops.*

2 NORMAN

Thousands of artifacts take visitors back into the ancient past at the **Oklahoma Museum of Natural History** on the University of Oklahoma campus. American Indian relics, dinosaur fossils, and Greek and Roman pieces are among the treasures on view.

The Cross Timbers, a heavy swath of oak forest that stretches across central Oklahoma, once served as a natural barrier between the Plains Indians to the west and the southeastern tribes. Lake Thunderbird in **Little River State Park,** east of Norman, offers an excellent view of the forest.

3 WEWOKA

Wewoka, named for the Seminole phrase for "barking water" after a nearby gurgling creek, was the end point of the forced march of the Seminoles from Florida. Today it is the capital of the Seminole Nation. The **Seminole Nation Museum** displays artifacts such as the patchwork clothing that the Seminoles are known for and shellshakers, which are leggings made of terrapin shells, worn by women during tribal dances. Works by prominent Seminole and Creek artists are also on view.

4 CHICKASAW NATIONAL RECREATION AREA

Jewel-toned waters flow like liquid emeralds in this lush playground near Sulphur. Waterfalls, creeks, and mineral and freshwater springs once lured bathers who believed in their restorative powers; today visitors still bring their water jugs to fill. Hiking trails wind through woods carpeted with wildflowers in summer. A nature center offers exhibits and nature walks, and two lakes afford swimming and fishing.

5 ARDMORE

Ardmore sits in the shadow of the Arbuckle Mountains, a hiker's paradise. The **Greater Southwest Historical Museum** traces the history of the area from its days as an Indian Territory to the 1930's. A re-created turn-of-the-century town includes a log cabin, general store, and blacksmith shop.

To the south lies the 6,500-acre lake that gives **Lake Murray State Park** its name. Oklahoma's largest state park, Murray was constructed as a WPA and Civilian Conservation Corps project during the Depression. Much of the park still retains its hand-hewn look.

6 LAWTON

Fort Sill was established as a cavalry post in 1869 in the middle of what was then Kiowa and Comanche land. Today the fort serves as an artillery school, and some of the frontier-era buildings are still in use. American Indian and military artifacts are displayed in the Fort Sill Museum. At Chief's Knoll, famed

A Wichita lodge at Indian City U.S.A. is made of cedar poles and swamp grass.

Indian leaders, including the Kiowa chiefs Satank and Kicking Bird, are buried. The Apache warrior Geronimo is buried in the post's Apache cemetery. Cannons, both vintage and modern, can be viewed along the Cannon Walk.

The 550-million-year-old Wichita Mountains are among the oldest in the country. Worn down over time to sculptured granite boulders, they are especially popular with hikers and mountain climbers. Most of the northeastern section, where the peaks are the tallest, is part of the **Wichita Mountains Wildlife Refuge.** Elk, bison, longhorn cattle, gray foxes, and bobcat are among the protected species living here. A three-mile road leads to the summit of Mount Scott, which boasts tales of ancient spirits, Spanish gold, and buried outlaw loot.

7 ANADARKO

Indian City U.S.A., two miles south of Anadarko, sits above a camp that still draws annual tribal gatherings. Visitors can tour authentic full-size reconstructions of seven Plains Indian villages. Members of various tribes perform dances in summer and on weekends.

Modern American Indian painting was born near this town with the work of a group known as the Kiowa Five. Theirs is among the art featured in the **Southern Plains Indian Museum and Craft Center.** Next door is the **National Hall of Fame for Famous American Indians,** where a sculpture garden showcases bronze busts of Olympic gold medalist Jim Thorpe, the Sioux chief Sitting Bull, and others.

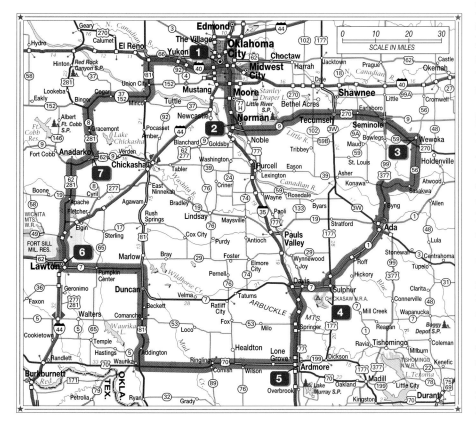

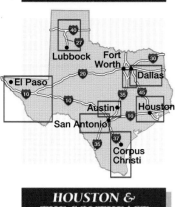

Texas

Beyond the legendary Texas of cowboys and oil-men is a land of rich diversity—from the wonderfully varied landscapes stretched out under endless skies to an extraordinary mix of cultures.

1 HOUSTON

America's fourth-largest city was founded by land speculators in 1836, the same year that Texas won its independence from Mexico. It has been a speculators' town ever since. An unplanned city with no zoning laws, Houston has an unpredictable urban landscape that is its charm to those who like the city and its curse to those who do not. Clusters of tall buildings rise arbitrarily from the prairie, forming mini-downtowns like the chic **Galleria** area on the West Loop, named for a popular multilevel indoor shopping mall. Another building that appears out of nowhere is the **Astrodome,** the world's first domed stadium (1965); tours are offered unless events are scheduled.

A building frenzy during the 1970's oil boom turned Houston into the very archetype of the shining Sun Belt city. Much of the "old" Houston survives in such neighborhoods as Freedmans Town, Houston Heights, and the old Sixth Ward. For a taste of affluent Houston, drive by the mansions on **River Oaks Boulevard,** a 1920's subdivision laid out for the first generation of Texas oil millionaires, or visit **Bayou Bend Collection and Gardens,** the estate of the late collector and patron who had one of the most remarkable names in the world: Miss Ima Hogg, the daughter of a former Texas governor.

Houstonians have gone in for art and architecture in a wholehearted way. Downtown you will find outdoor sculpture by Miró and Dubuffet. The tallest building, at 75 stories, is I. M. Pei's pentagonal **Texas Commerce Tower** (there's a public viewing area on the 60th floor), while the most innovative may be Philip Johnson's twin-towered black skyscraper, **Pennzoil Place.** Of the city's many art treasures, the two not to miss are the **Rothko Chapel,** with 14 large somber paintings by Abstract Expressionist Mark Rothko, and **The Menil Collection** museum, displaying the works assembled by art pa-

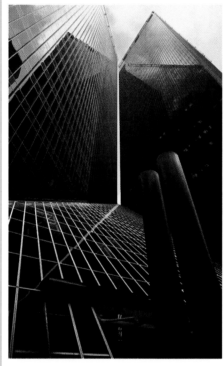

***Two trapezoids** soar into the sky at Philip Johnson's Pennzoil Place in Houston.*

trons John and Dominique de Menil. The Surrealist galleries displaying Magritte and others are the highlight here.

▶ *For a change of pace from driving, take the 90-minute boat tour of the Port of Houston (713-670-2576). This free trip on Buffalo Bayou is so popular that reservations must be made at least two months in advance.*

Space Center Houston is part theme park, part museum, and part educational center. You can try on a space helmet, visit Mission Control, see space artifacts, use a computer simulator to land a space shuttle, and watch films. Perhaps the exhibit with the biggest impact, though, is **Rocket Park,** where rockets used in the Mercury and Apollo programs are on display.

2 BRENHAM

The most popular place in Brenham may be the **Blue Bell Creamery,** where the tour ends with a scoop of the state's best ice cream. The town itself is idyllic and has a number of well-preserved 19th-century buildings; one is the 1870 **Giddings-Stone Mansion,** which can be toured by appointment.

3 WASHINGTON

The Texas Declaration of Independence was signed in this village, which was the capital of the Republic of Texas from 1842 to 1845. **Barrington,** the home of Anson Jones, the last president of the Republic, was moved to **Washington-on-the-Brazos State Historical Park** from a nearby rural site during the centennial celebration of Texas independence in 1936. The park also contains the old townsite and a replica of **Independence Hall,** constructed on the exact location of the original building.

4 HUNTSVILLE

Sam Houston's homestead was in Huntsville, and the **Sam Houston Memorial Museum** includes two of his mid-1840's homes—Woodland Home and Steamboat House, where he died; his grave is nearby in Oakwood Cemetery. Among the museum's displays is a saddle belonging to his foe, Santa Anna.

5 BIG THICKET

All that remains of the once-impenetrable wilderness that covered southeast Texas, the **Big Thicket National Preserve** is eight scattered woodlands and four water corridors totaling 86,000 acres. Early settlers found it virtually impossible to hack through the tangled forest; only criminals and draft dodgers

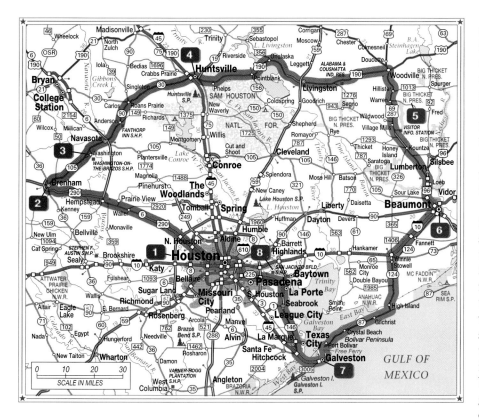

lived there. Now largely "farmed" for its lumber and replanted after harvest, the Thicket still shows remnants of its stubborn resistance to settlement.

▶ *A good introduction to the area is the 1½-mile main loop of the Kirby Nature Trail at the Big Thicket Visitor Information Station.*

6 BEAUMONT

The oil era began here in 1901 with the Spindletop gusher, which spewed out 800,000 barrels of oil in nine days before it could be controlled. Fortunes were made overnight here, but not by all. Visit the **Spindletop/Gladys City Boomtown Museum** to learn the sad story of a man the boom passed by: Pattillo Higgins. A self-taught geologist, Higgins saw signs of oil and gas at Spindletop Hill earlier, even taking his Sunday school class to the hill to see the tiny jets of gas he ignited after poking a hole in the ground with a stick. He drilled three times in the 1890's without success; the prize went to a man who carted rotary drilling equipment to the site in 1901 and brought in the gusher that had eluded Higgins.

The boomtown that briefly sprang up around the oil field, called Gladys City,

has been re-created at the museum. The original town was built on land that was held by Higgins's failed oil company and took its name from two little girls named Gladys—both of whom attended his Sunday school class.

7 GALVESTON ISLAND

Before September 8, 1900, Galveston was Texas's wealthiest and most beautiful city, a thriving port and seashore resort with wide boulevards and Victorian mansions. Then a killer hurricane destroyed much of the city and left more than 6,000 dead. Despite the construction of a massive seawall, Galveston never recovered economically from the

storm, but the surviving monuments to its 19th-century grandeur make it one of the state's most historic cities. Foremost among the prestorm mansions that are open to the public is the 1886 **Bishop's Palace**, a representative of the Romantic Revival style. The **Moody Mansion**, long occupied by one of Galveston's leading families, is also a museum, as is **Ashton Villa**, built before the Civil War.

A number of commercial buildings from Galveston's heyday have been restored on **The Strand**. Once known as the Wall Street of the Southwest, The Strand is now a shopping and tourist mecca. A trolley ride will take you to the beachfront **Hotel Galvez**, which was built to lure tourists back to Galveston's 32 miles of public beaches after the hurricane. **Moody Gardens**, at Offatts Bayou, is a garden fantasy that boasts the new Palm Beach and self-guided tours of a living rain forest enclosed in a 10-story-tall glass pyramid.

▶ *The Galveston visitor bureau (800-351-4237) will mail you a free discount coupon booklet for many of the island's attractions.*

8 SAN JACINTO BATTLEGROUND

Here a ragtag Texas army under Gen. Sam Houston defeated a Mexican force led by Gen. Antonio Lopez de Santa Anna and won independence for Texas in April 1836. A 570-foot monument, taller than the obelisk in Washington, at **San Jacinto Battleground State Historical Park** commemorates the heroes of the Texas Revolution.

Palm Beach is part of the 142-acre Moody Gardens complex on Galveston's Offatts Bayou. Its creamy white sand was shipped in by the bargeload from Florida.

1 SAN ANTONIO

One of the oldest cities in Texas, and once the largest and most cosmopolitan, this old town resonates with a romantic past. San Antonio is also a city intent on getting you lost. The downtown streets more or less follow the course of the San Antonio River, the ribbon that winds through downtown, and the path of the *acequias,* the old irrigation ditches the Spaniards used to water their crops. But no matter where you are, someone can point you toward **The Alamo,** Texas's most famous shrine, which sits in the middle of the city. It was first a mission and then a fort, but all that remains is the chapel, now a venerated museum, and the Long Barrack, once the living quarters for the priests.

Nestled on the east bank of the river is **La Villita,** the village that arose alongside the Alamo, then called Mission San Antonio de Valero. Today restaurants and bars abound, and festive tables are spread beneath the cypress trees. The **River Walk** is the best place to capture the feel of the city, whether you take a leisurely stroll or board one of the river taxis that float past the walk.

Four more missions in **San Antonio Missions National Historical Park** stand on the banks of the river; all are open daily for tours. **Mission Concepcion** is the largest unrestored mission in the U.S. Also in the park are the smaller **Mission San Juan** and **Mission Espada.** But the grandest of the old edifices is **Mission San José,** built two years after the Alamo in 1720, with a church, a granary, and Spanish and Indian quarters within the compound. One of the biggest attractions at Mission San José is the **Mariachi Mass,** which draws people from around the world; it is held every Sunday at noon.

▶ *Tour the missions in the first hour they open—9:00 A.M. in summer and 8:00 A.M in winter—so that the park rangers can give you a personal tour before the crowds come.*

For a look at Texas idiosyncrasy, stop in at the Lone Star Brewery to see its **Buckhorn Hall of Horns,** decorated with trophy heads from all over the world and 4,000 white-tailed-deer antlers, weighing two tons. There's also a **Hall of Fins,** dedicated to fish. And if you like, stop in at the **Buckhorn Saloon,** which serves a complimentary ice-cold Lone Star beer or root beer.

The city celebrates its cultural diversity each April at **Fiesta San Antonio,** an exuberant 10 days of lavish parades and nonstop music. Food stands sell everything from escargots to fried cactus to the best Tex-Mex food around as the strains of mariachi, Tejano, jazz, and rock music fill the air. The Battle of Flowers Parade, a century-old, crowd-pleasing tradition in San Antonio, offers brightly colored floats and marching bands; the Texas Cavaliers' River Parade cruises down the river; and the Fiesta Flambeau Parade, the largest nighttime parade in the nation, is a joyful spectacle worthy of Mardi Gras.

2 EAGLE PASS

This town on the Mexican border grew up around **Fort Duncan,** built in 1849.The part of the fort that still stands has been turned into a small museum. Artifacts from Indian-fighting days and from the Civil War, when the fort was occupied by Confederate soldiers, are on display.

Across the river is the larger Mexican city of **Piedras Negras,** where you can

bargain for handicrafts and folk art at **El Mercado,** about two blocks from the Eagle Pass bridge.

3 BRACKETTVILLE

A full replica of the Alamo in this tiny town shows you how the old mission might have looked in 1836. The battle was, in fact, re-created here in the 1950's for the filming of John Wayne's classic movie *The Alamo.*

You'll also see the adjacent **Alamo Village,** built for the movie and still used as a set for Western films, including television's *Lonesome Dove.* Tour the general store, stagecoach barn, jail, blacksmith shop, and bank. There's live entertainment here in summer, with staged gunfights in the streets and eight daily shows of music, singing, and Western comedy-melodramas.

4 UVALDE

This prosperous, inviting ranching community lies just at the point where the Hill Country fades into the south

Mission San José (left) is the most extensively renovated of the four missions in San Antonio's historical park. The city is the only one in the country that has five 18th-century missions— counting the Alamo—within its limits. Mariachi musicians (below) perform after a Sunday Mass.

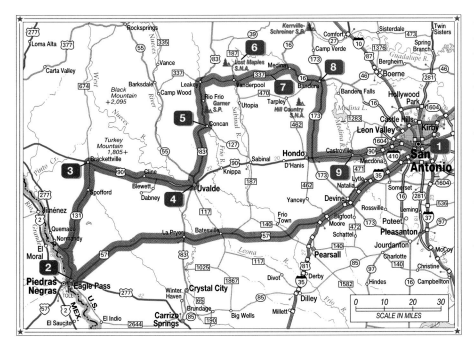

Texas brush country. The town, settled in 1853, was home to John Nance Garner. "Cactus Jack," as he was called, was a congressman from 1903 to 1932 and was vice president for FDR's first two terms. He retired from politics and returned to his hometown in 1941. The **Garner Museum,** with original furnishings, is open to the public.

5 CONCAN

This well-kept Hill Country secret, with spectacular scenery and a population of no more than 100 permanent residents, is located on the Frio River. Among the resorts that attract visitors is the venerable **Neal's Vacation Lodges,** with rustic cabins that look out on a swimming hole offering crystal-clear water, rapids, and tubing. The swimming hole is open to the public for a minimal fee.

Garner State Park, one of Texas's favorite playgrounds, is located seven miles up the Frio River and lures fun seekers with its excellent swimming and unparalleled tubing. Comfortable renovated cabins are available, each with a separate bedroom and kitchenette; most have fireplaces.

▶ *The 17 cabins at Garner State Park are in such demand that reservations for the year fill up quickly. Call the Texas State Park Central Reservation Center at 512-389-8900 as soon as possible after January 1.*

6 LOST MAPLES

Stands of bigtooth maples, the western species of maple that grows in sheltered canyon areas, line the banks of the Sabinal River and provide a splash of brilliant fall color in the first weeks of November. The **Lost Maples State Natural Area,** north of the tiny town of Vanderpool, covers 2,200 acres and has 11 miles of hiking trails that lead you through a number of different habitats with more than 350 plant species. Birdwatchers descend on the area in spring and summer to spot rare black-capped vireos, golden-cheeked warblers, and green kingfishers.

An interpretive exhibit in the park headquarters explains how the maples came to thrive in the Hill Country.

7 MEDINA RIVER SCENIC DRIVE

The 20-mile stretch of **Rte. 337** between the towns of Vanderpool and Medina is one of the most scenic in Texas. As you drive, you'll get glimpses of the quicksilver Medina River wending its way—sometimes at your side, sometimes in the distance—through secluded, rugged country.

8 BANDERA

Folks in Bandera aren't afraid to indulge in a good Texas brag. They have designated their town not only the Cowboy Capital of the World but also the Dude Ranch Capital of the World and the Trick and Fancy Ropers Capital of the World. Dude ranches do indeed surround this pleasant small town, which harbors some astonishing Texana. To see it firsthand, visit the **Frontier Times Museum,** established in 1933 by J. Marvin Hunter, publisher of the local *Frontier Times* magazine. Some 30,000 displays include a map of Texas crafted from rattlesnake rattles, a fireplace made of fossil snails, and bottles from Judge Roy Bean's saloon.

The 1891 **Bandera County Courthouse,** located on Main Street, sports a cowboy statue on its lawn, honoring all the cowboys in the land—but especially the seven national rodeo cowboy champions from Bandera County.

To enjoy Bandera to the fullest, pick up a free brochure guide to walking tours of more than 30 historic sites at the town's Chamber of Commerce.

▶ *An authentic small-town rodeo takes place every Tuesday and Saturday in Bandera, from Memorial Day to Labor Day. Tickets are only $4 for adults and $2 for children.*

9 CASTROVILLE

Settled by immigrants from the Alsace region of France in 1844, Castroville has kept much of its European flavor. More than 90 of its original mid-19th-century houses still stand, looking as if they were imported from villages along the Rhine River. Even the Alsatian dialect survived here for generations, spoken by many of the townspeople until well after World War II.

The town's main attraction is the **Landmark Inn,** which opened as a general store in 1849 and later added rooms. The Texas Parks and Wildlife Department runs the inn, which has eight rooms available to guests.

Also in this hamlet is an Alsatian bakery, St. Louis Catholic Church, and the former home of Henri Castro, the French-Portuguese impresario who brought Alsatian settlers to Texas. His home, **Castro House,** has been restored but is not open to the public. Another attraction is **St. Louis Day,** an Alsatian festival held each year on the Sunday closest to August 25.

1 AUSTIN

With its chalky white limestone hills, green lakes, hole-in-the wall Mexican cafés, and the shade of sprawling live oak trees, Austin is famous for its hedonistic ambience, lively politics, throngs of musicians and writers, and lively nightlife. Energized by the vast student population at the **University of Texas,** it is an oasis in the Southwest, the cultural and intellectual Athens of Texas, and an irresistible lure for those tired of faster-paced cities.

▶ *A trolley, the Capitol Metro 'Dillo, provides free transportation through downtown Austin and to the campus of the University of Texas.*

To savor Austin's past, stroll west on Seventh Street from downtown to the **Bremond Block,** a 19th-century enclave for one of Austin's leading merchant families. Because the Bremonds believed in togetherness, the parents and their grown children lived in six fine houses on the same city block. The homes range in architectural style from High Victorian opulence to antebellum charm, and their welcoming porches,

The Lone Star flag is proudly waved in Austin as a rodeo parade makes its way down Congress Avenue from the State Capitol. The pink granite of the building was quarried in the Texas Hill Country.

balustrades, turrets, and verandas bring back a more genteel era, when people stayed in touch by living close by.

To dip into Austin's nightlife, head east from Congress Avenue on **Sixth Street,** lined with clubs, bars, and restaurants. The feel here is a bit like Bourbon Street. The sidewalks are jammed at night, and the air is filled with music pouring out of front doors. If you raise your eyes above street level, you'll see the old native limestone buildings and storefronts of one of Austin's most historic streets.

No visit to Austin would be complete without a visit to the **State Capitol,** which, as Texans like to brag, is seven feet taller than the one in Washington.

The pink granite building is a trove of Texana and architectural details, and has been enlarged with a vast underground wing. For tours, start at the Capitol Complex Visitors Center on the southeast corner of the grounds.

The crown jewel and symbolic heart of Austin is **Barton Springs,** easily the best "swimmin' hole" in the world in the eyes of Texans. A thousand feet of shimmering turquoise water, the pool lies nestled between grassy sloping lawns, with downtown skyscrapers rising just above the dam. Crystal-clear springwater pours out of crevices in the rocky bank, keeping the pool a brisk 68°F year-round.

The massive white marble **Lyndon Baines Johnson Library and Museum,** standing on a hillside on the eastern edge of the University of Texas campus, is one of the grandest and most impressively stocked presidential libraries in the country. On its eighth floor is a replica of the oval office as it appeared when LBJ was president.

▶ *To break your tour of the huge presidential library, walk to the conference center just behind the building, where a café serves food and drinks from 11:00 A.M. to 2:00 P.M.*

2 SAN MARCOS

Many of the water parks found around the country are high-tech and glitzy, but beloved **Aquarena Springs** entertains its visitors the way it always has: with underwater ballets viewed from a glass wall that looks into a spring and a

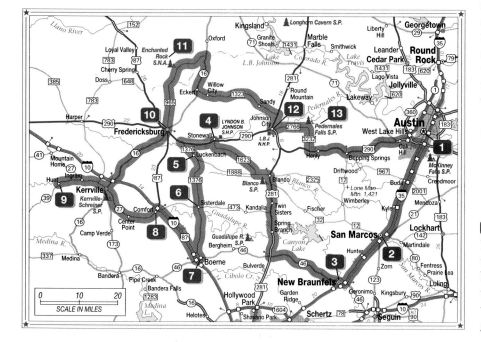

1930's atmosphere that hasn't changed since the park opened in 1929. Built on a crystal-clear lake fed by the head-springs of the San Marcos River, the park welcomes delighted visitors to the **Submarine Theater,** where the underwater performers present a lighthearted reenactment of the discovery of the spring by Indians. Other acts show synchronized swimming and Ralph, the famous Diving Pig.

Glass-bottom boats ferry tourists across the lake to gaze down at immense catfish. A sky lift connects the lake to a frontier village, where you'll find a Texas-style market, a Bavarian glassblower, hanging gardens, and the original **San Marcos Mission,** now restored. The **Historic Inn,** a two-story hotel built into the hillside, with balconies overlooking the spring, looks much as it did in the 1930's.

3 NEW BRAUNFELS

This town was founded in 1845 by Prince Carl of Solms-Braunfels as a stepping-stone colony for German immigrants in Texas—the Germans who would later establish the Hill Country towns to the west. A historic district, some of it still in the restoration stage, preserves the town's early buildings downtown. Two miles north, at Conservation Plaza, is the **Baetge House,** with a first floor furnished with pre-1860 pieces. Restored hotels are the **Faust Hotel** and the **Prince Solms Inn,** which give you a taste of early-20th-century Texas. The Faust, which became known as the Honeymoon Hotel soon after it opened in 1929, is one of the few authentically restored full-service hotels in the state. The Prince Solms is furnished with antiques and has a charming garden and a restaurant.

More than 75 beautifully crafted pieces of furniture, all made by German cabinetmakers in the mid-1800's, are on display at the **Museum of Texas Handmade Furniture,** located at the 1858 **Breustedt-Dillen Haus.**

The German heritage of New Braunfels is most evident at **Wurstfest,** a 10-day celebration in which 40,000 tons of sausage and 65,000 gallons of beer are consumed. It starts on the Friday before the first Monday of November.

4 STONEWALL

Just across Ranch Road One from the LBJ Ranch, the **Lyndon B. Johnson State Historical Park** makes a great introduction to the Texas Hill Country and its most famous native son. The visitor center displays presidential and boyhood memorabilia of Lyndon Johnson. Also in the center are exhibits that focus on the Hill Country and its people, and a video program that explains the influence of this unique part of Texas on the 36th president.

The park also contains the **Sauer-Beckmann Farmstead,** a living-history farm. Park employees dressed in period costumes run the farm just as it would have been operated by a German family at the turn of the century. In the spring they plant gardens, in summer they do canning, and in fall they make sausage.

Don't miss a drive on **Ranch Road One.** The LBJ ranch house is not open to the public, but you can see the ranch across the Pedernales River from this road. A tour bus takes you to the **Johnson Birthplace,** a white farmhouse just down the river. A replica, the house has

Tubers *float down the green ribbon of the Guadalupe River near New Braunfels.*

been furnished with many of the Johnson family's original possessions, including Johnson's childhood toys.

▶ *A free National Park Service bus tour of the LBJ Ranch takes you to the birthplace and provides a close-up view of the Texas White House.*

5 LUCKENBACH

The late Texas folk hero and storyteller Hondo Crouch bought this six-building town in 1970 and, poking fun at the country's rush toward sophistication, turned Luckenbach into a national media event by touting it as the only place to be. Another boost was given to the town's fame when singer Jerry Jeff Walker recorded *Viva Terlingua,* an epoch-making album, in Luckenbach's old dance hall, followed later by singer Waylon Jennings's *Luckenbach, Texas,* with its dose of plaintive nostalgia.

The town was founded in 1849 and provided little more than a post office and general store until Crouch took over. Unless you're there for the ladies' chili cook-off in October or a dance on a Saturday night, there's not much to do. Most visitors simply poke around in the atmospheric **General Store;** others might buy a long-neck beer and sit out under one of the live oaks to contemplate the tranquility of the place and to breathe the clean Hill Country air.

6 SISTERDALE

Sisterdale is little more than a wide spot in the road. On one side is the **Sisterdale General Store,** with an ornately carved 1900 bar, old beer signs, and mounted animal heads. Walking in is like stepping into the past. Across the street is **Sister Creek Vineyards and Winery,** whose Hill Country vintage is available for tasting and sales on Monday to Saturday afternoons.

7 BOERNE

Many sturdy German buildings still stand in Boerne, lending an Old World feeling to the center of this town. Boerne started as a stagecoach stop, but by the 1890's, after it was connected to San Antonio by rail, it had become a resort—famous for "the purest air God ever made for man or woman." Visitors still breathe the pristine air of the countryside, hike in the rugged hills, explore the caves along Cibolo Creek, and enjoy the cool springwater.

8 COMFORT

Located at the confluence of the Guadalupe River and Cypress Creek, this hamlet of 1,400 people was founded in 1854 by German freethinkers who came to the United States fleeing

Guadalupe River. Roads follow the curves of the river, so that you can admire the peaceful green stream, its banks lined with noble cypress trees.

10 FREDERICKSBURG

This German town, founded in 1846, has become a favorite of visitors drawn by the antique and gift shops, the German bakeries, the architecture, and the almost endless local celebrations that

Fredericksburg by Japanese donors.

Be sure to explore the side streets to see the old stone Sunday Houses, the charming small limestone and timber residences that ranchers and farmers built in town for weekend use.

▶ *The Fredericksburg visitor bureau, on Market Square, provides information about tours and local sights.*

11 ENCHANTED ROCK

The dramatic pink granite dome of **Enchanted Rock** dominates the surrounding landscape. Approaching the giant monolith from a distance, you can easily understand why the Indians attributed magical properties to the rock. In some lights, the flakes of shiny mica embedded in the granite give the dome an ethereal glow. After a rain, the bands of water coursing down the smooth sides shine like streams of silver.

The 425-foot climb up the smooth face to the top affords views of the surrounding valley—and a wonderful sense that the landscape has not changed for thousands of years.

Enchanted Rock, a massive dome of Precambrian pink granite more than a billion years old, is one of the oldest exposed rocks in North America. It is the center of a 1,643-acre natural park that is home to more than 500 varieties of plants.

both political and religious oppression.

Some 19th-century buildings still remain in this typical Hill Country town. Of special interest in Comfort are the **Faltin Homestead**, the **Faltin General Store**, the **Ingenhuett-Faust Hotel**, and the **Otto Brinkmann House**.

9 HUNT

The **Hunt Store** is probably the only combination café–grocery store–gas station in Texas that caters to cedar choppers and carries the Sunday *New York Times*—a clue to the character of the place. One of the most scenic parts of Texas, and long a summer retreat for children from Dallas, Houston, and abroad who attend the exclusive summer camps in the area, the countryside around Hunt is a combination of the rustic and the refined.

The main attraction here is the

feature beer, sausage, sauerkraut, and oompah bands. The early settlers made Main Street wide enough for a wagon pulled by a team of oxen to turn around, and built handsome stone buildings, many of which still stand. The **Vereins Kirche**, a small octagonal building, was the first church—nondenominational, so that all could share. The old county courthouse designed by Texas architect Alfred Giles has been lovingly restored and renovated as the **Public Library.** The **Pioneer Museum** offers the best look you'll get at domestic life in early Fredericksburg, and the **Admiral Nimitz Museum,** housed in the restored steamboat-shaped hotel built by Admiral Nimitz's grandfather, displays memorabilia from World War II. A pleasant surprise behind the old hotel is a Japanese peace garden built in 1976 by artisans who were sent to

12 JOHNSON CITY

The Johnsons moved into the modest **Johnson Boyhood Home** in 1913, when the future president was five years old. The house, with six rooms, a screened porch, and a porch swing, is typical of its time. Carefully restored and furnished with many of the family's belongings, the dwelling looks as if the family had just left, with toys scattered about Lyndon's and his brother Sam's room, and papers and magazines set out in the living room.

13 PEDERNALES FALLS

The falls at the north end of **Pedernales Falls State Park,** where the river pours through a tight gorge, cascade down two dams to spill gracefully into an emerald pool. Follow the nature trail downstream to twin waterfalls, where Regal and Bee creeks come together just before joining the Pedernales.

The 4,800-acre park stretches along the river for six miles. Trails take you up into a rugged canyon habitat where you can see ospreys, bald eagles, wild turkeys, and deer.

1 LUBBOCK

Behind the flat, treeless land of the Texas Panhandle is a rich pioneer history, an amusing taste for eccentricity, and even some classic Western scenery. The Panhandle's heritage is ranching, but today its economic base is farming. Cotton is king here: Lubbock, at the bottom of the Panhandle in the South Plains, handles about a fifth of the nation's output. For a thorough look at the crop's past, present, and future, tour the **International Textile Research Center**, a part of Texas Tech University. The Panhandle's quirky side is represented in Lubbock by **Mackenzie Park**, whose main attraction is a large prairie dog colony. You can feed the little critters bread if they're in the mood. And don't miss the **Ranching Heritage Center**, where more than 30 historic ranching structures, ranging from a one-room log cabin to Victorian homes, have been relocated on 16 acres and restored. On a more somber note, an oversize statue of Buddy Holly, complete with glasses and electric guitar, stands near the **Lubbock Memorial Civic Center**; the influential rock-and-roll star from Lubbock was killed in a 1959 plane crash.

Three local wineries offer tasting and tours: **Llano Estacado** and **Cap Rock** are in Lubbock; **Pheasant Ridge** is seven miles north, near New Deal.

Residents of Prairie Dog Town, housed in a Lubbock park, share a moment of play.

2 PALO DURO CANYON

Millions of years ago, more than 16,000 acres of colorful canyon were carved out by the Red River. Now part of **Palo Duro Canyon State Park**, the canyon is 120 miles long, more than 1,000 feet deep, and as much as 20 miles wide. Unceasing wind and winter storms have fashioned the red rock into delicate shapes. A good introduction to the park is the 30-minute ride on the narrow-gauge **Sad Monkey Railroad**.

3 AMARILLO

At the turn of the century, Amarillo was the cattle-shipping capital of the world. West of here was the largest spread ever to be fenced, the 3-million-acre XIT Ranch. But irrigation from the Ogallala Aquifer turned the region into farming country. Two reminders of the glory days are luxurious houses built by early cattle barons—**Harrington House** and the Lee Bivins home, now housing the Amarillo Convention and Visitors Bureau. Amarillo is also the site of two eccentric Texas monuments: the Pop Art sculpture of buried cars known as **Cadillac Ranch**, which is visible from Interstate 40 west of town, and the **Helium Monument** at the Amarillo Medical Center, a tribute to the fact that 90 percent of the world's supply of the gas is produced nearby.

The town of Canyon, 15 miles south of Amarillo, is home to the state-supported **Panhandle-Plains Historical Museum**, widely regarded as the best regional museum in Texas. Outstanding exhibits on petroleum, ranching, and Plains Indians are on view, along with a re-created 1900 Panhandle village and an art collection that includes paintings by Texas artist Frank Reaugh, a contemporary of Frederic Remington.

4 BOYS RANCH

In the era of the great cattle drives, Tascosa was a wild and woolly town that attracted gunslingers like Billy the Kid and Pat Garrett, the sheriff. Situated on the Canadian River in the badlands known as the Canadian Breaks, the town served as county seat for nine counties of the Texas Panhandle—until the railroad bypassed it in favor of Amarillo. That was the end of Tascosa; its official name is now **Boys Ranch**, after the facility that was established here in 1939. More than 5,000 boys have lived here; in 1992, the ranch went coed and now houses young men and women from 10 to 18 years of age.

▶ *Visitors are welcome to take a tour of the ranch and to join the residents for lunch. Donations are accepted.*

Also in the town is the **Old Courthouse**, now restored and open for tours. On display are more than 800 kinds of barbed wire, as well as branding irons, antique furnishings, saddles, and other artifacts. Nearby you can tour a restored one-room schoolhouse. Don't miss **Boot Hill Cemetery**, named for one in Dodge City, Kansas, the terminus of the cattle trail that passed through old Tascosa.

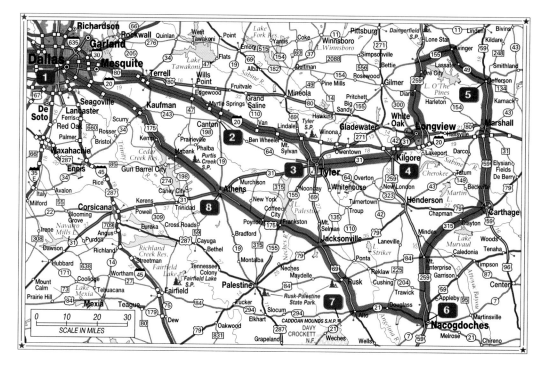

From the museum, you can walk to the **First Baptist Church.** The world's largest Baptist church covers five city blocks and boasts more than 25,000 members, one of whom will be glad to give you a tour. Another tour in town—one so popular you have to book it months in advance—is of the **Dr. Pepper** plant, home of the famous Texas soft drink.

To view Dallas in all its domestic glory, head toward **Highland Park,** an incorporated town of about 9,000 people near downtown. Residents refer to Highland Park as the Bubble. Its streets are lined with mansions that are home to many of Dallas's oldest and wealthiest families. One of the small jewels of the town is the **Meadows Museum** at nearby Southern Methodist University. The museum boasts a first-rate collection of Spanish masterpieces.

At night, Dallasites frequent the restaurants, shops, and nightclubs of the **West End,** the restored warehouse district on the west side of downtown,

 PANHANDLE SCENIC DRIVE

The roads from Borger to Lubbock take you through countryside straight out of a Western movie. On Rte. 136 southwest of Borger, you'll come to **Alibates Flint Quarries National Monument,** an archeological site first used by the Clovis people 11,500 years ago to make arrowheads and tools, and open to guided tours with a ranger. Below Claude on Rte. 207, you'll encounter breathtaking canyons, especially at the **Figure 3 Ranch** (six miles off Rte. 207 on Rte. 1258), which holds a Cowboy Morning gathering on a canyon rim—with an authentic chuck wagon breakfast and genuine Texas cowboys demonstrating roping and other skills.

▶ *Cowboy Morning is held from April to October, and occurs daily in June, July, and August. Make reservations in advance by calling 800-658-2613.*

At Silverton, turn east on Rte. 86 to find beautiful **Caprock Canyons State Park,** where the caprock—an abrupt drop-off that runs the length of the Panhandle—has been eroded into steep chasms that expose colorful streaks of mineral deposits. Farther along Rte. 207 and Rte. 62, from Floydada to Lubbock, you'll pass through sweeping cotton fields with windmills and the occasional patch of sunflowers.

DALLAS & THE EAST

DALLAS

Dallasites make it a point of pride that their city has no ostensible reason for existing, no geographical advantages, and no natural beauty. As Dallas boosters are quick to tell you, it is a city founded on hustle and free enterprise. A center of finance, banking, law, transportation, and merchandising, Dallas is easily Texas's most fashion-conscious city and the most conspicuous in its consumption of wealth.

To see Dallas, start in **Dealey Plaza,** where John F. Kennedy was assassinated. The sixth floor of the former **Texas School Book Depository** has been turned into a museum where photo collections and a 40-minute documentary film bring back one of the most tragic days of this century.

Downtown stands the massive **Dallas Museum of Art,** with a blue-chip collection of African, European, and contemporary art and a new Museum of the Americas wing with art dating from pre-Columbian times to 1945. The nearby **Morton H. Meyerson Symphony Center,** designed by I. M. Pei, is an architectural beauty whose acoustics are said to be among the best in the world.

Big Tex booms a welcome to visitors at the State Fair of Texas, the largest in the world.

or stroll along **Deep Elm** (pronounced EL-lum), the sector of east Elm Street where jazz clubs abound.

> ▶ *Save money on the color-coded Hop-a-Bus routes downtown. The Blue Bunny, Green Frog, and Red Kangaroo run each weekday, with a fare of only 25 cents and a free transfer.*

In early October the **State Fair of Texas**—the world's largest, of course, and the film set for a Rodgers and Hammerstein musical, *State Fair*, in 1962—welcomes some 3 million people to its thrill rides and its restored Art Deco exhibition halls, built for the Texas Centennial in 1936 at Fair Park.

Dallas is a city dedicated to shopping, and no trip would be complete without a stop at **Neiman Marcus**, the emporium that sets the tone for the city and for fashion-conscious families across Texas. For the full flavor, try the original store downtown at Main and Ervay or the one at **NorthPark**, one of the city's most attractive shopping centers.

2 CANTON

This is not only Texas's oldest flea market but also the largest, covering 133 acres, with antiques, quilts, farm implements, and anything else you might want to buy or swap. **First Monday Trade Days,** which attract as many as 4,500 exhibitors and 130,000 shoppers, are actually held not on Mondays—despite the name—but on the Friday, Saturday, and Sunday before the first Monday of every month.

3 TYLER

Tyler calls itself the Rose Capital of America, and with good reason: the town produces about 20 percent of the nation's commercial rose bushes. Visit the 14-acre **Tyler Municipal Rose Garden** to see gazebos, fountains, archways, and ponds ornamented with 30,000 rosebushes of 400 varieties; bloom time is late April to late October.

4 KILGORE

In 1930, after oil wildcatter C. L. (Dad) Joiner blew the lid off the vast East Texas Oil Field, the sleepy little farming town of Kilgore was suddenly turned into a booming tent city filled with some 10,000 drillers, roughnecks, and con men. The **East Texas Oil Museum** re-creates those days with vintage photographs from family albums, old clippings from the local newspaper, a 1932 movie made in the fields, and the taped recollections of old-timers. One of the original derricks still stands in town on a 1.2-acre tract where 24 derricks once rose side by side.

5 JEFFERSON

In the steamboat era, Jefferson was a bustling inland port of 12,000. As legend has it, the town might have become one of Texas's great cities had it not had the effrontery to reject the overtures of railroad tycoon Jay Gould. Gould swore that he would see grass grow in the streets of Jefferson, and he had his way, effectively killing the town by bypassing it with the Texas and Pacific Railroad. Fortunately, the lack of growth left many of Jefferson's handsomer buildings intact. The **Excelsior House Hotel** has been in continuous operation since 1850. Ulysses S. Grant, Rutherford B. Hayes, Oscar Wilde, and Jay Gould all signed the register. For a dollar, you can tour Gould's personal railroad car, luxuriously fitted out with four staterooms, a dining room, and a bathroom with a silver washbasin.

6 NACOGDOCHES

This pleasant town is surrounded by pine forests. First a village of the Nacogdoche Caddo Indians, then a Spanish mission founded in 1716, Nacogdoches is one of the oldest settlements in Texas. The **Sterne-Hoya Museum and Library** is housed in the former home of Adolphus Sterne, who built it in 1830 and later helped finance the Texas Revolution; it now contains Texas memorabilia. The **Stone Fort Museum,** a reconstruction of the Spanish fort and trading post built by Gil Y'Barbo, the town's founder, was headquarters for four unsuccessful attempts to establish the Republic of Texas.

7 CADDOAN INDIAN MOUNDS

East Texas is one of the few places in the state where you can savor the history of the early Indians. **Caddoan Indian Mounds State Historical Park,** near the town of Alto, is one of the better-developed sites. Between A.D. 500 and A.D. 1100, the Caddos built three large mounds here, two of which were for ceremonial purposes. The third mound was for burials.

8 ATHENS

The town that calls itself the pea-pickin' capital of the world celebrates its favorite crop on the third weekend of July with a **Black-eyed Pea Jamboree.** Among the attractions are beauty pageants, parades, a black-eyed pea cook-off, and a shelling contest. And in the pervading spirit of fun, the crowds that flock to the festival are quick to throw puns about with abandon, engaging in "reci-pea" trading and enjoying a "peatini"—a martini with no olive, but with a single black-eyed pea.

1 FORT WORTH

The City Where the West Begins: this has been Fort Worth's motto since local newspaper editor and visionary Amon Carter popularized it in the 1930's. For a town that started life as an outpost for settlers against Comanche attack, Fort Worth has flowered into an extraordinary home of the arts. Its cultural heart lies just beyond a magnificent series of public gardens and houses some of the world's greatest masterpieces of painting and sculpture, as well as a museum

Vaulted ceilings with dramatic skylights flood Fort Worth's Kimbell Art Museum (right) with natural light. The work of architect Louis I. Kahn, the building houses European and Asian works, including an elaborately decorated Buddha (detail below) from 12th-century Thailand.

devoted to representations of the folks Fort Worth first became famous for: the Plains Indian, the buffalo hunter, and the cowboy.

The Japanese Garden in the **Fort Worth Botanic Garden** complex is a 7½-acre enclosure of serene beauty situated in the midst of rose arbors and walking trails near the Trinity River banks. Inside the authentic architecture, shaded ponds, waterways, and springtime cherry blossoms transport one for an hour to Japan. The tranquil Moon Viewing Deck is copied from the Silver Pavilion Garden in Kyoto.

Drive on through the gardens to reach the cluster of museums that has gained renown across the world. The **Kimbell Art Museum**, a modern architectural gem, boasts the finest works of many major European and Asian artists. Its galleries are comfortable and intimate, and the traveling exhibitions that grace them are good complements to the outstanding permanent collection. Across the street is the **Amon Carter Museum.** Here the paintings and bronzes by Frederic Remington and Charles M. Russell bring back the atmosphere of the Old West with vivid clarity: dusty riders compete for a water hole, the sun beats down on an Indian war party. For more contemporary fare, the nearby

Modern Art Museum of Fort Worth presents the work of masters of the 20th century, while one block away the **Fort Worth Museum of Science and History** offers wonderful exhibits for children of any age to enjoy, with hands-on participation in everything from a voyage through the human body to a dinosaur dig. For a change of pace, **Sundance Square**, on the north edge of downtown, is a cluster of charming turn-of-the century buildings and red brick streets that now serve as a center for dining and entertainment.

Perhaps the most famous nickname

for Fort Worth—Cowtown—can still be exemplified by its **Stockyards.** Long the last major civilized outpost for cattle drivers heading up to Kansas City, this livestock center, located 2½ miles north of downtown, is still the place to see genuine riders 'n' ropers having fun. **Stockyard Stations**—once hog and sheep pens but now converted to shops that sell art, furniture, gourmet coffees, and all things Western—connect Eighth Avenue to downtown by the *Tarantula,* a genuine steam train from the 1890's.

Top cowboys and cowgirls compete year-round at the **Cowtown Coliseum Rodeo.** And don't miss the **Cowgirl Hall of Fame,** moving here in mid-1995 from the Panhandle.

▶ *In the 132-block Downtown Free Zone—from Belknap Street south to Lancaster Street and from Jones Street east to Henderson Street—you can hop on any city bus for free.*

2 WAXAHACHIE

If this town looks familiar, it's probably because so many movies—including *Places in the Heart* and *Tender Mercies*—have been filmed here to take advantage of the wonderfully preserved 19th-century ambience. Dominating the center of town is one of the most eccentric public structures ever built in Texas, the red sandstone and granite **Ellis County Courthouse.** The building rose in 1895 with the help of three stone carvers brought from Europe. Tucked among the gargoyles of the friezes is the repeated face of a young woman—the pretty Mabel Frame, the boardinghouse proprietor's daughter with whom one of the homesick carvers fell in love.

Houses, on the other hand, are decorated with gingerbread trim. The downtown, chock-full of antique shops and tearooms, prides itself on maintaining its Victorian air. Also here is the **Ellis County Museum,** with relics of the region's history, including toys, vintage photos, and furnishings. In October, the Waxahachie Community Theatre stages performances—sometimes of Broadway musicals—at the 1896 **Chatauqua Auditorium,** a timber hexagonal building where Will Rogers and John Philip Sousa performed.

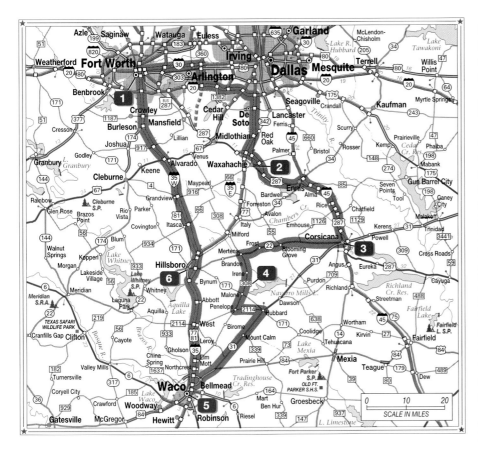

and now a community center. Farther north, in Jester Park, is a re-created **Pioneer Village** of old log cabins from the area, celebrating the life of early settlers.

4 BLACKLAND PRAIRIE SCENIC DRIVE

A 46-mile scenic drive through a swath of the state's fertile Blackland Prairie shows the north-central Texas landscape at its best. As you leave Corsicana on Rte. 22, you'll go through the tiny hamlets of Blooming Grove and Mertens, then turn left on Rte. 308 through Malone to Penelope; from here you'll follow Rte. 2114 to Hubbard to link up with the main highway, Rte. 31, to Waco. Fleets of clouds move across the huge sky, and barns and farmhouses are set on gently rolling land that in late summer presents a lovely patchwork of feathery mesquite, spent golden cornstalks, rust-colored milo, and emerald-green sorghum hay.

5 WACO

The Bosque and Brazos rivers converge in Waco, providing a beautiful setting for **Cameron Park,** with forested paths and limestone cliffs overlooking the water. Spanning the Brazos you will see the **Suspension Bridge** that was the largest in the world at the time of its construction, in 1870. Designed to be the prototype of the Brooklyn Bridge, it played a vital role in the Western movement: even the Chisholm Trail crossed over it, and you can too—by foot. Situated near the Brazos are several lovely restored Southern mansions, open to the public on weekends. On the riverbanks is **Fort Fisher Park Complex,** built to commemorate the original fort established by the Texas Rangers in 1837 and today the headquarters for Company F of the Rangers. It is also home to the **Texas Ranger Museum and Hall of Fame,** which displays a wide array of guns and Ranger equipment from Texas's early days.

A drive to the Baylor University campus a couple of blocks away will reward you with the **Armstrong Browning Library,** which holds one of the largest collections of the works and treasures of the Victorian poets Robert and Elizabeth Barrett Browning. Fifty-four

3 CORSICANA

Corsicana found its fortune as an oil boomtown early in the century. It was the site of the first commercial oil well west of the Mississippi, drilled in 1894 when the townsfolk were looking for water. Two major oil companies, Texaco and Mobil, got their starts here.

Today the towering derricks are gone, but the town has a second claim to fame: it is home to a fruitcake that has been shipped around the world since the early 1920's—officially known as the DeLuxe, but usually called simply the Corsicana fruitcake. The cake was created when a German immigrant, August Weidmann, arrived in town and tasted a pecan for the first time, added the nuts to his mother's recipe for white fruitcake, and with the aid of a businessman started selling the cakes— made both then and now with 27 percent pecans. Members of the visiting Ringling Brothers Circus discovered the delicacy in 1918 and shipped it to friends in other states and Europe. Today 4 million pounds of fruitcake are produced for the U.S. and 196 other countries. The **Collin Street Bakery,** on Rte. 31, has free guided tours from October to December; but you can buy cakes, pecan bread, 32 kinds of cookies, and other goodies any time of year.

▶ *Samples of the fruitcake and other bakery treats are free, and a fresh cup of coffee costs 10 cents.*

Just up 15th Street in Corsicana stands the small **Temple Beth-El,** a wooden synagogue built in 1900 with Russian-style onion domes—a unique beauty among Texas houses of worship

The DeLuxe fruitcake has been shipped in the famous Texas Star tin since 1945.

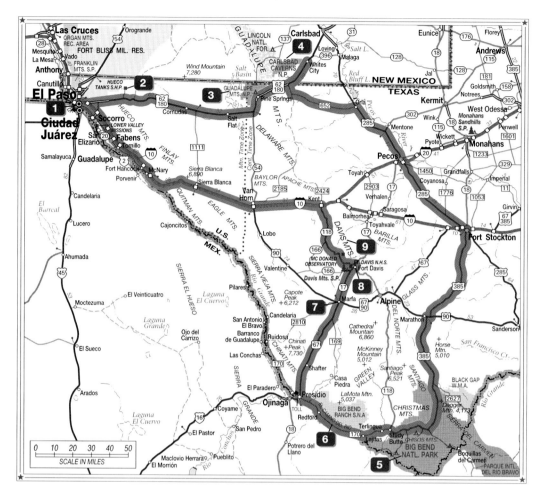

the range is crossed by **Transmountain Road,** which offers a good introduction to the high desert. The best city view is from **Murchison Park** on Scenic Drive, a favorite spot for sunset watching. West of the Franklins, the **University of Texas at El Paso** has some of the most unusual architecture of any university campus—buildings in the Bhutanese style of the Himalayas. The **Magoffin Home,** built of adobe scored to look like stone, is a fine example of late-19th-century architecture in far West Texas, and is open for tours.

East of downtown El Paso, in an area known locally as the Lower Valley, three missions survive from the Spanish colonial period of the 1600's: **San Elceario Church,** the **Mission Socorro,** and the **Mission Ysleta.**

stained-glass windows, each representing a Browning poem, decorate the Italian Renaissance–style building, and you can also view a number of Renaissance paintings and sculptures.

6 HILLSBORO

This charming old town is an antique lover's haven, and not even a furious fire has dimmed its charm. On New Year's Day in 1993, fire ravaged the 1893 limestone **Hill County Courthouse**—a building *The Saturday Evening Post* once called "a monstrosity" and *Harper's* said resembled "a cathedral in a town in France." The imposing walls remain, however, and work to restore the courthouse to its former glory will be complete in the mid-1990's.

Antique shops and malls now fill the vicinity of the courthouse square. The **Confederate Research Center and Museum** has an impressive collection of 3,500 books on the Civil War, as well as paintings, regimental histories, and other artifacts. Also in the center is the **Audie Murphy Gun Museum.**

1 EL PASO

In this fourth-largest city on the westernmost tip of Texas, you are closer to Phoenix than to Dallas, and closer to Los Angeles than to the state's eastern boundary. The city's economic and cultural interests are intertwined with those of the Mexican city of **Ciudad Juárez,** just across the Rio Grande. In Juárez you can take in a bullfight at the **Plaza Monumental** or shop for crafts from the interior of Mexico at the **Old City Market** on Avenida 16 de Septiembre, where you can try your hand at bargaining in the shopping stalls.

▶ *Americans do not need a visa to cross the bridge into Ciudad Juárez.*

One of the most striking features of El Paso is the Franklin Mountains, which penetrate deep into the heart of the city;

2 HUECO TANKS

West Texas has the state's tallest mountains east of the Rockies and the desolate northern reaches of the Chihuahuan Desert. The first stop on the edge of this remote landscape is the rocky outcrops of Hueco Mountains, where rock basins collect what little rainwater falls in this barren desert at **Hueco Tanks State Historical Park.** Another point of interest is the more than 3,000 pictographs in the caves and overhangs, left here by prehistoric visitors.

3 GUADALUPE MOUNTAINS NATIONAL PARK

The bluff profile of **El Capitan,** visible as far away as 50 miles, marks the southern end of the Guadalupe range. Also known as Sentinel Peak, the mountain was a landmark for every civilization that tried to tame this rugged land. The park contains the highest point in Texas, 8,749-foot **Guadalupe Peak,** and preserves rare desert microclimates. Lush springs, hidden canyons sheltered by 2,000-foot cliffs, and mountain forests of Douglas fir and pine are some of the park's major features. Hiking is the only way to see the interior of the park; a short side road leads to the mouth of **McKittrick Canyon**, the park's most popular trail.

4 CARLSBAD CAVERNS NATIONAL PARK

From Guadalupe Peak, it's a 40-mile drive over the New Mexico border to **Carlsbad Caverns**. The Big Room at Carlsbad is the largest underground chamber in the world—255 feet high, with enough area for 14 football fields. Immense formations hang down from the top of the chamber and build up from the floor, sometimes meeting to form one massive column. You can make the trip to the Big Room by elevator, or descend 829 feet below the surface on a steep trail that passes through four ornate chambers on the way.

5 BIG BEND NATIONAL PARK

Bigger than Rhode Island but lightly visited because of its remoteness and scarcity of accommodations, Big Bend is one of America's great national parks. The variety of attractions is astonishing: low desert, high desert, sheer canyons, a major river, dramatic mountains, evergreen forests, volcanic wastelands, and historic sites ranging from an old army post to an abandoned mercury mine. No view in Texas rivals the 100-mile arc of the Rio Grande that can be seen from the south rim of the Chisos Mountains, but the spot can be reached only by an arduous hike. The rest of Big Bend is extremely accessible, however, because of a road network that served ranchers who lived here before the area became a park. Among the attractions that can easily be reached by car are the mouth of **Santa Elena Canyon**, where the river emerges from a gorge that is 1,500 feet deep; the ruins of an unlikely resort called **Hot Spring**; and the **Basin of the Chisos**, surrounded by 7,000-foot peaks. Even the back-country roads to **Dagger Flat**—a forest of giant yuccas—and the **Grapevine Hills** can be used by ordinary passenger cars.

▶ The only hotel in Big Bend is the Chisos Mountain Lodge, and reservations must be made well in advance.

6 THE RIVER ROAD

Rte. 170 west from Big Bend may be the best scenic drive in Texas. It starts in the revived ghost town of **Terlingua**, where mercury miners once lived in adobe huts and where the first championship chili cook-off was staged, then goes to **Lajitas**, an odd mixture of an old trading post and a new resort. The road then follows the Rio Grande along the route the Spanish called the **Camino del Río**. On the way, you'll pass through 50 miles of canyons, rock formations, and Mexican villages before you reach **Presidio**, a border town best known for having the hottest summer temperatures in Texas.

7 MARFA

Just 60 miles north of scorched Presidio, Marfa (elevation 4,882 feet) has the coolest summer temperatures in the state. *Giant*, the 1956 screen epic about the good and bad sides of Texas culture, was filmed in the barren desert west of here, and the cast was housed in the El Paisano Hotel in downtown Marfa. But Marfa is best known for the **Marfa Lights**, an unexplained ghostly glow that appears frequently in the mountains east of town. The state highway department has provided a viewing area 7½ miles east of town on Rte. 90.

8 FORT DAVIS

Near this town is the Indian War fort that was established to protect the San Antonio–El Paso Stage Road. The restored **Fort Davis National Historic Site** includes many original buildings that have been refurbished to look as they did in the 1880's. A broadcast of the sounds of a dress parade, with commands, bugle calls, and military music, rings out periodically on the parade grounds. For some time after the Civil War, Fort Davis was home to several regiments of Buffalo Soldiers, most of whom in the beginning were freed slaves. South of town is the **Chihuahuan Desert Visitor Center**, which features the largest living collection of Chihuahuan Desert cacti.

9 DAVIS MOUNTAINS

A stunning contrast to the surrounding desert, the Davis Mountains are an island of mountain grassland that can be lush and green in the late summer rainy season. Their red-rock canyons and sculpted formations were considered for national park status at one time. A good introduction to the area is Skyline Drive in **Davis Mountains State Park**, west of Fort Davis. One of the most scenic canyons is along Limpia Creek on Rtes. 17 and 118. As you head back toward Interstate 10 on Rte. 118, don't miss a stop at the **University of Texas McDonald Observatory**, where you'll enjoy an unimpeded view of the mountains from the top of Mount Locke.

The Chisos Mountains form the backdrop for eroded rocks in Big Bend National Park.

1 CORPUS CHRISTI

The top attractions in Corpus Christi are related to the sea. The **Texas State Aquarium** features an exhibit on the underwater life found around an oil platform, the legs of which serve as an artificial reef for fish of all sizes, including sharks and rays. Near the aquarium is the **U.S.S. *Lexington,*** an aircraft carrier that saw action in World War II and is now permanently moored in Corpus Christi Bay. The self-guided tour includes vintage aircraft on the flight deck, the immense anchor chain in the forecastle, and the captain's chair on the bridge. Three smaller ships, the **Columbus Fleet,** are tied up under the high Harbor Bridge: the *Niña, Pinta,* and *Santa María.* Spain built these authentic replicas of Christopher Columbus's caravels to celebrate the 500th anniversary of his discovery of the western hemisphere, sailed them across the Atlantic, and chose Corpus Christi as their permanent home.

▶ *A $2 water taxi connects downtown with the U.S.S.* Lexington, *Texas Aquarium, and Columbus Fleet.*

2 PADRE ISLAND

If you're looking for a secluded beach, Padre Island is the place. For the most scenic route from Corpus Christi to the island, take Shoreline Drive, which turns into Ocean Drive and passes the stair-step seawall and many of the city's most palatial homes. Then turn onto Ennis Joslin Road and South Padre Island Drive. The beautiful **Padre Island National Seashore** runs for 70 miles on this barrier island, most of which is undeveloped and without any facilities. Once you're on the island, drive south as far as time and your gas tank will allow; it won't be long before the cars thin out and nothing is left except you, the water, and the dunes.

3 PORT ARANSAS

Only a narrow channel separates Padre Island from Mustang Island, its neigh-

bor to the north. Port Aransas, at the northern tip of Mustang, is a quaint fishing village in the cool months and a booming beach resort in the warm months. The quaintness quotient is highest at the **Tarpon Inn**, where fishermen once signed the scales of tarpon they caught and tacked them to the walls in the lobby; one signature from 1937 was penned by Franklin D. Roosevelt. The prime winter attraction is a boat trip to the **Aransas National Wildlife Refuge**, home, from November through March, of the magnificent but endangered whooping cranes. Tours of the refuge depart from Port Aransas and Rockport/Fulton.

4 ROCKPORT/FULTON

These small communities on a peninsula separating Copano and Aransas bays have become havens for artists, anglers, and bird-watchers. To see local artists' works, visit the galleries at the **Rockport Center for the Arts**, housed in a lovely 19th-century home at Rockport harbor. The imposing 29-room **Fulton Mansion State Historical Structure** is another beauty, built by an early cattle baron. It was equipped with conveniences unheard of in 1875: flush toilets, hot and cold running water, central heat and ventilation, and a system of circulating water to cool food.

On Fulton Beach Road, live oak trees have been twisted into contorted shapes by prevailing winds; across the causeway in **Goose Island State Park** is the Texas champion live oak, which is more than 1,000 years old, with a circumference of 35 feet and a crown spread of almost 90 feet.

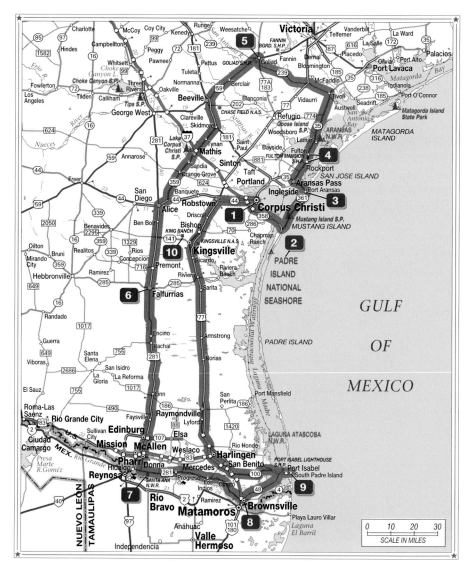

Whooping cranes find refuge near the town of Port Aransas on the Texas coast.

5 GOLIAD

This old town, where the Spanish established a mission and a fort in 1749, is a prime historic site. Texas rebels under Col. James Fannin sacrificed their lives in the 1836 war for independence from Mexico. But Goliad does not rank high in Texas mythology, because the revolutionaries here—unlike those at the Alamo—surrendered rather than fight to the death. They were soon executed. Both the fort, **Presidio La Bahía**, and the mission, **Espíritu Santo**, have been restored. The battle was fought nine miles east of town at **Fannin Battleground State Historic Park.**

6 FALFURRIAS

At the end of the last century, Don Pedrito Jaramillo was South Texas's most famous *curandero*, or folk healer, having arrived at the Los Olmos ranch near Falfurrias from his native Mexico in 1881. This "benefactor of humanity," as his epitaph describes him, accepted no pay for his prescriptions and provided food for locals when times were

hard. After he died in 1907, his tomb became the **Don Pedrito Shrine**; today it still attracts thousands who come to pray for aid, leaving pictures, flowers, candles, and crutches at the site.

7 SANTA ANA WILDLIFE REFUGE

Before farmers from the Midwest came to the fertile Rio Grande valley and cleared the land, the border was a thicket of subtropical vegetation. Now the 2,080-acre **Santa Ana Wildlife Refuge** is the only remnant of what the area looked like in the days before development, and is a home for wildcat ocelots and native chachalaca birds. A raised wooden walkway winds through the dense vegetation along the river.

▶ *The Audubon Society operates a tram tour during the winter, with views of hundreds of bird species.*

8 BROWNSVILLE

What remains of post–Civil War **Fort Brown** on the Mexican border is now part of the University of Texas campus at Brownsville. But the town that sprang from the fort still thrives, and shares a common culture with its older sister city across the border, **Matamoros.** Visitors shouldn't miss a trip across one of the Rio Grande bridges to take in the sights. Do your shopping at the **Mercado Juárez,** a colorful and crowded market made up of many shops; and don't be afraid to bargain. Back across the bridge, the biggest surprise in Brownsville is the **Gladys Porter Zoo,** where the use of natural habitats has earned it a ranking among the top small zoos in the United States.

9 SOUTH PADRE ISLAND

This is the Texas gold coast—a five-mile stretch of world-class beachfront hotels and condos on a 34-mile barrier reef. The international vacationers and tanned locals who flock to **South Padre Beach** all come for the same pleasures: the state's whitest sand, bluest water, and most reliable sunshine.

10 KING RANCH

Probably the most famous ranch in the world, the **King Ranch** is known for its size (it occupies some 825,000 acres), its cattle-raising operation (the Santa Gertrudis breed was developed here), and its audacity (founder Richard King moved the entire population of a Mexican village to the ranch more than a century ago). Much of the ranchland between the Rio Grande Valley and Kingsville is part of the King spread. The only way to see the ranch is to take one of the guided tours that begin at the visitor center.

In Kingsville the **King Ranch Museum** has an extensive collection of photographs depicting life on the ranch. There's also the **King Ranch Saddle Shop,** where saddles, bags, belts, and other leather goods are sold.

Padre Island (left) is the longest in the string of barrier islands that stretch for 113 miles along the Texas coast. Among the sea life found there is the curious ghost crab (above).

Texas • 251

New Mexico

A terra-cotta landscape bathed in a glorious light, the ridges and canyons of New Mexico hold the ruins of ancient cultures, the memory of a native people, and the monuments of the New World.

ALBUQUERQUE & INDIAN COUNTRY

1 ALBUQUERQUE

This Sun Belt boomtown began near the Rio Grande in 1706, almost a century after the Spanish built a governor's palace in Santa Fe. When the railroad passed nearby in the 1880's, the area around the tracks became known as New Town, as distinguished from Old Town, the original settlement. Today the remnants of Old Town have been reborn as shops, galleries, and restaurants cozily ensconced in restored adobes from the early 18th century. The cottonwood-shaded plaza dates back to 1780, and the **San Felipe de Neri Catholic Church** to 1793. The church is something of a metaphor for the transformation of Albuquerque from Spanish village to modern metropolis, as a succession of priests have added decidedly non-Spanish touches to the original structure—including Victorian bell towers.

Albuquerque has made many noteworthy architectural attempts to honor its heritage. The 1920's-era **KiMo Theater** is in the Pueblo Deco style: Art Deco with a Southwestern flavor. Originally a movie palace, it is now used for the performing arts. The **University of New Mexico** campus has three buildings designed by the noted architect John Gaw Meem, the foremost practitioner of the Pueblo style: **Scholes Hall**, the **Alumni Memorial Chapel**, and **Zimmerman Library.** Also on campus is the **Maxwell Museum of Anthropology,** with its model of a Neanderthal woman. Take the **Sandia Peak Aerial Tramway**—the world's longest such ride at 2.7 miles—to the top of the 10,378-foot mountain that looms over the city's east side. You can see far beyond the river into the western desert.

Cross the Rio Grande to see one of the most remarkable sites in the state. **Petroglyph National Monument** contains the artwork of Pueblo Indians who lived here 1,500 years ago. These prehistoric petroglyphs—rock etchings—of animals, birds, and the like are evidence of their occupation here. Civilization daily chips away at this fragile site, considered sacred by modern Indians; tread lightly.

2 ACOMA PUEBLO

Known as Sky City for its mesa-top location, Acoma Pueblo is a maze of narrow passageways and rock dwellings. In use for some 800 years, it is the oldest continuously occupied community in the country. Only 10 or so families remain to enjoy the spectacular views of fields, mesas, and immense sky; the rest of the population lives elsewhere on the reservation. The only way to see the pueblo is in the company of guides, who take groups to the mesa top by shuttle bus. The highlight of the guided tour is the handsome adobe-walled **San Esteban del Rey Mission.**

▶ *The only days you can visit Acoma Pueblo without a guide are September 2 and December 25-28. And note that video cameras are not allowed in the pueblo at any time.*

3 EL MALPAIS

Take a stroll on lava thousands of years old at **El Malpais National Monument and National Conservation Area.** The Spanish name translates as "bad land," an apt description for this rough-hewn valley. The lava beds lie between Rtes. 53 and 117, but the connecting road is not maintained and can be extremely rough. The best course—and a highly recommended scenic drive—is south about 20 miles on Rte. 117, passing the **Sandstone Bluffs** overlook and the **La Ventana** sandstone arch. Marked trails cross lava fields; self-guided maps are offered at the visitor centers in Grants and on Rte. 117. Wear sturdy shoes; the ground is rocky in patches.

The 1,500-foot-deep **Bandera Volcano,** about 25 miles south of Grants on Rte. 53, contributed some of the lava

Airborne whimsy: *Hot-air balloons fly high at the Albuquerque International Balloon Fiesta.*

Shiprock, a 1,700-foot-high geological formation on the Navajo Reservation, is considered sacred ground by the Navajo people. Climbers are not allowed to scale the rock.

to this forbidding landscape. Nearby, in the mysterious **Ice Cave**, water trapped in lava tubes has stayed frozen for untold centuries.

▶ *The temperature inside the Ice Cave never rises above 31°F. A climb is necessary to look into the volcano.*

4 EL MORRO

Known as Inscription Rock, **El Morro National Monument** is a 200-foot sandstone cliff that has for years been a message board for Indians and settlers who passed this way. Among the people who carved their words into immortality were Juan de Oñate, New Mexico's first governor, in 1605, and Diego de Vargas, who reconquered the area after a 1680 Pueblo revolt.

One of the largest Indian pueblos in the country, the **Zuni Pueblo**, is 34 miles west of El Morro. The Zuni tribe specializes in creating exquisite silver jewelry studded with turquoise and other native stones.

Traveling northward you'll be crossing the immense **Navajo Reservation,** which begins in New Mexico and sprawls across Arizona north and west to the Colorado River. Detour into Arizona to **Window Rock,** the capital of the Navajo nation. The octagonal shape of the tribal council house reflects the outline of a hogan, the traditional Navajo dwelling. The name "Window Rock" refers to the massive sandstone formation with a round hole near the top that is located in a nearby tribal park.

5 SHIPROCK PINNACLE

This famous landmark of the American West, whose outline vaguely resembles a tall ship, can be seen from 100 miles away. But for those who prefer a close-up view, the towering peak is located along Navajo Rte. 33, a scenic pathway south of the town of Shiprock that links Interstate 666 and Red Rock, Arizona.

6 AZTEC RUINS

The first Americans to discover what is now **Aztec Ruins National Monument** decided that the builders must have been influenced by the Aztecs of Mexico. They were wrong—the occupants were the now-vanished Anasazi—but the name stuck. A highlight of this 12th-century ruin is the **Great Kiva**, an underground ceremonial chamber.

7 CHACO CULTURE PARK

At one time the remarkable ruins of the **Chaco Culture National Historical Park** may have been the home of as many as 5,000 people. The ancient people known as the Anasazi lived here from approximately A.D. 800 to 1200. Ahead of their time socially and architecturally, the Anasazi built an extensive road system. The site's beautifully crafted buildings are among the best-preserved in the Southwest.

▶ *The park roads are unpaved; passage may be difficult in wet weather. Call ahead about road conditions.*

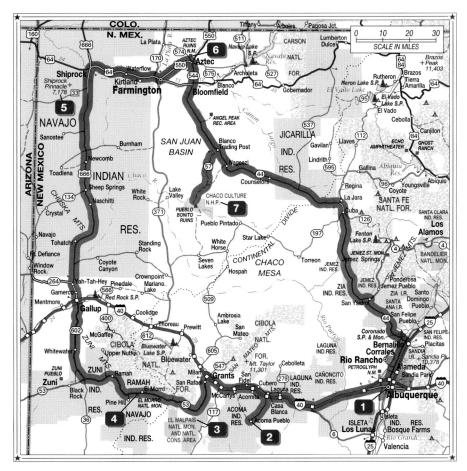

1 SANTA FE

Folks who say that Santa Fe has become too trendy and commercialized have got it all wrong: it's always been that way. The late artist Georgia O'Keeffe, who painted the landscapes of northern New Mexico, disliked the town's pretentiousness at first sight in 1917 and chose to live an hour away in tiny Abiquiu. Still, Santa Fe's charms make the city one of America's great destinations. Its setting at the foot of the Sangre de Cristo Mountains, its clean air and cool climate, its colorful Pueblo-style architecture and small-town scale, and its multiethnic mix of history, art, and food create a unique atmosphere.

The best thing to do here is just walk around the historic plaza and nearby blocks, browsing in shops and galleries and seeing attractions from the time when Santa Fe was the northernmost outpost of New Spain. Stop in at the adobe-walled **Palace of the Governors,** built by the Spanish in 1610 and now a state historical museum. The nearby Pueblo Revival–style **Museum of Fine Arts,** completed in 1917, boasts an open-door policy: local artists, regardless of reputation, are offered exhibition space. The permanent collection includes works by O'Keeffe and Robert Henri. The **Museum of International Folk Art,** two miles outside the city, has miniature Mexican villages, carved masks, and beaded Zuni dolls.

▶ *A one-price, three-day pass gains admittance to the aforementioned museums as well as to the Museum of Indian Arts and Culture.*

The intimate **Wheelwright Museum of the American Indian** has a collection of contemporary and historical American Indian art. Inside the Gothic 1873 **Loretto Chapel,** a seemingly unsupported spiral staircase swirls up to the choir loft.

Two of the top streets for strolling are **East De Vargas,** site of some of the city's oldest buildings—including the

Pulsating drumbeats accompany these Pueblo dancers in full tribal regalia as they stage a mock battle during the Eight Northern Indian Pueblo Craft Fair, held each July at a different pueblo. These dancers performed at the San Ildefonso Pueblo.

1610 **San Miguel Mission,** one of the oldest churches in the United States—and **Canyon Road,** home of some of the city's finest galleries. The **Fenn Gallery** is as much a museum as an art gallery, with a collection of works by Frederic Remington, Charles M. Russell, and other artists whose inspiration was the American West.

2 BANDELIER

In a region that boasts magnificent scenery at every turn in the road, the canyon known as **Bandelier National Monument** may top them all. Sheer walls, their faces pitted with ancient cliff dwellings, rise 600 feet above stands of pines on the canyon floor. A large circular ruin left some 800 years ago by the Anasazi stands in a clearing today. Nowhere in the American West is the sense of mystery about the Anasazi so poignant and strong: it is hard to imagine a people abandoning this heavenly location.

Zuni "needlepoint" bracelet, from the collection of the Wheelwright Museum in Santa Fe.

3 LOS ALAMOS

Across the Rio Grande you climb into canyon-and-mesa country to reach Los Alamos, a town that was built around the testing of the atomic bomb. Today it is an environmental, medical, and nuclear research center. Exhibits at the **Los Alamos Historical Museum** include correspondence of the physicist Albert Einstein and casings built to house the atomic bomb. Stop in at the **Bradbury Science Museum;** its exhibits center on the history and technology of the Manhattan Project, the U.S. Army organization that developed the atomic bomb.

4 ABIQUIU

Georgia O'Keeffe left a legacy of paintings that are Southwestern in both subject and spirit. An individualist who loved the solitude of the desert, she stipulated in her will that her two homes here remain closed to the public. What you can see, instead, is the sweeping countryside she couldn't stop painting. The drive to Abiquiu winds through the rugged Jemez Mountains. As it nears the town you enter O'Keeffe country, where canyon walls are washed in pastel striations.

Visitors are welcome at **Ghost Ranch,** 14 miles north on Interstate 84, where O'Keeffe painted many of her big-sky landscapes. It is now a Presbyterian conference center and contains two museums, one focusing on paleontology and the other on archeology.

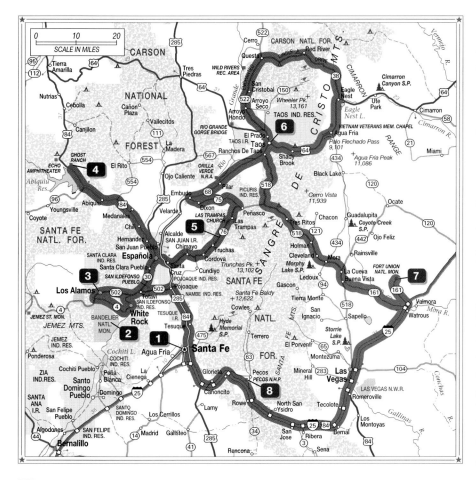

The **Taos Pueblo**, north of town, was the architectural inspiration for the builders of modern Taos and is still home to more than a thousand Indians.

From Taos, detour 11 miles north on Rte. 64 to the **Rio Grande Gorge Bridge**. The second-highest suspension bridge in the U.S. highway system offers a sublime view of the gorge below.

Back on Rte. 522 you'll be cruising the **Enchanted Circle Scenic Drive**, which slices spectacularly through the mountains north and east of Taos and passes **Wheeler Peak**, the highest point in the state at 13,161 feet. The view from **Bobcat Pass** looking down toward the town of Eagle Nest is stunning.

7 FORT UNION

East of the mountains, near what is now Interstate 25, lay the old Santa Fe Trail. From 1851 till the arrival of the railroad, the mission of Fort Union was to supply military posts and protect trailblazing traders and settlers. At the **Fort Union National Monument**, 100-year-old wagon ruts are still etched in the ground near the ruins of the old fort.

5 THE HIGH ROAD TO TAOS

This is yet another wonderful drive, some of it at elevations above 8,000 feet, past old churches and Spanish villages that remain almost untouched by the modern world. **Chimayó** is a weaving center with an adobe church that is venerated as the site of miraculous healings. **Cordova** is known for wood carving but lacks Chimayó's Old World charm. Robert Redford filmed *The Milagro Beanfield War* in **Truchas**, which offers vistas of the Sangre de Cristo and Jemez mountain ranges. **Las Trampas** has a circa-1760 mission church. The end of the route winds through a scented forest of spruce, fir, and aspen.

6 TAOS

Crystalline light and flawless teal skies drew artists here in the 1920's and 30's. Like Santa Fe, modern Taos has been largely commercialized. Although its mountain setting is superior to Santa Fe's—and its artistic past more authentic and its 80-odd art galleries a tad more affordable—the choice of activities in this smaller city is more limited.

Before entering the city, visit the 1815 **San Francisco de Asís Church**, a favorite subject of O'Keeffe's, in the town of Rancho de Taos, south of Taos on Rte. 68. Some of the original artists' and patrons' homes are now museums. Visit the **Mabel Dodge Luhan House**, where the socialite hosted a nonstop art salon. The **Ernest Blumenschein House** is a charming adobe eclectically decorated by the artist, who founded the Taos Society of Artists in 1915, and his wife.

8 PECOS NATIONAL HISTORICAL PARK

Here are the ruins of a Spanish Colonial mission and an ancient pueblo. The original church, damaged in the Pueblo Revolt of 1680, was rebuilt in 1717. Stroll the 1¼-mile self-guided trail among the ruins. The sight of the old mission standing alone in this great valley is a poignant symbol of Spain's futile attempt to hold onto the Southwest with priests rather than with settlers.

Classic adobe structures, like this handsome old church in Abiquiu, are often given protection from the elements by the addition of a layer of cement.

1 RUIDOSO

Southern New Mexico has one of America's harshest deserts, the land the Spanish called *Jornada del Muerto*: the Journey of Death. Its barrenness made it an ideal choice for the testing ground for the first atomic bomb. On either side of the desert, however, ponderosa and fir forests thrive and tiny lakes trap melting snow in 10,000-foot mountain ranges. Ruidoso is a year-round resort that offers skiing in the winter and horse racing in the summer. The world's richest horse race for quarter horses, the **All-American Futurity,** is the highlight of the racing season.

At the **Mescalero Apache Indian Reservation,** just south of Ruidoso, visitors may hunt for bear and elk. The Apache even offer guided deluxe hunts, combined with a stay at the tribe's **Inn of the Mountain Gods,** in Ruidoso.

One detour that's worth the trip is 22 miles west to view well-preserved drawings etched by ancient Indians onto rocks at **Three Rivers Petroglyph Site.**

2 ALAMOGORDO

With an air force base, a missile-testing range, and a landing strip for the space shuttle in the vicinity, this is a logical site for the International Space Hall of Fame. Here are sundry rockets, moon rocks, and detritus from deep space. A theater shows films on space travel, narrated by Walter Cronkite.

A tour to **Ground Zero,** the site where the first atomic bomb explosion took place, is conducted on the first Saturday in April and October. Contact the public affairs office at the White Sands Missile Range for details.

▶ *Although Ground Zero remains slightly radioactive, scientists consider the site harmless.*

For a scenic drive, take the 26-mile trip to the **Sunspot National Solar Ob-**

Prehistoric rock etchings, *or petroglyphs, can be seen at Three Rivers Petroglyph Site.*

servatory in the Sacramento Mountains; on the self-guided tour through the observatory you can see the massive telescopes and watch sunspots dance on video screens. The best desert view is the panorama from **Oliver Lee Memorial State Park,** 13 miles south of Alamogordo via Rte. 54.

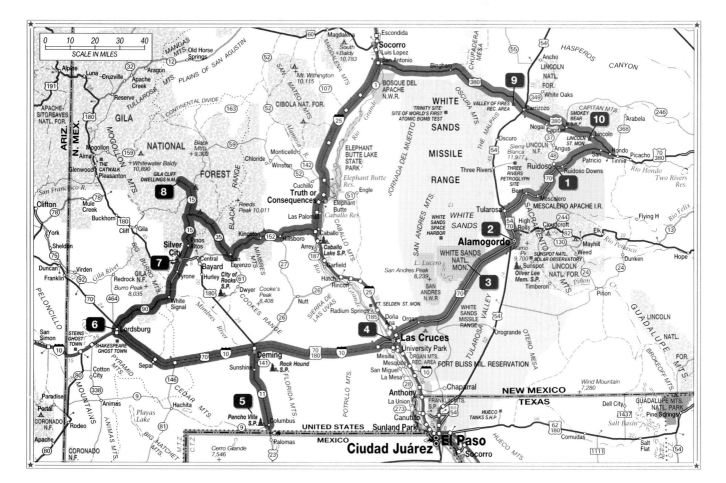

3 WHITE SANDS

Imagine an ocean of white sand, with 50-foot dunes for waves, spreading out as far as the eye can see. The **White Sands National Monument** is one park where you can frolic through the terrain with abandon or fling sand into the air; it matters not, because in a short time your footprints will disappear, and the wind will blow the sand into new shapes. One of the great views of the American West is of the snowcapped peak of 12,000-foot **Sierra Blanca,** to the northeast, seen from a dune in this desert desolation. A 13-mile drive takes visitors through the park. The best time to come is sunrise or sunset, when the dunes are bathed in cozy pink, gray, and purple tones. If you come during the middle of the day, the glare from the white gypsum dunes may overwhelm your eyes and your camera.

4 LAS CRUCES

The second-largest city in the state, Las Cruces lies on the Rio Grande and is the home of New Mexico State University. The adobe ruins of **Fort Selden State Monument,** built to protect settlers from the Apaches, are 13 miles north of town. Pull off the interstate and take scenic Rte. 185, which runs along the river. Just west of town is **Old Mesilla,** which consists of the plaza and original buildings of what was once an Arizona territorial capital and a Butterfield Overland Mail and Stage Line stop. The historic buildings endure, as elsewhere in the West, in their new incarnations as shops and restaurants.

5 PANCHO VILLA STATE PARK

The only invasion of mainland U.S. soil in the 20th century occurred in this barren landscape in March 1916. Pancho Villa, the Mexican bandit and rebel general, crossed the border near Columbus with about 600 men and killed 17 Americans. Although an expedition sent by President Woodrow Wilson chased Villa deep into Mexico, it failed to capture him. Today **Pancho Villa State Park** maintains original structures left over from U.S. army installations in the area. Across the highway a museum in the old railroad depot displays relics from the Villa raid.

6 LORDSBURG

Two of the state's best-preserved ghost towns lie near here. The 19th-century mining town of Shakespeare is just south, and the early-20th-century railroad crossing of Steins is 20 miles west. Billy the Kid, whose tracks can be found almost anywhere in this region, was a dishwasher at the still-standing **Stratford Hotel** in Shakespeare.

▶ *Both ghost towns lie on private property. Steins has been restored and is open daily, but tours of Shakespeare are limited to certain weekends.*

7 SILVER CITY

As the name suggests, Silver City is mining country. Open-pit copper mines and the remnants of old silver mines are very much in evidence. The town's hillside setting above a canyon is picturesque, as is the Victorian-era downtown. A marker designates the cabin site where the omnipresent Billy the Kid lived with his mother; he did his family proud by staging what may have been his first jailbreak here. The mountains to the north were the center of the ancient Mimbres culture, and a collection of highly valued Mimbres pottery is on display at the **Fleming Hall Museum** at New Mexico University.

A sea of sand is anchored by sturdy yucca plants at White Sands National Monument.

8 GILA CLIFF DWELLINGS

A small but dramatic ruin, **Gila Cliff Dwellings National Monument** is unique among the settlements scattered throughout the rugged Mogollon Mountains. Gila Cliff consists of a handful of natural caves sheltering a few rock buildings that were home to the Mogollon people in the 13th century. The wonder of Gila is that anyone would choose such an isolated and difficult domicile. This rough landscape later bred such fierce Indian warriors as the Apache leader Geronimo, born just east, near the forks of the Gila River. An elderly, defeated Geronimo later reminisced about his days as a boy here, when he "moved about like the wind" among the thorny cliffs and canyons rimmed with cottonwood trees.

▶ *Even the automobile cannot easily conquer the remoteness of Gila. The winding road is slow going, and after you arrive at the park, you must walk an uphill trail for almost a mile.*

9 VALLEY OF FIRES

The drive out of Gila through the Mimbres Valley and past the ghost town of **Kingston** is as scenic as any in New Mexico. Beyond Kingston is the Rio Grande and the vast desert terrain. On the other side is **Valley of Fires Recreation Area,** a landscape of black lava clumps and intermittent desert vegetation. Take the three-quarter-mile self-guiding trail that winds through this torturous landscape.

10 LINCOLN STATE MONUMENT

The Lincoln County War of 1878 is not as famous as the Gunfight at the OK Corral, but it lasted longer—six months instead of a few minutes—and proved deadlier. Billy the Kid worked for one faction; when its leader was ambushed, Billy and his cohorts killed many he deemed responsible, including the local sheriff. The general store from that era is part of the monument, and so is the courthouse where the Kid was held before his intended hanging. He escaped, leaving behind a bullet hole for a hundred years of tourists to look at. Nearly three months later, the Kid was killed by the next sheriff in town, Pat Garrett.

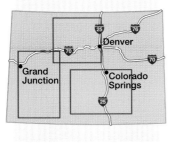

Colorado

The roads that were originally laid out to reach the gold and silver mines at the root of towering peaks now make it easy to see the purple mountains' majesty and colorful history of this state.

1 DENVER

Founded in 1859 to serve gold miners, Colorado's capital is a big city on a flat plain, which may surprise first-time visitors pursuing visions of Rocky Mountain highs. Denver skyscrapers rise below the truly skyscraping peaks of the Front Range to the west, best viewed in the morning from the big windows on the second floor of the **Denver Museum of Natural History** in City Park. The museum's most spectacular exhibit, opening in October 1995, is Prehistoric Journey, with walk-through dioramas of the history of life on earth through the last 3.5 billion years. The excellent **Denver Zoo** is also in City Park, and the **Denver Botanic Gardens** are a short drive away.

The blocky, solid-looking **U.S. Mint** downtown contrasts with the ethereal architecture of the **Denver Art Museum,** which has 28 sides and is home to one of the world's finest collections of American Indian artwork. The **Museum of Western Art** shows the works of more than 50 artists who captured the spirit of the American West. Also downtown is the **Denver Performing Arts Complex,** eight theaters and a symphony hall that surround a stunning block-long glass arch.

The gold-plated dome of Colorado's hilltop **State Capitol** shines above the city, and the 15th step at the west entrance marks exactly one mile above sea level. The nearby **Molly Brown House** gives you a look at the life and times of the unsinkable socialite who saved lives aboard the *Titanic.* Farther north, **Larimer Square** maintains the charm of the past in its cluster of shops and restaurants, all housed in beautifully restored Victorian buildings.

2 RED ROCKS PARK

Erosion and uplift have created a wonder just west of Denver: **Red Rocks Park,** where a 9,000-seat natural amphitheater is set amid gargantuan red sandstone slabs that have remarkable acoustics and provide the grandest possible concert setting.

Nearby are two trails: **Dinosaur Ridge Interpretive Trail,** notable for the dinosaur bones and tracks that can be seen in the sandstone strata, and, near Exit 259, the **I-70 Geological Cut Interpretive Trail,** where a 300-yard-long walkway above the highway provides a view of ancient multicolored rock layers. Signs along the cut explain the forces that created this hogback ridge 120 to 140 million years ago.

▶ *In Colorado's high country, warm means less cool than usual; in some places it may snow any day of the year. So travel with at least a sweater and wind-breaking rainwear.*

3 GEORGETOWN

Many of the more than 200 Georgetown buildings funded by 1863 silver strikes are restored to their Victorian elegance in Georgetown, now joined with the town of Silver Plume in the **Georgetown/Silver Plume National Historic District** to become the state's most picturesque mining town. The **Hamill House Museum** displays the residential luxury enjoyed by a silver baron: behind his 1879 home, a cupolaed outhouse reveals curious class distinctions: black walnut seats (two adult-sized, one child-sized) on the family's side of the partition and three of plain pine on the servants' side.

With tracks only three feet apart, narrow-gauge railroads negotiated tight curves when climbing to mountain mines. One of the most remarkable grades was a series of trestles and curves over which trains climbed 700 feet between Georgetown and Silver Plume. The towns were only two miles apart, but 4½ miles by the **Georgetown Loop Railroad,** which re-creates during the warm months the irresistible excitement of narrow-gauge railroading.

4 FRISCO

This town sits in the heart of Summit County, a winter sports hub with four major ski resorts—Arapahoe Basin, Keystone, Breckenridge, and Copper Mountain. Frisco's **Gold Rush Festival** in February (with a dogsled race called the Gold Mush) is a reminder of the area's mining past. Old mines lie beneath the waters of **Dillon Reservoir,**

T. Rex greets visitors to the Denver Museum of Natural History, where the Prehistoric Journey exhibit offers a walk-through environment of ancient plants, mammals, and dinosaurs.

A **camper** makes its way through the alpine tundra of Rocky Mountain National Park.

the 3,300-acre reservoir that supplies water to the dry east side of the Rocky Mountains through a 23-mile-long tunnel and provides cool summer recreation for water sports enthusiasts.

5 LEADVILLE

At 10,430 feet above sea level, Leadville is the nation's highest incorporated city. Rising south of town are Colorado's tallest peaks, Mount Elbert (14,433 feet) and Mount Massive (14,419 feet).

High living meant more than high elevation when Leadville boomed on silver wealth in the 1870's and 80's. Its downtown, restored to recall those high-spending days, is highlighted by the **Tabor Opera House,** built by mining magnate Horace Tabor. Tabor lived a soap opera, divorcing his loyal wife Augusta to marry young and beautiful Elizabeth McCourt (Baby) Doe. High living and falling silver prices impoverished the couple in the 1890's. On his deathbed in 1899, Horace urged Baby Doe to hang on to the **Matchless Mine.** Visitors to the mine shack see where she froze to death in 1935, waiting in vain for the Matchless to boom again.

Healy House, built in 1878 as the first substantial home in town, re-creates its 1899 status as a boardinghouse for lady schoolteachers: in summer, guides taking roles as teachers lead visitors through the house.

On your drive from Leadville to Steamboat Springs, stop at **Finger Rock,** a looming volcanic spire 350 feet tall along Rte. 131 between Toponas and Yampa. Twenty-four million to 8 million years ago, the towering rock was a conduit to the surface for molten lava. Eventually, the lava solidified and resisted the erosion that removed the surrounding sandstone.

▶ There is no access to the rock spire, but you can pull off Rte. 131 for a longer look or to take photos.

6 STEAMBOAT SPRINGS

A hot spring, noisily emitting spray like a steamboat's exhaust into the Yampa River, gave this ski resort its name. Though the spring has lost its dramatic emissions, more than 150 other springs still testify to the area's volcanic past. Some hot springs feed spas that ease skiers' sore muscles. This part of Colorado also attracts visitors to Fish Creek Falls and the flower-filled meadows along Rte. 40 where it crosses the Continental Divide at Rabbit Ears Pass.

7 ROCKY MOUNTAIN NATIONAL PARK

Colorado's most popular tourist attraction, this park is packed with mountain scenery crowned by 14,255-foot Longs Peak. Most summer visitors drive **Trail Ridge Road,** which climbs to 12,183

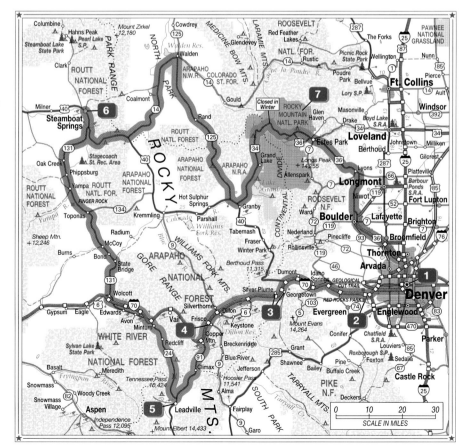

feet and meanders for 11 miles above the tree line. The road's vistas extend across flower- and snow-spangled meadows and glacier-carved precipices. The road is closed for as much as two-thirds of the year by winter winds that can approach 200 miles per hour. The nine-mile spur road to **Bear Lake** is open all year and is served by a free shuttle in summer that helps visitors to avoid fighting traffic. Nowhere in Colorado is wildlife so abundant or easy to see as in this park. Common sightings include mule deer, elk, and bighorn sheep, as well as coyotes, ground squirrels, chipmunks, and a wide variety of birds. The National Park Service offers free walks throughout the year to interpret the park's wildlife and scenery.

1 GRAND JUNCTION

Colorado National Monument boasts stone pillars rising from a maze of cliff-walled, 600-foot-deep canyons. Between the east and west entrances, 23-mile-long **Rim Rock Drive** twists past spectacular precipices sculpted by water and wind. Four miles from the west entrance, a visitor center contains displays explaining the scenery and the cultural history of the area. Scenic turnouts along Rim Rock Drive bear such appropriate names as Redlands, Grand View, and Cold Shivers Point.

In downtown Grand Junction, the **Dinosaur Valley Museum** features paleontology. Fossils, large photos of historic dinosaur-hunting expeditions, and half-sized animated models of dinosaurs form an impressive display.

▶ *Some of the shorter scenic trails in Colorado National Monument offer better views than does Rim Rock Drive. Longer trails are more arduous but take you into the canyons.*

2 RIFLE

North of this town, **Rifle Falls State Park** nestles in a narrow valley lined with red sandstone cliffs. Water from East Rifle Creek flows over an 80-foot cliff, forming a trio of waterfalls that plunge into a gentle stream meandering the length of the park. The creek also nourishes a lush environment of cottonwoods, ferns, and mosses.

Coyote Trail, one of the park's two hiking trails, begins at the base of the falls and takes you alongside the cliffs above the creek. Here you'll find numerous caves that you can explore.

3 GLENWOOD SPRINGS

This town takes its name from the largest outdoor mineral-hot-spring pool in the world—100 feet wide by 405 feet long. Emerging at 124°F., the spring's water mixes with surface water to average a comfortable 88° to 90°. A smaller therapy pool soothes its occupants at 104°. Because air temperature at Glenwood Springs is almost always cooler than the water, steam hangs above the pool most of the time; in winter it becomes dense fog.

The spring has a flow of 3.5 million gallons of water per day; the water in the big pool changes in six hours, and the water in the therapy pool in two.

4 REDSTONE

Redstone may be the quaintest village in Colorado. John Osgood, who built the town in 1903 for coal miners who worked for him, designed it to be delightful. Named for the colorful cliffs surrounding the narrow Crystal River valley, Redstone contains small, charming houses, each one architecturally unique. The **Redstone Inn,** now a ho-

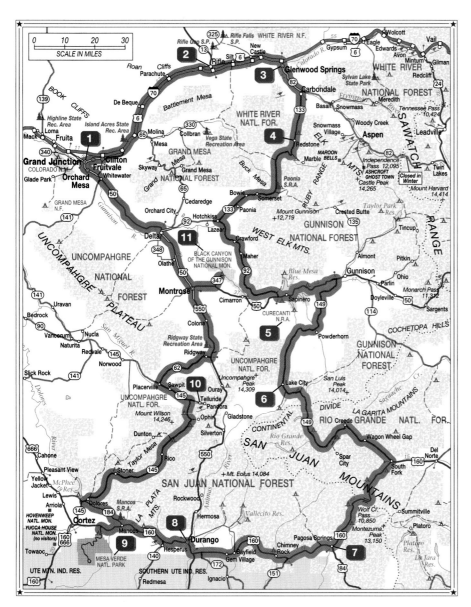

A narrow-gauge train chugs along the Animas River from Durango to Silverton.

tel, was built for unmarried miners and provided them with the amenities of an exclusive club. A short way upstream from his superb company town, Osgood built a residence for himself, the 42-room **Cleveholm Manor**, popularly called Redstone Castle—but spent little time living there. Today the mansion is open for tours; visitors can take a horse-drawn wagon or a sleigh ride to the mansion from town.

5 CURECANTI NATIONAL RECREATION AREA

Three reservoirs along the Gunnison River—Blue Mesa, Morrow Point, and Crystal—are part of the Colorado River Storage Project. Fishing is popular on **Blue Mesa**. During summer on **Morrow Point**, a National Park Service naturalist accompanies 90-minute boat tours to point out historic, scenic, and geological highlights of the lake's canyon setting. **Morrow Point Dam** is an engineering landmark, the nation's first double-curvature thin-arch concrete dam. Rte. 92, which cuts in and out of the recreation area, offers many fine views. Particularly notable is the dramatic 800-foot rock pillar called **Curecanti Needle**, which sits within Morrow Point Lake, separated from the canyon's 1,000-foot walls.

6 LAKE CITY

Lake San Cristobal is the second-largest natural lake in Colorado and certainly was the most quickly created. More than 700 years ago, the Slumgullion Earthflow (whose name comes from a local miner's stew the same color as the soil) blocked the Lake Fork of the Gunnison River. A huge mass of partially decomposed volcanic rock broke away from the towering **Cannibal Plateau**, at an elevation of 11,500 feet, and slumped four miles downhill to the Lake Fork.

Irreverent surveyors named Cannibal Plateau in 1874 for an adventurer, Alferd [sic] Packer, who killed, robbed, and ate his five traveling companions during a prolonged blizzard. The event is recounted on a marker 2½ miles south of Lake City, near the bridge where Rte. 149 crosses Lake Fork.

7 PAGOSA SPRINGS

Pagosa is a Ute Indian word meaning "healing waters," and the 153° F. water created Pagosa Springs' popularity as a spa in the late 1800's. **Treasure Falls**, named for a legendary lost gold cache, drops over a volcanic cliff a few steps away from Rte. 160, 15 miles north of Pagosa Springs.

Twenty miles west of the town, **Chimney Rock Archeological Area** marks the site of one of the most intriguing Anasazi Indian ruins. The Indians who lived here formed a community that seems to have functioned as an outpost of trade and an astronomy center rather than as a typical farming village.

▶ To visit Chimney Rock, take a Forest Service guided tour, conducted by the Pagosa Springs ranger office.

8 DURANGO

The **Durango and Silverton Narrow-Gauge Railroad**, belching steam and smoke and blasting its whistle, chugs out of the historic downtown area of Durango on a 3¼-hour trip through 44 miles of precipitous scenery to the little town of Silverton. Since 1882, this train has clickety-clacked through narrow rock cuts, along a ledge blasted 400 feet above the Animas River, and into deep gorges below jagged 13,000-foot peaks. Yellow passenger cars behind a coal-fired locomotive carry you back to the 1800's; open gondola cars bring up the rear. A two-hour layover in the mining town of Silverton provides time to roam the 19th-century streets.

▶ One of Colorado's premier attractions, this narrow-gauge trip usually fills to capacity in summer; reserve seats one to two months ahead.

9 MESA VERDE NATIONAL PARK

Suspended 2,000 feet above the Mancos and Montezuma valleys and preserved as a national park in 1906, the magical cliff dwellings, named "green table" by Spanish explorers because of the verdant tree cover and flatness of the ridges, are one of the world's most important archeological sites. A twisting mountain road of 21 miles separates the ruins from the outside world.

Mysterious Cliff Palace at Mesa Verde National Park has stood unoccupied for more than 700 years. The ruins are most beautiful around 6:00 P.M., when the sun's warm glow gives the best light for photographs.

Boomtown turned resort, Telluride today is a chic playground for skiers and tourists alike.

Chapin Mesa Archeological Museum sits on a canyon rim overlooking Spruce Tree House, a cliff dwelling. Other sites nearby include the largest of all the cliff dwellings, **Cliff Palace.**

▶ *Hiking is restricted, and it is forbidden to enter any cliff dwelling unless you're accompanied by a ranger.*

10 TELLURIDE

Because of their volcanic origin, the San Juan Mountains, whose 14,000-foot peaks encircle Telluride, contain deposits of gold and silver that created a brawling mining camp, sometimes pronounced to-hell-you-ride in the 1880's . In 1889 Butch Cassidy withdrew a reported $30,000 from the Telluride Bank at gunpoint. Restored Victorian buildings today contrast with modern condominiums, as Telluride takes advantage of the silver streams, golden aspen leaves, and glistening snow to draw tourists to the incomparable scenery of **Uncompahgre National Forest.**

11 BLACK CANYON OF THE GUNNISON

Extremely hard Precambrian rock enables the canyon walls bordering 12 miles of the Gunnison River to resist erosion and remain high and steep. Viewpoints on the opposite sides of

Black Canyon of the Gunnison National Monument sometimes are closer to each other (1,100 feet at Chasm View) than to the river 1,730 feet to 2,425 feet below. Dark rock and deep shadows gave the canyon its name—with a floor so dark, legend has it, that you can see the stars at noon. Hikes to the floor are arduous; vehicle access to the river from East Portal Road.

PLAINS & SOARING PEAKS

1 COLORADO SPRINGS

When railroad investor Gen. William J. Palmer founded Colorado Springs in 1871 specifically to serve tourists, he cleverly included the word *springs* to popularize his resort, even though there are no springs in the town. Nevertheless, **Manitou Springs** does bubble up nearby, its waters carbonated by passing through limestone.

Today the city boasts a number of other attractions, including the **Colorado Springs Fine Arts Center,** with an extensive collection of Hispanic, American Indian, and Western art. And on the western edge of town, the dramatic red sandstone pillars and cliffs in

the **Garden of the Gods,** a city park, are striking examples of free-form sculpture by wind and weather.

Rising above it all is **Pikes Peak,** the state's most famous mountain. Although its elevation of 14,110 feet ranks only in the mid-30's among the more than 50 Colorado peaks that tower 14,000 feet or higher, it attracts up to a million people to its summit each year. The sterling view from Pikes Peak inspired Katharine Lee Bates to write "America, the Beautiful," the nation's beloved patriotic hymn.

2 BENT'S OLD FORT

A short drive east of La Junta, **Bent's Old Fort National Historic Site** is a meticulous reconstruction of the adobe castle from which the Bent brothers, Charles and William, and Ceran St. Vrain ran a trading empire. Though some of the original fort burned down in 1849, National Park Service archeologists have rebuilt it with attention to detail that would fool Kit Carson and the other mountain men and Indians who knew the fort in the 1830's and 40's. Costumed in period dress accurate down to the buttons, interpreters relive for visitors the colorful activity of a frontier trading post in the mid 19th century, when the seeds of Manifest Destiny were taking root.

▶ *Cars must be parked several hundred yards from Bent's Old Fort. The Park Service provides transport for those unable to walk the distance.*

"Our Lady of the Rosary," in the Colorado Springs Fine Arts Center, was carved by a Hispanic artist in the 19th century.

3 FORT GARLAND

A farming community now surrounds **Fort Garland** in the San Luis Valley. The fort was built in 1858 to protect the area from Indian raids, and Col. Kit Carson was the commander here for two years. Abandoned in 1883, the atmospheric adobe fort now stands restored to its Carson-era appearance by the State Historical Society of Colorado.

spot and now covers 39 square miles at the base of the mountains. Constantly reshaped by the wind, some of the dunes rise as high as 700 feet.

5 ALAMOSA/MONTE VISTA NATIONAL WILDLIFE REFUGES

These refuges, named for nearby towns, are irresistibly attractive to sandhill cranes; thousands of these huge birds

an aerial tramway span the gorge, and an incline railway takes visitors to the bottom. From various viewing points along the rim, the Arkansas River at the bottom of the gorge looks like a tiny glittering ribbon, bordered by railroad tracks that are barely visible. The best—and least crowded—view of the gorge is from a picnic ground perched high above the river. To reach the spot, turn left at the short (.7-mile) side road that leaves County Rte. 3A. Early-morning light provides the best viewing.

7 CRIPPLE CREEK

An 1891 gold strike in the collapsed center of an ancient volcano made Cripple Creek the last of Colorado's mining boomtowns. By World War II its mines had dumped so much gold on world markets that the price fell, and diminished ores and fluctuating gold prices eventually ended Cripple Creek's prosperity. You can relive the glory days of the 1890's on tours that venture 1,000 feet deep into the **Mollie Kathleen Mine**, and in the **Cripple Creek District Museum**, where 12 rooms highlight the social life—and hard work—of this once-thriving mining

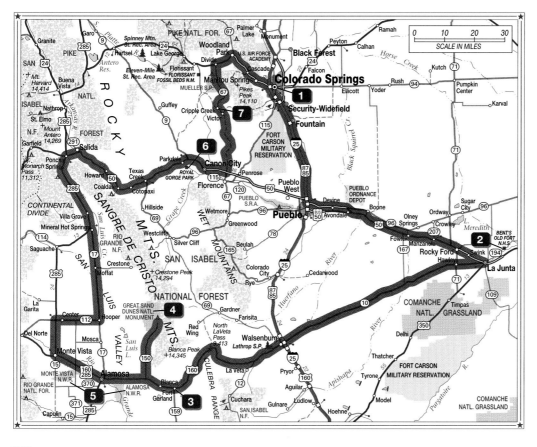

4 GREAT SAND DUNES

Great Sand Dunes National Monument is a little bit of the Sahara in Colorado. You'll feel the high winds in the wide, flat, dry San Luis Valley and observe the massive ridge of the Sangre de Cristo Mountains towering over the dunes. The ridge forms a windbreak, and as winds pass over it, they drop sand grains sucked from the valley.

▶ *Very early in the morning or in the evening are the best times to visit, when low light angles make the dunes particularly impressive.*

Over the course of 15,000 years, the sand has accumulated in this sheltered

drop in here to rest during their spring and fall migrations between Idaho and New Mexico. Accompanying them may be a few endangered whooping cranes. Also present are thousands of waterfowl and, in winter, abundant bald eagles.

The Monte Vista refuge offers a three-mile auto tour off Rte. 15, plus a dozen miles of county roads among its wetlands. Most of Alamosa's wildlife turns up near a bluff overlook along the two-mile road located off El Rancho Lane.

6 ROYAL GORGE

The Royal Gorge, near Canon City, is cut 1,053 feet deep by the Arkansas River. The world's highest suspension bridge, the **Royal Gorge Bridge**, and

town. The limited-stakes gambling that is permitted in Cripple Creek today helps recapture the rip-roaring mood of the town's boisterous boom days.

Three railroads hauled Cripple Creek's wealth at the height of its gold production. All are gone except for a four-mile stretch of the **Cripple Creek and Victor Narrow-Gauge Railroad,** which hauls visitors through an area of abandoned mines. The twisting routes of the other two railroads are now interesting unpaved—but passable—roads: the **Gold Camp Road** winds past several abandoned mines on its way to Colorado Springs, while the **Phantom Canyon Road** winds through a dramatic gorge to Canon City.

Wyoming

When you're in Wyoming, you're about as deep as you can get into the Old West. Savor the remarkable past of Cheyenne and Laramie and be amazed by the wonders of Yellowstone Park.

YELLOWSTONE & THE WEST

1 YELLOWSTONE NATIONAL PARK

In 1872, when the West was still wild, the world's first national park was established across an astounding natural wonderland in the northwest corner of the Wyoming Territory. The huge tract of more than 3,400 square miles spills over into adjacent Idaho and Montana, where—it may be noted for historical perspective—another four years would elapse before Custer's Last Stand. Clearly, our pioneering ancestors saw something unique and worthy of eternal preservation in this game-rich Canaan along the Continental Divide at elevations ranging up to almost 12,000 feet.

▶ *The park newspaper,* Yellowstone Today, *is essential reading for tips on safety, campgrounds, concessions, and ranger-led activities.*

The Grand Loop Road, shaped like a figure eight, traverses the park's major attractions in a 142-mile circuit. Many of the most famous geysers and hot springs lie along the western portion of this road, the 50 miles between **Mammoth Hot Springs** and **Old Faithful.** The trademark geyser, now spouting off at intervals averaging 75 minutes, is only the most glamorous of Yellowstone's galaxy of geothermal stars. The park's fumaroles, geysers, hot springs, and mud pots are the fascinating manifestations of water mixing with a seething volcanic mass down below— the remains of a giant caldera, or basin, a 47-mile-wide remnant of the last great volcanic explosion 600,000 years ago.

A visitor to the park is rarely out of sight of lakes and rivers of ethereal beauty. **Yellowstone Lake,** at 20 by 14 miles, is the largest mountain lake in North America. And the Yellowstone River's supreme spectacle, the **Grand Canyon of the Yellowstone,** unfolds

Elks *lounge on the white travertine ledges of Opal Terrace at Mammoth Hot Springs.*

from a variety of lookout points near Canyon Village. The 308-foot drop of the **Lower Falls** still looks as it did when such pioneer 19th-century landscape artists as Thomas Moran captured the beauties of the park for the world.

▶ *If you're camping in summer, choose a campsite before noon; the sites are usually filled by then.*

The park is not without significant hazards. Geothermal pools can exceed boiling temperatures; some lie hidden under fragile crusts. Boardwalks and sternly marked trails are there to protect environment and visitors alike. And no one should enter without a healthy respect for the fascinating animal population, especially the bears.

2 CODY

Named for its founder and promoter, the great frontiersman and showman William F. (Buffalo Bill) Cody, this handsome town astride Yellowstone's eastern gateway is home to one of America's great museums. The **Buffalo Bill Historical Center** is in fact four superb collections: the **Buffalo Bill Museum,** including Cody's personal memorabilia and such glamorous artifacts as the Deadwood Stage, a fixture of his shows; the **Whitney Gallery of West-**

The Yellowstone River *plunges over Lower Falls in the Grand Canyon of the Yellowstone.*

ern Art, with representative works by such major figures as Charles M. Russell and Frederic Remington; the **Cody Firearms Museum**, the preeminent collection of American firearms; and the **Plains Indian Museum**, a huge gathering of the rarest art and artifacts.

Yet another important museum stands just outside Cody on the Yellowstone Road. **Trail Town** is a collection of more than two dozen authentic Wyoming frontier structures, scores of horse-drawn vehicles, and other relics of the Old West.

3 THERMOPOLIS

Here's a town that delivers what its name (Greek for "Hot City") promises:

one of the world's largest mineral hot springs. Now a part of **Hot Springs State Park** on the edge of town, the natural wonder has been developed with a variety of water slides and indoor and outdoor swimming pools. Fanciers of Americana, recalling Butch Cassidy and the Sundance Kid, will want to visit the **Hot Springs County Museum and Cultural Center**, where they'll find the ornate saloon bar said to have dispensed cheer to the outlaws.

4 SOUTH PASS CITY

Founded in 1867 when prospectors struck gold nearby, South Pass City flowered for five years, its half-mile-long main street boasting seven hotels

and numerous saloons and sporting houses. The first boom ended in 1872, and South Pass City, after a series of booms and busts, became a ghost town. Today, preserved as **South Pass City State Historic Site**, this quintessential Wild West town retains about two dozen old buildings, some with museum displays and period rooms.

5 FLAMING GORGE

A 92-mile-long blue-water reservoir, winding through a landscape that ranges from desert to lush foothills to jagged mountains, is the centerpiece of **Flaming Gorge National Recreation Area**, the rugged playground on the Wyoming-Utah border. Two visitor centers, various marinas and campgrounds, and more than 100 miles of hiking trails lure the traveler who seeks the great outdoors and isn't afraid of a little strenuous activity. Other pursuits here are boating, water-skiing, and fishing—all excellent.

6 FORT BRIDGER

In 1843 the legendary frontiersman Jim Bridger, cashing in on the just-beginning flood of immigrants on the Oregon Trail, established a small fort, blacksmith shop, and supply depot beside the trail in the southwestern corner of Wyoming. Ten years later it was taken over by the Mormons, and in 1857 it became a U.S. Army outpost. By 1890 it had been abandoned. Historic preservation since the 1920's has culminated in today's restored setting, **Fort Bridger State Historic Site**, where some 20 buildings and other sites capture elements of all periods of Fort Bridger's brief and turbulent history. Two buildings that can be toured here are the reconstructed 1884 commanding officer's quarters, furnished in mid-1880's style, and a re-creation of **Jim Bridger's Trading Post**, where a costumed mountain man and his wife sell assorted trade goods—hats, knives, furs, beads, and more—to visitors.

7 FOSSIL BUTTE

Here at **Fossil Butte National Monument**, in a semiarid desert landscape of sagebrush and pale, flat-topped buttes, the silence of stone preserves a 50-mil-

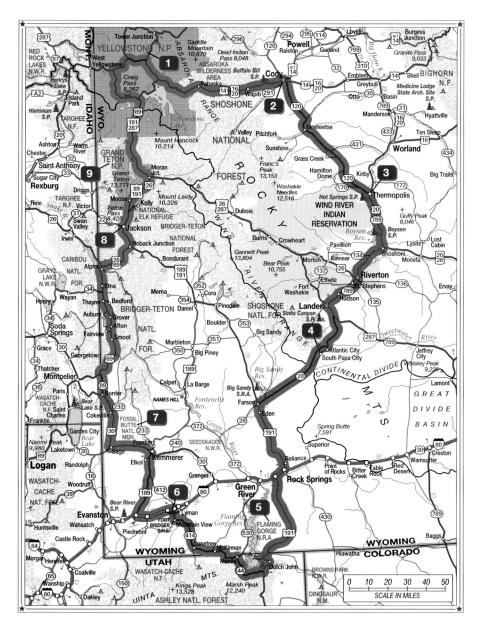

lion-year-old record of teeming animal and plant life. Fish, turtles, birds, flowers—their imprints have been found here by the millions over more than a century of digging by amateur and professional paleontologists. Such activity is tightly restricted today, but plenty of fossils are to be seen. The visitor center displays more than 20 species of fossilized fish, in addition to bats, crocodiles, and alligators, and an artist's rendition of how the region looked as a great lake in the Cenozoic Era.

8 JACKSON

Redolent of the Old West with its frontier architecture and memories of mountain men, rustlers, trappers, and Indians, the atmosphere-rich town of Jackson is a colorful tourist center. The **Wildlife National Art Museum** is an important stop, as is the **Jackson Hole Museum**, with its Western artifacts. Dude ranching, skiing, mountain climbing, and river float trips all are nearby. Among the West's great winter spectacles is the **National Elk Refuge**, where between November and May a herd averaging 8,000 of the majestic animals winters on the foothill meadows just outside town.

9 GRAND TETON NATIONAL PARK

Yellowstone's southern neighbor makes up for its smaller size with mountain panoramas of transcendent beauty, many of them easily viewed from the park-spanning John D. Rockefeller, Jr., Memorial Parkway. The **Teton Range**, jutting angularly upward to the 13,771-foot summit of Grand Teton, towers dramatically over the valley called Jackson Hole. Clear mountain lakes, sparkling rivers, and deep evergreen forests complete the picture. At the town of Moose, the National Park Service visitor center illuminates the natural history and geography of the region, aided by an easy half-mile-long trail of historic sights. On the northern end of the park, by Jackson Lake, the **Colter Bay Indian Arts Museum** displays Plains Indian artifacts and art. The region's vast menu of outdoor activities includes scenic drives, float trips, hiking, fishing, and horseback riding.

1 CHEYENNE

In 1867 a Union Pacific Railroad construction crew roared into a frontier crossroads and swiftly hammered up the rowdy archetype of frontier Western boomtowns that became Cheyenne. Unlike many others of the breed, this city would endure. By 1869, when the transcontinental railroad was finished, it was important enough to become the territorial capital. The present **State Capitol** dates from 1887, three years before statehood was achieved; beneath its golden-domed roof are murals depicting Wyoming's colorful history. A fuller account unfolds nearby at the **Wyoming State Museum**, where visitors trace the history of Plains Indians and the coming of settlers and railroads. The **Historic Governor's Mansion** was the first to shelter a woman governor, Nellie Tayloe Ross, in 1925.

▶ *Buy tickets at the convention bureau, located downtown on Lincoln Way, for a two-hour tour through Cheyenne's five historic districts.*

The town's past is linked inseparably and fondly to the pioneer spirit and Wyoming's ranching traditions. As early

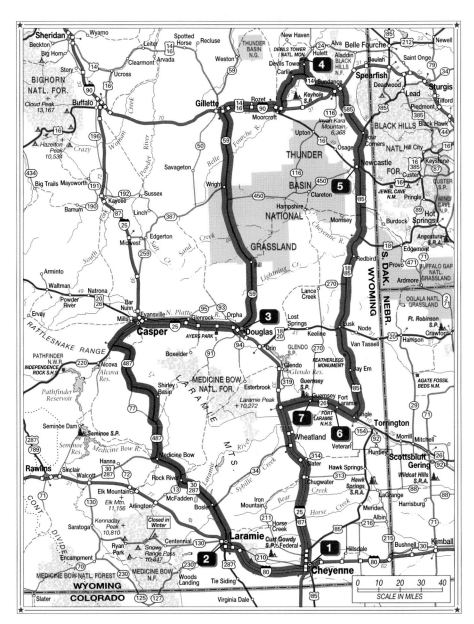

A bronco buster takes a tumble at the Cheyenne Frontier Days rodeo, known by cowboys as the "Daddy of 'em all." The rodeo, held every day of the festival, offers three hours of nonstop action.

as 1897, the region's ranchers and businessmen were growing worried at the rapid disappearance of the old frontier atmosphere, and to preserve it they began a great annual festival called **Frontier Days.** It continues today in the last full week of July. Lavish parades of Western riders, dances, a carnival, outdoor pancake breakfasts, and headline entertainment complement the main attraction: a gigantic daily rodeo at Frontier Park. The **Cheyenne Frontier Days Old West Museum** displays one of the largest collections of horse-drawn vehicles in the world, along with Western regalia and art.

2 LARAMIE

Like Cheyenne, Laramie boomed with the arrival of the Union Pacific; in 1868

Pancakes by the thousands satisfy the crowds at the Frontier Days festival.

the town was so wild that vigilantes introduced the attention-getting technique of multiple hanging. An echo of those brash days sounds at **Wyoming Territorial Park,** whose Western heritage theme is linked to the restored territorial prison of 1872. The park includes a frontier town, the National U.S. Marshals Museum, a dinner theater, and living-history programs.

Laramie's view of the future takes precedence at the 12,000-student University of Wyoming. The school welcomes visitors to its seven museums, where they may find particular interest in the **Fine Arts Center,** the **American Heritage Center,** and a fine geological museum. Nearby, the **Laramie Plains Museum** is housed in the grand Victorian Ivinson Mansion.

3 DOUGLAS

Douglas, site of the State Fair late each August, is visited year-round for its **Wyoming Pioneer Memorial Museum.** Its colorful and eclectic displays of relics range from the saddle of Tom Horn—a controversial range detective and gunman whose life ended on a Cheyenne gallows—to Victorian dresses and lamps. The museum's greatest strength is its collection of Indian artifacts and decorative arts.

4 DEVILS TOWER

This monstrous stumplike formation, rising 1,280 feet above the Belle Fourche River, is a many-columned volcanic plug that was left standing alone when the sedimentary rock

around it eroded away. President Theodore Roosevelt in 1906 declared the tower America's first national monument. Today the 1½-acre summit of **Devils Tower National Monument** is a popular rock-climbing destination.

5 NEWCASTLE

Like its namesake in England, Newcastle was a coal town. Now, however, this western gateway to the Black Hills puts an emphasis on oil. One of the leading attractions is the **Accidental Well,** said to be the nation's only hand-dug oil well. Guided tours show you drilling tools and pumps, and take you into a producing well.

6 FORT LARAMIE

Here, at **Fort Laramie National Historic Site,** is the real Old West: a major fur-trading and U.S. Army frontier outpost where the buglers sounded Boots and Saddles. In addition to guarding the Oregon, California, and Mormon trails, it was an important stop on the Overland Stage Line and the Pony Express, and a protector of the early transcontinental telegraph system.

▶ *The fort's bakery will show you how bread was made in the 1870's—and you may get a freshly baked sample.*

Fort Laramie played an important role for years in both conflicts and peace parleys with the Plains Indians. Today some 22 original buildings still stand, echoing those stirring days with living-history programs, period rooms, and museum exhibits.

7 GUERNSEY

Near Guernsey **Oregon Trail Ruts State Historic Site** shows the deep ruts that were gouged from sandstone outcroppings by thousands of lumbering pioneer wagons. The remains of the trail are today a silent memorial, heading eternally westward along the North Platte River. At nearby **Register Cliff,** the pioneers liked to record their names or initials and the date they passed by, sometimes adding the name of their hometown back east—a fascinating personal memento of the brave parade that was perhaps 350,000 souls long.

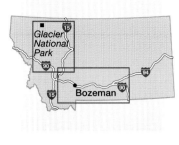

Montana

Stretch out in roomy Montana, from the open prairie under a "great house of sky" to the snow-dusted Rockies, where chinook winds snake down to warm the verdant valleys below.

SOUTH CENTRAL MONTANA

1 BOZEMAN

This university town looks much like a turn-of-the-century movie set, albeit marked by the trappings of modern life. Hundred-year-old stores sit beside bike shops and gourmet food stores. The study of the region's rich natural and cultural history thrives in this academic setting; each is handsomely represented in the city's number-one attraction, the

The Wild West *lives on in this reconstruction of the Dance & Stuart Store in Virginia City. Inside are goods typical of those sold in a 19th-century general store (above).*

Museum of the Rockies, on the Montana State University campus. On view is the pride of the museum: *Maiasaura peeblesorum,* a plant-eating dinosaur and the state fossil. Dioramas re-create a day in the life of a maiasaur some 80 million years ago, when the dinosaur roamed present-day Montana. The dinosaur *Tyrannosaurus rex* is here represented by the cast of a skull excavated in eastern Montana in 1991. Other museum highlights are a Sioux tepee and a 1930's service station.

Spreading from Bozeman 50 miles south to Yellowstone National Park is **Gallatin National Forest,** a vast woodland reserve. Take the scenic **Gallatin Canyon** road, Rte. 191, and trace the curving Gallatin River south through mountain country. Cross-country skiers can rent cozy, rustic cabins from the Forest Service for backwoods skiing on groomed trails. Montana's reputation as a fly fisherman's paradise is confirmed here in the icy headwaters of the Gallatin, Madison, and Yellowstone rivers.

Contact the Fishing Outfitters Association of Montana to engage a guide who can direct you to some of the clearest, frothiest streams and most spirited trout in the country.

▶ *Out-of-staters can buy two-day or season fishing licenses at most sporting-goods stores. The more than 300 public-access fishing sites are marked by a fish-and-hook sign. Maps are available from the Montana Department of Fish, Wildlife and Parks.*

2 VIRGINIA CITY/NEVADA CITY

It is said that Montana's 19th-century gold rush was so rich that a fortune hunter could "shake a dollar's worth of dust from an uprooted sagebrush." The raw frontier town of Virginia City glittered as Montana's gold capital in the 1860's and attracted not only gold hunters but cardsharps, prostitutes, and stagecoach robbers. Although the assorted riffraff swept out of Virginia City as quickly as they came, leaving a ghostly shell, a rakish boomtown flavor permeates the site today, where Old West structures line wooden sidewalks against a big-sky backdrop.

Just 1½ miles west, Nevada City is a living-history museum of an 1860's mining camp. The oldest standing post office in the state—a simple frame structure, its wood planks burnished by the elements—can be toured. Throughout the summer, the **Alder Gulch Work Train,** a narrow-gauge railroad, shuttles visitors between the two towns.

3 LEWIS AND CLARK CAVERNS

Hidden beneath the foothills of the Tobacco Root Mountains are connecting underground passageways created millions of years ago. At **Lewis and Clark Caverns State Park,** visitors can go down into the caves on two-hour, two-mile guided tours. Mineral deposits in the caverns have fashioned limestone formations into comely columns, pillows, and draperies.

4 WHITE SULPHUR SPRINGS

For centuries visitors have been drawn to these thermal mineral springs for recreation and possible relief from such sundry afflictions as arthritis, rheumatism, and stress. The springs lie in the center of town, where they are used to heat the water at the **Spa Hot Springs Motel,** which offers bathing in the two mineral pools. Between immersions, visit the **Castle,** an 1892 mansion and museum. Built from hand-cut blocks of granite quarried in the Castle Mountains, the Castle houses period furniture and antique clothes.

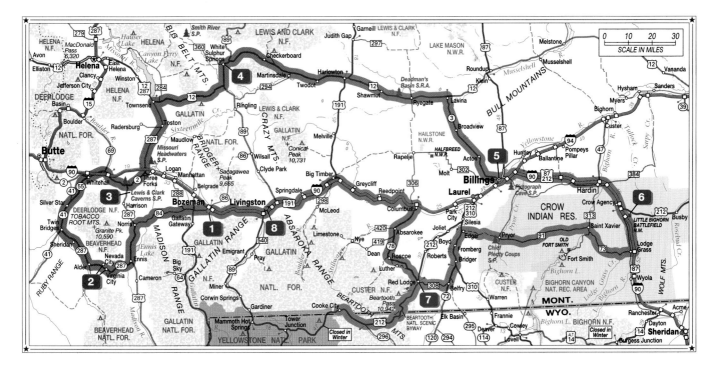

5 BILLINGS

As a bustling center of farming and the cattle trade, Montana's largest city swaggers with throngs of ropin' cowpokes and nonstop rodeo competition. This gateway to the New West is also the gateway to the Big Open country of eastern Montana—a vast, sweeping landscape that Montana writer Ivan Doig called "this great house of sky."

One of the state's most prominent turn-of-the-century bankers built a stunning mansion near the heart of the city. P. B. Moss died in 1947, but so many of his original furnishings remain at **Moss Mansion** that his presence is vividly felt. Inside, Moss's eclectic tastes are revealed in the mansion's Moorish entryway, Shakespearean library, Tudor dining room, and formal French parlor.

6 LITTLE BIGHORN BATTLEFIELD

On these sprawling fields of yellow-budded sweet clover, the last stand of Lt. Col. George Armstrong Custer was over in less than an hour. Dominating one of the final armed conflicts between northern Plains Indians and the U.S. cavalry, a much larger force of Sioux and Cheyenne warriors overwhelmed Custer and his troops on June 25, 1876. When it was over, the flamboyant cavalry officer and approximately 210 soldiers under his command lay dead on a knoll overlooking the Little

Bighorn Valley. The event is commemorated at **Little Bighorn Battlefield National Monument,** on the site of the battle. You can take self-guided auto and walking tours year-round.

Plains Indian powwows are held year-round at the seven reservations in Montana. The largest celebration is the **Crow Fair Powwow Rodeo and Race Meet,** at the Crow Reservation in Crow Agency every third weekend in August.

▶ *Follow powwow protocol: flash photography is not allowed during dance contests, and it is polite to ask before you flash at other events. Visitors can join in during the Round Dance, but at other times the dance area is sacred. Bring lawn chairs or blankets, as seating is usually limited.*

A powwow participant waits for her cue at the Crow Fair Powwow Rodeo and Race Meet.

7 RED LODGE

The switchbacks may seem serpentine and the heights formidable, but views from the **Beartooth National Scenic Byway** are among the most spectacular in America. Completed in 1936, the scenic road runs south from Red Lodge to Cooke City. Open only from late May to mid-October, the twisting 67-mile route takes at least 2½ hours to drive and climbs to elevations of up to 11,000 feet; it is definitely not for speeders. A number of pull-offs allow motorists to stop and admire a constantly changing panorama of glacial canyons and craggy peaks. In summer, wildflowers color the mountain slopes.

8 LIVINGSTON

This genial little town at the head of Paradise Valley was home to Calamity Jane. Of late it has attracted celebrities of the 20th-century variety, who have made this lush valley ringed by mountains their place of residence. The surrounding region is dude ranch country, where guests can snag hefty trout in blue-ribbon Yellowstone streams by day and dine by moonlight at night. Call the Montana Outfitters and Guides Association, in Helena, or the Dude Ranchers Association, in Laporte, Colorado, for best bets. In town, visit the **Depot Center,** an ornate Victorian train depot that displays rail exhibits.

1 GLACIER NATIONAL PARK

This geological wonderland encompasses 1,600 square miles of Rocky Mountain peaks, offering eye-popping vistas at every twist in the road. The sharpest turns occur on **Going-to-the-Sun Road,** a glorious thoroughfare cutting east-west through some of the park's boldest terrain. Snaking 50 miles, the road crosses the Continental Divide: water falling on one side drains toward the Pacific Ocean; on the other, toward the Atlantic.

▶ *The highest portions of Going-to-the-Sun Road are open only from June through October. The highway can be crowded in the summer.*

2 BROWNING

The tribal names of Crow, Blackfoot, Cheyenne, and Sioux evoke images of an era when bison roamed a rugged terrain that belonged to no one. The **Museum of the Plains Indian** brings this period alive through dioramas, murals, and Indian artifacts.

Between Browning and the town of Choteau, the highway becomes the dividing line between the contrasting landscapes of the East and West. This break in the terrain, where the snow-dusted peaks of the Rockies unfold into vast prairie land, is referred to as the **Rocky Mountain Front.** Here chinook winds swirl down from the mountains and rapidly warm the foothills.

The granite peaks of the Rocky Mountains dwarf Swiftcurrent Lake in Glacier National Park.

3 GREAT FALLS

The shortest river in the world lies just minutes from downtown Great Falls, so named for the cascade of falls encountered by Lewis and Clark in 1805. Roe River flows all of 67 showy yards before emptying into the Missouri River. The Roe's headwaters emerge from an underground spring at tree-shaded **Giant Springs Heritage State Park,** site of one of the world's largest freshwater springs and a trout hatchery.

In the heart of the city a museum has been created to honor one of the West's most beloved figures. Charles M. Russell gave up the genteel life for the frontier as a young man, and devoted himself to documenting what he considered a dying culture—the Old West. He felt disdain for the homestead movement—saying it turned the plains "grass side down"—and nothing but

"The Buffalo Hunt," by Charles M. Russell, is on display at the C. M. Russell Museum Complex in Great Falls. The self-taught artist depicted the last days of the Old West frontier in scenes like this one.

sympathy for the plight of the natives. The **C. M. Russell Museum Complex** includes the cowboy artist's 1900 home and his 1903 log cabin studio, filled with buffalo skulls and saddles. A museum houses the world's most extensive collection of his works—oil paintings, pen-and-inks, and illustrated letters.

4 GATES OF THE MOUNTAINS

From Great Falls to Helena you'll be traveling the **Lewis and Clark Trail,** lined with interpretive markers that retrace the explorers' footsteps. Just north of Helena, a two-hour boat cruise along seven breathtaking miles of the Missouri River gives you a sense of what this pioneering party must have felt on first discovering the steep-walled river gorge in 1805. Lewis and Clark named this spot the Gates of the Mountains for the 1,200-foot-high cliff walls that appear to swing open like a gate. The boat trip follows Lewis and Clark's course along the river, past Indian pictographs, mountain goats, and swooping eagles.

5 HELENA

Last Chance Gulch was just that for a group of prospectors digging for gold around present-day Helena in 1864. Tired and discouraged, they opted to try one more location—naming it Last Chance Gulch—and to give up if nothing panned out. Helena attributes its birth to what the gulch and its immediate environs eventually yielded: more than $25 million in gold. In the bargain the city's main street was gifted with the name it still bears: Last Chance Gulch.

For a perspective on this and other colorful aspects of Montana history, visit the **Montana Historical Society Museum.** Here are such diverse objects as Jim Bridger's Hawken rifle and Chief Joseph's stirrups. Across from the museum, the **Montana State Capitol** has a copper-clad dome and a Neoclassical exterior faced with Montana granite. Charles M. Russell paintings decorate the interior of the Capitol.

6 DEER LODGE

There is much to see and do in this old mining town along the Clark Fork River. The **Towe Ford Museum**'s collection of 100 vintage Fords and Lincolns includes the Ford Motor Company's first sports car. Horses were the favored mode of transportation for the cowboys who spent their days rounding up dogies on the local ranches. The **Grant-Kohrs Ranch National Historic Site,** in town, commemorates the cowpoke's calf-branding, maverick-roping, dust-eating lifestyle. Begun in 1862, the ranch had grown to 27,000 acres by 1900. You can tour much of the 23-room ranch house, as well as the bunkhouse. Summer finds cowboys demonstrating ranch skills of the past.

7 MISSOULA

Writers and musicians flock to this culturally energetic city, often cited as among the most livable in the country. Proximity to top recreation is one reason: a trout stream cuts through the center of town, and pristine mountain trails are within a stone's throw of the city limits. You have only to drive eight miles out of town to reach the hiking paths and rocky vistas of **Rattlesnake National Recreation Area and Wilderness.** Or simply unwind downtown at **Caras Park,** nestled along the Clark Fork River. Trolley train tours through the Victorian downtown are offered by **Discover Missoula Montana.**

▶ *Every Wednesday in summer is Out to Lunch day at Caras Park. Under the big tent are food, free music, and theatrical performances.*

8 MOIESE

Buffalo have the right-of-way at the **National Bison Range,** near Moiese. Motorists negotiating the refuge's 19-mile self-guided-tour route may find themselves waiting at a bison roadblock while a shaggy beast lies down and rubs its back in the road. The bison range was established in 1908 to protect the last of some 60 million bison that once roamed North America's grasslands.

9 POLSON

The white puffs of sail scudding across the horizon make a pretty picture at **Flathead Lake,** the largest natural freshwater lake west of the Mississippi. Take an excursion on the 41-foot *Port Polson Princess,* which offers narrated tours of the 28-mile-long lake, or one of the half-day white-water rafting trips, which leave from Riverside Park.

You can drive the 89-mile loop completely around the lake's edge. Stop in at **Bigfork,** as picturesque a village as any in America. In the summer a lively arts scene swells the tiny population; many come for the Broadway shows at the **Bigfork Summer Playhouse.** Just north of Polson, stop in for a wine tasting at **Mission Mountain Winery,** whose own Pinot Noir grapes are transformed into a ruby champagne.

10 KALISPELL

Entrepreneur Charles Edward Conrad not only founded this center of trade but also built its most elegant house. Conrad moved into his 26-room home in 1895. Today the **Conrad Mansion** appears much as it did then, when its owner entertained tribal chiefs in his sumptuous parlor. Conrad's tastes were expensive: his home is a showplace of Chippendale furniture and Tiffany stained-glass windows.

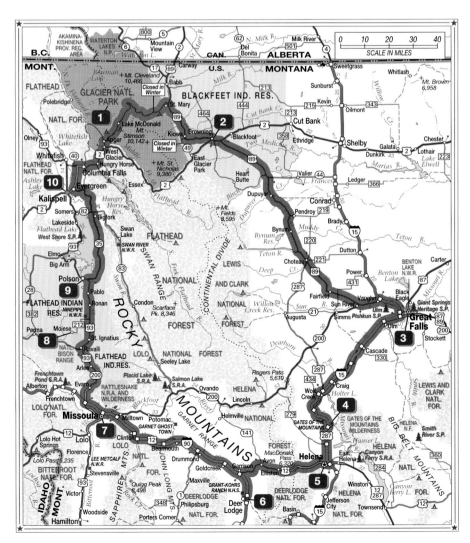

Idaho

With Hells Canyon, the Seven Devils Mountains, and the Snake River, Idaho offers more than just potatoes. Its landscape is dramatic—and far less forbidding than the names of its features imply.

SOUTHERN IDAHO

1 BOISE

Idaho's unassuming capital was christened by French fur traders delighted to encounter the wooded riverbanks here after a trying journey across the austere high desert of southern Idaho. Boise, from *boisé,* French for "wooded," boasts a verdant 13-mile greenbelt—a playground for pedestrians and bicyclers—along the Boise River, where it flows through the heart of the city.

Most of Boise's attractions cluster conveniently around the river. Within the lovely green expanse of Julia Davis Park is the **Idaho Historical Museum** and

Fly fishermen *wade into the shimmering calm of Silver Creek south of Sun Valley.*

its collection of pioneer-era homes; **Zoo Boise,** which boasts a large birds of prey collection; the hands-on **Discovery Center of Idaho;** and the **Boise Art Museum.**

Notorious husband-killer Lady Bluebeard was among the prisoners at the

Old Idaho Penitentiary, one of three territorial prisons still standing in the country. The inmates were given the task of tending the rose garden, planted in the early 1900's and still growing within the prison walls. Visitors can walk through four cell houses and see the charred evidence of the riot that finally caused the prison to be closed in 1973. Behind the penitentiary, fragrant flowers bloom in the **Idaho Botanical Garden,** made up of nine gardens with such themes as Butterfly-Hummingbird, Heirloom Rose, and Historical Iris.

Seven miles south of town one of the area's most popular attractions, the **World Center for Birds of Prey,** features the largest collection of birds of

prey in the Northwest. Birds such as the formidable harpy eagle, with six-inch talons and a wingspan of about seven feet, can be seen through a one-way glass behind the interpretive center, where peregrine falcons are regularly brought out for exhibition.

▶ *Avoid the Birds of Prey Center in April and May, when tours are given to schoolchildren, or visit after 2:30.*

2 IDAHO CITY

Rte. 21, known as the Ponderosa Pine Scenic Route, leads to Idaho City and the lush Sawtooth Wilderness beyond. Set in the middle of the Boise Basin, the city was born in a lucrative 1862 gold boom that drew 30,000 inhabitants to the area by 1865. It remains a well-preserved relic of the boisterous boom days, with sturdy brick buildings lining wood-plank sidewalks.

Pioneer businesses such as the Boise Basin Mercantile still operate along Main Street, where you can dine and drink in restaurants and saloons that date back to 1867. The **Boise Basin Museum,** housed in an 1867 post office, recalls the area's heyday. A mile south of town, **Warm Springs Resort** relaxes bathers with 97° F water from the same hot springs that soothed tired miners in the 1860's.

3 SAWTOOTH NATIONAL RECREATION AREA

Three jagged mountain ranges rising more than 10,000 feet cut across the skyline of this enchanting section of the Sawtooth National Forest. More than 300 well-hidden alpine lakes nestle amid the forested peaks. Of interest at the **Redfish Lake Visitor Center** near Stanley, with views of Redfish Lake, are the mounted examples of chinook, kokanee, and sockeye salmon. Other exhibits explain the flora, fauna, and geology of the area.

▶ *The visitor center lends cassette players and taped tours of the mountains keyed to mileposts on Rte. 75.*

Not far to the south lies the town of Ketchum, where Ernest Hemingway lived and is buried, and fashionable **Sun Valley,** the country's first ski resort, which now draws sophisticated leisure-seekers—including the Hollywood set—year-round.

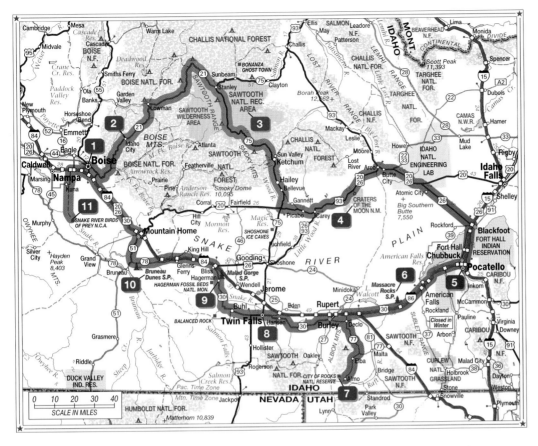

ons traversed a bleak sage desert, featureless for miles. Visual relief came in the form of massive granite outcroppings, some as tall as 60 stories, resembling a silent city. The usual emigrant reaction to such prominences along the trail was to carve messages in the rock. This granite proved too hard, so the inventive travelers smeared their inscriptions with axle grease instead.

8 TWIN FALLS

Located amid lush croplands that were covered with sagebrush before irrigation made the Magic Valley green, Twin Falls is named for a waterfall on the Snake River that boiled around a large rock outcropping. Now the Snake is used for irrigation and hydroelectricity, and the twin falls usually appear only in the city's name.

At **Shoshone Falls** northeast of town, however, the Snake still thunders in spring and fall with a power that Oregon Trail emigrants heard from three miles away. White waters plunge over a 212-foot precipice, hurling up mists and forming rainbows visible from a lookout point above. For a still more dazzling view, cross the **Perrine Memorial Bridge**, 486 feet high.

Don't miss the **Herrett Museum** at the College of Southern Idaho, known for its pre-Columbian artifacts from North, Central, and South America.

9 HAGERMAN

Hagerman Fossil Beds National Monument spreads for several miles along the steep cliffs of the Snake River and contains one of the world's best assemblages of fossils from the Pliocene epoch. Most famous among the fossils, which include fish and small mammal bones, are the 130 horse fossils discovered in the "horse quarry." A prehistoric horse skeleton dug up here is displayed at the **Hagerman Valley Historical Society Museum**. Less than a block away,

4 CRATERS OF THE MOON NATIONAL MONUMENT

This lunar landscape boasts one of the nation's highest concentrations of volcanic features, some formed as recently as 2,000 years ago. The lava flows and cinder cones were actually used for moon-walking practice by astronauts in the 1960's. A visitor center at the beginning of a scenic seven-mile loop road explains their creation and that of the ice caves and still more intriguing tree molds and lava bombs. Plant life includes a surprising carpeting of vivid wildflowers in summer.

▶ *The lava formations are sharp; wear sturdy shoes and stick to the trails. Carry a jacket and flashlight for exploring the lava tubes, some of which have ice on their floors.*

5 POCATELLO

A Shoshone chief named Pocatello lent his name to this town, part of the Fort Hall Indian Reservation. The government purchased some of the land to make way for a new north–south railroad, and a tent city sprang up in 1882 where this rail line intersected the

Union Pacific. Just off Main Street, the three-story 1915 **Oregon Short Line Depot** still stands. The **Bannock County Historical Museum** spotlights the town's railroading past and includes Shoshone and Bannock handicrafts.

In Upper Ross Park a replica of **Fort Hall** brings back the fur-trading era when the post was a booming commercial center. Bison, antelope, elk, and deer in a nearby field are reminders of the resources that fed the economy.

6 MASSACRE ROCKS

Massacre Rocks State Park, 10 miles southwest of American Falls, recalls a fatal day in 1862 when 10 Oregon Trail travelers were ambushed by a band of Indians. Thousands of other emigrants passed uneventfully through this break in the lava rocks, carving deep wagon ruts that created rolling swells still visible for miles. The park offers boating and fishing on the Snake River, and plenty of birds to be watched.

7 CITY OF ROCKS NATIONAL RESERVE

As California-bound emigrants branched from the main Oregon Trail, their wag-

the monument's **Visitor Center** offers displays including a camel skull and horse bones still imbedded in rock.

▶ *There is only one steep gravel road into the monument. Most visitors will want to view the area from the overlook. Just past 1,000 Springs, before the bridge, turn left at the sign for Bell Rapids, then drive for 2½ miles.*

10 BRUNEAU DUNES

Mammoth sand dunes at **Bruneau Dunes State Park** include the largest single structured sand dune in North America, towering 470 feet high. A five-mile self-guided nature trail climbs the dune and explains the area's geology. Three pretty lakes afford fishing.

11 SNAKE RIVER BIRDS OF PREY AREA

The largest concentration of breeding raptors in North America inhabits the volcanic cliffs along 81 miles of the Snake River in the **Snake River Birds of Prey National Conservation Area.** Abundant nesting sites and nearby prey make this an ideal spot for feeding young eagles, hawks, and falcons.

Spy their perches from the overlook at **Dedication Point** or from the river itself: boat trips through the conservation area are offered by outfitters based in Boise. But be sure to visit April through June, when the birds are nesting.

THE PANHANDLE

1 LEWISTON

Lewis and Clark floated down the Clearwater River until it met the Snake River; there they camped, in the shadow of the Bitterroot Mountains. This spot today is Lewiston, one of the most beautiful towns in the state and an important inland port. Oceangoing vessels steam up the Columbia River to the Snake and back to the Pacific.

A very different type of craft, speedy aluminum jet boats, carry visitors up the Snake to explore **Hells Canyon.** Daylong tours offer a return trip by boat or raft, and longer trips are available. **Hells Gate State Park,** at the outlet of the canyon, offers camping, swimming, and excursion boat tours.

2 MOSCOW

Beautiful fields of white wheat spread before you on the road from Lewiston to Moscow as you traverse a region of rolling hills and river valleys known as Palouse country. The striking Appaloosa horse—"a Palouse" horse—originated here in what was once Idaho's Nez Perce territory. At the **Appaloosa**

Museum you'll find such artifacts as a Nez Perce woman's saddle, with a horn in front from which a cradleboard hung. One or two of the handsome horses are on view in summer.

3 COEUR D'ALENE

French fur traders, unable to swindle the American Indians here out of valuable pelts with cheap trinkets, dubbed them Coeur d'Alene, or "Heart of the Awl," for their sharpness. The **Museum of North Idaho** chronicles the history of the area and its people. Today the popular resort city and antiques hub is a gateway to the lush playgrounds of the Idaho Panhandle.

Coeur d'Alene Lake, reputedly one of the most beautiful lakes in the world, reflects the forested mountains that surround it. The glacier-gouged lake attracts anglers and bird-watchers, along with one of the nation's largest populations of nesting ospreys, and bald eagles that plunge for salmon in winter. Cruises depart from the city dock.

4 SANDPOINT

The town of Sandpoint sits at the tip of **Pend Oreille Lake,** made long and skinny by the glaciers that carved the adjacent peaks. Fishermen sink their lines in hopes of huge returns from one of the largest natural lakes in the U.S.

There aren't just wheels at the **Vintage Wheel Museum** but the horse-drawn carriages and antique cars attached to them. Some of these relics may once have traveled over the Cedar Street Bridge, now a shopping arcade with lake and mountain views.

The Appaloosa, a descendant of the horses brought over by the Spanish in the 1500's, was bred by the Nez Perce of Idaho, Washington, and Oregon. Their horses were so fine that they were regularly stolen by other tribes.

5 KOOTENAI NATIONAL WILDLIFE REFUGE

In fall some 40,000 ducks descend on this refuge along the Kootenai River, along with a dozen or so bald eagles. Large white tundra swans take up residence in spring, accompanied by tiny songbirds that make themselves just as conspicuous with their rapturous melodies. Gaggles of Canada geese can be seen year-round, along with white-tailed deer. A 4½-mile driving tour, three observation points, and several trails provide views.

▶ *Drive as close to the edge of the road as possible to avoid the logging trucks that come barreling through.*

6 MOYIE FALLS

Jammed within the canyon walls of the Moyie River, this noisy white torrent is one of the area's most impressive falls. An overlook just off Rte. 2 provides views, as does the Moyie River Bridge, 450 feet above the canyon.

7 SPALDING

Named for a missionary to the Indians, Spalding is the headquarters of **Nez Perce National Historical Park,** which includes 38 sites scattered across north central Idaho and parts of Oregon, Washington, and Montana. A brochure outlining self-guided tours is available.

The **Spalding Site** marks the location of a mission built by Henry and Eliza Spalding in 1838, where they set up the state's first printing press, sawmill, and gristmill. The adjacent Spalding Site Visitor Center contains exhibits about Lewis and Clark, the Nez Perce, and early missionaries. Beautiful articles of Nez Perce clothing are on view.

8 WHITE BIRD BATTLEFIELD

The Nez Perce were friendly toward whites from the time of first contact by Lewis and Clark, but war broke out when gold seekers attempted to take over tribal lands in Oregon. The first battle of the Nez Perce Indian War was fought at White Bird Canyon, and went down in history as a decisive victory for the Nez Perce. But the ensuing conflict, which lasted four months and covered 1,400 miles, became the longest fighting retreat in American military history. It came to an end in Bear's Paw Battleground in Montana, where Chief Joseph uttered his famous words, "I will fight no more forever." The brochure available in Spalding outlines a driving tour of the battlefield over verdant rolling hills offering heavenly pastoral views.

9 HELLS CANYON NATIONAL RECREATION AREA

Carved by the mighty Snake River, Hells Canyon is North America's deepest gorge, plunging a mile and more into the earth. With sheer cliffs and swift rapids, this is remote and wild territory indeed. Most access is by boat. By car, the best road into the canyon is Rte. 71, which leads to the Hells Canyon Dam at the bottom of the gorge. From here you can take a powerboat up the canyon to various trailheads, or drive one of the Hells Canyon Scenic Byway roads—which are gravel and steep—to the rim.

▶ *The gravel roads are open only in warm weather. Check with the Forest Service office in Riggins for information about road conditions.*

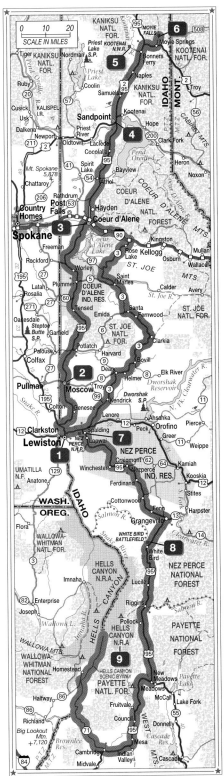

Hells Canyon is the handiwork of the swift-running Snake River, whose devilish rapids surge beneath the rubber rafts and high-powered jet boats that tour the gorge. Steep walls of basalt press in close on either side, making this one of the narrowest chasms, as well as the deepest, on the continent.

For hikers, the recreation area includes parts of the soaring **Seven Devils Mountains,** where snow lingers in summer even while temperatures top 100° F on the canyon floor. For those interested in faster, wetter travel, float and jet-boat trips of various lengths originate from the Hells Canyon Dam.

Utah

Settled by hardy Mormon pioneers, Utah is a land of majestic mountains and desert canyons ablaze with wildflowers and bedecked with rock formations seemingly inspired by the divine.

SALT LAKE CITY & THE NORTH

1 SALT LAKE CITY

Mormon leader Brigham Young knew that he had found the "right place" in 1847, while standing at the mouth of Emigration Canyon in what is now **Pioneer Trail State Park**. In the park is a monument to the Mormons' settlement of Utah and a re-created pioneer town.

Utah visitors seem to confirm Young's judgment of the Salt Lake Valley: Salt Lake City's **Temple Square** is said to be the most popular attraction in the state. In the square soars the six-spired **Mormon Temple**, topped by a golden statue of the angel Moroni. The temple is used for sacred ceremonies, and only members of the Mormon church—officially the Church of Jesus Christ of Latter-day Saints—may enter it. The nearby **Mormon Tabernacle** is open to the public and seats about 6,500 people for Sunday morning performances by the Mormon Tabernacle Choir. Daily organ concerts show off one of the finest organs in the world, which features more than 11,000 pipes.

Across the street are the **Family History Library**, which houses the world's largest collection of genealogical information, and the **Beehive House**, the restored adobe residence of Brigham Young. A wooden beehive, a symbol of industriousness and unity, sits atop the house. Only one of Young's 27 wives lived here while he was alive; another house, closed to the public, housed many of his other wives and children.

▶ *A visitor center offers guided tours of Temple Square, leaving every 15 minutes. If you can't be there for the Sunday morning Mormon Tabernacle Choir performance, you can hear them rehearse on Thursday night.*

Brigham Young stands before the Mormon Temple, which took 40 years to build.

Great Salt Lake, about 17 miles west of downtown, is the largest lake west of the Mississippi and is second only to the Dead Sea in salinity. The lake's water is eight times saltier than seawater.

2 OGDEN

Neatly laid out by Mormon pioneers, Ogden began as a gathering place for trappers and hunters and grew into a railroad center. **Union Station** now houses several museums, including the State Railroad Museum, the Browning Firearms Museum, and a collection of some of the world's largest locomotives. The station is part of **Historic 25th Street**, a restored commercial district.

A different sort of transportation is the focus of the **Hill Aerospace Museum** at Hill Air Force Base. More than 50 historic military aircraft are on display.

A considerable amount of flying goes on, too, at **Ogden Bay Waterfowl Management Area**, where some 2,000 ducks, 400 Canada geese, and thousands of other shore- and water-birds nest each year. In fall more than a million birds migrate through the area.

At **Fort Buenaventura State Park**, a former trading post and site of the first white settlement in the state, guides discuss the history of the reconstructed fort and the lives of the trappers and traders who did business here. A mountain man rendezvous takes place on Labor Day and Easter weekends.

The **Daughters of the Utah Pioneers Hall Museum** preserves bits of pioneer history with artifacts, photos, and the 1846 **Miles Goodyear Cabin**, built by the state's first settler. On the same block sits **Ogden Tabernacle Square**, where the local Mormon temple boasts a cluster of spires reaching as high as 185 feet. The temple is closed to the public, but visitors are welcome to browse through the exhibits in the neighboring tabernacle.

3 GOLDEN SPIKE NATIONAL HISTORIC SITE

Promontory, Utah, was the center of national attention when the last spike of the transcontinental railroad that bound East and West together was driven here on May 10, 1869. In summer, working replicas of the two steam locomotives that met where the rails joined are on view. A visitor center offers exhibits, and a 1½-mile loop trail follows the old railroad grade to points of interest.

4 RONALD V. JENSEN LIVING HISTORICAL FARM

In autumn vine maples paint a red backdrop for this re-created Mormon farm in Cache Valley, so named because mountain men hid their beaver pelts in underground caves here. Original farm buildings, including an 1875 farmhouse, have been moved to the site and are surrounded by fields, orchards, and livestock. "Workers" demonstrate farm skills, from cow-milking to sheep-shearing. The farm also displays pioneer farming artifacts and an amazing variety of farm implements, including a battalion of steam tractors.

5 HARDWARE RANCH

The best place to see Utah's state animal, the elk, is Hardware Ranch, a state wildlife management area east of Hyrum. As many as 800 wild elk gather here from November to March, when horse-drawn sleighs carry hay to the herds. This offering encourages the animals to halt their seasonal descent from the Wasatch-Cache National Forest here, rather than continue to the Cache Valley, where they would feed on orchard fruit trees and hay intended for dairy cows. Visitors too can ride the sleighs right to the feeding grounds to see the animals at close range.

6 OGDEN RIVER SCENIC BYWAY

Rte. 39 cuts through a stunning section of land in and around the **Wasatch-Cache National Forest**, past rolling hills dotted with picturesque farms and open meadows. A yellow canopy of quaking aspens tops 9,000-foot Monte Cristo in fall, and a scenic overlook takes in distant snowcapped peaks. At Huntsville look for **Pine View Reservoir**, a major recreation area in Utah.

7 HEBER CITY

Set in the Heber Valley and ringed by soaring mountains, Heber City couldn't enjoy a prettier setting. The **Heber Railroad Museum** boasts more antique railroading gear and steam locomotives than any other place in Utah. But visitors remember most fondly the Heber Valley Railroad, affectionately known as the Heber Creeper, the train that steams

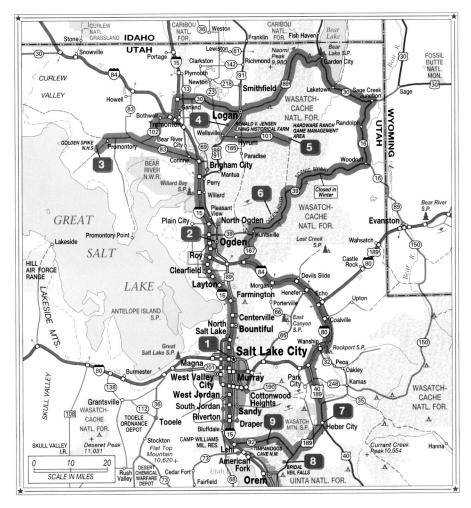

through the Heber Valley on a 32-mile excursion past impressive views of Mount Timpanogos and into the craggy depths of Provo Canyon.

8 BRIDAL VEIL FALLS

This double-tiered cascade drops 607 feet down the rugged walls of Provo Canyon. It thunders beneath riders on the Skytram, the steepest passenger tram in the world, offering views of the Utah Valley and Mount Timpanogos.

9 TIMPANOGOS CAVE NATIONAL MONUMENT

Located along the Alpine Scenic Drive (Rte. 92) in American Fork Canyon, these three small but spectacular limestone caverns in the flank of Mount Timpanogos are connected by man-made tunnels. Accessible only by a difficult 1½-mile path, the caves sit 1,065 feet up the mountainside. Inside are exotic, twisting helictites, delicate crystals, and stalactites and stalagmites. Note that you must purchase your ticket at the visitor center on the canyon floor before making the climb to the caves.

▶ *The temperature inside the caves is a constant 45° F. Bring a jacket, and bring water for the trail. Tours are often filled by midmorning. Try to arrive early or buy tickets in advance.*

At the Golden Spike *National Historic Site, the annual May 10 Last Spike Ceremony reenacts the driving of the spike—probably made of iron— that heralded the end of the Western frontier.*

1 ARCHES NATIONAL PARK

The world's largest concentration of natural arches—which, unlike natural bridges, never spanned streams—numbers more than 2,000 in this bizarre, desolate landscape. The sandstone structures range from 3 to 306 feet wide. Although many of the dramatic arches, windows, balanced rocks, and other erosion sculptures rise within view along the park roads, the most famous features—Delicate Arch, Landscape Arch, and Double Arch—require some walking for a close look. The trails range from an easy stroll to a steep mile-and-a-half climb.

► *Especially on warm days, reserve walking for early morning or evening, when the arches are most beautiful. Ask the visitor center staff what time of day offers the best light for the feature you want to see.*

2 DEAD HORSE POINT

An arrowhead-shaped promontory overlooking the Colorado River some 2,000 feet below, **Dead Horse Point State Park** is reached by a narrow neck about 90 feet wide. The 40-acre expanse was given its grim name after a group of cowboys (or thieves, according to one version of the story) corralled a herd of mustangs here and failed to return for them before the horses died of thirst on the waterless mesa.

The park's highlight is the juniper-framed view across 5,000 square miles of multicolored canyons bounded by mountains. Dominating this vista a dizzying distance below are the red canyons of the Colorado River, imprisoned in a twisting labyrinth as it flows into Canyonlands National Park.

3 CANYONLANDS NATIONAL PARK

Endless mesas, deeply eroded canyons, and stunning rock formations dazzle visitors to this largely undeveloped park. The mighty Green and Colorado rivers meet in the middle of the park and divide it into three sections.

► *The park's districts have separate access roads. The map on p. 279 takes you to Island in the Sky. Needles is reached by Rte. 211; the Maze, by a long dirt road off Rte. 24, accessible only to four-wheel-drive vehicles.*

The **Island in the Sky** district is a vast mesa isolated by the canyons of the two rivers. After passing over a 40-foot-wide isthmus called The Neck, park roads lead to spectacular desert panoramas at Green River Overlook and aptly named Grandview Point. Short, easy trails lead from the roads to such awe-inspiring natural creations as Mesa Arch and Upheaval Dome. Be sure to bring plenty of drinking water.

The **Needles** district offers spectacular multihued rock spires. **The Maze** is a remote section with excellent American Indian pictographs; it is for the serious hiker, not the casual traveler.

A dinosaur bone fossil intrigues a paleontologist at Dinosaur National Monument.

After leaving the park, be sure to fill your gas tank in the town of Green River on the way to Price.

4 NINE MILE CANYON

Fremont Indian artists had a particular liking for the rock panels of Nine Mile Canyon. Myriad petroglyphs and pictographs of hunting scenes and wildlife line the dirt road and some of the side canyons here. Ancient grain storage structures hide on ledges for the interest of sharp-eyed travelers; binoculars are helpful. Artifacts of more recent settlement include iron telegraph poles, abandoned stage stations, and cabins.

► *The Nine Mile Canyon turnoff from Rte. 191 turns to dirt after about 12 miles. The unpaved section should pose no problem in dry weather for vehicles no longer than 22 feet. Start out with a full tank of gas.*

5 PRICE

More dinosaur skeletons are displayed at the **Cleveland-Lloyd Dinosaur Quarry**, 30 miles south of Price by an unpaved road, than at any other site in the world. Most are remains of the fierce predator allosaurus, a mounted example of which stands in the quarry visitor center. When the quarry is open, Memorial Day through Labor Day, you may witness more bones being unearthed—bones that are likely to go the way of the 12,000 or so that have already been supplied to museums.

In its Hall of Dinosaurs, the **College of Eastern Utah Prehistoric Museum**

Delicate Arch at Arches National Park stands 45 feet high and 33 feet wide. One of nature's most spectacular formations, it is reached by way of a fairly strenuous three-mile round-trip trail.

displays four mounted skeletons from the quarry as well as footprints, an egg, and dinosaur-age plants. Another notable exhibit features artifacts of the Fremont Indian culture, including clay figurines 800 to 900 years old.

6 HELPER

Heavily loaded coal trains need help from extra locomotives to make the grade to Soldier Summit—hence Helper's name. At the **Western Mining and Railroad Museum** photos, model railroads, and coal mine models tell the area's history. Just as interesting are the items that recall the daily life of the members of nearly 20 ethnic groups who settled here. There are turn-of-the-century crocks used by the Germans to make sauerkraut and by the Spaniards to cure olives, and a beauty salon with a permanent-wave machine that plugs into the wall. Outside sit mining equipment and a red 1917 caboose. Also here is one of the largest displays of Depression-era WPA artwork in the country.

7 OURAY NATIONAL WILDLIFE REFUGE

Desert, marsh, and eroded bluffs are home to a wide variety of birds, mammals, and endangered fish at this refuge along the Green River. A brochure available at the kiosk at the entrance guides you on a 12-mile auto tour. Bald and golden eagles are common in winter; look for golden eagles nesting on rock ledges. In spring and fall, sandhill cranes pass through, accompanied by fewer and fewer huge, endangered whooping cranes. Watch year-round for great blue herons.

8 DINOSAUR NATIONAL MONUMENT

A wall of dinosaur fossils inside the **Dinosaur Quarry Visitor Center** displays a jumble of more than 1,600 partially exposed bones, left just as a long-gone river dumped them on a riverbed 145 million years ago. Bone hunters for various museums have removed hundreds of tons of fossils from the quarry here.

Though named for this unique bone bed, most of Dinosaur National Monument preserves the canyon wilderness carved by the Green and Yampa rivers.

Private companies offer one- to five-day raft trips. Superb views unfold from a 31-mile road that leads to an easy mile-long walking trail offering views of the rivers more than 1,700 feet below.

9 TRAIL THROUGH TIME

At mile marker 2 along Rte. 70, look for the exit for Rabbit Valley/Dinosaur Quarry, then follow the signs for Trail Through Time. This 1½-mile nature trail loops past 14 points of interest, including the fossilized neck and thigh bones of a 50-foot camarasaur. A brochure leads visitors back 140 million years to the age when this high desert was swampland. Fossils removed from the site are on display at **Dinosaur Valley**, a museum in nearby Grand Junction, Colorado, featuring half-size animated dinosaur models.

1 ZION NATIONAL PARK

Vivid cliffs of Navajo sandstone, originally wind-deposited sand dunes covered and then exposed by a retreating sea, rise 2,000 feet in Zion, carved by the Virgin River and eroded into fanciful arches and massive monoliths. This geological wonderland still inspires the awe reflected in the names of many of its prominent features: Altar of Sacrifice, Great White Throne, Temple of Sinawava, and Angels Landing.

Zion's early explorers predicted that only winged immortals would ever set foot atop the pinnacle of Angels Landing. But a steep 2½-mile trail, part of a

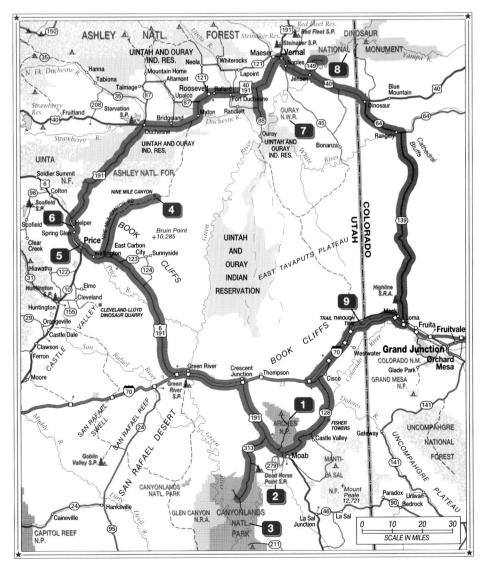

well-developed trail system, winds through a section called Walters Wiggles to the top. Throughout the park an amazing desert flora clings to the cliffs and grows on the canyon floor. Much of Zion's scenery can be viewed from the 5.2-mile **Kolob Canyons Road** in the park's northern section, as well as the 11-mile **Zion Mount Carmel Highway** and the 7-mile **Zion Canyon Scenic Drive** in the south.

2 IRON MISSION STATE PARK

Miners from the British Isles established the first iron foundry in the West near Cedar City. Later, Mormon converts arrived to strengthen the "iron mission," deemed vital to the success of Utah's Mormon settlements. Today the old foundry site is the final resting place for all manner of horse-drawn vehicles, including some with rubber tires. The collection includes farm implements and wagons, and a stagecoach reputedly shot up by Butch Cassidy.

Dioramas in the park's museum commemorate the beginnings of Cedar City's iron industry. Pioneer and American Indian artifacts are also displayed.

3 CEDAR BREAKS NATIONAL MONUMENT

No cedars grow here. Early pioneers confused junipers with the cedars of the Bible, which do not grow in North America. They used the word *breaks* to describe a natural amphitheater eroded in the side of a plateau. This three-mile-wide amphitheater displays an unrivaled palette of colors—red, white, gold, and violet. Junipers, pines, and Douglas firs add a touch of green, and aspens glow gold in fall. Summer brings a vibrant wildflower display. A five-mile scenic drive offers excellent views.

4 BRYCE CANYON NATIONAL PARK

Bryce Canyon is not a canyon. Its 36,000 acres contain a 20-mile escarp-

ment on the edge of a plateau, indented by a dozen dramatic alcoves. Within these alcoves rise unimaginable hoodoos, spires, arches, and other monuments intricately carved by erosion, all painted brilliant shades of red, yellow, white, and purple by iron and manganese in the rocks. Water continues to eat back the cliff edges at the rate of about one foot every 65 years.

Bryce's 20-mile-long main road has turnouts to stunning overlooks, and trails descend from the rim into the interior. The towers can also be viewed from below from turnouts on Rte. 12, where it enters the park from the east.

▶ *The best views of the canyon are from Sunset Point and Bryce Point.*

5 KODACHROME BASIN STATE PARK

Even in a land where fantastic desert landscapes are commonplace, this spot is remarkable. Kodachrome Basin was

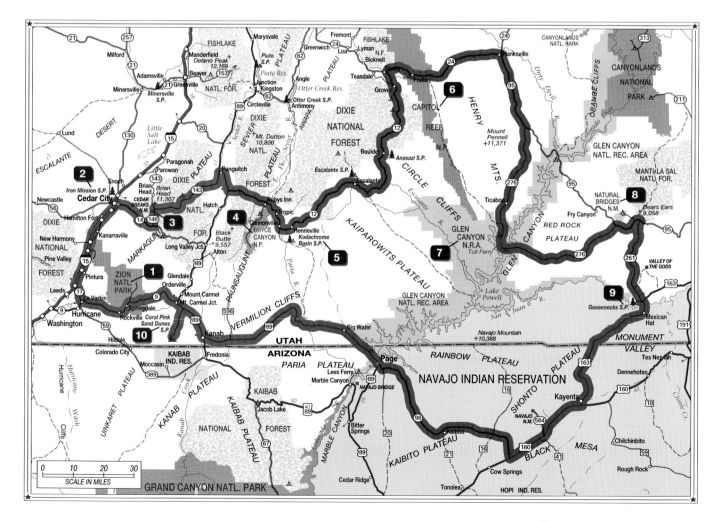

named by National Geographic Society explorers after a film they deemed good for recording the area's brilliant colors. Its mysterious rock towers are geologically unique, their formation controversial. Some believe they mark conduits to the surface of ancient springs, which eventually filled in and were made harder than the surrounding rock by particularly tough cement carried in the water. Erosion by wind and water eventually stripped away the softer rock surrounding these "petrified" springs.

6 CAPITOL REEF NATIONAL PARK

Paiute Indians called this the Land of the Sleeping Rainbow. Its layered, multihued ramparts blocked travel, and prospectors dubbed it a reef after the coral barriers at sea. Its domes, eroded by infrequent but intense rains beating on white sandstone, reminded them of the U.S. Capitol.

Hiking trails, such as the easy one-mile trail to Capitol Gorge, take visitors to points of interest on a more human scale, including petroglyphs and natural water tanks, or unusual pockets in the rock that hold water when it rains.

At the turn of the century Mormon orchardists formed a community called **Fruita** that lies within the park. The National Park Service offers tours of the historic buildings and orchards in summer. Visitors can compete with mule deer for the apples, pears, and other fruit on the trees in summer and fall.

▶ *This park and others on this loop are in Utah's slickrock country. Watch your step on the sandstone rocks.*

7 GLEN CANYON NATIONAL RECREATION AREA

A blue-green oasis and the second-largest man-made lake in the United States, Lake Powell stretches behind the Glen Canyon Dam. The colorful Navajo sandstone cliffs that rise above the surface paint a dramatic backdrop enjoyed by lovers of many water sports.

The lake affords easy access to the formerly remote **Rainbow Bridge National Monument,** on the eastern shore. Boat trips followed by a quarter-mile stroll lead to the world's largest and perhaps most beautiful natural bridge, 290 feet high and 275 feet across. These trips are available from the Bullfrog, Halls Crossing, and Wahweap marinas. The John Atlantic Burr Ferry transports vehicles between the Halls Crossing and Bullfrog marinas.

Sunlight casts *a golden glow on the formations of Queen's Garden in Bryce Canyon.*

8 NATURAL BRIDGES NATIONAL MONUMENT

Three natural bridges, each in a different stage of development, are visible from an eight-mile circle drive. Trails lead to **Sipapu,** a mature bridge no longer being undercut by floodwaters; it is the second-largest natural bridge in the world. Floodwaters are still carving **Kachina,** downstream. The third bridge, **Owachomo,** is so eroded that its delicate beauty seems fleeting. As they widen, the bridges will one day collapse under their own weight.

Hiking trails link the bridges and pass multiroom cliff dwellings abandoned by Anasazi Indian farmers some 650 years ago. A visitor center features a museum and native plant walkway.

▶ *On the way to Goosenecks State Park, Rte. 261 is unpaved for three miles as it climbs Cedar Mesa. Scenic turnouts offer views of Valley of the Gods and Monument Valley, but drive with extra caution because of the steep dropoffs.*

9 GOOSENECKS STATE PARK

A four-mile paved road leads to **Goosenecks Overlook,** perched about 1,000 feet above the San Juan River. Far below is the world's most spectacular example of an incised meander. Seven times within a straight-line mile the river doubles back, winding for more than five river miles. The San Juan carved this pattern for itself when it meandered slowly over flat land millions of years ago. Geological uplift was so gradual that it never increased its speed enough to run straight. In future ages, though, the river may leave dry horseshoe-shaped bridges behind like those found in White Canyon in Natural Bridges National Monument.

10 CORAL PINK SAND DUNES

Red and white cliffs of Navajo sandstone border the road to **Coral Pink Sand Dunes State Park.** Originally laid down as dunes that eventually solidified into rock, the Navajo sandstone is reverting to its old form as wind, precipitation, and frost gradually wedge apart the colorful rock and deposit the grains into new dunes. The pinkish dunes may eventually become rock again, but in the meantime they draw an appreciative crowd that includes the Jeep and dune buggy set. Wildflowers bloom in the park in June and July.

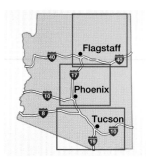

Arizona

A landscape studded with spectacular red canyons and tall saguaro cactus is the backdrop for this state's romantic blend of American and Hispanic cultures, architecture, and cuisine.

FLAGSTAFF &
GRAND CANYON

1 FLAGSTAFF

Humphreys Peak—the highest mountain in Arizona at 12,633 feet—towers above this pleasant university town, the starting point for one of the great scenic drives in the world. The **Museum of Northern Arizona** helps explain the geological processes that created the Colorado Plateau, as well as the history and culture of the native peoples who have lived there. Privately endowed **Lowell Observatory**, where the planet Pluto was discovered, has public tours and hours for viewing through its telescopes; check schedules, which vary, in advance. East of town are two extensive and very different Indian ruins: **Walnut Canyon National Monument**, where cliff dwellings are tucked into a secluded gorge, and **Wupatki National Monument**, a large village of rock houses with a ball court of the kind more often found in Mexico. Near Wupatki is **Sunset Crater Volcano National Monument**, an extinct volcano surrounded by lava beds eroded into weird shapes.

2 SOUTH RIM, GRAND CANYON NATIONAL PARK

The vastness of the Grand Canyon is almost beyond comprehension. It is so long, so wide, so deep, so improbable, that you cannot avoid being overwhelmed. The main activity here, of course, is looking; the canyon never changes, and yet it never looks the same, as the changing interplay of light and rock brings out remarkable hues.

The best introduction to the canyon is to drive the roads that extend east and west along the rim from the main commercial area, known as **Grand Canyon Village**. The eight-mile **West Rim Drive** follows the edge of the canyon closely and has numerous overlooks, including one aptly called The Abyss. Late afternoon is the best time to make the tour. The overlooks are also connected by a trail on the rim, which is paved and heavily used near the Village but offers more solitude as you go west.

▶ *Go to the Grand Canyon off season; in summer the park is very crowded. Also note that West Rim Drive is closed to car traffic in summer, when visitors must use a free shuttle.*

The **East Rim Drive** is longer and has fewer overlooks, but its canyon vistas are more colorful. You can see long stretches of the Inner Gorge and the Colorado River at **Grandview Point** and **Lipan Point.** The best time to watch the changing light is early morning. You can also see the canyon from an airplane or helicopter, from the back of a mule, from a raft on the Colorado River, or on foot. If you want to take a break from gazing at the scenery, there is an IMAX theater at Tusayan and a prehistoric Tusayan Anasazi ruin on the East Rim Drive near Lipan Point.

▶ *The best view of the canyon from the West Rim Drive is in late afternoon; at the East Rim, early morning.*

3 NORTH RIM, GRAND CANYON

Though it is 10 miles away across the chasm as the crow flies, the North Rim's only lodge is 214 miles from Grand Canyon Village by car. The North Rim is much less crowded than the South Rim, more than 1,000 feet higher in elevation, and set farther back from the river. The views here are mainly of side canyons; you get a much better sense

The Colorado River carved the most magnificent natural wonder on earth into the Colorado Plateau over the course of 5 to 10 million years. First a home to the Anasazi, the 277-mile long stretch of incomparable beauty known as the Grand Canyon was first seen by Europeans on Coronado's expedition of 1540.

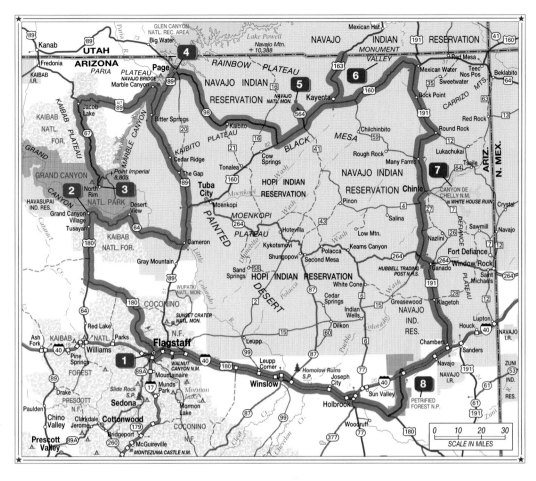

Monument Valley the universal image of the American West: fantastical shapes of buttes, mesas, and spires, rising from an otherwise flat and empty land. You will find these monoliths familiar—if not from the old Westerns, then from modern TV commercials. For a closer look at the monuments, take the 17-mile scenic drive in the tribal park operated by the Navajo Nation. The dirt road is slow going but not hazardous.

7 CANYON DE CHELLY

Its colors, clean lines, and proportions are so perfect that **Canyon de Chelly National Monument** (pronounced d-SHAY) seems to have been handcrafted. The canyon has sheer red walls, a white sandy bottom, occasional groves of greenery, and a meandering creek. The cliffs meet the canyon floor at right angles; only rarely does rubble or talus slope blur the intersection. The 20-mile drive along the rim leads to **Spider Rock**, an 800-foot spire. Pullouts provide views of cliff dwellings; a relatively easy trail at **White House Overlook** descends about 600 feet to a ruin on the canyon floor.

8 PETRIFIED FOREST NATIONAL PARK

A 28-mile scenic drive with frequent turnoffs provides access to all of this park's main features. The drive can be divided into three sections. To the north is the **Painted Desert**, where minerals have streaked the badlands with white and gray, red and rust. In the center are petroglyphs and other remnants of ancient civilizations at **Newspaper Rock** and **Puerco Ruin**. The southern section has most of the petrified wood. Two easy nature trails explore the transformed trees at their biggest—the **Long Logs Trail** and the more colorful **Crystal Forest Trail**.

---

on the North Rim of how erosion has carved the Grand Canyon and how huge the place really is. The forest is bigger too; instead of the pinyon and juniper that predominate on the South Rim, fir, spruce, and aspen are found on the North Rim. To get the best views, take the paved roads to **Cape Royal**, **Vista Encantada**, and **Point Imperial** or the dirt road, which can be rough, to **Point Sublime**.

▶ *The North Rim's Grand Canyon Lodge is closed from late October to early May because of heavy snow.*

4 PAGE

This town began life as a construction camp for the **Glen Canyon Dam** project in 1957. Now it is the center for recreation on **Lake Powell,** which is named for John Wesley Powell, who led early expeditions down the Colorado River. The **Powell Museum** contains information about the voyages. Visitors may rent boats at nearby Wahweap Marina or take tours of the gargantuan lake, which is 186 miles long.

5 NAVAJO NATIONAL MONUMENT

After leaving Page, Rtes. 98 and 160 go through the Navajo Indian Reservation, which occupies all of northeastern Arizona and spills over into Utah and New Mexico. The well-preserved cliff dwellings of the **Navajo National Monument** rank among the most stunning sights in Arizona. Unfortunately, they are also among the most isolated, requiring long treks to the ruins at Betatakin (5 miles round trip) and Keet Seel (17 miles round trip). Fortunately, Betatakin's magnificent setting in a sandstone canyon can be viewed from an overlook that is just a half-mile walk from the visitor center. The ruins are framed by an arch 452 feet high.

▶ *You can rent horses from a Navajo family for a trip to Keet Seel. Only 20 visitors a day are allowed.*

6 MONUMENT VALLEY/ NAVAJO TRIBAL PARK

Hollywood Westerns like *Stagecoach* and *She Wore a Yellow Ribbon* made

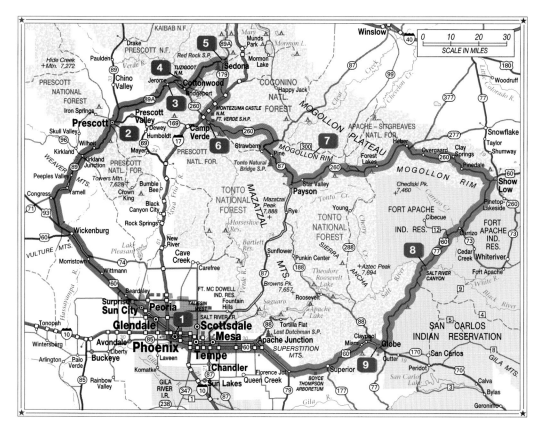

few historic buildings survive. An earlier Arizona lifestyle can be found at the **Pioneer Arizona Living History Museum**, a reconstituted frontier town in the desert north of Phoenix, which presents live exhibits on early Arizona life. Among the buildings is the first frame house in Arizona.

The turn-of-the-century territorial capitol building is now the **Arizona State Capitol Museum**, where a wax likeness of the first governor, George W. P. Hunt, sits behind his roll-top desk. **Heritage Square** is a collection of eight 19th-century homes, including the elegant Victorian **Rosson House**. An even earlier period of Arizona history is represented at the **Heard Museum**, whose exhibits on the American Indian cultures of the Southwest are regarded as the best in Arizona. If the modern urban landscape leaves you longing for natural scenery, head out to **South Mountain Park**—more than 20,000 acres of desert hills, rock formations, and tall saguaro cacti.

PHOENIX & MOGOLLON RIM

1 PHOENIX

In a state that is known the world over for its natural beauty, the charms of Phoenix are mostly man-made. The Valley of the Sun is home to some of the nation's priciest resorts and shopping areas, many of which are not actually in Phoenix itself but in the eastern suburb of **Scottsdale.** If staying in a resort is beyond your budget, plan to drop in for a meal just to ogle the landscaping and the people; the resorts are the most intriguing attractions in the Phoenix area. But the town is not all glitz; it is also the site of **Taliesin West,** Frank Lloyd Wright's western home, studio, and school, open year-round.

▶ *Scottsdale Road is a shopping magnet. Old Scottsdale and Fifth Avenue feature Western art and clothing, Indian jewelry, and crafts.*

In Phoenix proper the 1929 Arizona Biltmore, which Frank Lloyd Wright helped design, remains famous for its dramatic architecture and impeccable gardens. A modern rival is The Phoenician, built by financier Charles H. Keating, Jr., before the collapse of his savings and loan empire in the early 1990's. No extravagance was spared; one pool is lined with mother-of-pearl.

Phoenix grew so fast that most traces of its past have been obliterated, but a

Zuni women perform an Olla maiden dance in the amphitheater of the Heard Museum.

2 PRESCOTT

Prescott was Arizona's first territorial capital, and the town is one of the few places in Arizona that retain an old, gracious air. The **Sharlot Hall Museum** is named for a territorial historian who collected memorabilia from furniture to stagecoaches as the frontier disappeared before her eyes. Located in a downtown park, it includes the reconstructed governor's mansion—although cabin would be a more accurate word.

3 JEROME

This former mining boomtown is the best—and liveliest—ghost town in Arizona. Once it had 15,000 residents and a reputation as "the wickedest town in the West"; now it is making a comeback as a tourist center and art colony. Jerome is reached by a switchback road that winds through the town, which clings to the mountainside like a medieval Italian village. As you enter Jerome, one of the great vistas in Arizona unfolds to the north: the red rocks of Sedona appear beyond the barren hills north of the Verde River; then, as you reach the highest ground, the snowfields of the San Francisco peaks are revealed, some 50 miles to the north. In 1916 copper magnate James Douglas built his home on land next to his mine to capture this view; the estate is now the **Jerome State Historic Park.**

4 TUZIGOOT NATIONAL MONUMENT

Long before Europeans came to Arizona, this area was inhabited first by the Hohokam people, then by the Sinagua. Tuzigoot is the remains of a large Sinagua hilltop pueblo, which was begun about A.D.1125 and abandoned about A.D.1400.

The **Verde River Canyon Excursion Train** operates out of nearby Clarkdale, on Rte. 89A. The four-hour trip goes through high desert country accessible only by rail. Trains operate daily, except Tuesday, in the spring and fall; during the rest of the year, the trains run Wednesday through Sunday.

5 SEDONA

It is hard to imagine a more idyllic setting for a town. Situated on the banks of Oak Creek, nestled among red sandstone buttes and pinnacles whose color changes with the light, Sedona looks like a movie set; and it has often been one, beginning with the filming of Zane Grey's novel *The Call of the Canyon* in 1923. The town population of 9,000 is almost entirely devoted to making use of the red rocks. Visitors drive and hike in them, resident artists paint and photograph them, and New Age followers worship them. Indeed, Sedona has become a kind of New Age mecca, with New Age shops and even New Age Jeep tours to the "vortices"—regarded as sacred places where the energy of the earth is said to be focused.

▶ *The best driving routes for seeing the red rocks are Schnebly Hill Road, Dry Creek Road, and as you might expect, Red Rock Loop Road.*

Cathedral Rock *casts the reflection of its red spires onto Oak Creek, near Sedona.*

6 CAMP VERDE

The western end of a line of cavalry forts was located here during the Indian Wars of the 1860's to the 1890's. At Fort Verde, now **Fort Verde State Historic Park,** only a few of the original buildings remain; but a tour of the officers' quarters gives a good indication of how rank had its privileges, even on the frontier. Nearby, at **Montezuma Castle National Monument,** is a cliff dwelling that is unusual because of its five-story height. The name reflects the erroneous belief of early settlers that the structure had been built by Aztecs fleeing the Spanish conquerors of the 1520's.

7 THE MOGOLLON RIM

The Mogollon Rim (pronounced mo-ga-YONE) is one of the most important geological features of Arizona, an uplift of about 2,500 feet that angles across the center of the state, separating the forested plateaus and mountains of the north from the desert to the south. Rim-top towns like **Show Low** and **Pinetop-Lakeside** are resort centers for fishing, hunting, and skiing. You reach the rim just south of Show Low, so named because the town is located on land that was won in a poker game; the main street, Deuce of Clubs, honors the winning card. The descent from the rim as you approach Payson presents anoth-

er unforgettable panorama, especially at sunset, when rows of distant mountains are silhouetted against the orange glow.

8 SALT RIVER CANYON

In any other state the beautiful Salt River Canyon would be regarded as a scenic wonder, but in Arizona the competition is too strong. Still, the sight of the little river cutting its way through the rough backcountry is one of the best panoramas in the state. A dirt road just off Rte. 77/60 that is usually suitable for passenger cars follows the canyon downstream (westbound) for about four miles to **Cibecue Creek.** The road continues another 3½ miles to the **Salt Banks,** an area of colorful formations. You will, however, need a rough-terrain vehicle on this stretch. And if endangered bald eagles are nesting in the area, the Apache Indians who administer the canyon will not allow vehicles beyond Cibecue Creek.

▶ *Obtain a permit to use the road to the Salt Banks at the Salt River Canyon Store on Rte. 77/60.*

9 GLOBE

The drive into copper-mining country passes by the Superstition Mountains —according to legend, the home of the Lost Dutchman gold mine—and climbs through Queen Creek Canyon before reaching Globe and its sister cities of Miami and Claypool. Globe is the most interesting of the three towns. The main thoroughfare, **Broad Street,** looks like something out of the 1940's, with a billiard hall, a washateria, small cafés, and blocky commercial buildings. Also on Broad Street are the remains of the once-lucrative **Old Dominion Mine,** with a display of old mining machinery.

Thirty miles from Globe, on your way back to Phoenix, stop at the **Boyce Thompson Arboretum,** founded by a former copper magnate, to learn how to recognize the plants that manage to thrive in the Sonoran, Chihuahuan, and Mojave deserts of the American West. A cool, shaded canyon walk is an unexpected pleasure. After the arboretum, the scenery gradually changes as you reach the copper mines, where heaps of black tailings line the highway.

1 TUCSON

The atmosphere here is Old Arizona. Tucson is much more leisurely and less suburban than Phoenix, and much more in harmony with its desert surroundings than any other city in the southwestern United States. Dry *arroyos*—water-carved gulleys—course through the city, surging with water when it rains. The flanks of the moun-

Teddy bear cholla cacti catch the afternoon sun at Organ Pipe National Monument (right). One of the denizens of this flourishing desert is the collared lizard (below).

tains that ring the city are covered with thick stands of the distinctive saguaro cactus. Front yards proudly display cacti, paloverde, and other desert species instead of grass.

The first stop in Tucson should be the **Arizona-Sonora-Desert Museum,** which is part zoo and part arboretum, as well as a natural history museum. Here you will learn that saguaro grow 50 feet high, live 200 years, and don't start to develop arms until they have been around for three-quarters of a century. You'll see them yourself on the nine-mile drive through the western part of **Saguaro National Monument.**

The most popular route into the mountains is **Sabino Canyon,** in the formidable Santa Catalina Mountains, which form the northern boundary of the city. A tram will take you into the canyon, where you can hike into a federally protected wilderness or walk out the way you came in, catching the tram at one of its frequent stopping points. The downtown **El Presidio Historic District** is where old Tucson began, but the original adobes are hardly recognizable since their conversion to galleries, shops, and restaurants. One magnificent building that does survive from the Spanish colonial period, however, is **Mission San Xavier del Bac,** a gleaming white structure in the desert south of town. Its simple exterior is balanced by an intricately designed façade and an interior rich in old Spanish frescoes, carvings, and statuary.

▶ *Don't be alarmed by the monsoon rains that often hit Tucson in late summer. They clear the air of dust and rarely last more than 30 minutes.*

2 CHIRICAHUA NATIONAL MONUMENT

The Apache Indians called the Chiricahua Mountains "land of standing-up rocks." Thousands of rock columns etched with swirling patterns have turned the mountains into fantasy castles with spires and towers. Erosion has left many of the formations so precariously balanced that they seem to defy the laws of physics. Geronimo eluded U.S. soldiers for years in this maze before surrendering in 1886. A paved road climbs through Bonita Canyon to provide the best view, at **Massai Point.**

3 BISBEE

Buildings totter precariously on the sides of steep canyons in this old mining town, once the largest city between St. Louis and San Francisco. Walk up **Brewery Gulch,** Bisbee's onetime alley of sin, and stop in at any of the rejuvenated hotels for a cold one. Even the havoc that mining wreaked has become an attraction here: almost 400 million tons of earth were removed from **Lavender Pit Mine,** a man-made terraced canyon open for viewing on Rte. 80. The scar is a mile long.

4 TOMBSTONE

Touted as "the town too tough to die," Tombstone owes its survival less to an act of will than to America's unending fascination with the West's most famous shootout. It was 1881 when Wyatt Earp, his brothers, and Doc Holliday settled their differences with the Clantons and the McLowrys at the O.K. Corral, and cinematic versions of the gunfight are still being made in the 1990's. Flooding of the silver mines and two fires brought Tombstone's boom years to a premature end, but many landmarks of the early years have survived, including the **O.K. Corral** and **Boothill Cemetery.** Today you can count the bullet holes in the walls of the **Bird Cage Theater,** see the original office and equipment of the *Tombstone Epitaph,* and have a drink in the 1879 **Crystal Palace Saloon.**

5 NOGALES

Visitors come to this border town to shop on the Mexican side for authentic crafts at bargain prices. Two buildings of note stand on the American side: the **Pimeria Alta Historical Society Museum** (the old city hall, complete with

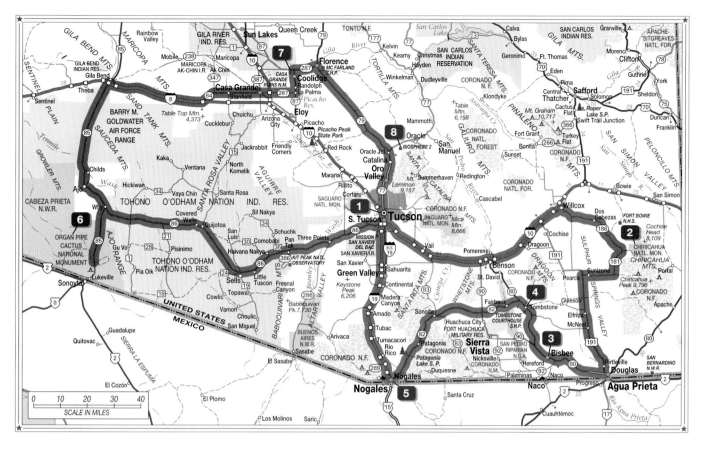

clock tower and jail cells), and, on a hillside, the Neoclassical silver-domed **1904 Court House,** gradually being restored to its former splendor.

6 ORGAN PIPE CACTUS NATIONAL MONUMENT

The long drive through the desert to this remote park on the Mexican border is worth the effort, because this is the only place in the United States to see the unusual organ pipe cactus. The plant's name comes from the tall, thick stems that can grow in clusters to heights of more than 20 feet. Two well-maintained scenic dirt roads loop through the park's classic desert terrain.

7 CASA GRANDE RUINS

When the Jesuit priest Eusebio Kino came here in 1694 he took one look at the Hohokam ruins, now **Casa Grande Ruins National Monument,** and gave them the Spanish name for "big house." The reference is to the massive central building surrounded by smaller ruins— a ceremonial center that is the largest freestanding prehistoric structure in Arizona, with 4½-foot-thick walls that rise a full four stories.

8 BIOSPHERE 2

Part serious science, part New Age dream, Biosphere 2 is a strange apparition in the high desert north of Tucson. Inside a gleaming structure of glass, scientists attempted to replicate and study the natural processes of the earth in a controlled, sealed environment. Its name is derived from the original Biosphere 1—that is, the earth itself.

In the original experiment, eight Biospherians who made their home in the dome from 1991 to 1993 were to rely on mini-environments that included a desert, a rain forest, an ocean, a marsh, even a farm. Although the attempt at creating self-sufficiency was not entirely successful, the project has a new goal: to use the dome as a laboratory for more wide-ranging scientific research. It has yet to be determined what the future holds for this striking structure.

A tour of Biosphere 2 involves a film and a self-guided walk around the structure. Visitors can peer through the glass but cannot go inside.

A cluster of cowboys, known around town as the Vigilantes, mill about in Tombstone, getting ready for a staged shootout on Allen Street. Actors also re-create the gunfight at the O.K. Corral.

Nevada

The great neon noise that is Las Vegas is only one of the facets of Nevada. Elsewhere, ghost towns stand in dusty sagebrush landscapes and remote alpine meadows burst into glorious bloom.

LAS VEGAS & LOW DESERT

1 LAS VEGAS

Think of it as a giant theme park, and the theme is excess. On Las Vegas's fabled Strip, you can find billion-dollar hotels, an erupting volcano, a pirate battle at sea, a replica of the Sphinx, jungles, fountains, and casinos with neon signs that turn the night into day. Inside the casinos, daylight is eliminated altogether, and in the dark reaches of the vast carpeted rooms you hear the ringing and clanging of slot machines, the siren call to gamblers.

If gambling doesn't appeal to you, keep in mind that Vegas can be as much fun for a spectator as for a participant. The hotels are fantasylands: the **Luxor** is ancient Egypt, **Caesar's Palace** is ancient Rome, the **Mirage** is the South Pacific—and no expense has been spared to carry out the themes. The white Siberian tiger habitat at the Mirage, the top-dollar **Forum Shops at Caesar's,** and the display of $1 million in cash at **Binion's Horseshoe** downtown are some of the more famous sights. But the best attraction of all is the people, most of whom act as if every day were New Year's Eve.

Away from the big hotels, the most-visited place is the **Liberace Museum,** where the late pianist's gaudy costumes and rhinestone-studded piano are on display. The **Gambler's Book Club** may be the world's strangest bookstore, devoted entirely to games of chance and the mobsters who once ran them. If you find yourself wondering what Thomas Jefferson would have thought of all this, unwind by taking a cruise on sparkling Lake Mead to **Hoover Dam.**

Venture out of the city on day trips to such spectacular nearby attractions as the **Grand Canyon.** Or point your car westward on Charleston Boulevard and motor out of town to **Red Rock Canyon,** where a 13-mile scenic drive takes you deep into Joshua tree country and pristine desertlands.

▶ *To avoid the smoky atmosphere found in most casinos, contact the Las Vegas Convention and Visitors Authority, which will tell you where to find smoke-free casinos.*

2 MOUNT CHARLESTON

The Spring Mountains, a geological island that reaches almost 12,000 feet in elevation, rise out of the barren Mojave Desert. You can drive as high as 8,500 feet on Mount Charleston, Nevada's third-highest peak, by way of Kyle Canyon and Lee Canyon. Take one of the short trails on the mountain to stands of bristlecone pines, considered the oldest living things on earth, or to **Cathedral Rock** or **Desert View.** Or simply enjoy the cool shade of the **Toiyabe National Forest;** these will be the last trees you'll see for a long time as you continue your drive.

3 DEATH VALLEY

The drive to **Death Valley National Monument** passes by the nation's atomic testing grounds—visitors not welcome! Much of Death Valley lies just across the state line in California. Despite its forbidding name, the valley is a beautiful place to tour, particularly when the weather is temperate, from October to April. But diehards who disdain crowds like it just fine in the summer, when temperatures top 100° F and you can drive for miles without encountering a soul. This is the kind of dry heat that reduces fresh bread to dusty crumbles. The desert landscape includes a salt bed known as **Devil's Golf Course** and a real oasis, fed by underground springs, called **Furnace Creek.** Among the scenic drives are **Mustard Canyon** and **Artist's Drive.**

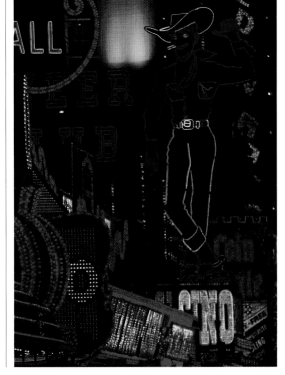

The lights of Las Vegas can be seen blazing for many desert miles. Up close, the Vegas Strip is a noisy jumble of clanging slot machines, flashing neon, and the whoops and hollers of gamblers who have struck gold. The famous cowboy at left has beckoned visitors into the Pioneer Club casino since 1951. Below, a patron wrestles a giant slot machine.

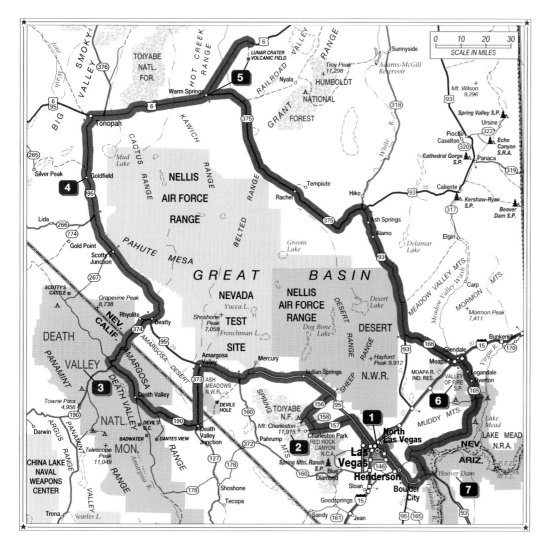

training here. This is the heart of the Great Basin desert, where ghost towns and a tortured terrain are all that remain. Yet the very emptiness of the landscape is its triumph; here is that rare place that mortal man cannot tame.

The southbound turnoff off Rte. 6 is a well-maintained dirt road that first passes **Easy Chair Crater,** a 600-foot-high hill that resembles an armchair. Six miles south is 3,800-foot-wide **Lunar Crater.** From the rim you can look down on the site of a volcanic explosion from eons past. Then travel back to Rte. 6, cross, and stop a mile away at the **Black Rock Lava Flow,** where you can walk among black lava boulders.

▶ *If you are not in a four-wheel-drive, take care in exploring side roads. You may get stuck in a dust pot—pits of talc so fine that a car will get mired in them.*

You can stand at the lowest point in the United States, 282 feet below sea level, and gaze across the valley at towering **Telescope Peak.** Abandoned dwellings and old mining equipment tell of the days when men mined borax in this harshest of environments.

Come up for air and supplies in **Beatty,** a charming Old West village. Nearby **Rhyolite,** a crumbling ghost town, is fascinating. The 1906 **Cook Bank Building,** now merely a two-story stone façade, may be the most photographed structure in the West. You'll also see the rock and mud ruins of the town prostitutes' "cribs"—tiny one-room "offices" lined up side by side.

▶ *If you're driving through Death Valley in the summer, fill your tank with gas and carry lots of water, for both you and your car. On hiking trails, wear long pants for protection against snakes and prickly bushes.*

4 GOLDFIELD

It has been said that if Nevada were a country, it would be the fourth-largest gold-producing nation in the world. Plenty of gold remains in these hills, but the boom is over for Goldfield. In the early 1900's it was the largest town in Nevada, but today most of the turn-of-the-century buildings are empty. Still functioning, though, is the handsome **Esmeralda County Court House,** which is all that saves the town from oblivion. Less handsome, but also surviving, is the old **Santa Fe Saloon**—somewhat of a town museum, with old photographs and newspaper headlines.

5 WARM SPRINGS/ LUNAR CRATER

This abandoned hamlet, with one lone ranch house and a stone corral, is the junction for **Rte. 6,** which takes you to Lunar Crater, a volcanic field so rugged that the Apollo astronauts considered

6 VALLEY OF FIRE STATE PARK

This was Nevada's first state park—a line of massive sandstone cliffs that have been eroded into such odd shapes as **Elephant Rock.** A short walk leads to some Indian petroglyphs; another easy trail passes by petrified logs. At certain times, when the light is just right, the rocks glow a fiery red.

7 HOOVER DAM

The lights of the Las Vegas Strip glittering on the desert floor are powered in part by the engineering muscle of this modern marvel. The **Hoover Dam** created vast Lake Mead, which provides several Western states with water and power by impounding the mighty Colorado River as it exits the Grand Canyon. A tour of Hoover Dam offers strolls through tunnels decorated with tilework and glimpses of seven-story-high generators.

❶ CARSON CITY

In 1858, Abe Curry bought a piece of land in the Eagle Valley and named it after the legendary mountain man Kit Carson. Months later, the discovery of the silver-rich Comstock Lode set off a mineral boom. In turn, the need for lumber to build mines set off a timber boom in the forests around Lake Tahoe, and Carson City happily prospered.

The town was designated the state capital in 1864, and in 1869 the U. S. Mint was opened here, ultimately producing $50 million in gold and silver coins by the time of its closing in 1893. The Mint is now the **Nevada State Museum,** where artifacts from Nevada's mining days—Carson City dollars, a handsome Gatling gun, a gambling wheel—are on display. The **Nevada State Railroad Museum** boasts three steam engines and equipment belonging to the Virginia & Truckee Railroad, which hauled ore between 1869 and 1938. Mining riches raised elegant homes for the men who made their fortunes here. You can take a guided tour of the **Bowers Mansion,** an 1864 Victorian house built of gray granite.

❷ GENOA

The first permanent white settlement in Nevada was founded here in 1850 by Mormons, who saw the site as an ideal trading stop for westward-bound gold seekers. **Mormon Station State Historic Monument** preserves this tradition with a rebuilt log stockade replicating one that protected an 1851 trading post. Genoa was also a picturesque resting place for Pony Express riders and travelers crossing the Sierra Nevada into California. Artifacts from those days can be seen in the lovely 1865 **Genoa Courthouse.**

❸ LAKE TAHOE

Mark Twain called it "a noble sheet of blue water…walled in by a rim of snow-clad mountain peaks…the fairest picture the whole earth affords." The Nevada side of this still-heavenly body of azure water is today studded with sprawling resorts and Vegas-style casinos. But the snowy peaks remain, as do thousands of acres of shimmering forest and lots of elbow room for both roulette players and nature lovers. Take a cruise on the **M.S. Dixie II** from Zephyr Cove to Emerald Bay, on the California side of the lake. See where the TV program *Bonanza* was filmed at the **Ponderosa Ranch** in Incline Village. Here the original ranch house stands in a Western theme park.

▶ *The drive on Interstate 80 from Reno to Carlin Canyon is a long, fairly uneventful stretch of road. Take along books on tape or your favorite music to pass the time.*

❹ CARLIN CANYON

Eons ago, the Humboldt River flowed across a gentle plain. Mountain-building forces upheaved the surrounding landscape at the same rate that the river eroded its bed downward. Eventually, high canyon walls trapped the river in what geologists call an "entrenched me-

The Silver Queen *adorns a Virginia City bar, wearing a gown of 3,000 silver coins.*

ander," bending the river into a snaky, slow-moving pattern as opposed to the pattern of a straightforward, fast-moving highland stream. Detour from Interstate 80 through Carlin Canyon from the Central exit or the East Carlin exit.

❺ LAMOILLE

The Ruby Mountains are often called the most spectacular range in Nevada. Ancient glaciers sculpted canyons into the 11,000-foot rocky peaks now dotted with crystalline lakes and lush meadows within **Humboldt National Forest.** The easiest way to experience these splendors is along **Lamoille Canyon Scenic Byway.** This 12-mile paved road carries visitors as high as 8,800 feet at Roads End, a trailhead for the 40-mile **Ruby Crest Trail.**

❻ GREAT BASIN
NATIONAL PARK

No mere sagebrush desert this: the Great Basin National Park is more a landscape of alpine meadows and glaciated mountains. One, **Wheeler Peak,** rises to 13,063 feet. On its flanks dwell gnomelike bristlecone pines from 3,000 to 4,000 years old. The easiest way to reach these ancient pines is to follow the 12-mile **Wheeler Peak Scenic Drive** to its end at 10,000 feet.

Within the limestone base of the national park are **Lehman Caves.** Guided 1½-hour tours lead visitors through illuminated passageways past awesome stalagmites and stalactites. A candlelight tour—where everyone carries old-fashioned candle lanterns—is offered every evening in the summer season at 6 P.M.

Dubbed "the loneliest road in America," **Rte. 50** runs westward from Great Basin National Park all the way to Carson City. But boring it is not. You'll drive past mountain ranges and desert lands, cattle country, and historic mining towns. Dig for garnet stones at **Garnet Hill,** just south of Ely on Rte. 6. The pink-tinged rocks found in the hillsides contain the semiprecious garnets, which in their raw state resemble raisins. Between Cold Springs and Fallon is **Sand Mountain,** a giant sand dune. Send for a "Highway 50 Survival Kit" from either the Fallon, Austin, Eureka, or Ely chambers of commerce.

The oldest living trees, *bristlecone pines brace a rocky, windy terrain on the slopes of Mount Washington in Great Basin National Park.*

7 AUSTIN

The boom never really ended for this old mining town, where stores of silver have been unearthed since the 1860's. The restored **Reuel Gridley General Store** is now a museum displaying local historical artifacts. **Stokes Castle**, a tower of granite, is the remnant of a grand summer home built in the 1890's for Eastern financier Anson Phelps Stokes. The tower looks out over a 60-mile radius of desert and mountains.

8 COLD SPRINGS

On a 1,966-mile Pony Express route that was littered with hardship and danger, this stretch of Nevada country was one of the most dangerous. Rte. 50 follows the route of the Express, whose riders on horseback carried mail between St. Joseph, Missouri, and Sacramento in the early 1860's. The remnants of the **Cold Springs Pony Express Station**, where fresh mounts waited for hard-riding expressmen, rest on the south side of the highway. In 1860 Paiute Indian raiders killed the station keeper, ran off the stock, and burned whatever would go up in flames. The station is a fairly strenuous 1½-mile hike from the highway. On the opposite side of the road, behind a chain-link fence, lie the ruins of freight and telegraph relay stations.

9 FORT CHURCHILL

Nevada boasts many ghost towns, but **Fort Churchill State Historic Park** has the state's only ghost fort. The terra-cotta remnants of the adobe fort today rest in a landscape of sage and dust. The U.S. Army built this fort in 1860 to guard against Indian attacks; 10 years later it was deserted. A visitor center nearby reconstructs its history.

10 VIRGINIA CITY

The discovery of the Comstock Lode's store of silver and gold drew a motley assortment of 30,000 people to this rocky terrain. Among those drawn here was Mark Twain, who wrote for the *Territorial Enterprise,* the first newspaper in Nevada. He had much to report: the saloon count in Virginia City's heyday reached 110, and the boom brought to town such state-of-the-art technology as the only elevator between San Francisco and Chicago.

Virginia City retains its boomtown feel. Several museums filled with gold rush minutiae line the creaky wooden boardwalks along **C Street.** Opulent mansions built for the mining elite perch on the slopes of Mount Davidson. A colonnaded veranda rings **Mackay Mansion,** first lived in by William Randolph Hearst's father, George.

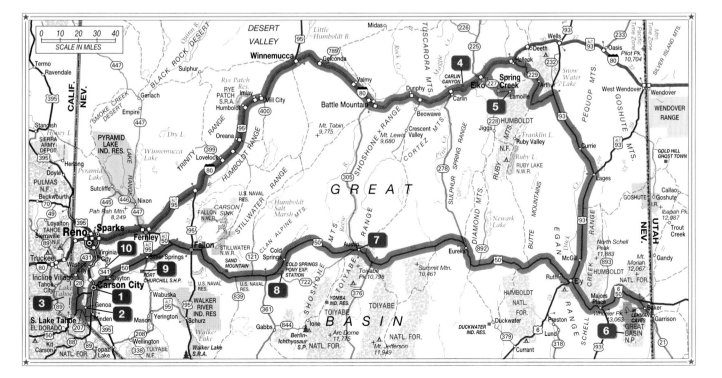

FAR WEST & HAWAII

*F*rom a nostalgic stroll along Hollywood's Walk of Fame to a cruise up the Yukon River, from the towering heights of California's redwoods to the moonscape of Haleakala Volcano in Maui, these five states—Washington, Oregon, California, Alaska, and Hawaii—offer an extraordinary diversity of both landscape and culture.

In the Pacific Northwest you'll explore the ravaged landscape of Mount St. Helens, spot frolicking sea lions in the frothy surf of Depoe Bay, and watch as imaginary kingdoms are fashioned at the sandcastle contest on Cannon Beach. Farther south you'll gaze out over the blue of San Francisco Bay and relive California's past at adobe Spanish missions.

In Alaska you'll marvel at Denali's wind-swept glaciers and visit a fishing village whose culture speaks of the state's Russian heritage. Far across the sea, in Hawaii, you'll relish the serenity of Kauai and the bustle of Honolulu. Prepare for a grand trip on 17 tours through the rich variety of America's last frontier.

Big Sur coastline

Washington

Washington is actually two landscapes. West of the Cascade Range abundant rainfall nourishes ancient forests that edge the Pacific. To the east is a vast land of farms and quaint small towns.

SEATTLE & OLYMPIC PENINSULA

1 SEATTLE

The folk who dwell in this rain-kissed emerald city carry on an open love affair with their town. To Seattleites, living on a tree-lined hillside—with icy mountain vistas and a backyard of flowering dogwoods, all within the city limits of a major metropolis is living well indeed. To best appreciate the city's setting, visit the **Space Needle** to see the Olympic Mountains to the west, the Cascade Range to the east, and island-dotted Puget Sound all around. This Seattle landmark, with a revolving restaurant and lounge, offers stunning 360° views. On the rare days when the sun splits open the pewter sky, snow-capped Mount Rainier makes a grand showing. When "the mountain is out," as they say in Seattle, the populace is doubly content.

Seattle is a city of water. Some 161 bridges pass over inlets and rivulets often swollen with rainwater. On days when skies are gray and drizzly, locals head for one of the best public libraries in the country or to the city's famed bookstore, the **Elliot Bay Book Company.** Or they drink coffee—pots of it. This is, after all, the city that originated the coffee-bar craze.

Gray skies or no, Seattle is abuzz with activity. An antique streetcar shuttles passengers along its route from Pier 70 to the **International District.** Visit the **Seattle Aquarium** to catch the antics of harbor seals at feeding time. Up the hill is what some say is the soul of Seattle: **Pike Place Market.** At this four-block soundside warren you can forage for fresh produce and fixings, banter with mischievous seafood dealers—beware of "low-flying" fish—or scour alleyways for free samplings of homemade jams.

***The futuristic Space Needle** was constructed for the 1962 Seattle World's Fair.*

The historic neighborhood known as **Pioneer Square Historic District** was once the prosperous hub of 19th-century Seattle. In the 1920's, this 31-block district of Romanesque Revival structures fell into a state of near ruin: it was the original Skid Row, so named for the local sawmills' practice of sliding lumber down the street onto loading docks. In the 1970's, the neighborhood was dusted off and restored, and now gleaming cafés and galleries line its cobblestone streets. You can revisit the Seattle of the Victorian era in the **Underground Tours,** 1½-hour guided tours of the now-subterranean old establishments of Pioneer Square. After the great fire of 1889, the city was built at a higher level for better drainage and these street-level floors were sealed off.

► *Downtown traffic in Seattle can be heavy, so park the car and tour on foot. Or take the Metro bus, which offers free rides anywhere downtown from 6 A.M. to 7 P.M.*

2 TACOMA

Bing Crosby's birthplace has two historic districts, fine Victorian residences, and much to do. The **Broadway Center for the Performing Arts** includes two old restored vaudeville halls.

The pioneer, Indian, and Alaskan collections at the **Washington State Historical Society Museum** are the largest on the Pacific Coast. **Point Defiance Park,** 700 acres of gardens and old-growth forest, has a zoo and aquarium.

3 OLYMPIA

This pretty-as-a-picture state capital has parks of all stripes: harborside parks, historic parks, and the **Capitol Campus,** one of the finest capitol grounds in the nation. The elegant **Legislative Building** bears more than a passing resemblance to the U.S. Capitol; it's even surrounded by flowering cherry trees.

On arriving here in 1805, Lewis and Clark feasted on what they described as "giant salmon" and tiny but savory oysters. The once-plentiful Olympia oyster has been nearly exterminated in modern times by pollutants, imported pests, and its own delicate temperament—and somewhat upstaged by the bigger, hardier Pacific oyster. Strictly farm-raised now, the Olympia remains prized for its salty, pungent flavor. You can take a crash course in oyster farming at **Taylor United, Inc.,** 10 miles northwest, on one-hour plant tours; reserve ahead. Both Olympia and Pacific oysters are sold on-site.

4 ABERDEEN/HOQUIAM

These twin cities share bustling **Grays Harbor,** named for Capt. Robert Gray, who first charted this land in 1792. The shipyard in Aberdeen's **Grays Harbor Historical Seaport** often includes a replica of Gray's ship, the *Lady Washington.* The museum offers seasonal cruises aboard the ship along the Chehalis, a nationally designated wild and scenic river.

Stop in **Kalaloch** on your drive up the coast, where short, well-marked trails lead to the beach. Literally thousands of

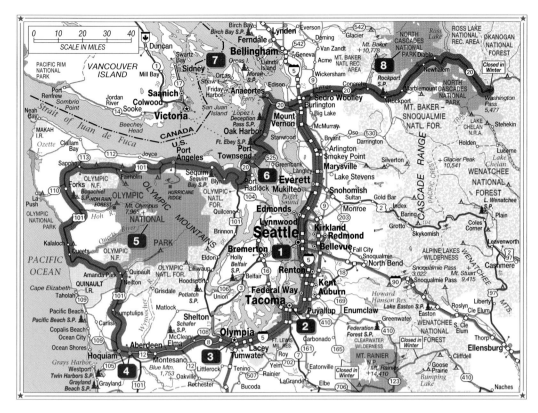

on the vegetation-shrouded three-quarter-mile **Hall of Mosses Loop Trail.**

Take the 14-mile road just west of Fairholm south to the steaming sulfur pools of **Sol Duc Hot Springs.** This rustic spa resort dates back to 1910; a three-quarter-mile hike leads to **Sol Duc Falls.**

The **Port Angeles** entrance to the park takes you through subalpine meadows of spring-blooming avalanche lilies and purple lupine. Seventeen miles south is **Hurricane Ridge,** which affords spectacular views of glacier-mantled **Mount Olympus.**

6 PORT TOWNSEND

A haven for writers and artists, Port Townsend boasts more Victorian architecture than any community north of San Francisco. Landmark buildings along Water Street and gingerbread houses perched on a hill overlooking the harbor recall the town's late-19th-century heyday. To spend the night in a stately Victorian home along Officers' Row in **Fort Worden State Park,** you must reserve well in advance. The park bustles with arts festivals in the summer and contains a handsome lighthouse.

You'll be taking a 30-minute ferry from Port Townsend to Keystone, on pastoral **Whidbey Island.** From here you'll drive over the Deception Pass bridge to **Anacortes.** The San Juan Islands can be reached by car ferry from this charming seaside town.

7 SAN JUAN ISLANDS

The 172 evergreen islands dotted along the San Juan County waterways are prized for their beauty and recreational choices but especially for their low-key pace. Four of the islands can be reached by ferry from the town of Anacortes. Try to visit off-season; these popular islands can be crowded in summer.

With relatively few hills, **Lopez Island** is a favorite of cyclists, who leisurely cruise past orchards, weath-

live starfish, plump and colorful, cling to seaside rocks. Bone-white drift logs are strewn along the beach, carried here from upriver streams and picked clean by the elements. Check the tide chart before you go beachcombing, however. High tides can sweep in quickly, sending these huge timbers rolling about.

5 OLYMPIC NATIONAL PARK

Some of the most diverse landscapes in the United States make up this magnificent 1,441-square-mile park, from pastoral meadows to forests of gargantuan Douglas firs to snowy peaks.

▶ *Several entrances lead into the park. These roads do not link up within the park, so you must return to Rte. 101 to reach another road. Most charge an entrance fee in the summer. A park pass is good for one year.*

The **Hoh River Road** takes you into fairy-tale rain forest country. The entrance is 25 miles north of Kalaloch; then drive east 19 miles to reach the park. Here in the **Hoh Rain Forest,** two nature trails meander through the cathedral gloom of a temperate rain forest. In the morning, elk may be spotted

Wet and wild: Attired in a rain slicker, a visitor takes a stroll through the luxuriant Hall of Mosses, a winding trail in the temperate Hoh Rain Forest of Olympic National Park.

ered barns, and velvety pastures. **Friday Harbor**, on **San Juan Island**, is a popular sailors' anchorage. Rent a bike and pedal to the **Whale Museum**, to study orca lore. To see the real thing, visit the **Lime Kiln Point Lighthouse** at **Lime Kiln Point State Park**, 10 miles west, where in the summer you can spy pods of orca whales feeding close to shore. The largest and most rugged of the islands is **Orcas Island**. Here **Mount Constitution** in **Moran State Park** offers panoramas of the surrounding islands.

8 NORTH CASCADES

The gateway to the North Cascade mountains is **Skagit Valley**, one of the world's premier flower bulb–producing regions. The first two weeks in April are reserved for the **Skagit Valley Tulip Festival** in Mount Vernon. Dial 1-800-4-TULIPS for peak bloom updates.

You'll be traveling east on Rte. 20, the sublime **North Cascades Scenic Highway**. Hiking trails to mountain aeries are a mere pull-off away. **North Cascades National Park** preserves a vast domain of old-growth forests, subalpine meadows, and snowcapped peaks. Rocky cliffs rim chilly **Diablo Lake**; in the summer the waters turn a deep green hue from icy glacial runoff.

CASCADES & PACIFIC COAST

1 MOUNT RAINIER

Known to the local Indians as Tahoma—the Great Mountain—14,411-foot Mount Rainier is one of the world's most massive volcanoes. It dominates the skyline for more than 100 miles around, easily dwarfing the neighboring 6,000-foot behemoths in the Cascades. Flanking Rainier are 26 massive glaciers. Start your trip at **Elbe**, aboard the **Mount Rainier Scenic Railroad**, pulled by 1920's steam locomotives that travel for miles through lush alpine forests and over the Nisqually River. At **Paradise**, in the south-central park, gentle hills framed by Rainier's snowy dome are blanketed with wild-

flowers in the warm months. You can get great views of **Mount Rainier National Park** at the visitor center in Paradise. Take the 1½-mile **Nisqually Vista Trail** here for equally superb views of Rainier and the Nisqually Glacier. Thousand-year-old Douglas fir, western red cedar, and western hemlock line the 1.3-mile **Grove of the Patriarchs** nature trail, near the park's southeastern entrance. Detour off the designated loop eight miles northwest to the visitor center at **Sunrise**, where you can see Rainier from the highest auto-accessible point in the park.

▶ *Call ahead for road conditions; highways are often closed in the winter.*

Sunrise on Reflection Lake casts a mirror image of Mount Rainier on the icy waters.

2 YAKIMA

Often cited as one of America's most livable cities, Yakima offers a sunny, lively environment close to Cascades recreation. Sagebrush-dusted hills surround the irrigated fields of the **Yakima Valley**, where nearly half of the nation's fresh apple harvest is grown. But you won't have to drive far to reap the seasonal bounty from roadside farm stands. This is a city where farmers happily bring their cherries, peaches, and pears directly to town.

In town, a trolley takes visitors to such sites as the **Capitol Theatre**, an opulent performing-arts hall restored to its 1920's splendor. The **Yakima Valley Museum** contains a replica of the Supreme Court office of Justice (and native son) William O. Douglas.

3 TOPPENISH

Murals depicting scenes from Toppenish history blanket the sides of buildings in this award-winning city. See them by taking a narrated **Mural Tour** in a horse-drawn Conestoga wagon. A seven-story winter lodge dominates the **Yakama Nation Cultural Center**, which chronicles the history of the Yakama (also spelled Yakima) nation.

The fertile volcanic soil of the Yakima Valley has been a boon to grape growers, spawning a wine industry that is world renowned. A loosely strung necklace of 23 wineries, from **Wapato** to **Benton City**, follows the flow of the Yakima River. Visit the last weekend in April for the **Yakima Valley Winegrowers' Spring Barrel Tasting**.

From the town of Paterson west to Vancouver you'll be driving the **Lewis and Clark State Highway** (Rte. 14) through the **Columbia River Gorge**. A national scenic area astride the river protects many of the same cliffs, waterfalls, and forests that Lewis and Clark encountered in 1805.

4 MARYHILL

The palatial mansion built by the railroad heir Samuel Hill stands in splendid isolation on a bluff overlooking the Columbia River. Here, miles from any other town, Hill in the 1920's created the **Maryhill Museum of Fine Arts**, with its rich collection of European and American art. In the Queen Marie Room are a throne and coronation gown and icons—items Queen Marie of Romania donated in gratitude for American aid after World War I.

5 NORTH BONNEVILLE

Beacon Rock, just west, is a massive remnant from an ancient volcano. Hiking trails wind through a state park surrounding the 848-foot-high rock. Just east, the **Bonneville Dam** combines the oldest (1937) powerhouse on the river and the newest (1986), but both follow the same mission: to harness hydropower from the Columbia. Chinook salmon and steelhead trout can be seen struggling up fish ladders from lighted underwater windows at the **North Shore Visitor Center.**

6 VANCOUVER

This vigorous port city with a multi-ethnic populace is within striking distance of fir-shrouded mountains and brisk river breezes. Visit 19th-century Vancouver, when it was described as "the New York of the Pacific," at the reconstructed **Fort Vancouver National Historic Site,** furnished as the fur-trading center it was in 1845.

A collection of 21 Victorian homes built for military personnel have been restored as the **Officers' Row National Historic District.** Open to the public are the 1886 **Marshall House,** once the quarters of Gen. George C. Marshall, and the 1850 **Grant House.**

In Battle Ground, 15 miles northeast, hop aboard the **Lewis & Clark Railway.** Its 2½-hour seasonal weekend trips roughly follow the route of the pioneers past scenic vistas. In the summer you can take a dip in Yacolt Creek; in December a Christmas-tree train will carry you up the mountain to bring back your own fresh-cut tree.

The fertile volcanic soil of the Yakima Valley produces one of the country's largest apple crops, and vast vineyards supply the region's burgeoning wine industry.

7 MOUNT ST. HELENS

On May 18, 1980, after 123 years of silence, this "ice-cream cone in the sky" blew its top. Today a million visitors a year come to the 110,000-acre **Mount St. Helens National Volcanic Monument** to gape at a devastated landscape that was once a snowy summit.

From Cougar, a 60-mile network of national forest roads, most of them paved, links many of the sites within the monument. You can drive Rte. 83 literally onto the slope of the volcano and then get out and hike even higher up (4,800 feet) to **Climbers Bivouac** for spectacular vistas.

Those who can't get enough of Mount St. Helens should return to Interstate 5 and detour north to Castle Rock. Take Rte. 504 east five miles to the **Mount St. Helens National Volcanic Visitor Center** at Silver Lake. Here is a walk-in model of the volcano, as well as a continuously running 22-minute video and slide program of the actual eruption. Slated to open in late 1996 is the **Johnston Ridge Observatory,** 45 miles east, where you can stare down into the volcano's gaping crater; call the monument headquarters for the opening date.

▶ *No shade exists in devastated areas and trails are dry, so wear sunscreen or a hat and bring water. And get a weather update; the Cascades have notoriously unpredictable weather.*

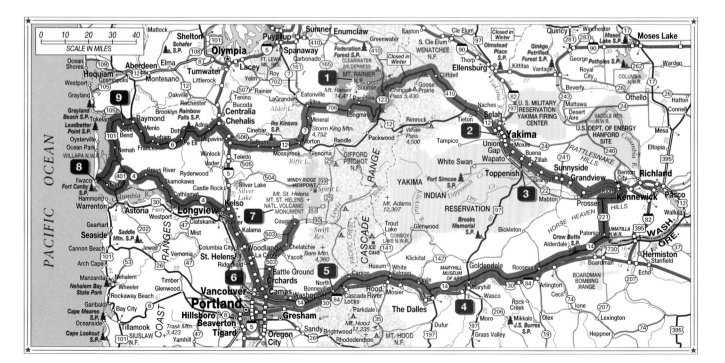

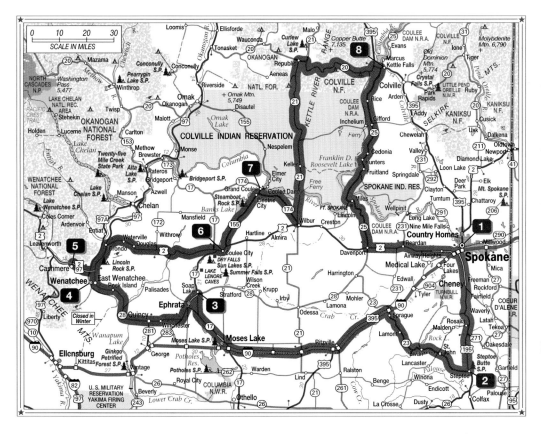

has one of America's finest collections of Indian arts and handicrafts. Next door, the restored **Campbell House** recalls Spokane's late-19th-century Age of Elegance, when local captains of commerce built themselves extravagant mansions.

A self-guided driving tour winds through the woodlands of **Turnbull National Wildlife Refuge,** a breeding area for diving ducks, some 20 miles southwest of Spokane. Tundra swans occasionally appear in spring.

2 STEPTOE

The drive from Spokane to Steptoe is a lovely one, tripping over the undulating patchwork hills of Palouse country. The 3,612-foot **Steptoe Butte** in Steptoe Butte State Park needs no advertising to entice people to come; the view from this ancient mountaintop, of waving green and gold wheat fields, sells itself.

3 SOAP LAKE

Known as Smokiam ("healing waters") to local Indians, the resort lake of this small town contains alkaline waters with high concentrations of 16 minerals and salts. The name is derived from the sudsy froth on the lake's surface. These waters have long drawn believers, who claim a good soak relieves arthritis, psoriasis, and sundry other ailments.

► *Many local motels pipe lake water into bathtubs and pools; otherwise, you can take the waters from the source itself, at the numerous public beaches along Soap Lake.*

4 WENATCHEE

The sun-kissed Wenatchee Valley became one of the world's largest apple-growing regions once irrigation was established here in 1903. Since 1919, Wenatchee has thrown a party for its most important crop with an **Apple Blossom Festival** from late April

8 ILWACO

Fort Canby State Park has a dramatic setting at the tip of Cape Disappointment, where the Columbia pours into the Pacific. The 1856 **Cape Disappointment Lighthouse** stands guard over one of the most treacherous river bars in the world.

The **Willapa National Wildlife Refuge** protects 11,200 acres of salt marsh, sand dunes, and freshwater wetlands. One unit of the refuge encompasses **Long Island,** a naturalist's paradise that can only be reached by private boat. Once there, hike to **Cedar Grove,** a stand of virgin cedar forest, undisturbed for 4,000 years. Or birdwatch at the goose pasture in the **Riekkola Unit,** where beds of grass are grown for the pleasure of Canada geese.

9 SOUTH BEND

Since the 1890's this little port has been known as the Oyster Capital of the West. Still-pristine Willapa Bay produces one-sixth of the entire country's harvest. Visit during the four-day **Oyster Stampede,** held on Memorial Day weekend, when you can reserve a tour of the **Coast Oyster Company,** the world's largest oyster-processing plant.

1 SPOKANE

Washington's second-largest city is the unofficial capital of the Inland Northwest—a densely forested, hilly landscape in the rain shadow of the Cascades. Thousands of years ago this region was shaped by a devastating flood; hence the sculpted terrain. Watered by irrigation from the Spokane Aquifer, the fertile volcanic soil produces bumper harvests of wheat, apples, and hops.

Much of Spokane's splendid park system was designed by Frederick Law Olmsted. **Riverfront Park,** once the city railroad yard, was established following the Expo '74 World's Fair. This 100-acre greensward has a river island, midway rides, and a 1909 hand-carved carousel. The 80-foot **Spokane Falls,** beautifully illuminated at night, thunders in the background.

Formal rose and lilac gardens and greenhouses teeming with exotic plants make up **Duncan Gardens** in Manito Park. The **Cheney Cowles Museum**

through early May. Orchards of apricots, cherries, and pears line roadsides, brightening the valley in springtime with pink and white blossoms. Visit the **Washington Apple Commission Visitor Center** for exhibits, a film, and a sampling of apples and juices.

The **North Central Washington Museum**, situated in a landmark post office building, depicts native and pioneer life here with such exhibits as "Mainstreet 1910" and "The River Sings," a multimedia show recounting the cultural history of the American Indians who lived here.

Ohme Gardens, three miles north of town, is perched on a rocky bluff above the Wenatchee Valley, offering views of the Cascade Range and the Columbia and Wenatchee rivers. Six decades of cultivation by the Ohme family have transformed nine acres of desert scrub into terraced alpine gardens. Stone pathways meander among fern-bordered pools and shady glens of towering evergreens.

5 CASHMERE

This historic mission town in the orchard-covered hills of the Wenatchee Valley has an old-fashioned main street with replica 19th-century buildings. The **Chelan County Historical Museum** re-creates a pioneer village with some 20 structures, most built between 1872 and 1910 and assembled here from the surrounding area. Downtown, tours and tastings are offered at the **Aplets & Cotlets Candy Factory**, which has been producing candies made of fresh fruit and walnuts for more than 70 years.

Fresh-picked apples are readied for market in the orchards of the Wenatchee Valley.

On your drive from Cashmere, stop at **Dry Falls**, six miles south of Coulee City. Stepped basalt cliffs rise 800 feet above a canyon floor. More than half a million years ago a waterfall twice as high and five times as wide as Niagara Falls roared over the precipice. The course of the Columbia River ultimately shifted, leaving the cataract high and dry. Hiking trails wind through nearby **Sun Lakes State Park**, which contains nine small lakes in the canyon gouged by the waters of Dry Falls.

6 COULEE CITY

Established at the junction of railroad and stagecoach lines, this pioneer community is the only place between Seattle and Spokane where those traveling Rte. 2 can cross the broad, 50-mile-long trough called the **Grand Coulee**, which was formed at the end of the last Ice Age by the rushing glacial meltwater of the Spokane Flood .

The drive north on Rte. 155 along Grand Coulee's eastern rim presents a starkly rugged beauty familiar from countless Westerns: a big sky, sagebrush countryside, and craggy cliffs. **Steamboat Rock**, a butte that rises 1,000 feet above Banks Lake, was a landmark to Indians and settlers. Try the moderate 45-minute hike to the top of this flat-topped promontory, where you can poke about on 640 relatively flat acres and see for 20 miles.

► *Bring along insect repellent to Steamboat Rock in the warmer months; mosquitoes can be bothersome.*

7 GRAND COULEE

As tall as a 61-story building and nine blocks long, **Grand Coulee Dam** is one of the engineering marvels of the world. This massive concrete structure harnesses Columbia River waters to bring irrigation, power, flood control, and recreation to this arid region. An outside elevator at the third power plant rises at a 45° angle, affording spectacular views of the spillway. In the summertime the spillway is used as a giant screen for one of the world's largest laser light shows.

8 KETTLE FALLS

Once Kettle Falls tumbled 33 feet in less than half a mile. Now they lie submerged beneath **Lake Roosevelt**, a 130-mile-long reservoir formed by Grand Coulee Dam. The **Coulee Dam National Recreation Area** encompasses 100,000 acres from the dam north along Lake Roosevelt practically to the Canadian border. The recreation area is popular with anglers, boaters, waterskiers, and swimmers.

One of the state's oldest churches rests beneath the pines just north of town. Built in 1845, the restored **St. Paul's Mission** was used for services by native Indians who came here to fish for salmon in the Columbia River.

Rocky coulees, steep basalt cliffs, and a broken necklace of glistening lakes combine to give Dry Falls, just south of Coulee City, a sinuous beauty.

Oregon

Oregon's famous coastal scenery is spectacular indeed—but you haven't seen the state until you've also laid eyes on the beautiful Columbia River Gorge and the deepest lake in America.

PORTLAND & THE NORTHWEST

1 PORTLAND

Lush and livable, albeit wet, Portland is one of the country's newest hot spots, buoyed by a burgeoning arts scene and nature at its back door. Visit the City of Roses in June, when the blooms of more than 10,000 rosebushes in the **International Rose Test Gardens** unfold. Don't miss the view of snow-capped Mount Hood in the distance. An open-air shuttle will take you to the **Japanese Gardens**, which visitors from Japan have pronounced exquisite. Catch the Zooliner, a charming steam train, for a ride to the **Metro Washington Park Zoo**, where a rain forest exhibit regularly soaks its crocodiles with steamy downpours. More famous is the zoo's collection of Asian elephants, one of the largest in the country.

Downtown Portland, sprinkled with fountains, parks, and cafés, also has its share of shops and museums and a smattering of Postmodern architecture sure to elicit an opinion. Atop one such structure, the Portland Building, is a hammered-copper sculpture, **Portlandia**, second in size only to the Statue of Liberty. A harbor in stormy weather is **Powell's City of Books**, one of the largest bookstores in the country. At the **Portland Art Museum**, make it a point to see the Northwest Coast Indian art, which joins works from around the world spanning 35 centuries. In **Old Town** 19th-century cast-iron buildings like those in SoHo in New York house artists' studios, eateries, and shops.

▶ *The Saturday Market operates Saturdays and Sundays, March through December, in Old Town. It is the largest outdoor crafts fair in the country, with food and music too.*

2 COLUMBIA RIVER GORGE NATIONAL SCENIC AREA

An engineering feat, the **Columbia River Scenic Highway** (Rtes. 30 and 84) follows the largest river in the West for 22 miles past volcanic cliffs, over which dozens of waterfalls plummet. **Crown Point**, a 720-foot bluff, offers a dramatic preview of the gorge. Next you'll encounter an 11-mile stretch containing 11 waterfalls, culminating in the two-tiered postcard-perfect **Multnomah Falls**, the second-highest year-round waterfall in the country, which drops a total of 620 feet. Footpaths lead to the top of the lower falls, and a stone lodge at the bottom serves as a restaurant and visitor center.

3 MOUNT HOOD

A nearly symmetrical volcanic cone, Mount Hood is Oregon's highest peak at 11,235 feet. Only an hour and a half from Portland, it is the core of a play-ground that offers year-round skiing and magnificent hiking trails. The **Mount Hood Loop Highway** affords a barrage of scenic views as it circles the mountain via the towns of **Government Camp**, a resort village, and **Hood River**, a windsurfers' mecca. Near the top of the mountain looms the rustic stone-and-timber **Timberline Lodge**, built in the 1930's as a New Deal WPA project. Its massive beams, intricate woodwork, and enormous fireplaces offer a warm welcome to weary skiers. Visitors can hike from the lodge to an alpine meadow or take the chairlift to a winding interpretive trail.

▶ *Don't miss the beautiful sunset view of the Cascade Range from the bar on the third floor of the lodge.*

Pioneer Courthouse Square *in downtown Portland is a prime spot for people-watching.*

4 OREGON CITY

The Oregon Trail ended in Oregon City, the first state capital, nestled in the lush Willamette Valley downstream from the 40-foot **Willamette Falls**. The Municipal Free Elevator will hoist you up a cliff to an observation platform for a bird's-eye view.

The stately clapboard **John McLoughlin House National Historic Site** recalls the fur-trading days when the Hudson's Bay Company representative now known as the Father of Oregon lived here. The **Oregon Trail Interpretive Center** honors the intrepid journey west by the 300,000 immigrants who came in wagons and on horseback in the 1840's and 1850's.

5 DEPOE BAY

Seals and sea lions have claimed the coast around Depoe Bay for their own. Whale-watching cruises depart from the pint-size harbor here, one of the smallest harbors anywhere. North of the harbor are the **Spouting Horns**, cracks in the rocks that convert crashing waves into waterspouts, most active after storms. Six miles south, storms and rising tides cause waves to surge and boil at **Devil's Punch Bowl State Park.** Outgoing tides reveal starfish, sea urchins, and other glistening creatures in the adjacent **Marine Gardens Ocean Shore Preserve.**

6 TILLAMOOK

At Pacific City the **Three Capes Scenic Loop** winds west from Rte. 101 to Tillamook. The three capes—Kiwanda, Lookout, and Meares—sum up the Oregon coast's singular beauty: crashing waves, sparkling white sand dunes, beaches strewn with sculptured driftwood and lustrous agates, and wildlife including seals, sea lions, and comical tufted puffins. Near the **Cape Meares Lighthouse** grows the **Octopus Tree,** a weathered Sitka spruce with six trunks.

In Tillamook visitors can tour the famed **Tillamook Cheese Factory** and sample some of the country's best Cheddars. Head south on Rte. 101 for an easy one-mile hike to the **Munson Creek Falls,** which tumble 266 feet over mossy cliffs.

7 CANNON BEACH

Cannon Beach, dubbed the Carmel of the Oregon coast, epitomizes the stunning scenery for which the shoreline is famous. A haven for artists, it boasts some of the finest galleries and shops on the West Coast, and the granddaddy of sandcastle contests, held in early summer. Almost synonymous with Cannon Beach is **Haystack Rock,** at

Sand sculpture goes well beyond castle building at the annual contest on Cannon Beach.

235 feet one of the tallest coastal monoliths in the world. It is framed by wind-shaped trees and is best viewed from the beach at **Ecola State Park.** Scan the sea closely in April and May and you may spot a whale or two.

8 FORT CLATSOP

Lewis and Clark camped here for three months during the rainy winter of 1805–06 before embarking on their journey back east. A replica of their fort at **Fort Clatsop National Memorial** is staffed in summer by buckskin-clad rangers who show how the expedition passed the time by tanning hides, rendering lard for candles, crafting canoes, and fashioning lead bullets.

9 ASTORIA

A constant parade of fishing boats passes the waterfront of Astoria, originally a fur-trading post named for John Jacob Astor. Astoria is not only the oldest permanent settlement west of the Mississippi; it is a genuine maritime town, perched on the banks of the Columbia River. Most prominent among the Victorian homes here is the Queen Anne–style **Flavel House,** built by a sea captain who surveyed his fleet from the cupola. The 125-foot **Astoria Column** looks out over the coast, the river, and the surrounding mountains.

Salvaged treasures at the **Columbia River Maritime Museum** are part of a collection that has been called one of the best on the West Coast. On display is the historic lightship *Columbia*.

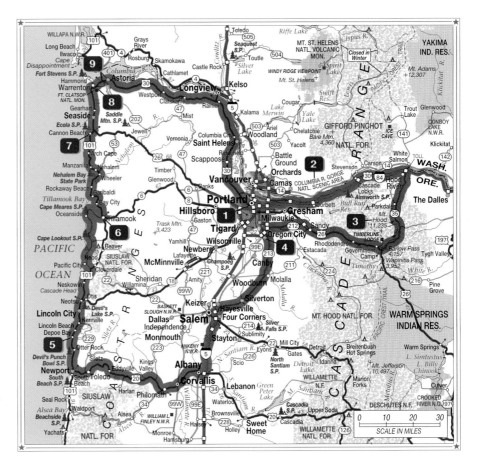

1 CRATER LAKE NATIONAL PARK

The sapphire glow of Crater Lake, at 1,932 feet deep the deepest lake in the country, is almost unreal. Astonishingly clear, the lake was formed in a caldera created by a monumental volcanic explosion. Rain and snow later filled the crater to within 1,000 feet of the rim.

The 33-mile **Rim Drive** offers more than a dozen scenic viewpoints. A two-mile trail leads from the road to the top of **Mount Scott**, the highest point in the park, where an observation point affords sweeping views of the lake and the surrounding forested peaks. The steep, mile-long **Cleetwood Trail** is the only way to reach the lake itself. (Be aware that the climb back up is quite strenuous.) Boats depart from the shore for a two-hour tour with a stop at **Wizard Island**, a 760-foot cinder cone within the crater. Back on land, the lovely three-quarter-mile **Castle Crest Wildflower Trail** may leave you breathless—but only because of its beauty. It is most colorful in July.

▶ *The Rim Trail is open late June through October. The hiking trails are usually blocked by snow from October to July. Boat tours are available July through mid-September.*

2 JACKSONVILLE

In the charming streets of Jacksonville, founded in an 1852 gold rush, it might as well still be the 19th century. After fires repeatedly reduced the town to ashes, merchants learned to rebuild in brick. When the gold boom went bust and the railroad passed the town by in the 1880's, the sturdy buildings remained. Pick up a walking-tour map at the **Jacksonville Museum**, filled with historical exhibits. In summer the acclaimed **Britt Festivals** feature first-rate jazz, classical, and popular musicians.

3 OREGON CAVES NATIONAL MONUMENT

Fantastic draperies of marble and other petrified embellishments led the poet Joaquin Miller to call this cavern the Marble Halls of Oregon. Arrive early and dress warmly for a walking tour that reveals the cave's stony secrets. Nearby trails wind through the Siskiyou National Forest past wide fields of wildflowers and along cliffs that overlook mountain vistas. Don't miss the king-size Douglas fir that measures more than 40 feet around at its base.

4 GOLD BEACH

At Gold Beach the raging Rogue River makes its way into the Pacific. The estuary attracts seals and sea lions that lie in wait for the fish that swim seaward from April through July. Jet boat trips offer views of the estuary from the river, famed for its salmon and steelhead. At **Cape Sebastian State Park**, seven miles south, rocky headlands rise more than 700 feet above an ocean accented with dramatic sea stacks that tower offshore. A trail lined with irises, orchids, and other wildflowers in spring leads to the ocean.

5 PORT ORFORD

The rockbound coast at Port Orford, viewed from the promontory known as **Battle Rock**, ranks among the most picturesque stretches on the Oregon coast—and also the rainiest. Once you reach **Cape**

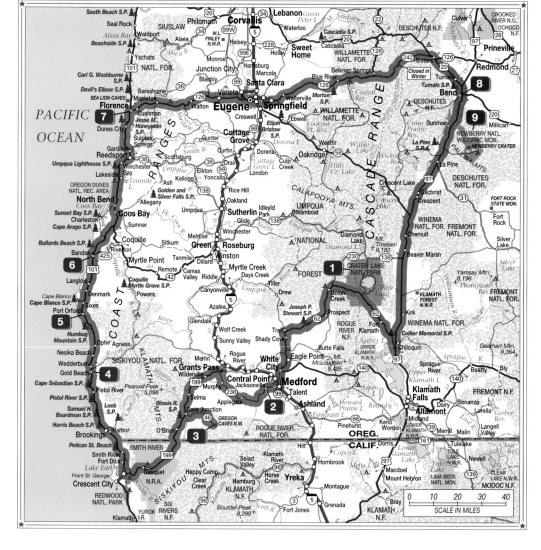

Pacific harbor seals like this happy rock-sitter are found all along the Oregon coast.

Blanco six miles north, you can go no farther west: this is the westernmost headland in the lower 48 states accessible by car. From **Cape Blanco State Park**, photographers shoot the oldest lighthouse in Oregon, built in 1870. Sea lions gather on the rocks offshore.

6 BANDON

The cranberry capital of Oregon, set on yet another gorgeous spot on the coast, Bandon bursts with flaming rhododendrons and flowering Scotch brooms in spring. Drive **Beach Loop Road** to take in natural offshore rock sculptures with names such as Face Rock, Elephant Rock, and Table Rock. A scenic road through **Bullards Beach State Park** leads to the octagonal **Coquille Lighthouse**. After the frequent storms, Bandon's beaches sparkle with agates and other semiprecious treasures.

7 FLORENCE

Forty miles south of Florence begins a drastic shift from rocky coast to the sand dunes of the **Oregon Dunes National Recreation Area**, some of which rise as high as 400 feet. The dunes actually dam rivers, creating a series of coastal lakes favored by windsurfers and sailors as well as by a variety of wildlife, including tundra swans in winter. At the **Oregon Dunes Overlook**, 10 miles south of Florence, an easy stroll leads to observation decks that offer the most accessible views. At **Jesse M. Honeyman State Park** you can actually slide down a sand dune into sparkling Cleawox Lake. The park is especially beautiful in May, when the rhododendrons are in bloom.

See even more of the colorful shrubs on **Rhododendron Drive**. Late May and June are the best times to view the carnivorous cobra lilies at **Darlingtonia Botanical Wayside**, where boardwalks lead you through the boggy habitat of these deceptively harmless-looking plants. When you break for civilization, head to waterfront **Old Town**, a turn-of-the-century neighborhood of coffee shops, antique stores, and restaurants.

Eleven miles north of Florence at **Sea Lion Caves**, an elevator descends to a wave-excavated grotto favored by Steller's sea lions. In spring and summer look for these playful creatures on the rocky ledges outside the cave. In the distance rises **Heceta Head Lighthouse**, reputedly the most photographed beacon in the U.S. For excellent whale-watching, take a detour 13 miles north to **Cape Perpetua**.

8 BEND

Where the high desert meets the Cascade mountains you'll find Bend, named for its location at a bend on the Deschutes River. Racing toward the Columbia River, the Deschutes whisks scores of rubber-rafting adventurers with it. For a scenic overview, follow the road that spirals around **Pilot Butte** to the top of this isolated cinder cone. From here the city and the Cascade peaks spread before you.

At the **High Desert Museum**, six miles south of town, visitors can compare the amenities of a Paiute Indian camp with those of a fur trapper's. Bats fly in the Desertarium, and raptors, otters, and porcupines carry on in naturalistic settings outside.

9 NEWBERRY NATIONAL VOLCANIC MONUMENT

The volcanic history of this area is written plainly in cinder cones, lava flows, and masses of obsidian (black volcanic glass) scattered over the landscape. The five-mile-wide **Newberry Crater** boasts two lakes, prime for trout and salmon fishing. Paulina Peak, the highest point on the rim, offers the best view into the gaping caldera. The **Lava Lands Visitor Center** interprets the surreal topography, which you can view from a lookout tower atop **Lava Butte.**

▶ *In summer the road to the top of Lava Butte is closed to private vehicles, but an inexpensive shuttle will take you up and back.*

Near Lava Butte is **Lava River Cave**, a mile-long tube of volcanic curiosities that you can explore with your own flashlight or a rented lantern. Bring a jacket: the temperature hovers between 35° F and 40° F. The cave is usually closed in winter. In **Lava Cast Forest** stand the eerie molds of pine trees long ago engulfed by molten rock.

Heceta Head Lighthouse perches protectively on a treacherous stretch of rocky coast.

Mendocino
San Francisco
Sacramento
Santa Cruz
Los Angeles
San Diego

California

A land of movie stars, gold rushes, redwoods, and astonishing beauty, California has captured the imagination of the world ever since Americans first trekked westward to this Golden State.

SAN DIEGO & THE DESERT

1 SAN DIEGO

Famous for its year-round sparkling weather and relaxed living, San Diego is full of distractions: cultural, athletic, and scenic, with spectacular desert and canyon areas to one side and the Pacific coastline ever beckoning to the West.

A good introduction to this seductive city is **Balboa Park,** the landscaped setting for a number of attractions, including the world-famous **San Diego Zoo.** The zoo has some 3,200 animals living in natural habitats. Moving sidewalks, guided tours, and the Skyfari Aerial Tramway make it easy to get around.

Hop on the park's free tram service to the **San Diego Museum of Art,** where you'll find classics of American and European painting and other art treasures, as well as cutting-edge works by California artists. A short stroll away is the **San Diego Museum of Man,** considered one of the best anthropological museums in the country. The galleries feature artifacts and folklore from ancient times to the present, with a special focus on the Southwest, Mexico, and Latin America. Next door to the museum, check to see what's playing at the **Old Globe Theatre**—an institution known around the world. Then pay a visit to the **San Diego Aerospace Museum,** a sleek structure that includes the Aerospace Hall of Fame. Hanging in the building's rotunda is a model of Charles A. Lindberg's *Spirit of St. Louis.*

When you leave Balboa Park, drive west to the tip of Point Loma to the **Cabrillo National Monument,** which commemorates Juan Rodríguez Cabrillo, the first European explorer to reach the California coast. The overlook offers stunning panoramic views of the blue Pacific—and, from December through February, the chance to spot whales.

A short hop on the highway takes you to **Old Town San Diego State Historic Park,** where many of San Diego's original adobe buildings bring the city's rich Mexican heritage to life.

▶ *For an intimate look at Old Town San Diego, take a free guided walking tour, offered daily at 2:00 P.M.*

A Mexican dancer from Jalisco celebrates San Diego's colorful heritage at Old Town.

Get another taste of the Southwest by wandering through the park's market area; the lively restaurants serve some of the tastiest—and most generous—Mexican meals around. Before leaving the city, don't miss the 1769 **Mission San Diego de Alcalá,** the state's oldest mission that still holds church services.

To the west is **La Jolla.** Its name—Spanish for "the jewel"—is fitting for this elegant and cosmopolitan town set along glistening beaches bordered by dramatic bluffs. Stroll down Girard or Prospect streets to see its luxurious boutiques and stylish cafés.

2 LAGUNA BEACH

This picturesque Southern California beach town has long enjoyed a reputation as a magnet for artists. The streets are dotted with art galleries and craft stores, along with the requisite surfing hangouts you expect to see in any Southern California beach town. Arts festivals are held throughout the year. The most impressive is the summertime **Pageant of the Masters,** where life literally imitates art: local models' faces gaze through carefully designed backgrounds in re-creations of famous paintings. The **Laguna Beach Museum of Art** features American art, with an emphasis on work by California artists.

3 SAN JUAN CAPISTRANO

Nestled in the hills between the Santa Ana Mountains and the coast, this historic town developed around **Mission San Juan Capistrano.** Among the most elaborate and beautiful of the California missions until much of it collapsed in the 1812 earthquake, it is most famous for the swallows that arrive promptly each St. Joseph's Day (March 19). After they hatch and rear their young, they depart for their 6,000-mile journey south on the Feast of St. John of Capistrano (October 23). If you miss the swallows' sojourn, you can still enjoy the chapel and the town's courtyards, museums, and old adobe houses.

4 TEMECULA

Virtually unknown to tourists until the mid-1980's, Temecula is a true California boomtown. This breezy spot in the high chaparral has become a modern city in just a matter of years. It is, in fact, the oldest continuously-inhabited town in the country (it was long an important Indian settlement), and a stroll through **Old Town Temecula** will give you a taste of the charm of its rugged past. The city is also proud of its dozen-plus top-notch wineries—among them

Joshua trees, *said to have been named for the prophet by Mormons, stretch heavenward.*

the **Thornton Winery** and the family-owned **Cilurzo Vineyard and Winery**—most of which offer tastings and tours, often free of charge.

5 RIM OF THE WORLD DRIVE

This winding 40-mile road high in the San Bernardino Mountains affords magnificent vistas of the San Bernardino Valley as it leads to **Big Bear Lake,** a popular spot for fishing and water sports in the summer and skiing and ice-skating in the winter.

▶ *Don't miss the gold rush sites in the Big Bear area. The Holcomb Valley Gold Fever Auto Tour guide is available at the Big Bear ranger station.*

6 PALM SPRINGS

With its beautiful desert setting and steady sunshine, this fashionable resort is the vacation retreat or residence for numerous celebrities; you may glimpse a familiar face or two on the golf course or browsing in the shops. In town the **Palm Springs Desert Museum** has exhibits that range from Matisse to arts and treasures of the Old West. The **Palm Springs Aerial Tramway** takes you on a thrilling 2½-mile ascent into the forests of Mount San Jacinto State Park for a spectacular overview of the vast desert area. The 20-minute ride lifts you from desert heat into cool mountain air. And the three nearby **Indian Canyons**—Palm, Andreas, and Murphy—offer a restful oasis, with tree-shaded walking trails.

7 JOSHUA TREE NATIONAL MONUMENT

This huge expanse of nearly untouched land is where the high (Mojave) desert and the low (Colorado) desert meet in a fortunate convergence of unusual geological formations and plants. Camping, picnicking, and hiking facilities abound here. The **Oasis Visitor Center,** in the town of Twentynine Palms, has fact-sheets and maps to help you interpret the landscape. **Key's View** has one of the best views; on clear days you can see all the way south to the Salton Sea.

8 ANZA-BORREGO DESERT

With 600,000 acres of desert splendor, **Anza-Borrego Desert State Park** showcases the beauty of the arid landscape—particularly in the spring, when flowers turn the ground into a brief but vibrant celebration of color. The willowy ocotillo, vivid red in flower and up to 20 feet tall, and the elephant tree, gray and wrinkly like the animal's trunk, are among the unusual plants you'll see. Within the park is **Agua Caliente Hot Springs,** where spring-fed natural pools, one indoors and one outdoors, provide a welcome respite from the dry landscape.

On your way back to San Diego on Rte. 78, stop in **Julian,** a center for the 1869 Gold Rush and now known for its lovely Victorian houses, spring flowers, and autumn apple harvests.

1 WESTSIDE

When people speak of Westside in LA, they may mean any of several neighborhoods in particular or all of the city west of La Brea and east of the Santa Monica city line. No matter; what the Westside lacks in geographical definition it makes up for in state of mind. Upscale, energetic, and easily navigable, the neighborhoods of Westwood, West Hollywood, and Beverly Hills are an excellent introduction to the inimitable Southern California lifestyle.

Westwood, once a small college town, is now a busy hub of restaurants, shops, theaters—and home of the sprawling campus of UCLA, one of the nation's leading research universities and perhaps the most beautiful, where grand Romanesque buildings give way to sleek modern facilities, all in a park-like setting. At the north end of the campus the **Franklin Murphy Sculpture Garden** features works by Henry Moore and Gaston Lachaise, and in the southeast corner the **Mildred Mathias Botanic Garden** is a horticulturalist's delight, with a range of unusual plants.

▶ *Stroll the campus with a self-guiding map, available at the information kiosks, or check into the visitor center for a weekday tour schedule.*

To the north the UCLA campus abuts one of LA's most famous thoroughfares, **Sunset Boulevard,** where you'll find sidewalk vendors hawking maps of the stars' homes—maps that are sometimes reliable and sometimes not. But rest assured that the stars' homes are all about you, especially in **Beverly Hills,** where mansions line Beverly Drive and ascend into the hills above. The best way to explore this oasis is simply to wander—up into the hills to see the most expensive real estate and through the shopping district between Santa Monica and Wilshire boulevards. **Rodeo Drive,** one of the most lavish shopping streets in the world, runs south from Sunset just east of the **Beverly Hills Hotel.**

East of Beverly Hills, **West Hollywood** offers some of LA's best people-watching. Stroll trendy **Melrose Avenue** between La Brea and Fairfax avenues, then browse the **Farmers Market** and eat at **Canter's Deli,** both on Fairfax. Or visit **Beverly Center,** a Westside shopping mall that boasts hundreds of restaurants and shops.

Starstruck tourists *gaze at the brass stars on the Hollywood Walk of Fame. Adjacent is a forecourt where the famous have left footprints and signatures in wet cement.*

Just south of West Hollywood proper, on Wilshire Boulevard, is one of LA's most famous and improbable sites: the **La Brea Tar Pits.** Formed 40,000 years ago, the oily lagoons lured countless prehistoric creatures to their death.

Next door is the Los Angeles County Museum of Art, a world-class museum complex by any standard, with works by Picasso and Rembrandt and a new pavilion for Japanese art.

2 HOLLYWOOD

Although most studios have relocated to other parts of Los Angeles, Hollywood is still synonymous with the entertainment industry, and ground zero for film nostalgia. It's not hard to find: just look up for the **Hollywood Sign,** high in the Hollywood Hills above Sunset Boulevard, or look down as you stroll the **Hollywood Walk of Fame,** where the names of 2,000 entertainment industry luminaries have been embedded in the sidewalks on brass plaques. And even though few film stars frequent Hollywood anymore, you can glimpse the next best thing at the **Hollywood Wax Museum.**

The grandest of the studio tours is at **Universal Studios Hollywood,** a veritable television and movie theme park. The tour lasts six hours and includes encounters with King Kong and a 30-foot robotic shark, and a simulated earthquake with a magnitude of 8.3. On a quieter note, a small museum celebrates the life and work of Lucille Ball.

In nearby Glendale, **Forest Lawn Memorial Park,** both a cemetery and an outdoor museum, has a vast collection of marble statuary and a stained-glass replica of Leonardo da Vinci's *The Last Supper.* Errol Flynn and Walt Disney are buried here, as are Nat King Cole and Clark Gable.

Near **Griffith Park,** Forest Lawn–Hollywood Hills has its own share of Hollywood's famous. Griffith Park also offers some of the best views of the city from its observatory, as well as planetarium and laser shows. Two other attractions in the park are the **Los Angeles Zoo,** where the koalas are perennial favorites, and the **Gene Autry Western Heritage Museum,** where an exhibit of Western movie memorabilia is housed in a charming mission–style building.

3 PASADENA

Known to the world as the home of the Tournament of Roses Parade and the Rose Bowl, the gracious suburb of

lusion captures the imagination at **Fantasmic!**, a spellbinding extravaganza of special effects.

▶ *Crowds are thinner at Disneyland on weekdays. On a weekend, choose Sunday.*

6 LONG BEACH

Long Beach, settled early in this century as a summer beach resort for movie stars, still beckons visitors to wander its waterways, streets, and marinas. Begin exploring the area in the **Naples** section of Long Beach, a quiet residential neighborhood of Victorian and Mission-Revival homes distinguished by the unlikely presence of tidal canals. For an adventure, try a whale-watching cruise. But the biggest maritime attraction of all, at 81,237 tons, is berthed in Long Beach: the **Queen Mary.** Visitors can explore all of her magnificent decks, from engine room to staterooms to bridge, and dine in one of the many restaurants on board.

7 SANTA CATALINA ISLAND

Catalina is a splendid hideaway, about one hour by ferry from Long Beach, San Pedro, or Newport Beach. There are no freeways here, and only one town, the beach and harbor hamlet of **Avalon.** The round 1929 **Casino Building**, with open galleries and a red tile roof, sits at the entrance of the harbor. Its ballroom is still used for dancing, and the downstairs movie theater has been restored to its 1930's glory.

Most of the island is a nature conservancy, with a variety of exotic sea life and free-roaming goats, boar, and buffalo transplanted to the island in 1924 for the filming of a movie.

8 THE BEACH CITIES

In the national imagination, Southern California is its beaches, and the best way to explore them is to sample them one by one. Start by rounding the **Palos Verdes Peninsula**, stopping to look for

Pasadena also offers some of LA's most intriguing architecture, museums, and historic sites, including one of the world's great cultural repositories: **The Huntington Library, Art Gallery and Botanical Gardens.** Built by railroad magnate Henry Huntington at the turn of the century, the complex is a vast storehouse of treasures and is worth a day-long visit. The library owns 3 million books, prints, and maps and some of the world's most important manuscripts, including a Gutenberg Bible, first editions of Shakespeare, and the earliest-known edition of Chaucer's *Canterbury Tales.* Not to be outdone, the Huntington's 150-acre botanical display boasts the world's largest assemblage of camellias, a Japanese garden, and more than 1,000 varieties of roses.

Also in Pasadena is the **Norton Simon Museum,** with Cubist and Impressionist paintings and Rodin sculptures. Close by, **Old Pasadena,** a recently restored sector of historic buildings that now house restaurants and music clubs makes for pleasant strolling.

4 DOWNTOWN

As vast as it is, Los Angeles seems barely to need a downtown, but it is here, where rail met river, that the "City of Angels" was born. Now a gleaming center of international banking and commerce, Downtown also has its own historic and cultural sites. The locus of the original 1781 settlement has been lost, but its spirit is preserved at **El Pueblo de Los Angeles,** a 44-acre urban park that includes pre-1900 structures, a busy Mexican market on Olvera Street, and Ávila Adobe (1818), reputedly the oldest standing structure in Los Angeles. Visitors will also recognize many buildings from film and television, including **Los Angeles City Hall, Union Station,** and the magnificent five-story glass courtyard of the **Bradbury Building,** which now houses law offices. At the northern end of downtown, **Little Tokyo** is a bustling area of Japanese businesses, restaurants, and culture. And the new **Museum of Contemporary Art** displays—under pyramidal skylights—a fine collection of Modern and Postmodern work since 1940.

5 DISNEYLAND

The theme park whose innovative attractions amazed the world when it opened in 1955 still offers pleasures for young and old: the high-tech, neck-snapping thrills of **Space Mountain,** the hologram-filled **Haunted Mansion,** and the crowd-pleasing **Pirates of the Caribbean.** Newer attractions include the **Indiana Jones Adventure** and **Mickey's ToonTown.** The world of il-

whales at one of the many turnoffs on the bluffs, and proceed north on Highland Avenue through the south bay towns of **Redondo**, **Hermosa**, and **Manhattan Beach**, each with a lively scene around its pier. Continue north through **Marina del Rey**, then turn west on Venice Boulevard into the heart of **Venice Beach**, the exotic seaside community adopted in recent years by an eclectic mix of artists, street performers, and eccentrics of various stripes. The Venice boardwalk is a sight to behold, with troubadours on rollerskates, fire-eaters, freelance psychics, and clusters of bodybuilders energetically pumping iron by the sea.

North of Venice is **Santa Monica**, a charming city by the sea with lovely hotels and homes and upscale shopping and dining. Farther north, **Pacific Palisades** is home to **Will Rogers State Historic Park**, where the humorist's home is open for tours. Just past Sunset Boulevard, at the southern edge of **Malibu**, the **J. Paul Getty Museum** contains the philanthropist's mammoth collection of classical antiquities, decorative art, and major paintings from every period, all housed in an astounding copy of a first-century Roman villa.

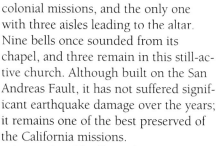

1 SANTA CRUZ
Earthquakes have been hard on California missions—among them Mission Santa Cruz (1791), of which only one adobe building remains. A one-third-scale replica of the original mission now stands on the grounds of Holy Cross Church as a testament to the importance of missions in early California: **Santa Cruz State Historic Park**, with traditional statues and vestments hand-carved from local sandstone.

2 SANTA CLARA
Mission Santa Clara de Asis, founded in 1777, is well known today for its lovely gardens. The current mission building is a replica of the fifth in the series of missions in Santa Clara, which was built in 1825. Nearby is the **de Saisset Museum**, which includes displays on early California history.

3 SAN JUAN BAUTISTA
Founded in 1797, **Mission San Juan Bautista** had the largest church of the colonial missions, and the only one with three aisles leading to the altar. Nine bells once sounded from its chapel, and three remain in this still-active church. Although built on the San Andreas Fault, it has not suffered significant earthquake damage over the years; it remains one of the best preserved of the California missions.

Across the old village plaza, **San Juan Bautista State Historic Park** reflects a different era, when Americans rushed to find California gold in the 1850's. Among the well-preserved buildings are the 1858 **Plaza Hotel**, created from the barracks of Mexican soldiers. In those days, when Mexico governed California, the local headquarters was in the **Castro-Breen Adobe**, originally constructed in 1840; it is open for tours.

4 SAN JOAQUIN VALLEY SCENIC DRIVE
Rte. 25, a two-lane road that winds from Hollister to Fresno, goes through the bucolic rolling hills of the San Joaquin (wa-KEEN) Valley, dotted with vineyards, orchards, and—in spring—a brilliant mantle of wildflowers. Along the way, between Paicines and Bitterwater, you can stop off at a striking contrast: **Pinnacles National Monument**, an amazingly rugged landscape of towering, erosion-sculpted volcanic rock spires.

▶ *Be sure to fill your gas tank at Hollister; there are no gas stations on Rte. 25 until Coalinga, 100 miles away.*

5 FRESNO
Surrounded by 1 million irrigated acres in the San Joaquin Valley, Fresno thrives on agriculture. The **Fresno County Blossom Trail**, driven in spring, is a self-guided tour that winds through 67 miles of orchards in spectacular flower. After the yearly harvest, roadside stands overflow with succulent strawberries, citrus fruits,

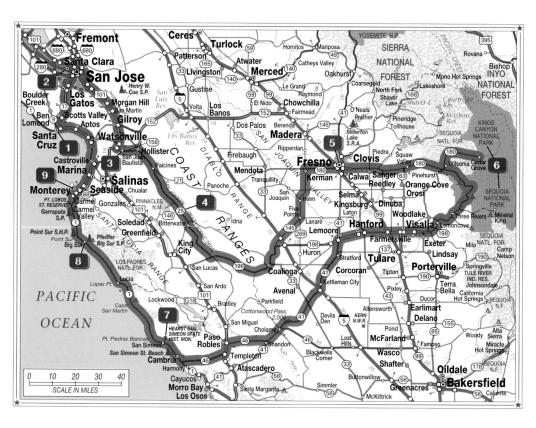

The incomparable coastline of Big Sur was sculpted by nature into a veritable work of art.

pistachios, and other produce.

In Fresno, **Forestiere Underground Gardens** is an astonishing labyrinth of 50 underground rooms dug out of the hardpan soil by a prosperous vintner from Sicily. Fruit trees grow through skylights, and the living quarters are surrounded by numerous patios, grottoes, and courts connected by tunnels.

6 SEQUOIA AND KINGS CANYON NATIONAL PARKS

About 2,200 years ago a feathery sprout broke the ground in what would become Sequoia National Park, and the **General Sherman Tree** began to reach for the sky. Measured by volume it is the most massive tree on earth, a growing behemoth with a 1,385-ton trunk. The **Generals Highway** takes you through forests of incomprehensibly grand sequoias. Breaks in the forest reveal panoramas of granite monoliths and immense canyons.

Lush green meadows, waterfalls, and broad, glaciated valleys bordered by rounded granite domes highlight the beautiful sister national park, Kings Canyon. Its peaks culminate in **Mount Whitney,** at 14,494 feet the highest mountain in the lower 48. The canyon that gives the park its name is deeper than the Grand Canyon—8,200 feet from its lowest point to its highest.

7 HEARST CASTLE

The **Hearst San Simeon State Historical Monument** preserves the home that publisher William Randolph Hearst named La Cuesta Encantada, "The Enchanted Hill." The centerpiece of this estate, appropriately named La Casa Grande, is a big house indeed, with 165 rooms, gardens, terraces, and pools. Commonly called Hearst Castle, the house was built between 1919 and 1947 to display Hearst's huge collection of Spanish and Italian antiques. With mansions for guest houses, the castle overlooks 123 landscaped acres, the sea, and the town of San Simeon.

8 BIG SUR

Monterey Peninsula has one of the loveliest shoreline drives in America and includes the jewel called Big Sur. Inland are the rugged Santa Lucia Mountains; seaward are the often fog-shrouded, eternally wave-pounded

A glass bubble provides an intimate view of a shark at the Monterey Bay Aquarium.

cliffs that afford unparalled views of the untamed sea. At **Pfeiffer Big Sur State Park** a redwood forest contrasts with a beach considered by locals to be Big Sur's most beautiful: the incomparable **Pfeiffer Beach,** bounded by towering sea stacks. One of the best places to watch the sun go down is at **Nepenthe,** the venerable restaurant perched on a cliff overlooking the Pacific.

▶ *Look for the Nepenthe sign 63 miles up the road from Hearst Castle on Rte. 1. To find Pfeiffer Beach, continue two miles north on Rte. 1 and make a sharp left on the paved road a half mile past Big Sur Post Office.*

9 MONTEREY PENINSULA

Point Lobos State Reserve has been called, with little exaggeration, the "greatest meeting of land and water in the world." Fulfilling this promise are dramatic headlands, magnificent groves of rare Monterey cypress, endangered brown pelicans, and perhaps America's most charming mammal, the rare and remarkable sea otter.

Carmel features many art galleries, markets, shops, and a particularly appealing beach. At **Carmel Mission** spectacular gardens declare the glory of God as fervently as did pioneer missionary Junípero Serra. Founder of many California missions, Padre Serra established this one in 1770–71 and made it his headquarters until his death in 1784. His grave is under the floor of the church.

The **Seventeen Mile Drive** toll road along the peninsula coast from Carmel to Pacific Grove boasts magnificent seaside scenery, including such highlights as Seal Rock and Bird Rock, as well as stately mansions and lush golf courses.

Pelicans, seals, gulls, and sea otters are on view at **Monterey Harbor,** the setting for John Steinbeck's 1945 novel, *Cannery Row.* Overfishing destroyed the sardine industry, and shops now line Cannery Row, surrounding the acclaimed **Monterey Bay Aquarium.** Close by, the **Monterey State Historic District** preserves acres of adobe buildings near the shops and restaurants on **Fisherman's Wharf,** where noisy northern sea lions bellow for handouts.

1 SAN FRANCISCO

Millions of travelers have indeed left their hearts in this city by the bay—enthralled by its natural beauty, colorful architecture, and inventive cuisine. Much of the city's appeal lies in its setting: San Francisco sprawls over some 40 hills that rise, like an Atlantis, from the deep blue water of San Francisco Bay, with the slender span of the Golden Gate Bridge as an elegant grace note.

The hills make for spectacular scenery but unnerving driving. Steep, switchbacked **Lombard Street** is the ultimate amateur driving experience for intrepid motorists. Try riding the nifty century-old cable cars instead. Or take a 20-minute ferryboat ride to **Alcatraz Island** or **Angel Island** and gaze back at the white city skyline shimmering against the bay waters. Stroll in 1,017-acre **Golden Gate Park** and see the classic 1879 **Conservatory of Flowers**.

Bridge with a view: *Morning traffic snakes into San Francisco on the Golden Gate Bridge.*

Bring cool-weather garb to this splendid city, caught in an eternal spring except when the fog rolls in. "The coldest winter I ever spent," said Mark Twain, "was the summer I spent in San Francisco." And bring a hearty appetite as well: it's practically impossible to eat a mediocre meal here, where innovative chefs draw from the region's rich supplies of farm-fresh produce, Pacific seafood, world-renowned wines, and multicultural culinary influences to create edible masterworks. **Fisherman's Wharf**, overlooking the bay, draws as many people for its seafood restaurants as for the live sea lions lounging leisurely on the docks.

▶ *Never stand behind the conductor on a cable car: an inadvertent elbow punch may come your way during the constant maneuvering of the operating levers.*

San Francisco is a city of cultural diversity as well. In **Nob Hill** the upper crust frequent the elegant **Fairmont Hotel**. A ride in the hotel's outdoor glass elevator to the Fairmont Crown provides a sublime view of the city. Save a morning for a **Flower Power Haight-Ashbury Walking Tour**, which whimsically recalls the neighborhood's hippie era while reveling in its gentrified Victorian architecture. Soak up the city's Asian heritage, dating from gold rush days, on a historical and culinary tour of **Chinatown**, one of the largest settlements of its kind east of Asia. The Japanese influence is on display in April, during the **Cherry Blossom Festival** in **Japantown** and at Golden Gate Park's lovely **Japanese Tea Garden**.

This is a city of colors: rambling Victorian homes are playfully splashed in pastels, and pearl-white granite buildings gleam under the quintessential California blue sky. The architecture is colorful as well. Following the devastating earthquake of 1906, many of the city's Beaux Arts structures were rebuilt with a modernist tilt. One that survived was the **Haas-Lilienthal House,** a handsome turn-of-the-century home that is open for tours. Visit the 1915 **City Hall,** a French Renaissance–style gem whose dome was modeled after that of the U.S. Capitol.

2 GOLDEN GATE NATIONAL RECREATION AREA

San Franciscans need drive only minutes to reach pristine trails and beaches. The **Golden Gate National Recreation Area** is an expansive coastal preserve that once contained the region's numerous military posts. The recreation area encompasses Alcatraz Island as well as 5,000 green city acres. In Marin County alone are 20 miles of cliffside beaches and redwood stands.

The recreation area includes the 550-acre **Muir Woods National Monument,** 12 miles northwest of the Golden Gate Bridge. Here live true American giants: old-growth, unlogged redwood trees. The tallest is 252 feet; the oldest is more than 1,000 years old. At the north end of the recreation area lies the 65,000-acre **Point Reyes National Seashore.** Its steep, craggy coastline conceals grassy meadows and an old lighthouse that offers terrific views.

On your way up the coast, stop at **Bodega Bay,** whose cool green hillsides formed the backdrop for Alfred Hitchcock's 1963 film *The Birds.*

3 POINT ARENA

Some of California's most dramatic scenery parallels cliff-hugging **Rte. 1,** where pounding surf lashes jagged shoreline. The chilly, moist weather nurtures the region's coastal redwoods. Here is where Californians go to pursue simple pleasures: fishing, hiking, surfing, whale-watching, collecting driftwood, diving for abalone, exploring tide pools, and visiting quaint, still largely unspoiled villages.

Up the coast at **Point Arena** a historic lighthouse guards the windswept, foggy coastline. The 1870 **Point Arena Lighthouse** was replaced in 1907 after suffering damage in the 1906 earthquake. Tours to the top provide fine vistas.

4 UKIAH

Rte. 253 leaves the cool coastline behind and rambles through redwood stands, emerging in fertile farm and wine country. Chosen the number one small town in California, Ukiah boasts some 30 wineries, more modest in scale than those in the Napa and Sonoma valleys but producing premium, award-winning wines nonetheless. The area is also known for its mineral springs. The

The rolling vineyards of Napa and Sonoma have fast become world-class wine producers.

only naturally carbonated, naturally warm mineral baths in North America, **Vichy Springs Resort,** offers resort guests and day-trippers a soothing soak in the opaque, sulfurous water.

5 CALISTOGA

More stress-calming mineral and mud baths await at Calistoga, "the original hot springs of the West." This resort town was founded in 1859 by Samuel Brannan, who hailed from Saratoga, New York, and who was thus well acquainted with the restorative powers of mineral waters. Upon settling in California, Brannan is said to have been tipsy when he named the town he hoped to turn into a spa center "the Calistoga of Sarafornia." The town's name, needless to say, stuck.

6 ST. HELENA

St. Helena is considered the heart of the Napa Valley wine country. Some of the valley's oldest wineries are situated in this town of Victorian charm and chic eateries. Before you take a tasting tour, become wine-savvy at the **Napa Valley Wine Library.** If too much viticultural data has your head swimming, simply gaze out the library's picture windows at the view of gently rolling vineyards.

7 NAPA/SONOMA

In contrast to the raw, rugged splendor of the Pacific Coast, California's wine country presents a serene, pastoral landscape. In these verdant valleys, broken only by the Mayacamas Mountains, the weather is so mild, clear, and steady that hot-air balloonists compete for air space. This moderate climate makes possible the cultivation of grapes that have made the names Napa and Sonoma synonymous with fine wines.

The Napa Valley's more than 240 wineries are located along a 30-mile stretch of Rte. 29 called **Winery Row.**

▶ *Visit in the off-season, from mid-November to late April, when the roads, wineries, and tasting rooms are less congested than during the early autumn harvest celebrations.*

Ride in Pullman dining cars while sipping crisp California wines on the **Napa Valley Wine Train,** which makes a 36-mile excursion through lush countryside between Napa and St. Helena.

Sonoma Valley is home to three dozen wineries; the county has 130. Rustic-looking **Buena Vista** is the state's oldest premium winery. The pretty town of **Sonoma** has an expansive and shady civic plaza and was the center of a short-lived rebellion that briefly proclaimed the independent Republic of California in 1846. The historic landmark district is also famous as the site of the last and most northern of the 21

Spanish missions, the restored 1823 **Mission San Francisco de Solano.**

North of Sonoma, redwoods and lean Douglas firs frame a memorial to the writer who called this land his Beauty Ranch. The **Jack London State Historic Park** contains the immense skeletal ruins of **Wolf House,** the 26-room mansion that mysteriously burned to the ground just before London's occupancy. Here too is the author's grave and the little cottage where he died in 1916, at the age of 40. The one-mile **Lake Trail** gently weaves through a stand of redwoods to the lake. Nearby, a fairly strenuous three-mile **Mountain Trail** winds 2,300 feet up **Sonoma Mountain.** Here you will see grand views of the **Valley of the Moon.** According to local legend, Wappo Indians traveling on horseback from Sonoma to Kenwood reported watching the moon drop from sight and rise again between the hills seven times. Today, slowly driving on Rte. 12 on a clear, moonlit night, you can witness the rise and fall of seven moons over the Mayacamas.

SACRAMENTO & SIERRA NEVADA

1 SACRAMENTO

In 1839 Capt. John Sutter built a fort near the confluence of the Sacramento and American rivers on a 48,000-acre Mexican land grant. Nine years later he laid out the town of Sacramento, which became the state capital after booming as a supply center for gold miners. Explore the rebuilt **Sutter's Fort** with a self-guided-tour map.

Old Sacramento, a renovated 10-block commercial district of shops, restaurants, and museums along the Sacramento River, carries visitors back to the gold rush era. The **Central Pacific Passenger Station** has been reconstructed to its 1876 appearance. Built of glass and steel, the **California State Railroad Museum** houses more than 20 restored locomotives and train cars.

More prosaic but tastier than gold, the region's almond crop exemplifies the agricultural riches that surround the city, the potential that Sutter dreamed of exploiting instead of gold. At **Blue Diamond Growers** you'll receive what gold mines fail to offer: free samples.

2 CAMINO

As early as the 1850's, fruit orchards were planted in the Sierra Nevada foothills, blessed with cool nights and warm days. Orchards by the dozens still blanket **Apple Hill,** a well-marked region strewn with fruit farms along

Rte. 50. Camino is the heart of orchard country. Visit in September or October during the harvest.

▶ *Tourist traffic during the fall harvest can be heavy on weekends. Leave your car behind and hitch a ride to the apple ranches on the Apple Bus, which leaves from Placerville. Or visit the orchards on a weekday.*

3 COLOMA

Flecks of gold metal seen glittering in the millrace of John Sutter's new sawmill on January 24, 1848, may have done more to change the landscape of the American West than any other single event. The region was part of Mexico when gold was discovered and was sparsely populated. But soon the rush was on. Thirty-one months after gold was found at Sutter's Mill, California officially entered the union as a state. Unfortunately, the men who discovered the bonanza failed to strike it rich. Sawmill worker James Marshall, who first noticed the glittering dust, went from job to job with only modest success, and a bitter John Sutter later petitioned the U.S. government for compensation for land he lost to squatters. At **Marshall Gold Discovery State Historic Park,** a statue of Marshall and his restored 1860 log cabin stand near a working replica of **Sutter's Mill.** A self-guiding map leads you down marked, well-maintained trails.

4 AUBURN

Hitching posts and wooden sidewalks give the streets of historic **Old Auburn** the look of a Western movie set. Many of Old Auburn's turn-of-the-century buildings owe their longevity to the firefighters from the **Auburn Hook & Ladder Company,** the oldest volunteer fire department in California. Peer into its former quarters, an 1839 wooden firehouse with a pointed bell tower. This and the **Auburn Post Office,** which has been in use since July 1853, were among the handful of buildings to survive the terrible fire of 1855.

At the 1894 **Placer County Courthouse,** live court cases are held in a reconstructed 1800's courtroom, outfitted with vintage benches and ornate lighting. Downstairs, a replicated 1850's sheriff's office has been filled with the original office furniture of the county's gold rush–era sheriff, whose belongings—right down to the pictures on the wall—were kept in mint condition for more than 100 years by his family.

5 GRASS VALLEY

Prospector George McKnight literally stumbled onto hefty stores of gold in 1850 when he stubbed his toe on a chunk of rock streaked with gold. At **Empire Mine State Historic Park** you can step down into an old mine shaft that continued to produce gold until its closing in 1957. Over a 100-year span nearly 6 million ounces of gold was unearthed here. Daily guided tours take you past restored buildings made of waste rock from the mines and into **Bourn Cottage,** a mansion retreat for mine executives. Easy to moderate hiking trails lace the 777-acre site, taking trekkers into forested backcountry and past the remains of old mining claims and stamp mills, where rock was crushed to retrieve the gold within.

6 LAKE TAHOE

True to its name, Lake Tahoe, a Washo Indian word for "big water," sprawls 22 miles long and 12 miles wide. It is beautiful too: deep, clear, and blue-green. The lake is 6,300 feet above sea level and ringed by a crown of mountain ridges. In the early 1900's, the wealthy began retreating to Tahoe for its remoteness and cool beauty. Today big-name entertainers headline at the luxury resorts and casinos that line the Nevada shoreline (a third of the lake lies in Nevada). But Lake Tahoe—whose waters, at 99.9 percent purity, are likened to distilled—is much more than simply Vegas on the Water. Pris-

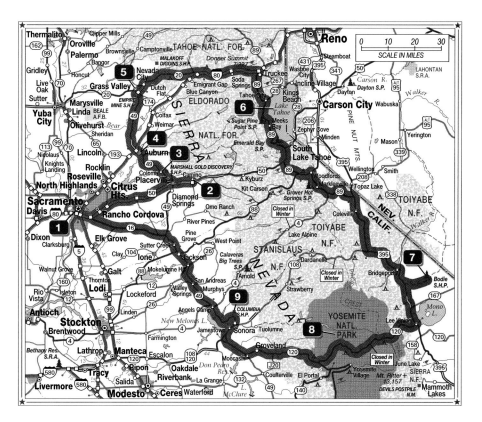

tine state parks provide superb recreation. Take the 72-mile shoreline drive around the lake; spring and fall are the best times to go, when traffic thins. The beautiful green hue of the water can be appreciated from a cliffside perch overlooking **Emerald Bay.** At **Sugar Pine Point State Park** is the **Ehrman Mansion,** a 1903 summer palace in the Queen Anne style.

The Tahoe Basin is one of the top downhill-ski regions in the country, and many of the state parks groom cross-country ski trails as well. Trams at **Squaw Valley USA** and **Heavenly** ski resorts offer fine views of Lake Tahoe and the forested landscape. Take a cruise on the lake past mansion homes on the *Tahoe Queen,* a stern-wheeler with a glass-bottom viewing area.

7 BODIE

The passage of time has been suspended at **Bodie State Historic Park,** where some 150 Old West structures exist in a state of "arrested decay." No glitzy restorations, no modern refreshment stands jolting you back to the 20th century; what you see is pretty much what the town of Bodie looked like when it was abandoned in 1942. Peer through dusty windows at turn-of-the-century furniture, dishes, and dry goods. You'll even see 1870's slot machines in the old casino. The town is haunted as well by its reputation as one of the West's most lawless mining camps, when, in its heyday in 1879, it held 6,000 assorted settlers and renegades. "Good-bye, God, I'm going to Bodie," wrote a little girl upon her family's move to the town.

▶ *This relatively noncommercial park has no gas, food, or lodging and only a limited selection of film.*

Emerald Bay, on the California shore of Lake Tahoe, offers breathtaking vistas from cliffside pull-offs. Cruise boats transport passengers on daily sightseeing trips in and out of Emerald Bay.

8 YOSEMITE NATIONAL PARK

Rather ordinary geological processes over time conspired to create some rather extraordinary scenery in Yosemite. This is one formidable park: 1,169 square miles, 263 miles of roadway, and 800 miles of trails. Visitors tend to concentrate in **Yosemite Valley,** amid granite domes and cliffs that soar thousands of feet up from the valley floor. Free shuttle buses to the east end of this seven-mile-long cul-de-sac allow you to park your car instead of driving the often congested roads.

Many of the world's most impressive waterfalls are here. The highest single falls in Yosemite, **Ribbon Falls,** cascades 1,612 feet. Short walks to Vernal Falls, Yosemite Falls, and Bridalveil Falls are easy and worthwhile.

▶ *Visit the falls in the off-season, as trails can be crowded in summer and some falls dry up in the hot months.*

The park also preserves groves of giant sequoias. Easily accessible by car is the Mariposa grove; the Tuolumne grove is easy to get to by trail. In the Mariposa grove you'll encounter **Grizzly Giant,** the oldest tree in the grove, at 210 feet tall. At **Glacier Point** you'll get an unsurpassed view of Yosemite Valley below and of **Half Dome,** the 2,000-foot-tall sheer face of a split rock that is the unofficial symbol of the park.

9 COLUMBIA STATE HISTORIC PARK

No more aptly named highway in California exists than **Rte. 49,** which slashes through the mother lode of gold country. One mining town that never died lies along this road. Columbia's five square blocks of historic commercial district appear much as they did in the gold rush era from 1850 to 1870, when this was one of California's brassiest boomtowns. Now a state park, the town is largely uncommercialized, although you can do business inside the Old West stores. Sip a sarsaparilla soda in one of two saloons or simply browse in the shops. The town may seem familiar to you; much of the TV series *Little House on the Prairie* was filmed here and in the surrounding dusty scrubland.

MENDOCINO & THE REDWOODS

1 MENDOCINO

California may be the nation's most populous state, but you'd never know it from exploring Mendocino and points north. Here is a fog-shrouded wilderness of little towns and big trees, jagged coastlines and rugged mountains, a land as different from that of its fast-paced southern neighbors as night is from day. The severity of nature—fierce winds and surf along the coast and volcanic explosions inland—has created a powerfully unique landscape.

The picturesque art colony and former lumber town of Mendocino is a favorite getaway of city dwellers from the Bay area. The town looks more like a Cape Cod village than a California seacoast town, and for good reason: Mendocino was settled by New England lumber-mill workers in the 19th century. They built tidy clapboard houses and picket fences among majestic redwood stands. A stroll about town reveals quaint cubbyholes of galleries and old-time bars and the venerable **Mendocino Hotel,** a grand Victorian built in 1878.

2 HUMBOLDT REDWOODS STATE PARK

After a stunning drive up the coast, where you pass rock-strewn coves and trees sculpted by the elements into odd shapes, you head inland to the land of the tall trees. Old-growth redwoods are unimaginably huge—they exceed 300 feet in height, 18 feet in diameter. Exit from the highway onto the 32-mile scenic **Avenue of the Giants** for access to 51,000 acres of redwood groves, by far the largest park concentration of redwoods in California. Frequent pull-outs and easy trails let you get up close to the big trees. Stop at the visitor center, where a cross section of a redwood trunk reveals the big tree's age; tree

Like babes in the woods, *a mother and child are dwarfed by several towering patriarchs in Redwood National (left). The largest undisturbed old-growth tract of redwoods on earth shelters a wide variety of plant life, such as sorrel and blossoming trillium (above).*

rings are labeled with dates that go back to the time of Charlemagne.

The biggest trees are in **Rockefeller Forest,** toward the center of the park. Here is the densest acreage on earth. The **Founder's Grove** can be easily reached on a short, level trail that takes you by the massive 362-foot **Dyerville Giant,** which toppled over in 1991. Even on its side, the tree is so high (more than 17 feet) that you can't see over the top of the trunk.

Driving north, turn off Rte. 101 onto twisting **Mattole Road,** which curves along **Cape Mendocino,** a remote, sparsely populated region of pastoral meadows, cliffside beaches, and rock-strewn river waters. Don't be put off by reports of Mattole Road's snaking curves; this scenic two-lane road is well-maintained. Commercial activity is scarce, however, so gas up in Weott and bring along supplies before venturing out on the four-hour trip.

3 FERNDALE

You will cross velvety cow pastures to reach this lovely small town, whose elaborate "butterfat palaces," built by the immigrant dairymen who settled here, have been so immaculately restored that locals refer to Ferndale as the Victorian Village. One, the **Gingerbread Mansion,** is a bed-and-breakfast; you can stroll in its formal garden.

After leaving Ferndale, detour down Rte. 101 to **Scotia,** a neat little lumbermill town of pastel bungalows. Scotia is owned by the Pacific Lumber Company, which operates one of the last of the working redwood plants in the Northwest. Free tours are offered at the mill, where huge logs are reduced to rough lumber in less than five minutes.

4 EUREKA

With a population of almost 30,000, this is the biggest coastal city north of San Francisco. But Eureka has the feel of small-town, Main Street America. The chief attraction is **Old Town,** which includes one of the finest Victorian homes in the country, the ornate **Carson Mansion.** Once a lumber baron's home, it is now a private club.

5 REDWOOD NATIONAL PARK

This park's worthy draws include **Tall Trees Grove,** which boasts the world's first-, third-, and sixth-tallest redwoods. It can be reached only by hiking—the shortest route is a mile-and-a-half hike downhill to Redwood Creek—and trail access through a gate is limited to 35 vehicles a day. More accessible is **Lady Bird Johnson Grove,** with a mile-long nature walk. The visitor center, two miles south of **Orick,** has permits for entry into Tall Trees Grove.

Included in the 113,200 acres of parkland are miles of beautiful coastline.

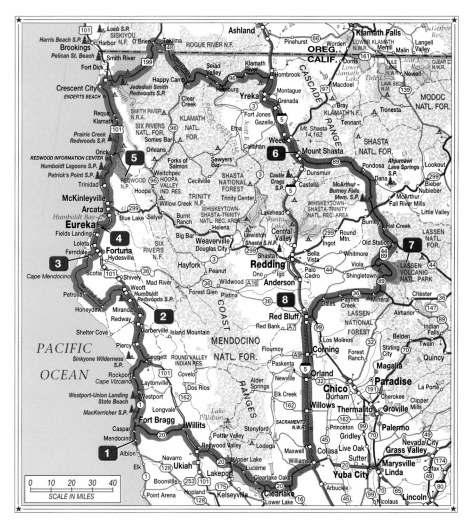

About two miles north of Orick is Davison Road, a turnout that leads to **Gold Bluffs Beach.** Here yellow cliffs tower over the road, which ends at a narrow gash called **Fern Canyon,** lushly overgrown with ferns, mosses, and vines.

Follow Rte. 101 to Rte. 199 into **Jedidiah Smith Redwoods State Park,** an inland preserve of silence, solitude, and light where you can picnic, hike, or float in the **Smith River**—the last wild river in California.

6 MOUNT SHASTA

It's called a stratovolcano, and for sheer mass, nothing can match this mountainous amalgamation of many volcanos. Called "the white mountain" by the native Indians, who revere it, snow-covered **Mount Shasta** rises over 14,000 feet and stands alone, with no other peak to supply competition. The **Everett Memorial Highway** will take you up 7,800 feet for an unforgettable view of hundreds of miles.

7 LASSEN VOLCANIC NATIONAL PARK

Unlike Mount Shasta, considered a dormant volcano, **Lassen Peak** had its last big eruption in 1915. **Lassen Park Road** cuts across the peak's west face, from which you can walk to bubbling mudpots like **Bumpass Hell,** an area of fumaroles, superheated steam vents, and hot springs. It's a one-mile walk to the overlook point, for a bird's-eye view. Gather information at the **Loomis Museum,** an orientation site.

8 RED BLUFF

Here lived the only president of the Bear Flag Republic. At the **William B. Ide Adobe State Historic Park** you'll see Ide's 1850's adobe home. The Red Bluff town park hugs the **Sacramento River,** whose waters rush down from the icy peaks of Mount Shasta, carrying salmon and steelhead trout. Drop a line in and picnic by the river. Southward, you'll pass olive orchards near Corning.

Alaska

The call of the wild rings out in Alaska, where caribou outnumber people and brown bears hunt salmon like eager fishermen. Once considered a frozen wasteland, this is America's last frontier.

ANCHORAGE & THE INTERIOR

1 ANCHORAGE

Sprawling at the base of the Chugach Mountains, Anchorage is home to half of the state's population and is anything but typical of the rest of Alaska. Midway between Tokyo and New York, it was originally a tent city for railroad workers, who enjoyed its relatively mild climate. Today Anchorage offers an excellent base from which to venture out into the Alaskan hinterlands.

The **Anchorage Museum of History and Art** holds the state's best collection of fine arts and Native Alaskan crafts. Works by Alaskan artists include a 6- by 10-foot oil painting of Mount McKinley by Sydney Laurence. Dioramas in the Alaska Gallery chronicle the state's history. At **Earthquake Park** displays recall the 1964 earthquake—the largest ever in North America—which rearranged south central Alaska. Walk along the Coastal Trail for stunning views of active volcanoes to the southwest, and to the north, if the weather permits, Mounts McKinley and Foraker, North America's highest and third-highest peaks.

Chugach State Park perches on the brink of the Alaskan wilderness, embracing glacier-carved lakes and viewing areas for spying on Dall sheep and moose. Twice a day you can witness the wavelike tidal bore in Turnagain Arm, which surges as high as six feet.

About 20 miles south, via Rte. 1, the five-mile-long **Portage Glacier** is Alaska's most-visited site. A visitor center overlooks the icy mass, and a ferry carries passengers to the glacier's face.

▶ *On the way to Portage Glacier, stay near the road. The mudflats along Turnagain Arm are like quicksand.*

2 HATCHER PASS

The drive to Hatcher Pass leads through one of the most picturesque stretches of the beautiful Matanuska Valley, where long hours of daylight in summer produce startling 70-pound cabbages. A well-maintained gravel road, closed in winter, climbs the pass to reveal stunning alpine scenery, culminating in sweeping views of the valley and the Chugach Mountains. Wooden mining camp buildings sit deserted at **Independence Mine State Historical Park**, the remains of a fortune-making gold mine that operated from the 1930's to 1951. A visitor center offers exhibits and tours of some of the buildings.

3 TALKEETNA

Once the hub of the Talkeetna Mountains mining district, this quaint village is the jumping-off point for climbers headed for Mount McKinley and other Alaska Range peaks. Talkeetna is also the place for booking a breathtaking

Mt. McKinley forms the snowy backdrop for a lone caribou at Denali National Park.

flight around the mountain with one of several "flightseeing" companies. This is your chance to skim over a glacier and even make a glacier landing. The flights, over an hour long, are reasonably affordable and worth every penny.

4 DENALI NATIONAL PARK

Long before you enter Denali, its central feature looms unmistakably before you. Many come to scale Mount McKinley—called Denali, or the "Great One," by the Tanaina Indians—and inevitably a few fail to return. But there are many other reasons to visit the park named for the tallest peak in North America, most notably the wildlife.

Denali is one of the best places to see and photograph the denizens of Alaska's wilderness—grizzly bears, moose, caribou, Dall sheep, and wolves. Between Memorial Day and mid-September the park roads are closed to private vehicles, so to see the animals you'll have to hike or take the park's shuttle bus, which leaves from the **Visitor Center**. Allow a full day for the 170-mile round-trip tour. Private companies also offer wildlife tours narrated by naturalists. Reservations are necessary. Or leave the buses behind and opt for a float trip on the Nenana River. Save time for the sled-dog demonstration at **Park Headquarters**.

▶ *The park's shuttle bus rides, available mid-May through September, are popular. You will be given a ticket for the next available tour, which in July and August may be the next day.*

5 FAIRBANKS

Unlike Anchorage, Fairbanks, surrounded by hundreds of miles of arctic bush, is everything you'd expect of an Alaskan city. Its best-loved attractions are the northern lights, which decorate the night sky from September through April. In summer, when daylight stretches its stay to 22 hours, temperatures can soar to 90°F. In winter four halfhearted hours of sunshine accompany average temperatures of -10° F.

Tour boats skirt the icy-toothed Columbia Glacier, most of which is below sea level.

A real treat is the four-hour narrated **Riverboat Discovery** stern-wheeler tour on the Chena and Tanana rivers, with a stop at an Athabascan village. You'll also want to visit the **University of Alaska Museum** for its Arctic wildlife displays, Russian artifacts, and gold collection. Finally, indulge in the mouthwatering salmon bake at **Alaskaland,** a theme park that re-creates Alaska's gold rush days with 29 authentic pioneer buildings. If gazing at so many glaciers and snowy mountaintops has given you the chills, warm your bones with a side trip to **Chena Hot Springs,** some 60 miles east.

6 RICHARDSON HIGHWAY

In the early 1900's the Richardson Trail was the main winter route into the interior. No longer a path for horse-drawn sleighs and dogsleds, the Richardson is a modern highway connecting Fairbanks to Valdez, winding through the foothills of the Alaska Range and the Chugach Mountains, with historical markers and scenic pullouts along the way. Keep your eyes peeled as you near **Delta Junction** for the large herd of bison here, best viewed from the turnoff at mile 241.3 (mileposts mark most Alaska highways). The highway parallels the Trans-Alaska Pipeline; you can photograph that inspiring feat of American engineering from a lookout at mile 205.7, past **Black Rapids Glacier.**

7 COPPER CENTER

Fishwheels—large revolving wheels suspended in the water with nets attached—still scoop salmon from the silt-laden **Copper River** as they have for more than a century. When the salmon are running, June through August, you just might see one tumble down the chute into the fish box.

In the charming village of Copper Center, nestled within view of the soaring Wrangell Mountains, stop at **Wrangell–St. Elias National Park Visitor Center.** There rangers can advise you of current conditions on the 96-mile drive to **Kennicott,** a wonderfully preserved copper-mining town with picturesque mining ruins, and neighboring **McCarthy,** where the miners went to eat, drink, and be merry.

8 VALDEZ

Lined with glacial waterfalls and snow-covered mountains, the last leg of the Richardson Highway through the Chugach Mountains to Valdez is truly stunning. Watch for the turnoff to **Worthington Glacier,** which you can actually touch. **Thompson Pass,** covered with wildflowers in early summer, provides sweeping views of the area.

Set against a backdrop of icy peaks, Valdez, the terminus of the Trans-Alaska Pipeline and the snowiest town in North America, was unfortunately made famous by the biggest oil spill in history. (To see exhibits about the spill, stop in the **Valdez Museum.**) Charter boats depart from Valdez for an unfor-

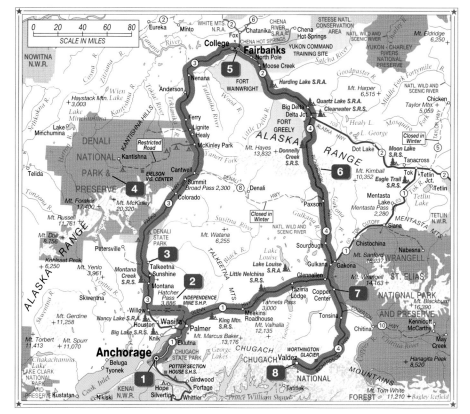

gettable eight-hour cruise to the immense **Columbia Glacier** in Prince William Sound. The creeping blue-white slab is the largest tidewater glacier in North America. Raft and kayak trips of the sound are available, and outfitters also offer trips through the gorgeous **Keystone Canyon** on the Lowe River.

An alternative route back to Anchorage is by the Alaska Marine Highway ferry from Valdez to Whittier through Prince William Sound. From Whittier you can drive your car onto a train to Portage. Reservations are required for both the train and the ferry.

▶ *The Marine Highway ferry to Whittier passes the Columbia Glacier and is a less expensive alternative to the private cruises, though the charter boats offer a longer and closer look.*

SOUTHEAST & THE YUKON

1 HAINES

Nestled snugly between the Lynn Canal—the longest and deepest fjord in North America—and the 6,500-foot-high Chilkat Range, Haines boasts perhaps the most majestic setting of any town in Alaska.

Fort William H. Seward, Alaska's first permanent Army post, was named for the secretary of state who engineered the Alaska Purchase. A salmon bake sizzles nightly here in the Indian Tribal House. Tlingit carvers craft traditional masks and totem poles at Alaskan Indian Arts, housed in the old hospital. And at the Chilkat Center for the Arts, Chilkat Dancers perform in summer wearing the exquisite blankets, woven of cedar bark and mountain goat hair, for which the tribe is known.

If you miss the dancers you can still see the blankets at the **Sheldon Museum,** which also offers such artifacts as a sawed-off shotgun that belonged to Jack Dalton, the arm-twisting entrepreneur who created a toll road to the Klondike. Fishing boats cruise the picturesque **Small Boat Harbor** across the street.

On the way to Canada you'll pass the **Alaska Chilkat Bald Eagle Preserve,** 10 miles north of Haines on the Chilkat River. Late fall sees the largest bald eagle gathering in the country, drawn by a run of chum salmon. Even in summer there are some 200 resident eagles. Best views are on the Haines Highway between miles 18 and 22; float trips are available through outfitters in Haines.

▶ *Canadian and U.S. customs on the Haines Highway close nightly. Check their hours, and remember that Canadian time is one hour ahead.*

2 HAINES JUNCTION

The Haines Highway runs along the eastern edge of **Kluane National Park** to Haines Junction, at the foot of the massive Kluane Range. The **Kluane Park Visitor Reception Centre** will help orient you to the park. Hidden behind the dramatic ridges to the west are the world's largest nonpolar icefields and glaciers, and Mount Logan, Canada's highest peak, at 19,545 feet. To see Logan you'll have to fly, as you will to see just about any of the park, whose few roads are open only to four-wheel-drive vehicles. Flightseeing tours are available in several places, including Burwash Lodge near the north end of **Kluane Lake,** 40 miles north of town and one of the true gems of the Yukon.

3 WHITEHORSE

Capital of the Yukon Territory, this is the largest city in northern Canada. Just up the Yukon River are the infamous Whitehorse Rapids of **Miles Canyon,** which claimed the lives of several stampeders on their way to Dawson City before the Mounties required Klondikers to portage or hire skilled rivermen for this stretch. A two-hour narrated cruise through the canyon is not to be missed.

A thorough look at the Yukon—its animals, peoples, and history—can be had without leaving the **MacBride Museum.** The poetry of Robert Service, the

Haines, *nestled beneath snow-covered peaks on a scenic fjord, encapsulates Alaska's rugged beauty. It was founded as a Presbyterian mission at the site of a Chilkat portage, and is known for—of all things—its strawberries. The local strawberry festival eventually became the state fair.*

North's most famous bard and author of "The Spell of the Yukon," rings out at Sam McGee's cabin on the grounds. Another relic of Yukon history, the **SS Klondike** stern-wheeler, hauled goods up the Yukon River and can be toured.

Takhini Hot Springs, 17 miles northwest, and **Lake Laberge,** 17 miles north and the setting for Robert Service's "Cremation of Sam McGee," make excellent half-day or evening side trips.

4 CARCROSS

Carcross (short for "caribou crossing"), a picturesque village of Tlingit natives and artists in the Yukon Territory, straddles the outlet of Lake Bennett, the headwaters of the Yukon River. A rough road climbs nearly 3,000 feet up **Mon-**

Juneau is surely the only capital with a glacier in its backyard: the **Mendenhall Glacier,** which sweeps down from the mammoth Juneau Icefield. Trails on both sides offer views.

It was gold that first drew outsiders to Juneau, and today hiking trails wind through old mining areas, including **Gold Creek Valley** and **Douglas Island.** Some of the trails lead to prime fishing spots where you can hook the king salmon of your dreams. An assortment of things Alaskan—a walrus-hide whaling boat, a stuffed grizzly, and the Bald Eagle Nesting Tree—is on display at the **Alaska State Museum.**

From Juneau it's a short flight to **Gustavus,** a quaint community just outside **Glacier Bay National Park and Preserve.** Crowding the bay speckled with blue-tinged bergs is the world's largest concentration of tidewater glaciers. The *Spirit of Adventure* tour boat is your ticket to a show that may include views of humpback whales and the crash of ice chunks breaking off the glaciers, creating floating docks for harbor seals.

tana Mountain, which boasts views of the beautiful Windy Arm and its islands, feather-footed ptarmigans, and a resident band of caribous. Victims of gold fever en route to the Klondike stayed at the **Caribou Hotel,** said to be the Yukon's oldest operating hotel.

5 SKAGWAY

The last stretch of the Klondike Highway from White Pass to Skagway takes in some of Alaska's grandest scenery. Skagway, at the northern tip of the Inside Passage, was a gateway to the Klondike goldfields. A century later it still exudes that frontier aura, and many of its gold rush stores, gambling houses, and saloons still stand. The **Klondike Gold Rush National Historical Park Visitor Center** offers walking tours.

Thousands of horses—unfed and poorly packed—perished on the steep and narrow trail over White Pass on their way to the Yukon headwaters. The **White Pass & Yukon Route Railroad** parallels the route they took, hugging precipitous cliffs and chugging over dramatic gorges and past waterfalls. This is the very scenery that inspired both Jack London and Robert Service.

6 JUNEAU

Leave it to Alaska to have as its capital a city accessible only by boat or plane—a capital that can easily be called the most scenic in America, nestled at the foot of Mount Juneau. The ferry ride down the Lynn Canal from Skagway is unsurpassed; reservations are necessary.

Tlingit totem *poles at Sitka National Historical Park guard Sitka's native heritage.*

7 SITKA

Fishing boats depart from the historic harbors of Sitka, a short flight or nine-hour ferry ride from Juneau. This former capital of Russian America boasts magnificent mountain backdrops and **Mount Edgecumbe,** a volcano resembling a miniature Mount Fuji.

▶ *The ferries often stop in Sitka for three hours, time enough for the bus tour that begins at the dock and includes the major attractions.*

Sitka's highlight is **Sitka National Historical Park,** which commemorates the final battle between the Russians and the local Tlingits and celebrates both cultures. Its highlight is a forested trail lined with 11 striking totem poles. Native carvers practice their craft at the visitor center.

Onion-domed **St. Michael's Cathedral** is filled with Russian Orthodox art, icons, and vestments saved by local residents from a fire that destroyed the original church. At the **Sheldon Jackson Museum,** Native artifacts from spirit masks to canoes are on display.

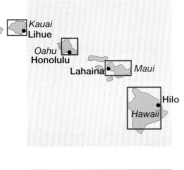

Kauai
Lihue
Oahu
Honolulu
Lahaina — Maui
Hilo
Hawaii

Hawaii

Prepare to lose your heart to the 50th state, where volcanoes, mist-shrouded uplands, and crystalline waters form the backdrop for a spirited blending of Polynesia and the West.

1 HONOLULU

Honolulu is a city, a county, a capital, and the most underrated attraction in Hawaii. The County of Honolulu is the entire island of Oahu, an angular mass of mountain, valley, and shoreline graced with two incomparably beautiful mountain ranges, Koolau and Waianae.

The **Bernice Pauahi Bishop Museum** in Kalihi, the world's most respected repository of Hawaiian and Pacific artifacts, sets the tone for the Hawaii experience. Feather cloaks, prehistoric tools, crafts, and implements bring to life Hawaii's Polynesian past and people.

In downtown Honolulu, stark highrises and historic buildings blend easily with ethnic neighborhoods like **Chinatown.** A walk among the noodle shops, herb shops, lei stands, fish markets, and Chinese, Thai, and Vietnamese eateries yields distinctively local sights and smells. Today this ethnic beehive shows no signs of the Great Chinatown Fire of January 1900, when some 4,000 were left homeless by a government-set fire intended to control the bubonic plague.

A half-mile walk across town takes you to the last official residence of Hawaiian royalty, **Iolani Palace,** which stands as a baleful reminder of the overthrow of the Hawaiian monarchy by American sugar interests in 1893. Its koa stairway, gilded furniture, chandeliers, and crown jewels bespeak a time of heightened European influence.

▶ *Perfect excuse for a picnic: the Royal Hawaiian Band's free noontime concerts on the Iolani Palace lawn on Fridays—held every month but August.*

Four miles from downtown Honolulu, amid the waterfalls of Manoa Valley, the 194-acre **Lyon Arboretum** is an oasis of calm, with hybrid sandalwood, taro, palms, heliconias, spices, and ferns nestled along the lower portions of the Koolau mountain walls.

From the waterfalls of Manoa, head seaward to the waters of Waikiki. **Kapiolani Park,** 220 green acres in the shadow of **Diamond Head,** includes among its attractions the popular **Waikiki Aquarium,** where headliners include monk seals in an outdoor habitat and sharks in a 35,000-gallon tank.

A religious icon, thought to represent Ku, one of the four major Hawaiian deities, is among the Polynesian artifacts displayed at the Bishop Museum.

2 MAKAPU'U

In east Oahu the extinct volcano and natural aquarium called **Hanauma Bay** teems with tropical fish—and people. Don't be discouraged; you don't have to snorkel to enjoy the view from the top of the crater. At the nearby **Halona Blowhole,** clear days offer views of Maui, Molokai, and Lanai. The surfing magnet called **Sandy Beach** unfurls along the shoreline, crowded with daring bodysurfers and curious spectators.

The easternmost spit on Oahu, Makapu'u appears suddenly only minutes from Sandy Beach. Don't miss the views from the overlook: surfers and two offshore islands, the **Makapu'u Lighthouse** to the right, the Mokulua Islands in the distance, and the sweeping, white-sand **Waimanalo Beach** snaking along the windward shoreline. Then look up to see the sharp, chiseled cliffs of the **Koolau Mountains** at your elbow, falling to the road like a curtain.

▶ *The 45-minute hike to the Makapu'u Lighthouse begins at the gate before the lookout. It's hot and mostly uphill, but the spectacular ocean views may include whales in the winter.*

3 NUUANU PALI

In 1795 Kamehameha the Great won a decisive battle by pushing his opponents over the 1,000-foot precipice called the **Nuuanu Pali.** Today the spectacular views from the lookout make it a top Hawaii attraction. On the way, visit the **Queen Emma Summer Palace,** built in 1847 and used later as a summer retreat of Queen Emma and Kamehameha IV. You can get very close to the artifacts, among them the koa wood cradle of Albert, the royal couple's son who died at age four. To savor the beauty of the rain forest, take **Nuuanu Pali Drive** and meander along ginger-flanked streams and gracious *kama'aina* (local resident) estates.

4 KAILUA

The anchor of this suburban coastal community is the 35-acre **Kailua Beach Park,** a playground for windsurfers, fishermen, sailors, and beachgoers. The beach includes ancient fishing grounds, seaweed-harvesting grounds, and some excellent swimming areas.

Venturing north, you'll pass fruit stands and sleepy villages like Waiahole, Waikane, and Kaaawa, where farmers grow taro and papaya and struggle to preserve their rural lifestyle.

Hanauma Bay, a reef haven for fish, draws snorkelers and sunbathers to its sandy beach—a half-mile crescent of Polynesian paradise.

In Kahana Bay and the valley, native Hawaiians still fish, farm, and weave as their ancestors did centuries ago.

▶ *Look for mangoes (Pirie and Hayden are the best) and litchis at Oahu fruit stands in summer months, and pomelos and papayas year-round.*

5 LAIE/KAHUKU

As the North Shore's theme park, the **Polynesian Cultural Center** in Laie enlightens visitors with its sprawling South Seas villages and cultural demonstrations. A few miles north of this North Shore gateway you'll find yourself in Kahuku, a plantation town with aquaculture and papaya farms and one of Oahu's most pleasing parks, **Malaekahana State Recreation Area,** a small cluster of state cabins on a crescent bay ringed with ironwoods.

6 SUNSET BEACH

Sunset Beach begins the string of legendary North Shore beaches—Ehukai, Banzai, Waimea—that ring this part of the island. During summer months, Sunset is wide, gentle, and inviting. In the winter swells, only professional and seasoned surfers dare enter the water.

High on a hill in Pupukea, about two miles down Rte. 83, is one of the most stunning views on the North Shore: the **Pu'u O Mahuka Heiau,** overlooking Waimea Valley, Waimea Bay, and **Waimea Falls Park,** where guided night walks are given on full-moon nights and ancient hula is performed

regularly. A place of human sacrifice in pre-Western days, the stone structure, a marvel of masonry, remains a haunting remnant of the past.

Some seven miles south of Waimea Falls, **Haleiwa** town brims with offbeat attractions, from tropically flavored shave ice (the local rage and much like snow cones) to *saimin* (a Japanese noodle soup) and plate-lunch counters.

7 PEARL HARBOR

As you approach Honolulu, stop at Pearl Harbor, the site of the **U.S.S. Arizona Memorial.** A white concrete and steel structure spans the hull of the sunken ship, a casualty of the attack on Pearl Harbor in 1941. The monument, in which more than 1,100 servicemen are entombed, is a silent reminder of one of the most fateful days in history.

1 LAHAINA

Lahaina has always been favored—first by Hawaiian kings, then by whalers, missionaries, and tourists. The Hawaiian kingdom's political center until 1845, today the town is chockablock with captivating galleries, shops, restaurants, and historic sites. The **Baldwin House** recounts the story of Rev. Dr. Dwight Baldwin, who arrived in the mid-1830's and established a strong Christian foothold on Maui. Other notable sites in Lahaina include the 1832 **Waiola Church** (formerly Waine'e Church) and the **Holy Innocents Episcopal Church**, founded in 1862 by Queen Emma and Kamehameha IV. As Asian immigrants arrived to work the sugarcane fields in the late 1800's, they, too, built their temples, among them the **Lahaina Jodo Mission** and the 1912 **Wo Hing Temple.**

You can obtain free maps and more information from the **Lahaina Restoration Foundation,** located next to the Baldwin House. On the second and last Thursdays of the month, senior citizens make and sell leis in front of the Baldwin House in what has become one of Lahaina's most endearing traditions.

And although the whalers may be gone, Lahaina still welcomes humpback whales every year from December through April.

▶ *Among the great whale-watching vantage points near Lahaina are Launiupoko Wayside, just south of town, and the Papawai Point lookout, just before you reach Maalaea.*

2 KAANAPALI

Built in the early 1960's, Hawaii's first master-planned resort is cradled between three miles of shoreline and fields of sugarcane on the flanks of the West Maui Mountains. You can chug the three miles between Lahaina and Kaanapali on a rebuilt 1890 vintage sugarcane train. Six hotels, assorted shops and restaurants, and two 18-hole golf courses that were once taro fields are spread out over 1,200 Kaanapali acres. You can enjoy a stroll along the shoreline path that runs the length of the resort and gaze at the islands of Lanai and Molokai in the distance. Sheraton Maui's steep cliff, **Puu Kekaa** (black rock), marks a spectacular swimming and snorkeling spot—and the place from which Hawaiians believed the souls of the dead made their leap into the spirit land of their ancestors.

Pristine pools descend to the sea on an ancient lava bed at O'heo Gulch near Kipahulu.

3 KAPALUA

Century-old pine trees, rolling pineapple fields, and one of America's best beaches add to the allure of this 1,500-acre resort. Two hotels, sprawling villas, three golf courses, two tennis complexes, and chic restaurants and shops make up Kapalua. From **Napili Bay** to the south to **Kapalua Bay**, the coastline offers the kind of swimming, snorkeling, and picnic spots that tourists prize. All of the beaches have public access, and most have restroom and shower facilities. At **Kapalua Beach** at the Kapalua Bay Hotel, you'll find the best nearshore snorkeling on the island.

Note that road conditions prohibit driving rental cars more than three miles past the beach, so you must return the same way, on Rte. 30.

▶ *The Kapalua Wine Symposium is an institution—a weekend in July of wine tastings, gourmet dinners, and lofty debates on gastronomy.*

4 WAILUKU

Wailuku, the county seat, is flush against the West Maui Mountains; there's hardly a more fetching spot on the island. Stop at the **Maui Historical Museum at the Bailey House,** a 19th-century structure housing Hawaiian quilts, stone and shell implements, cordage, and feather work. Continue three miles to Iao Valley, where the 2,250-foot-high **Iao Needle** rises green and velvety next to a gushing stream. Kamehameha the Great defeated his Maui rivals in a bloody massacre there in 1790, clogging the stream with fallen bodies. The tranquillity of this valley today overshadows that distant event.

5 WAILEA

South Maui's Wailea is the island's newest resort, with five upscale hotels and numerous condominiums strung along five crescent bays. This is the area for five-star dining, tennis, and golf. Although lined with hotels, the beaches—**Polo, Wailea, Ulua, Mokapu,** and the northernmost and least encumbered **Keawakapu**—are still accessible to the public. Look west and Kahoolawe, Molokini, and the West Maui Mountains come into view. Look east to see the slopes of the Haleakala volcano.

6 MAKENA BEACH

Drive past Wailea on Wailea Alanui and you'll come upon Makena Beach, the last great beach of the South Shore accessible by car. When hotel development took hold in Wailea, beachgoers went farther south and wound up at this quintessential tropical beach. Stock up before venturing to Makena Beach; it's hot, and there are no amenities.

The road continues south to the **Ahihi-Kinau Natural Area Reserve,** and past it to **La Perouse Bay,** nirvana for seasoned snorkelers. From here you'll have to backtrack up Rte. 31 and Rte. 30 all the way to Wailuku before you continue your tour into Maui's upcountry and Haleakala National Park.

7 HALEAKALA NATIONAL PARK

Dress warmly and start early if you want to be in this volcano-centered park for sunrise. The road to Haleakala's summit—10,023 feet high—winds for hours through the uplands of Kula until you reach the **Haleakala Visitor Center.** If the weather cooperates, you'll see the sun illuminate the moonlike terrain and ghostly silversword plants in a world of complete stillness. On the way down, treat yourself to breakfast at one of the lodges in Kula and watch as the shadows move down the hillside and West Maui comes into sunlight. Then visit a flower farm in Kula, to witness the potency of volcanic soil.

▶ *To beat the sun to the summit, call the visitor center for sunrise time, and ask a ranger or hotel concierge for the estimated driving time.*

8 MAKAWAO

Chic boutiques, New Age health food stores, restaurants, bakeries, and art galleries mark this *paniolo* (cowboy) town. The Maui Roping Club's 4th of July **Makawao Rodeo** is the state's most celebrated; the rest of the year the town is a pleasantly laid-back stop for dining and shopping, with attractions that include the **Hui No'eau Visual Arts Center,** a nine-acre, Mediterranean-style estate turned art center, built in 1917.

The 'i'iwi is a brilliantly hued native bird.

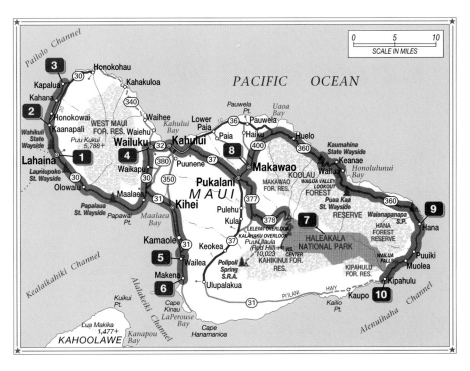

9 HANA

It's a good idea to tackle the 54-mile drive to Hana with mosquito repellent, a full tank, water, and a picnic lunch. You'll twist and turn around waterfalls, over taro-covered peninsulas, past 19th-century churches, and through dense tropical rain forest. The head of the **Waiakamoi Ridge Trail,** the **Kaumahina Stream** wayside, and **Keanae Lookout** are among dozens of scenic picnic spots along the way. In Hana, the black sand cove at **Waianapanapa State Park** beckons from the shoreline. Ten minutes down the main road, the single small room of the **Hana Cultural Center** is filled with war implements, carved idols, fishing gourds, and other artifacts.

10 KIPAHULU

Twelve miles past Hana, Kipahulu's **O'heo Gulch** has pool after pool cascading to the ocean in neat terraces sculpted from an ancient lava flow. Part of Haleakala National Park, the Kipahulu Valley is one of Hawaii's most remote and scenic regions, relatively undisturbed by humankind and flourishing with birds and vegetation.

▶ *For further information on hiking trails and cultural demonstrations, pay a visit to the Kipahulu ranger station at Haleakala National Park.*

KAUAI

1 LIHUE

The cultural history of this lushest of Hawaiian islands is presented in the two simple stone buildings that make up the **Kauai Museum.** Within are artifacts from Kauai's pre-Western and plantation cultures. Five minutes away is the **Grove Farm Homestead,** an 80-acre complex of orchards, cottages, and gardens. Originally part of a working plantation established by George Wilcox in 1864, the homestead today is a museum. It's something of a time warp: lying about are old hats, soap tins, silver-handled hairbrushes, a 100-year-old stove, and other impeccably preserved plantation memorabilia that recall the plantation's heyday. Tours are by advance reservation only.

2 POIPU

Although devastated by Hurricane Iniki in 1992, the town of Poipu has made a remarkable recovery. On your drive to the sunshine-filled South Shore, you'll pass through a tunnel of sky-high eucalyptus trees resembling a cathedral ceiling of shimmering green. The **Tunnel of Trees,** on Rte. 520, suffered damage by Iniki but has grown back as full and luxurious as before. Before reaching Poipu, you'll pass the little town of **Koloa**, where Hawaii's first sugar plantation was established, in 1835. Beneath the monkeypod trees are lovingly restored 19th-century storefronts.

▶ *For the best in fresh produce, seasonal fish, crafts, and other Kauai finds, seek out the county-sponsored Sunshine Markets, which move about from town to town.*

Beach lovers flock to **Poipu Beach Park**, where snorkeling in a sheltered lagoon and witnessing Technicolor sunsets are top attractions. But the star of the South Shore is the 186-acre **Lawai Gardens**, in Lawai, headquarters garden of the **National Tropical Botanical Garden**, the most highly respected botanical research facility in Hawaii. All manner of plants flourish in this storybook setting, from the rare to the indigenous. Since Hurricane Iniki damaged the garden in 1992, restoration is being done in stages. But you can still visit; call the visitor center for updates.

3 WAIMEA

Each year, in either February or October, the **Waimea Town Celebration** takes over this old plantation town, with a festive parade, local foods, arts, crafts, and entertainment; call the West Kauai Main Street office for dates.

For a lovely coastal detour, trace the 2½ miles of black-sand coastline west to Kekaha, where the sand turns bone white. From here to Polihale stretches 12½ miles of beach along the Mana Coastal Plain. It ends at **Polihale Beach**, where desertlike sands make a fine cushion for sunbathing and gazing out at lovely **Niihau**, whose residents are virtually all native Hawaiians. In the summer, Polihale is a spectacular swimming beach; in the winter, however, surf can be deceptively treacherous, so it's not advisable to swim at that time.

▶ *Road access to Polihale Beach is through Polihale State Park. From Waimea to Mana you'll travel westward on Rte. 50 and then take a five-mile dirt road to reach the park.*

While in Waimea, it's smart to pick up a picnic lunch and fill your gas tank and water bottles before you head for the surrealistic heights of **Waimea Canyon.** As the road winds uphill, western Kauai unfolds below and the island of Niihau, looking like a large purple

A young dancer at Poipu Beach displays her traditional grass skirt and headdress.

whale, dominates the horizon. Forty-five miles later, you'll hear the bleating of goats echoing against chiseled canyon walls colored every shade of purple, gold, green, and red. Above the gorges, streams, and waterfalls of this 10-mile valley glide graceful white-tailed tropic birds. Stop gaping long enough to snap a picture—not surprisingly, the canyon is one of the state's most photographed landscapes.

4 KOKEE STATE PARK

Between 3,000 and 4,000 feet above sea level, Kokee State Park offers a cool alternative to the warmer tropical valleys below. A light jacket or sweater is often needed in the crisp upcountry air. The 4,345-acre park contains many hiking trails and the most striking vista on the island, of beautiful **Kalalau Valley**, the largest—and perhaps the lushest—valley on the Na Pali coast.

▶ *The view of Kalalau Valley is usually clearest in the early morning, before the clouds have gathered.*

Stop in at the 41-year-old **Kokee Natural History Museum**, where you can linger among books, detailed topographical maps, and displays of rare honeycreepers and other fauna. The museum's programs include everything from summer Wonder Walks to a his-

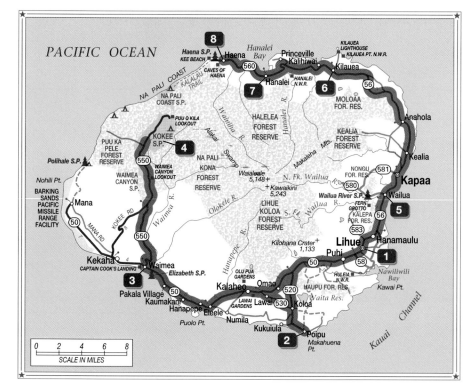

torical festival in the fall honoring Queen Emma, who in 1871 stopped on a remote Kokee hillside to dance the hula and honor the land. Next door, the **Kokee Lodge** offers hearty meals and 12 rustic cabins to rent.

No highway crosses the island's difficult northwestern terrain, so a complete loop along the Kauai coastline is impossible. To reach Wailua you must backtrack eastward past Lihue—hardly a hardship in this spectacular scenery.

5 WAILUA

Wailua Beach, located on the north side of the Wailua River, and **Lydgate Beach Park,** on the south, are stunning complements to the hau tree–lined waterway that curves inland up the flanks of Mount Wai'ale'ale. Despite the riverboats delivering tourists by the hundreds to the verdant **Fern Grotto**—a popular site for wedding ceremonies—the Wailua River has retained the mystique that made it a favorite place of Hawaiian royalty.

Sacred pre-Western stone temples, called *heiau,* ran from the mouth of the Wailua River to the top of Mount Wai'ale'ale in ancient times. Of those that exist today, three are accessible and can be seen in **Wailua River State Park.** If you start at Lydgate Beach Park at the mouth of the river (great for a picnic too) and take Rte. 580 *ma uka* (Hawaiian for "toward the mountain"), you'll pass numerous cultural and scenic treasures. **Poli'ahu** is a *heiau* of immense size, where an interpretive station describes the cultural and historic significance of Wailua. The royal birthing stones, **Holoholoku,** are where royal mothers came to give birth to future *ali'i*—royalty. When you stop at the rainbowed **Opaekaa Falls,** cross the street for a view of the Wailua River—it will take your breath away. Recover with a picnic at the **Keahua Arboretum,** an idyllic streamside behind **Sleeping Giant Mountain.**

6 KILAUEA

Kilauea would be simply one long stretch of beach tucked into the folds of high cliffs if it were not for the national historic landmark **Kilauea Point Lighthouse** and **Kilauea Point National Wildlife Refuge,** a sanctuary for seabirds and a resting area for nene geese, the endangered state bird. You'll see not only swooping birds but a lovely vista and, if you're lucky, humpback whales, monk seals, or green turtles— all endangered species—cavorting off Kilauea Point. Along the way stop at the 100-year-old **Kong Lung Center,** a former plantation, to browse and dine.

7 HANALEI

Hanalei's crazy quilt of taro patches sprawls beneath the lookout just past the sumptuous Princeville Resort. Besides producing much of Hawaii's poi—a Hawaiian staple made of taro— the valley is a national wildlife refuge for four species of endangered waterbirds. Among this laid-back town's

The Waioli Huiia Church, built in 1912, boasts a lush tropical setting in Hanalei. To the right is the original mission church, now the Waioli Social Hall, constructed in 1841.

many charms is the **Waioli Mission House Museum,** built in 1837. The grounds about the cottage are filled with shaded gardens, making it a splendid place for quiet contemplation. Close by is the **Waioli Huiia Church,** a charming timber structure painted the bright green of the islands.

Driving on, you'll cross several turn-of-the-century one-lane bridges. At Hanalei Bay, you'll see the oft-filmed marvels of **Na Molokama Mountain** and its fabled waterfalls.

8 HAENA

Haena Beach is a vision, with glistening waves lapping at white shores. Nearby is the **Maniniholo Dry Cave,** actually a long, sandy lava tube tucked beneath a cliff. Beyond it lie two wet caves: **Waikapalae** is a short hike uphill, and **Waikanaloa** is by the roadside. The **Limahuli Gardens,** another branch of the National Tropical Botanical Garden, is the pot of gold at the end of the road. The gardens contain 15 acres of rare and native plants as well as 1,000-year-old Hawaiian terraces and a pristine stream stocked with colorful indigenous fish. Towering above the gardens is **Makana.** In pre-Western times, island youths scaled this 1,280-foot cliff in spectacular nighttime flame-throwing celebrations. Be sure to call the state tourist bureau for the current tour schedule; access to the site is limited, and reservations are required.

At **Kee Beach,** the end of the highway, the 11-mile **Kalalau Trail** reverberates with the echoes of the ancients. The first two miles of the trail are accessible only by foot and lead to **Hanakapiai,** a velvety green valley with a sparkling white-sand beach. Swimming at Hanakapiai Beach is not recommended, however, because currents can be treacherous and unpredictable.

1 HILO

Hilo, the county seat of Hawaii Island (more often called the Big Island), is a town of quiet local color. From Coconut Island in Hilo Bay you can glimpse the world's largest active volcano, **Mauna Loa,** through the billowing clouds and watch boats hauling the day's catch into the **Suisan Fish Market.** At the **Hilo Farmers Market,** open Wednesday and Saturday mornings, vendors sell everything from fish to fern shoots to anthuriums of every color.

For a taste of Big Island history, pore over the Hawaiian pili grass structures and missionary memorabilia at the **Lyman Museum and Mission House,** a restored home built for a family of missionaries in 1839, filled with the 19th-century remnants of their time here. And if you're here in spring, take note: the week-long **Merrie Monarch Festival,** starting on Easter Sunday, includes the world's premier hula competition.

2 HAWAII VOLCANOES NATIONAL PARK

This 229,277-acre park ranges from sea level to the summit of 13,677-foot-high **Mauna Loa.** A 30-mile drive from Hilo takes you to the visitor center, where you can gather maps and updates on access and road conditions—information that is critical because of **Kilauea Volcano**'s ongoing eruption.

▶ *At an elevation of 4,000 feet, the park can be cold and rainy; be sure to bring a jacket and raingear.*

The **Thurston Lava Tube, Kilauea Iki Trail** (a 4½-mile loop), and **Kipuka Puaulu** (a one-mile loop) wind through native forests where honeycreepers feast on lehua blossoms. Pele, the volcano goddess of lore, is said to dwell in **Halemaumau,** Kilauea's crater. Take **Crater Rim Drive,** an 11-mile circle around Kilauea, and ask a ranger about conditions on the 20-mile **Chain of Craters Road;** on some days, you can see steam rising where the lava meets the Pacific.

3 NAALEHU

Heading south from the park, stop at **Punaluu Beach,** ringed by coconut trees set in jet-black sand. Traces remain of the spring-fed ponds that surrounded the bay before development and tidal waves altered the shoreline. The Hawaiians used to dive into the ponds carrying calabashes and fill them with fresh water from the springs bub-

Kilauea, *the centerpiece of Hawaii Volcanoes National Park, remains active today.*

bling on the ocean floor. About 15 minutes from Punaluu, you'll pass **Naalehu** and its wonderful roadside fruit stand; don't pass up the sweet Ka'u navel oranges. Beyond it, at the end of a barely paved 11-mile drive south from Rte. 11, is **South Point,** the southernmost point in the United States and the first landfall of the Polynesian voyagers.

4 PU'UHONUA O HONAUNAU NATIONAL HISTORICAL PARK

Under the pre-Western Hawaiian system, lawbreakers who entered this sanctuary escaped death or punishment by being absolved by a priest. Today Pu'uhonua O Honaunau is a 180-acre park of pristine tidal pools, thatched structures, house foundations, burial caves, and archeological wonders.

Five minutes north on the coastline at **Kealakekua Bay,** a tall white pillar marks the site where Capt. James Cook died in a skirmish with natives, who had considered him a reincarnated god.

5 HOLUALOA

The drive north meanders through coffee-growing countryside and past charming towns with unpronounceable names. At the town of **Captain Cook,** stop at the **Kona Historical Society Museum,** housed in the 1870's Greenwell Store, and the 12-acre **Amy B. H. Greenwell Ethnobotanical Garden,** which has the world's finest collection of Hawaiian bananas, dozens of taro varieties, and more than 100 species of native Hawaiian and Polynesian-introduced plants. Then follow Rte. 180 to the artists' village of **Holualoa** and explore its galleries and coffeehouses perched 1,500 feet above the shoreline.

6 KAILUA-KONA

Although bustling and deluged with visitors, Kailua-Kona remains a significant historical town. The Hawaiian chieftain Kamehameha the Great died at the **Ahu'ena Heiau** building, and Hawaii's first Christian church, **Mokuaikaua,** on Ali'i Drive, was founded in 1820. Governor John Adams Kuakini, brother-in-law of Kamehameha the Great, built the Victorian-style **Hulihee Palace,** across the street, in 1838. The palace houses priceless heirlooms from the Hawaiian monarchy.

In May, the Kona Outdoor Circle puts on its annual **Pua Plantasia** festival, where Kona coffee, flowers and nursery products, food, and Hawaiian entertainment flow freely.

7 KOHALA COAST

The landscape from North Kona to South Kohala is one long stretch of black lava. The area was rocked by volcanic eruptions in 1801 and 1859. Coconut trees at the shoreline and golf courses along the way flash brief patches of green. The coastline is peppered with exquisite beaches, but the access to most is through private property. One lovely beach that is accessible is **Anaehoomalu Bay,** a 20-minute drive north of the Kona Airport. Surrounded by fish ponds and palm fronds, Anae-hoomalu belies the tall tale that the Big Island has a shortage of prime beaches.

For a close-up view of Hawaiian petroglyphs—pictures etched in stone—drive 10 minutes north to the **Puako Petroglyphs Archaeological Preserve** in the Mauna Lani Resort. Five minutes north of the preserve is lovely **Hapuna Beach,** where frothy cobalt waves reign supreme. Taking a dip in the rough Hapuna surf, however, is discouraged for nonswimmers.

8 KAWAIHAE

Cutting an impressive silhouette high on the hill over Kawaihae is the **Pu'uko-hola Heiau.** The stone temple was built by Kamehameha the Great in 1790–91 and was dedicated to his war god, Kukailimoku. This national historic site lies near **Spencer Beach Park,** a camping and recreational spot much loved by locals. Twelve miles north, wander along the coral beach and among the canoe sheds and stone platforms of **Lapakahi State Historical Park,** a beautifully restored ancient fishing village.

9 HAWI

His name, Kamehameha, meant "the lonely one," and his massive frame stood over six feet tall. A detour off Rte. 270 takes you to the birthplace of the chieftain who, through his tough, autocratic rule, managed to unify the Hawaiian Islands. Also here is the **Mookini Heiau,** built centuries ago from stones said to have been passed hand to hand in a single night from 14 miles away. The stillness is haunting; the view, sublime.

Past tiny Hawi, in the town of Kapaau, the original **King Kamehameha I Statue** stands before the courthouse. Made in Italy, the statue sank with a ship off the Falklands, was miraculously recovered, and was sent to the king's homeland. At the end of the road, breathtaking **Pololu Valley** begins the series of inaccessible northern valleys.

10 WAIMEA

To reach Waimea, an oasis of velvety green cinder cones, flower farms, and vegetable farms (as well as some of the Big Island's best restaurants), you will

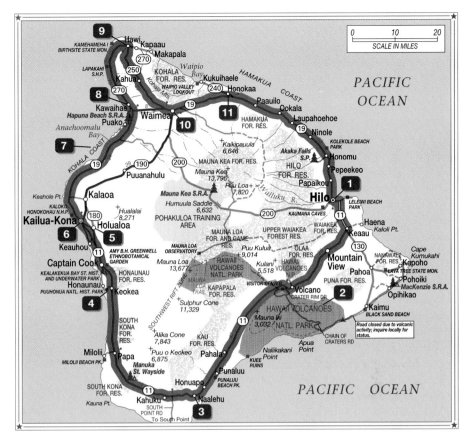

drive through the Kohala Mountains, the oldest mountain range on the island and a wonderland of ironwood forests and pastureland 4,000 feet in elevation. Many consider Rte. 250, known as the **Kohala Mountain Road,** to be the finest drive on the island.

Waimea is the home of the **Parker Ranch Visitor Center and Museum,** on the grounds of one of the largest privately owned ranches in the United States. Begun in 1809 by sailor John Palmer Parker, who tamed a wild herd of cattle on the Big Island, Parker Ranch today consists of 225,000 acres of land,

Fragrant plumeria *is used to fashion leis.*

where Hawaiian cowboys, or *paniolos,* spend their days rounding up more than 55,000 head of cattle.

11 HONOKAA

Macadamia nuts, the quintessential Hawaiian crop, are grown in orchards throughout the islands. In the town of Honokaa, you can tour **Hawaiian Macadamia Plantations, Inc.,** where you'll see the nuts swiftly separated from their shells and roasted to a toasty brown. After the tour, freshly roasted samples are yours to eat.

Honokaa is the gateway to the Waipio Valley, once a cultural center for pre-Western Hawaiians. From the **Waipio Lookout** you can see the eight-mile-long valley, the switchback trail up its northern flank, and the black-sand shore. The **Hamakua Coast** drive back to Hilo is a fitting finale to your tour: an odyssey through sugarcane fields, waterfall-laced valleys, and plantation villages. In the midst of the wrenching beauty of **Laupahoehoe,** a peninsula and park, is a memorial honoring the 24 people who died here in a 1946 tsunami, or tidal wave—a reminder of the fragility of these lovely islands.

Where to Find It

Consult the regional headings on the next four pages for the locations of attractions that interest you most: grand houses, beautiful gardens, nature preserves, military sites, out-of-the-ordinary museums, or festivals. For more general information, check with the national parks or state tourism bureaus listed on pages 332–333; both will be glad to answer your questions by mail or by telephone.

ESTATES & GRAND HOUSES

The houses in this list are open for tours. Schedules vary from place to place: from late fall to early spring many sites are either closed or open only by appointment. Call ahead for the latest information.

New England

Colonel Black Mansion, Ellsworth, Maine, 40
Nickels-Sortwell House, Wiscasset, Maine, 43
Victoria Mansion, Portland, Maine, 42
Castle in the Clouds, Moultonborough, N.H., 45
Goodwin Mansion, Portsmouth, N.H., 48
Wentworth-Coolidge Mansion, Portsmouth, N.H., 48
Hildene, Manchester, Vt., 50
Wilson Castle, Proctor, Vt., 51
Chesterwood, Stockbridge, Mass., 58
Jeremiah Lee Mansion, Marblehead, Mass., 56
The Mount, Lenox, Mass., 58
Blithewold Mansion, Bristol, R.I., 63
The Breakers, Newport, R.I., 60
John Brown Mansion, Providence, R.I., 62
Gilette Castle, Hadlyme, Conn., 67
Shaw-Perkins Mansion, New London, Conn., 66

▼

NBP National Battlefield Park, NHP National Historic Park, NMP National Military Park, NWR National Wildlife Refuge, SHP State Historic Park, SP State Park

Mid-Atlantic

Boldt Castle, Alexandria Bay, N.Y., 84
Boscobel, Garrison, N.Y., 72
Coe Hall, Oyster Bay, N.Y., 73
Home of Franklin D. Roosevelt, Hyde Park, N.Y., 78
Kykuit, North Tarrytown, N.Y., 72
Lyndhurst, Tarrytown, N.Y., 72
Olana, Hudson, N.Y., 77
Old Westbury Gardens, Old Westbury, N.Y., 72
Philipsburg Manor, North Tarrytown, N.Y., 72
Prouty-Chew House, Geneva, N.Y., 83
Rose Hill Mansion, Geneva, N.Y., 83
Sagamore Hill, Oyster Bay, N.Y., 73
Schuyler Mansion, Albany, N.Y., 77
Van Cortlandt Manor, Croton-on-Hudson, N.Y., 72
Vanderbilt Mansion, Hyde Park, N.Y., 78
Ford Mansion, Morristown, N.J., 89
Glenmont, West Orange, N.J., 89
Kuser Farm Mansion, Hamilton, N.J., 91
Ringwood Manor, Ringwood, N.J., 89
Smithville Mansion, Mount Holly, N.J., 91
Asa Packer Mansion, Jim Thorpe, Pa., 97
Baldwin-Reynolds House, Meadville, Pa., 103
Clayton, Pittsburgh, Pa., 100
Grey Towers, Milford, Pa., 96
Hoyt West, New Castle, Pa., 103

Pennsbury Manor, Morrisville, Pa., 95
Tara, Clark, Pa., 103
Nemours Mansion, Wilmington, Del., 104
Winterthur, Wilmington, Del., 104
Hampton, Towson, Md., 107

Southeast

Centre Hill, Petersburg, Va., 117
Hermitage Foundation, Norfolk, Va., 117
Oatlands, Leesburg, Va., 115
Blennerhassett Mansion, Parkersburg, W.Va., 121
L.S. Good House, Wheeling, W.Va., 120
Waldomore, Clarksburg, W.Va., 121
Ashland, Lexington, Ky., 126
Hunt-Morgan House, Lexington Ky., 126
Belle Meade Plantation, Nashville, Tenn., 134
Hermitage, Nashville, Tenn., 134
Oaklands, Murfreesboro, Tenn., 134
Rock Castle, Hendersonville, Tenn., 135
Smith-Trahern Mansion, Clarksville, Tenn., 135
Biltmore Estate, Asheville, N.C., 143
Hope Plantation, Windsor, N.C., 140
Tryon Palace, New Bern, N.C., 140
Battery homes, Charleston, S.C., 144
Hopsewee Plantation, Georgetown, S.C., 145
Hay House, Macon, Ga., 146
Isaiah Davenport House, Savannah, Ga., 148
Jekyll Island mansions, Ga., 149
Owens-Thomas House, Savannah, Ga., 148
Swan House, Atlanta, Ga., 146
Ca' d'Zan, Sarasota, Fla., 154
Vizcaya, Miami, Fla., 150
Arlington, Birmingham, Ala., 160
Sturdivant Hall, Selma, Ala., 161
Oakleigh, Mobile, Ala., 162
Columbus pilgrimage homes, Miss., 166
Stanton Hall, Natchez, Miss., 165
Vicksburg pilgrimage homes, Miss., 164
Houmas House, Burnside, La., 171
Melrose, Natchitoches, La., 173
Nottoway, La., 171
Oak Alley, La., 172
San Francisco, La., 172
St. Francisville pilgrimage homes, La., 171
Shadows-on-the-Teche, New Iberia, La., 169
Tezcuco, Burnside, La., 171

Midwest

Henry Ford Estate, Dearborn, Mich., 176
Honolulu House, Marshall, Mich., 177
Governor's Mansion, Marshall, Mich., 177
Mac-O-Chee, West Liberty, Ohio, 181
Mac-A-Cheek, West Liberty, Ohio, 181
Stan Hywet Hall and Gardens, Akron, Ohio, 180
Hillforest, Aurora, Ind., 184
James Lanier Home, Madison, Ind., 185
Magnolia Manor, Cairo, Ill., 191
Pierre Menard Home, Chester, Ill., 191
Queen Anne Mansion, Eureka Springs, Ark., 193
Felix Valle House, Ste. Genevieve, Mo., 196
Maison Guibourd-Valle, Ste. Genevieve, Mo., 196
Hoyt Sherman Place, Des Moines, Iowa, 200
Salisbury House, Des Moines, Iowa, 200
Terrace Hill, Des Moines, Iowa, 200
Fairlawn Mansion, Superior, Wis., 208
Pabst Mansion, Milwaukee, Wis., 204
James J. Hill House, St. Paul, Minn., 210
Glensheen, Duluth, Minn., 212

Great Plains & Mountains

Frank Phillips Home, Bartlesville, Okla., 234
Ashton Villa, Galveston, Tex., 237
Bayou Bend, Houston, Tex., 236
Bishop's Palace, Galveston, Tex., 237
Fulton Mansion, Fulton, Tex., 250
Giddings-Stone Mansion, Brenham, Tex., 236
Harrington House, Amarillo, Tex., 243
Moody Mansion, Galveston, Tex., 237
Southern mansions, Waco, Tex., 247
Castle, White Sulphur Springs, Mont., 268
Conrad Mansion, Kalispell, Mont., 271
Moss Mansion, Billings, Mont., 269
Jerome State Historic Park, Jerome, Ariz., 285
Rosson House, Phoenix, Ariz., 284
Bowers Mansion, Carson City, Nev., 290
Mackay Mansion, Virginia City, Nev., 291

NOVEL MUSEUMS

Most museums are devoted to art, history, or science. But the museums in this list have their own delightful focus, tracing the history of everything from mustard to teddy bears to the lives of famous people.

HALLS OF FAME

The champions of sports, music, and other domains live on in the museums that pay them homage.

MILITARY SITES

The commemorative sites of the Revolutionary and Civil wars are concentrated in the eastern U S. In the West are the remains of the forts that protected the pioneers.

National Parks and State Tourism Bureaus

National Park	Address	Phone Number
Acadia	P.O. Box 177, Bar Harbor, ME 04609	207-288-3338
Arches	P.O. Box 907, Moab, UT 84532	801-259-8161
Badlands	P.O. Box 6, Interior, SD 57750	605-433-5361
Big Bend	P.O. Box 129, Big Bend National Park, TX 79834	915-477-2251
Biscayne	P.O. Box 1369, Homestead, FL 33090	305-247-7275
Bryce Canyon	Bryce Canyon, UT 84717	801-834-5322
Canyonlands	West Resource Blvd., Moab, UT 84532	801-259-7164
Capitol Reef	HC 70 Box 15, Torrey, UT 84775	801-425-3791
Carlsbad Caverns	3225 National Parks Hwy., Carlsbad, NM 88220	505-785-2232
Channel Islands	1901 Spinnaker Dr., Ventura, CA 93001	805-658-5730
Crater Lake	P.O. Box 7, Crater Lake, OR 97604	503-594-2211
Denali	P.O. Box 9, Denali Park, AK 99755	907-683-2294
Dry Tortugas	P.O. Box 6208, Key West, FL 33041	305-242-7700
Everglades	40001 State Rd. 9336, Homestead, FL 33034	305-242-7700
Gates of the Arctic	P.O. Box 74680, Fairbanks, AK 99707	907-692-5494
Glacier Bay	P.O. Box 140, Gustavus, AK 99826	907-697-2230
Glacier	West Glacier, MT 59936	406-888-5441
Grand Canyon	P.O. Box 129, Grand Canyon, AZ 86023	602-638-7888
Grand Teton	P.O. Drawer 170, Moose, WY 83012	307-739-3300
Great Basin	Baker, NV 89311	702-234-7331
Great Smoky Mountains	107 Park Headquarters, Gatlinburg, TN 37738,	615-436-1200
Guadalupe Mountains	H.C. 60 Box 400, Salt Flat, TX 79847	915-828-3251
Haleakala	P.O. Box 369, Makawao, HI 96768	808-572-9306
Hawaii Volcanoes	P.O. Box 52, Hawaii National Park, HI 96718	808-967-7311
Hot Springs	P.O. Box 1860, Hot Springs, AR 71902	501-623-1433
Isle Royale	800 E. Lakeshore Dr., Houghton, MI 49931	906-482-0984
Katmai	P.O. Box 7, King Salmon, AK 99613	907-246-3305
Kenai Fjords	P.O. Box 1727, Seward, AK 99664	907-224-3175
Kobuk Valley	P.O. Box 1029, Kotzebue, AK 99752	907-442-3890
Lake Clark	4230 University Dr., Suite 311, Anchorage, AK 99508	907-781-2218
Lassen Volcanic	38050 Hwy. 36 East, Mineral, CA 96063	916-595-4444
Mammoth Cave	Mammoth Cave, KY 42259	502-758-2328
Mesa Verde	P.O. Box 8, Mesa Verde, CO 81330	303-529-4465
Mount Rainier	Tahoma Woods, Star Route, Ashford, WA 98304	206-569-2211
North Cascades	2105 Hwy. 20, Sedro Woolley, WA 9828	206-856-5700
Olympic	600 East Park Ave., Port Angeles, WA 98362	206-452-0330
Petrified Forest	P.O.Box 2217, Petrified Forest National Park, AZ 86028	602-524-6228
Redwood	1111 Second St., Crescent City, CA 95531	707-464-6101
Rocky Mountain	Estes Park, CO 80517	303-586-1206
Sequoia–Kings Canyon	Three Rivers, CA 93271	209-565-3134
Shenandoah	Rte. 4, Box 348, Luray, VA 22835	703-999-2266
Theodore Roosevelt	P.O. Box 7, Medora, ND 58645	701-623-4466
Voyageurs	3131 Hwy. 53, International Falls, MN 56649	218-283-9821
Wind Cave	RR 1 Box 190, Hot Springs, SD 57747	605-745-4600
Wrangell–St. Elias	P.O. Box 29, Glennallen, AK 99588	907-822-5235
Yellowstone	P.O. Box 168, Yellowstone National Park, WY 82190	307-344-7381
Yosemite	P.O. Box 577, Yosemite National Park, CA 95389	209-372-0200
Zion	Springdale, UT 84767-1099	801-772-3256

State Tourism Bureau	Address	Phone Number
Alabama Bureau of Tourism and Travel	P.O.Box 4309, Montgomery, AL 36103	205-242-4169 or 800-ALABAMA
Alaska Division of Tourism	P.O. Box 110801, Juneau, AK 99811	907-465-2010
Arizona Office of Tourism	1100 West Washington, Phoenix, AZ 85007	602-542-8687 or 800-842-8257
Arkansas Dept. of Parks and Tourism	One Capitol Mall, Little Rock, AR 72201	501-682-7777 or 800-NATURAL
California Division of Tourism	801 K St., Suite 1600,Sacramento, CA 95814	916-322-2881 or 800-862-2543
Denver Metro Convention and Visitors Bureau	225 W. Colfax, Denver, CO 80202	303-892-1112 or 800-645-3446
Connecticut Tourism Division	865 Brook St., Rocky Hill, CT 06067	203-258-4355 or 800-CT-BOUND
Delaware Tourism Office	99 Kings Hwy., Box 1401, Dover, DE 19903	302-739-4271 or 800-441-8846
Florida Division of Tourism	126 West Van Buren St., Tallahassee, FL 32399	904-487-1462
Georgia Dept. of Industry, Trade and Tourism	P.O. Box 1776, Atlanta, GA 30301	404-656-3590 or 800-VISIT-GA
State of Hawaii Tourist Information	P.O. Box 2359, Honolulu, HI 96804	808-586-2550
Idaho Division of Tourism Development	700 West State St., Boise, ID 83720	208-334-2470 or 800-VISIT-ID
Illinois Bureau of Tourism	100 West Randolph St., Suite 3-400, Chicago, IL 60601	312-814-4732 or 800-223-0121
Indiana Dept. of Commerce/Tourism	One North Capitol Ave., Suite 700, Indianapolis, IN 46204	317-232-8860 or 800-382-6771
Iowa Division of Tourism	200 East Grand Ave., Des Moines, IA 50309	515-242-4705 or 800-345-4692
Kansas Travel & Tourism Division	700 SW Harrison St., Suite 1300, Topeka, KS 66603	913-296-2009 or 800-2-KANSAS
Kentucky Dept. of Travel Development	2200 Capitol Plaza Tower, 500 Mero St., Frankfort, KY 40601	502-564-4930 or 800-225-8747
Louisiana Office of Tourism	P.O. Box 94291, Baton Rouge, LA 70804	504-342-8119 or 800-33-GUMBO
Maine Office of Tourism	33 Stone St., Augusta, ME 04333	207-287-5711 or 800-533-9595
Maryland Office of Tourism Development	217 East Redwood St., 9th Fl., Baltimore, MD 21202	410-333-6611 or 800-445-4558
Massachusetts Office of Travel and Tourism	100 Cambridge St., 13th Fl., Boston, MA 02202	617-727-3201 or 800-447-MASS
Michigan Travel Bureau	P.O. Box 30226, Lansing, MI 48909	517-373-0670 or 800-5432-YES
Minnesota Office of Tourism	121 7th Place East, Suite 100, St. Paul, MN 55101	612-296-5029 or 800-657-3700
Mississippi Division of Tourism Development	P.O. Box 849, Jackson, MS 39205	601-359-3297 or 800-927-6378
Missouri Division of Tourism	P.O. Box 1055, Jefferson City, MO 65102	314-751-4133 or 800-877-1234
Travel Montana	800 Conley Lake Rd., Deer Lodge, MT 59722	406-444-2654 or 800-VISIT-MT
Nebraska Travel and Tourism Division	Dept. of Econ. Dev., P.O. Box 94666, Lincoln, NE 68509	402-471-3796 or 800-228-4307
Nevada Commission of Tourism	5151 S. Carson St., Carson City, NV 89710	702-687-4322 or 800-237-0774
New Hampshire Office of Travel and Tourism	P.O. Box 1856, Concord, NH 03302	603-271-2343
New Jersey Division of Travel and Tourism	20 West State St., CN 826, Trenton, NJ 08625	800-JERSEY-7
New Mexico Dept. of Tourism	491 Old Santa Fe Trail, Santa Fe, NM 87503	505-827-7400 or 800-545-2040
New York State DED Division of Tourism	One Commerce Plaza, Albany, NY 12245	518-474-4116 or 800-225-5697
North Carolina Travel and Tourism Division	430 North Salisbury St., Raleigh, NC 27611	919-733-4171 or 800-847-4862
North Dakota Tourism	204 East Blvd., Liberty Memorial Bldg., Bismarck, ND 58505	701-224-2525 or 800-HELLO-ND
Ohio Division of Travel and Tourism	P.O. Box 1001, Columbus, OH 43216	800-BUCKEYE
Oklahoma Tourism and Recreation Dept.	2401 Lincoln Blvd., Rm. 500, Oklahoma City, OK 73105	405-521-3981 or 800-652-6552
Oregon Economic Dev. Dept., Tourism Div.	775 Summer St. NE, Salem, OR 97310	503-986-0000 or 800-547-7842
Pennsylvania Office of Travel Marketing	Rm. 453, Forum Bldg., Harrisburg, PA 17120	717-787-5453 or 800-VISIT-PA
Rhode Island Tourism Division	7 Jackson Walkway, Providence, RI 02903	401-277-2601 or 800-556-2484
South Carolina Dept. of Parks, Rec., & Tourism	Box 71, Room 902, Columbia, SC 29202	803-734-0122
South Dakota Dept. of Tourism	711 East Wells Ave., Pierre, SD 57501	800-732-5682
Tennessee Dept. of Tourism Development	P.O. Box 23170, Nashville, TN 37202	615-741-2158 or 800-836-6200
Texas Dept. of Commerce, Tourism Division	P.O. Box 12728, Austin, TX 78711	512-462-9191 or 800-888-8839
Utah Travel Council	Council Hall/Capitol Hill, Salt Lake City, UT 84114	801-538-1030 or 800-UTAH-FUN
Vermont Dept. of Travel and Tourism	134 State St., Montpelier, VT 05602	802-828-3236 or 800-VERMONT
Virginia Tourism	901 E. Byrd St., Richmond, VA 23219	804-786-4484 or 800-VISIT-VA
Washington State Tourism Development Division	P.O. Box 42500, Olympia, WA 98504	206-586-2088 or 800-544-1800
West Virginia Division of Tourism and Parks	2101 Washington St. East, Charleston, WV 25305	304-558-2286 or 800-225-5982
Wisconsin Division of Tourism	P.O. Box 7606, Madison, WI 53707	608-266-2161 or 800-432-8747
Wyoming Division of Tourism	I-25 at College Dr., Cheyenne, WY 82002	307-777-7777 or 800-225-5996

Page numbers in **bold type** refer to illustrations.

Page numbers in **bold type** refer to illustrations.

Page numbers in **bold type** refer to illustrations.

Page numbers in **bold type** refer to illustrations.

Johnson City, Tex., 242
Johnson Victrola Museum, Dover, Del., 105
Johnstown, Pa., 100
John Strong Mansion, Middlebury, Vt., 52
Joshua Tree NM, Calif., 14, 305, **305**
Joslyn Art Museum, Omaha, Nebr., 224
J. Paul Getty Museum, Malibu, Calif., 308
Juárez, Chihuahua, Mexico, 248
Judy Garland Historical Center, Grand Rapids, Minn., 212
Jugtown, N.C., 140
Julian, Calif., 305
Juliette Gordon Low Birthplace, Savannah, Ga., 148
Junction City, Kans., 229
Juneau, Alaska, 319
Jungle Gardens, Avery Island, La., 170
Jungle Larry's Zoological Park and Caribbean Gardens, Naples, Fla., 153

K

Kaanapali, Hawaii, 322
Kahuku, Hawaii, 321
Kailua, Hawaii, 320–321
Kailua-Kona, Hawaii, 326
Kalalau Trail, Hawaii, 326
Kalaloch, Wash., 294–295
Kalamazoo, Mich., 177
Kalispell, Mont., 271
Kanapaha Botanical Gardens, Gainesville, Fla., 157
Kansas City, Mo., 37, 198–199
Kansas Cosmosphere and Space Center, Hutchinson, Kans., 231
Kansas Museum of History, Topeka, Kans., 228
Kansas State University, Manhattan, Kans., 230
Kapalua, Hawaii, 322
Kapiolani Park, Honolulu, Hawaii, 320
Kate Chopin Home Bayou Folk Museum, Cloutierville, La., 173
Kauai, Hawaii, 323–324
Kauai Museum, Lihue, Hawaii, 323
Kauffman Museum, Newton, Kans., 231
Kaumahina Stream, Hawaii, 323
Kawaihae, Hawaii, 327
Kaw Mission, Council Grove, Kans., 229
Keahua Arboretum, Hawaii, 325

Kealakekua Bay, Hawaii, 326
Keanae Lookout, Hawaii, 323
Kearney, Nebr., 225
Keawakapu Beach, Hawaii, 322
Keene, N.H., 47
Keeneland Race Course, Lexington, Ky., 126, **126**
Kelleys Island, Ohio, 182
Kennebunkport, Maine, 42, **42**
Kennedy Compound, Hyannis Port, Mass., 57
Kennedy Museum, Hyannis, Mass., 57
Kennesaw Mountain National Battlefield Park, Marietta, Ga., 147
Kent, Conn., 65
Kentucky Center for the Arts, Louisville, Ky., 128
Kentucky Derby, Louisville, Ky., 128
Kentucky Horse Park, Lexington, Ky., 126
Kettle Falls, Wash., 299
Keuka Lake Winery Route, N.Y., 82
Keystone Canyon, Alaska, 318
Kilauea Volcano, Hawaii, 326, **326**
Kilgore, Tex., 245
Kill Devils Hills, N.C., 138–139
Kimbell Art Museum, Fort Worth, Tex., 246, **246**
Kingfisher, Okla., 233
King Ranch, Kingsville, Tex., 251
Kings Canyon NP, Calif., 309
Kingsley Plantation, Fort George Island, Fla., 156
Kingston, N.Mex., 257
Kingston, N.Y., 78
Kingston, R.I., 61–62
Kingsville, Tex., 251
King-Tiddell Cottage, Savannah, Ga., 148
Kinsman Notch, N.H., 45
Kipahulu, Hawaii, 323
Kirkpatrick Center Museum Complex, Oklahoma City, Okla., 234
Kisatchie NF, La., 172, **172**
Kismet, N.Y., 74
Klondike Gold Rush NHP, Skagway, Alaska, 15, 319
Kluane NP, Alaska, 318
Knife River Indian Villages, N.Dak., 218
Knox College, Galesburg, Ill., 189
Knoxville, Tenn., 130
Kodachrome Basin SP, Utah, 280–281
Kohala Coast, Hawaii, 326–327
Kohala Mountain Road, Hawaii, 327
Kokee SP, Hawaii, 324–325
Koloa, Hawaii, 324

Kona Historical Society Museum, Captain Cook, Hawaii, 326
Konza Prairie, Kans., 230
Koolau, Hawaii, 320
Koolau Mountains, Hawaii, 320
Kootenai NWR, Idaho, 274
Krohn Conservatory, Cincinnati, Ohio, 182
Kuser Farm Mansion, Hamilton, N.J., 91
Kutztown, Pa., 97

L

Lac du Flambeau, Wis., 209
Lackawanna Coal Mine Tour, Scranton, Pa., 96
Lackawaxen, Pa., 96
Ladew Topiary Gardens, Monkton, Md., 107
Lafayette, La., 170
Laguna Beach, Calif., 304
Lahaina, Hawaii, 322
Laie, Hawaii, 321
Lajitas, Tex., 249
Lake Champlain Islands, Vt., 53
Lake Champlain Maritime Museum, Basin Harbor, Vt., 52
Lake City, Colo., 261
Lake Dardanelle, Ark., 192
Lake Erie Islands, Ohio, 181–182
Lake Ferguson, Miss., 167
Lake George, N.Y., 81, **81**
Lake Jackson Mounds, Fla., 158
Lake Laberge, Yukon Territory, Canada, 318
Lake Lure, N.C., 142
Lake McConaughy, Nebr., 226
Lake Mead, Ariz., 14
Lake Murray SP, Okla., 235
Lake of the Ozarks, Mo., 199
Lake Pepin, Minn., 211
Lake Placid, N.Y., 37, 80
Lake Powell, Ariz., 35, 283
Lakeridge Winery and Vineyards, Clermont, Fla., 155
Lake Roosevelt, Wash., 299
Lake Sakakawea, N.Dak., 217
Lake San Cristobal, Colo., 261
Lakes Art Center, Okoboji, Iowa, 201
Lake Sharpe, S.Dak., 222
Lake Tahoe, Calif.-Nev., 35, 290, 313, **313**
Lake Wales, Fla., 153
Lambertville, N.J., 91
Lamoille, Nev., 290
Lamoille Canyon Scenic Byway, Nev., 290
Lancaster, Pa., 99
Land Between the Lakes, Tenn., 135
Landis Valley Museum, Lancaster, Pa., 99
Lansing, Mich., 178

Lapakahi, Hawaii, 327
Laramie, Wyo., 267
Las Cruces, N.Mex., 257
Lassen Volcanic NP, Calif., 315
Las Trampas, N.Mex., 255
Las Vegas, Nev., 37, 288, **288**
Laupahoehoe, Hawaii, 327
Laura Ingalls Wilder–Rose Wilder Lane Home and Museum, Mansfield, Mo., 199
Lavender Pit Mine, Ariz., 287
La Ventana, El Malpais, N.Mex., 252
Lawai Gardens, Hawaii, 324
Lawrence, Kans., 228–229
Lawrenceburg, Tenn., 135
Lawton, Okla., 235
Lead, S.Dak., 221
Leadville, Colo., 259
Leaming's Run Gardens, Swainton, N.J., 92
Lebanon, Ohio, 182
Leesburg, Va., 115
Leestown Company, Frankfort, Ky., 127
Lenox, Mass., 58
Le Perouse Bay, Hawaii, 322
Letchworth SP, N.Y., 87
Level Cross, N.C., 141
Lewes, Del., 105
Lewis and Clark Caverns SP, Mont., 268
Lewis & Clark Railway, Wash., 297
Lewis and Clark SP, N.Dak., 217
Lewis and Clark State Highway, Wash., 296
Lewis and Clark Trail, Mont., 270
Lewisburg, W.Va., 125
Lewiston, Idaho, 274
Lewiston, N.Y., 86
Lexington, Ky., 126, **126**
Lexington, Mass., 54
Lexington, N.C., 143
Lexington, U.S.S., **Corpus Christi,** Tex., 250
Lexington, Va., 119
Liberace Museum, Las Vegas, Nev., 288
Libraries, 10
Library of Congress, Washington, D.C., 108
Life-Saving Museum of Virginia, Virginia Beach, Va., 117
Lightner Museum, St. Augustine, Fla., 157, **157**
Lightship Museum, Portsmouth, Va., 117
Lihue, Hawaii, 323
Lily Bay SP, Maine, 41
Limahuli Gardens, Hawaii, 325
Lime Kiln Point SP, Wash., 296
Lincoln, Nebr., 226
Lincoln County Historical Society Museum, North Platte, Nebr., 226
Lincoln Heritage House, Elizabethtown, Ky., 129

Page numbers in **bold type** refer to illustrations.

Page numbers in **bold type** refer to illustrations.

Page numbers in **bold type** refer to illustrations.